Glencoe Literature

Internet resources are just a click away!

STEP 1 ▶ Go to glencoe.com

STEP 2 ▶ Connect to resources by entering **QuickPass** codes.

GL39770u1   Enter this code with appropriate unit numbers.

STEP 3 ▶ Access your **Online Student Edition**, handheld downloads, games, and more:

Literature and Reading Resources

- Author Search
- Literature Classics
- Big Question Web Quests
- Literary and Text Elements eFlashcards and Games
- Interactive Reading Practice

Selection Resources

- Audio Summaries
- Selection Quizzes
- Selection Vocabulary eFlashcards and Games
- Reading-Writing Connection Activities

Vocabulary and Spelling Resources

- Academic and Selection Vocabulary eFlashcards and Games
- Multi-Language Glossaries
- Spelling Games

Writing, Grammar, and Research Resources

- Interactive Writing Models
- Writing and Research Handbook
- Graphic Organizers
- Sentence Combining Activities
- Publishing Options

Media Literacy, Speaking, Listening, and Viewing Resources

- Media Analysis Guides
- Project Ideas and Templates
- Presentation Tips and Strategies

Assessment Resources

- End of Unit Assessment
- Test-Taking Tips and Strategies

Glencoe

Literature

COURSE 3

Program Consultants

Jeffrey D. Wilhelm, Ph.D.

Douglas Fisher, Ph.D.

Kathleen A. Hinchman, Ph.D.

David G. O'Brien, Ph.D.

Taffy Raphael, Ph.D.

Cynthia Hynd Shanahan, Ed.D.

McGraw Hill **Glencoe**

Acknowledgments

Grateful acknowledgment is given authors, publishers, photographers, museums, and agents for permission to reprint the following copyrighted material. Every effort has been made to determine copyright owners. In case of any omissions, the Publisher will be pleased to make suitable acknowledgments in future editions.

Acknowledgments continued on page R75.

Send all inquiries to:
Glencoe/McGraw-Hill
8787 Orion Place
Columbus, OH 43240-4027

ISBN: 978-0-07-877977-0
MHID: 0-07-877977-4

Printed in the United States of America.

8 9 10   QVR/LEH 13 12 11

Program Consultants

Senior Program Consultants

Jeffrey D. Wilhelm, Ph.D. Jeffrey Wilhelm is Professor of English Education at Boise State University and Director of the Boise State Writing Project. He specializes in reading and adolescent literacy and does research on ways to engage readers and writers. A middle and high school teacher for thirteen years, Wilhelm is author or coauthor of eleven books, including the award-winning works *You Gotta BE the Book* and *Reading Don't Fix No Chevys.*

Douglas Fisher, Ph.D. Douglas Fisher is Professor of Language and Literacy Education at San Diego State University. He is also Director of the award-winning City Heights Educational Pilot, a project for improving urban adolescent literacy. Fisher has published many articles on reading and literacy and has coauthored *Improving Adolescent Literacy: Strategies That Work.*

Program Consultants

Kathleen A. Hinchman, Ph.D. Kathleen Hinchman is Professor and Chair, Reading and Language Arts Center, School of Education, Syracuse University. A former middle school English and reading teacher, Hinchman researches social perspectives toward literacy. She is coauthor of three books on reading and literacy, including *Principled Practices for a Literate America: A Framework for Literacy and Learning in the Upper Grades.*

David G. O'Brien, Ph.D. David O'Brien is Professor of Literacy Education at the University of Minnesota and a former classroom teacher. O'Brien's research explores reading in content areas as well as ways to motivate learners to engage in school-based literacy tasks. He is conducting studies on the use of technology-based literacy, using computers and related technology.

Taffy Raphael, Ph.D. Taffy Raphael is Professor of Literacy Education at the University of Illinois at Chicago (UIC). She does literacy research on upper elementary and middle school students and has coauthored several books, including *Book Club: A Literature-Based Curriculum* and *Book Club for Middle School.* She has received the International Reading Association (IRA) Outstanding Educator Award and is in the IRA Hall of Fame.

Cynthia Hynd Shanahan, Ed.D. Cynthia Hynd Shanahan is Professor in the Reading, Writing, and Literacy program at the University of Illinois at Chicago (UIC). She is also a consultant with the Center for Literacy at UIC. Hynd Shanahan has been a classroom teacher and has taught reading instruction to elementary-level through college-level teachers. She has authored a chapter in the book *Engaged Reading,* edited by John T. Guthrie and Donna Alverman.

Advisory Board

Special Consultants

Donald R. Bear, PhD.
Donald R. Bear is Professor, Department of Curriculum and Instruction Director, E. L. Cord Foundation Center for Learning and Literacy at the University of Nevada, Reno. He is the author of *Words Their Way* and *Words Their Way with English Learners.*

Jana Echevarria, PhD.
Jana Echevarria is Professor, Educational Psychology, California State University, Long Beach, and Principal Researcher, National Research and Development Center of English Language Learners. She is the author of *Making Content Comprehensible for English Learners: The SIOP Model.*

Dinah Zike, M.Ed.
Dinah Zike was a classroom teacher and a consultant for many years before she began to develop Foldables®—a variety of easily created graphic organizers. Zike has written and developed more than 150 supplemental books and materials used in classrooms worldwide. Her *Big Book of Books and Activities* won the Teacher's Choice Award.

The Writers' Express®
Immediate Impact. Lasting Transformation.   wex.org

Glencoe National Reading and Language Arts Advisory Council

Wanda J. Blanchett, Ph.D.
Associate Dean for Academic Affairs and Associate Professor of Exceptional Education, School of Education
University of Wisconsin-Milwaukee
Milwaukee, Wisconsin

William G. Brozo, Ph.D.
Professor of Literacy
Graduate School of Education, College of Education and Human Development
George Mason University
Fairfax, Virginia

Nancy Drew, Ed.D.
LaPointe Educational Consultants
Corpus Christi, Texas

Susan Floria-Ruane, Ed.D.
Professor, College of Education
Michigan State University
East Lansing, Michigan

Nancy Frey, Ph.D.
Associate Professor of Literacy in Teacher Education
School of Teacher Education
San Diego State University
San Diego, California

Kimberly Lawless, Ph.D.
Associate Professor
Curriculum, Instruction and Evaluation
College of Education
University of Illinois at Chicago
Chicago, Illinois

Sharon Fontenot O'Neal, Ph.D.
Associate Professor
Texas State University
San Marcos, Texas

William Ray, M.A.
Lincoln-Sudbury Regional High School
Sudbury, Massachusetts

Victoria Gentry Ridgeway, Ph.D.
Associate Professor
Reading Education
Clemson University
Clemson, South Carolina

Janet Saito-Furukawa, M.Ed.
English Language Arts Specialist
District 4
Los Angeles, California

Bonnie Valdes, M.Ed.
Independent Reading Consultant
CRISS Master Trainer
Largo, Florida

Teacher Reviewers

Bridget Agnew
St. Michael Middle School
Chicago, IL

Monica Araiza
Garcia Middle School
Brownsville, TX

Katherine R. Baer
Howard County Public Schools
Ellicott City, MD

Tanya Bateson
Amundsen High School
Chicago, IL

Yolanda Conder
Owasso Mid-High School
Owasso, OK

Gwenn de Mauriac
The Wicasset Schools
Wicasset, ME

Joseph F. Hutchinson
Toledo Public Schools
Toledo, OH

Dianne Konkel
Cypress Lake Middle School
Fort Myers, FL

Patricia Lee
Radnor Middle School
Wayne, PA

Heather S. Lewis
Waverly Middle School
Lansing, MI

Sandra C. Lott
Aiken Optional School
Alexandria, LA

Lori Howton Means
Fulton Junior High School
O'Fallon, IL

Claire C. Meitl
Howard County Public Schools
Ellicott City, MD

Paul C. Putnoki
Torrington Middle School
Torrington, CT

Stephanie L. Robin
N.P. Moss Middle School
Lafayette, LA

Fareeda J. Shabazz
Paul Revere Elementary School
Chicago, IL

Molly Steinlage
Brookpark Middle School
Grove City, OH

Barry Stevenson
Garnet Valley Middle School
Glen Mills, PA

Book Overview

UNIT ONE

How Do You Stay True to Yourself? 1

Reading Skills: Analyze Characters, Determine Main Idea and Supporting Details, Identify Sequence

Literary Elements: Narrator and Point of View, Plot, Repetition, Character, Style, Conflict, Theme, Setting, Narrative Poetry

Writing Product: Narrative

Vocabulary: Word Usage, Context Clues

Grammar: Concrete and Abstract Nouns, Personal and Possessive Pronouns and Antecedents, Main/Helping Verbs

UNIT TWO

Reading: What's in It for You? 145

Reading Skills: Analyze Cultural Context, Analyze Evidence, Identify Cause-and-Effect Relationships, Recognize Author's Purpose, Analyze Plot

Literary Elements: Theme, Author's Purpose, Informational Text, Description, Simile, Suspense, Mood, Diction, Setting

Writing Product: Functional Document

Vocabulary: Synonyms, Context Clues

Grammar: Irregular Verbs, Agreement with Indefinite Pronouns, Present and Past Perfect Tense

UNIT THREE

What's More Important, the Journey or the Destination? 305

Reading Skills: Analyze Style, Analyze Setting, Analyze Historical Context, Identify Cause-and-Effect Relationships, Analyze Theme, Analyze Characterization

Literary Elements: Conflict, Stanza, Speaker, Myth, Rhyme and Rhyme Scheme, Metaphor, Characterization, Rhythm and Meter, Assonance and Consonance, Onomatopoeia and Alliteration, Motivation, Imagery, Sonnet

Writing Product: Response to Literature

Vocabulary: Word Usage, Context Clues, Synonyms

Grammar: Common and Proper Nouns, Reflexive and Intensive Pronouns, Future Tense, Adjectives and Adverbs, Modifying Phrases and Clauses, Comparative and Superlative

Reading Skills: Distinguish Fact and Opinion, Analyze Evidence, Compare and Contrast Information, Analyze Cause-and-Effect Relationships, Analyze Conflict

Literary Elements: Argument, Thesis, Style, Author's Perspective, Parallelism, Text Structure, Ode, Tone, Symbol, Dialogue, Theme

Writing Product: Persuasive Essay

Vocabulary: Word Usage

Grammar: Double Negatives, Capitalization of Sentences, Misplaced/Dangling Modifiers, Demonstrative Adjectives, Direct Objects, Indirect Objects

Reading Skills: Analyze Diction, Analyze Mood, Analyze Cultural Context, Analyze Tone, Analyze Description, Analyze Text Structure

Literary Elements: Flashback, Voice, Elegy, Free Verse, Description, Simile and Metaphor, Irony, Foreshadowing, Tone

Writing Product: Research Report

Vocabulary: Synonyms, Context Clues, Word Usage

Grammar: Subject-Verb Agreement, Commas with Appositives, Commas with Relative Clauses

Reading Skills: Analyze Plot, Make Generalizations About Theme, Analyze Text Features

Literary Elements: Act and Scene, Drama, Stage Directions, Voice, Speaker

Writing Product: Expository Essay

Vocabulary: Context Clues, Synonyms, Word Usage

Grammar: Commas to Prevent Misreading or Confusion

Part 2 *Believing in Yourself*

Part 2 *Reading for Enjoyment*

UNIT THREE

WHAT'S More Important, the Journey or the Destination?

Part 1 — *Difficult Paths*

Part 2 *Memorable Places*

UNIT FOUR

WHAT'S Worth Fighting For?

BQ Explore the **BIG** Question

Part 1 — Society and the World

Part 2 *Freedom and Fairness*

UNIT FIVE

WHAT
Really Matters?

BQ Explore the **BIG** Question

Part 1 *Personal Connections*

Part **2** *Social Issues*

Part 3 · Scientific Matters

HOW Do You Keep from Giving Up?

BQ Explore the **BIG** Question

Finding Strength from Within

Speaking, Listening, and Viewing Workshop

Unit Challenge

Reference Section

Selections by Genre

Fiction

Poetry

Drama

Folktales and Myths

Graphic Story

Nonfiction

Essays

Features

Skills Workshops

How to Use *Glencoe Literature*

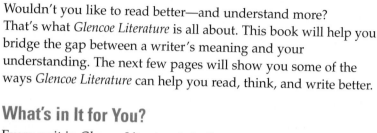

Wouldn't you like to read better—and understand more? That's what *Glencoe Literature* is all about. This book will help you bridge the gap between a writer's meaning and your understanding. The next few pages will show you some of the ways *Glencoe Literature* can help you read, think, and write better.

What's in It for You?

Every unit in *Glencoe Literature* is built around a **Big Question,** a question that you will want to think about, talk about, maybe even argue about, and finally answer. The unit's reading selections will help you come up with your answers.

Organization

Each unit contains:

- A **Unit Opener** that introduces and helps you explore the unit's Big Question. A short reading selection uses the themes of the unit's **Parts** to guide you through ways of approaching the Big Question.

- **Literature selections** such as short stories, poems, plays, and biographies.

- **Informational texts** such as nonfiction; newspaper, online, and magazine articles; textbook lessons; and interviews.

- A **Genre Focus** that guides you through the features of a main genre from the unit.

- **Functional documents** such as signs, schedules, letters, and instructions.

- A **Comparing Literature** feature that gives you a chance to compare and contrast pieces of writing.

- A **Writing Workshop** to help you express your ideas about the Big Question through a specific form of writing.

- A **Speaking, Listening, and Viewing Workshop** to help you make oral presentations and become a better listener.

- A **Unit Challenge** where you'll answer the Big Question.

Reading and Thinking

As an active reader, you'll use *Glencoe Literature* to develop your reading and thinking skills.

BEFORE YOU READ sets the stage for the selection and previews the skills and strategies that will guide your reading.

MEET THE AUTHOR introduces you to the real-life story of the writer whose work you will read and write about. ·······················

The **LITERARY ELEMENT** and the **READING SKILL** or **STRATEGY** give you the basic tools you will use to read and analyze the selection. ···········

As you read the **LITERATURE SELECTIONS**, you will see that parts of the text are highlighted in different colors. On the side of the page are ········· color-coded questions that help you think about and understand the highlighted text.

VOCABULARY A new vocabulary word is in **bold** type when it first appears in the reading selection. ....

VOCABULARY The word and its pronunciation, part of speech, and definition appear at the bottom of the same page. ....

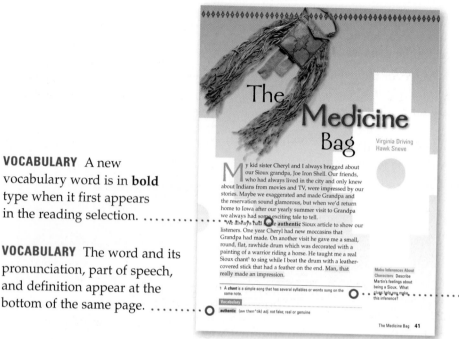

The Medicine Bag

Virginia Driving Hawk Sneve

My kid sister Cheryl and I always bragged about our Sioux grandpa, Joe Iron Shell. Our friends, who had always lived in the city and only knew about Indians from movies and TV, were impressed by our stories. Maybe we exaggerated and made Grandpa and the reservation sound glamorous, but when we'd return home to Iowa after our yearly summer visit to Grandpa we always had some exciting tale to tell.

We always had some **authentic** Sioux article to show our listeners. One year Cheryl had new moccasins that Grandpa had made. On another visit he gave me a small, round, flat, rawhide drum which was decorated with a painting of a warrior riding a horse. He taught me a real Sioux chant[1] to sing while I beat the drum with a leather-covered stick that had a feather on the end. Man, that really made an impression.

Make Inferences About Characters Describe Martin's feelings about being a Sioux. What clues help you make this inference?

1 A *chant* is a simple song that has several syllables or words sung on the same note.

Vocabulary

authentic (aw then´tik) *adj.* not fake; real or genuine

The Medicine Bag   **41**

FOOTNOTES Selection footnotes explain words or phrases that you may not know to help you understand the story.

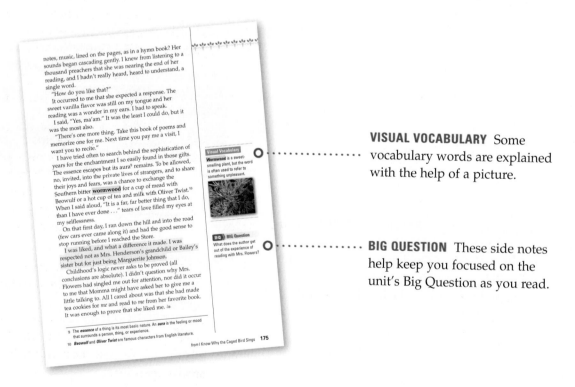

notes, music, lined on the pages, as in a hymn book? Her sounds began cascading gently. I knew from listening to a thousand preachers that she was nearing the end of her reading, and I hadn't really heard, heard to understand, a single word.

"How do you like that?"

It occurred to me that she expected a response. The sweet vanilla flavor was still on my tongue and her reading was a wonder in my ears. I had to speak.

I said, "Yes, ma'am." It was the least I could do, but it was the most also.

"There's one more thing. Take this book of poems and memorize one for me. Next time you pay me a visit, I want you to recite."

I have tried often to search behind the sophistication of years for the enchantment I so easily found in those gifts. The essence escapes but its aura[9] remains. To be allowed, no, invited, into the private lives of strangers, and to share their joys and fears, was a chance to exchange the Southern bitter **wormwood** for a cup of mead with Beowulf or a hot cup of tea and milk with Oliver Twist.[10] When I said aloud, "It is a far, far better thing that I do, than I have ever done . . ." tears of love filled my eyes at my selflessness.

On that first day, I ran down the hill and into the road (few cars ever came along it) and had the good sense to stop running before I reached the Store.

I was liked, and what a difference it made. I was respected not as Mrs. Henderson's grandchild or Bailey's sister but for just being Marguerite Johnson.

Childhood's logic never asks to be proved (all conclusions are absolute). I didn't question why Mrs. Flowers had singled me out for attention, nor did it occur to me that Momma might have asked her to give me a little talking to. All I cared about was that she had made tea cookies for *me* and read to *me* from her favorite book. It was enough to prove that she liked me.

Visual Vocabulary
Wormwood is a sweet-smelling plant, but the word is often used to refer to something unpleasant.

BQ Big Question
What does the author get out of the experience of reading with Mrs. Flowers?

9   The *essence* of a thing is its most basic nature. An *aura* is the feeling or mood that surrounds a person, thing, or experience.

10 *Beowulf* and *Oliver Twist* are famous characters from English literature.

from *I Know Why the Caged Bird Sings*   **175**

VISUAL VOCABULARY Some vocabulary words are explained with the help of a picture.

BIG QUESTION These side notes help keep you focused on the unit's Big Question as you read.

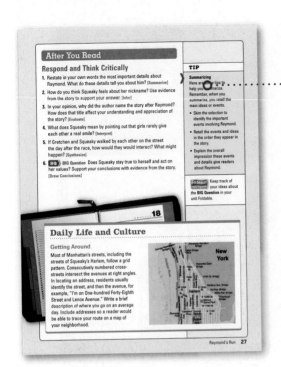

Wrap up the selection with **AFTER YOU READ**. Explore what you have learned through a wide range of reading, thinking, vocabulary, and writing activities.

Vocabulary

VOCABULARY WORDS may be new to you or seem difficult, but they are important words. Vocabulary words from each selection are introduced on the **BEFORE YOU READ** page. Each word is accompanied by its pronunciation, its part of speech, its definition, and the page number on which it first appears. The vocabulary word is also used in a sample sentence. The first appearance of each

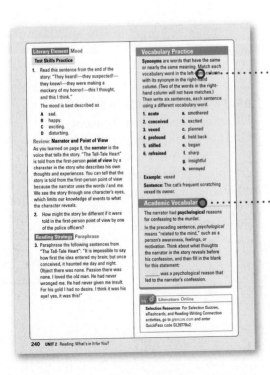

VOCABULARY PRACTICE On the **AFTER YOU READ** pages, you will be able to practice using the vocabulary words in an exercise. This exercise will show you how to use a vocabulary strategy to understand new or difficult words.

ACADEMIC VOCABULARY Many of the **AFTER YOU READ** pages also introduce you to examples of academic vocabulary. These are words that you come across in your schoolwork. You will be asked to use these words to answer questions.

Organizing Information

FOLDABLES For every unit, you'll be shown how to make a *Foldable* that will help you keep track of your thoughts about the Big Question. See page R8 for more about Foldables. ·····························

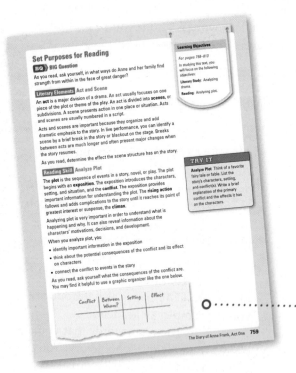

GRAPHIC ORGANIZERS In *Glencoe Literature*, you will use different kinds of graphic organizers to help you arrange information. These graphic organizers include, among others, Venn diagrams, compare and contrast charts, cluster diagrams, and chain-of-events charts.

Writing Workshops

Each unit in *Glencoe Literature* includes a Writing Workshop. The workshop walks you through the writing process as you work on an extended piece of writing related to the unit.

- You will use helpful strategies to meet writing goals.

- You will learn tips and polish your critical thinking skills as you analyze workshop models.

- You will focus on mastering specific aspects of writing, including organization, grammar, and vocabulary.

- You will use a writing plan to evaluate your own writing.

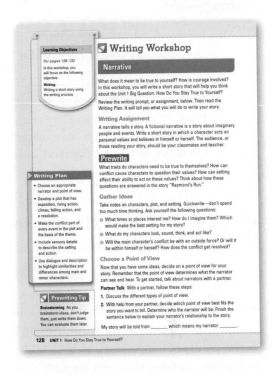

Assessment

Following each unit, you will be tested on the literature, reading, and vocabulary skills you learned. This test will give you the practice you need to succeed while providing an assessment of your understanding of the unit objectives.

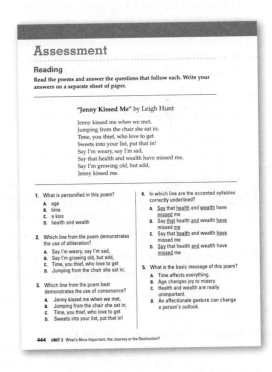

Reading and Thinking with Foldables®

by Dinah Zike, M.Ed., Creator of Foldables®

Foldables® are three-dimensional interactive graphic organizers for taking notes and organizing your ideas. They're also fun! You will fold paper, cut tabs, write, and manipulate what you have made in order to organize information; review skills, concepts, and strategies; and assess your learning.

Using Dinah Zike's Foldables in Reading and Literature Classes

Use Foldables before, during, and after reading selections in *Glencoe Literature*.

- **Before you read:** Your unit Foldable will help you focus on your purpose for reading by reminding you about the Big Question.

- **During reading:** Your unit Foldable will help you stay focused and engaged. It will also help you track key ideas and your thoughts about each selection to help you answer the Big Question. Using the Foldable will also encourage you to use higher level thinking skills in approaching text.

- **After you read:** Your unit Foldable will help you review your thoughts from your reading

and analyze, interpret, and evaluate various aspects of the Big Question. Your Foldable notes will also help you with your unit challenge. These notes can stimulate rich group discussions and inquiry as well.

 **FOLDABLES®** **Study Organizer**

As you read, you'll make notes about the Big Question. Later, you'll use these notes to complete the Unit Challenge. See pages R8–R9 for help with making Foldable 1. This diagram shows how it should look. ○ ⋯

> **Become an active reader. Track and reorganize information so that you can better understand the selection.**

1. Make one page for each selection. At the end of the unit, you'll staple the pages together into one Foldable.

2. Label the front of the fold-over page with the selection ○ ⋯⋯⋯ title.

> **Practice reading and following step-by-step directions.**

3. Open the fold-over page. On the right side, write the label My Purpose for Reading.

4. Open the Foldable all the way. At the top center, write the label The Big Question.

Selection title here

> **Use the illustrations that make the directions easier to follow.**

Be Computer Safe and Smart

Cyber Safety

As you explore the *Glencoe Literature* program, you will have many opportunities to go online. When you use the Internet at school or home, you enter a kind of community—the cyber world. In this online world, you need to follow safety rules and to protect yourself. Here are some tips to keep in mind:

- ☑ Be a responsible cyber citizen. Use the Internet to share knowledge that makes people's lives better. Respect other people's feelings and do not break any laws.

- ☑ Beware of cyber bullying. People can be hurt and embarrassed by comments that have been made public. You should immediately tell your teacher or counselor if you feel threatened by another student's computer postings.

- ☑ Do not give out personal information, such as your address and telephone number, without your parents' or guardians' permission.

- ☑ Tell your teacher, parent, or guardian right away if you find or read any information that makes you feel uneasy or afraid.

- ☑ Do not e-mail your picture to anyone.

- ☑ Do not open e-mail or text messages from strangers.

- ☑ Do not tell anyone your Internet password.

- ☑ Do not make illegal copies of computer games and programs or CD-ROMs.

Words To Know

cyber world the world of computers and high-tech communications

cyber safety actions that protect Internet users from harm

cyber ethics responsible code of conduct for using the Internet

cyber bully a person who uses technology to frighten, bother, or harm someone else

cyber citizen a person who uses the Internet to communicate

LOG ON ▶ **Literature** Online

For more about Internet safety and responsibility, go to glencoe.com.

Reading Handbook

The What, Why, and How of Reading

You'll need to use the skills and strategies in the following chart to respond to questions and prompts in the selections. As you begin a new lesson, look carefully at the **Reading Skill or Strategy** on the **Before You Read** pages. Then find those skills and strategies in this chart and read about what they are, how to use them, and why they're important. The more you refer to the chart, the more these active reading skills and strategies will become a natural part of the way you read.

What is it?	Why is it important?	How to do it
Preview Previewing is looking over a selection before you read.	Previewing lets you begin to see what you already know and what you'll need to know. It helps you set a purpose for reading.	Look at the title, illustrations, headings, captions, and graphics Look at how ideas are organized. Ask questions about the text.
Skim Skimming is looking over an entire selection quickly to get a general idea of what the piece is about.	Skimming will tell you what a selection is about. If the selection you skim isn't what you're looking for, you won't need to read the entire piece.	Read the title of the selection and quickly look over the entire piece. Read headings and captions and maybe part of the first paragraph to get a general idea of the selection's content.
Scan Scanning is glancing quickly over a selection in order to find specific information.	Scanning helps you pinpoint information quickly. It saves you time when you have a number of selections to look at.	As you move your eyes quickly over the lines of text, look for key words or phrases that will help you locate the information you're looking for.
Predict Predicting is taking an educated guess about what will happen in a selection.	Predicting gives you a reason to read. You want to find out if your prediction and the selection events match, don't you? As you read, adjust or change your prediction if it doesn't fit what you learn.	Combine what you already know about an author or subject with what you learned in your preview to guess what will be included in the text.
Set a Purpose Setting a purpose for reading is deciding why you are reading.	Setting a purpose for reading helps you decide on the reading strategies you use with a text.	Ask yourself if you are reading to understand new information, to find specific information, or to be entertained.

What is it?	Why is it important?	How to do it
Clarify Clarifying is looking at difficult sections of text in order to clear up what is confusing.	Authors often build ideas one on another. If you don't clear up a confusing passage, you may not understand main ideas or information that comes later.	Go back and reread a confusing section more slowly. Look up words you don't know. Ask questions about what you don't understand. Sometimes you may want to read on to see if further information helps you.
Question Questioning is asking yourself whether information in a selection is important. Questioning is also regularly asking yourself whether you've understood what you've read.	When you ask questions as you read, you're reading strategically. As you answer your questions, you're making sure that you'll get the gist of a text.	Have a running conversation with yourself as you read. Keep asking: Is this idea important? Why? Do I understand what this is about? Might this information be on a test later?
Visualize Visualizing is picturing a writer's ideas or descriptions in your mind's eye.	Visualizing is one of the best ways to understand and remember information in fiction, nonfiction, and informational text.	Carefully read how a writer describes a person, place, or thing. Then ask yourself: What would this look like? Can I see how the steps in this process would work?
Monitor Comprehension Monitoring your comprehension means thinking about whether you're understanding what you're reading.	The whole point of reading is to understand a piece of text. When you don't understand a selection, you're not really reading it.	Keep asking yourself questions about main ideas, characters, and events. When you can't answer a question, review, read more slowly, or ask someone to help you.
Identify Sequence Identifying sequence is finding the logical order of ideas or events.	In a work of fiction, events are usually presented in chronological (time) order. With nonfiction, understanding the logical sequence of ideas in a piece helps you follow a writer's train of thought. You'll remember ideas better when you know the logical order a writer uses.	Ask yourself what the author is trying to do: Tell a story? Explain how something works? Present information? Look for clues or signal words that might point to time order, steps in a process, or order of importance.
Connect Connecting means linking what you read to events in your own life or to other selections you've read.	You'll "get into" your reading and recall information and ideas better by connecting events, emotions, and characters to your own life.	Ask yourself: Do I know someone like this? Have I ever felt this way? What else have I read that is like this selection?

What is it?	Why is it important?	How to do it
Summarize Summarizing is stating the main ideas of a selection in your own words and in a logical sequence.	Summarizing shows whether you've understood something. It teaches you to rethink what you've read and to separate main ideas from supporting information.	Ask yourself: What is this selection about? Answer who, what, where, when, why, and how? Put that information in a logical order.
Determine Main Idea Determining an author's main idea is finding the most important thought in a paragraph or in a selection.	Finding main ideas gets you ready to summarize. You also discover an author's purpose for writing when you find the main ideas in a selection.	Think about what you know about the author and the topic. Look for how the author organizes ideas. Then look for the one idea that all of the sentences in a paragraph or all the paragraphs in a selection are about.
Respond Responding is telling what you like, dislike, or find surprising or interesting in a selection.	When you react in a personal way to what you read, you'll enjoy a selection more and remember it better.	As you read, think about how you feel about story elements or ideas in a selection. What's your reaction to the characters in a story? What grabs your attention as you read?
Review Reviewing is going back over what you've read to remember what's important and to organize ideas so you'll recall them later.	Reviewing is especially important when you have new ideas and a lot of information to remember.	Filling in a graphic organizer, such as a chart or diagram, as you read helps you organize information. These study aids will help you review later.
Interpret Interpreting is when you use your own understanding of the world to decide what the events or ideas in a selection mean. It's more than just understanding and remembering the facts.	Every reader constructs meaning on the basis of what he or she understands about the world. Finding meaning as you read is all about you interacting with the text.	Think about what you already know about yourself and the world. Ask yourself: What is the author really trying to say here? What larger idea might these events be about?
Infer Inferring is when you use your reason and experience to guess what an author does not come right out and say.	Making inferences is a large part of finding meaning in a selection. Inferring helps you look more deeply at characters and points you toward the theme or message in a selection.	Look for clues the author provides. Notice descriptions, dialogue, events, and relationships that might tell you something the author wants you to know.

What is it?	Why is it important?	How to do it
Draw Conclusions Drawing a conclusion is using a number of pieces of information to make a general statement about people, places, events, and ideas.	Drawing conclusions helps you find connections between ideas and events. It's another tool to help you see the larger picture.	Notice specific details about characters, ideas, and events as you read. Can you make a general statement on the basis of these details? For example, do a character's actions lead you to conclude that he or she is kind?
Analyze Analyzing is looking at separate parts of a selection in order to understand the entire selection.	Analyzing helps you look critically at a piece of writing. When you analyze a selection, you'll discover its theme or message, and you'll learn the author's purpose for writing.	To analyze a story, think about what the author is saying through the characters, the setting, and the plot. To analyze nonfiction, look at how the writer has organized main ideas. What do those ideas suggest?
Synthesize Synthesizing is combining ideas in order to reach a new understanding.	Synthesizing helps you move to a higher level of thinking. Creating something new of your own goes beyond remembering what you learned from someone else.	Think about the ideas or information you've learned in a selection. Ask yourself: Do I understand something more than the main ideas here? Can I create something else from what I now know?
Evaluate Evaluating is making a judgment or forming an opinion about something you have read. You can evaluate a character, an author's purpose, or the reliability of information in an article or text.	Evaluating can help you become a wise, sensible reader. Many selections—especially text you read online—require careful judgments about an author's qualifications and about the reliability of information presented.	As you read, ask yourself: Is this character realistic and believable? Is this author qualified to write on this subject? Is this author biased? Does this author present opinions as facts?

HOW Do You Stay True to Yourself?

THE **BIG** Question

> " *If you don't understand yourself, you don't understand anybody else.* "
>
> —NIKKI GIOVANNI

FOLDABLES®
Study Organizer

Unit 1 Big Question

How Do You Stay True to Yourself?

Throughout Unit 1, you will read, write, and talk about the **BIG** Question— "How Do You Stay True to Yourself?" Use your Unit 1 **Foldable**, shown here, to keep track of your ideas as you read. Turn to the back of this book for instructions on making this **Foldable.**

HOW Do You Stay True to Yourself?

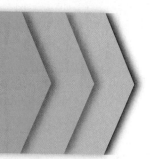

You have read about understanding yourself in the Nikki Giovanni quotation on page 1. Your values and beliefs define who you are. When you face tough choices, your principles may give you the best guidance in making good decisions. By staying true to yourself, you can conquer the toughest challenges.

Think about ways to stay true to yourself:

○ Acting on Your Values

○ Believing in Yourself

What You'll Read

What can you learn from **short fiction,** brief works about imaginary people and events? As you read, think about how characters deal with problems similar to yours. How do they decide what's right? In what ways do they act on their values? In this unit, you will read different types of short fiction, including literary sketches, short stories, and folktales that provide answers to the question: How do you stay true to yourself?

What You'll Write

As you explore the Big Question, you'll write notes in your Unit 1 **Foldable.** Later, you'll use these notes to complete two writing assignments related to the big question.

1. **Write a Narrative**

2. **Choose a Unit Challenge**

   ○ **On Your Own Activity: Create a Values Chart**

   ○ **Group Activity: Perform and Videotape a Scene**

What You'll Learn

Literary Elements

narrator and point of view

plot

repetition

character

style

short fiction

conflict

theme

setting

narrative poetry

Reading Skills and Strategies

make predictions about plot

monitor comprehension

visualize

make inferences about characters

activate prior knowledge

analyze characters

preview

determine main idea and supporting details

identify sequence

summarize

MIRACLE MAN

SAM BLAIR

In the next 24 seconds, one team would be crowned the college football national champions. The University of Southern California needed just one more defensive play to win the title. The University of Texas needed something just short of a miracle. A miracle—or a special play by Texas's do-it-all quarterback, Vince Young. Texas, trailing by 5 points in the 2006 Rose Bowl game, faced fourth down on the Southern Cal eight-yard line. Everyone in burnt orange—Longhorn fans, players, coaches—was worried. But Young had it all under control.

"I had my angels behind me," he says. "I had my team and my fans behind me. I really don't get nervous."

NEVER GIVE UP

Young, now in his first season with the National Football League's Tennessee Titans, received the snap from center. He retreated several steps, watching his receivers spread across the field. . . . "I stayed poised and relaxed," Young says. "Then I saw an opening and scored."

Young swerved right, eluding one desperate tackler around the five-yard line, then took two long, almost casual strides into the end zone for a touchdown. A successful 2-point conversion with 19 seconds left gave the Longhorns a 41–38 lead and the national championship. The Trojans, the defending champions, were stunned.

Other top teams had been stunned by Young, too.

In the 2005 Rose Bowl, Texas beat Michigan, 38–37, after Young moved his team into field-goal range just before time expired. Last September, the Longhorns

Set a Purpose for Reading

Read to discover how Vince Young stays true to himself.

BQ BIG Question

Vince Young has plenty of confidence. In what way can confidence help you stay true to yourself?

beat Ohio State, 25–22, on Young's touchdown pass to Limas Sweed with 2:37 left.

ON THE WRONG PATH

Young felt great pressure earlier in his life, but it wasn't on a football field.

At 7, he had a head-on collision with a car while riding his bike without a helmet. He underwent surgery to repair internal injuries and shortly after the accident starred in a public-service announcement encouraging kids on bikes to wear helmets.

At 12, his life really exploded. Young was arrested and handcuffed for fighting on the campus of Dick Dowling Middle School.

Felicia Young, struggling to raise Vince and his two older sisters alone for the most part, was steaming mad when she arrived to take her son home.

"Keep going the way you're going and you'll end up in the hospital, in jail, or dead!" she screamed.

That was Vince's wake-up call.

CHANGE FOR THE BETTER

"I started concentrating more on football and other sports and trying to educate myself in my books," Young says. "Things took off from there."

His coaches and uncles helped him along. Then he entered James Madison High School as a freshman and met a father figure in football coach Ray Seals.

Today Seals sits in his small office in the Madison boys' gymnasium and proudly talks about his best athlete in 40 years of coaching.

"Vincent was like most kids—playful and mischievous,"[1] Seal says. "He came in to talk a lot. Not about football, about life. We talked about the potential he had and how you work it right. He just believed he could do anything."

Young's mom had a spiritual conversion the summer before he entered Madison that changed her children's lives as well as her own. Felicia Young returned to her

BQ ▶ **BIG Question**
In what way did poor decisions threaten Vince Young's future?

BQ ▶ **BIG Question**
How did Vince Young act on his values?

---

1 A **mischievous** (mis′ chə vəs) kid is playful in a harmful or annoying way.

old church, Mount Horeb Missionary Baptist, with her children, looking for guidance and support.

KEEPING IT REAL

The church is in the heart of the Fourth Ward, a community established by former slaves shortly after they learned of the Emancipation Proclamation[2] on June 19, 1865. Dr. Samuel Smith Jr. has served as pastor there for 42 years.

Dr. Smith, coach Seals, and Young's coaches at Texas say they are proud of his work with young people. On a lovely spring Saturday morning, Young and his pastor walked together, leading a parade of youngsters through the aging neighborhood to their church. . . . Young posed for photos and autographed white T-shirts bearing the words, "Keeping It Real With Vince Young."

Young told the kids how proud he was to be there and gave them some advice: "Stay in school. Work hard. Be respectful. Have fun—but in a good way."

Young received similar advice when he was in school. The adviser: Steve McNair, the quarterback the Titans traded to Baltimore this summer to make room for Young.

"I've learned a lot from Steve," Young says. "Off the field I try to carry myself in the same way: humble, giving back to the community. On the field, I'll be strong and competitive all the time—especially when the team really needs me."

ONE OF THE GREATS

Now expectations are high as Young continues his career in the NFL.

"We're very excited about the things he can do," Titans coach Jeff Fisher says. "The arm strength, the leadership qualities, all the intangible things."

Texas coach Mack Brown expects another outstanding chapter in Young's career.

"He competes as hard as anyone I've ever been around," Brown says. "There's no downside. If he stays healthy, he'll be one of the great ones to ever play."

Vince Young of the Tennessee Titans

BQ ▸ **BIG Question**

How does Vince Young stay true to himself both on and off the playing field?

---

2 On January 1, 1863, President Abraham Lincoln issued the ***Emancipation Proclamation,*** which freed all enslaved people living in the Confederate states.

After You Read

Respond and Think Critically

1. In your own words, restate the most important points in the article. Then compare your work with the article, making sure that you have included the article's main ideas, critical details, and the underlying meaning. **[Summarize]**

2. What does it mean when the writer says that Vince's "life really exploded" at age 12? **[Interpret]**

3. What do you suppose is the writer's opinion of Vince Young? **[Infer]**

4. Based on what you've learned about Young, list some actions you could take in order to reach such admirable goals. **[Synthesize]**

Writing

Write a Journal Entry Think about Vince Young's efforts to stay true to himself. How does reading about Vince help you think about your own values and beliefs? Record your thoughts in a short journal entry. You may want to begin with this sentence:

"I have always felt that _____, until _____."

Think about what's important to you. What lessons can you learn from the way Vince Young has lived his life?

Learning Objectives

For page 6

In this assignment, you will focus on the following objectives:

Reading: Analyzing and evaluating biography.

Connecting to contemporary issues.

Writing: Writing a journal entry.

Vince Young waits on the sidelines.

 Literature Online

Unit Resouces For additional skills practice, go to glencoe.com and enter QuickPass code GL39770u1.

Acting on Your Values

Tree Planting. Artist Unknown.

BQ **BIG Question** **How Do You Stay True to Yourself?**

How are the people in the picture showing that they value the environment?
What actions might you take to show the things you value in your community?

My Name and *Bums in the Attic*

Learning Objectives

For pages 8–12

In studying this text, you will focus on the following objective:

Literary Study: Analyzing narrator and point of view.

Connect to the Short Fiction

Think about something you would like to do but are not sure how, such as changing your name or moving to an exotic new place.

Quickwrite Describe in a few sentences something you dream about doing in the future. Tell how you might achieve your dream.

Build Background

"My Name" and "Bums in the Attic" are literary sketches from the book *The House on Mango Street* by Sandra Cisneros. The main character, a teenager named Esperanza, tells stories about growing up in a Latino neighborhood in Chicago.

- The literary sketches describe the people Esperanza meets while growing up on Mango Street.

- *The House on Mango Street* reflects the life experiences of the author, Sandra Cisneros.

Set Purposes for Reading

BQ ▶ **BIG Question**

Read "My Name" and "Bums in the Attic" to find out what Esperanza values.

Literary Elements Narrator and Point of View

The **narrator** is the person who tells the story. The narrator's point of view depends on his or her relationship to the story. In **first-person** point of view, the narrator is a character in the story and tells the story in his or her own words. In **third-person** point of view, the narrator is someone outside the story. If a story is told from a **third-person omniscient,** or all-knowing, point of view, the narrator sees into the minds of multiple characters. If events are described from a **third-person limited** point of view, the narrator relates the thoughts, actions, and feelings of only one character.

Meet Sandra Cisneros

Storyteller and Poet Sandra Cisneros was born in Chicago, the only daughter in a family with seven children. Her family frequently moved between the United States and Mexico. As a result, Cisneros often felt lonely and unsettled. Throughout her childhood, she spent much of her time reading and writing.

Literary Works Cisneros is the author of many poems, stories, and novels. Her first book of fiction, *The House on Mango Street* (1984), is her most highly praised work. *Caramelo* (2002) is her most recent novel.

Sandra Cisneros was born in 1954.

My Name

Sandra Cisneros

Portrait of Virginia, 1929. Frida Kahlo. Oil on canvas, 76.5 x 59.5 cm. ©Banco de Mexico Trust. ©ARS, NY.

*I*n English my name means hope. In Spanish it means too many letters. It means sadness, it means waiting. It is like the number nine. A muddy color. It is the Mexican records my father plays on Sunday mornings when he is shaving, songs like sobbing.

It was my great-grandmother's name and now it is mine. She was a horse woman too, born like me in the Chinese year of the horse—which is supposed to be bad luck if you're born female—but I think this is a Chinese lie because the Chinese, like the Mexicans, don't like their women strong.

<u>View the Art</u> Consider the colors the artist has chosen to use in this painting. What message do the colors help to convey about the girl's personality?

Narrator and Point of View
The narrator uses the words *my, mine,* and *me* to refer to herself. Based on this information, what is the point of view of this story?

My great-grandmother. I would've liked to have known her, a wild horse of a woman, so wild she wouldn't marry. Until my great-grandfather threw a sack over her head and carried her off. Just like that, as if she were a fancy chandelier.[1] That's the way he did it.

And the story goes she never forgave him. She looked out the window her whole life, the way so many women sit their sadness on an elbow. I wonder if she made the best with what she got or was she sorry because she couldn't be all the things she wanted to be. Esperanza. I have inherited her name, but I don't want to inherit her place by the window.

At school they say my name funny as if the syllables were made out of tin and hurt the roof of your mouth. But in Spanish my name is made out of a softer something, like silver, not quite as thick as sister's name—Magdalena— which is uglier than mine. Magdalena who at least can come home and become Nenny. But I am always Esperanza.

I would like to baptize myself under a new name, a name more like the real me, the one nobody sees. Esperanza as Lisandra or Maritza or Zeze the X. Yes. Something like Zeze the X will do. 🔊

BQ **BIG Question**
In what way do Esperanza's feelings about her name reflect her ability to stay true to herself and her values?

---

1 A *chandelier* is a fancy light fixture that hangs from the ceiling.

Bums in the Attic

Sandra Cisneros

Peyrlebade, 1896–97. Odilon Redon. Oil on canvas. Musee d'Orsay, Paris.

I want a house on a hill like the ones with the gardens where Papa works. We go on Sundays, Papa's day off. I used to go. I don't anymore. You don't like to go out with us, Papa says. Getting too old? Getting too stuck-up, says Nenny. I don't tell them I am ashamed—all of us staring out the window like the hungry. I am tired of looking at what we can't have. When we win the lottery[2] . . . Mama begins, and then I stop listening.

People who live on hills sleep so close to the stars they forget those of us who live too much on earth. They don't look down at all except to be content to live on hills. They have nothing to do with last week's garbage or fear of rats. Night comes. Nothing wakes them but the wind.

One day I'll own my own house, but I won't forget who I am or where I came from. Passing bums will ask, Can I come in? I'll offer them the attic, ask them to stay, because I know how it is to be without a house.

Some days after dinner, guests and I will sit in front of a fire. Floorboards will squeak upstairs. The attic grumble.

Rats? they'll ask.

Bums, I'll say, and I'll be happy. 🦢

---

2 A *lottery* is a drawing of numbered tickets. People buy tickets to win. A drawing is held to pick the winning numbers.

Narrator and Point of View
What details tell you that this story is written from the first-person point of view?

BQ **Big Question**
How does Esperanza plan to remain true to herself and her values?

After You Read

Respond and Think Critically

1. Using your own words, describe Esperanza's feelings about her name. [Summarize]

2. What does Esperanza mean when she says she does not want to inherit her great-grandmother's place by the window? [Interpret]

3. What type of person is Esperanza? Use details from both literary sketches to support your opinion. [Synthesize]

4. According to Esperanza, what difficulties do she and her family face in trying to fit in with society? Support your answer with examples. [Analyze]

5. **Literary Elements** Narrator and Point of View Consider why Sandra Cisneros uses a first-person point of view in these works. Why might it be better to have Esperanza, and not an outsider, tell her story?

6. **BQ** BIG Question Explain in your own words how Esperanza stays true to her values while wanting to have a better life away from Mango Street. [Draw Conclusions]

Academic Vocabulary

In "Bums in the Attic," Esperanza decides that a **priority** in her life is to someday own a home.

Using context clues and an example from the story, try to figure out the meaning of the word *priority* in the sentence above. Check your guess in the dictionary.

 Writing

Write a Journal Entry What has gone well for you during the past week? What has been disappointing? Write about the good and bad things you have recently experienced. What did you learn from them? Could things have been better or worse?

TIP

Interpreting
Here are some tips to help you interpret. Remember when you interpret, you think about what the author is communicating through her use of language.

- Skim the selection to see how Esperanza describes her great-grandmother.

- Think about the ideas the author is communicating through Esperanza's description of her great-grandmother.

- Tell what you learned about Esperanza's viewpoint from this description.

FOLDABLES Keep track of
Study Organizer your ideas about
the **BIG Question** in your
unit Foldable.

Selection Resources
For Selection Quizzes, eFlashcards, and Reading-Writing Connection activities, go to glencoe.com and enter QuickPass code GL39770u1.

Raymond's Run

Connect to the Short Story

The nicknames that usually stick to a person are the ones that capture a distinctive trait, good or bad. Think about how a nickname can sum up a person in a word or two.

Quickwrite Freewrite for a few minutes about a nickname that would irritate you and one that would suit you perfectly. Why would a certain nickname annoy you? How might another nickname tell people what you're all about? Would you feel differently about the names depending on who used them, when, and where? What are some pitfalls of using nicknames, whether those names emphasize positive or negative traits?

Build Background

"Raymond's Run" is a short story about a young African-American girl who prides herself on being the fastest runner in the neighborhood.

- This modern story takes place in Harlem, a section of New York City.
- A fast runner might earn the nickname "Mercury" after the Roman god known for speed. Statues show Mercury with a winged hat and winged sandals.

Vocabulary

liable (lī′ ə bəl) *adj.* likely; apt (p. 18). *A person who is afraid of spiders is liable to scream at the sight of a tarantula.*

sidekicks (sīd′ kiks) *n.* close friends or companions (p. 18). *The magician's sidekicks are always on stage.*

reputation (rep′ yə tā′ shən) *n.* what people generally think about the character of a person or thing; good name (p. 19). *A reputation for kindness can take a lifetime of good deeds to build.*

static (stat′ ik) *n.* crackling or hissing sounds that interrupt normal sounds, such as those from a microphone (p. 23). *Static crackles as you try to tune in to a radio station with a weak signal.*

Meet Toni Cade Bambara

"I write because I really think I've got hold of something, that if I share it, . . . might lift someone's spirits, or enable someone to see more clearly."
—Toni Cade Bambara

Making a Difference Toni Cade Bambara's writing presents a rich portrayal of African-American life. Her works also show the unfair treatment of women and minorities. Bambara was a professor and a civil rights activist.

Literary Works Bambara is the author of a novel, short stories, essays, and screenplays. "Raymond's Run" was first published in 1971 in *Tales and Stories for Black Folks*.

Toni Cade Bambara was born in 1939 and died in 1995.

 Literature Online

Author Search For more about Toni Cade Bambara, go to glencoe.com and enter QuickPass code GL39770u1.

Set Purposes for Reading

BQ BIG Question

What beliefs, values, or ideas have the strongest influence on how you act? Is honesty your greatest value? Or is it courage or kindness? As you read, think about the values that the narrator's words, thoughts, and actions show.

Literary Element Plot

Plot is the sequence of events in stories. Most plots include the following five parts, or stages. A plot begins with the **exposition,** which introduces the story's main characters, setting and situation. The **rising action** adds complexity to the story's conflicts, or problems. The **climax** is the point of greatest interest or suspense. The **falling action** shows the result of the climax and brings the story to a close. The **resolution** presents the story's final outcome.

As you read "Raymond's Run," identify each plot element.

Reading Strategy Make Predictions About Plot

When you **make predictions about plot,** you consider details about the characters, setting, and situation and make educated guesses about what will happen. As you read, look for clues that suggest what might happen next and then make predictions. Later, as you continue to read, verify or adjust your predictions.

A graphic organizer like the one below can help you make predictions about the plot and check your predictions. As you read, note each new situation and make a prediction based on clues from the story. Then check to see if your prediction was correct.

Situation	Prediction	What Really Happens

TRY IT

Two of your friends argue about a science project they are working on. They have been good friends for a long time, but they have been arguing about a lot of things lately. What do you predict will happen between them? Explain your prediction.

Raymond's Run

Toni Cade Bambara

I don't have much work to do around the house like some girls. My mother does that. And I don't have to earn my pocket money by hustling; George runs errands for the big boys and sells Christmas cards. And anything else that's got to get done, my father does. All I have to do in life is mind my brother Raymond, which is enough.

Sometimes I slip and say my little brother Raymond. But as any fool can see he's much bigger and he's older too. But a lot of people call him my little brother cause he needs looking after cause he's not quite right. And a lot of smart mouths got lots to say about that too, especially when George was minding him. But now, if anybody has anything to say to Raymond, anything to say about his big head[1], they have to come by me. And I don't play the dozens[2] or believe in standing around with somebody in my face doing a lot of talking. I much rather just knock

Make Predictions About Plot Based on this clue, what predictions can you make about conflicts that may arise for the narrator?

Beatrice's Trainers. Emily Patrick. Oil on panel. Private Collection.

---

1 Raymond's **big head** may be the result of *hydrocephaly* (hī′ drə sef′ ə lē), a condition in which fluid is trapped around the brain, damaging the brain and enlarging the skull.

2 **Play the dozens** refers to an exchange of insulting remarks.

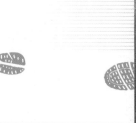

Petite Fille, 1982. Lois Mailou Jones. Watercolor, 24 x 30 in. Courtesy of the artist.

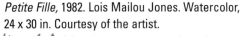 **View the Art** In what way or ways does the subject of this painting remind you of Squeaky? Explain your thoughts.

you down and take my chances even if I am a little girl with skinny arms and a squeaky voice, which is how I got the name Squeaky. And if things get too rough, I run. And as anybody can tell you, I'm the fastest thing on two feet.

There is no track meet that I don't win the first place medal. I used to win the twenty-yard dash when I was a little kid in kindergarten. Nowadays, it's the fifty-yard dash. And tomorrow I'm subject to run the quarter-meter relay all by myself and come in first, second, and third. The big kids call me Mercury cause I'm the swiftest thing in the neighborhood. Everybody knows that—except two people who know better, my father and me. He can beat me to Amsterdam Avenue with me having a two fire-hydrant headstart and him running with his hands in his pockets and whistling. But that's private information. Cause can you imagine some thirty-five-year-old man stuffing himself into PAL shorts to race little kids? So as far as everyone's concerned, I'm the fastest and that goes for Gretchen, too, who has put out the tale that she is going to win the first-place medal this year. Ridiculous. In the second place, she's got short legs. In the third place, she's got freckles. In the first place, no one can beat me and that's all there is to it.

Plot Which stage of the plot is this sentence part of? How can you tell from this sentence and the rest of the paragraph?

I'm standing on the corner admiring the weather and about to take a stroll down Broadway so I can practice my breathing exercises, and I've got Raymond walking on the inside close to the buildings, cause he's subject to fits of fantasy and starts thinking he's a circus performer and that the curb is a tightrope strung high in the air. And sometimes after a rain he likes to step down off his tightrope right into the gutter and slosh around getting his shoes and cuffs wet. Then I get hit when I get home. Or sometimes if you don't watch him he'll dash across traffic to the island in the middle of Broadway and give the pigeons a fit. Then I have to go behind him apologizing to all the old people sitting around trying to get some sun and getting all upset with the pigeons fluttering around them, scattering their newspapers and upsetting the waxpaper lunches in their laps. So I keep Raymond on the inside of me, and he plays like he's driving a stage coach which is o.k. by me so long as he doesn't run me over or interrupt my breathing exercises, which I have to do on account of I'm serious about my running, and I don't care who knows it.

Now some people like to act like things come easy to them, won't let on that they practice. Not me. I'll high-prance down 34th Street like a rodeo pony to keep my knees strong even if it does get my mother uptight so that she walks ahead like she's not with me, don't know me, is all by herself on a shopping trip, and I am somebody else's crazy child. Now you take Cynthia Procter for instance. She's just the opposite. If there's a test tomorrow, she'll say something like, "Oh, I guess I'll play handball this afternoon and watch television tonight," just to let you know she ain't thinking about the test. Or like last week when she won the spelling bee for the millionth time, "A good thing you got 'receive,' Squeaky, cause I would have got it wrong. I completely forgot about the spelling bee." And she'll clutch the lace on her blouse like it was a narrow escape. Oh, brother. But of course when I pass her house on my early morning trots around the block, she is practicing

BQ BIG Question

How does the author show that Squeaky is honest with herself and others?

the scales on the piano over and over and over and over. Then in music class she always lets herself get bumped around so she falls accidently on purpose onto the piano stool and is so surprised to find herself sitting there that she decides just for fun to try out the ole keys. And what do you know—Chopin's[3] waltzes just spring out of her fingertips and she's the most surprised thing in the world. A regular prodigy. I could kill people like that. I stay up all night studying the words for the spelling bee. And you can see me any time of day practicing running. I never walk if I can trot, and shame on Raymond if he can't keep up. But of course he does, cause if he hangs back someone's **liable** to walk up to him and get smart, or take his allowance from him, or ask him where he got that great big pumpkin head. People are so stupid sometimes.

So I'm strolling down Broadway breathing out and breathing in on counts of seven, which is my lucky number, and here comes Gretchen and her **sidekicks**: Mary Louise, who used to be a friend of mine when she first moved to Harlem from Baltimore and got beat up by everybody till I took up for her on account of her mother and my mother used to sing in the same choir when they were young girls, but people ain't grateful, so now she hangs out with the new girl Gretchen, and talks about me like a dog; and Rosie, who is as fat as I am skinny and has a big mouth where Raymond is concerned and is too stupid to know that there is not a big deal of difference between herself and Raymond and that she can't afford to throw stones.[4] So they are steady coming up Broadway and I see right away that it's going to be one of those Dodge City scenes cause the street ain't that big and they're close to the buildings just as we are. First I think

Plot While making the story's conflict more complex, the **rising action** also increases reader interest. How does this sentence achieve both results?

---

3 **Chopin** (shō′pan) was a nineteenth-century Polish composer famous for his short but difficult piano pieces.

4 The narrator is referring to the saying, "People who live in glass houses shouldn't **throw stones.**" It warns people not to criticize others for something that they themselves might also be criticized for.

Vocabulary ....

liable (lī′ə bəl) *adj.* likely; apt

sidekicks (sīd′kiks) *n.* close friends or companions

I'll step into the candy store and look over the new comics and let them pass. But that's chicken and I've got a **reputation** to consider. So then I think I'll just walk straight on through them or even over them if necessary. But as they get to me, they slow down. I'm ready to fight, cause like I said I don't feature a whole lot of chit-chat, I much prefer to just knock you down right from the jump and save everybody a lotta precious time.

"You signing up for the May Day races?" smiles Mary Louise, only it's not a smile at all. A dumb question like that doesn't deserve an answer. Besides, there's just me and Gretchen standing there really, so no use wasting my breath talking to shadows.

"I don't think you're going to win this time," says Rosie, trying to signify with her hands on her hips all salty,[5] completely forgetting that I have whupped her behind many times for less salt than that.

"I always win cause I'm the best," I say straight at Gretchen who is, as far as I'm concerned, the only one talking in this ventriloquist-dummy routine. Gretchen smiles, but it's not a smile, and I'm thinking that girls never really smile at each other because they don't know how and don't want to know how and there's probably no one to teach us how, cause grown-up girls don't know either. Then they all look at Raymond who has just brought his mule team to a standstill. And they're about to see what trouble they can get into through him.

"What grade you in now, Raymond?"

"You got anything to say to my brother, you say it to me, Mary Louise Williams of Raggedy Town, Baltimore."

"What are you, his mother?" sasses Rosie.

"That's right, Fatso. And the next word out of anybody and I'll be *their* mother too." So they just stand there and Gretchen shifts from one leg to the other and so do they.

Plot Identify the stage of the plot. How does the dialogue add to the conflict at this stage?

Make Predictions About Plot The May Day race could have one of two outcomes for Squeaky. Which outcome do you predict, and how do you think Squeaky will react?

---

5 Here, *signify* is slang for "to stir things up; cause trouble for fun." This is what Rosie is trying to do by being *salty*, or critical and sarcastic.

Vocabulary

reputation (rep′yə tā′shən) *n.* what people generally think about the character of a person or thing; good name

Harlem Jig, 2001. Colin Bootman. Private Collection.
View the Art How does this scene in the painting compare with the way you imagine the setting of the story? Explain.

Then Gretchen puts her hands on her hips and is about to say something with her freckle-face self but doesn't. Then she walks around me looking me up and down but keeps walking up Broadway, and her sidekicks follow her. So me and Raymond smile at each other and he says, "Gidyap" to his team and I continue with my breathing exercises, strolling down Broadway toward the ice man on 145th with not a care in the world cause I am Miss Quicksilver[6] herself.

---

6 **Quicksilver** is another name for the metal mercury, which was named for the swift Roman god. At room temperature, the silver-colored metal is liquid and flows rapidly.

I take my time getting to the park on May Day because the track meet is the last thing on the program. The biggest thing on the program is the May Pole dancing, which I can do without, thank you, even if my mother thinks it's a shame I don't take part and act like a girl for a change. You'd think my mother'd be grateful not to have to make me a white organdy[7] dress with a big satin sash and buy me new white baby-doll shoes that can't be taken out of the box till the big day. You'd think she'd be glad her daughter ain't out there prancing around a May Pole getting the new clothes all dirty and sweaty and trying to act like a fairy or a flower or whatever you're supposed to be when you should be trying to be yourself, whatever that is, which is, as far as I am concerned, a poor Black girl who really can't afford to buy shoes and a new dress you only wear once a lifetime cause it won't fit next year.

I was once a strawberry in a Hansel and Gretel pageant when I was in nursery school and didn't have no better sense than to dance on tiptoe with my arms in a circle over my head doing umbrella steps and being a perfect fool just so my mother and father could come dressed up and clap. You'd think they'd know better than to encourage that kind of nonsense. I am not a strawberry. I do not dance on my toes. I run. That is what I am all about. So I always come late to the May Day program, just in time to get my number pinned on and lay in the grass till they announce the fifty-yard dash.

I put Raymond in the little swings, which is a tight squeeze this year and will be impossible next year. Then I look around for Mr. Pearson, who pins the numbers on. I'm really looking for Gretchen if you want to know the truth, but she's not around. The park is jam-packed. Parents in hats and corsages and breast-pocket handkerchiefs peeking up. Kids in white dresses and light-blue suits. The parkees[8] unfolding chairs and chasing the rowdy kids from Lenox[9] as if they had no right to be there.

---

7 **Organdy** is a lightweight fabric, usually made of cotton.

8 The city's park employees are the **parkees.**

9 **Lenox** is an avenue that runs through Harlem.

The big guys with their caps on backwards, leaning against the fence swirling the basketballs on the tips of their fingers, waiting for all these crazy people to clear out the park so they can play. Most of the kids in my class are carrying bass drums and **glockenspiels** and flutes. You'd think they'd put in a few bongos or something for real like that.

Then here comes Mr. Pearson with his clipboard and his cards and pencils and whistles and safety pins and fifty million other things he's always dropping all over the place with his clumsy self. He sticks out in a crowd because he's on stilts. We used to call him Jack and the Beanstalk to get him mad. But I'm the only one that can outrun him and get away, and I'm too grown for that silliness now.

"Well, Squeaky," he says, checking my name off the list and handing me number seven and two pins. And I'm thinking he's got no right to call me Squeaky, if I can't call him Beanstalk.

"Hazel Elizabeth Deborah Parker," I correct him and tell him to write it down on his board.

"Well, Hazel Elizabeth Deborah Parker, going to give someone else a break this year?" I squint at him real hard to see if he is seriously thinking I should lose the race on purpose just to give someone else a break. "Only six girls running this time," he continues, shaking his head sadly like it's my fault all of New York didn't turn out in sneakers. "That new girl should give you a run for your money." He looks around the park for Gretchen like a periscope in a submarine movie. "Wouldn't it be a nice gesture if you were . . . to ahhh . . ."

I give him such a look he couldn't finish putting that idea into words. Grownups got a lot of nerve sometimes. I pin number seven to myself and stomp away, I'm so burnt. And I go straight for the track and stretch out on the grass while the band winds up with "Oh, the Monkey Wrapped His Tail Around the Flag Pole," which my teacher calls by some other name. The man on the loudspeaker is calling everyone over to the track and I'm on my back looking at the sky, trying to pretend I'm in the country, but I can't,

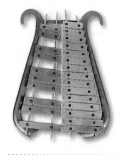
Make Predictions About Plot How does this sentence affect your prediction about whether Squeaky will win the May Day race?

because even grass in the city feels hard as sidewalk, and there's just no pretending you are anywhere but in a "concrete jungle" as my grandfather says.

The twenty-yard dash takes all of two minutes cause most of the little kids don't know no better than to run off the track or run the wrong way or run smack into the fence and fall down and cry. One little kid, though, has got the good sense to run straight for the white ribbon up ahead so he wins. Then the second-graders line up for the thirty-yard dash and I don't even bother to turn my head to watch cause Raphael Perez always wins. He wins before he even begins by psyching[10] the runners, telling them they're going to trip on their shoelaces and fall on their faces or lose their shorts or something, which he doesn't really have to do since he is very fast, almost as fast as I am. After that is the forty-yard dash which I used to run when I was in first grade. Raymond is hollering from the swings cause he knows I'm about to do my thing cause the man on the loudspeaker has just announced the fifty-yard dash, although he might just as well be giving a recipe for angel food cake cause you can hardly make out what he's sayin for the **static**. I get up and slip off my sweat pants and then I see Gretchen standing at the starting line, kicking her legs out like a pro. Then as I get into place I see that ole Raymond is on line on the other side of the fence, bending down with his fingers on the ground just like he knew what he was doing. I was going to yell at him but then I didn't. It burns up your energy to holler.

Every time, just before I take off in a race, I always feel like I'm in a dream, the kind of dream you have when you're sick with fever and feel all hot and weightless. I dream I'm flying over a sandy beach in the early morning sun, kissing the leaves of the trees as I fly by. And there's always the smell of apples, just like in the country when I

Make Predictions About Plot Do you think Squeaky or Gretchen will win the race? Why?

---

10 **Psyching** the runners means scaring or intimidating them.

Vocabulary ....

static (stat′ik) *n.* crackling or hissing sounds that interrupt normal sounds, such as those from a microphone

was little and used to think I was a choo-choo train, running through the fields of corn and chugging up the hill to the orchard. And all the time I'm dreaming this, I get lighter and lighter until I'm flying over the beach again, getting blown through the sky like a feather that weighs nothing at all. But once I spread my fingers in the dirt and crouch over the Get on Your Mark, the dream goes and I am solid again and am telling myself, Squeaky you must win, you must win, you are the fastest thing in the world, you can even beat your father up Amsterdam if you really try. And then I feel my weight coming back just behind my knees then down to my feet then into the earth and the pistol shot explodes in my blood and I am off and weightless again, flying past the other runners, my arms pumping up and down and the whole world is quiet except for the crunch as I zoom over the gravel in the track. I glance to my left and there is no one. To the right, a blurred Gretchen, who's got her chin jutting out as if it would win the race all by itself. And on the other side of the fence is Raymond with his arms down to his side and the palms tucked up behind him, running in his very own style, and it's the first time I ever saw that and I almost stop to watch my brother Raymond on his first run. But the white ribbon is bouncing toward me and I tear past it, racing into the distance till my feet with a mind of their own start digging up footfuls of dirt and brake me short. Then all the kids standing on the side pile on me, banging me on the back and slapping my head with their May Day programs, for I have won again and everybody on 151st Street can walk tall for another year.

"In the first place . . ." the man on the loudspeaker is clear as a bell now. But then he pauses and the loudspeaker starts to whine. Then static. And I lean down to catch my breath and here comes Gretchen walking back, for she's overshot the finish line too, huffing and puffing with her hands on her hips taking it slow, breathing in steady time like a real pro and I sort of like her a little for

Plot The most important turning point, the **climax** starts to make the outcome of the conflict clear. What do these lines begin to tell you about the outcome of Squeaky and Gretchen's rivalry?

the first time. "In first place . . ." and then three or four voices get all mixed up on the loudspeaker and I dig my sneaker into the grass and stare at Gretchen who's staring back, we both wondering just who did win. I can hear old Beanstalk arguing with the man on the loudspeaker and then a few others running their mouths about what the stopwatches say. Then I hear Raymond yanking at the fence to call me and I wave to shush him, but he keeps rattling the fence like a gorilla in a cage like in them gorilla movies, but then like a dancer or something he starts climbing up nice and easy but very fast. And it occurs to me, watching how smoothly he climbs hand over hand and remembering how he looked running with his arms down to his side and with the wind pulling his mouth back and his teeth showing and all, it occurred to me that Raymond would make a very fine runner. Doesn't he always keep up with me on my trots? And he surely knows how to breathe in counts of seven cause he's always doing it at the dinner table, which drives my brother George up the wall. And I'm smiling to beat the band cause if I've lost this race, or if me and Gretchen tied, or even if I've won, I can always retire as a runner and begin a whole new career as a coach with Raymond as my champion. After all, with a little more study I can beat Cynthia and her phony self at the spelling bee. And if I bugged my mother, I could get piano lessons and become a star. And I have a big rep as the baddest thing around. And I've got a roomful of ribbons and medals and awards. But what has Raymond got to call his own?

So I stand there with my new plans, laughing out loud by this time as Raymond jumps down from the fence and runs over with his teeth showing and his arms down to the side, which no one before him has quite mastered as a running style. And by the time he comes over I'm jumping up and down so glad to see him—my brother Raymond, a great runner in the family tradition. But of course everyone thinks I'm jumping up and down because the men on the loudspeaker have finally gotten themselves

together and compared notes and are announcing "In first place—Miss Hazel Elizabeth Deborah Parker." (Dig that.) "In second place—Miss Gretchen P. Lewis." And I look over at Gretchen wondering what the "P" stands for. And I smile. Cause she's good, no doubt about it. Maybe she'd like to help me coach Raymond; she obviously is serious about running, as any fool can see. And she nods to congratulate me and then she smiles. And I smile. We stand there with this big smile of respect between us. It's about as real a smile as girls can do for each other, considering we don't practice real smiling every day, you know, cause maybe we too busy being flowers or fairies or strawberries instead of something honest and worthy of respect . . . you know . . . like being people. ❧

Plot Coming at the end of a narrative, the **resolution** reveals the outcome of the conflict. Is the resolution of the plot the most important part of this story? Why or why not?

Make Predictions About Plot Verify your predictions about the resolution of the plot. In what ways are the actual events of the story similar to or different from what you had expected?

Spring Reservoir, 1997. Max Ferguson. Oil on canvas. Private Collection.

View the Art What parts of this painting reflect the May Day setting of the story?

After You Read

Respond and Think Critically

1. Restate in your own words the most important details about Raymond. What do these details tell you about him? [Summarize]

2. How do you think Squeaky feels about her nickname? Use evidence from the story to support your answer. [Infer]

3. In your opinion, why did the author name the story after Raymond? How does that title affect your understanding and appreciation of the story? [Evaluate]

4. What does Squeaky mean by pointing out that girls rarely give each other a real smile? [Interpret]

5. If Gretchen and Squeaky walked by each other on the street the day after the race, how would they would interact? What might happen? [Synthesize]

6. **BQ** BIG Question Does Squeaky stay true to herself and act on her values? Support your conclusions with evidence from the story. [Draw Conclusions]

TIP

Summarizing
Here are some tips to help you summarize. Remember, when you summarize, you retell the main ideas or events.

- Skim the selection to identify the important events involving Raymond.

- Retell the events and ideas in the order they appear in the story.

- Explain the overall impression these events and details give readers about Raymond.

FOLDABLES **Study Organizer** Keep track of your ideas about the **BIG Question** in your unit Foldable.

Daily Life and Culture

Getting Around

Most of Manhattan's streets, including the streets of Squeaky's Harlem, follow a grid pattern. Consecutively numbered cross-streets intersect the avenues at right angles. In locating an address, residents usually identify the street, and then the avenue, for example, "I'm on One-hundred Forty-Eighth Street and Lenox Avenue." Write a brief description of where you go on an average day. Include addresses so a reader would be able to trace your route on a map of your neighborhood.

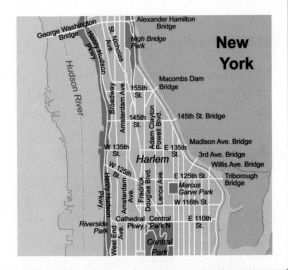

Literary Element Plot

Test Skills Practice

1. What conflict does Squeaky face and how is it resolved? Support your answer with details and information from the story.

2. What other conflicts can you see in the story? In what way or ways do additional conflicts make the story more interesting? Support your answer with details and information from the story.

Review: Narrator and Point of View

As you learned on page 8, a **narrator** is the person or character who tells a story.

Point of view is the relationship of the narrator to the story. In a story with **first-person point of view,** the story is told by one of the characters. The reader generally sees everything through that character's eyes.

3. Which item below tells the narrator and point of view of "Raymond's Run"?
   A   Raymond, first person
   B   outside narrator, third person
   C   Squeaky, first person
   D   Squeaky, third person

Reading Strategy

Make Predictions About Plot

Test Skills Practice

4. Which quotation from the story helps you predict that Raymond will become a runner?
   A   "he needs looking after, cause he's not quite right."
   B   "Doesn't he always keep up with me on my trots?"
   C   "he's subject to fits of fantasy and starts thinking he's a circus performer."
   D   "I've got Raymond walking on the inside close to the buildings."

Vocabulary Practice

Choose the sentence that uses the vocabulary word correctly.

1. **A.** You are **liable** to feel hungry if you skip lunch.

   B. I knew that Maria would arrive at the celebration on time because she is very **liable**.

2. **A.** The police chief immediately sent a **reputation** of the best officers to the crime scene.

   B. Tomas feared that a bad grade in his biology class would ruin his **reputation**.

3. **A.** The brand new car was badly damaged after **sidekicks** with a huge truck.

   B. Teresa really believed that she and Dominique would be best friends and **sidekicks** for life.

4. **A.** William turned on the radio to hear the basketball game, but all he could get was **static.**

   B. Donell had done so well in school and at sports that he felt quite **static.**

Academic Vocabulary

After she ran the May Day race, Squeaky's **perspective** on her future changed.

In the preceding sentence, *perspective* means outlook. Think about a time when your outlook or view of the world changed. What caused the change in your perspective?

LOG ON ▶ **Literature** Online

Selection Resources For Selection Quizzes, eFlashcards, and Reading-Writing Connection activities, go to glencoe.com and enter QuickPass code GL39770u1.

Respond Through Writing

Research Report

Investigate the Science of Running In a research report, investigate the science of running. Include details, ideas, and direct quotations about how runners can prepare by stretching, how muscles work during a run, and the effect of brain chemicals during a run. If you find varying perspectives, paraphrase or summarize them. Use primary sources (such as a runner's account) and secondary sources (such as a book on the science of running). Be sure to distinguish between primary and secondary sources.

Understand the Task In your report, you will explain changes that occur in a runner's body during and after a run.

Prewrite To help organize your research, fill out a graphic organizer like the one below. List questions you would like to answer. As you do your research, write answers to your questions.

Before Running	During Running	After Running
Why is it important to stretch?	What happens to a runner's muscles?	Why do runners often feel better after they run?

Draft Sometimes it's helpful to use sentence frames as you draft a report. For instance, your introduction will include a thesis statement that tells the purpose of your paper, which might be stated as follows:

Many changes occur in a runner's body during a run, including _____, _____, and _____.

Your body paragraphs will discuss the topics you've introduced in your thesis, such as the following:

The first change a runner experiences is _____.

Revise Trade papers with a partner. Ask your partner to underline your thesis statement. Then ask your partner to highlight two changes that a runner experiences. If your partner has difficulty finding this information, you may need to revise your writing to clarify your thesis.

Edit and Proofread Proofread your paper, correcting any errors in spelling, grammar, and punctuation. Review the Grammar Tip in the side column for information on correct capitalization.

Learning Objectives

For page 29

In studying this text, you will focus on the following objectives:

Writing:
Write a research report using primary and secondary sources.

Record and organize ideas during research.

> **Grammar Tip**

Capitalization
Look at these two sentences. One drink name is capitalized and the other is not. Why?

Many runners like Gorpo because it comes in a powder form that they can mix with enough water to get a taste they prefer.

Bottles of lemonade can also give runners energy, and water can be added if the taste is too strong.

Capitalize brand names and trademarks of specific products. Names of nonspecific products, such as lemonade, are not capitalized.

And Ain't I a Woman?

Connect to the Speech

Think about a time when you learned of a situation in which someone wasn't being treated fairly.

Quickwrite Freewrite for a few minutes from the point of view of the person who wasn't treated fairly. What could you say to encourage others to treat you differently?

Build Background

Sojourner Truth gave the speech "And Ain't I a Woman?" at a women's rights convention in Ohio in 1851.

- At the time of the convention, women did not have the right to vote in elections.

- On the second day of the convention, a number of male ministers insisted that women were too weak and not smart enough to vote. One man gave religious reasons against the right of women to vote.

- Sojourner Truth's speech is her answer to these men.

Vocabulary

borne (bôrn) v. given birth to (p. 33).
She has borne four children.

intellect (int′əl ekt′) n. power of mind to know, understand, and reason (p. 33).
She was a woman of intellect.

obliged (ə blījd′) v. to be grateful (p. 33).
I am much obliged to you for your kindness.

Meet Sojourner Truth

A Traveling Preacher
Born into slavery, Sojourner Truth endured backbreaking work and cruel treatment. At age 29, she escaped from slavery. At age 46, she took the name Sojourner Truth. A sojourner is a person who never stays in one place very long. As a traveling preacher, Truth began speaking against slavery and in support of women's rights.

Helping the Nation During the Civil War, Truth helped gather supplies for African-American volunteer regiments. Toward the end of the war, Truth moved to Washington, D.C. There she worked with the National Freedmen's Relief Association, counseling former enslaved people.

Sojourner Truth was born in 1797 and died in 1883.

 Literature Online

Author Search For more about Sojourner Truth, go to glencoe.com and enter QuickPass code GL39770u1.

Set Purposes for Reading

BQ BIG Question

Your values are what you find important in your life and part of what makes you who you are. As you read, identify the values that are most important to Sojourner Truth. How does she act on her values?

Literary Element Repetition

Repetition is the repeating of sounds, words, phrases, or lines in a piece of writing. Repetition is often used in persuasive speeches to emphasize a speaker's point.

In speeches, repetition strengthens the message by reminding the audience of the main idea. Repetition can also build a speech to a climax that raises emotions or moves the audience to action.

As you read, think about the idea Sojourner Truth emphasizes through repetition.

Reading Strategy Monitor Comprehension

When you **monitor comprehension,** you think about whether you're understanding what you're reading. Imagine you are reading instructions on how to put together a model airplane. If you do not understand what you have read, you will not be able to assemble the model correctly.

To monitor your comprehension, pause to think about what you have read.

- Ask questions about what you do not understand.
- Write notes about what you *do* know.
- Read ahead to look for a main idea.

As you read the speech, use a graphic organizer like the one below. If you find something confusing, write a question. Look for details in the speech that help answer your question. Write your answer and identify the detail or details that you used.

Question:

Answer:

Detail:

TRY IT

Monitor Comprehension Read to understand the paragraph below about light from a star. On a sheet of paper, write questions about what you do not understand or would like to know more about. Then reread more slowly to clarify.

When you look at a star, you see light that left the star many years ago. The light that you see travels fast. Still, the distances across space are so great that it takes years for the light to reach Earth— sometimes millions of years.

And Ain't I a Woman?

In Sojourner Truth I Fought for the Rights of Women as Well as Blacks, 1947. Elizabeth Catlett. Linocut, 15 x 22.5 cm. Private Collection. Art ©Elizabeth Cattlet/Licensed by VAGA, New York, NY.

View the Art Based on this image, what qualities does Sojourner Truth seem to possess? Explain your answer.

That man over there says that women need to be helped into **carriages,** and lifted over ditches, and to have the best place everywhere. Nobody ever helps me into carriages, or over mud-puddles, or gives me any best place! And ain't I a woman? Look at me! Look at my arm. I have ploughed and planted, and gathered into barns, and no man could head[1] me! And ain't I a woman? I could work as much and eat as much as a man—when I could get it—and bear

---

1 In this speech, *head* means "to do something better than someone else."

Visual Vocabulary

A **carriage** (kar′ ij) is a wheeled, usually horse-drawn vehicle designed to carry people.

the lash as well! And ain't I a woman? I have **borne** thirteen children, and seen them most all sold off to slavery, and when I cried out with my mother's grief, none but Jesus heard me! And ain't I a woman?

Then they talk about this thing in the head; what's this they call it? [**Intellect,** someone whispers.] That's it, honey. What's that got to do with women's rights or Negroes[2] rights? If my cup won't hold but a pint, and yours holds a quart, wouldn't you be mean not to let me have my little half-measure full?

Then that little man in black there, he says women can't have as much rights as men, 'cause Christ wasn't a woman! Where did your Christ come from? Where did your Christ come from? From God and a woman! Man had nothing to do with Him.

If the first woman God ever made was strong enough to turn the world upside down all alone, these women together ought to be able to turn it back, and get it right side up again! And now they is asking to do it, the men better let them.

Obliged to you for hearing me, and now old Sojourner ain't got nothing more to say. 🐚

Repetition Why do you think Sojourner Truth repeats this question?

Monitor Comprehension Reread to clarify. What point about equality is Sojourner Truth trying to make with this question?

BQ **BIG Question** What actions does Sojourner Truth support in this paragraph? Explain how these actions relate to Truth's values.

---

2 The term ***Negroes*** meant "African Americans" at the time Truth made this speech. Truth is referring to the rights of African Americans.

Vocabulary ....

borne (bôrn) *v.* given birth to

intellect (int′ əl ekt′) *n.* power of mind to know, understand, and reason

obliged (ə blījd′) *v.* to be grateful

This photograph was taken in Belton, South Carolina, in 1899. These women did not have the right to vote, and their husbands and sons were denied their legal rights, too.

After You Read

Respond and Think Critically

1. What three main ideas about women is Sojourner Truth responding to in this speech? **[Summarize]**

2. What is Truth really saying each time she repeats "And ain't I a woman"? **[Infer]**

3. What does Truth mean by the sentence, "If the first woman God ever made was strong enough to turn the world upside down all alone, these women together ought to be able to turn it back, and get it right side up again!"? **[Interpret]**

4. **Literary Element** Repetition Truth repeats the question "And ain't I a woman?" What other question does she repeat? Would her speech have had the same impact without those questions? Explain. **[Evaluate]**

5. **Reading Strategy** Monitor Comprehension Truth says, "And now they is asking to do it, the men better let them." Think of one question and one detail that would help you understand that sentence. Then explain what the sentence means. **[Examine]**

6. **BQ** **BIG Question** In what ways were you affected by Sojourner Truth's speech? What did it show you about the importance of acting on your values? Explain your opinion. **[Connect]**

Vocabulary Practice

Choose the sentence that uses the vocabulary word correctly.

1. **A.** Amalia was **borne** in July 1998.

   B. Katherine had **borne** five children before she was 40.

2. **A.** Manuel was filled with **intellect** about his exams.

   B. Claire's **intellect** showed in her academic achievements.

3. **A.** Ethan was **obliged** when he forgot his keys.

   B. Elena was **obliged** to babysit her sister.

Writing

Write a Letter Do you ever feel like your rights are not respected because you are a teenager? Make a list of ways in which teenagers' rights are not respected. Then choose one or two of those rights. Write a persuasive letter that you would send to a newspaper arguing in favor of the right or rights for teenagers. Use repetition in your letter to emphasize your point.

TIP

Inferring
Inferring is using your reason and experience to figure out what an author does not come right out and say directly. When you infer, you do the following:

- Look for details that direct you toward what you want to know.

- Look more deeply at the selection's main message.

 Keep track of your ideas about the **BIG Question** in your unit Foldable.

 Literature Online

Selection Resources
For Selection Quizzes, eFlashcards, and Reading-Writing Connection activities, go to glencoe.com and enter QuickPass code GL39770u1.

from Sojourner Truth:
Ain't I a Woman?

By Patricia C. and Fredrick McKissack

Coretta Scott King Award

Set a Purpose for Reading

Read to understand the impact of Sojourner
Truth's speech at the Ohio convention.

Build Background

In this excerpt, some words from Sojourner
Truth's speech are slightly different from those in
the version you've just read. Truth never wrote
down the speech, so different versions survive.

Reading Strategy Visualize

The **setting** of a piece of writing is the time and
place in which the events occur. When you
visualize the setting, you create a picture of it in
your mind. As you read, use a chart like the one
below to note details the writers use to help you
visualize the setting. Then note the feeling, or
mood, that these details create.

Detail	Feeling

Sojourner was lecturing in Ohio
when someone told her there
was going to be a Woman's Rights
Convention in Akron, Ohio, organized
by Mrs. Frances Gage.[1] Sojourner
decided to attend.

Hundreds of men and women
gathered at a local church to hear what
the various speakers had to say. Clearly
the audience was of mixed opinions on
the subject of women's rights. Most of
the men had come with unyielding[2]
prejudices, clergymen mostly who tried
to discredit the women's movement as
anti-Christian. A few women had come
accompanied by their enlightened
husbands or male companions. Some
women came alone, but with their

---

1   Mrs. *Frances Gage* was a vocal participant in the
    antislavery and women's rights movements in Ohio in
    the mid-1800s.

2   Here, *unyielding* means "inflexible."

husband's or father's "permission." Then there were the seasoned feminists who came because, at last, their goals and aspirations were being addressed.

The gathering was large but for the most part congenial. Suddenly, the doors swung open and a tall, proud figure stood framed in the doorway. "It's Sojourner Truth," someone whispered. Slowly Sojourner walked to the front of the church, noticing she was the only black person there. Since there were no seats left, she took a seat on the steps to the pulpit. She folded her arms and listened.

Soon the room was buzzing. Was a black woman going to speak?

One speaker after another came to the podium, each trying to impress his or her opinion upon the crowd. Several preachers tried to disrupt the meeting by encouraging women "who feared God" to leave immediately. When that didn't work, the preachers used the same tired logic that had been used for centuries to oppress women and blacks. *God created women to be weak and blacks to be a subservient[3] race.*

One clergyman argued that Jesus was a man and that if God had intended women to be equal He "would have at that time made some gesture to show his intent."

Another man quoted a newspaper article which suggested that "a woman's place is at home taking care of her children." (*What?* thought

A painted portrait of Sojourner Truth.

Sojourner. *Nobody ever gave me that opportunity.*)

Then, of course, there was the persistent argument that woman had sinned first and therefore revealed her inferiority.

During a brief intermission, a group of women cornered Frances Gage and questioned whether Sojourner would be allowed to speak. They were afraid that having a black woman speak might confuse the issues and even discredit their cause. After all, *what has women's rights to do with abolition?*[4]

---

3 Here, **subservient** means "in a position of slavery."

4 Here, **abolition** refers to the ending of the enslavement of African Americans in the United States.

Some of the "leading"[5] ladies were threatening to leave.

"Let's just see," Mrs. Gage answered, making no commitment either way.

When the next session began, Sojourner approached the pulpit. "No, no, don't let her speak," several men and women called out.

Sojourner turned to the chairwoman asking for permission. Gage hesitated momentarily, then simply introduced her, "Sojourner Truth." That's all that was needed.

By then Sojourner was used to facing hostile crowds. Fearlessly, but gently, she took control of the situation. First, she removed her sunbonnet, folded it neatly and set it aside. Her slow deliberate movements had a calming affect on the audience.

All morning she'd listened to preachers—men who ought to know better—use the Bible to support their own dead-end purposes. She was furious and ready to do battle using God's own truth. With no prepared speech in front of her she began in a deep, husky voice:

"Well, Children, where there is so much racket, there must be somethin' out of kilter. . . . The white men will be in a fix[6] pretty soon. But what's all this about anyway?

"That man over there," she said pointing to a minister who had said a woman's place was to be mother, wife and companion, good sister, and loving niece. Among other things he also said women were the "weaker sex."

To this Sojourner took issue. "He says women need to be helped into carriages and lifted over ditches and to have the best everywhere. Nobody ever helps me into carriages, over mud puddles, or gets me any best places."

And raising herself to her full height, she asked, "And ain't I a woman?"

Sojourner turned to the men who were seated behind her. "Look at me!" She bared her right arm and raised it in the air. The audience gasped as one voice. Her dark arm was muscular, made strong by hard work. "I have ploughed. And I have planted." No doubt she was remembering the year she had worked for John Dumont to earn early freedom. "And I have gathered into barns. And no man could head[7] me. " She paused again and asked this time in a whisper. "And ain't I a woman?"

"I have borne [thirteen] children and seen them sold into slavery, and when I cried out in a mother's grief, none heard me but Jesus. And ain't I a woman?" (No doubt Sojourner was thinking about her mother but used "I" instead. Sojourner only had five children.)

---

5 In this context, *leading* means "most important."

6 The expression *in a fix* means "in a difficult situation."

7 In this speech, *head* means "to do something better than someone else."

Then one by one she took on the male religious pedants.[8] "You say Jesus was a man so that means God favors men over women. Where did your Christ come from?" She asked again. "Where did he come from?" Then she answered her own question. "From God and a woman. Man had nothing to do with him."

She challenged the widely held belief that women were less intelligent than men, and blacks had no intellect at all. "Suppose a man's mind holds a quart, and woman's don't hold but a pint; if her pint is full, it's as good as a quart." Her common sense ripped at the core of male hypocrisy.[9]

Sojourner directed her conclusion to the women in the audience. "If the first woman God ever made was strong enough to turn the world upside down all alone, these women together ought to be able to turn it back and get it right-side up again and now that they are asking to do it, the men better let 'em."

Few listeners at the time could understand the full import[10] of what Sojourner Truth was really saying in that hard-hitting "Ain't I a Woman?" speech. It is doubtful the rural farm community was ready to accept the claim that took women's rights across the boundaries of race, class, and the bondage of slavery.

Sojourner's "truth" was simple. Racism and sexism were unacceptable to people of good reason. 🐚

---

8 **Pedants** are people who present their ideas in a dull and rigid manner with too much emphasis on rules and unimportant details.

9 **Hypocrisy** means "dishonesty."

---

10 **Import** means "meaning."

Respond and Think Critically

1. Write a summary of the main events in this excerpt. [Summarize]

2. Think about the comments of the preachers who tried to disrupt the meeting. What general statements can you make about these men and the ideas they were trying to express? [Draw Conclusions]

3. A number of people didn't want to let Truth speak at the convention. Some of the women even wondered, "what has women's rights to do with abolition?" The writers do not come right out and answer this question. What do you think their answer would be? [Infer]

4. **Text-to-Text** The writers explain that Sojourner Truth did not prepare a speech. How does knowing she was influenced by the speakers before her help you better understand the speech "And Ain't I a Woman?" [Connect]

5. **Reading Strategy** Visualize List at least two details that helped you visualize the setting. What feeling, or mood, did each detail create? Use the notes in your chart to help you answer. [Examine]

6. **BQ** **BIG Question** What obstacles did Sojourner Truth face in staying true to herself? How did her words and attitude show that she believed in herself? [Make Judgments]

The Medicine Bag

Connect to the Short Story

Think about a tradition that has been passed down through your family.

Partner Talk With a partner, talk about your family tradition. Is it something you enjoy or does it just seem like something you have to do? Do you think this family tradition is worth keeping? Share your ideas with the class.

Build Background

In "The Medicine Bag," Martin, a suburban teenager, connects with his family traditions during a visit from his Sioux great-grandfather.

- The Sioux are a Native American people who live in the Great Plains. The Plains, a vast stretch of prairie land, extend from Montana to Texas.

- Martin's great-grandfather lives on a reservation, a designated area that the United States government set aside for Native Americans to live on after they were forced from their land.

Vocabulary

authentic (aw then′ tik) *adj.* not fake; real or genuine (p. 41). *The painting in the museum was an authentic work of Pablo Picasso.*

stately (stāt′ lē) *adj.* impressive or dignified (p. 42). *A new suit and tie gave Mr. Crawford a very stately appearance.*

embrace (em brās′) *v.* to clasp in the arms; hug (p. 43). *The mother and daughter wanted to embrace after not seeing each other for some time.*

sheepishly (shēp′ ish lē) *adv.* with embarrassment; with a feeling of being at fault (p. 44). *The student sheepishly offered an apology to the teacher for coming to biology class late.*

Meet Virginia Driving Hawk Sneve

"I try to present an accurate portrayal of American Indian life as I have known it."

—Virginia Driving Hawk Sneve

Native American Roots Virginia Driving Hawk Sneve grew up on the Rosebud Reservation in South Dakota. She left the reservation to attend a boarding high school. After college, she became a teacher. Sneve says her grandmothers gave her a love of Indian traditions and storytelling.

Literary Works Sneve has written many books about the history and culture of Native American peoples. "The Medicine Bag" was published in 1975.

Virginia Driving Hawk Sneve was born in 1933.

 Literature Online

Author Search For more about Virginia Driving Hawk Sneve, go to glencoe.com and enter QuickPass code GL39770u1.

Set Purposes for Reading

BQ BIG Question

We all have values—what we believe to be right or worthwhile. As you read, identify the values of each main character. What's important to the character? Are the character's actions in keeping with his or her values?

Literary Element Character

A **character** is a person, an animal, or an imaginary creature in a literary work. Characters can either be dynamic or static. **Dynamic characters** grow and change during a story. **Static characters** remain the same throughout a story.

Pay attention to what characters think, feel, and do. You will find that main characters are often dynamic characters. They are described in detail, so readers learn not only about their appearance and actions but their hopes and fears.

As you read "The Medicine Bag," ask yourself which characters are static and which are dynamic.

Reading Strategy Make Inferences About Characters

When you **make inferences,** you are making a guess based on clues. You use clues in the text and your own knowledge to figure out something that the writer does not tell you directly.

Making inferences is important because it helps you understand characters and situations much more deeply than you would otherwise.

To make inferences about characters, focus on how the character acts, how the character looks, what the character says, and what others say about the character. As you read, use a graphic organizer like the one below to help you make inferences about characters.

Type of Clue	Example	Inferences
• Character's Action	• constantly jingles keys	• nervous
• Character's Appearance	• hair isn't combed and clothes are wrinkled	• messy
• What Character Says	• "Don't ask questions. Just do as I say."	• bossy
• What Other Characters Say	• "Be careful what you tell him."	• untrustworthy

TRY IT

Make Inferences About Characters A new student is introduced to your class. When you talk to her, you notice that she always looks down at the ground and mumbles when she answers questions. What can you infer about the new girl?

The Medicine Bag

Virginia Driving
Hawk Sneve

My kid sister Cheryl and I always bragged about our Sioux grandpa, Joe Iron Shell. Our friends, who had always lived in the city and only knew about Indians from movies and TV, were impressed by our stories. Maybe we exaggerated and made Grandpa and the reservation sound glamorous, but when we'd return home to Iowa after our yearly summer visit to Grandpa we always had some exciting tale to tell.

We always had some **authentic** Sioux article to show our listeners. One year Cheryl had new moccasins that Grandpa had made. On another visit he gave me a small, round, flat, rawhide drum which was decorated with a painting of a warrior riding a horse. He taught me a real Sioux chant[1] to sing while I beat the drum with a leather-covered stick that had a feather on the end. Man, that really made an impression.

---

1 A *chant* is a simple song that has several syllables or words sung on the same note.

Make Inferences About Characters Describe Martin's feelings about being a Sioux. What clues help you make this inference?

Vocabulary ....

authentic (aw then′tik) *adj.* not fake; real or genuine

We never showed our friends Grandpa's picture. Not that we were ashamed of him, but because we knew that the glamorous tales we told didn't go with the real thing. Our friends would have laughed at the picture, because Grandpa wasn't tall and **stately** like TV Indians. His hair wasn't in braids, but hung in stringy, gray strands on his neck and he was old. He was our great-grandfather, and he didn't live in a **tipi,** but all by himself in a part log, part tar-paper shack on the Rosebud Reservation in South Dakota. So when Grandpa came to visit us, I was so ashamed and embarrassed I could've died.

There are a lot of yippy poodles and other fancy little dogs in our neighborhood, but they usually barked singly at the mailman from the safety of their own yards. Now it sounded as if a whole pack of mutts were barking together in one place.

I got up and walked to the curb to see what the commotion was. About a block away I saw a crowd of little kids yelling, with the dogs yipping and growling around someone who was walking down the middle of the street.

I watched the group as it slowly came closer and saw that in the center of the strange procession was a man wearing a tall black hat. He'd pause now and then to peer at something in his hand and then at the houses on either side of the street. I felt cold and hot at the same time as I recognized the man. "Oh, no!" I whispered. "It's Grandpa!"

I stood on the curb, unable to move even though I wanted to run and hide. Then I got mad when I saw how the yippy dogs were growling and nipping at the old man's baggy pant legs and how wearily he poked them away with his cane. "Stupid mutts," I said as I ran to rescue Grandpa.

When I kicked and hollered at the dogs to get away, they put their tails between their legs and scattered. The kids ran to the curb where they watched me and the old man.

"Grandpa," I said and felt pretty dumb when my voice cracked. I reached for his beat-up old tin suitcase, which was tied shut with a rope. But he set it down right in the street and shook my hand.

Character Describe how the narrator's feelings change. What do you learn about him?

Vocabulary

stately (stāt´lē) *adj.* impressive or dignified

♦♦♦

"*Hau, Takoza,* Grandchild," he greeted me formally in Sioux.

All I could do was stand there with the whole neighborhood watching and shake the hand of the leather-brown old man. I saw how his gray hair straggled from under his big black hat, which had a drooping feather in its crown. His rumpled black suit hung like a sack over his stooped frame. As he shook my hand, his coat fell open to expose a bright-red, satin shirt with a beaded **bolo tie** under the collar. His getup wasn't out of place on the reservation, but it sure was here, and I wanted to sink right through the pavement.

"Hi," I muttered with my head down. I tried to pull my hand away when I felt his bony hand trembling, and looked up to see fatigue in his face. I felt like crying. I couldn't think of anything to say so I picked up Grandpa's suitcase, took his arm, and guided him up the driveway to our house.

Mom was standing on the steps. I don't know how long she'd been watching, but her hand was over her mouth and she looked as if she couldn't believe what she saw. Then she ran to us.

"Grandpa," she gasped. "How in the world did you get here?"

She checked her move to **embrace** Grandpa and I remembered that such a display of affection is unseemly to the Sioux and would embarrass him.

"*Hau,* Marie," he said as he shook Mom's hand. She smiled and took his other arm.

As we supported him up the steps the door banged open and Cheryl came bursting out of the house. She was all smiles and was so obviously glad to see Grandpa that I was ashamed of how I felt.

"Grandpa!" she yelled happily. "You came to see us!"

Grandpa smiled and Mom and I let go of him as he stretched out his arms to my ten-year-old sister, who was still young enough to be hugged.

"*Wicincala,* little girl," he greeted her and then collapsed.

He had fainted. Mom and I carried him into her sewing room, where we had a spare bed.

Visual Vocabulary

A **bolo tie** is a type of necktie made of cord and fastened with a decorative clasp.

Vocabulary

embrace (em brās') *v.* to clasp in the arms; hug

After we had Grandpa on the bed Mom stood there helplessly patting his shoulder.

"Shouldn't we call the doctor, Mom?" I suggested, since she didn't seem to know what to do.

"Yes," she agreed with a sigh. "You make Grandpa comfortable, Martin."

I reluctantly moved to the bed. I knew Grandpa wouldn't want to have Mom undress him, but I didn't want to, either. He was so skinny and frail that his coat slipped off easily. When I loosened his tie and opened his shirt collar, I felt a small leather pouch that hung from a thong[2] around his neck. I left it alone and moved to remove his boots. The scuffed old cowboy boots were tight and he moaned as I put pressure on his legs to jerk them off.

I put the boots on the floor and saw why they fit so tight. Each one was stuffed with money. I looked at the bills that lined the boots and started to ask about them, but Grandpa's eyes were closed again.

Mom came back with a basin of water. "The doctor thinks Grandpa is suffering from heat exhaustion,"[3] she explained as she bathed Grandpa's face. Mom gave a big sigh, *"Oh hinh,* Martin. How do you suppose he got here?"

We found out after the doctor's visit. Grandpa was angrily sitting up in bed while Mom tried to feed him some soup.

"Tonight you let Marie feed you, Grandpa," spoke my dad, who had gotten home from work just as the doctor was leaving. "You're not really sick," he said as he gently pushed Grandpa back against the pillows. "The doctor said you just got too tired and hot after your long trip."

Grandpa relaxed, and between sips of soup he told us of his journey. Soon after our visit to him Grandpa decided that he would like to see where his only living descendants lived and what our home was like. Besides, he admitted **sheepishly,** he was lonesome after we left.

Make Inferences About Characters What does Grandpa's behavior reveal about his personality?

---

2 A ***thong*** is a narrow strap of leather or other material.

3 ***Heat exhaustion*** is dizzinesss and faintness from being in the sun too long.

Vocabulary ....

sheepishly (shēp′ish lē) *adv.* with embarrassment; with a feeling of being at fault

✦✦✦

I knew everybody felt as guilty as I did—especially Mom. Mom was all Grandpa had left. So even after she married my dad, who's a white man and teaches in the college in our city, and after Cheryl and I were born, Mom made sure that every summer we spent a week with Grandpa.

I never thought that Grandpa would be lonely after our visits, and none of us noticed how old and weak he had become. But Grandpa knew and so he came to us. He had ridden on buses for two and a half days. When he arrived in the city, tired and stiff from sitting for so long, he set out, walking, to find us.

He had stopped to rest on the steps of some building downtown and a policeman found him. The cop, according to Grandpa, was a good man who took him to the bus stop and waited until the bus came and told the driver to let Grandpa out at Bell View Drive. After Grandpa got off the bus, he started walking again. But he couldn't see the house numbers on the other side when he walked on the sidewalk so he walked in the middle of the street. That's when all the little kids and dogs followed him.

I knew everybody felt as bad as I did. Yet I was proud of this 86-year-old man, who had never been away from the reservation, having the courage to travel so far alone.

"You found the money in my boots?" he asked Mom.

"Martin did," she answered, and roused herself to scold. "Grandpa, you shouldn't have carried so much money. What if someone had stolen it from you?"

Grandpa laughed. "I would've known if anyone tried to take the boots off my feet. The money is what I've saved for a long time—a hundred dollars—for my funeral. But you take it now to buy groceries so that I won't be a burden to you while I am here."

"That won't be necessary, Grandpa," Dad said. "We are honored to have you with us and you will never be a burden. I am only sorry that we never thought to bring you home with us this summer and spare you the discomfort of a long trip."

Grandpa was pleased. "Thank you," he answered. "But do not feel bad that you didn't bring me with you for I would not have come then. It was not time." He said this in such a way that no one could argue with him. To Grandpa and the

Sioux, he once told me, a thing would be done when it was the right time to do it and that's the way it was.

"Also," Grandpa went on, looking at me, "I have come because it is soon time for Martin to have the medicine bag."

We all knew what that meant. Grandpa thought he was going to die and he had to follow the tradition of his family to pass the medicine bag, along with its history, to the oldest male child.

"Even though the boy," he said still looking at me, "bears a white man's name, the medicine bag will be his."

I didn't know what to say. I had the same hot and cold feeling that I had when I first saw Grandpa in the street. The medicine bag was the dirty leather pouch I had found around his neck. "I could never wear such a thing," I almost said aloud. I thought of having my friends see it in gym class, at the swimming pool, and could imagine the smart things they would say. But I just swallowed hard and took a step toward the bed. I knew I would have to take it.

But Grandpa was tired. "Not now, Martin," he said, waving his hand in dismissal, "it is not time. Now I will sleep."

So that's how Grandpa came to be with us for two months. My friends kept asking to come see the old man, but I put them off. I told myself that I didn't want them laughing at Grandpa. But even as I made excuses I knew it wasn't Grandpa that I was afraid they'd laugh at.

Nothing bothered Cheryl about bringing her friends to see Grandpa. Every day after school started there'd be a crew of giggling little girls or round-eyed little boys crowded around the old man on the patio, where he'd gotten in the habit of sitting every afternoon.

Grandpa would smile in his gentle way and patiently answer their questions, or he'd tell them stories of brave warriors, ghosts, animals, and the kids listened in awed silence. Those little guys thought Grandpa was great.

Finally, one day after school, my friends came home with me because nothing I said stopped them. "We're going to see the great Indian of Bell View Drive," said Hank, who was supposed to be my best friend. "My

BQ BIG Question

Why do you think Martin did not want to bring his friends to see Grandpa?

brother has seen him three times so he oughta be well enough to see us."

When we got to my house Grandpa was sitting on the patio. He had on his red shirt, but today he also wore a fringed leather vest that was decorated with beads. Instead of his usual cowboy boots he had solidly beaded moccasins on his feet that stuck out of his black trousers. Of course, he had his old black hat on—he was seldom without it. But it had been brushed and the feather in the beaded headband was proudly erect, its tip a brighter white. His hair lay in silver strands over the red shirt collar.

I stared just as my friends did and I heard one of them murmur, "Wow!"

Grandpa looked up and when his eyes met mine they twinkled as if he were laughing inside. He nodded to me and my face got all hot. I could tell that he had known all along I was afraid he'd embarrass me in front of my friends.

"*Hau, hoksilas,* boys," he greeted and held out his hand.

My buddies passed in a single file and shook his hand as I introduced them. They were so polite I almost laughed. "How, there, Grandpa," and even a "How-do-you-do, sir."

"You look fine, Grandpa," I said as the guys sat on the lawn chairs or on the patio floor.

"*Hanh,* yes," he agreed. "When I woke up this morning it seemed the right time to dress in the good clothes. I knew that my grandson would be bringing his friends."

"You guys want some lemonade or something?" I offered. No one answered. They were listening to Grandpa as he started telling how he'd killed the deer from which his vest was made.

Grandpa did most of the talking while my friends were there. I was so proud of him and amazed at how respectfully quiet my buddies were. Mom had to chase them home at supper time. As they left they shook Grandpa's hand again and said to me:

Sioux vest, Plains Indian. British Museum, London.

Character Review the actions of Martin's friends. Do they appear as static or dynamic characters?

The Medicine Bag **47**

"Martin, he's really great!"

"Yeah, man! Don't blame you for keeping him to yourself."

"Can we come back?"

But after they left, Mom said, "No more visitors for a while, Martin. Grandpa won't admit it, but his strength hasn't returned. He likes having company, but it tires him."

That evening Grandpa called me to his room before he went to sleep. "Tomorrow," he said, "when you come home, it will be time to give you the medicine bag."

I felt a hard squeeze from where my heart is supposed to be and was scared, but I answered, "OK, Grandpa."

All night I had weird dreams about thunder and lightning on a high hill. From a distance I heard the slow beat of a drum. When I woke up in the morning I felt as if I hadn't slept at all. At school it seemed as if the day would never end and, when it finally did, I ran home.

Grandpa was in his room, sitting on the bed. The shades were down and the place was dim and cool. I sat on the floor in front of Grandpa, but he didn't even look at me. After what seemed a long time he spoke.

"I sent your mother and sister away. What you will hear today is only for a man's ears. What you will receive is only for a man's hands." He fell silent and I felt shivers down my back.

"My father in his early manhood," Grandpa began, "made a vision quest[4] to find a spirit guide for his life. You cannot understand how it was in that time, when the great Teton Sioux[5] were first made to stay on the reservation. There was a strong need for guidance from *Wakantanka*, the Great Spirit. But too many of the young men were filled with despair and hatred. They thought it was hopeless to search for a vision when the glorious life was gone and only the hated confines of a reservation lay ahead. But my father held to the old ways.

Make Inferences About Characters What do you learn about Martin based on his actions in these lines?

---

4 A ***vision quest*** was a special trip made by young Sioux men to receive a dream that gave them a song or an object that protected and guided them in life.

5 The ***Teton Sioux*** are the largest Sioux tribe. They were traditionally buffalo hunters.

Portrait of an Indian, 1900.
Charles Craig.

View the Art Which
character in the story
might this person be?
Explain your answer.

"He carefully prepared for his quest with a purifying
sweat bath and then he went alone to a high butte top to
fast and pray. After three days he received his sacred
dream—in which he found, after long searching, the white
man's iron. He did not understand his vision of finding
something belonging to the white people, for in that time
they were the enemy. When he came down from the butte
to cleanse himself at the stream below, he found the
remains of a campfire and the broken shell of an iron
kettle. This was a sign which reinforced his dream. He
took a piece of the iron for his medicine bag, which he had
made of elk[6] skin years before, to prepare for his quest.

"He returned to his village, where he told his dream to
the wise old men of the tribe. They gave him the name
Iron Shell, but neither did they understand the meaning of
the dream. This first Iron Shell kept the piece of iron with
him at all times and believed it gave him protection from
the evils of those unhappy days.

"Then a terrible thing happened to Iron Shell. He and
several other young men were taken from their homes by

6 An *elk* is a very large type of deer with broad antlers.

the soldiers and sent far away to a white man's boarding school.[7] He was angry and lonesome for his parents and the young girl he had wed before he was taken away. At first Iron Shell resisted the teachers' attempts to change him and he did not try to learn. One day it was his turn to work in the school's blacksmith[8] shop. As he walked into the place he knew that his medicine had brought him there to learn and work with the white man's iron.

"Iron Shell became a blacksmith and worked at the trade when he returned to the reservation. All of his life he treasured the medicine bag. When he was old, and I was a man, he gave it to me, for no one made the vision quest any more."

Grandpa quit talking and I stared in disbelief as he covered his face with his hands. His shoulders were shaking with quiet sobs and I looked away until he began to speak again.

"I kept the bag until my son, your mother's father, was a man and had to leave us to fight in the war across the ocean. I gave him the bag, for I believed it would protect him in battle, but he did not take it with him. He was afraid that he would lose it. He died in a faraway place."

Again Grandpa was still and I felt his grief around me.

"My son," he went on after clearing his throat, "had only a daughter and it is not proper for her to know of these things."

He unbuttoned his shirt, pulled out the leather pouch, and lifted it over his head. He held it in his hand, turning it over and over as if memorizing how it looked.

"In the bag," he said as he opened it and removed two objects, "is the broken shell of the iron kettle, a pebble from the butte, and a piece of the sacred sage."[9] He held the pouch upside down and dust drifted down.

"After the bag is yours you must put a piece of prairie sage within and never open it again until you pass it on to your son." He replaced the pebble and the piece of iron, and tied the bag.

---

7 A **boarding school** is a school where students live together as well as go to school.

8 A **blacksmith** makes iron objects, such as horseshoes, kettles, and door hinges.

9 **Sage** is a sweet-smelling plant. Different varieties are used for medicine or as seasoning.

I stood up, somehow knowing I should. Grandpa slowly rose from the bed and stood upright in front of me holding the bag before my face. I closed my eyes and waited for him to slip it over my head. But he spoke.

"No, you need not wear it." He placed the soft leather bag in my right hand and closed my other hand over it. "It would not be right to wear it in this time and place where no one will understand. Put it safely away until you are again on the reservation. Wear it then, when you replace the sacred sage."

Grandpa turned and sat again on the bed. Wearily he leaned his head against the pillow. "Go," he said, "I will sleep now."

"Thank you, Grandpa," I said softly and left with the bag in my hands.

That night Mom and Dad took Grandpa to the hospital. Two weeks later I stood alone on the lonely prairie of the reservation and put the sacred sage in my medicine bag.

BQ **BIG Question**

What values has Martin gained in the story? Tell how you think he will act on these values in the future.

After You Read

Respond and Think Critically

1. What reasons for coming does Grandpa give? Do you think these are good reasons for his visit? Explain your thoughts. **[Recall and Make Judgments]**

2. How is it possible for Martin to feel both shame and pride about his grandfather? **[Interpret]**

3. At the end of the story, is Martin ready to receive his great-grandfather's gift? Give reasons why or why not. **[Evaluate]**

4. What qualities or character traits suggest that Martin is a dynamic character? Use details from the story to support your answer. **[Analyze]**

5. Grandpa tells Martin he does not have to wear the medicine bag. What can you infer about Grandpa's character from this gesture? **[Infer]**

6. **BQ** **BIG Question** In the story, Martin has difficulty accepting his family's Sioux traditions. He struggles to be true to himself. Have you ever struggled to be true to yourself? Explain. **[Connect]**

TIP

Analyzing
All characters have character traits, but dynamic characters change and develop during the course of a story.

- How would you describe Martin at the beginning of the story? How does he act when he sees his great-grandfather down the street?

- How does Martin feel about his great-grandfather and his Sioux heritage at the end of the story?

FOLDABLES Study Organizer Keep track of your ideas about the **BIG Question** in your unit Foldable.

Connect to the Art

When Grandpa meets with Martin's friends, Grandpa wears beaded moccasins, a beaded headband with a feather in it, and a deerskin vest. Grandpa tells Martin's friends the story of how he killed the deer his vest is made from. Find out more about how the Sioux crafted their clothing, including how they made colorful beads and tanned leather. Create a presentation with images and descriptions and share it with the class.

Literary Element Character

1. Explain whether Martin is a dynamic or a static character. Support your answer with details from the story.

Review: Plot

Plot can be divided into five parts. The **exposition** introduces characters, setting, and conflict. During the **rising action,** complications arise as the main character faces the conflict. The **climax** is the most emotional or suspenseful point. The **falling action** shows how the conflict will probably work out. The **resolution** provides the conflict's outcome.

2. Which excerpt best illustrates the resolution of "The Medicine Bag"?

   A "Grandpa decided that he would like to see where his only living descendants lived . . ."

   B "I was proud of this 86-year-old man, who had never been away from the reservation . . ."

   C "one day after school, my friends came home with me . . ."

   D "I . . . put the sacred sage in my medicine bag."

Reading Strategy
Make Inferences About Characters

3. Which of the following would you infer about Martin at the very beginning of the story?

   A He is ashamed of his great-grandfather.
   B He is proud of his great-grandfather.
   C He wants his great-grandfather to visit.
   D He wants his friends to meet his great-grandfather.

Vocabulary Practice

Choose the sentence that uses the vocabulary word correctly.

1. **A.** The museum sent out letters searching for **authentic** Arabic art.

   B. **Authentic** materials do not repel water as well as natural ones.

2. **A.** Jack's **stately** old backpack had a sour smell after he left his lunch in it for a few days.

   B. The freshly mowed lawn gave the new home a **stately** appearance.

3. **A.** Tony was so angry with Lynette that he wanted to **embrace** her.

   B. Julie gave her little sister an **embrace** before she left for her first day of school.

4. **A.** Monica **sheepishly** admitted that she had eaten the last cookie.

   B. Lions in the exhibit have been known to **sheepishly** roar at people who pass by.

Academic Vocabulary

On page 45, Martin's father tells Grandpa, "We are honored to have you with us and you will never be a burden." He offers Grandpa **assurance** that he will not be a burden to the family. Using context clues (hints in nearby words and sentences), try to figure out the meaning of *assurance*. Check your guess in a dictionary.

 Literature Online

Selection Resources For Selection Quizzes, eFlashcards, and Reading-Writing Connection activities, go to glencoe.com and enter QuickPass code GL39770u1.

Respond Through Writing

Summary

Report Story Events A story is composed of a series of events that take place in a specific order. In a brief essay, summarize the story events in "The Medicine Bag." Make sure you tell what happens in the right order.

Understand the Task

- When you summarize, you include the most important events in a story.

- A summary should not include unnecessary or minor details—details you could leave out and still understand the story.

Prewrite To help you organize your essay, fill out a graphic organizer like the one below. Add as many rows as you need. Be sure to list events in the order in which they occur.

> **1**
>
> Martin explains that his family visits his Sioux great-grandfather every year.
>
> **2**
>
> He likes to tell his friends Grandpa's stories but is worried they will laugh at Grandpa if they meet him.

Draft One way to draft your summary is by using sentence frames. For instance, to start off your summary, include a sentence that shares the main idea of the story.

"The Medicine Bag" is a story about _____.

As you write your summary, use transition words and phrases. These are words and phrases—such as *in the beginning, first, next, then, after that,* or *finally*—that help tell the sequence of events.

In the beginning of the story, _____.
Then, _____. *Finally,* _____.

Revise Trade papers with a partner. Ask your partner to number the events in your summary and compare it to the original story. If your partner finds events that are out of order, you may need to revise your summary.

Edit and Proofread Proofread your papers, correcting any errors in spelling, grammar, and punctuation. Review the Grammar Tip in the side column for information on correct grammar use.

Grammar Tip

Verb Tense
The tense, or time, of a verb tells when an action is occurring.

Past tense:
I walked to the store.

Present tense:
I walk to the store.

Future tense:
I will walk to the store.

Unlike historical events, which you discuss in the past tense because they are set in time, fictional events come alive again whenever someone reads about them. For that reason, story summaries are written in the **literary present tense.** We would say, "In the beginning of the story, Robert rows across a lake." The action is told in present tense ("rows") instead of past tense ("rowed").

Vocabulary Workshop

Context Clues

Connection to Literature

"I reluctantly moved to the bed. I knew Grandpa wouldn't want to have Mom undress him, but I didn't want to, either."

—Virginia Driving Hawk Sneve, "The Medicine Bag"

Learning Objectives

For page 55

In this assignment, you will focus on the following objective:

Vocabulary: Understanding words by using context clues.

You can often figure out the meaning of a word from **context clues.** The context of a word is the sentence or passage in which it appears. For example, in the quotation above, the words *I didn't want to* give a clue to the meaning of the word *reluctantly* (*reluctantly* means "in an unwilling or hesitant way"). Some common kinds of context clues include definitions, restatements, examples, comparisons, and contrasts.

Here are context clues for some other words from "The Medicine Bag."

Word	Context Clue	How It Helps
quest	Grandpa's father prepared for his quest—or *search*—for a vision.	gives a definition
confines	The Sioux lived within the confines of the reservation. They had to stay within *these borders.*	provides a restatement
commotion	*Yelling kids* and *barking dogs* can cause a commotion.	gives examples
sacred	It was *not an ordinary* dream. It was a sacred dream.	provides a contrast

TRY IT: Use context clues to define the underlined words.

1. Grandpa's <u>getup</u> included a rumpled suit, satin shirt, and boots.
2. The odd <u>procession</u> marched down the street, a noisy parade of children, dogs, and Grandpa.
3. Grandpa <u>collapsed</u> like a roof breaking under a heavy snow.

Tip

Vocabulary Terms Context clues are words in a surrounding sentence or passage that help you figure out the meaning of an unfamiliar word.

Test-taking Tip Look before and after an unknown word for a synonym or definition, a restatement, a comparison or contrast, or a description or action associated with the word.

LOG ON ▶ **Literature** Online

Vocabulary For more vocabulary practice, go to glencoe.com and enter the QuickPass code GL39770u1.

Waters of Gold

Connect to the Folktale

Think about a time when you acted generously toward a friend, a family member, or your community.

Partner Talk With a partner, talk about why you chose to be generous. How did others benefit from your actions? Also discuss any factors that made you hesitate before acting. Share your ideas with the class.

Build Background

A **folktale** is a traditional story that has been passed from generation to generation by oral retelling. "Waters of Gold" is a written version of an ancient Asian folktale. This story takes place in a small farming village.

- In the farming village where the story is set, wealth and leisure are rare. Water has to be hauled from a well. Survival depends on hard work.

- In folktales, it is common for everyday life to be turned around by a magical person or force.

- Folktales teach lessons about human nature, featuring characters who choose right over wrong, gain wisdom, or live out their values.

Meet Laurence Yep

"I was an American child— so relentlessly so that my grandmother became hesitant to talk about Chinese things with me."

—Laurence Yep

Inspired by His Heritage
As a child, Laurence Yep wasn't very interested in his heritage or in writing. "Back then," he said, "I thought of myself as a scientist." In high school, he began writing science fiction stories. Later, he returned to his heritage—Chinese history and legends—to write his award-winning works.

Literary Works Yep is the author of many novels, including *Dragonwings* and *Dragon's Gate*. "Waters of Gold" is one of the tales in *Tongues of Jade*.

Laurence Yep was born in 1948.

 Literature Online

Author Search For more about Laurence Yep, go to glencoe.com and enter QuickPass code GL39770u1.

Set Purposes for Reading

BQ BIG Question

As you read, identify the values revealed by each character's words and actions.

Literary Element Style

Style is the distinctive way an author writes. Two important elements of style are word choice, or diction, and sentence structure.

- **Word Choice** is an author's use of specific, vivid words to express certain ideas or feelings.

- **Sentence Structure** refers to the way a sentence is put together. Short sentences can speed readers through the story's action. Longer sentences with phrases provide depth of detail.

Simple words and sentences are typical in folktales—they help make the stories easier to remember and recite.

As you read, ask yourself, how does the author's style help me imagine and understand the folktale?

Reading Strategy Activate Prior Knowledge

When you **activate prior knowledge,** you recall what you already know. When someone mentions a topic, you're likely to think of facts, processes, or experiences related to that topic. Connecting to what you know can help you make sense of new information.

For example, think of some folktales that you've heard or read. Folktales include animal stories, trickster tales, fairy tales, myths, legends, and tall tales. What do these stories have in common?

As you read, you can use a graphic organizer like the one below to help you activate prior knowledge about the setting, characters, or vocabulary in the folktale.

New Topic:	Folktales
Facts I Know	They usually take place in the past ("Once upon a time"), involve magic, and teach a lesson.
Events I Know	Although the characters face challenges, the story usually ends with "happily ever after."
Experiences I've Had	When I was younger, I saw cartoons based on these stories.

TRY IT

Activate Prior Knowledge
Use a graphic organizer like the one shown to activate your prior knowledge about Asia. Think about what you know about the food, countries, and geographical features of Asia.

Waters of Gold

Laurence Yep

The Emperor Kiang Hsi on Tour in the Southern Provinces, 1699. Chinese School. Pen, watercolor, and gouache on silk. British Museum, London.

Many years ago, there lived a woman whom everyone called Auntie Lily. She was Auntie by blood[1] to half the county and Auntie to the other half by friendship. As she liked to say, "There's a bit of Heaven in each of us." As a result, she was always helping people out.

Because of her many kind acts, she knew so many people that she couldn't go ten steps without meeting someone who wanted to chat. So it would take her half the day to go to the village well and back to her home.

Eventually, though, she helped so many people that she had no more money. She had to sell her fields and even her house to her neighbor, a rich old woman. "If you'd helped yourself instead of others, you wouldn't have to do this," the neighbor said smugly.[2] "Where are all those other people when you need them?"

"That isn't why I helped them," Auntie Lily said firmly. She wound up having to pay rent for the house she had once owned. She supported herself by her **embroidery**; but since her eyes were going bad, she could not do very much.

One day an old beggar entered the village. He was a ragbag of a man—a trash heap, a walking pig wallow. It was impossible to tell what color or what shape his clothes had once been, and his hair was as muddy and matted as a bird's nest. As he shuffled through the village gates, he called out, "Water for my feet. Please, water for my feet. One little bowl of water—that's all I ask."

Everyone ignored him, pretending to concentrate on their chores instead. One man went on replacing the shaft of his hoe. A woman swept her courtyard. Another woman fed her hens.

The beggar went to each in turn, but they all showed their backs to him.

After calling out a little while longer, the beggar went to the nearest home, which happened to belong to the rich old woman. When he banged at her door, he left the dirty outline of his knuckles on the clean wood. And when the

Visual Vocabulary

Embroidery is the art of using needle and thread to sew decorative designs on cloth.

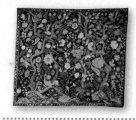

---

1 If you are connected to someone **by blood**, you are related to him or her.

2 Someone who acts **smugly** appears overly confident, as though he or she is superior to others.

rich woman opened her door, his smell nearly took her breath away.

Now it so happened that she had been chopping vegetables when the beggar had knocked. When the beggar repeated his request, she raised her cleaver menacingly. "What good would one bowl of water be? You'd need a whole river to wash you clean. Go away."

"A thousand pardons," the old beggar said, and shambled[3] on to the next house.

Though Auntie Lily had to hold her nose, she asked politely, "Yes?"

"I'd like a bowl of water to wash my feet." And the beggar pointed one grimy finger toward them.

Her rich neighbor had stayed in her doorway to watch the beggar. She scolded Auntie Lily now. "It's all your fault those beggars come into the village. They know they can count on a free meal."

It was an old debate between them, so Auntie Lily simply said, "Any of us can have bad luck."

"Garbage," the rich old woman declared, "is garbage. They must have done something bad, or Heaven wouldn't have let them become beggars."

Auntie Lily turned to the beggar. "I may be joining you on the road someday. Wait here."

Much to the neighbor's distress, Auntie Lily went inside and poured water from a large jar in her kitchen into a bucket. Carrying it in both hands, she brought it outside to the beggar and set it down.

The beggar stood on one leg, just like a crane, while he washed one callused, leathery sole over the bucket. "You can put mud on any other part of me, but if my feet are clean, then I feel clean."

As he fussily continued to cleanse his feet, Auntie Lily asked kindly, "Are you hungry? I don't have much, but what I have I'm willing to share."

The beggar shook his head. "I've stayed longer in this village than I have in any other. Heaven is my roof, and the whole world my house."

Auntie Lily stared at him, wondering what she would look like after a few years on the road. "Are you very

Style What does this simple statement suggest about Auntie Lily's attitude toward the beggar?

Activate Prior Knowledge Think of a TV or movie character whose attitude is similar to the rich old woman's. What words would you use to describe this character?

---

3 **Shambled** means "walked slowly or awkwardly; shuffled."

tired? Have you been on the road for very long?"

"No, the road is on me," the beggar said, and held up his hands from his dirty sides. "But thank you. You're the first person to ask. And you're the first person to give me some water. So place the bucket of water by your bed tonight and do not look into it till tomorrow morning."

As the beggar shuffled out of the village again, Auntie Lily stared down doubtfully at the bucket of what was now muddy water. Then, even though she felt foolish, she picked it up again. "You're not really going to take that scummy water inside?" laughed the rich neighbor. "It'll probably breed mosquitoes."

"It seemed important to him," she answered. "I'll humor[4] him."

"Humoring people," snapped the neighbor, "has got you one step from begging yourself."

However, Auntie Lily carried the bucket inside anyway. Setting it down near her sleeping mat, she covered the mouth of the bucket with an old, cracked plate so she wouldn't peek into it by mistake, and then she got so caught up in embroidering a pair of slippers that she forgot all about the beggar and his bucket of water.

She sewed until twilight, when it was too dark to use her needle. Then, because she had no money for oil or candles, she went to sleep.

The next morning Auntie Lily rose and stretched the aches out of her back. She sighed. "The older I get, the harder it is to get up in the morning."

She was always saying something like that, but she had never stayed on her sleeping mat—even when she was sick. Thinking of all that day's chores, she decided to water the herbs she had growing on one side of her house.

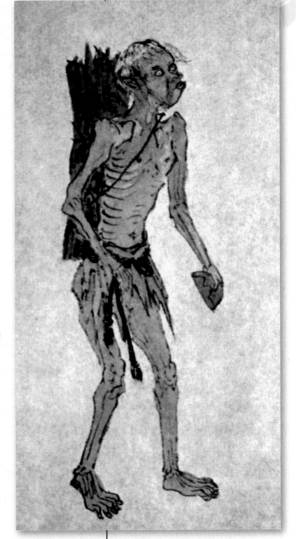

Two Beggars (detail), 1500. Chou Ch'en, Ming Dynasty. Watercolor.
View the Art In what ways is this image of a Chinese beggar similar to the character described in the folktale?

---

4 To *humor* someone is to go along with the person's request, even if it doesn't seem to make sense.

Her eyes fell upon the beggar's bucket with its covering plate. "No sense using fresh water when that will do as well. After all, dirt's dirt to a plant."

Squatting down, she picked up the bucket and was surprised at how heavy it was. "I must have filled it fuller than I thought," she grunted.

She staggered out of the house and over to the side where rows of little green herbs grew. "Here you go," she said to her plants. "Drink deep."

Taking off the plate, she upended the bucket; but instead of muddy brown water, there was a flash of reflected light and a clinking sound as gold coins rained down upon her plants.

Auntie Lily set the bucket down hastily and crouched, not trusting her weak eyes. However, where some of her herbs had been, there was now a small mound of gold coins. She squinted in disbelief and rubbed her aching eyes and stared again; but the gold was still there.

She turned to the bucket. There was even more gold inside. Scooping up coins by the handful, she freed her little plants and made sure that the stalks weren't too bent.Then she sat gazing at her bucket full of gold until a farmer walked by. "Tell me I'm not dreaming," she called to him.

The farmer yawned and came over with his hoe over his shoulder. "I wish I were dreaming, because that would mean I'm still in bed instead of having to go off to work."

Auntie Lily gathered up a handful of gold coins and let it fall in a tinkling, golden shower back into the bucket. "And this is real?"

The farmer's jaw dropped. He picked up one coin with his free hand and bit into it. He flipped it back in with the other coins. "It's as real as me, Auntie. But where did you ever get that?"

So Auntie Lily told him. And as others woke up and stepped outside, Auntie told them as well, for she still could not believe her luck and wanted them to confirm that the gold was truly gold. In no time at all, there was a small crowd around her.

Style How do the words the author uses help you visualize the scene?

Activate Prior Knowledge You may have seen movies with pirates or gold diggers who bite gold. Based on what you've seen, why do you think the farmer bites the gold coin?

If the bucket had been filled with ordinary copper cash, that would have been more money than any of them had ever seen. In their wildest dreams, they had never expected to see that much gold. Auntie Lily stared at the bucket uncomfortably. "I keep thinking it's going to disappear the next moment."

The farmer, who had been standing there all this time, shook his head. "If it hasn't disappeared by now, I don't think it will. What are you going to do with it, Auntie?"

Auntie Lily stared at the bucket, and suddenly she came to a decision. Stretching out a hand, she picked up a gold coin. "I'm going to buy back my house, and I'm going to get back my land."

The farmer knew the fields. "Those old things? You could buy a valley full of prime land with half that bucket. And a palace with the other half."

"I want what I sweated for." Asking the farmer to guard her bucket, Auntie Lily closed her hand around the gold coin. Then, as the crowd parted before her, she made her way over to her neighbor.

Now the rich old woman liked to sleep late; but all the noise had woken her up, so she was just getting dressed when Auntie knocked. The old woman yanked her door open as she buttoned the last button of her coat. "Who started the riot? Can't a person get a good night's sleep?"

With some satisfaction, Auntie Lily held up the gold coin. "Will this buy back my house and land?"

"Where did you get that?" the old woman demanded.

"Will it buy them back?" Auntie Lily repeated.

The rich old woman snatched the coin out of Auntie Lily's hand and bit into it just as the farmer had. "It's real," the old woman said in astonishment.

"Will it?" Auntie asked again.

"Yes, yes, yes," the old woman said crabbily. "But where did you ever get that much gold?"

When Auntie Lily told her the story and showed her the bucket of gold, the rich old woman stood moving her mouth like a fish out of water. Clasping her hands together, she shut her eyes and moaned in genuine pain. "And I sent him away. What a fool I am. What a fool."

BQ BIG Question

How does Auntie Lily's comment show that she stands by her values?

Landscape, Mid-Edo.
Ike Gyokuran. Hanging
scroll; ink and colors on
silk, 44 1/8 x 19 3/16 in. Gift
of the Asian Art Foundation
of San Francisco, The
Avery Brundage Collection.
Asian Art Museum of San
Francisco, CA. B76 D3.
Licensed by VAGA, NY.

And the old woman beat her head with her fists.

That very afternoon, the beggar—the ragbag, the trash heap, the walking pig wallow—shuffled once more through the village gates with feet as dirty as before. As he went, he croaked, "Water for my feet. Please, water for my feet. One little bowl of water—that's all I ask."

This time, people dropped whatever they were doing when they heard his plea. Hoes, brooms, and pots were flung down, hens and pigs were kicked out of the way as everyone hurried to fill a bucket with water. There was a small riot by the village well as everyone fought to get water at the same time. Still others rushed out with buckets filled from the jars in their houses.

Style In what way does the length of this sentence and its one-syllable words convey the feeling of this scene?

"Here, use my water," one man shouted, holding up a tub.

A woman shoved in front of him with a bucket in her arms. "No, no, use mine. It's purer."

They surrounded the old beggar, pleading with him to use their water, and in the process of jostling one another, they splashed a good deal of water on one another and came perilously[5] close to drowning the beggar. The rich old woman, Auntie Lily's neighbor, charged to the rescue.

"Out of the way, you vultures," the rich old woman roared. "You're going to trample him." Using her elbows, her feet, and in one case even her teeth, the old woman fought her way through the mob.

No longer caring if she soiled her hands, the old woman seized the beggar by the arm. "This way, you poor, misunderstood creature."

Fighting off her neighbors with one hand and keeping her grip on the beggar with the other, the old woman hauled him inside her house. Barring the door against the rest of the village, she ignored all the fists and feet thumping on her door and all the shouts.

"I really wasn't myself yesterday, because I had been up the night before tending a sick friend. This is what I meant to do." She fetched a fresh new towel and an even newer bucket and forced the beggar to wash his feet.

When he was done, he handed her the now filthy towel. "Dirt's dirt, and garbage is garbage," he said.

However, the greedy old woman didn't recognize her own words. She was too busy trying to remember what else Auntie Lily had done. "Won't you have something to eat? Have you traveled very far? Are you tired?" she asked, all in the same breath.

The old beggar went to the door and waited patiently while she unbarred it. As he shuffled outside, he instructed her to leave the bucket of water by her bed but not to look into it until the morning.

That night, the greedy old woman couldn't sleep as she imagined the heap of shiny gold that would be waiting for her tomorrow. She waited impatiently for the sun to rise

Style Though the beggar repeats the old woman's words from earlier in the story, in what way is the meaning different?

---

5 *Perilously* means "dangerously," referring to risky or threatening circumstances.

and got up as soon as she heard the first rooster crow.

Hurrying to the bucket, she plunged her hands inside expecting to bring up handfuls of gold. Instead, she gave a cry as dozens of little things bit her, for the bucket was filled not with gold but with snakes, lizards, and ants.

The greedy old woman fell sick—some said from her bites, some claimed from sheer[6] frustration. Auntie Lily herself came to nurse her neighbor. "Take this to heart: Kindness comes with no price."

The old woman was so ashamed that she did, indeed, take the lesson to heart. Though she remained sick, she was kind to whoever came to her door.

One day, a leper[7] came into the village. Everyone hid for fear of the terrible disease. Doors slammed and shutters banged down over windows, and soon the village seemed deserted.

Only Auntie Lily and her neighbor stepped out of their houses. "Are you hungry?" Auntie Lily asked.

"Are you thirsty?" the neighbor asked. "I'll make you a cup of tea."

The leper thanked Auntie Lily and then turned to the neighbor as if to express his gratitude as well; but he stopped and studied her. "You're looking poorly, my dear woman. Can I help?"

With a tired smile, the rich old woman explained what had happened. When she was finished, the leper stood thoughtfully for a moment. "You're not the same woman as before: You're as kind as Auntie Lily, and you aren't greedy anymore. So take this humble gift from my brother, the old beggar."

With that, the leper limped out of the village; and as he left, the illness fell away from the old woman like an old, discarded cloak. But though the old woman was healthy again, she stayed as kind as Auntie Lily and used her own money as well and wisely as Auntie Lily used the waters of gold. ❦

 **BQ** ❱❱ **BIG Question**

What do the old woman's actions reveal about how her values have changed?

---

6 Here, *sheer* means "complete" or "absolute."

7 A *leper* is a person with a severe, disabling skin disease.

After You Read

Respond and Think Critically

1. How does Auntie Lily know the rich old woman? [Identify]

2. Auntie Lily states, "There's a bit of Heaven in each of us." What does this tell you about her attitude toward other people? [Infer]

3. Why does the rich old woman find snakes, lizards, and ants in her bucket instead of gold? [Draw Conclusions]

4. Find words or phrases that indicate this story is a folktale. Why do you think the author chose to convey his main message about values in a folktale instead of another type of story? [Analyze]

5. Think about the endings of other folktales you know. Are the endings of these stories different than the ending of "Waters of Gold"? Explain your ideas. [Evaluate]

6. **BQ** BIG Question What actions show that Auntie Lily and, later, her rich old neighbor live out the values of generosity and compassion? What are some other ways people show that they believe in these values? [Connect]

Academic Vocabulary

After she became rich, Auntie Lily did not want to **reside** in a new place. To become more familiar with the word *reside*, complete the graphic organizer below.

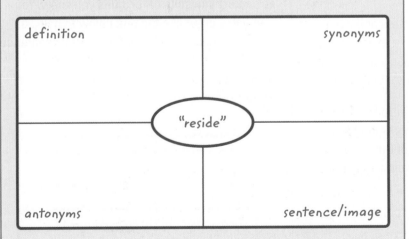

definition	synonyms
	"reside"
antonyms	sentence/image

TIP

Analyzing
Here are some tips to help you analyze. Remember that when you analyze, you look at individual parts of the selection in order to understand the entire selection.

- Skim the selection for words or phrases that are usually found in folktales.

- Identify how these phrases help the author tell the story.

- Locate phrases and sentences that the author uses to teach a lesson.

 Keep track of your ideas about the **BIG Question** in your unit Foldable.

 Literature Online

Selection Resources
For Selection Quizzes, eFlashcards, and Reading-Writing Connection activities, go to glencoe.com and enter QuickPass code GL39770u1.

1. Describe Yep's writing style, including word choice and sentence structure, in "Waters of Gold." Support your observations with examples from the selection.

2. Why do you think most folktales reflect a similar style?

Review: **Narrator and Point of View**

Every story has a storyteller, or **narrator**. **Point of view** is the relationship of the narrator to the story.

- In the **first-person** point of view, the narrator is a character in the story who refers to himself or herself as "I" or "me."

- In the **third-person** point of view, the narrator is not a character in the story and does not take part in events. He or she stands apart from the action and describes what is happening.

3. Who is telling the story in "Waters of Gold"? What clues did you use to help you determine the narrator and the point of view?

Reading Strategy
Activate Prior Knowledge

4. In what ways did the characters and events of "Waters of Gold" meet your expectations? In what ways did they surprise you? Use the notes in your graphic organizer to help you.

5. Think of the setting in another folktale you've read. What qualities does this setting share with the setting of "Waters of Gold"? Use a Venn Diagram like the one below to help you respond.

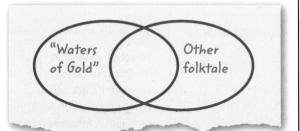

Grammar Link

Concrete and Abstract Nouns Nouns tell who or what a sentence is about. Nouns can be concrete or abstract.

Concrete Nouns name things that you can see or touch. *Tree* and *shoe* are examples of concrete nouns.

Abstract nouns name ideas, qualities, and feelings—things you cannot see and touch. *Friendship, satisfaction,* and *freedom* are abstract nouns.

Practice Make a list of concrete nouns and a list of abstract nouns from the folktale. Then add your own examples of each type of noun to the lists.

Write with Style

Apply Sentence Length Think of a lesson you would like to convey as a folktale. Your story can take place during modern times, or it can take place long ago. You can use people or animals as characters. Try to use simple sentences to capture the style of folktales you know. You can use a chart like the one below to help you construct your sentences. First write a sentence from "Waters of Gold." Then write your own sentence, imitating the structure and length of Yep's sentence.

> Many years ago, there lived a woman whom everyone called Auntie Lily.

> Long, long ago, there lived a man named _____.

Part 2
Believing in Yourself

Woman Holding Trophy. Artist Unknown.

BQ > **BIG Question** **How Do You Stay True to Yourself?**

The figure in the picture stands in the center of sunrays. How might the picture represent the power of believing in yourself? What can you achieve by believing in yourself?

Learning Objectives

For pages 70–71

In studying this text, you will focus on the following objectives:

Literary Study: Analyzing plot, character, setting, point of view, and theme.

Genre Focus:
Short Fiction

F iction is writing about imaginary people and events. **Short fiction** consists of stories meant to be read in about one sitting. Like longer works of fiction, short fiction includes such literary elements as plot, characters, setting, point of view, and theme.

Short stories, folktales, legends, myths, and literary sketches are all examples of short fiction.

Literary Elements

Plot The **plot** is the series of events showing how a conflict or problem is resolved. The plot usually unfolds in five steps. The **exposition** introduces the story's setting and characters and sets up the conflict, or problem. The **rising action** develops the story's conflict and builds suspense. The **climax** is the point of greatest emotion and interest. The **falling action** shows what happens to the characters after the climax. The **resolution** completes the falling action and reveals the final outcome of the conflict.

Characters A **character** is a person, animal, or imaginary creature that appears in a literary work. Usually a story is built around a **main character. Minor characters** move the action along by interacting with the main character and providing background information.

Characterization includes all the methods an author uses to develop a character. In **direct characterization,** the story's narrator makes statements about a character's personality. In **indirect characterization,** a character's personality is revealed through his or her words and actions and through what others think and say about him or her.

Authors use **dialogue** and **description** to bring characters to life. Dialogue is conversation between two or more characters. Through description, the author creates an impression of a setting, a person, an animal, an object, or an event by appealing to one or more of the five senses.

Setting The **setting** is the time and place in which story events occur. The setting includes the historical period, geographic region, and season. The culture in which the characters develop is also part of setting.

Narrator and Point of View The **narrator** is the person who tells the story. In fiction, the narrator may be a character in the story. The **point of view** is the relationship of the narrator to the story.

Theme The **theme** of a story is its main message. Sometimes the theme is stated directly by the narrator or by a character. Sometimes, however, the reader must figure out the theme by examining the characters, the plot, and literary devices such as symbolism and mood.

TRY IT

Using graphic organizers like those on the next page, identify the characteristics of a work of short fiction in this unit.

Characteristics of the Genre

To better understand literary elements in short fiction and how authors use literary elements to create effects and achieve their purposes, look at the story map and characterization chart below. The story map examines elements of "Raymond's Run." The characterization chart looks at characters in both "Raymond's Run" and "The Medicine Bag."

Story Map

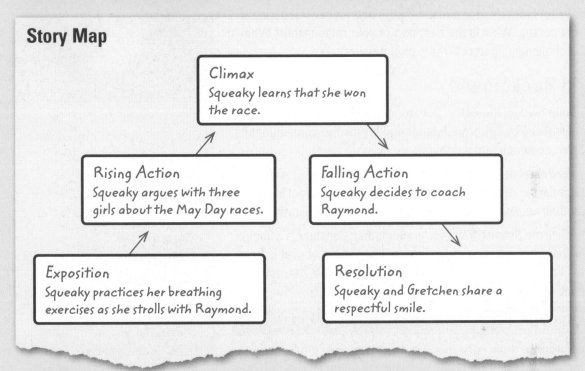

Climax
Squeaky learns that she won the race.

Rising Action
Squeaky argues with three girls about the May Day races.

Falling Action
Squeaky decides to coach Raymond.

Exposition
Squeaky practices her breathing exercises as she strolls with Raymond.

Resolution
Squeaky and Gretchen share a respectful smile.

Characterization Chart

Main Character	Revealing Thought or Action	Character Trait
Squeaky	"I give him [Mr. Pearson] such a look he couldn't finish putting that idea into words. Grownups got a lot of nerve sometimes."	Proud of her running ability
Martin	"His getup wasn't out of place on the reservation, but it sure was here, and I wanted to sink right through the pavement."	Embarrassed by his heritage

Literature Online

Literature and Reading For more selections in this genre, go to glencoe.com and enter QuickPass code GL39770u1.

Abuela Invents the Zero

Connect to the Short Story

Think about a relationship you have with an older person, such as a grandparent, another relative, or a neighbor.

Quickwrite Freewrite for a few minutes about your relationship with this person. What is the best part of your relationship? What are the challenging parts? Write a brief answer.

Build Background

In "Abuela Invents the Zero," Constancia, a New Jersey teenager, is embarrassed by her grandmother and learns the consequences of making someone feel worthless.

- *Zero* is a number that is neither negative nor positive. It is another way of saying *nothing* or *none*. If people make you feel like a zero, they make you feel like you have no value, or worth.

- *Abuela* is the Spanish word for grandmother. Constancia's abuela is in New Jersey to see snow. Puerto Rico, where Abuela is from, is too warm for snow to form, which is why Abuela has never seen it.

Vocabulary

compromise (kom′ prə mīz′) *n.* a settlement of differences reached by each side giving in on certain demands (p. 75). *My sister and I made a compromise—I could choose the television show if she could choose the snack.*

retrieve (ri trēv′) *v.* to bring back (p. 76). *I had to retrieve my coat from the hall closet.*

inconvenient (in′ kən vēn′ yənt) *adj.* not easy to do, use, or reach (p. 77). *My brother left the cereal in an inconvenient place on the shelf.*

congregation (kong′ grə gā′ shən) *n.* an assembly of persons who meet for worship (p. 77). *The congregation stood up and sang a hymn.*

 Literature Online

Author Search For more about Judith Ortiz Cofer, go to glencoe.com and enter QuickPass code GL39770u1.

Meet Judith Ortiz Cofer

"The memories of [childhood and my parents] emerge in my poems and stories like time-travelers popping up with a message for me."

—Judith Ortiz Cofer

Mastering the English Language

English was not Judith Ortiz Cofer's first language. Born in Puerto Rico, she learned English after her family moved to the United States mainland. "It was a challenge," she said, "not only to learn English, but to master it enough to teach it and—the ultimate goal—to write poetry in it." Cofer's writing reflects the differences between her two childhood homes: the island of Puerto Rico and the United States mainland.

Literary Works Cofer writes fiction and poetry for young adults. Her novel, *The Meaning of Consuelo,* was on the New York Public Library's Books for the Teen Age 2004 List.

Judith Ortiz Cofer was born in 1952.

Set Purposes for Reading

BQ BIG Question

As you read, decide if Constancia's actions show that she is self-confident or if she is worried about what others think.

Literary Element Conflict

Conflict is the central struggle between opposing forces in a story. A character may face an external conflict, an internal conflict, or both.

- An **external conflict** occurs when a character struggles against an outside force, such as another character, society, or nature.

- An **internal conflict** is a struggle within the mind of a character. Internal conflicts often involve a decision a character must make or a fear he or she must face.

As you read "Abuela Invents the Zero," identify Constancia's external and internal conflicts. Note the character that she struggles with and how that struggle makes Constancia feel. Evaluate the ways in which the conflicts are or are not resolved. Would you have acted in the same way to resolve the conflicts?

Reading Skill Analyze Characters

When you **analyze characters,** you look closely at their thoughts, words, and actions to determine their personality traits. For example, based on the things a character says or does, you might decide that he or she is brave, fearful, generous, or selfish.

- A **dynamic character** usually has many sides to his or her personality. The character grows and changes as the story progresses.

- A **static character** usually has one main characteristic. He or she stays the same throughout the story.

As you read, use a chart like the one below to help you analyze the characters. Note the characters' thoughts, words, and actions and then decide whether the characters are static or dynamic.

Name of Character	Thoughts, Words, Actions	Analysis: Static or Dynamic?
Constancia		
Abuela		
Constancia's mother		
Constancia's father		

Learning Objectives

For pages 72–79

In studying this text, you will focus on the following objectives:

Literary Study: Analyzing conflict.

Analyzing characters.

TRY IT

Analyze In a few words, describe a friend or family member. Use that person's words and actions to help you analyze what he or she is like. In the past year, would you say the person has been static or dynamic? Explain.

Abuela Invents the Zero

Judith Ortiz Cofer

Portrait of a Woman. Henry Lamb. Private Collection, ©Agnew's, London.

"You made me feel like a zero, like a nothing," she says in Spanish, *un cero, nada.* She is trembling, an angry little old woman lost in a heavy winter coat that belongs to my mother. And I end up being sent to my room, like I was a child, to think about my grandmother's idea of math.

It all began with Abuela coming up from the Island[1] for a visit—her first time in the United States. My mother and father paid her way here so that she wouldn't die without seeing snow, though if you asked me, and nobody has, the dirty slush in this city is not worth the price of a ticket. But I guess she deserves some kind of award for having had ten kids and survived to tell about it. My mother is the youngest of the bunch. Right up to the time when we're supposed to pick up the old lady at the airport, my mother is telling me stories about how hard times were for la familia on la isla,[2] and how *la abuela* worked night and day to support them after their father died of a heart attack. I'd die of a heart attack too if I had a troop like that to support. Anyway, I had

Analyze Characters Abuela says these words that begin the story. What do they tell you about her?

---

1 The *Island* is what the narrator calls Puerto Rico, an island about 1,000 miles southeast of Miami, Florida.

2 *La familia* (lä fä mē′lē ä) is Spanish for "the family," and *la isla* (lä ēs′lä) is Spanish for "the island."

seen her only three or four times in my entire life, whenever we would go for somebody's funeral. I was born here and I have lived in this building all my life. But when Mami says, "Connie, please be nice to Abuela. She doesn't have too many years left. Do you promise me, Constancia?"—when she uses my full name, I know she means business. So I say, "Sure." Why wouldn't I be nice? I'm not a monster, after all.

So we go to Kennedy to get la abuela and she is the last to come out of the airplane, on the arm of the cabin attendant, all wrapped up in a black shawl. He hands her over to my parents like she was a package sent airmail. It is January, two feet of snow on the ground, and she's wearing a shawl over a thin black dress. That's just the start.

Once home, she refuses to let my mother buy her a coat because it's a waste of money for the two weeks she'll be in *el Polo Norte,* as she calls New Jersey, the North Pole. So since she's only four feet eleven inches tall, she walks around in my mother's big black coat looking ridiculous. I try to walk far behind them in public so that no one will think we're together. I plan to stay very busy the whole time she's with us so that I won't be asked to take her anywhere, but my plan is ruined when my mother comes down with the flu and Abuela absolutely *has* to attend Sunday mass or her soul will be eternally damned. She's more Catholic than the Pope.[3] My father decides that he should stay home with my mother and that I should escort la abuela to church. He tells me this on Saturday night as I'm getting ready to go out to the mall with my friends.

"No way," I say.

I go for the car keys on the kitchen table: he usually leaves them there for me on Friday and Saturday nights. He beats me to them.

"No way," he says, pocketing them and grinning at me.

Needless to say, we come to a **compromise** very quickly. I do have a responsibility to Sandra and Anita, who don't

Analyze Characters What character traits, or qualities, does the girl demonstrate in these lines?

Conflict Why is her father's decision likely to be a problem for Constancia?

---

3 The **Pope** is the spiritual leader of the Roman Catholic Church.

Vocabulary ....

compromise (kom′ prə mīz′) *n.* a settlement of differences reached by each side giving in on certain demands

drive yet. There is a fashion show at Brookline Square that we *cannot* miss.

"The mass in Spanish is at ten sharp tomorrow morning, entiendes?"[4] My father is dangling the car keys in front of my nose and pulling them back when I try to reach for them. He's really enjoying himself.

"I understand. Ten o'clock. I'm out of here." I pry his fingers off the key ring. He knows that I'm late, so he makes it just a little difficult. Then he laughs. I run out of our apartment before he changes his mind. I have no idea what I'm getting myself into.

Sunday morning I have to walk two blocks on dirty snow to **retrieve** the car. I warm it up for Abuela as instructed by my parents, and drive it to the front of our building. My father walks her by the hand in baby steps on the slippery snow. The sight of her little head with a bun on top of it sticking out of that huge coat makes me want to run back into my room and get under the covers. I just hope that nobody I know sees us together. I'm dreaming, of course. The mass is packed with people from our block. It's a holy day of obligation[5] and everyone I ever met is there.

I have to help her climb the steps, and she stops to take a deep breath after each one, then I lead her down the aisle so that everybody can see me with my bizarre grandmother. If I were a good Catholic, I'm sure I'd get

Church Steeple and Rooftops. Edward Hopper.

BQ BIG Question

Does Constancia stay true to herself and to her family? Explain.

Conflict What details in these lines suggest that Constancia experiences an external conflict?

---

4 **Entiendes?** (en tyen′dās) is Spanish for "do you understand?"

5 A **holy day of obligation** is a day on which people who practice the Roman Catholic faith are required to attend mass.

Vocabulary ....

retrieve (ri trēv′) *n.* to bring back

some purgatory[6] time taken off for my sacrifice. She is walking as slow as Captain Cousteau[7] exploring the bottom of the sea, looking around, taking her sweet time. Finally she chooses a pew, but she wants to sit in the *other* end. It's like she had a spot picked out for some unknown reason, and although it's the most **inconvenient** seat in the house, that's where she has to sit. So we squeeze by all the people already sitting there, saying, "Excuse me, please, *con permiso*, pardon me," getting annoyed looks the whole way. By the time we settle in, I'm drenched in sweat. I keep my head down like I'm praying so as not to see or be seen. She is praying loud, in Spanish, and singing hymns at the top of her creaky voice.

I ignore her when she gets up with a hundred other people to go take communion. I'm actually praying hard now—that this will all be over soon. But the next time I look up, I see a black coat dragging around and around the church, stopping here and there so a little gray head can peek out like a **periscope** on a submarine. There are giggles in the church, and even the priest has frozen in the middle of a blessing, his hands above his head like he is about to lead the **congregation** in a set of jumping jacks.

I realize to my horror that my grandmother is lost. She can't find her way back to the pew. I am so embarrassed that even though the woman next to me is shooting daggers[8] at me with her eyes, I just can't move to go get her. I put my hands over my face like I'm praying, but it's really to hide my burning cheeks. I would like for her to disappear. I just know that on Monday my friends, and my enemies, in the barrio[9] will have a lot of senile-

Conflict Review Constancia's difficulties with her grandmother. What details suggest that Constancia suffers both external and internal conflicts?

---

6 In the Roman Catholic faith, **purgatory** is a place where people go after death to free their souls from sin before going to heaven.

7 **Captain Cousteau** refers to Jacques Cousteau, a French researcher who explored the ocean.

8 If people are **shooting daggers** at you, they are looking at you in an angry way.

9 **Barrio** (bä′ rē ō) is the Spanish word for *neighborhood*.

Vocabulary

inconvenient (in′kən vēn′yənt) *adj.* not easy to do, use, or reach

congregation (kong′grə gā′shən) *n.* an assembly of persons who meet for worship

grandmother jokes to tell in front of me. I am frozen to my seat. So the same woman who wants me dead on the spot does it for me. She makes a big deal out of getting up and hurrying to get Abuela.

The rest of the mass is a blur. All I know is that my grandmother kneels the whole time with *her* hands over her face. She doesn't speak to me on the way home, and she doesn't let me help her walk, even though she almost falls a couple of times.

When we get to the apartment, my parents are at the kitchen table, where my mother is trying to eat some soup. They can see right away that something is wrong. Then Abuela points her finger at me like a judge passing a sentence on a criminal. She says in Spanish, "You made me feel like a zero, like a nothing." Then she goes to her room.

I try to explain what happened. "I don't understand why she's so upset. She just got lost and wandered around for a while," I tell them. But it sounds lame, even to my own ears. My mother gives me a look that makes me cringe and goes in to Abuela's room to get her version of the story. She comes out with tears in her eyes.

"Your grandmother says to tell you that of all the hurtful things you can do to a person, the worst is to make them feel as if they are worth nothing."

I can feel myself shrinking right there in front of her. But I can't bring myself to tell my mother that I think I understand how I made Abuela feel. I might be sent into the old lady's room to apologize, and it's not easy to admit you've been a jerk—at least, not right away with everybody watching. So I just sit there not saying anything.

My mother looks at me for a long time, like she feels sorry for me. Then she says, "You should know, Constancia, that if it wasn't for this old woman whose existence you don't seem to value, you and I would not be here."

That's when *I'm* sent to *my* room to consider a number I hadn't thought much about—until today. 🔖

Analyze Characters In what ways has Constancia's experience affected her?

After You Read

Respond and Think Critically

1. Retell the events that make Abuela feel like a zero. [Summarize]

2. As the story ends, Constancia realizes that what she did was wrong. What lesson or lessons do you think Constancia has learned from this incident? Explain. [Infer]

3. Do you think the author was effective at making Constancia a believable character? Explain. [Evaluate]

4. **Literary Element** Conflict What internal conflict does Constancia face at the end of the story? Explain her conflict. [Analyze]

5. **Reading Skill** Analyze Characters Is Constancia a static or dynamic character? Support your answer with details from the story and with notes from your graphic organizer. [Analyze]

6. **BQ** BIG Question Constancia is worried about what others think of her. As a result, she treats her grandmother in a way that makes her feel like a zero. How can caring too much about what others think about you prevent you from believing in yourself? [Connect]

Vocabulary Practice

Answer these questions.

1. Which is a **compromise**—getting popcorn at the movies or getting to go to the movies if you wash the dog?

2. Which would you need to **retrieve**—the keys on the table in front of you or a sweater you left at your friend's house?

3. Which is **inconvenient**—having to walk to school in the rain or getting dropped off in front of your classroom on a sunny day?

4. Which is a **congregation**—a large group of people worshipping or two friends playing a game?

Writing

Write a Scene Write a scene between Abuela and Constancia in which Constancia apologizes to Abuela and explains what she has learned and how she has changed. Your scene should show how their conflict has been resolved.

TIP

Evaluating
When a question asks you to evaluate, you will need to combine text information with your own knowledge and experience to form a judgment.

- Think about the things Constancia says and does.

- Ask yourself whether Constancia's words and actions seem like things a teenager might say and do.

- Consider whether Constancia reminds you of yourself or of other people you know.

- Use the text details and your own knowledge to decide whether Constancia is a believable character.

FOLDABLES Keep track of
Study Organizer your ideas about the **BIG Question** in your unit Foldable.

 Literature Online

Selection Resources
For Selection Quizzes, eFlashcards, and Reading-Writing Connection activities, go to glencoe.com and enter QuickPass code GL39770u1.

Learning Objectives

For pages 80–81

In this workshop, you will focus on the following objective:

Grammar: Combining sentences.

Sentence Combining

In the following quotation, Judith Ortiz Cofer combines several ideas into one sentence.

> *"She doesn't speak to me on the way home, and she doesn't let me help her walk, even though she almost falls a couple of times."*
>
> —Judith Ortiz Cofer, "Abuela Invents the Zero"

If Cofer had not combined the ideas into one sentence, she might have written:

> *She doesn't speak to me on the way home. She doesn't let me help her walk. She almost falls a couple of times.*

In your own writing, you can make similar choices about sentence length and structure. As you combine short sentences into longer ones, you begin to develop your own writing style. Study the following solutions to help you combine sentences and make your writing more interesting.

Examples

Solution 1 Use a **coordinating conjunction** to join words or groups of words in a sentence. Coordinating conjunctions include words such as *and, but, or, nor, so, for,* and *yet.* Two or more simple sentences (independent clauses) can be combined into a **compound sentence** with a coordinating conjunction.

Original sentence: Constancia went into her room. She thought about what she had done. Her mother was still angry with her.

Combined: Constancia went into her room and thought about what she had done, but her mother was still angry with her.

Solution 2 Use a **subordinating conjunction** to join two clauses, or ideas, to make one dependent on the other. Subordinating clauses include words such as *after, although, as, because, if, since,* and *when.*

Original sentence: I think that Constancia will finally apologize to Abuela. That's the right thing to do.

Combined: I think that Constancia will finally apologize to Abuela because that's the right thing to do.

Watch Out!

When two main clauses are connected by a coordinating conjunction, the first main clause often ends with a comma. You can also use a semicolon to join main clauses.

Helpful Hint

To identify subordinate clauses, look for subordinating conjunctions followed by a subject and verb. Other subordinating conjunctions include *while, although, as though, if, since, so long as, unless,* and *until.*

Solution 3 Use a **prepositional phrase,** a group of words that begins with a preposition and ends with a noun or pronoun.

Original sentence: Abuela glared at Constancia. Her eyes showed her great anger.

Combined: Abuela glared at Constancia with eyes that showed great anger.

Solution 4 Use an **adjective clause,** a group of words with a subject and predicate that modifies a noun or a pronoun. Adjective clauses begin with *who, whom, whose, that,* and *which.*

Original sentence: Abuela was due to arrive at the airport. She was coming from Puerto Rico.

Combined: Abuela, who was coming from Puerto Rico, was due to arrive at the airport.

Solution 5 Use an **appositive** or an **appositive phrase.** An appositive is a noun placed next to another noun to identify it or give additional information about it. An appositive phrase includes an appositive and other words that describe it.

Original sentence: The narrator of this story is Constancia. She is the granddaughter of Abuela.

Combined: The narrator of this story is Constancia, the granddaughter of Abuela.

TRY IT: Sentence Combining

Write a sentence that combines each group of elements.

1. Constancia had to take Abuela to church. She wanted to go out with her friends.

2. Constancia finally agreed to take Abuela to church. Her father promised to let her use the car.

3. Abuela walked through the church. She had a lost look on her face.

4. Constancia wished she were somewhere else. She was embarrassed of being with Abuela.

5. Constancia was a high-school age girl. She did not treat her abuela very well.

Literature Online

Grammar For more grammar practice, go to glencoe.com and enter QuickPass code GL39770u1.

Who Can Be Born Black and Saying Yes

Connect to the Poems

Think about all the things that form your identity—your heritage, your family, your interests, your friends, and your hometown.

List Create a detailed list of things that form your identity. Note whether each item belongs to a specific category. Some examples of possible categories include people, places, or interests.

Build Background

The United States has often been called a "melting pot" because it is home to people from many different countries.

- Mari Evans identifies both the challenges and pleasures of being an African American in the United States.

- Diana Chang describes moving between China and the United States as being "translated" from one culture to another.

Set Purposes for Reading

BQ ▶ **BIG Question**

Read the poems to find out how recognizing their identity helps people believe in themselves.

Literary Element Theme

The **theme** of a literary work is the main message that occurs throughout the work. To identify the theme, ask yourself, what is the main message of this poem?

Meet the Authors

Mari Evans

Mari Evans's works celebrate her African-American heritage and criticize the injustice of racism. She believed in herself and had poetry, plays, children's books, and musicals published.

Mari Evans was born in 1923.

Diana Chang

Diana Chang's Chinese heritage inspires much of her poetry and fiction. She was born in New York City but spent part of her childhood in China before returning to the United States.

Diana Chang was born in 1934.

Who Can Be Born Black

Mari Evans

Thinking, 1990. Carlton Murrell. Oil on board. Private Collection.

Who
can be born black
and not
sing
5   the wonder of it
the joy
the challenge

And/to come together
in a coming togetherness
10   vibrating with the fires of pure knowing
reeling with power
ringing with the sound above sound above sound
to explode/in the majesty of our oneness
our comingtogether
15   in a comingtogetherness

Who
can be born
black
and not exult[1]

---

1   *Exult* means "to rejoice or to leap for joy."

Theme What do the words *joy* and *challenge* convey about the speaker's understanding of life for most African Americans?

Saying Yes

Diana Chang

*Asian Woman with Hair
Comb.* Todd Davidson.

"Are you Chinese?"
"Yes."

"American?"
"Yes."

5   *Really* Chinese?"
"No . . . not quite."

"*Really* American?"
"Well, actually, you see . . ."

But I would rather say
10   yes

Not neither-nor,
not maybe,
but both, and not only

The homes I've had,
15   the ways I am

I'd rather say it
twice,
yes

Theme What theme about
identity is expressed in lines
11–13?

BQ BIG Question

In what way does the
repetition of the word *yes* in
lines 2, 4, 10, and 18 reflect
the speaker's belief in
herself?

After You Read

Respond and Think Critically

1. What are five words or expressions that the speaker uses to describe her feelings about her heritage in "Who Can Be Born Black"? In your own words, describe these feelings. [Paraphrase]

2. What two parts of the speaker's identity are discussed in "Saying Yes"? [Recall and Identify]

3. What does the word *really* mean in lines 5 and 7 of "Saying Yes"? Why does the speaker in the poem hesitate when the questioner uses that word? [Interpret]

4. What is the questioner in "Saying Yes" trying to do by repeatedly asking the same questions in different ways? What can you infer about the type of answer the questioner is looking for? [Infer]

5. In what way do the speaker's answers to "Who Can Be Born Black" convey the poem's theme? [Analyze]

6. BIG Question In what way do these two poems show that the speakers share a similar belief in themselves? [Compare]

TIP

Interpreting
Here is a tip to help you interpret. Use what you know about the world to think about why the speaker wanted to emphasize the word *really*. Think about what point the speaker is trying to make.

FOLDABLES
Study Organizer Keep track of your ideas about the **BIG Question** in your unit Foldable.

Academic Vocabulary

In "Who Can Be Born Black," the speaker's attitude toward her cultural heritage might be described as **energetic.** To become more familiar with the word *energetic,* create a graphic organizer like the one below and fill in the boxes.

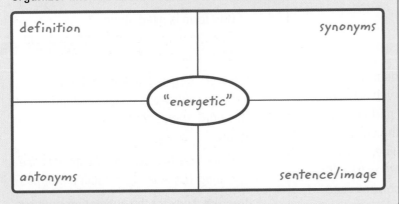

definition   synonyms

"energetic"

antonyms   sentence/image

 Writing

Write a Stanza Use the words or phrases that you entered in the list on page 82 and what you have learned from reading the poems to write a short, one-stanza poem about an occasion when you demonstrated self-confidence.

LOG ON **Literature** Online

Selection Resources
For Selection Quizzes, eFlashcards, and Reading-Writing Connection activities, go to glencoe.com and enter QuickPass code GL39770u1.

1. A **recurring theme** is a message about life or human nature found across different texts. What recurring theme is common to both poems? Support your answer with textual evidence.

2. Which poem best expresses the recurring theme? In your response, consider the different speakers and the way each presents her thoughts and feelings.

Review: **Repetition**

Both poems use the **repetition** of words and phrases to emphasize meaning and to create rhythm, or a musical quality.

3. What words or phrases in "Who Can Be Born Black" are repeated? In what way do they help create rhythm and feeling in the poem?

4. In "Who Can Be Born Black," the speaker combines words to make bigger words (that aren't standard English words). What effect do these "word creations" have on the rhythm of the poem?

5. What words or phrases in "Saying Yes" are repeated? In what way do they contribute to the meaning of the poem?

Listening and Speaking

Performance Read one of the poems aloud to your classmates. You may work with a partner. If you choose "Saying Yes," one partner can read the questioner's lines and the other partner can read the answering lines. If you choose "Who Can Be Born Black," work with two other classmates. Each person can read one stanza. Practice reading your stanza until you can read it with appropriate pace, tone of voice, rhythm, and gestures. Then read the poem as a group, with each member reading the stanza he or she practiced.

Grammar Link

Personal Pronouns, Possessive Pronouns, and Antecedents A pronoun is a word that takes the place of one or more nouns. A personal pronoun refers to a specific person or thing. Personal pronouns replace nouns that are subjects or objects in sentences.

Mr. and Mrs. Larson enjoy flowers. Every spring they plant a big garden. (They replaces the subject of the first sentence, Mr. and Mrs. Larson.)

The teacher praised Jim for his report. The teacher told him he did a good job. (Him replaces the object of the first sentence, Jim.)

You may use pronouns in place of possessive nouns also. A possessive pronoun is a pronoun that shows who or what has something. Possessive pronouns have two forms.

One form of the possessive pronoun is used before a noun.
Carol's class wrote a play. Her class also performed the play.

One form is used alone.
The students voted on the best poem. Mine won the prize.

The word or group of words that a pronoun refers to is called its *antecedent*. The word *antecedent* means "going before."

Mark likes baseball, but he doesn't like fishing. (Mark is the antecedent of he.)

Practice Look for the subject pronouns in "Saying Yes." In what way does the speaker's use of these pronouns suggest a conversation? What is the antecedent of the object pronoun *it* at the end of this poem?

Learning Objectives

For pages 87–90

In studying this text, you will focus on the following objectives:

Reading: Determining main idea and supporting details.

Set a Purpose for Reading

Read to discover what the writer reveals about the value of staying true to yourself.

Preview the Article

1. Read the *deck*, or subtitle, beneath the article's title. What do you suppose is the answer to this question?

2. Scan the captions that accompany the photographs. What do they tell you about the writer's conclusions?

Reading Skill

Determine Main Idea and Supporting Details

The most important idea in a paragraph or passage is called the **main idea**. **Supporting details** explain the main idea. Look at the section headings in the selection. Identify the main idea of each section. Write your ideas in a graphic organizer like the one below.

Main Idea:

Detail 1

Detail 2

Detail 3

TIME

The Question of Popularity

How much does popularity matter?

By TAMARA EBERLEIN

Being popular means that other kids think you're cool. It doesn't mean (as many parents may think) that the cool kids are especially well liked or nice or admired for their smarts. Popular kids may be envied for their cool factor, but they may not have a lot of close friends.

If you're like most middle schoolers, you've probably thought about how much (or perhaps how little) popularity matters to you. It's not unusual to want to fit in. But it's more important to have a few close friends, accept yourself for who you are, and be comfortable with the people you do hang out with.

The In Crowd

Kids know that in most schools there is an "in crowd" of kids who are the most popular. Emily Kaplan, a middle schooler in Larchmont, New York, describes her school's in crowd this way: "The girls are kind of snobby, the boys obnoxious. If you laugh at something, they just go, 'That's not funny.' [But] when you're alone together, the popular girls are really nice." Emily's friend Liana Diamond adds, "When they're with their other friends, they don't talk to you."

Who is popular varies from place to place. And of course, not every popular kid is obnoxious or a snob or unfriendly. Believe it or not, for some kids who are popular, it's hard work to stay that way. Trying to stay on top can cause stress and insecurity because who's popular and who's not can change daily.

The Middle Group

The majority of kids fall somewhere in between the top and the bottom—and many adults say that kids in the middle group may be happiest and best off. "These kids have several close friends and are also part of a larger group that explores their interests, like soccer or music. They aren't overly caught up in the popularity game,"

Being popular isn't as important as having a few close friends who accept you for who you are.

Sean Murphy/Stone/Getty Images

says Sandy Sheehy, who has written a book about friendships. "What's important is not [if you get] invited to the 'right' sleepovers. It's whether [you have] a few close friends."

Margaret Sagarese, coauthor of a book about cliques, has a tip for kids who are trying to figure out where they belong. She suggests that you keep a list of what you like about yourself. "Social acceptance and personal acceptance are two very different things. [You] need to see that liking [yourself] is more important than being part of the in crowd," she says. If being a part of the in group means acting in ways that you wouldn't normally act or want to act, then stay true to yourself. Make decisions according to your own values. Don't be afraid to be you.

The Free Thinkers

What makes a kid less than popular? Sometimes it's the "wrong" clothes. Sometimes it's an embarrassing incident that a young person can't live down. And sometimes there's just no way of knowing.

"My friends and I are kind of the geeky group," says Zach McGraw,* a middle schooler in South Bend, Indiana. "I've wished I could be popular millions of times. But I've managed to find a good group to hang out with."

---

* Name and location have been changed to protect privacy.

Kids like Zach might find a new friend or a group to hang out with outside of school—at church, synagogue,[1] martial arts classes, book clubs, or summer camps. Seeking out others with similar interests is often a good place to start trying to fit in and to develop relationships.

Having one good friend whom you can connect with makes a world of difference. When you like who that person is and can trust that person—then you have a true friendship that will last. Good friends build us up and help us feel confident about ourselves. They will most likely be around long after the in crowd is just a memory.

---

1 A *synagogue* is a Jewish house of worship.

In Their Own Words:

Kids Talk About Popularity

Want to know what other teens really think about cliques, geeks, and being cool? Read on for the innermost thoughts of middle schoolers.

BABYJOHN: "At my old school I didn't have many friends. When I moved, I was suddenly accepted into the in crowd. But I have bad memories of being unpopular, and I sometimes worry that my closest friends will exclude me."

RIVERRUNNER: "I had no real friends for about one-third of the year. When I finally thought I had found a true friend, she said to me that a different girl we hang out with was 'popular,' that she was 'semipopular,' and that 'no offense, but you're a total geek.' Now we just don't ever talk, and I am more happy with the not-so-popular group. And I have a few friends outside of school that I hang out with."

CHERRY-COLA: "Lately, I have been feeling so unhip. I buy clothes and jewelry that make me seem more like everyone else. I feel as though I have to keep updating myself so that other people won't think I'm a loser. How you dress has everything to do with who you are."

TESTSCHIK182: "My best friend of five years was put in classes with all of the popular people. She'll do anything to be in the in crowd. I am definitely not a dork, but I'm not popular. [My best friend] has started to ignore me in the hall. How can I talk to her without feeling like an idiot? Her new friends aren't true friends at all."

MARISSA: "At the beginning of this year, the most popular guy in school liked me. I had tons of friends. But toward the middle of the year, Mr. Popular dumped me. Now I'm really lonely, I get made fun of a lot, and most kids don't like me."

Having several close friends and being part of a larger group may make kids happiest and best off.

HAPPY DUDE: "I get teased, hit, punched. I don't know if I should hit them back or just run away; I feel that rips apart my courage and self-confidence. I don't know what to do."

SHORTY11: "During the school year, I was rejected and not invited to parties, movies, etc. But once the summer began, I met new people who accepted me for who I was, not for the clothing I wore or for my looks. So my advice to other kids is to hang on to the friends you've got and make an effort to meet new people." 🖱

Respond and Think Critically

1. According to the writer, what three groups do middle school students fall into? [Recall]

2. Do parents' and kids' definitions of *cool* differ? What does this say about parents and kids? [Interpret]

3. Which group of kids does Eberlein say are usually happiest? Do you agree? Why or why not? [Make Judgments]

4. Do you think teen popularity is a topic an adult writer can understand? Why or why not? [Respond]

5. **Reading Skill** Determine Main Idea and Supporting Details When you analyzed the selection, what evidence did you find to support its main ideas? Did your analysis make you think there should be more evidence? Use your graphic organizer to help you answer. [Analyze]

6. **BQ** BIG Question Is it possible to stay true to yourself and still be popular? Why or why not? [Evaluate]

The People Could Fly

Connect to the Folktale

Remember a time when you wanted to make a situation better.

Partner Talk With a partner, talk about the problem you faced and how you overcame it. Share your thoughts with the class.

Build Background

This story takes place on a plantation in the United States during slavery times.

- The practice of kidnapping Africans and bringing them to North America as enslaved people began in 1619. Africans were brought to the United States on large ships like the one shown below. Slavery was allowed to continue in parts of the country until the end of the Civil War in 1865.

- "The People Could Fly" is a folktale loosely based on fact. In the early 1800s, a group of enslaved West Africans rose up against the slave agents that were carrying them from one part of Georgia to another by boat. The agents were killed, and the West Africans were never found.

- Local slave owners believed that the West Africans drowned themselves to escape bondage. But enslaved people on the plantations had a very different explanation of what happened. That explanation is reflected in "The People Could Fly."

Meet Virginia Hamilton

"In the background of much of my writing is the dream of freedom tantalizingly out of reach."

—Virginia Hamilton

Stories of Escape Virginia Hamilton's works celebrate her African-American ancestry and culture. "The People Could Fly" is based on a folktale told since the time of slavery. Hamilton's own grandfather escaped from slavery by crossing the Ohio River. As Hamilton and her characters show, storytelling is a way to preserve cultural heritage.

Literary Works Hamilton is the author of many award-winning books for young people. *The People Could Fly: American Black Folktales* was published in 1985.

Virginia Hamilton was born in 1936 and died in 2002.

 Literature Online

Author Search For more about Virginia Hamilton, go to glencoe.com and enter QuickPass code GL39770u1.

Set Purposes for Reading

▶ BQ ▶ BIG Question

As you read, think about what "believe in yourself" means to the characters. How does it affect the choices they make?

Literary Elements ▸ Setting and Mood

Setting is the time and place in which a story occurs. The setting includes any elements in which the action occurs: the historical period; geographic region; season; weather; and spaces, such as rooms and landscapes. The culture of the characters is also part of the setting. **Mood** is the feeling created by the time, place, or events of a story. For example, if a story takes place in a dark, broken-down house, the setting will create a gloomy mood.

Setting and mood shape the way we feel about a story, helping us understand—and sympathize with—the characters.

As you read "The People Could Fly," think about how the setting affects the mood of the story.

Reading Skill ▸ Identify Sequence

The order in which thoughts and actions are arranged is called **sequence.** To identify sequence, note the order in which one event follows another.

For example, you arrive at your grandmother's house. Then you get in the car with your family to drive there. How could that happen? You have to travel to a place first before you can arrive there. In a story, events usually take place in **chronological order**, or time order.

As you read, try using a graphic organizer like the timeline below to help you keep track of the sequence of events within the folktale.

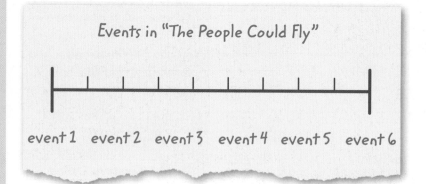

TRY IT

Identify Sequence You plan to write a report on Frederick Douglass. In what order would you perform the following tasks?

- Revise report
- Conduct research on the topic
- Draft report

The People Could Fly

Virginia Hamilton

The People Could Fly, 1985. Leo and Diane Dillon. Pastel and watercolor. Private collection.

They say the people could fly. Say that long ago in Africa, some of the people knew magic. And they would walk up on the air like climbin up on a gate. And they flew like blackbirds over the fields. Black, shiny wings flappin against the blue up there.

Then, many of the people were captured for Slavery. The ones that could fly shed their wings. They couldn't take their wings across the water on the slave ships. Too crowded, don't you know.

The folks were full of misery, then. Got sick with the up and down of the sea. So they forgot about flyin when they could no longer breathe the sweet scent of Africa.

Say the people who could fly kept their power, although they shed their wings. They kept their secret magic in the land of slavery. They looked the same as the other people from Africa who had been coming over, who had dark skin. Say you couldn't tell anymore one who could fly from one who couldn't.

Setting and Mood What do you learn about the setting of the folktale from these lines?

One such who could was an old man, call him Toby. And standin tall, yet afraid, was a young woman who once had wings. Call her Sarah. Now Sarah carried a babe tied to her back. She trembled to be so hard worked and scorned.

The slaves labored in the fields from sunup to sundown. The owner of the slaves callin himself their Master. Say he was a hard lump of clay. A hard, glinty coal. A hard rock pile, wouldn't be moved. His Overseer[1] on horseback pointed out the slaves who were slowin down. So the one called Driver cracked his whip over the slow ones to make them move faster. That whip was a slice-open cut of pain. So they did move faster. Had to.

Sarah hoed and chopped the row as the babe on her back slept.

Say the child grew hungry. That babe started up bawling too loud. Sarah couldn't stop to feed it. Couldn't stop to soothe and quiet it down. She let it cry. She didn't want to. She had no heart to croon[2] to it.

"Keep that thing quiet," called the Overseer. He pointed his finger at the babe. The woman scrunched low. The Driver cracked his whip across the babe anyhow. The babe hollered like any hurt child, and the woman fell to the earth.

The old man that was there, Toby, came and helped her to her feet.

"I must go soon," she told him.

"Soon," he said.

Sarah couldn't stand up straight any longer. She was too weak. The sun burned her face. The babe cried and cried, "Pity me, oh, pity me," say it sounded like. Sarah was so sad and starvin, she sat down in the row.

"Get up, you black cow," called the Overseer. He pointed his hand, and the Driver's whip snarled around Sarah's legs. Her sack dress tore into rags. Her legs bled onto the earth. She couldn't get up.

Toby was there where there was no one to help her and the babe.

Identify Sequence Identify three events that have happened to Sarah. List the events in order.

Setting and Mood What does the burning sun tell readers about the setting? Explain the mood, or feeling, this detail creates.

---

1 During slavery times, the **overseer** directed the enslaved people.

2 To **croon** is to hum or sing in a low, soft tone.

"Now, before it's too late," panted Sarah. "Now, Father!"

"Yes, Daughter, the time is come," Toby answered. "Go, as you know how to go!"

He raised his arms, holding them out to her. *"Kum . . . yali, kum buba tambe,"* and more magic words, said so quickly, they sounded like whispers and sighs.

The young woman lifted one foot on the air. Then the other. She flew clumsily at first, with the child now held tightly in her arms. Then she felt the magic, the African mystery. Say she rose just as free as a bird. As light as a feather.

The Overseer rode after her, hollerin. Sarah flew over the fences. She flew over the woods. Tall trees could not snag her. Nor could the Overseer. She flew like an eagle now, until she was gone from sight. No one dared speak about it. Couldn't believe it. But it was, because they that was there saw that it was.

Say the next day was dead hot in the fields. A young man slave fell from the heat. The Driver come and whipped him. Toby come over and spoke words to the fallen one. The words of ancient Africa once heard are never remembered completely. The young man forgot them as soon as he heard them. They went way inside him. He got up and rolled over on the air. He rode it awhile. And he flew away.

Another and another fell from the heat. Toby was there. He cried out to the fallen and reached his arms out to them. *"Kum kunka yali, kum . . . tambe!"* Whispers and sighs. And they too rose on the air. They rode the hot breezes. The ones flyin were black and shinin sticks, wheelin above the head of the Overseer. They crossed the rows, the fields, the fences, the streams, and were away.

"Seize the old man!" cried the Overseer. "I heard him say the magic *words.* Seize him!"

The one callin himself Master come runnin. The Driver got his whip ready to curl around old Toby and tie him up. The slaveowner took his hip gun from its place. He meant to kill old, black Toby.

But Toby just laughed. Say he threw back his head and said, "Hee, hee! Don't you know who I am? Don't you know some of us in this field?" He said it to their faces. "We are ones who fly!"

And he sighed the ancient words that were a dark promise. He said them all around to the others in the field under the whip, ". . . *buba yali . . . buba tambe . . . .*"

There was a great outcryin. The bent backs straighted up. Old and young who were called slaves and could fly joined hands. Say like they would ring-sing. But they didn't shuffle in a circle. They didn't sing. They rose on the air. They flew in a flock that was black against the heavenly blue. Black crows or black shadows. It didn't matter, they went so high. Way above the plantation, way over the slavery land. Say they flew away to *Free-dom.*

And the old man, old Toby, flew behind them, takin care of them. He wasn't cryin. He wasn't laughin. He was the seer.[3] His gaze fell on the plantation where the slaves who could not fly waited.

"Take us with you!" Their looks spoke it but they were afraid to shout it. Toby couldn't take them with him. Hadn't the time to teach them to fly. They must wait for a chance to run.

"Goodie-bye!" The old man called Toby spoke to them, poor souls! And he was flyin gone.

So they say. The Overseer told it. The one called Master said it was a lie, a trick of the light. The Driver kept his mouth shut.

The slaves who could not fly told about the people who could fly to their children. When they were free. When they sat close before the fire in the free land, they told it. They did so love firelight and *Free-dom,* and tellin.

They say that the children of the ones who could not fly told their children. And now, me, I have told it to you. 🐦

---

3 A *seer* is a prophet or someone who is unusually wise.

Setting and Mood What details within this passage indicate that the mood of the folktale has changed?

BQ **BIG Question**
How do the enslaved people demonstrate they believe in themselves? Explain what happens to them as a result of their strong belief.

Identify Sequence Recall the events that happened after the enslaved people flew and before the speaker tells the story to us.

After You Read

Respond and Think Critically

1. Explain how the enslaved people lost their wings. [Summarize]

2. Why was it important for the enslaved people who were left behind to tell this story to their children? [Evaluate]

3. Why is Toby the one who knows the magic words? [Infer]

4. Toby helps a young man fly away. What happens before this? What happens afterwards? [Recall]

5. "The People Could Fly" takes place aboard a ship, in the fields of a plantation, and in the air above and beyond the plantation. In what way does the mood change from the beginning to the end of the folktale? [Analyze]

6. **BIG Question** The enslaved people had to believe in themselves in order to fly. What does "believe in yourself" mean to you? How can you show that you believe in yourself? [Connect]

TIP

Evaluating
Traditions are the most valued practices or beliefs within a culture.

- Like character traits, they help define a culture.

- They provide a sense of history, linking one generation to the next.

Folktales are one way in which traditions are passed down.

FOLDABLES Keep track of
Study Organizer your ideas about
the **BIG Question** in your
unit Foldable.

Connect to Social Studies

Until 1865, when all enslaved people in the United States were freed, millions of people of African descent toiled on plantations. They lived under harsh conditions and were forced to raise crops like cotton and tobacco. Although enslaved people grew and harvested the crops, the plantation owner sold the crops and kept any profit. This system was known as a "plantation economy." Why did the plantation economy exist for so many years? Who benefited from this system? Present what you learned to the class.

Literary Elements Setting and Mood

Test Skills Practice

1. In what century, and in what part of the United States, does the story occur? What details offer clues on when and where the story takes place?

Review: Theme

Theme is the main message about life or human nature that the author shares with the reader. Sometimes a theme is **stated** directly, for example, "Be honest," or "Respect your elders."

When a theme is not stated directly, it is **implied**—indicated or suggested by what happens in the story. In that case, you have to figure out the implied theme by analyzing the story's other elements, such as plot, setting, and character.

Test Skills Practice

2. In your own words, write the theme of the story. Then find a passage in the story that expresses the theme.
3. Is the theme of "The People Could Fly" implied or stated? Support your answer with evidence from the story.

Reading Skill Identify Sequence

Test Skills Practice

4. The Master "come runnin" when
   - **A** we first meet the Overseer.
   - **B** Sarah flies away.
   - **C** Toby helps the other slaves fly.
   - **D** Toby flies away.

Academic Vocabulary

The West Africans underwent a **transformation** when they were captured and lost their wings. In the preceding sentence, *transformation* means change. Think about a time when you underwent a *transformation*. How did you change? What caused the change? What were the results of the change? You might use a web like the one below to organize your answer.

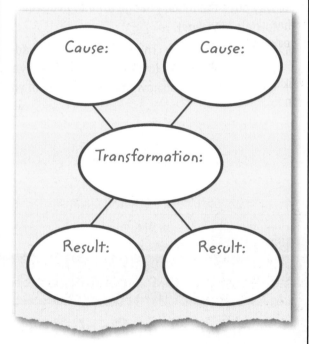

 **Literature** Online

Selection Resources For Selection Quizzes, eFlashcards, and Reading-Writing Connection activities, go to glencoe.com and enter QuickPass code GL39770u1.

Respond Through Writing

Short Story

Apply Plot Development "The People Could Fly" is a folktale in which the characters overcome the terrors of slavery by flying away. In your own folktale, create an exciting plot (with all five plot elements) in which characters develop a unique way of overcoming a problem. Make your characters come alive by using dialogue and by describing their movements and gestures. In your story, show the significance of, or your attitude about, the subject.

Understand the Task A folktale usually explains how or why something in nature or in a culture happened. It can include events that aren't possible in real life or characters with traits that aren't realistic, such as people flying or animals talking.

Prewrite To help you organize your story, fill out a graphic organizer like the one below. Add as many rows as you need. Be sure each event in the story leads to the next one.

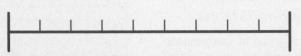

Long ago, some people in Africa had wings and could fly.

They lost their wings when they were captured and enslaved.

Draft You may want to use sentence frames as you draft your folktale. For instance, to begin your folktale, write a sentence describing the setting—where and when the story takes place.

Long, long ago, deep in a dark forest _____.

As you write your folktale, use words and phrases that give details about the setting. Also, add dialogue, movements, and gestures to help bring your characters to life.

It was so long ago, the animals could still _____. One day, under the tallest, thickest trees, the animals gathered for a meeting. They _____.

Revise Trade papers with a partner. Ask your partner to number the events in your folktale. If your partner thinks the events are out of order, work together to rearrange them in a logical sequence.

Edit and Proofread Proofread your folktale, correcting any errors in spelling, grammar, and punctuation. Review the Grammar Tip in the side column for information on correct grammar use.

> **Grammar Tip**

Quotation Marks
Look at these two sentences from "The People Could Fly." In both, we see a speaker's words followed by a speaker tag that identifies who is talking. How is the punctuation different?

"Now, before it's too late," panted Sarah.

"Seize the old man!" cried the Overseer.

In the first sentence, the quote ends in a comma to separate the quote from the speaker tag. In the second sentence, the quote ends in an exclamation mark, so a comma isn't needed to separate the Overseer's words from the speaker tag. Remember that the punctuation at the end of the quote always goes within, not outside, the quotation marks.

Barbara Frietchie

Connect to the Poem

Think about a time when you stood up for something you believed in.

Quickwrite Describe in a few sentences what you believed in and supported. Why was this issue important to you? How did you show your support? Did others respect your ideas?

Build Background

"Barbara Frietchie" is a poem about a legendary American heroine who reportedly defied Confederate soldiers during the Civil War. As they marched through her town, she waved the American flag from an upper window of her home.

- Barbara Frietchie lived in Frederick, Maryland, which was a crossroads during the Civil War. Both Confederate and Union troops passed through Frederick on their way to battles.

- Stonewall Jackson, shown below, led a group of Confederate troops that occupied Frederick, Maryland. Confederate and Union troops were moving toward the Battle of Antietam in 1862, the bloodiest one-day battle of the Civil War.

 Literature Online

Author Search For more about John Greenleaf Whittier, go to glencoe.com and enter QuickPass code GL39770u1.

Meet John Greenleaf Whittier

Poet and Slavery Opponent
John Greenleaf Whittier was eighteen years old when his sister secretly sent one of his poems to a local paper in Massachusetts. Not only did the editor of the paper print the poem, but he also encouraged the shy farmer's son to educate himself and develop his talent. After two terms of high school, Whittier went on to work as a journalist and writer. He wrote for forty years before achieving financial success with his poetry. He also became heavily involved in the anti-slavery movement at the local, state, and national levels.

Literary Works Whittier published many volumes of poetry, articles, reviews, and one novel. "Barbara Frietchie" was first published in 1863.

John Greenleaf Whittier was born in 1807 and died in 1892.

Set Purposes for Reading

BQ BIG Question

As you read, think about Barbara Frietchie's brave action. Why do you think her courage helped her stay true to herself?

Literary Element Narrative Poetry

A **narrative poem** tells a story in poetic form. Like traditional stories, it has characters, a setting, and a plot. **Characters** are the people in a story. The **setting** is the time and place in which the events happen. **Plot** is the sequence of related events in a story.

It is important to read narrative poetry so you can appreciate its rhythm and rhyme and understand the similarities and differences it has with other types of stories. Narrative poetry about historical events and figures can also teach readers valuable lessons about the past.

As you read "Barbara Frietchie," identify the characters, the setting, and the plot.

Reading Strategy Summarize

When you **summarize,** you restate the main ideas of something you read using your own words. For example, when a friend asks you what happened in a book, don't explain every detail. Instead, just describe the parts that help your friend understand what happened.

Summarizing will help you understand what you read and retell the important points of a story. As you read,

- observe information about the characters and setting
- notice the problem and the events that lead to its resolution
- summarize by tying together the information about the characters, setting, and plot

You may find it helpful to use a graphic organizer like the one below to help you summarize.

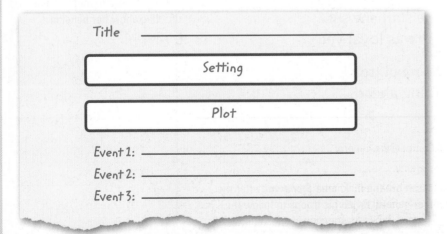

Title _____

Setting

Plot

Event 1: _____
Event 2: _____
Event 3: _____

Learning Objectives

For pages 100–106

In studying this text, you will focus on the following objectives:

Literary Study:
Analyzing narrative poetry.

Summarizing the events of a narrative poem.

TRY IT

Summarize Think about something that happened in the last few days. Describe what happened to a partner, telling only the most important events and details.

BARBARA FRIETCHIE

John Greenleaf Whittier

Up from the meadows rich with corn,
Clear in the cool September morn,

The clustered spires of Frederick stand
Green-walled by the hills of Maryland.

5   Round about them orchards sweep,
Apple and peach tree fruited deep,

Fair as the garden of the Lord
To the eyes of the famished rebel horde,[1]

On that pleasant morn of the early fall
10 When Lee[2] marched over the mountain wall;

Over the mountains winding down,
Horse and foot, into Frederick town.

Forty flags with their silver stars,
Forty flags with their crimson bars,

15 Flapped in the morning wind: the sun
Of noon looked down, and saw not one.

Up rose old Barbara Frietchie then,
Bowed with her fourscore[3] years and ten;

Bravest of all in Frederick town,
20 She took up the flag the men hauled down

In her attic window the staff she set,
To show that one heart was loyal yet.

Up the street came the rebel tread,
Stonewall[4] Jackson riding ahead.

Narrative Poetry What details does the speaker use to describe the **setting** at Frederick? How might the town of Frederick symbolize the United States?

BQ **BIG Question**
In what way does Barbara Frietchie's reaction to the flag show her belief in herself?

---

1 A **horde** is a large group.

2 **Robert E. Lee** was the most famous Confederate general.

3 One **score** is twenty, so **fourscore** is eighty.

4 Confederate General Thomas J. Jackson got the nickname **Stonewall** after the First Battle of Bull Run in 1861. Another general urged his troops to follow the example of Jackson, exclaiming, "There is Jackson, standing like a stone wall."

25   Under his slouched
       hat left and right
   He glanced; the old
       flag met his sight.

   "Halt!"—the dust-
       brown ranks
       stood fast.
   "Fire!"—out blazed
       the rifle-blast.

   It shivered the
       window, pane
       and sash;
30 It rent the banner with seam and gash.

   Quick, as it fell, from the broken staff
   Dame[5] Barbara snatched the silken scarf.

   She leaned far out on the window-sill,
   And shook it forth with a royal will.

35 "Shoot, if you must, this old gray head,
   But spare your country's flag," she said.

   A shade of sadness, a blush of shame,
   Over the face of the leader came;

   The nobler nature within him stirred
40 To life at that woman's deed and word;

   "Who touches a hair of yon gray head
   Dies like a dog! March on!" he said.

   All day long through Frederick street
   Sounded the tread of marching feet:

Summarize In your own words, summarize the events that caused Barbara Frietchie to snatch up the flag.

Narrative Poetry Why is Stonewall Jackson's change in attitude important to the **plot** of the poem?

---

5 ***Dame*** is a title formerly used for the woman in charge of a household.

45 All day long that free flag tost[6]
Over the heads of the rebel host.[7]

Ever its torn folds rose and fell
On the loyal winds that loved it well;

And through the hill-gaps sunset light
50 Shone over it with a warm good-night.

Barbara Frietchie's work is o'er,
And the Rebel rides on his raids no more.

Honor to her! and let a tear
Fall, for her sake, on Stonewall's bier.[8]

55 Over Barbara Frietchie's grave,
Flag of Freedom and Union, wave!

Peace and order and beauty draw
Round thy symbol of light and law;

And ever the stars above look down
60 On thy stars below in Frederick town! ✤

Summarize List three main points that explain why Barbara Frietchie is thought of as a heroine.

---

6 **Tost** is an old spelling of *tossed*.

7 **Host**, here, means "army."

8 A **bier** (bēr) is a stand on which a coffin is placed before it is buried.

After You Read

Respond and Think Critically

1. What does Barbara Frietchie do after the soldiers shoot at her flag? [Identify]

2. Why does the speaker make a point to include Barbara Frietchie's age in the poem? [Draw Conclusions]

3. In lines 20–22, what is the speaker's attitude toward all of the townspeople except Barbara Frietchie? Explain your thoughts. [Infer]

4. Identify patterns of rhyming words in the poem. Why do you think the author chose to write "Barbara Frietchie" as a poem rather than as narrative prose? [Analyze]

5. Describe briefly the events that occur after Barbara Frietchie tells Stonewall Jackson "Shoot, if you must, this old gray head, / But spare your country's flag." [Summarize]

6. **BIG Question** In what way do Barbara Frietchie's actions show that she believes in herself? What are some other ways people show that they believe in themselves? [Connect]

Academic Vocabulary

Barbara Frietchie's actions were **symbolic** for the Union during the Civil War.

In the preceding sentence, *symbolic* means "to act as a symbol." A symbol is an object, person, place, or experience that represents something larger than itself. Think about something in your life that is symbolic for you. What is it, and why is it symbolic?

TIP

Inferring
To answer the question, think about what Barbara Frietchie did that the other people in the town did not do. How does the poet feel about Barbara Frietchie's accomplishments?

FOLDABLES Study Organizer Keep track of your ideas about the **BIG Question** in your unit Foldable.

 Literature Online

Selection Resources
For Selection Quizzes, eFlashcards, and Reading-Writing Connection activities, go to glencoe.com and enter QuickPass code GL39770u1.

Literary Element Narrative Poetry

1. Based on lines 53–54, "Honor to her! and let a tear / Fall, for her sake, on Stonewall's bier," how does the speaker view Stonewall Jackson at the end of the poem?

2. What mood does Whittier create in the first sixteen lines of the poem? Support your answer with descriptions from the poem.

Review: Setting and Mood

As you learned on page 92, the **setting** of a story is the time and place in which the events happen. The words a writer uses to describe the setting often create a **mood** or emotion. For example, a description of a bright, warm kitchen might create a pleasant mood, while a description of a dark, damp forest creates a somber mood.

3. The first sixteen lines of the poem establish the setting. What mood does Whittier create by beginning the poem in this way?

Reading Strategy Summarize

4. Use your own words to describe events that lead up to Barbara Frietchie's confrontation with Stonewall Jackson.

Use a graphic organizer like the one below to fill in descriptive details from the narrative poem and then form a conclusion about the mood based on those details.

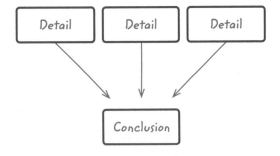

Grammar Link

Main Verbs and Helping Verbs Verbs are words that show action or a state of being. Verbs of two or more words are called **verb phrases**. The most important verb in a verb phrase is the **main verb**. The other verbs in the phrase are called **helping verbs**. They help the main verb tell *when* an action or a state of being occurs, or they help the main verb tell *whether* an action or state of being will occur.

> **One-word verb:** I <u>play</u> basketball.
> (*Play* is the main verb.)

> **Verb phrase:** I <u>have been</u> excited.
> (*Been* is the main verb; *have* is a helping verb.)

> **Verb phrase:** I <u>will be shooting</u> baskets.
> (*Shooting* is the main verb; *will be* is a helping verb.)

Practice Write three sentences about what happened in the poem "Barbara Frietchie." Be sure to use both main and helping verbs. Underline the main verbs once and the helping verbs twice.

Listening and Speaking

Literature Group Make a list of famous people who have stayed true to themselves and whose actions could be subjects of narrative poems.

Comparing Literature

from *Tom Sawyer* and *Born Worker*

Learning Objectives

For pages 107–127

In studying these texts, you will focus on the following objectives:

Literary Study: Analyzing characters.

Reading: Comparing and contrasting characters.

Writing: Writing a comparison.

BQ **BIG Question**

As you read these paired selections, think about how the main characters in *Tom Sawyer* and "Born Worker" try to stay true to themselves.

Literary Element **Character**

A **character** is a person, an animal, or an imaginary creature in a literary work. **Characterization** refers to the ways a writer develops a character. As you read each selection, pay attention to the main characters' actions, words, and thoughts to better understand each character's personality.

Also pay attention to what the narrator or other characters think or say about that character.

Reading Skill **Compare and Contrast**

Have you ever met a person who reminded you of someone else? The two people may have many similarities, but they probably also have differences. When you compare and contrast one person with another, you are recognizing ways in which they are alike and different.

You can understand literature better when you compare and contrast literary elements, such as characters. On the following pages, you'll compare and contrast the characters in *Tom Sawyer* and "Born Worker." You'll also consider their reactions and motivations. Use a graphic organizer like this one to help you.

Character	Character's Words, Thoughts, and Actions	What the narrator or other characters think or say
Tom Sawyer		
Ben		
José		
Arnie		

Meet the Authors

Mark Twain

Mark Twain wrote novels, stories, and essays. He was born in 1835 and died in 1910.

Gary Soto

Gary Soto grew up in California. He has published more than thirty books.

 Literature Online

Author Search For more about Mark Twain and Gary Soto, go to glencoe.com and enter QuickPass code GL39770u1.

from Tom Sawyer

Mark Twain

Saturday morning was come, and all the summer world was bright and fresh, and brimming with life. There was a song in every heart; and if the heart was young the music issued at the lips. There was cheer in every face, and a spring in every step. The locust trees were in bloom, and the fragrance of the blossoms filled the air.

Cardiff Hill, beyond the village and above it, was green with vegetation, and it lay just far enough away to seem a Delectable Land, dreamy, reposeful, and inviting.

Tom appeared on the sidewalk with a bucket of whitewash[1] and a long-handled brush. He surveyed the fence, and the gladness went out of nature, and a deep melancholy settled down upon his spirit. Thirty yards of board fence nine feet high! It seemed to him that life was hollow, and existence but a burden. Sighing he dipped his brush and passed it along the topmost plank; repeated the operation; did it again; compared the insignificant whitewashed streak with the far-reaching continent of unwhitewashed fence, and sat down on a tree-box discouraged. . . .

He began to think of the fun he had planned for this day, and his sorrows multiplied. Soon the free boys would come tripping along on all sorts of delicious expeditions, and they would make a world of fun of him for having to work—the very thought of it burnt him like fire. He got out his worldly

---

1 **Whitewash** is a white paint-like substance used to coat fences.

Tom Sawyer Whitewashing Fence. Worth Brehm.

View the Art Study the details of the painting on page 109. Then read on and decide which boy is Tom Sawyer. Give reasons for your answer.

Comparing Literature
What do Tom's thoughts, feelings, and actions tell you about his character up to this point? Add these details to your chart.

wealth and examined it—bits of toys, marbles, and trash; enough to buy an exchange of work maybe, but not enough to buy so much as half an hour of pure freedom. So he returned his straitened means to his pocket, and gave up the idea of trying to buy the boys. At this dark and hopeless moment an inspiration burst upon him. Nothing less than a great, magnificent inspiration. He took up his brush and went tranquilly to work. Ben Rogers hove in sight presently, the very boy of all boys whose ridicule he had been dreading. Ben's gait was the hop, skip, and jump—proof enough that his heart was light and his anticipations high. He was eating an apple, and giving a long melodious whoop at intervals, followed by a deep-toned ding dong dong, ding dong dong, for he was personating a steamboat! As he drew near he slackened speed, took the middle of the street, leaned far over to starboard, and rounded-to[2] ponderously, and with laborious pomp and circumstance, for he was personating the *Big Missouri,* and considered himself to be drawing nine feet of water[3]. He was boat, and captain, and engine-bells combined, so he had to imagine himself standing on his own hurricane-deck[4] giving the orders and executing them:

'Stop her, sir! Ling-a-ling-ling.' The headway ran almost out, and he drew up slowly towards the sidewalk. 'Ship up to back! Ling-a-ling-ling!' His arms straightened and stiffened down his sides. 'Set her back on the stabboard! Ling-a-ling-ling! Chow! ch-chow-wow-chow!' his right hand meantime, describing stately circles, for it was representing a forty-foot wheel. 'Let her go back on the labboard! Ling-a-ling-ling! Chow-ch-chow-chow!' The left hand began to describe circles.

Comparing Literature Why do you think Ben pretends to be a steamboat? Consider what this tells you about his character and add these details to your chart.

---

2 **Rounded-to** (used with ships) means "turned."

3 When a ship is **drawing nine feet of water,** it means it requires a depth of nine feet of water in order to float.

4 The **hurricane-deck** of a passenger ship is its light upper deck.

'Stop the stabboard! Ling-a-ling-ling! Stop the labboard! Come ahead on the stabboard! Stop her! Let your outside turn over slow! Ling-a-ling-ling! Chow-ow-ow! Get out that head-line! Lively, now! Come—out with your spring-line—what're you about there? Take a turn round that stump with the bight of it! Stand by that stage now—let her go! Done with the engines, sir! Ling-a-ling-ling!

'Sht! s'sht! sht!' (Trying the gauge-cocks[5].)

Tom went on whitewashing—paid no attention to the steamer. Ben stared a moment, and then said:

'Hi-yi! You're up a stump[6], ain't you!'

No answer. Tom surveyed his last touch with the eye of an artist; then he gave his brush another gentle sweep, and surveyed the result as before. Ben ranged up alongside of him. Tom's mouth watered for the apple, but he stuck to his work. Ben said:

'Hello, old chap, you got to work, hey?'

'Why, it's you, Ben! I warn't noticing.'

'Say, I'm going in a swimming, I am. Don't you wish you could? But of course, you'd druther work, wouldn't you? 'Course you would!'

Tom contemplated the boy a bit, and said:

'What do you call work?'

'Why, ain't that work?'

Tom resumed his whitewashing, and answered carelessly:

'Well, maybe it is, and maybe it ain't. All I know is, it suits Tom Sawyer.'

'Oh, come now, you don't mean to let on that you like it?'

The brush continued to move.

'Like it? Well, I don't see why I oughtn't to like it. Does a boy get a chance to whitewash a fence every day?'

Comparing Literature
What additional information have you learned about Ben's character at this point? Add this information to your chart.

---

5 A **gauge cock** is a valve used to determine the water level in a steam boiler.

6 **Up a stump** means "in a difficult situation."

That put the thing in a new light. Ben stopped nibbling his apple. Tom swept his brush daintily back and forth—stepped back to note the effect—added a touch here and there—criticized the effect again, Ben watching every move, and getting more and more interested, more and more absorbed. Presently he said:

'Say, Tom, let me whitewash a little.'

Tom considered: was about to consent; but he altered his mind: 'No, no; I reckon it wouldn't hardly do, Ben. You see, Aunt Polly's awful particular about this fence—right here on the street, you know—but if it was the back fence I wouldn't mind, and she wouldn't. Yes, she's awful particular about this fence; it's got to be done very careful; I reckon there ain't one boy in a thousand, maybe two thousand, that can do it the way it's got to be done.'

'No—is that so? Oh, come now; lemme just try, only just a little. I'd let you, if you was me, Tom.'

'Ben, I'd like to, honest injun; but Aunt Polly—well, Jim wanted to do it, but she wouldn't let him. Sid wanted to do it, and she wouldn't let Sid. Now, don't you see how I am fixed? If you was to tackle this fence, and anything was to happen to it—'

'Oh, shucks; I'll be just as careful. Now lemme try. Say—I'll give you the core of my apple.'

'Well, here. No, Ben; now don't; I'm afeard—'

'I'll give you all of it!'

Tom gave up the brush with reluctance in his face, but alacrity in his heart. And while the late steamer Big Missouri worked and sweated in the sun, the retired artist sat on a barrel in the shade close by, dangled his legs, munched his apple, and planned the slaughter of more innocents[7]. There was no lack of material; boys happened along every little while; they came to jeer, but remained to whitewash. By the time

Comparing Literature What is the first thing you learn about Ben Rogers? Think about why this fact about Ben is important.

---

7 *Planned the slaughter of more innocents* means Tom planned to acquire the possessions of all other gullible, or easily fooled, boys who would arrive.

Ben was fagged out[8], Tom had traded the next chance to Billy Fisher for a kite in good repair; and when he played out, Johnny Miller bought in for a dead rat and a string to swing it with; and so on, and so on, hour after hour. And when the middle of the afternoon came, from being a poor poverty-stricken boy in the morning Tom was literally rolling in wealth. He had, besides the things I have mentioned, twelve marbles, part of a jew's harp, a piece of blue bottle-glass to look through, a spool-cannon, a key that wouldn't unlock anything, a fragment of chalk, a glass stopper of a decanter, a tin soldier, a couple of tadpoles, six fire-crackers, a kitten with only one eye, a brass door-knob, a dog-collar—but no dog—the handle of a knife, four pieces of orange-peel, and a dilapidated old window sash. He had had a nice, good, idle time all the while—plenty of company—and the fence had three coats of whitewash on it! If he hadn't run out of whitewash he would have bankrupted every boy in the village.

Tom said to himself that it was not such a hollow world after all. He had discovered a great law of human action, without knowing it, namely, that in order to make a man or a boy covet a thing, it is only necessary to make the thing difficult to attain. If he had been a great and wise philosopher, like the writer of this book, he would now have comprehended that work consists of whatever a body is obliged to do, and that play consists of whatever a body is not obliged to do. And this would help him to understand why constructing artificial flowers, or performing on a tread-mill, is work, whilst rolling nine-pins or climbing Mont Blanc is only amusement. There are wealthy gentlemen in England who drive four-horse passenger-coaches twenty or thirty miles on a daily line, in the summer, because the privilege costs them considerable money; but if they were offered wages for the service that would turn it into work, then they would resign. ❧

Comparing Literature
Explain the trick that Tom plays on all the other boys. In what way does this trick affect your opinion of Tom and the other boys?

---

8 **Fagged out** means "tired out."

BORN WORKER

Gary Soto

They said that José was born with a ring of dirt around his neck, with grime under his fingernails, and skin calloused from the grainy twist of a shovel. They said his palms were already rough by the time he was three, and soon after he learned his primary colors, his squint was the squint of an aged laborer. They said he was a born worker. By seven he was drinking coffee slowly, his mouth pursed the way his mother sipped. He wore jeans, a shirt with sleeves rolled to his elbows. His eye could measure a length of board, and his knees genuflected[1] over flower beds and leafy gutters.

They said lots of things about José, but almost nothing of his parents. His mother stitched at a machine all day, and his father, with a steady job at the telephone company, climbed splintered, sun-sucked poles, fixed wires and looked around the city at tree level.

"What do you see up there?" José once asked his father.

"Work," he answered. "I see years of work, *mi'jo.*[2]"

José took this as a truth, and though he did well in school, he felt destined to labor. His arms would pump, his legs would bend, his arms would carry a world of earth. He believed in hard work, believed that his strength was as ancient as a rock's.

Comparing Literature
The narrator begins by telling readers what other people think about José. As you read, list these details about José on your chart.

---

1. To *genuflect* (jen′yoo flekt′) is to kneel respectfully, as in church.
2. The contraction *mi'jo* (mē′hō) stands for the Spanish phrase *mi hijo,* which means "my son."

"Life is hard," his father repeated from the time José could first make out the meaning of words until he was stroking his fingers against the grain of his sandpaper beard.

His mother was an example to José. She would raise her hands, showing her fingers pierced from the sewing machines. She bled on her machine, bled because there was money to make, a child to raise, and a roof to stay under.

One day when José returned home from junior high, his cousin Arnie was sitting on the lawn sucking on a stalk of grass. José knew that grass didn't come from his lawn. His was cut and pampered, clean.

"José!" Arnie shouted as he took off the earphones of his CD Walkman.

"Hi, Arnie," José said without much enthusiasm. He didn't like his cousin. He thought he was lazy and, worse, spoiled by the trappings³ of being middle class. His parents had good jobs in offices and showered him with clothes, shoes, CDs, vacations, almost anything he wanted. Arnie's family had never climbed a telephone pole to size up the future.

---

3 The **trappings** of middle class are the things Arnie's family owns that show they have a comfortable life.

Comparing Literature
How is Arnie different from José? Add details about Arnie to your chart.

To make money for her family, José's mother sewed until her fingers bled.

Arnie rose to his feet, and José saw that his cousin was wearing a new pair of high-tops. He didn't say anything.

"Got an idea," Arnie said cheerfully. "Something that'll make us money."

José looked at his cousin, not a muscle of curiosity twitching in his face.

Still, Arnie explained that since he himself was so clever with words, and his best cousin in the whole world was good at working with his hands, that maybe they might start a company.

"What would you do?" José asked.

"Me?" he said brightly. "Shoot, I'll round up all kinds of jobs for you. You won't have to do anything." He stopped, then started again. "Except—you know—do the work."

"Get out of here," José said.

"Don't be that way," Arnie begged. "Let me tell you how it works."

The boys went inside the house, and while José stripped off his school clothes and put on his jeans and a T-shirt, Arnie told him that they could be rich.

"You ever hear of this guy named Bechtel?"[4] Arnie asked.

José shook his head.

"Man, he started just like us," Arnie said. "He started digging ditches and stuff, and the next thing you knew, he was sitting by his own swimming pool. You want to sit by your own pool, don't you?" Arnie smiled, waiting for José to speak up.

"Never heard of this guy Bechtel," José said after he rolled on two huge socks, worn at the heels. He opened up his chest of drawers and brought out a packet of Kleenex.

Arnie looked at the Kleenex.

"How come you don't use your sleeve?" Arnie joked.

Comparing Literature
Consider what you already know about Arnie. Why might you not trust him in his deal with José?

---

4 **Bechtel** is probably Stephen D. Bechtel (1900–1989), who was president of a large and famous construction and engineering company.

José thought for a moment and said, "I'm not like you." He smiled at his retort.

"Listen, I'll find the work, and then we can split it fifty-fifty."

José knew fifty-fifty was a bad deal.

"How about sixty-forty?" Arnie suggested when he could see that José wasn't going for it. "I know a lot of people from my dad's job. They're waiting for us."

José sat on the edge of his bed and started to lace up his boots. He knew that there were agencies that would find you work, agencies that took a portion of your pay. They're cheats, he thought, people who sit in air-conditioned offices while others work.

"You really know a lot of people?" José asked.

"Boatloads," Arnie said. "My dad works with this millionaire—honest—who cooks a steak for his dog every day."

He's a liar, José thought. No matter how he tried, he couldn't picture a dog grubbing[5] on steak. The world was too poor for that kind of silliness.

"Listen, I'll go eighty-twenty," José said.

"Aw, man," Arnie whined. "That ain't fair."

José laughed.

"I mean, half the work is finding the jobs," Arnie explained, his palms up as he begged José to be reasonable.

José knew this was true. He had had to go door-to-door, and he disliked asking for work. He assumed that

View the Photograph Which of these two would you say is José and which is Arnie? Think about the reasons for your choice.

---

5 **Grub** is slang for food, so grubbing is eating.

it should automatically be his since he was a good worker, honest, and always on time.

"Where did you get this idea, anyhow?" José asked.

"I got a business mind," Arnie said proudly.

"Just like that Bechtel guy," José retorted.

"That's right."

José agreed to a seventy-thirty split, with the condition that Arnie had to help out. Arnie hollered, arguing that some people were meant to work and others to come up with brilliant ideas. He was one of the latter. Still, he agreed after José said it was that or nothing.

In the next two weeks, Arnie found an array of jobs. José peeled off shingles from a rickety garage roof, carried rocks down a path to where a pond would go, and spray-painted lawn furniture. And while Arnie accompanied him, most of the time he did nothing. He did help occasionally. He did shake the cans of spray paint and kick aside debris so that José didn't trip while going down the path carrying the rocks. He did stack the piles of shingles, but almost cried when a nail bit his thumb. But mostly he told José what he had missed or where the work could be improved. José was bothered because he and his work had never been criticized before.

But soon José learned to ignore his cousin, ignore his comments about his spray painting, or about the way he lugged rocks, two in each arm. He didn't say anything, either, when they got paid and Arnie rubbed his hands like a fly, muttering, "It's payday."

Then Arnie found a job scrubbing a drained swimming pool. The two boys met early at José's house. Arnie brought his bike. José's own bike had a flat that grinned like a clown's face.

"I'll pedal," José suggested when Arnie said that he didn't have much leg strength.

With Arnie on the handlebars, José tore off, his pedaling so strong that tears of fear formed in Arnie's eyes.

Comparing Literature
What do Arnie's words reveal about his personality? Write words that describe Arnie on your graphic organizer.

Comparing Literature
Think again about the ways in which José and Arnie are different. What details show these differences? Add any new details to your comparison chart.

"Slow down!" Arnie cried.

José ignored him and within minutes they were riding the bike up a gravel driveway. Arnie hopped off at first chance.

"You're scary," Arnie said, picking a gnat from his eye. José chuckled.

When Arnie knocked on the door, an old man still in pajamas appeared in the window. He motioned for the boys to come around to the back.

"Let me do the talking," Arnie suggested to his cousin. "He knows my dad real good. They're like this." He pressed two fingers together.

José didn't bother to say OK. He walked the bike into the backyard, which was lush with plants—roses in their last bloom, geraniums, hydrangeas, pansies with their skirts of bright colors. José could make out the splash of a fountain. Then he heard the hysterical yapping of a poodle. From all his noise, a person might have thought the dog was on fire.

"Hi, Mr. Clemens," Arnie said, extending his hand. "I'm Arnie Sanchez. It's nice to see you again."

José had never seen a kid actually greet someone like this. Mr. Clemens said, hiking up his pajama bottoms, "I only wanted one kid to work."

"Oh," Arnie stuttered. "Actually, my cousin José really does the work and I kind of, you know, supervise."

Mr. Clemens pinched up his wrinkled face. He seemed not to understand. He took out a pea-sized hearing aid, fiddled with its tiny dial, and fit it into his ear, which was surrounded with wiry gray hair.

"I'm only paying for one boy," Mr. Clemens shouted. His poodle click-clicked and stood behind his legs. The dog bared its small crooked teeth.

"That's right," Arnie said, smiling a strained smile. "We know that you're going to compensate[6] only one of us."

Mr. Clemens muttered under his breath. He combed his hair with his fingers. He showed José the pool,

---

6 To compensate (kom′pən sāt′) is to pay someone for his or her work.

Comparing Literature
Based on what you already know about Arnie, what does his response to the bike ride tell you about his character?

Comparing Literature
In what way do Arnie's words support what you already know about him?

which was shaped as round as an elephant. It was filthy with grime. Near the bottom some grayish water shimmered and leaves floated as limp as cornflakes.

"It's got to be real clean," Mr. Clemens said, "or it's not worth it."

"Oh, José's a great worker," Arnie said. He patted his cousin's shoulders and said that he could lift a mule.

Mr. Clemens sized up José and squeezed his shoulders, too.

"How do I know you, anyhow?" Mr. Clemens asked Arnie, who was aiming a smile at the poodle.

"You know my dad," Arnie answered, raising his smile to the old man. "He works at Interstate Insurance. You and he had some business deals."

Think about how difficult it would be to clean this pool.

Mr. Clemens thought for a moment, a hand on his mouth, head shaking. He could have been thinking about the meaning of life, his face was so dark.

"Mexican fella?" he inquired.

"That's him," Arnie said happily.

José felt like hitting his cousin for his cheerful attitude. Instead, he walked over and picked up the white plastic bottle of bleach. Next to it were a wire brush, a pumice stone, and some rags. He set down the bottle and, like a surgeon, put on a pair of rubber gloves.

"You know what you're doing, boy?" Mr. Clemens asked.

José nodded as he walked into the pool. If it had been filled with water, his chest would have been wet. The new hair on his chest would have been floating like the legs of a jellyfish.

"Oh, yeah," Arnie chimed, speaking for his cousin. "José was born to work."

José would have drowned his cousin if there had been more water. Instead, he poured a bleach solution into a rag and swirled it over an area. He took the wire brush and scrubbed. The black algae[7] came up like a foamy monster.

"We're a team," Arnie said to Mr. Clemens.

Arnie descended into the pool and took the bleach bottle from José. He held it for José and smiled up at Mr. Clemens, who, hands on hips, watched for a while, the poodle at his side. He cupped his ear, as if to pick up the sounds of José's scrubbing.

"Nice day, huh?" Arnie sang.

"What?" Mr. Clemens said.

"Nice day," Arnie repeated, this time louder. "So which ear can't you hear in?" Grinning, Arnie wiggled his ear to make sure that Mr. Clemens knew what he was asking.

Mr. Clemens ignored Arnie. He watched José, whose arms worked back and forth like he was sawing logs.

Comparing Literature
What does Arnie's behavior toward Mr. Clemens reveal about Arnie's character?

---

7 **Algae** (al´jē) are plants, such as pond scum, that grow in water.

"We're not only a team," Arnie shouted, "but we're also cousins."

Mr. Clemens shook his head at Arnie. When he left, the poodle leading the way, Arnie immediately climbed out of the pool and sat on the edge, legs dangling.

"It's going to be blazing," Arnie complained. He shaded his eyes with his hand and looked east, where the sun was rising over a sycamore, its leaves hanging like bats.

José scrubbed. He worked the wire brush over the black and green stains, the grime dripping like tears. He finished a large area. He hopped out of the pool and returned hauling a garden hose with an attached nozzle. He gave the cleaned area a blast. When the spray got too close, his cousin screamed, got up, and, searching for something to do, picked a **loquat** from a tree.

"What's your favorite fruit?" Arnie asked.

José ignored him.

Arnie stuffed a bunch of loquats into his mouth, then cursed himself for splattering juice on his new high-tops. He returned to the pool, his cheeks fat with the seeds, and once again sat at the edge. He started to tell José how he had first learned to swim. "We were on vacation in Mazatlán.[8] You been there, ain't you?"

José shook his head. He dabbed the bleach solution onto the sides of the pool with a rag and scrubbed a new area.

"Anyhow, my dad was on the beach and saw this drowned dead guy," Arnie continued. "And right there, my dad got scared and realized I couldn't swim."

Arnie rattled on about how his father had taught him in the hotel pool and later showed him where the drowned man's body had been.

"Be quiet," José said.

"What?"

"I can't concentrate," José said, stepping back to look at the cleaned area.

Visual Vocabulary
A **loquat** is a yellow or orange plumlike fruit that has a slightly acid taste.

Comparing Literature
Based on everything that has happened at Mr. Clemens's house, has your opinion changed about the differences between José and Arnie? Explain, and add any new details to your chart.

---

8 **Mazatlán** (mä sä tlän) is a seaport in western Mexico. It is popular with tourists who like beaches and fishing.

Arnie shut his mouth but opened it to lick loquat juice from his fingers. He kicked his legs against the swimming pool, bored. He looked around the backyard and spotted a lounge chair. He got up, dusting off the back of his pants, and threw himself into the cushions. He raised and lowered the back of the lounge. Sighing, he snuggled in. He stayed quiet for three minutes, during which time José scrubbed. His arms hurt but he kept working with long strokes. José knew that in an hour the sun would drench the pool with light. He hurried to get the job done.

Arnie then asked, "You ever peel before?"

José looked at his cousin. His nose burned from the bleach. He scrunched up his face.

"You know, like when you get sunburned."

"I'm too dark to peel," José said, his words echoing because he had advanced to the deep end. "Why don't you be quiet and let me work?"

Arnie babbled on that he had peeled when on vacation in Hawaii. He explained that he was really more French than Mexican, and that's why his skin was sensitive. He said that when he lived in France, people thought that he could be Portuguese or maybe Armenian, never Mexican.

José felt like soaking his rag with bleach and pressing it over Arnie's mouth to make him be quiet.

Then Mr. Clemens appeared. He was dressed in white pants and a flowery shirt. His thin hair was combed so that his scalp, as pink as a crab, showed.

"I'm just taking a little rest," Arnie said.

Arnie leaped back into the pool. He took the bleach bottle and held it. He smiled at Mr. Clemens, who came to inspect their progress.

"José's doing a good job," Arnie said, then whistled a song.

Mr. Clemens peered into the pool, hands on knees, admiring the progress.

"Pretty good, huh?" Arnie asked.

Mr. Clemens nodded. Then his hearing aid fell out,

Comparing Literature
What do you learn here about José's feelings toward Arnie? Think about the ways José's words and thoughts help readers understand the character of Arnie.

Comparing Literature
Evaluate the truthfulness of Arnie's statement. What does it reveal about his personality?

and José turned in time to see it roll like a bottle cap toward the bottom of the pool. It leaped into the stagnant water with a plop. A single bubble went up, and it was gone.

"Dang," Mr. Clemens swore. He took shuffling steps toward the deep end. He steadied his gaze on where the hearing aid had sunk. He leaned over and suddenly, arms waving, one leg kicking out, he tumbled into the pool. He landed standing up, then his legs buckled, and he crumbled, his head striking against the bottom. He rolled once, and half of his body settled in the water.

"Did you see that!" Arnie shouted, big-eyed.

José had already dropped his brushes on the side of the pool and hurried to the old man, who moaned, eyes closed, his false teeth jutting from his mouth. A ribbon of blood immediately began to flow from his scalp.

"We better get out of here!" Arnie suggested. "They're going to blame us!"

José knelt on both knees at the old man's side. He took the man's teeth from his mouth and placed them in his shirt pocket. The old man groaned and opened his eyes, which were shiny wet. He appeared startled, like a newborn.

"Sir, you'll be all right," José cooed, then snapped at his cousin. "Arnie, get over here and help me!"

"I'm going home," Arnie whined.

"You punk!" José yelled. "Go inside and call 911."

Arnie said that they should leave him there.

"Why should we get involved?" he cried as he started for his bike. "It's his own fault."

José laid the man's head down and with giant steps leaped out of the pool, shoving his cousin as he passed. He went into the kitchen and punched in 911 on a telephone. He explained to the operator what had happened. When asked the address, José dropped the phone and went onto the front porch to look for it.

"It's 940 East Brown," José breathed. He hung up and looked wildly about the kitchen. He opened up the

Comparing Literature
In what ways do José and Arnie react differently to Mr. Clemens's accident? What does each character's reaction tell you about his personality? Record the traits you identify on your comparison chart.

Quickly, José called 911 to get help for Mr. Clemens.

refrigerator and brought out a plastic tray of ice, which he twisted so that a few of the cubes popped out and slid across the floor. He wrapped some cubes in a dish towel. When he raced outside, Arnie was gone, the yapping poodle was doing laps around the edge of the pool, and Mr. Clemens was trying to stand up.

"No, sir," José said as he jumped into the pool, his own knees almost buckling. "Please, sit down."

Mr. Clemens staggered and collapsed. José caught him before he hit his head again. The towel of ice cubes dropped from his hands. With his legs spread to absorb the weight, José raised the man up in his arms, this fragile man. He picked him up and carefully stepped toward the shallow end, one slow elephant step at a time.

"You'll be all right," José said, more to himself than to Mr. Clemens, who moaned and struggled to be let free.

The sirens wailed in the distance. The poodle yapped, which started a dog barking in the neighbor's yard.

"You'll be OK," José repeated, and in the shallow end of the pool, he edged up the steps. He lay the old man in the lounge chair and raced back inside for more ice and another towel. He returned outside and placed the bundle of cubes on the man's head, where the blood flowed. Mr. Clemens was awake, looking about. When the old man felt his mouth, José reached into his shirt pocket and pulled out his false teeth. He fit the teeth into Mr. Clemens's mouth and a smile appeared, something bright at a difficult time.

"I hit my head," Mr. Clemens said after smacking his teeth so that the fit was right.

José looked up and his gaze floated to a telephone pole, one his father might have climbed. If he had been there, his father would have seen that José was more than just a good worker. He would have seen a good man. He held the towel to the old man's head. The poodle, now quiet, joined them on the lounge chair.

A fire truck pulled into the driveway and soon they were surrounded by firemen, one of whom brought out a first-aid kit. A fireman led José away and asked what had happened. He was starting to explain when his cousin reappeared, yapping like a poodle.

"I was scrubbing the pool," Arnie shouted, "and I said, 'Mr. Clemens, you shouldn't stand so close to the edge.' But did he listen? No, he leaned over and . . . Well, you can just imagine my horror."

José walked away from Arnie's jabbering. He walked away, and realized that there were people like his cousin, the liar, and people like himself, someone he was getting to know. He walked away and in the midmorning heat boosted himself up a telephone pole. He climbed up and saw for himself what his father saw—miles and miles of trees and houses, and a future lost in the layers of yellowish haze. &

Comparing Literature
Explain why Arnie does not tell the truth to the fireman. What does this tell you about his character?

Comparing Literature
What has José learned about himself? Explain why he thinks he is different than Arnie.

Comparing Literature

BQ **BIG Question**

Now use the unit Big Question to compare and contrast *Tom Sawyer* and "Born Worker." Think about Tom and Ben in *Tom Sawyer* and José and Arnie in "Born Worker." With a group of classmates discuss questions such as,

- What are each character's values and beliefs?

- Does each character stay true to his values and beliefs? Explain your opinion.

- In these two stories, what are the results of a character staying true to himself?

Support each answer with evidence from the readings.

Literary Element Character

Use the details you wrote in your compare-and-contrast chart to compare and contrast the characters in *Tom Sawyer* and "Born Worker." With a partner, answer the following questions:

1. In what ways are Tom Sawyer and José different? Do you see any similarities between these two characters?

2. In what ways are Tom Sawyer and Arnie similar? Do you see any differences between them? Think about the reasons behind each character's actions.

3. In what ways are José and Ben similar and different?

Write to Compare

In one or two paragraphs, compare and contrast the ways that Mark Twain and Gary Soto characterize Tom Sawyer and José. You might focus on these questions as you write.

- What does the narrator of each story tell readers about the character?

- What do each character's main words, thoughts, and actions reveal about him?

- Did you like either Tom Sawyer or José? Explain how each author's way of describing the character affected your opinion of that character.

 Writing Tip

Comparative Adjectives As you write, use comparative adjectives. Most adjectives with one syllable, and some with two, form the comparative by adding the suffix *-er*. For most adjectives with two or more syllables, the comparative is formed by adding *more* before the adjective. Some adjectives have irregular comparatives. For example, for both *good* and *well,* the comparative is *better.*

 Literature Online

Selection Resources
For Selection Quizzes, eFlashcards, and Reading-Writing Connection activities, go to glencoe.com and enter QuickPass code GL39770u1.

Learning Objectives

For pages 128–133

In this workshop, you will focus on the following objective:

Writing:
Writing a short story using the writing process.

Narrative

What does it mean to be true to yourself? How is courage involved? In this workshop, you will write a short story that will help you think about the Unit 1 Big Question: How Do You Stay True to Yourself?

Review the writing prompt, or assignment, below. Then read the Writing Plan. It will tell you what you will do to write your story.

Writing Assignment

A narrative tells a story. A fictional narrative is a story about imaginary people and events. Write a short story in which a character acts on personal values and believes in himself or herself. The audience, or those reading your story, should be your classmates and teacher.

Prewrite

What traits do characters need to be true to themselves? How can conflict cause characters to question their values? How can setting affect their ability to act on these values? Think about how these questions are answered in the story "Raymond's Run."

Gather Ideas

Take notes on characters, plot, and setting. Quickwrite—don't spend too much time thinking. Ask yourself the following questions:

- What times or places interest me? How do I imagine them? Which would make the best setting for my story?

- What do my characters look, sound, think, and act like?

- Will the main character's conflict be with an outside force? Or will it be within himself or herself? How does the conflict get resolved?

Choose a Point of View

Now that you have some ideas, decide on a point of view for your story. Remember that the point of view determines what the narrator can see and hear. To get started, talk about narrators with a partner.

Partner Talk With a partner, follow these steps:

1. Discuss the different types of point of view.

2. With help from your partner, decide which point of view best fits the story you want to tell. Determine who the narrator will be. Finish the sentence below to explain your narrator's relationship to the story.

My story will be told from _____ which means my narrator _____.

Writing Plan

- Choose an appropriate narrator and point of view.

- Develop a plot that has exposition, rising action, climax, falling action, and a resolution.

- Make the conflict part of every event in the plot and the basis of the theme.

- Include sensory details to describe the setting and action.

- Use dialogue and description to highlight similarities and differences among main and minor characters.

 Prewriting Tip

Brainstorming As you brainstorm ideas, don't judge them, just write them down. You can evaluate them later.

Get Organized

Use your notes to make a characterization chart and a plot diagram.

Characterization Chart		
Details	**Personality Trait**	**Direct or Indirect**
Roland says, "I'm twice the actor Axel is."	pride	direct characterization (Roland's statement)

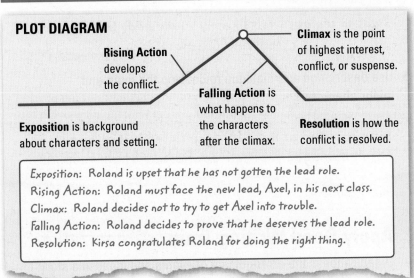

PLOT DIAGRAM

Rising Action develops the conflict.

Climax is the point of highest interest, conflict, or suspense.

Falling Action is what happens to the characters after the climax.

Exposition is background about characters and setting.

Resolution is how the conflict is resolved.

Exposition: Roland is upset that he has not gotten the lead role.
Rising Action: Roland must face the new lead, Axel, in his next class.
Climax: Roland decides not to try to get Axel into trouble.
Falling Action: Roland decides to prove that he deserves the lead role.
Resolution: Kirsa congratulates Roland for doing the right thing.

Draft

Organize your ideas and add more details to develop your draft.

Get It On Paper

- Review your notes. Look at your story plan.
- Open your story with something surprising or engaging.
- Tell the events in your story plan in the order in which they occur.
- Don't worry about spelling, grammar, or punctuation right now.

Develop Your Draft

1. Use correct pronouns for the **point of view** and **narrator** you chose.

"I'm twice the actor Axel is!"

2. Determine which events are important for each stage of your **plot**.

I was stunned that I hadn't gotten the lead role in the play.

Literature Online

Writing and Research For prewriting, drafting, and revising tools, go to glencoe.com and enter QuickPass code GL39770u1.

Writing Tip

Use signal words like *first,* *then,* and *later* to make the order of events in your plot clear.

TRY IT

Analyzing Cartoons Think about what the one woman is saying about the other woman's resume. With a partner, decide what the cartoon suggests about organization.

3. Make sure the plot's events add to the **conflict**. As you write, ask "What does this event have to do with the conflict and theme?"

> Unfortunately, Axel was in my next class. As soon as I got there, I saw him beaming with excitement.

4. Add **sensory details** to describe the setting and action clearly.

> I was so jealous I felt like my whole body was on fire.

5. Use description and dialogue to develop the **main and minor characters**.

> Kirsa scowled at me. "It's nice to see this setback hasn't damaged your self-confidence at all, Roland."

Apply Good Writing Traits: Organization

Organization is the arrangement of events and ideas in a story. Strong, clear organization guides readers through your story and makes your writing easier to follow.

Read the sentences below from "Raymond's Run." Which words help you understand the order of events?

> First I think I'll step into the candy store and look over the new comics and let them pass.

> Then they all look at Raymond who has just brought his mule team to a standstill.

> After that is the forty-yard dash which I used to run when I was in first grade.

As you draft your story, decide which words will clearly show the order of events. After you finish, read your draft and ask yourself if any events are missing or seem out of place.

Analyze a Student Model

"Understudy? I have to be the understudy? To Axel Armistead? I'm twice the actor Axel is!" I was stunned that I hadn't gotten the lead role in the play.

Kirsa scowled at me. "It's nice to see this setback hasn't damaged your self-confidence at all, Roland." I was about to retort, but I knew class would start soon and there was no time for a long discussion.

"I've got to go now," said Kirsa when the bell rang. "There's nothing you can do about it, anyway, so you're going to have to accept it." I didn't want to hear that, but Kirsa was probably right. Unless Axel was really terrible or got sick, I'd never be the lead. I'd just have to get over it.

Unfortunately, Axel was in my next class. As soon as I got there, I saw him beaming with excitement. I was so jealous I felt like my whole body was on fire.

"I heard the news about the play," my friend Joel whispered to me as we waited for class to start. "You know, I've never liked Axel, either. Maybe we can find a way to get him into some trouble. Why not say you saw Axel looking at my paper during the test?"

I thought about that. After being accused of cheating, Axel would be in big trouble. He might even get kicked out of the play, making me the lead. My heart started beating faster at the thought. I kept thinking about Joel's plan all during class.

When the bell rang, I sighed, shrugged my shoulders, and told Joel that I didn't want to win by hurting someone else. I knew I deserved the lead role. I'd just have to prove it. Then I'd have something to be really proud of.

"You did the right thing," admitted Kirsa when I told her after school about Joel's idea and my decision. "Now let's get to play practice so you can beat Axel fairly."

Point of View and Narrator

The story is told in first-person point of view. You can tell because the narrator is a character and refers to himself as "I."

Plot

Notice the background information about Roland and his situation. Also notice the rising action, or events that develop the conflict.

Conflict

Roland's external conflict is between him and Axel for the lead. His internal conflict occurs when he is tempted to get Axel into trouble.

Sensory Details

Details like this description help readers understand what the character is feeling.

Dialogue

The way characters speak tells readers about their personalities.

Revising Tip

Speaker Tags Use precise words that give clues about a character's tone of voice. Occasionally replace *said* with words such as *admitted, explained, whispered,* or *cooed.* Be careful about overusing alternatives though.

Revise

Now it's time to revise your draft so your ideas really shine. Revising is what makes good writing great, and great writing takes work!

Peer Review Trade drafts with a partner. Use the chart below to review your partner's draft by answering the questions in the *What to do* column. Talk about your peer review after you have glanced at each other's drafts and written down the answers to the questions. Next, follow the suggestions in the *How to do it* column to revise your draft.

Revising Plan

What to do	How to do it	Example
Can the reader easily identify the narrator and the point of view?	Use the pronouns *I* and *me* for the first-person point of view and *he, she, him,* and *her* for the third-person point of view.	He ˄I was stunned that he ˄I hadn't gotten the lead role in the play.
Did you include all stages of the plot?	Make sure background information is provided and that events develop the conflict and eventually lead to a resolution.	I'd just have to get over it. ˄Unfortunately, Axel was in my next class.
Is the conflict part of every event and the basis of the theme?	Provide details that connect the event to the conflict.	After being accused of cheating, Axel would be in big trouble. He might even get kicked out of the play, ~~which would make him sad~~ ˄making me the lead.
Can readers experience the setting and action for themselves?	Choose specific, concrete words that help readers see, hear, smell, taste, or feel the scene.	I was so jealous ˄I felt like my whole body was on fire.
Does the reader know the characters better through your use of dialogue and description?	Write dialogue that shows how a character thinks or feels.	Kirsa scowled at me. "~~You are being egotistical.~~" ˄"It's nice to see this setback hasn't damaged your self-confidence at all, Roland."

Edit and Proofread

For your final draft, read your narrative one sentence at a time. The **Editing and Proofreading Checklist** inside the back cover of this book can help you spot errors. Use this resource to help you make any necessary corrections.

Grammar Focus: Punctuation of Dialogue

Be sure to use quotation marks for dialogue and apply other punctuation rules so readers know when characters are speaking. Below are some examples of problems with the punctuation of dialogue and possible solutions from the Workshop Model.

Problem: It is unclear which words are spoken.

You did the right thing admitted Kirsa when I told her after school about Joel's idea and my decision.

Solution: Place quotation marks before and after the spoken words and place a comma or any end punctuation mark inside the quotation marks.

"You did the right thing," admitted Kirsa when I told her after school about Joel's idea and my decision.

Problem: Punctuation for the quotation is used incorrectly.

"I've got to go now said Kirsa when the bell rang."

Solution A: Put a comma and a quotation mark at the end of the spoken words. Remove the quotation mark from the end of the sentence.

"I've got to go now," said Kirsa when the bell rang.

Solution B: Reorder the sentence. Put the speaker tag in front of the quotation, and follow it with a comma. Then enclose the spoken words and end punctuation in quotation marks.

When the bell rang, Kirsa said, "I've got to go now."

Present

It's almost time to share your writing with others. Write your narrative neatly in print or cursive on a separate sheet of paper. If you have access to a computer, type your narrative on the computer and check your spelling. Save your document to a disk and print it out.

Speaking, Listening, and Viewing Workshop

Narrative Presentation

Activity

Connect to Your Writing Deliver an oral presentation of a narrative to your classmates. You might adapt the narrative you wrote for the Writing Workshop on pages 128–133. Remember that you focused on the Unit 1 Big Question: How Do You Stay True to Yourself?

Plan Your Presentation

Reread your story and highlight sections to include in your presentation. Your narrative presentation should have a plot with a beginning, middle, and end and describe a specific setting. Explain the significance of the events you are relating and your attitude about what occurred in the story. Include dialogue and descriptive details. Use action verbs, precise language, and appropriate colorful modifiers. Avoid the passive voice, for example, *the race was run.* Speak in the active voice.

Rehearse Your Presentation

Practice your presentation several times. Rehearse in front of a mirror to watch your movements and facial expressions. You may use note cards to remind you of the story's important events, but practice enough times so that you won't lose eye contact with your audience.

Deliver Your Presentation

- Speak clearly and precisely.
- Adjust your speaking style to fit individual characters.
- Change the pace of your speaking to help emphasize important moments throughout your story.
- Change your tone or volume for emotion or to build suspense.

Listen to Appreciate

As you listen to another student's presentation, take notes about what you like about the story and its delivery. Use statement frames to share your opinions with the storyteller.

- I liked the gestures/voices you used because _____.
- The mood of the story is _____. You created that mood by _____.
- I think the theme of the story is _____. It reminds me of _____.

▶ Presentation Checklist

Answer the following questions to evaluate your presentation:

- ❏ Did you speak clearly and precisely—and in a style that fits your characters?
- ❏ Did you change the pace of your speaking to fit with the story's events?
- ❏ Did you vary the tone or volume of your voice to add interest to the story?
- ❏ Did you make and hold eye contact with your audience?

Literature Online

Speaking, Listening, and Viewing For project ideas, templates, and presentation tips, go to glencoe.com and enter QuickPass code GL39770u1.

Unit Challenge

Answer the BIG Question

In Unit 1, you explored the Big Question through reading, writing, speaking, and listening. Now it's time for you to complete one of the Unit Challenges below with your answer to the Big Question.

HOW Do You Stay True to Yourself?

Learning Objectives

For page 135

In this assignment, you will focus on the following objectives:

Writing:
Creating a prewriting chart.

Writing an essay.

Writing a narrative.

Technology:
Creating and presenting a video.

Use the notes you took in your Unit 1 **Foldable** to complete the Unit Challenge you have chosen.

Before you present your Unit Challenge, be sure it meets the requirements below. Use this first plan if you chose to make a values chart to help you figure out things you need to remember in order to stay true to yourself.

On Your Own Activity: Create a Values Chart

❏ Make a chart with two columns, the first labeled *Important Values* and the second labeled *Explanations*.

❏ In the first column, list at least five values that are important to you. Order your list by how important each value is to you.

❏ In the second column, explain why each is important to you.

❏ Using your chart, write a brief paper that explains how your values help you stay true to yourself in everyday life.

❏ Revise your work and share it with a partner before turning it in.

Use this second plan if you chose to perform and videotape a scene.

Group Activity: Perform and Videotape a Scene

❏ With a group, come up with a clear, realistic situation that relates to the Big Question—How do you stay true to yourself?

❏ Act out the situation several times. Discuss which parts of the performance best addressed the Big Question.

❏ Use this information to write a script for an extended version of the situation. Include specific actions, physical descriptions, background information, and dialogue.

❏ Videotape your scene and present it to the class.

Independent Reading

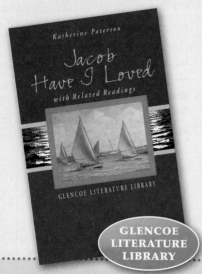

Fiction

To explore the Big Question in other works, choose one of these books from your school or local library.

Jacob Have I Loved

by Katherine Paterson

As the United States enters World War II, thirteen-year-old Sara Louise Bradshaw is growing up in the shadow of her twin sister, Caroline. Blaming Caroline for her unhappiness, Sara struggles to find her own identity. She learns to work on the water with her father on the island where they live.

GLENCOE LITERATURE LIBRARY

Dogsong

by Gary Paulsen

Fourteen-year-old Russel Susskit is unhappy with modern life in his native Alaska and yearns for the simpler life of his Inuit ancestors. Inspired by a wise man, Russel sets out across the ice in a dogsled on a voyage of self-discovery.

GLENCOE LITERATURE LIBRARY

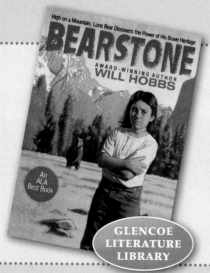

GLENCOE LITERATURE LIBRARY

Bearstone

by Will Hobbs

When Cloyd Atcitty, a Native American boy, gets kicked out of a group home for troubled youths, he is sent to work on a farm in Colorado owned by an old white man. At first, his new situation seems unbearable, but the farm is near the ancestral home of the boy's people, the Utes. Life-changing experiences help Cloyd come to terms with his heritage, himself, and his attitude towards the future.

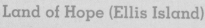

Land of Hope (Ellis Island)

by Joan Lowery Nixon

Rebekah Levinsky and her family are the main characters in this story about the American immigrant experience of the early 1900s. The author tells of the Levinsky family's voyage from Russia to America and their struggle to survive on New York's Lower East Side.

Nonfiction

The Voice That Challenged a Nation: Marian Anderson and the Struggle for Equal Rights

by Russell Freedman

In the 1920s and 1930s, Marian Anderson became world famous for her singing voice. At home in the United States, however, this African American woman had to fight for the right to perform in concert halls that were restricted to whites. This is the account of a talented and determined artist who stood up for herself and ultimately for all African Americans.

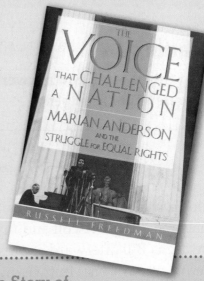

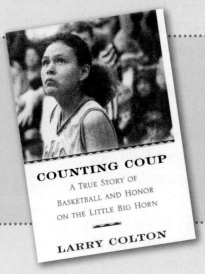

Counting Coup: A True Story of Basketball and Honor on the Little Big Horn

by Larry Colton

Counting Coup is the Native American tradition when a warrior gains glory by touching his enemy and living to tell the tale. Battling racism, alcoholism, and domestic violence, the girls on the Hardin High School basketball team learn how to be winners on and off the court and to be true to themselves.

No Body's Perfect

by Kimberly Kirberger

This collection of poems, essays, and stories written by teenagers explores issues surrounding body image, food, and self-esteem. The book helps young people to accept themselves for who they are and offers insight as well as hope.

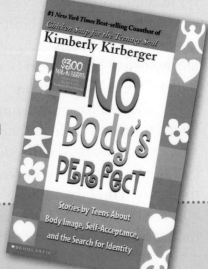

Write a Review

Write a book review for your classmates. Be sure to explain what you found interesting, unusual, exciting, or even puzzling in the book. Include specific examples and descriptive details to support your ideas.

Assessment

Reading

Read the passage and answer the questions. Write your answers on a separate sheet of paper.

---

from **"The Ransom of Red Chief"** by O. Henry

It looked like a good thing, but wait till I tell you. We were down South, in Alabama—Bill Driscoll and myself—when this kidnapping idea struck us. It was, as Bill afterward expressed it, "during a moment of temporary mental apparition"; but we didn't find that out till later.

There was a town down there, as flat as a flannel cake, and called Summit, of course. It contained inhabitants of as undeleterious[1] and self-satisfied a class of peasantry as ever clustered around a maypole.

Bill and me had a joint capital of about six hundred dollars, and we needed just two thousand dollars more to pull off a fraudulent town-lot scheme in western Illinois. We talked it over on the front steps of the hotel. Philoprogenitiveness,[2] says we, is strong in semi-rural communities; therefore, and for other reasons, a kidnapping project ought to do better there than in the radius of newspapers that send reporters out in plain clothes to stir up talk about such things. We knew that Summit couldn't get after us with anything stronger than constables and, maybe, some lackadaisical bloodhounds and a diatribe or two in the *Weekly Farmers' Budget*. So, it looked good.

We selected for our victim the only child of a prominent citizen named Ebenezer Dorset. The father was respectable and tight, a mortgage fancier[3] and a stern, upright collection-plate passer and forecloser. The kid was a boy of ten, with bas-relief freckles, and hair the color of the cover of the magazine you buy at the newsstand when you want to catch a train. Bill and me figured that Ebenezer would melt down for a ransom of two thousand dollars to a cent. But wait till I tell you.

---

1 This is a made-up word. The narrator means that the townspeople are harmless.

2 *Philoprogenitiveness* is a rarely used word meaning "love of one's children."

3 The narrator means to say that Dorset is a *financier*, one who arranges mortgages.

About two miles from Summit was a little mountain, covered with a dense cedar brake. On the rear elevation of this mountain was a cave. There we stored provisions.

One evening after sundown, we drove in a buggy past old Dorset's house. The kid was in the street, throwing rocks at a kitten on the opposite fence.

"Hey, little boy!" says Bill, "would you like to have a bag of candy and a nice ride?"

The boy catches Bill neatly in the eye with a piece of brick.

"That will cost the old man an extra five hundred dollars," says Bill, climbing over the wheel.

That boy put up a fight like a welter-weight cinnamon bear; but, at last, we got him down in the bottom of the buggy and drove away. We took him up to the cave, and I hitched the horse in the cedar brake. After dark I drove the buggy to the little village, three miles away, where we had hired it, and walked back to the mountain.

Bill was pasting court-plaster over the scratches and bruises on his features. There was a fire burning behind the big rock at the entrance of the cave, and the boy was watching a pot of boiling coffee, with two buzzard tail-feathers stuck in his red hair. He points a stick at me when I come up, and says:

"Ha! cursed paleface, do you dare to enter the camp of Red Chief, the terror of the plains?"

---

1. How can a reader tell that the story is written in the first person?
   A. The style is informal.
   B. The story uses some words incorrectly.
   C. The narrator is a character in the story.
   D. The narrator reveals the thoughts of a character.

2. O. Henry creates a comic effect by
   A. writing in the first person.
   B. varying his sentence length.
   C. including passages of dialogue.
   D. creating a narrator who enjoys using long words.

3. Read this sentence from the passage.

   It looked like a good thing, but wait till I tell you.

   This sentence is an example of

   A. irony.
   B. allusion.
   C. foreshadowing.
   D. figurative language.

Literature Online

Assessment For additional test practice, go to glencoe.com and enter QuickPass code GL39770u1.

4. Read this sentence from the passage.

> **Bill and me had a joint <u>capital</u> of about six hundred dollars, and we needed just two thousand dollars more to pull off a fraudulent town-lot scheme in western Illinois.**

The word <u>capital</u> in this sentence means

A. debt.
B. plan of attack.
C. requirement.
D. supply of money.

5. Read this sentence from the passage.

> **There was a town down there, as flat as a flannel cake, and called Summit, of course.**

The irony present in this sentence is obvious to a reader who knows that

A. the word <u>summit</u> means "highest point."
B. the town of Summit is completely fictional.
C. no town is actually as flat as a flannel cake.
D. a pancake is called a "flannel cake" only in certain regions.

6. Read this sentence from the passage.

> **The kid was in the street, throwing rocks at a kitten on the opposite fence.**

From this scene, it appears that the "kid"

A. is good at games.
B. is probably a troublemaker.
C. likes dogs more than cats.
D. will enjoy being kidnapped.

7. Which sentence best summarizes this passage?

A. Two criminals think of a plan to make money.
B. A tough little boy shows he has a mean streak.
C. Two criminals kidnap a tough little boy to raise money.
D. Violent crime strikes the quiet Alabama town of Summit.

8. From the scene at the cave that ends this passage, a reader can infer that both Bill and the narrator

A. have short tempers.
B. enjoy caring for children.
C. can be pushed around by the boy.
D. are good at making long-term plans.

9. What is ironic in the plot of this story so far?

A. The kidnapping victim bullies the crooks.
B. The crooks successfully capture their victim.
C. The crooks rent a buggy instead of stealing one.
D. A wealthy and respectable man has a troublesome child.

Write your answer to the following question on a separate sheet of paper.

10. What can you tell about the kind of person the narrator is? Support your answer with evidence from the passage.

Vocabulary Skills

On a separate sheet of paper, write the numbers 1–14. Next to each number, write the letter of the word or phrase that means about the same as the underlined word.

1. among the <u>congregation</u>

    A. doctors   **C.** workers
    B. church goers   **D.** students

2. <u>liable</u> to speak out in class

    A. unlikely   **C.** forbidden
    B. encouraged   **D.** expected

3. <u>authentic</u> local cooking

    A. good   **C.** modern
    B. actual   **D.** old-fashioned

4. a strong <u>intellect</u>

    A. reason   **C.** argument
    B. effort   **D.** mental ability

5. to <u>reside</u> together

    A. dwell   **C.** work
    B. travel   **D.** struggle

6. walking <u>sheepishly</u>

    A. with others   **C.** very slowly
    B. with a purpose   **D.** in a guilty way

7. the cowboy's <u>sidekick</u>

    A. spurs   **C.** horse
    B. buddy   **D.** saddle

8. to feel <u>obliged</u>

    A. sympathetic   **C.** rewarded
    B. unfortunate   **D.** appreciative

9. to <u>embrace</u> a relative

    A. hug   **C.** dislike
    B. welcome   **D.** invite

10. that <u>inconvenient</u> location

    A. nearby   **C.** surprising
    B. unfamiliar   **D.** not handy

11. a <u>stately</u> gesture

    A. rude   **C.** formal
    B. clear   **D.** mysterious

12. to <u>retrieve</u> a ball

    A. get   **C.** throw
    B. kick   **D.** inflate

13. annoying <u>static</u>

    A. heat   **C.** noise
    B. nasty smell   **D.** harsh lights

14. to lose one's <u>reputation</u>

    A. temper   **C.** sense of humor
    B. pride   **D.** respectability

Writing Strategies

The following is a rough draft of part of a student's report. It contains errors. Read the passage. Then answer the questions on a separate sheet of paper.

---

(1) Usually, a good writer thinks about what they hope to accomplish in their work. (2) If O. Henry hoped to accomplish entertainment, he certainly succeeded. (3) His stories are known for their humor. (4) They are also known for their surprise endings. (5) Many a reader has looked up at the end of a story and said, "Well, I didn't see that coming!" (6) In addition, O. Henry was extremely skilled at developing characters. (7) His characters are usually ordinary people. (8) They sometimes do extraordinary things.

1. How should sentence 1 be rewritten to reflect the use of correct grammar?
   A. Usually, good writers think about what they hope to accomplish in their work.
   B. Usually, good writers think about what he or she hope to accomplish in their work.
   C. Usually, a good writer thinks about what they hope to accomplish in his or her work.
   D. Usually, a good writer thinks about what he or she hopes to accomplish in their work.

2. How can sentences 3 and 4 best be combined?
   A. For humor and for surprise endings, his stories are known.
   B. His stories are known for their humor and surprise endings.
   C. Humor and also surprise endings are some things his stories are known for.
   D. His stories are known for their humor, and they are also known for surprise endings.

3. Read this sentence.

   Many a reader has looked up at the end of a story and said, "Well, I didn't see that coming!"

   What is the helping verb in this sentence?
   A. has   C. said
   B. looked   D. see

4. How can sentences 7 and 8 best be combined?
   A. His characters are usually ordinary people, and they sometimes do extraordinary things.
   B. His characters are usually ordinary people because they sometimes do extraordinary things.
   C. His characters are usually ordinary people so they sometimes do extraordinary things.
   D. His characters are usually ordinary people, but they sometimes do extraordinary things.

Writing Product

Read the prompt in the box below and follow the "Directions for Writing." Use one piece of paper to jot down ideas and organize your thoughts. Then neatly write your essay on another sheet. You may not use a dictionary or other reference materials.

Writing Situation:

Although you have read only the beginning of "The Ransom of Red Chief," you have been asked to predict what will happen in the rest of the story.

Directions for Writing:

Write a short essay that explains what you think will happen in the rest of "The Ransom of Red Chief." Explain how hints in the excerpt you have read make your predictions reasonable.

Keep these hints in mind when you write.

- Concentrate on what the prompt tells you to write.
- Organize the way you will present your ideas.
- Provide good, clear support for your ideas.
- Use different kinds of sentence structures.
- Use precise words that express your ideas clearly.
- Check your essay for mistakes in spelling, grammar, and punctuation.

READING: What's in It for You?

THE **BIG** Question

> " *To read is to voyage through time.* "
>
> —**CARL SAGAN**

FOLDABLES®
Study Organizer

Throughout Unit 2, you will read, write, and talk about the **BIG** Question— "Reading: What's in It for You?" Use your Unit 2 **Foldable,** shown here, to keep track of your ideas as you read. Turn to the back of this book for instructions on making this **Foldable.**

Reader Response
Journal
Unit 2
Big
Question
What's In
It for You?

READING:
What's in It for You?

There are lots of reasons to read. Reading can teach you new things, spark your emotions, and take your imagination to new places. As you've read on page 145, reading can even take you on a voyage through time. What reasons can you think of to read? Explore what reading can do for you.

Think about different reasons to read:

- Reading for Knowledge
- Reading for Enjoyment

What You'll Read

You can benefit from reading many different kinds of texts. In this unit, you'll read **informational texts** that will show you how reading can help you learn about interesting people, places, and things. You will also read short stories, poetry, and other texts that can lead you to discover answers to the Big Question.

What You'll Write

As you explore the Big Question, you'll write notes in your Unit 2 **Foldable.** Later, you'll use these notes to complete two writing assignments related to the Big Question.

1. **Write a Functional Document**
2. **Choose a Unit Challenge**
   - **On Your Own Activity: Create a Reading Chart**
   - **Group Activity: Write a Reading Plan**

What You'll Learn

Literary Elements

theme

author's purpose

informational text

text features

text structure

simile

suspense

mood

diction

setting

Reading Skills and Strategies

preview

summarize

analyze cultural context

analyze evidence

skim and scan

identify cause-and-effect relationships

visualize

paraphrase

recognize author's purpose

analyze plot

compare and contrast

from
Zoya's Story

Zoya with John Follain
and Rita Cristofari

At the head of the Khyber Pass, when we reached the border with Afghanistan at Torkham,[1] our car stopped short of the Taliban checkpoint. Before getting out of the car, my friend Abida helped me to put the *burqa* on top of my shirt and trousers and adjusted the fabric until it covered me completely. I felt as if someone had wrapped me in a bag. As best I could in the small mountain of cheap blue polyester, I swung my legs out of the car and got out.

The checkpoint was a hundred yards away, and I stared for a moment at my homeland beyond it. I had been living in exile in Pakistan[2] for five years, and this was my first journey back to Afghanistan. I was looking at its dry and dusty mountains through the bars of a prison cell. The mesh of tiny holes in front of my eyes chafed against my eyelashes. I tried to look up at the sky, but the fabric rubbed against my eyes.

In order to get into Afghanistan, Zoya had to wear a burqa (bur´ kə), a cloth garment that covers a woman's entire body and has mesh holes to allow the woman to see.

Set a Purpose for Reading

Read the excerpt from *Zoya's Story*. Think about what you gain from reading a real-life story like this one.

---

1 The **Khyber Pass** is a 33-mile passage that connects Pakistan with **Afghanistan** (af gan´ i stan´), which is a mountainous country in central Asia. **Torkham** is a town on the border between Pakistan and Afghanistan.

2 **Pakistan** (pak´ i stan´) is a country in south Asia that shares borders with India, China, Iran, and Afghanistan.

The *burqa* weighed on me like a shroud.[3] I began to sweat in the June sunshine and the beads of moisture on my forehead stuck to the fabric. The little perfume—my small gesture of rebellion—that I had put on earlier at once evaporated. Until a few moments ago, I had breathed easily, instinctively, but now I suddenly felt short of air, as if someone had turned off my supply of oxygen.

I followed Javid, who would pretend to be our *mahram*, the male relative without whom the Taliban refused to allow any woman to leave her house, as he set out for the checkpoint. I could see nothing of the people at my side. I could not even see the road under my feet. I thought only of the Taliban edict[4] that my entire body, even my feet and hands, must remain invisible under the *burqa* at all times. I had taken only a few short steps when I tripped and nearly fell down.

When I finally neared the checkpoint, I saw Javid go up to one of the Taliban guards, who was carrying his Kalashnikov rifle slung jauntily over his shoulder. He looked as wild as the Mujahideen, the soldiers who claimed to be fighting a "holy war," whom I had seen as a child: the crazed eyes, the dirty beard, the filthy clothes. I watched him reach to the back of his head, extract what must have been a louse, and squash it between two fingernails with a sharp crack. I remembered what Grandmother had told me about the Mujahideen: "If they come to my house, they won't even need to kill me. I'll die just from seeing their wild faces."

I heard the Taliban ask Javid where he was going, and Javid replied, "These women are with me. They are my daughters. We traveled to Pakistan for some treatment because I am sick, and now we are going back home to Kabul." No one asked me to show any papers. I had been told that for the Taliban, the *burqa* was the only passport they demanded of a woman.

If the Taliban had ordered us to open my bag, he would have found, tied up with string and crammed

---

3 A cloth placed over a dead body is called a ***shroud***.

4 An ***edict*** (eʹ dikt) is a rule or an order.

BQ ▶ **BIG Question**

What have you learned about the burqa?

BQ ▶ **BIG Question**

What have you learned about the Taliban up to this point?

Taliban fighters sit outside of the American embassy in Kabul, Afghanistan, in 2001.

View the Photograph How do the men in this photo compare with Zoya's description of the Taliban?

at the bottom under my few clothes, ten publications of the clandestine[5] association I had joined, the Revolutionary Association of the Women of Afghanistan. They documented, with photographs that made my stomach churn no matter how many times I looked at them, the stonings to death, the public hangings, the amputations performed on men accused of theft, at which teenagers were given the job of displaying the severed limbs to the spectators, the torturing of victims who had fuel poured on them before being set alight, the mass graves the Taliban forces left in their wake.

These catalogs of the crimes perpetrated by the Taliban guard's regime had been compiled on the basis

5 A *clandestine* (klan des′ tin) association is a secret organization.

of reports from our members in Kabul. Once they had been smuggled to the city, they would be photocopied thousands of times and distributed to as many people as possible.

But the Taliban made no such request. Shuffling, stumbling, my dignity suffocated, I was allowed through the checkpoint into Afghanistan.

As women, we were not allowed to speak to the driver of a Toyota minibus caked in mud that was waiting to set out for Kabul, so Javid went up to him and asked how much the journey would cost. Then Abida and I climbed in, sitting as far to the back as we could with the other women. We had to wait for a Taliban to jump into the minibus and check that there was nothing suspicious about any of the travelers before we could set off. For him, even a woman wearing white socks would have been suspicious. Under a ridiculous Taliban rule, no one could wear them because white was the color of their flag and they thought it offensive that it should be used to cover such a lowly part of the body as the feet.

The longer the drive lasted, the tighter the headband on the *burqa* seemed to become, and my head began to ache. The cloth stuck to my damp cheeks, and the hot air that I was breathing out was trapped under my nose. My seat was just above one of the wheels, and the lack of air, the oppressive heat, and the smell of gasoline mixed with the stench of sweat and the unwashed feet of the men in front of us made me feel worse and worse until I thought I would vomit. I felt as if my head would explode.

We had only one bottle of water between us. Every time I tried to lift the cloth and take a sip, I felt the water trickle down my chin and wet my clothes. I managed to take some aspirin that I had brought with me, but I didn't feel any better. I tried to fan myself with a piece of cardboard, but to do so I had to lift the fabric off my face with one hand and fan myself under the *burqa* with the other. I tried to rest my feet on the back of the seat in front of me

BQ ▶ **BIG Question**

Why do you think Zoya wanted the photocopied documents to be "distributed to as many people as possible"?

BQ ▶ **BIG Question**

What are your feelings about the Taliban so far in your reading?

so as to get some air around my legs. I struggled not to fall sideways as the minibus swung at speed around the hairpin bends, or to imagine what would happen if it toppled from a precipice[6] into the valley below.

I tried to speak to Abida, but we had to be careful what we said, and every time I opened my mouth the sweat-drenched fabric would press against it like a mask. She let me rest my head on her shoulder, although she was as hot as I was.

It was during this journey that I truly came to understand what the *burqa* means. As I stole glances at the women sitting around me, I realized that I no longer thought them backward, which I had as a child. These women were forced to wear the *burqa*. Otherwise they face lashings, or beatings with chains. The Taliban required them to hide their identities as women, to make them feel so ashamed of their sex that they were afraid to show one inch of their bodies. The Taliban did not know the meaning of love.

The mountains, waterfalls, deserts, poor villages, and wrecked Russian tanks that I saw through the *burqa* and the mud-splattered window made little impression on my mind. I could only think ahead to when my trip would end. For the six hours that the journey lasted, we women were never allowed out. The driver stopped only at prayer time, and only the men were allowed to get out of the minibus to pray at the roadside. Javid got out with them and prayed. All I could do was wait.

BQ BIG Question

What details have you learned in this paragraph and the previous paragraph to help you understand Zoya's difficult journey?

BQ BIG Question

What have you learned about the treatment of women in Afghanistan under Taliban rule?

BQ BIG Question

What did you get out of reading about Zoya's journey?

6 A *precipice* (pres′ ə pis) is the edge of a cliff.

After You Read

Respond and Think Critically

1. Use your own words to briefly tell the most important events in Zoya's dangerous journey to Afghanistan. [Summarize]

2. What can you infer about the status of women in Pakistan? [Infer]

3. Why do you think Zoya has been living in exile in Pakistan? [Synthesize]

4. Do you think Zoya effectively gets her message across to readers of this excerpt? Explain with details from the text. [Evaluate]

Writing

Write a Short Essay Write an essay of two to three paragraphs analyzing "Zoya's Story." When you analyze, you look at separate parts in order to understand the entire piece. Your essay should show your own insight and interpretation into the ways in which "Zoya's Story" reflects her heritage, traditions, attitudes, and beliefs—as well as the political situation she describes. Support your analysis and interpretations with references to the text, to other authors, or to your personal knowledge. You may want to use this topic sentence to get started:

After reading "Zoya's Story," I now understand that _____.

Learning Objectives

For page 152

In this assignment, you will focus on the following objectives:

Literary Study: Analyzing and evaluating informational text.

Connecting to contemporary issues.

Writing: Writing a short essay.

LOG ON ▶ **Literature** Online

Unit Resources For additional skills practice, go to glencoe.com and enter QuickPass code GL39770u2.

Reading for Knowledge

Portrait of Erasmus of Rotterdam. Quentin Massys or Metsys. Oil on canvas.
Palazzo Barberini, Rome.

BQ **BIG Question** **Reading: What's in It for You?**

The painting shows Erasmus, a great thinker who wrote about religious education and other topics during the early 1500s. What details in the portrait suggest Erasmus's devotion to reading and writing? What would you read to help you know more about ideas that interest you?

Before You Read

There is no Frigate like a Book and *Because of Libraries We Can Say These Things*

Connect to the Poems

Think about a time when you read a story or a poem that captured your imagination and made you feel like you were part of it.

List Create a list of places you would like to visit or adventures you would like to have. Then make a list of books or poems you have read that let you imagine these experiences.

Build Background

The United States has more than 9,000 public libraries, which are free and available to all residents. The first official public library in the United States was established in 1854 in Boston, Massachusetts, when Emily Dickinson was in her twenties.

Set Purposes for Reading

BQ BIG Question

Read "There is no Frigate like a Book" and "Because of Libraries We Can Say These Things" to find out how reading can transport you to another reality and enrich your life.

Literary Element Theme

A **theme** is the main message of a story, poem, novel, or play, often expressed as a general statement about life. Some works have a stated theme, which is expressed directly. More commonly, works have an implied theme, which is revealed gradually. **Recurring themes** are ideas or concepts that are repeated within a work or in more than one work. As you read, look for a theme that appears in both poems.

Literature Online

Author Search For more about Emily Dickinson and Naomi Shihab Nye, go to glencoe.com and enter QuickPass code GL39770u2.

Meet the Authors

Emily Dickinson

Emily Dickinson wrote more than 1,700 poems in her life. As a writer, she is known for her distinct lyrical style, her passion, and her wit. She lived from 1830 to 1886.

Naomi Shihab Nye

Born to an American mother and a Palestinian father, Naomi Shihab Nye often gets her inspiration for her poems from everyday events. She was born in 1952.

THERE IS NO FRIGATE LIKE A BOOK

Emily Dickinson

La Roche Guyon, 1891. Theodore Robinson. Oil on canvas. Brooklyn Museum of Art, NY.

There is no Frigate° like a Book
To take us Lands away
Nor any Coursers° like a Page
Of prancing Poetry—
5   This Traverse may the poorest take
Without oppress of Toll—
How frugal is the Chariot
That bears the Human soul.

---

1   A *frigate* is an old-style sailing ship.

3   *Coursers* are swift or spirited horses.

5   To *traverse* is to move across or journey through.

Theme What is the theme of the poem as stated in lines 1–4?

BQ **BIG Question**

What do lines 5–8 tell you about how books benefit everyone?

The Mill Library, 1990. James McDonald. Oil on canvas. Private Collection, Bourne Gallery, Reigate, Surrey, UK.

View the Art What can you infer about the books in this painting based on their appearance?

Because of Libraries
We Can Say These Things

Naomi Shihab Nye

She is holding the book close to her body,
carrying it home on the cracked sidewalk,
down the tangled hill.
If a dog runs at her again, she will use the book as
   a shield.

5 She looked hard among the long lines
of books to find this one.
When they start talking about money,
when the day contains such long and hot places,
she will go inside.
10 An orange bed is waiting.
Story without corners.
She will have two families.
They will eat at different hours.

She is carrying a book past the fire station
15 and the five-and-dime.
What this town has not given her
the book will provide; a sheep,
a wilderness of new solutions.
The book has already lived through its troubles.
20 The book has a calm cover, a straight spine.°

When the step returns to itself
as the best place for sitting,
and the old men up and down the street
are latching their clippers,°

25 she will not be alone.
She will have a book to open
and open and open.
Her life starts here.

Theme In what way is the theme expressed in lines 10–15 similar to the theme expressed in Dickinson's poem?

BQ **BIG Question**
In lines 16–20, what does the girl understand about how reading a book can enhance her life?

---

20 The **spine** is the part of the book where all the pages are attached; the title and the author's and publisher's names usually appear on a book's spine.

24 When the old men **latch their clippers**, the poet means that the men close their cutting devices, which they are using to trim shrubs.

After You Read

Respond and Think Critically

1. In your own words, retell what the girl experiences in the Nye poem. [Summarize]

2. Why do you think Dickinson used capital letters in an unusual way in her poem? [Interpret]

3. Based on details in the poem by Nye, what can you infer about the young girl's neighborhood? [Infer]

4. What do you think the young girl in the Nye poem would think of the ideas expressed by Dickinson in her poem? Explain your answer. [Analyze]

5. **Literary Element** **Theme** Think about the recurring theme in these two poems. How is the theme presented differently in each poem? [Compare]

6. **BQ** **BIG Question** In your opinion, which poem best conveys the idea that reading is a very beneficial thing for all people to do? Explain your answer. [Evaluate]

Spelling Link

Patterns in Words of Two or More Syllables The following spelling rule will help you recognize when to double consonants.

Rule: Words of more than one syllable have their consonants doubled **only** when the final syllable is stressed.

Examples:

begin	beginning	prefer	preferred
open	opening	listen	listened

Practice On a separate sheet of paper, add a suffix, such as *-ing, -ed,* or *-er,* to each of the following words, deciding first whether or not to double the final consonant.

shorten, defer, offer, submit

 Writing

Write a Blurb Your local library asks you to write a blurb—a short, persuasive paragraph—about why it's important to have a good library. The blurb is to be published on your community's Web site. Use examples and details to persuade the people in your community to support the library so that it can continue to provide good books and other reading material to residents.

TIP

Inferring
Here are some tips to help you infer information from what you read. Remember, when you infer, you use text clues and your own knowledge to figure out something that is not directly stated.

- Identify the lines that have clues about where the young girl lives.

- Think about neighborhoods you have seen that look similar.

- Use these hints to describe the girl's neighborhood in your own words.

FOLDABLES **Study Organizer** Keep track of your ideas about the **BIG Question** in your unit Foldable.

 **Literature** Online

Selection Resources
For Selection Quizzes, eFlashcards, and Reading-Writing Connection activities, go to glencoe.com and enter QuickPass code GL39770u2.

Set a Purpose for Reading

Read to learn about three young immigrants to the United States. As you read, focus on their challenges and gains.

Preview the Article

1. Skim the **subheads**—the headings that break the article into parts. What do you predict the writer will discuss in each part?

2. Read the **deck**, or the sentence beneath the title. What information does the deck provide?

3. Scan the images' **captions**. What do they tell you?

Reading Strategy

Summarize When you summarize, you state the main ideas of a text in your own words and in a logical order. As you read, write each section's main idea in a graphic organizer like the one below.

Section	Main Ideas

TIME

Coming to AMERICA

The nation's newest immigrants share a time-honored dream with groups from the past.

By JOE MCGOWAN, MARISA WONG, VICKIE BANE, and LAURIE MORICE

Waves of Immigrants

The United States is a nation built by immigrants. From 1840 to 1870, the first wave of immigrants came from Ireland, England, Germany, and China to dig waterways and lay railroad tracks. From 1890 to 1924, a second wave crashed over Ellis Island,[1] the historic immigration station in New York Harbor, from countries such as Italy and Russia. These newcomers toiled in factories and built cities.

Now, a new wave of immigrants is coming to America. Over 31 million immigrants live in the U.S. They make up about 11.5% of the population. Like those who came before, these immigrants are arriving in hopes of building their own version of the American Dream.

---

[1] During these years, more than 17 million immigrants entered the United States through *Ellis Island*, a small island off the southern tip of Manhattan.

PLEDGING ALLEGIANCE: Proud, brand-new American citizens

A New Era with New Challenges

Since the terrorist attacks of September 11, 2001, America has been rethinking its immigration policy. Some people want to limit the number of new immigrants to 300,000 a year. All foreign visitors face new delays, including high-tech screening and longer waiting periods.

Once here, immigrants need help. "Family is always the first resource," says Lily Woo, the principal of Public School 130, in New York City, where many Chinese newcomers attend school. Extended immigrant families help one another find housing and work. Other support groups, like churches and community centers, are not as strong as they once were. As a result, about 25% of immigrant households receive government assistance, typically for health care and school for their children. Some 30% of immigrants have not graduated high school, and many have low-paying jobs.

Early immigrants quickly took on all aspects of American culture. But, today, many immigrants have one foot in the U.S. and one foot in their native land. With cell phones and the Internet, it's now easier for newcomers to keep in touch with the country they left behind.

"I'm the luckiest kid in the world," says Prudence Simon, 10, who now lives in New York. "I have two homes, Trinidad and the U.S.A."

Only the future will reveal how the new immigrants will build their American Dream. But one thing is certain, they have a rich history on which to lay a foundation.

OPEN DOORS: Immigrants arrive at Ellis Island, in New York Harbor, in 1920. Nearly 14 million foreign-born people were living in the United States that year.

Corbis Bettmann

Immigrants Past and Present

They may come from different places, but immigrants share similar experiences. Starting over in a new country often takes time and can be hard. Here's a look at how three young immigrants dealt with their new American lives.

Jin Hua Zhang

When she was 11 years old, Jin Hua's father brought his family to New York City. Although Jin Hua has made friends and is doing well in school, she still misses her home in China.

In my hometown of Ting Jiang, in southeastern China, people always said that America was very good, like some kind of wonderland. They said you could have a good life here. So when my mother, my brother, and I flew into New York City's LaGuardia Airport, I was so happy. It was night, and I thought, "This city is so good, so beautiful." I knew at that moment my life would be changing. I thought it would be great.

But then I came to my apartment. I was shocked. In China, my parents were bosses at a company that made bricks. We had a big house; it was very comfortable. Here, there were four of us squeezing into two small rooms [in Chinatown]. Everything is shared—I can't do anything in private. The next day, when I went down to the street, it was so noisy. And, oh, my gosh, so stinky! Starting school was hard too. In China, I'd been a good student—I completed every exam perfectly. Here, I didn't understand what the teacher was saying. It was the [toughest] time I've ever had.

Jin Hua shares this bedroom with her parents and older brother.

Erin Patrice O'Brien

all the time, every morning until midnight, [because they] want me to go to college [instead of] working in a factory like most Chinese immigrants [we know]. But I feel like I have less. I don't know if I consider myself an American. I feel like I'm really more Chinese.

Sonia Diaz

In 1994, Sonia's family moved to Asheboro, North Carolina, from the tiny town of San Francisco de Asis, Mexico. Caught between two worlds, she struggled to stay loyal to her Hispanic heritage while making the most of her new life in America.

I wasn't ready for the racism I found when I started school here. In seventh grade, kids used to laugh at my accent when the teacher asked me to read in front of the class. By the time I was in ninth grade, my Mexican friends didn't like to talk to American people. They were scared of having people laugh. So they didn't want to get involved in anything, no clubs, no sports. I wanted to, but I never could because no other Hispanics were.

Then in 11th grade, I got put in mostly honors classes, because I had good grades. Back then, it was all Americans in those classes. So I needed to talk to them, and we made friends. My Hispanic friends would get mad—they'd say that I didn't know who I was. But after a while I was like, I'm going to talk to

But the biggest difference between China and here was that I was lonely. Some Americans look at you differently [if you're an immigrant]; they look down on you. I had to make all new friends. In China, teenagers come together as a group and go out to play. Here, my parents didn't want me to hang out outside; they thought I could get lost or [might] hang out with bad people.

I know that my family decided to come here so my brother and I could get a better education. In China, they made money more easily, but they never felt like it was enough; they always wanted more. Now, they work

whomever I want to. And I did. I made American friends, and I had Mexican friends. I even have an American boyfriend.

Things are different at my school now. There are lots more Mexican kids, and they're more involved, more open. The soccer team used to be mostly white; now it's mostly Hispanic. Looking back, I wish I could do high school over again. I'd take every honors class, join every club. I missed so many things because I didn't want people to make fun of me. I'm glad it's not like that anymore.

Sonia (with her little brother Jose Luis) strikes a pose in front of her house in Asheboro, North Carolina.

Jason Dewey

Peter Deng

Peter was one of Sudan's "Lost Boys," thousands of boys who were separated from their families by the ongoing civil war in their country, and then walked by themselves for months before finally finding safety at a refugee camp in Kenya. In March 2001, he was allowed to emigrate[2] to the United States, where he's building a brand-new life.

When I first came to Denver, [Colorado,] I had never slept in a bed. I had never seen television or snow. Even women in shorts—that's not so common in Africa.

I was born in the village of Jale, in the southern part of Sudan. Our homes were huts made out of long grasses. So the first week [that the Lost Boys were in Denver], we stayed inside, not coming out. There were eight of us sharing a house, two to a room. Ecumenical Refugee Services [who helped sponsor the Lost Boys] gave us a television. They also bought us clothes and groceries for the first two months and showed us how to cook.

There were so many things—the stove, the refrigerator—that we didn't know how to use. I was one of the first Lost Boys to get a job, as a warehouse clerk, processing customer orders. When I got my first paycheck, I didn't know what to do with it. I kept it under the bed for two weeks—until

---

2 If you **emigrate**, you leave a country or region to live somewhere else.

[somebody] told me I had to put it in the bank.

Now I write checks. I've even bought a car. I love the United States. I like to watch basketball. I've started college, and I have friends—some African, some American.

Sometimes we get together for parties. People are so friendly and polite, and nobody discriminates or takes advantage of you. My mother died in 1998, but my younger brother is still in the camp in Kenya. I want to bring him here, to get the same opportunities as me. This is a very free life. It's very, very exciting.

Peter stands tall at his school, the University of Colorado.

Gerard Gaskin

Respond and Think Critically

1. What do you think the writer means by the statement "Today, many immigrants have one foot in the U.S. and one foot in their native land"? **[Interpret]**

2. When you skimmed before reading, what did you predict you would learn in the sections featuring a person's name as a subhead? How accurate was your prediction? **[Analyze]**

3. Which of the three young people do you feel is the happiest? Explain why you feel this way. **[Evaluate]**

4. **Text-to-Self** Which one of the young people's issues do you identify with most directly? Explain why you chose this person. **[Connect]**

5. **Reading Strategy** Summarize Write a summary of this article. Check your work against the article to make sure that you have included all important ideas and details. For help on writing a summary, see page 54. **[Summarize]**

6. **BQ** **BIG Question** What did you learn from reading about the experiences of Jin Hua, Sonia, and Peter? **[Respond]**

from *I Know Why the Caged Bird Sings*

Connect to the Autobiography

Think about a person who has had an important effect on your life.

Quickwrite Describe this person. What have you learned from him or her? What effect has the person had on your life?

Build Background

This excerpt from Maya Angelou's autobiography *I Know Why the Caged Bird Sings* takes place in rural Stamps, Arkansas, in the 1930s. Stamps was segregated at that time. Young Marguerite and her brother Bailey are living with their grandmother, whom they call Momma.

- In the late 1870s Jim Crow laws were passed in the South requiring separation of whites from blacks in public transportation and schools. The laws expanded to theaters, restaurants, and other public places.

- In 1954 the Supreme Court in *Brown vs. Board of Education of Topeka* overturned the "separate but equal" doctrine of racial segregation in public schools, and this ruling extended to other public places.

Vocabulary

aristocrat (ə ris′ tə krat) *n.* a member of the upper class (p. 167). *The librarian had the manners and elegance of an aristocrat.*

persistently (pər sis′ tənt lē) *adv.* enduring; continuing for a long time (p. 168). *She looked cool even during the worst of the persistently hot summer.*

competently (kom′ pət ənt lē) *adv.* done ably, with the necessary ability (p. 170). *I can sew competently enough to repair a small tear.*

intolerant (in tol′ ər nət) *adj.* unwilling to allow or endure differences of opinion or practice (p. 173). *Because she was intolerant of her brother's constant singing, she didn't want to sit next to him on the bus.*

Meet Maya Angelou

"There is a kind of strength . . . in black women. It's as if a steel rod runs right through the head down to the feet."

—Maya Angelou

A Person of Many Talents Born Marguerite Johnson, the author later changed her name to Maya Angelou. As a child, she survived racism, poverty, her parents' divorce, and a traumatic event that left her unable to speak for many years. She went on to become an author, poet, playwright, editor, educator, and professional stage and screen performer.

Literary Works Angelou is the author of many books, including *I Know Why the Caged Bird Sings,* which was published in 1970.

Maya Angelou was born in 1928.

 Literature Online

Author Search For more about Maya Angelou, go to glencoe.com and enter QuickPass code GL39770u2.

Set Purposes for Reading

BQ BIG Question

As you read, try to identify what Maya Angelou, as Marguerite, learns from her relationship with Mrs. Flowers. Then ask yourself whether you've learned something similar from reading her story. Explain.

Literary Element Author's Purpose

The **author's purpose** is his or her reason for writing a particular work. An author usually writes for one of the following four reasons: to explain, to inform, to persuade, or to entertain. Authors of engaging autobiographies, such as *I Know Why the Caged Bird Sings,* often have more than one reason for writing about their life experiences.

When you know why an author wrote something, you can better understand and evaluate what you are reading. To help you identify the author's purpose, think about the details that the author is sharing and his or her choice of words.

As you read, ask yourself what Maya Angelou hoped to accomplish by sharing her personal story.

Reading Skill Analyze Cultural Context

The customs, beliefs, relationships, and traditions that are typical of a certain region and time period are the **cultural context** in a story.

Understanding the cultural context of an autobiography is important because a person's thoughts and actions may be affected by his or her culture. The cultural context of the rural South during the 1930s is important in this excerpt from *I Know Why the Caged Bird Sings.*

As you read, list details that suggest the cultural context of Angelou's autobiography. Use a graphic organizer like the one below to help you.

Details	What They Tell Me
Mrs. Flowers wore printed dresses, flowered hats, and gloves.	She dresses like a lady. She appears more formal than the other townspeople.
_____	_____
_____	_____
_____	_____

Learning Objectives

For pages 165–177

In studying this text, you will focus on the following objectives:

Literary Study: Analyzing author's purpose.

Reading: Analyzing cultural context.

from *I Know Why the* Caged Bird Sings

Maya Angelou

Portrait of Alma Thomas, c. 1945. Laura Wheeler Waring. Oil on canvas, 30 x 25 1/8 in. Gift of Vincent Melzac. Smithsonian American Art Museum, Washington, DC.

Mrs. Bertha Flowers was the **aristocrat** of Black Stamps. She had the grace of control to appear warm in the coldest weather, and on the Arkansas summer days it seemed she had a private breeze which swirled around, cooling her. She was thin without the taut look of wiry people, and her printed voile[1] dresses and flowered hats were as right for her as denim overalls for a farmer. She was our side's answer to the richest white woman in town.

Analyze Cultural Context
What does this sentence tell you about the town where the author lives?

---

1 **Voile** is a light cotton fabric.

Vocabulary

aristocrat (ə ris′ tə krat′) *n.* a member of the upper class

Her skin was a rich black that would have peeled like a plum if snagged, but then no one would have thought of getting close enough to Mrs. Flowers to ruffle her dress, let alone snag her skin. She didn't encourage familiarity. She wore gloves too.

I don't think I ever saw Mrs. Flowers laugh, but she smiled often. A slow widening of her thin black lips to show even, small white teeth, then the slow effortless closing. When she chose to smile on me, I always wanted to thank her. The action was so graceful and inclusively benign.[2]

She was one of the few gentlewomen I have ever known, and has remained throughout my life the measure of what a human being can be.

Momma had a strange relationship with her. Most often when she passed on the road in front of the Store, she spoke to Momma in that soft yet carrying voice, "Good day, Mrs. Henderson." Momma responded with "How you, Sister Flowers?"

Mrs. Flowers didn't belong to our church, nor was she Momma's familiar. Why on earth did she insist on calling her Sister Flowers? Shame made me want to hide my face. Mrs. Flowers deserved better than to be called Sister. Then, Momma left out the verb. Why not ask, "How *are* you, *Mrs.* Flowers?" With the unbalanced passion of the young, I hated her for showing her ignorance to Mrs. Flowers. It didn't occur to me for many years that they were as alike as sisters, separated only by formal education.

Although I was upset, neither of the women was in the least shaken by what I thought an unceremonious greeting. Mrs. Flowers would continue her easy gait up the hill to her little bungalow, and Momma kept on shelling peas or doing whatever had brought her to the front porch.

Occasionally, though, Mrs. Flowers would drift off the road and down to the Store and Momma would say to me, "Sister, you go on and play." As I left I would hear the beginning of an intimate conversation. Momma **persistently** using the wrong verb, or none at all.

Author's Purpose Why do you think Angelou opens this selection with a detailed description of Mrs. Flowers?

Analyze Cultural Context Think about what these sentences tell you about the meaning of the word *sister* in this culture. Does the author think it is the proper way to address Mrs. Flowers? Explain.

---

2 Here, **benign** means "kind."

Vocabulary

persistently (pər sis′tənt lē) *adv.* enduring; continuing for a long time

"Brother and Sister Wilcox is sho'ly the meanest—" "Is," Momma? "Is"? Oh, please, not "is," Momma, for two or more. But they talked, and from the side of the building where I waited for the ground to open up and swallow me, I heard the soft-voiced Mrs. Flowers and the textured voice of my grandmother merging and melting. They were interrupted from time to time by giggles that must have come from Mrs. Flowers (Momma never giggled in her life). Then she was gone.

She appealed to me because she was like people I had never met personally. Like women in English novels who walked the moors[3] (whatever they were) with their loyal dogs racing at a respectful distance. Like the women who sat in front of roaring fireplaces, drinking tea incessantly[4] from silver trays full of scones and crumpets.[5] Women who walked over the "heath" and read morocco-bound books and had two last names divided by a hyphen. It would be safe to say that she made me proud to be Negro, just by being herself.

She acted just as refined as whitefolks in the movies and books and she was more beautiful, for none of them could have come near that warm color without looking gray by comparison.

It was fortunate that I never saw her in the company of powhitefolks. For since they tend to think of their whiteness as an evenizer, I'm certain that I would have had to hear her spoken to commonly as Bertha, and my image of her would have been shattered like the unmendable Humpty-Dumpty.

One summer afternoon, sweet-milk fresh in my memory, she stopped at the Store to buy provisions. Another Negro woman of her health and age would have been expected to carry the paper sacks home in one hand, but Momma said, "Sister Flowers, I'll send Bailey up to your house with these things."

She smiled that slow dragging smile, "Thank you, Mrs. Henderson. I'd prefer Marguerite, though." My name was

---

3 A *moor* is a stretch of open rolling land.

4 *Incessantly* means "constantly."

5 A *scone* is a biscuit, usually shaped like a triangle, and a *crumpet* is a small round bread, like an English muffin.

beautiful when she said it. "I've been meaning to talk to her, anyway." They gave each other age-group looks.

Momma said, "Well, that's all right then. Sister, go and change your dress. You going to Sister Flowers's."

The **chifforobe** was a maze. What on earth did one put on to go to Mrs. Flowers' house? I knew I shouldn't put on a Sunday dress. It might be sacrilegious.[6] Certainly not a house dress, since I was already wearing a fresh one. I chose a school dress, naturally. It was formal without suggesting that going to Mrs. Flowers' house was equivalent to attending church.

I trusted myself back into the Store.

"Now, don't you look nice." I had chosen the right thing, for once.

"Mrs. Henderson, you make most of the children's clothes, don't you?"

"Yes, ma'am. Sure do. Store-bought clothes ain't hardly worth the thread it take to stitch them."

"I'll say you do a lovely job, though, so neat. That dress looks professional."

Momma was enjoying the seldom-received compliments. Since everyone we knew (except Mrs. Flowers, of course) could sew **competently,** praise was rarely handed out for the commonly practiced craft.

"I try, with the help of the Lord, Sister Flowers, to finish the inside just like I does the outside. Come here, Sister."

I had buttoned up the collar and tied the belt, apronlike, in back. Momma told me to turn around. With one hand she pulled the strings and the belt fell free at both sides of my waist. Then her large hands were at my neck, opening the button loops. I was terrified. What was happening?

"Take it off, Sister." She had her hands on the hem of the dress.

"I don't need to see the inside, Mrs. Henderson, I can tell . . ." But the dress was over my head and my arms were stuck in the sleeves. Momma said, "That'll do. See here, Sister Flowers, I French-seams around the armholes."

Visual Vocabulary

A **chifforobe** is a type of dresser. It has drawers and a place to hang clothes.

---

6 If something is **sacrilegious**, it shows disrespect for something sacred.

Vocabulary

competently (kom′ pət ənt lē) *adv.* done ably, with the necessary ability

Somewhere in America, c. 1933–34. Robert Brackman. Oil on canvas, 30 1/8 x 25 1/8 in. Smithsonian American Art Museum, Washington, DC.

Through the cloth film, I saw the shadow approach. "That makes it last longer. Children these days would bust out of sheet-metal clothes. They so rough."

"That is a very good job, Mrs. Henderson. You should be proud. You can put your dress back on, Marguerite."

"No ma'am. Pride is a sin. And 'cording to the Good Book, it goeth before a fall."

"That's right. So the Bible says. It's a good thing to keep in mind."

I wouldn't look at either of them. Momma hadn't thought that taking off my dress in front of Mrs. Flowers would kill me stone dead. If I had refused, she would have thought I was trying to be "womanish" and might have remembered St. Louis. Mrs. Flowers had known that I would be embarrassed and that was even worse. I picked up the groceries and went out to wait in the hot sunshine. It would be fitting if I got a sunstroke and died before they came outside. Just dropped dead on the slanting porch.

Analyze Cultural Context Consider what this paragraph tells you about Momma's culture. How is it different from the world Marguerite wants to live in?

Author's Purpose Think about why the author describes her feelings in this way. For what reason would she write about this in such a dramatic manner?

There was a little path beside the rocky road, and Mrs. Flowers walked in front swinging her arms and picking her way over the stones.

She said, without turning her head, to me, "I hear you're doing very good school work, Marguerite, but that it's all written. The teachers report that they have trouble getting you to talk in class." We passed the triangular farm on our left and the path widened to allow us to walk together. I hung back in the separate unasked and unanswerable questions.

"Come and walk along with me, Marguerite." I couldn't have refused even if I wanted to. She pronounced my name so nicely. Or more correctly, she spoke each word with such clarity that I was certain a foreigner who didn't understand English could have understood her.

"Now no one is going to make you talk—possibly no one can. But bear in mind, language is man's way of communicating with his fellow man and it is language alone which separates him from the lower animals." That was a totally new idea to me, and I would need time to think about it.

"Your grandmother says you read a lot. Every chance you get. That's good, but not good enough. Words mean more than what is set down on paper. It takes the human voice to infuse them with the shades of deeper meaning."

I memorized the part about the human voice infusing words. It seemed so valid and poetic.

She said she was going to give me some books and that I not only must read them, I must read them aloud. She suggested that I try to make a sentence sound in as many different ways as possible.

"I'll accept no excuse if you return a book to me that has been badly handled." My imagination boggled at the punishment I would deserve if in fact I did abuse a book of Mrs. Flowers'. Death would be too kind and brief.

The odors in the house surprised me. Somehow I had never connected Mrs. Flowers with food or eating or any other common experience of common people. There must have been an outhouse, too, but my mind never recorded it.

Analyze Cultural Context
Think about why the author pays so much attention to the way Mrs. Flowers speaks. What does this reveal about the culture in which the author lives?

The sweet scent of vanilla had met us as she opened the door.

"I made tea cookies this morning. You see, I had planned to invite you for cookies and lemonade so we could have this little chat. The lemonade is in the icebox."

It followed that Mrs. Flowers would have ice on an ordinary day, when most families in our town bought ice late on Saturdays only a few times during the summer to be used in the wooden ice-cream freezers.

She took the bags from me and disappeared through the kitchen door. I looked around the room that I had never in my wildest fantasies imagined I would see. Browned photographs leered or threatened from the walls and the white, freshly done curtains pushed against themselves and against the wind. I wanted to gobble up the room entire and take it to Bailey, who would help me analyze and enjoy it.

"Have a seat, Marguerite. Over there by the table." She carried a platter covered with a tea towel. Although she warned that she hadn't tried her hand at baking sweets for some time, I was certain that like everything else about her the cookies would be perfect.

They were flat round wafers, slightly browned on the edges and butter-yellow in the center. With the cold lemonade they were sufficient for childhood's lifelong diet. Remembering my manners, I took nice little lady-like bites off the edges. She said she had made them expressly for me and that she had a few in the kitchen that I could take home to my brother. So I jammed one whole cake in my mouth and the rough crumbs scratched the insides of my jaws, and if I hadn't had to swallow, it would have been a dream come true.

As I ate she began the first of what we later called "my lessons in living." She said that I must always be **intolerant** of ignorance but understanding of illiteracy. That some people unable to go to school were more educated and even more intelligent than college professors. She encouraged me to listen carefully to what country people called mother wit.

Vocabulary

intolerant (in tol′ər ənt) *adj.* unwilling to allow or endure differences of opinion or practice

Deirdre's Kitchen III.
Pam Ingalls.

That in those homely sayings was couched[7] the collective wisdom of generations.

When I finished the cookies she brushed off the table and brought a thick, small book from the bookcase. I had read *A Tale of Two Cities*[8] and found it up to my standards as a romantic novel. She opened the first page and I heard poetry for the first time in my life.

"It was the best of times and the worst of times . . ." Her voice slid in and curved down through and over the words. She was nearly singing. I wanted to look at the pages. Were they the same that I had read? Or were there

---

7 Here, **homely** means "ordinary." **Couch**, as a verb, means "to say."

8 **A Tale of Two Cities** is a novel by Charles Dickens that describes English people who get caught up in the French Revolution.

notes, music, lined on the pages, as in a hymn book? Her sounds began cascading gently. I knew from listening to a thousand preachers that she was nearing the end of her reading, and I hadn't really heard, heard to understand, a single word.

"How do you like that?"

It occurred to me that she expected a response. The sweet vanilla flavor was still on my tongue and her reading was a wonder in my ears. I had to speak.

I said, "Yes, ma'am." It was the least I could do, but it was the most also.

"There's one more thing. Take this book of poems and memorize one for me. Next time you pay me a visit, I want you to recite."

I have tried often to search behind the sophistication of years for the enchantment I so easily found in those gifts. The essence escapes but its aura[9] remains. To be allowed, no, invited, into the private lives of strangers, and to share their joys and fears, was a chance to exchange the Southern bitter **wormwood** for a cup of mead with Beowulf or a hot cup of tea and milk with Oliver Twist.[10] When I said aloud, "It is a far, far better thing that I do, than I have ever done . . ." tears of love filled my eyes at my selflessness.

On that first day, I ran down the hill and into the road (few cars ever came along it) and had the good sense to stop running before I reached the Store.

I was liked, and what a difference it made. I was respected not as Mrs. Henderson's grandchild or Bailey's sister but for just being Marguerite Johnson.

Childhood's logic never asks to be proved (all conclusions are absolute). I didn't question why Mrs. Flowers had singled me out for attention, nor did it occur to me that Momma might have asked her to give me a little talking to. All I cared about was that she had made tea cookies for *me* and read to *me* from her favorite book. It was enough to prove that she liked me.

Visual Vocabulary

Wormwood is a sweet-smelling plant, but the word is often used to refer to something unpleasant.

BQ **BIG Question**

What does the author get out of the experience of reading with Mrs. Flowers?

---

9 The *essence* of a thing is its most basic nature. An *aura* is the feeling or mood that surrounds a person, thing, or experience.

10 *Beowulf* and *Oliver Twist* are famous characters from English literature.

After You Read

Respond and Think Critically

1. Use your own words to retell what happens after Mrs. Flowers and the author leave Momma. [Summarize]

2. When Mrs. Flowers tells the author that she should always be intolerant of ignorance but understanding of illiteracy, what does she mean? [Interpret]

3. Why does Mrs. Flowers stand out from other people in the town? [Infer]

4. What do you think is the author's purpose for writing about her experiences with Mrs. Flowers? [Draw Conclusions]

5. Using details from the story that you have collected in your graphic organizer, describe the culture of the people the author knows in her town. [Analyze]

6. **BQ** **BIG Question** What did you learn about becoming who you want to be from reading this excerpt from Maya Angelou's autobiography? [Connect]

Vocabulary Practice

Answer the following questions.

1. Where would you expect to find an **aristocrat**—a poor part of town or a rich part of town?

2. If a neighbor **persistently** plays the drums, is the noise constant or rare?

3. If a plumber **competently** fixes a leak, is his work good or bad?

4. When people are **intolerant,** are they open to change or resistant to new ideas?

Academic Vocabulary

Mrs. Flowers's fine clothing **implied** that she came from a wealthy family.

In the preceding sentence, *implied* means "expressed or suggested." Think about how Mrs. Flowers's appearance affects Marguerite's impression of her, and then fill in the blank below:

_____ implied that Marguerite took care in choosing a dress to wear to visit Mrs. Flowers.

TIP

Analyzing
Here are some tips to help you analyze. Remember when you analyze, you look at separate parts of a selection in order to understand the entire selection.

- Think about the customs, beliefs, traditions, and relationships in the story.

- Identify how the characters' words and actions are affected by their culture.

- Think about what your analysis suggests about the culture.

 FOLDABLES **Study Organizer** Keep track of your ideas about the **BIG Question** in your unit Foldable.

LOG ON **Literature** Online

Selection Resources
For Selection Resources, eFlashcards, and Reading-Writing Connection activities, go to glencoe.com and enter QuickPass code GL39770u2.

Test Skills Practice

1. What is the purpose of the following passage about Mrs. Flowers?

   "She was one of the few gentlewomen I have ever known, and has remained throughout my life the measure of what a human being can be."

   A. to contrast typical behavior with that of Mrs. Flowers
   B. to give an example of a gentlewoman
   C. to give reasons for admiring Mrs. Flowers
   D. to show the narrator's admiration and respect for Mrs. Flowers

Review: Theme

The **theme** is the main message of a literary work. Some works have a **stated theme,** as in, "Be yourself" or "Do unto others as you would have them do unto you." Sometimes there is an **implied theme** that readers must figure out by analyzing the characters and events.

2. What is the theme of this autobiography? Choose the passage that you think best illustrates this theme.

Reading Skill Analyze Cultural Context

The cultural context in Maya Angelou's autobiography helps readers understand the customs and traditions in rural Stamps, Arkansas, in the 1930s.

3. Why does Marguerite feel shame when she listens to the intimate conversation between Momma and Mrs. Flowers? Think about how the customs in her community affect her opinion of what's right and wrong.

Grammar Link

Irregular Verbs It is important to learn how to form verb tenses so you can use verbs correctly in a sentence.

For **regular verbs,** you form the past tense and the past participle by adding -d or -ed to the verb's base form.

The past tense and past participle of **irregular verbs** do not follow the pattern of regular verbs. Several patterns are used for irregular verbs. With time and practice, you'll remember them. Here is the pattern for the verb *be.*

- I am going to *be* in Stamps, Arkansas. (base form)

- I *was* in Stamps, Arkansas. (past tense)

- I have *been* in Stamps, Arkansas. (past participle)

Practice Look at the way the author uses verbs in *I Know Why the Caged Bird Sings.* Find examples of verbs used incorrectly and explain why the author chose to do this in the autobiography.

Research and Report

Internet Connection Research more about what life was like for African Americans in the South in the 1930s and 1940s. Organize your notes in a web like the one below.

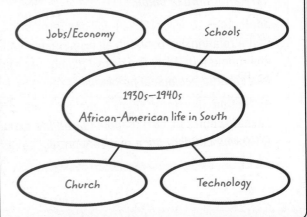

Huge, Freed Pet Pythons Invade Florida Everglades

Connect to the Informational Text

If you read a story about a talking snake, would you think the snake was real or imaginary? If you read a science article about snakes, would the snakes be real?

List Make two lists about snakes. Title one *Real* and the other *Imaginary*. Under *Real*, list facts about snakes. Under *Imaginary*, include characteristics of snakes in fictional stories and movies.

Build Background

Many people think that it's fun to have an exotic pet such as a snake, a lizard, or a large spider. However, when these animals get too big, some people release them into the wild. This practice is dangerous for native plants and animals in the area.

- Pythons are some of the longest snakes in the world. They can grow to 20 feet long. They kill their prey by wrapping around it and constricting its flow of oxygen.

- Pythons and other exotic pets released into the wild feed on the animals and plants in the area, damaging the ecosystem.

Vocabulary

horde (hôrd) *n.* a large crowd of people or animals (p. 180). *Each spring, a horde of termites flies out of that old tree trunk.*

invasive (in vā′ siv) *adj.* having a tendency to spread and have harmful effects (p. 181). *The invasive disease attacked herd after herd of cattle.*

ecological (ē′ kəl oj′ i kəl) *adj.* concerning the pattern of the relationship between all living things and their environment (p. 181). *The destruction of the rain forests has created ecological problems.*

extinction (iks tingk′ shən) *n.* the dying out of a plant or animal species (p. 181). *People feared the extinction of the California condor until a recovery project saved it.*

Meet Stefan Lovgren

World News Reporter
As a writer for *National Geographic News*, Stefan Lovgren has reported on earthquakes in the South Pacific, killer asteroids from space, and ancient treasure in Egypt. Lovgren is also a contributor to the news Web site MSNBC.com.

 Literature Online

Author Search For more about Stefan Lovgren, go to glencoe.com and enter QuickPass Code GL39770u2.

Set Purposes for Reading

BQ BIG Question

Read "Huge, Freed Pet Pythons Invade Florida Everglades" to find out how exotic animals are getting into places they shouldn't be and why these animals are creating a crisis. As you read, ask yourself, what am I learning from this article?

Literary Elements Text Features

Text features are visual clues that help readers find and understand information. Common text features are titles, headings, photographs, captions, tables, charts, and diagrams.

Text features are important because they highlight points the writer wants to emphasize in the text. For example, **bold** or *italic* letters may signal important words. Graphics such as maps, charts, diagrams, and photographs help illustrate or summarize key information. Captions or labels next to graphic aids help explain why those features are important to the main idea.

As you read, note ways in which each text feature helps communicate the writer's ideas.

Reading Skill Analyze Evidence

When you analyze a piece of writing, you look at its separate parts to understand the entire piece. One part to analyze is the **evidence**—the detailed information the writer uses to support ideas and opinions.

Evidence should support the writer's idea or opinion and offer reliable information from sources readers trust, such as encyclopedias or university Web sites. Reliable evidence is important if the writer wants readers to agree with his or her main points.

Evidence comes in many forms. It can include

- statistics, or numbers, based on information gathered from many sources
- expert opinions from people who have studied a topic carefully
- results of studies or conclusions based on research of a topic

To analyze evidence, you might use a chart like the one below.

Writer's Important Points	Supporting Evidence
Everglades National Park is being overrun by Burmese pythons	Alligators seen fighting with pythons (eyewitness accounts)

Learning Objectives

For pages 178–184

In studying this text, you will focus on the following objectives:

Reading:
Understanding text features.

Analyzing evidence.

TRY IT

Analyze Evidence Read the following paragraph. Then analyze the evidence that supports the writer's main point.

The National Park Service has gathered information and created reports on the invasion of exotic fish in Everglades National Park. The National Park Service found that fish such as tilapia, Mayan cichlids, and oscars have been imported from Africa and South America. The exotic fish compete with the Florida largemouth bass and other native fish for nesting beds and food.

Huge, Freed Pet Pythons
Invade Florida Everglades

Stefan Lovgren

This 12-foot Burmese python was recently caught in the backyard of a south Florida home.

In February, a group of tourists at the Pa-hay-okee Overlook in Florida's Everglades National Park stumbled upon a battle between an alligator and a python. The stunned onlookers watched as the snake wrapped itself around the alligator, only to see its opponent counter by rolling over and grabbing the snake in its mouth and swimming off with the snake in its jaw.

It was not the first such battle. In January of last year, a **horde** of tourists watched another epic contest between an alligator and a python at the park's Anhinga Trail. After more than 24 hours in the jaws of the alligator, that snake broke free and moved off into the marsh.

For now, the alligators in the Florida Everglades are holding their ground against the invading snakes. But the odds may be changing. The park is being overrun with

Vocabulary

horde (hôrd) *n.* a large crowd of people or animals

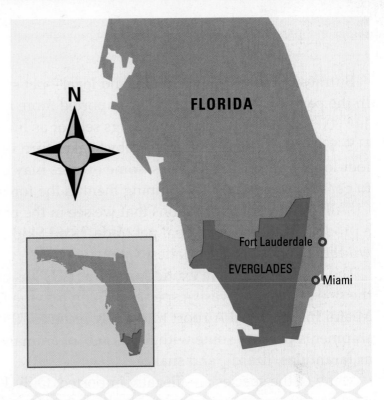

Burmese pythons, one of the world's largest snakes. These pythons can grow to be more than 20 feet (6 meters) long in their natural habitat in Southeast Asia.

The Burmese python is just one of thousands of non-native animal and plant species that have invaded the United States in the last decades. Florida teems with exotic creatures that have no business living there. . . . The economic toll from damage by **invasive** species— and the costs of trying to control them—is enormous: U.S. $137 billion a year, according to a 1999 Cornell University study.

The **ecological** outlook is equally grim. Second only to habitat loss, invasive species are a leading cause of species endangerment and **extinction** both in the United States and worldwide. Almost half of the species on the U.S. endangered species list are threatened wholly or partly by introduced species. Steven A. Williams, director of the U.S. Fish and Wildlife Service, calls invasive species the number one environmental threat to the United States.

Some invasive species may be "stowaway" organisms that arrive here inside packing materials, or micro-critters that are dumped from ships' water tanks. But many plants and animals also enter the U.S. as part of the booming trade in exotic pets or food.

Analyze Evidence In what way does this evidence support the writer's claims about the economic cost of this problem? Think about how reliable this evidence might be.

Vocabulary . . . .

invasive (in vā´siv) *adj.* having a tendency to spread and have harmful effects

ecological (ē´kəl oj´i kəl) *adj.* concerning the pattern of the relationship between all living things and their environment

extinction (iks tingk´shən) *n.* the dying out of a plant or animal species

Burmese pythons are popular—and legal—pet snakes. In the past five years, the U.S. has imported more than 144,000 Burmese pythons. Hatchlings sell for as little as U.S. $20. But once the cute little baby snakes turn into 15-foot-long (5-meter-long) beasts, some owners may decide to get rid of their pets by dumping them in the forest.

"All of the Burmese pythons that we see in the park are a product of the international pet trade," said Skip Snow, a wildlife biologist at Everglades National Park. . . .

The booming trade in exotic animals as pets has opened the floodgates for invasive species coming into the U.S. Miami International Airport reportedly receives 70 foreign shipments per day, some with thousands of animals, such as **tarantulas,** lizards, and snakes.

Many of the species are illegally imported. Only 1 to 2 percent of cargo containers are actually opened and checked. But many of the exotic animals are perfectly legal to bring into the country. U.S. residents, for example, can legally own 22 of the 24 pythons found around the world. . . .

Snow, the Everglades National Park biologist, appeals to pet owners who may have grown tired of their exotic animals: "Please don't release them into the wild."

BQ **BIG Question**

What are you learning about the python population in Florida from this article? Read on to the end and write your answer on your Big Question Foldable.

Analyze Evidence In what way does this evidence support the writer's claims about the illegal importing of pythons?

An American crocodile swims in the waters of Florida's Everglades National Park.

View the Photograph Compare this photo to the one at the beginning of the article. How do these images help you understand why the author calls the fight between these animals an "epic contest"?

After You Read

Respond and Think Critically

1. Other than through being imported, what are some ways invasive organisms enter the United States? Why do you think this has become a worldwide problem? [Recall and Infer]

2. Alligators and pythons are predators with few natural enemies. What could be the outcome for both species if the python population continues to grow in the Everglades? [Infer]

3. Stefan Lovgren concludes this article with a quotation from Skip Snow, a biologist. Is Snow a reliable or unreliable source of information? Explain your thoughts. [Analyze]

4. Why do you think the problem of freed exotic pets might be especially severe in Florida? [Draw Conclusions]

5. A farmer notices that many of his unplanted fields have fewer and fewer native grasses and wildflowers. What is the most likely cause of the disappearance of native grasses and flowers? [Synthesize]

6. **BQ** BIG Question What are the most important facts or lessons you have learned from this article? Explain. [Evaluate]

TIP

Synthesizing
When you **synthesize** information, you apply what you learned to a new idea.

- Skim the selection to learn what happens when an invasive species enters a new habitat.

- Think about how the information could apply to any invasive species, including vegetation.

- Create new ideas based on what you have learned.

 FOLDABLES **Study Organizer** Keep track of your ideas about the **BIG Question** in your unit Foldable.

Connect to Science

Statistics is a mathematical science. It involves collecting, analyzing, and presenting information, or data. Statistics are also facts presented as a number or a percentage.

One way scientists keep track of changes in an ecosystem such as the Everglades is by gathering and studying statistics. For example, the United States Environmental Protection Agency (EPA) is involved in a research project to determine the condition of the Everglades and what may need to be done to restore it. From 1993 to 1996 and again in 1999, researchers collected samples of Everglades freshwater. The samples were used to determine the condition of more than 750 miles of canals and 3,000 square miles of freshwater marsh. Scientists found that chemical pollutants were increasing. About 44% of the canal system and 4% of the marsh area exceeded acceptable chemical levels.

On Your Own Answer the following questions on a separate sheet of paper.

1. How did scientists discover that the level of chemicals in freshwater parts of the Everglades had increased from 1996 to 1999?

2. Why are scientific studies important to the future of the Everglades?

Literary Elements Text Features

1. Do you think that the title "Huge, Freed Pet Pythons Invade Florida Everglades" would make readers want to read this article? Why or why not?

2. How does the map of Florida help readers better understand the information presented in this passage of the text?

Review: Author's Purpose

The author's purpose is the intention of the author. An author generally writes for one or more of these reasons: to inform or explain, to express feelings, to persuade, and to entertain.

3. Stefan Lovgren's main purpose for writing this article is to inform the reader of a problem, but does he have another purpose? Explain your thoughts.

Reading Skill Analyze Evidence

4. Review the chart of important points and supporting evidence you compiled as you read the article.

   a. What evidence does the writer use to support his statements that invasive species are taking a toll on local species and the environment?

   b. How reliable is the writer's evidence? Explain your thoughts.

Vocabulary Practice

Match each boldface vocabulary word with the word or words from the right column that have the same meaning. Two of the words in the right column will not have matches. Then use each vocabulary word in a sentence or draw or find a picture that represents the word.

1. **horde**
2. **invasive**
3. **ecological**
4. **extinction**

a. expectations
b. survival
c. intruding
d. crowd
e. environmental
f. permanent disappearance

Academic Vocabulary

According to the writer, many people do not understand the **implications** of having exotic species as pets. In this sentence, *implications* means "the natural consequences of some act or decision." Think about the ideas expressed by the writer in the passage. Then fill in the blank for this statement: _____ is one of the implications of owning and caring for an exotic lizard.

Literature Online

Selection Resources For Selection Quizzes, eFlashcards, and Reading-Writing Connection activities, go to glencoe.com and enter QuickPass code GL39770u2.

Respond Through Writing

Summary

Report Main Ideas and Events In "Huge, Freed Pet Pythons Invade Florida Everglades," the writer provides evidence to support one main idea. The main idea of a work of nonfiction is also called its thesis. Summarize Lovgren's main idea, or thesis, and how he supports it.

Understand the Task To find the **main idea**, review the article and look for the one idea present throughout the text. To show the writer's ownership of his ideas, use apostrophes as the Grammar Tip explains.

Prewrite Review the chart you made that shows the important ideas and supporting details. Then review the article to see if you have missed any important ideas. You might want to reorganize your information into a graphic organizer like the one below, or you might create one that better fits your own way of organizing ideas.

> Important Idea:
>
> ↓
>
> Supporting detail or details:
>
> ↓

Draft Study your graphic organizer to determine the one main idea that all the evidence supports. Then start with an introductory paragraph to explain the main idea of the article. Add a paragraph about each of the important points that support the main idea. Your conclusion should summarize the main idea and the most persuasive supporting details. After you figure out your plan, write a thesis sentence to get started. This sentence frame may help you:

> Stefan Lovgren's thesis in the article is _____; he believes _____.

Revise Read your first draft carefully to determine whether your paragraphs follow a logical order and present a consistent main idea. If necessary, rearrange and rewrite text to make the ideas flow. Each idea should lead to the ideas expressed in the next paragraph. Make sure ideas are concisely stated and supported by details.

Edit and Proofread Proofread your paper, correcting any errors in spelling, grammar, and punctuation. Review the Grammar Tip in the side column for information on apostrophes.

Grammar Tip

Apostrophes
An **apostrophe (')** shows when a noun is possessive. It also shows where letters are missing from contractions.

Maya's jeans are in the washing machine. (The apostrophe and the *s* show that Maya possesses, or owns, the jeans.)

Maya wasn't planning on wearing those jeans today. (The apostrophe shows where the letter *o* was taken out to make the words *was* and *not* into one word—*wasn't*.)

Use an apostrophe after the final *s* to form the possessive of a plural noun that ends in *s*.

The players' scores were posted in the school paper.

To form a possessive of a plural noun that does not end in *s,* add an apostrophe and *s* (*'s*).

The women's soccer team won the championship.

Genre Focus:
Informational Text

The main purpose of an **informational text** is to share knowledge about a particular subject. Most informational texts tell you *who* did something or *why* something has happened. Some examples, also called **functional documents,** tell you *how* to do something. To conduct research on a topic, you need to consult informational texts.

Nonfiction works such as history and science textbooks, reference books, news articles, and reports are examples of informational texts.

Informational Elements

Text Structure refers to the way a writer arranges ideas and information within a piece of writing. There are several common patterns of organization:

- **Main Idea and Supporting Details** presents the key idea of a topic and additional information to back it up.

- **Chronological Order** is the arrangement of events in the order in which they happen in time.

- **Cause-and-Effect Organization** explores the causal, or connecting, relationships between events and ideas.

- **Problem-and-Solution Organization** examines a specific issue and presents one or more possible solutions.

- **Compare-and-Contrast Organization** describes the similarities and differences between two or more items.

Text Features are visual clues that help readers quickly locate or understand information in a text. Within the text, you might find:

- **Headings and Subheadings** that convey the main topic and secondary topics in the text.

- **Boldface Words or Phrases**—ideas that the writer wishes to emphasize.

Outside the text, you might find:

- **Illustrations,** such as photographs and art, that help you visualize what's discussed in the text.

- **Graphics,** such as diagrams, graphs, charts, and maps, to deepen your understanding of the text.

- **Captions**—short descriptions or titles used to explain an illustration or graphic.

- **Footnotes**—brief notes at the bottom ("foot") of the page that correspond to, and clarify the meaning of, words in the text.

TRY IT

Using diagrams like the ones on the next page, identify the characteristics of some informational selections in this unit.

Characteristics of the Genre

To better understand text structure and text features in informational works, look at the cause-and-effect diagram and the compare-and-contrast diagram below.

The following chart uses examples from "Huge, Freed Pet Pythons Invade Florida Everglades." Create a diagram like the one below to examine cause-and-effect order in "Zoya's Story," "Coming to America," or "Hollywood's Rise to Fame."

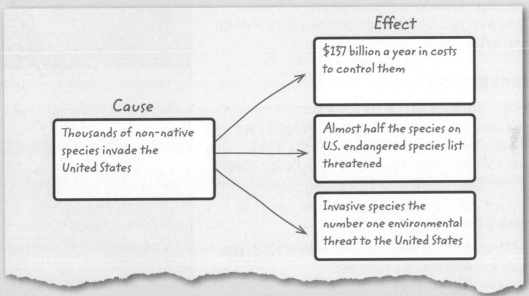

Effect

$137 billion a year in costs to control them

Cause

Thousands of non-native species invade the United States

Almost half the species on U.S. endangered species list threatened

Invasive species the number one environmental threat to the United States

Compare and contrast the text features of two of the bike documents.

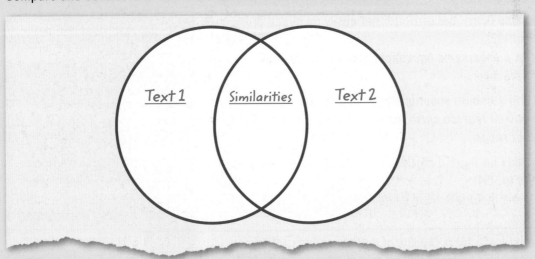

Text 1   Similarities   Text 2

LOG ON ▶ **Literature** Online

Literature and Reading For more selections in this genre, go to glencoe.com and enter QuickPass code GL39770u2.

Before You Read

from *The Great Fire*

Connect to the Informational Text

What would you do if you saw a blazing fire in your neighborhood?

Partner Talk With a partner, talk about ways to be prepared for a fire and what you would do if a fire ever broke out in your neighborhood. What are some ways to be prepared for a fire? How would you warn your family, friends, and neighbors and help them get to safety?

Build Background

On the evening of October 8, 1871, a fire broke out near the barn of Katherine O'Leary at 137 DeKoven Street in Chicago. By the time the fire was under control a day and a half later, it had destroyed much of one of America's largest cities. People began to call it the Great Chicago Fire.

- About three-and-one-half square miles and more than 18,000 structures were destroyed by the fire.

- The Great Chicago Fire was responsible for at least 300 deaths and left more than 90,000 people homeless.

Vocabulary

cumbersome (kum′bər səm) *adj.* not easily managed or carried (p. 192).
The large, cumbersome backpacks made progress quite slow for the hikers.

singe (sinj) *v.* to burn superficially or lightly; scorch (p. 192).
If you put your feet too close to the campfire, the fire may singe your shoes.

inflammable (in flam′ə bəl) *adj.* capable of being set on fire easily (p. 194).
Inflammable materials always need to be handled with great care.

velocity (vi los′ə tē) *n.* rapidity of motion; speed (p. 195).
The second-place runner could not match the velocity of the winner.

Meet Jim Murphy

"History is an endless succession of fascinating stories just waiting to be discovered."
—Jim Murphy

Children As Heroes Jim Murphy often writes about young people involved in historic events. According to Murphy, "Children weren't just observers of our history. They were actual participants and sometimes did amazing and heroic things."

Literary Works Murphy has written many award-winning books. *The Great Fire*, first published in 1995, won many awards, including being chosen as a Newbery Honor Book in 1996. To find out about the Great Chicago Fire, Murphy read letters and articles by people who were caught in the fire.

Jim Murphy was born in 1947.

 Literature Online

Author Search For more about Jim Murphy, go to glencoe.com and enter QuickPass code GL39770u2.

Set Purposes for Reading

BQ BIG Question

As you read, ask yourself what you can learn from reading about other people's mistakes.

Literary Element Description

Writers use **description,** or vivid details, to help readers imagine what a person, place, or thing is like. Good description can appeal to the five senses: seeing, hearing, touching, tasting, and smelling.

Description is important because it helps readers create a picture in their mind which can help them understand unfamiliar subjects or topics. Also, authors can use description to set the tone and mood of their writing and make characters come alive.

As you read, ask yourself, which details are especially vivid and original? How does description create a mood in this selection?

Reading Strategy Draw Conclusions About Events

When you **draw conclusions,** you combine clues from the writing with your own knowledge and experience to figure out what the writer is saying. Drawing conclusions about events means using a number of pieces of information to form general ideas of or make general statements about specific events.

Drawing conclusions about events is important because you don't have to rely on the author to point out connections between events for you. You can draw conclusions to make the connections between events yourself, which helps you see the "big picture."

When you draw conclusions about events, you

- notice details about events and anything related to them, such as characters

- use what you already know about the event in question or similar events

- check your conclusion against the details in the text to make sure they support it

As you read, ask yourself, "What conclusions can I draw about the events in the text?" You may find it helpful to use a graphic organizer like the one below to help you keep track of your ideas.

Details	What I Know	Conclusions

Learning Objectives

For pages 188–198

In studying this text, you will focus on the following objectives:

Literary Study: Analyzing description.

Reading: Drawing conclusions about events.

TRY IT

Draw Conclusions About Events Think of a recent event in your community. What conclusions can you draw about that event? For example, maybe your local grocery store closed after a new supermarket opened nearby. What conclusions could you draw from this situation? With a partner, try to think of more events to draw conclusions about.

THE GREAT FIRE

JIM MURPHY

On duty at the Courthouse[1] that night was forty-year-old Mathias Schaffer. Schaffer was showing some visitors around the tower when one of them pointed to smoke in the distance. Schaffer glanced at the smoke, but dismissed the sighting. It was just the smoldering embers from the previous night's fire, he assured them. Nothing to worry about.

Several minutes passed before Schaffer looked up from what he was doing and saw flames leaping wildly into the black sky. The light *was* from a different fire after all; he'd been fooled because this new blaze was almost directly behind the still-flickering remnants of the Saturday October 7 fire.

He studied the flames, trying to determine their exact location. This wasn't easy because of the distance and tall

Courthouse Square becoming engulfed in flames during the Chicago Fire, 1871. *Hand-colored woodcut.*

Description How does the way the author describes the fire here emphasize how serious the fire was?

---

1 The ***Courthouse*** was a building with a high tower that was used to watch for fires. When a fire was sighted, a watchman in the tower sent an alarm to a firehouse near the blaze.

buildings between him and the flames. In addition, the moonless sky was made even murkier[2] by the swirling, smoky haze. Schaffer signaled down the speaking tube[3] and had his assistant strike Box 342.[4] This sent engines rumbling through the streets—to a location almost a mile away from the O'Leary's barn.

Schaffer's first signal went out at 9:30. Several minutes later, Schaffer realized his mistake and ordered Box 319 struck. This was still seven blocks away from the O'Learys', but close enough that firefighters could see the flames and alter their course. Unfortunately, Schaffer's young assistant, William J. Brown, stubbornly refused to strike Box 319, saying he was afraid it would confuse the situation. Brown was so stubborn about his decision that even after the fire he was able to write arrogantly[5] in a letter that "I am still standing the watch[6] that burned Chicago."

These errors had two fatal consequences. The most obvious was that a number of engines and dozens of firefighters were sent on a wild-goose chase[7] and did not get to the fire for many minutes. More critical is that it kept fire companies located near DeKoven[8] Street in their stations. Several had seen the eerie, dancing glow beyond the rooftops near them and, even without official notice from Schaffer, prepared to respond. When they heard Box 342 rung, however, they assumed the fire was out of their territory and unhitched the horses. Only two fire companies were not fooled by the misleading alarm.

The clang of bells and the sound of pounding hooves could be heard above the roar of the fire. *America* arrived on

Description What sense do the descriptions "clang of bells," "pounding hooves," and "roar of the fire" appeal to? How do they help you picture the scene?

---

2 **Murky** means "hazy" or "hard to see through." It was even harder for the watchman to see because the smoke from the earlier fires made the sky **murkier.**

3 A **speaking tube** was a pipe made to carry a voice from one part of a building to another.

4 Watchmen at the courthouse sent alarms to local fire stations by hitting numbered boxes that were linked to the local stations. The station linked to **Box 342** was a mile from the fire.

5 When you act **arrogantly,** you act like you think you're smarter or more important than other people.

6 **Standing the watch** means "being on guard duty."

7 A **wild-goose chase** is a search that has no chance of success.

8 The fire started near 137 **DeKoven** Street.

the scene first, closely followed by *Little Giant*. Hoses were rolled out, attached to water outlets, and the water turned on. Unfortunately, *America* was a hose cart and could not throw water any great distance, while *Little Giant* was eleven years old (the oldest engine in service). Their limited range forced firefighters to stand very close to the flames. The newer, more powerful pumping engines were either a mile away searching for a phantom fire, or still in their stations.

The fire had begun near the corner of DeKoven and Jefferson and quickly fanned out thanks to increasingly gusty winds. One tongue traveled north up Jefferson, while the other headed east toward Lake Michigan. There was no way firefighters from two engines could contain a wind-driven fire with such a wide front. Still, they did their best.

Two men hauled the **cumbersome** canvas hose as close to the flames as possible and aimed a stream of water at the burning building. The water hissed and boiled when it struck the burning wood, sending up a vapor of white steam. The firefighters held their position until the fierce heat began to **singe** the hair on their heads and arms, and their clothes began to smolder. When the pain became unbearable, they staggered back from the flames for a moment's relief, then lunged forward again.

Draw Conclusions About Events What conclusions can you draw about the firefighters who were battling the blaze?

More engines began arriving at the scene, as did the department's Chief Marshal Robert A. Williams. A common fire-fighting technique of the time was to surround a blaze with engines and use a flood of water to stop it from spreading. Williams immediately set about repositioning engines, hoping to halt the fire's advance until all the missing equipment could get to the scene.

The firefighters were already engulfed in a wave of withering heat, and the flames were reaching out toward them. "Marshal," one of the men yelled, "I don't believe we can stand it here!"

Description How does the author use description to set the mood of this scene?

"Stand it as long as you can," Williams told them, before hurrying to another engine. Along the way he noticed that several houses were smoking and on the verge of igniting.

Vocabulary
....

cumbersome (kum′bər səm) *adj.* not easily managed or carried

singe (sinj) *v.* to burn superficially or lightly; scorch

Flaming buildings and boats along the Chicago River during the Great Fire, 1871. Hand-colored woodcut.

 View the Art How do you think people in Chicago felt as they saw buildings and boats aflame along the Chicago River?

He came upon the driver of *America* and its foreman, John Dorsey. "Turn in a second alarm!" Williams ordered Dorsey. "This is going to spread!" A second alarm would bring in additional engines and men.

Meanwhile, Chamberlin[9] had retreated several blocks in the face of the advancing flames. "I stepped in among some sheds south of Ewing Street; a fence by my side began to blaze; I beat a hasty retreat, and in five minutes the place where I had stood was all ablaze. Nothing could stop that conflagration there. It must sweep on until it reached a broad street, and then, everybody said, it would burn itself out."

The heat and dry air had left twelve-year-old Claire Innes tired and listless all day. She went to bed sometime between eight and eight-thirty only to be startled awake later when a horse-and-wagon clattered past her window at high speed. This was followed by loud voices from the street below her window.

"I was only half awake and not inclined to get up when I heard a man outside say that a fire was burning in the West Division. Father went to the door and asked about the fire

Draw Conclusions About Events What conclusion can you draw about the fire from Chamberlin's account?

---

9 One of the first people to reach the fire was Joseph E. ***Chamberlin,*** a reporter for the *Chicago Evening Post.*

and the man repeated what he had told his companions, but this time he added that the fire was a big one and that they were going to have a look at it. Father came inside and said something to Mother. . . . His voice did not sound unusual, [so] I turned over and closed my eyes again."

Claire and her family were staying in the South Division of the city, many blocks from the fire. There really was no reason for them to become alarmed. In fact, most citizens would see the glowing nighttime sky and dismiss it as nothing important. Not even the warning words in that day's *Chicago Tribune* drew much attention: "For days past alarm has followed alarm, but the comparatively trifling losses have familiarized us to the pealing of the Courthouse bell, and we [have] forgotten that the absence of rain for three weeks [has] left everything in so dry and **inflammable** a condition that a spark might set a fire which would sweep from end to end of the city."

But no one seemed very concerned. This was evident by what Alfred L. Sewell observed while strolling through the city at around 9:30 that night. "Many people were just returning from the Sunday evening services at the various churches when the general alarm was given, but, beyond the immediate vicinity of the beginning of the conflagration, no unusual fear or solicitude was felt by the citizens. The German beerhouses were filled with merry crowds, and as it was a warm evening, the streets all over the city were filled with joyful idlers and promenaders, in their Sunday apparel. A pleasanter, quieter, or a happier evening than was that one is seldom known in a great city."

And despite his own paper's editorial, not even the editor in chief of the *Chicago Tribune*, Horace White, smelled a good story in the smoke that was blowing into his neighborhood. "I had retired to rest, though not to sleep [that night], when the great bell struck the alarm; but fires had been so frequent of late, and had been so speedily extinguished, that I did not deem it worthwhile to get up and look at it, or even to count the strokes of the bell to learn where it was."

Description How does the description of people throughout the city contrast to the descriptions of what is happening at the fire?

Vocabulary

inflammable (in flam′ə bəl) *adj.* capable of being set on fire easily

As the rest of the city went about its business, fireman Dorsey was racing through the streets to the closest signal box, which happened to be at Goll's drugstore. He opened the small door on the box and used his thumb to pull down the lever. Dorsey then headed back to the scene of the fire, not realizing that he'd made a mistake—he had forgotten to pull down the lever four times, a special signal that would have made it a true second alarm. At the Courthouse, Schaffer and Brown would hear Dorsey's alarm, but, assuming it was simply another signal telling them about the original fire, they failed to call out more engines. The fire had now been burning for over an hour, and the wind was increasing in **velocity**.

Despite this, Chief Marshal Williams had managed to get a thin circle of engines around the fire. He had five steamers at the scene now, plus three hose carts and a hook-and-ladder wagon, all of them pumping water into the fire at various locations. Spectators were asked to help and many responded by chopping up fences and sidewalks, hoping to deprive the fire of fuel.

Draw Conclusions About Events What can you conclude about the construction of Chicago at the time of the fire?

Meanwhile the heat was beginning to wear down some of the firemen. Charles Anderson remembered when his friend Charles McConners came by and said, "Charley, this is hot!"

"It is, Mac," Anderson replied.

His friend disappeared for a few moments, then returned carrying a wooden door, which he positioned like a warrior's shield between Anderson and the fire.

I have it now, Anderson thought. I can stand it a considerable time.

Anderson no sooner thought this when the door caught fire and burned McConners' hand. McConners flung the door down and then Anderson's clothes began to smoke. The heat was so intense that his leather hat began to twist out of shape.

Description How does the description in this paragraph appeal to different senses?

Williams came by and issued new orders. "Charley, come out as fast as possible. Wet the other side of the street or it will burn!"

Vocabulary ....

velocity (vi los′ ə tē) *n.* rapidity of motion; speed

The Great Chicago Fire, 8–10 October, 1871. Currier & Ives. Lithograph.

With the help of onlookers, Anderson began to reposition his hose. He hadn't gotten it very far when water pressure suddenly dropped and only a trickle of liquid came from the hose. A powerful steam engine had arrived at the fire and had simply removed Anderson's hose from its water plug. This was routine procedure, done under the assumption that a steamer would always be more effective than a simple hose cart. Sadly, the steamer did not drag its hose to Anderson's position and he had to watch as four or five houses across the street caught fire.

At the same moment that Anderson's hose stopped, another steamer malfunctioned and its water also gave out. A well-aimed rap of a hammer got the engine working again, but then, at about 10:30, an old section of hose burst and the flow of water stopped again. Two valuable links in the chain of defense were gone, and there was nothing to stop the fire in these locations.

Williams rushed to get the water going and to reposition his engines, but it was too late. The wind had pushed the fire past his circle, a wind that was blowing directly toward the heart of the city.

Later at the official inquiry, all of the mistakes and missed chances that occurred in the opening minutes of the fire would be discussed in great detail. As one firefighter put it, "From the beginning of that fatal fire, everything went wrong!" 🔔

BQ **BIG Question**

What can be accomplished by reviewing mistakes that were made during a situation? What have you gotten out of reading about the mistakes made during the Chicago fire?

After You Read

Respond and Think Critically

1. When the fire first started, what mistakes kept fire trucks from going to the right location? [Recall and Identify]

2. Why does the author write that Brown was "stubborn" and that Brown wrote "arrogantly" about his decision? [Interpret]

3. Why do you think that the citizens of Chicago were so unconcerned about the fire blazing through the city? Explain your answer. [Infer]

4. Which of the many mishaps during the fire were due to bad luck? Which were the result of human error? [Analyze]

5. What conclusion can you draw about firefighting equipment at the time of the Great Chicago Fire? [Draw Conclusions]

6. **BQ** BIG Question Think about how the firefighters responded. What can you get out of reading about such behavior? [Connect]

Vocabulary Practice

Synonyms are words that have the same or nearly the same meaning. Match each boldfaced vocabulary word with its synonym in the right-hand column. Two of the words in that column will not have matches. Then write sentences using each vocabulary word.

1. **cumbersome**
2. **singe**
3. **inflammable**
4. **velocity**

a. combustible
b. acceleration
c. unwieldy
d. convenient
e. sear
f. swiftness

Academic Vocabulary

In "The Great Fire," the blaze raged **unrestrained** through the city. In this sentence, *unrestrained* means "not under control." To become more familiar with the word *unrestrained,* create a graphic organizer like the one below and fill in the boxes.

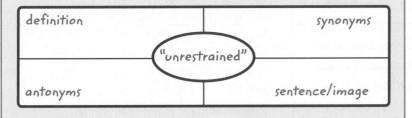

definition	synonyms
"unrestrained"	
antonyms	sentence/image

TIP

Analyzing
Here are some tips to help you analyze. Remember when you analyze, you break a selection into parts to see how they work together to convey an overall idea.

- Make a list of the mishaps that occur in the narrative.

- Examine the circumstances surrounding each mishap.

- Determine whether the mishap was caused by bad luck or human error.

 FOLDABLES Study Organizer Keep track of your ideas about the **BIG Question** in your unit Foldable.

 Literature Online

Selection Resources
For Selection Quizzes, eFlashcards, and Reading-Writing Connection activities, go to glencoe.com and enter QuickPass code GL39770u2.

Literary Element Description

1. Which words or phrases from "The Great Fire" appeal to the sense of sight? Which words or phrases appeal to the sense of hearing? Make two lists, one of memorable sights and the other of sounds.

2. What description in the text do you feel is the most successful in conveying what it was like to be in the middle of the Great Chicago Fire? Explain what exactly makes it so successful to you.

Review: Conflict

Remember that in a text **conflict** is the struggle between opposing forces. When a character clashes with another character, with nature, with society, or with fate, that character is involved in an **external conflict.** The conflicts in "The Great Fire" are external conflicts.

3. What is the central conflict in "The Great Fire"? Which of the following does this central conflict involve: people, nature, society, or fate?

4. What other conflicts can you find within the text? Identify the type of each external conflict you find. Explain whether each conflict is resolved in the selection, and if so, how it is resolved.

Reading Strategy
Draw Conclusions About Events

5. Think about how people such as Mathias Schaffer, the newspaper editor, and many of the citizens of Chicago initially react to the fire. Based on what you have read about their behavior, what conclusion or conclusions can you draw about how common fires were in the city at this time?

6. After reading his account of the events of the Great Chicago Fire, what can you conclude about the author's purpose for writing about this event? Support your answer with evidence from the text.

Grammar Link

Agreement with Indefinite Pronouns
An **indefinite pronoun** is a noun substitute that does not refer to a specific person, place, or thing. Certain indefinite pronouns are always singular, or equal to *he, she,* or *it.* Study the list below.

anybody	**everybody**	**no one**
anyone	**everyone**	**nothing**
anything	**everything**	**somebody**
each	**neither**	**someone**
either	**nobody**	**something**

For example:
   No one is to blame for the fire.

In the sentence above, *No one* is singular, meaning it is equal to *he, she,* or *it.* So the right verb form is *is.*

Practice Write the correct verb form for each sentence.

1. Each of the firefighters (is, are) singed.

2. Nobody (was, were) able to find a way to stop the fire.

3. Everyone (think, thinks) the fire will be quickly extinguished.

4. Somebody (fail, fails) to pull the alarm.

5. Everything (is, are) destroyed in the fire.

Research and Report

Visual/Media Presentation Using the library or the Internet, research art and photographs depicting the Great Chicago Fire and the rebuilding effort that followed. Draw a picture or make a collage that shows the devastation caused in Chicago by the Great Fire and the efforts to rebuild the city after the fire. Remember to credit the sources you use as inspiration for your presentation.

Before You Read

Functional Documents

Learning Objectives

For pages 199–207

In this assignment, you will focus on the following objectives:

Reading: Skimming and scanning.

Writing: Writing technical directions.

Connect to the Functional Documents

Think about a time you wanted to buy something important for yourself. What did you want to buy? Why did you feel you needed it?

Partner Talk With a classmate, talk about what you considered buying. What information did you gather to help you decide whether to buy the item or which brand or type of item to buy?

Build Background

If you have the money and desire to purchase something important or expensive, such as a bicycle, you'll want to look for the best value for your money. You can turn to **functional documents** for information.

- **Consumer choice articles** are newspaper, magazine, or Internet articles that provide useful information about products and often compare popular brands or models.

- When you purchase your bicycle, you'll receive a **product warranty.** It explains which parts the manufacturer is willing to repair or replace if the part breaks during a given period of time.

- If you need to make an adjustment or a repair, **technical directions** will describe the process, and list the tools, for doing the work.

Set Purposes for Reading

BQ **BIG Question**

Read these functional documents to learn how to choose, purchase, and operate important things you buy, such as a bicycle.

Reading Strategies **Skim and Scan**

Skilled readers often **skim** and **scan** functional documents to locate key information. When you skim, you look quickly over a document to get a general idea of the structure and subject. When you scan, you look for a particular piece or type of information. You skim *before* you read the document. You scan *after* you've read the document. As you read, follow these tips:

- Skim through the entire document, noting any text features that stand out—headings, subheadings, charts, or words in bold print or italics.

- Scan the document, looking only for key words or phrases that have to do with the information you seek.

Understand Consumer Choice Articles

"Today, a vast variety of models are offered in a wide range of prices."

This line frames a challenge that all shoppers face: trying to choose a specific product when there are so many types of that product available. To choose what's best for you, you need to determine which features you value most, then find the products that have those features. People read consumer choice articles to become better informed about a product before purchasing it. By comparing one product to another, consumer choice articles can tell you what to look for and where to find it.

Choosing a Bike

You couldn't pick a better time to shop for a new bike. Today, a vast variety of models are offered in a wide range of prices. From super-plush comfort bikes to knobby tire mountain bikes, from pure road machines to sturdy cruisers, your local shop has two-wheelers perfect for just about everything.

So many attractive choices can be overwhelming. But a large selection is a wonderful thing because it greatly increases the likelihood of finding the perfect bike. Plus, at the bicycle store, you'll be able to ask questions, learn about different bike types, even test a few.

Just be sure to go in equipped with a little knowledge about yourself, the cycling you'd like to do, and some basic information about bike models that have already caught your fancy. That way, you'll be able to answer the questions from the shop's staff and you'll get a bike you really enjoy.

To help, we recommend a little self analysis (not required).

Analyze Yourself

Consider how many times a week or month you might ride. If you're new to biking, think about your other sports experiences. Did you participate mostly for fun or did you take it seriously? Your tendencies can tip you off as to whether you'll be satisfied with a basic model or whether you'll need something better that your enthusiasm won't outgrow.

Think about your tendencies in purchasing other things, too. For example, do you consistently demand the highest quality, or are you more apt to look for reasonable quality and lower cost? Do you dig high-tech gadgets or are you

Skim Look quickly through the article. Based on the headings, what topics are addressed?

satisfied with simpler designs? If you're joining a cycling club, will you want a bike that outshines all the others? Or will any two-wheeler that does the job be just fine?

Where you live plays a major role in what type of bike to get. You'll ride more if your new machine matches your riding opportunities. For example, if you're surrounded by beautiful trails, an off-road bike might be a better choice than a pavement pounder (assuming you don't also have great road rides, in which case, you might need two bikes!).

Mind Your Budget

Additionally, it helps to know about how much you want to spend because that's a quick way to focus the selection process on the appropriate models. Like computers and other modern appliances, it's best (and cheapest) to purchase the most appropriate model at the start than to gamble on a make-do bike and buy another later. Regardless of the type, as you spend more, bicycles get slightly lighter (easier to ride) and are equipped with more features and more efficient components or parts.

While it's always possible to upgrade parts down the road, bike components are much more affordable when they're included as standard equipment on the new bike. So, it's most economical to get what you want when you buy your new bike.

When calculating how much you'd like to spend on that new machine, remember that you may need some extras. Common purchases include helmets, locks, pumps, tool kits, cycling shorts, and shoes.

Know the Bike Types

Here's a rundown of the six major bike types available with descriptions of their intended use and common features. Use these descriptions to determine which type is right for you.

If you're not sure, keep in mind that most bicycle shops offer test rides, which is an excellent way to see how types differ. You might also ask friends who ride if you can try their bikes. Ride both on and off road (on the appropriate models) to experience the difference.

ROAD SPORT BIKES	
Use	Built for use on pavement, these models have plenty of get-up-and-go and are perfect for centuries,[1] touring, longer commutes, fitness riding, and pledge rides.
Common Features	Efficient-pedaling lightweight frames and wheels; drop or flat handlebars; low gearing and excellent braking; narrow, high-pressure tires.
MOUNTAIN BIKES	
Use	Sometimes called All-Terrain Bikes (ATB) or Off-Road Bikes, these amazing vehicles could also be called Go-everywhere/Do-everything bikes. From cliff-like dropoffs to shoe-drenching stream crossings, almost no obstacle can stop a skilled rider.
Common Features	Upright riding position; flat or riser handlebars; high-traction, flat-resistant tires; low gearing; excellent braking; rugged frames, wheels, and components; suspension for control and comfort on rough terrain.
HYBRID BIKES	
Use	A hybrid[2] of the mountain bike and the road bike, these practical machines are ideal for city riding, commuting, touring, and fitness riding.
Common Features	Upright riding position; flat handlebars; low gearing for easy hill climbing; powerful brakes; light, lively wheels with flat-resistant tires; load-carrying capacity.
COMFORT BIKES	
Use	Designed for easy pedaling and the least amount of stress on the body, comfort bikes are perfect for leisurely town riding, cruising by the shore, vacation outings, and any ride where you're out more for fun than for speed.
Common Features	Upright riding position; wide handlebars; wide, comfortable seats; flat-resistant tires; easy pedaling; soft ride.

Skim Glance at the chart. How is the information organized?

---

1 ***Centuries*** are 100-mile-long biking trips or events.

2 A ***hybrid*** combines qualities or features from two different sources.

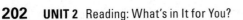

CRUISERS	
Use	Rolling on soft "balloon" tires and equipped with comfy wide seats and handlebars, these models are great for leisurely spins to school, pedaling to the shore with your surfboard under your arm, or just for coasting around the neighborhood.
Common Features	Comfortable upright riding position; shock-absorbing fat tires; foot-friendly rubber pedals; sweet seat and spacious handlebars; usually feature from 1 to 7 speeds.
RECUMBENTS	
Use	Resembling lawn chairs on wheels, these impressive and ultra-comfortable rigs are great for most road uses, including touring, commuting, fitness riding, and pledge rides.
Common Features	Unique frames that provide a comfy reclining riding position; seats with full support and backrests for amazing comfort; low gearing and excellent braking.

Now that you know a little more about yourself and your bicycle choices, you're ready to hit the shops. Enjoy selecting that new two-wheeler. Soon, you'll be spinnin' and grinnin'.

Understand Warranties

What is a warranty and why is it important? A warranty is a guarantee from the maker (manufacturer) of the product, indicating which parts of the product the maker is willing to repair or replace—under what conditions and for what period of time—should a part break or fail. In short, the warranty tells you what the maker "owes" you after you buy the item.

Sample Bike Warranty

Warranty Statement

Bob's Bicycles warrants only to the original purchaser / consumer of this product that such products and parts thereof, when used for normal riding purposes by a person that properly fits and is capable of riding and controlling this bicycle, are free of defects in workmanship and material. This warranty does not apply to any part thereof which may fail due to improper assembly, accident, abuse, neglect, or normal wear and tear.

Scan Review the bicycle types. Which types are best for leisurely riding?

Skim Read the headings. What topics are covered in the warranty?

Warranty Parts

For one year from the date of purchase, when properly assembled as detailed in the owner's manual, Bob's Bicycles will replace any defective part which results when this cycle is used in a normal manner.

Warranty on Frame

For the usable life of this cycle, Bob's Bicycles will replace the frame at no charge should it fail in any weld point when the cycle has been used in a normal manner and as determined by our inspection. Claims under this warranty must be made through the authorized[1] Bob's Bicycles dealer. Proof of purchase is required. A warranty registration card must be completed and received by Bob's Bicycles before a warranty claim may be processed.

Our warranties do not apply to any unit that has been abused, misused, altered by component parts or substitutions, or used for rental or other commercial[2] uses. Labor charges incurred in[3] the replacement of parts are not covered by this warranty.

The Following Exclusions Apply to All Bob's Bicycles Models

This warranty does not apply to any unit that has been used for stunt riding, bicycle moto-cross, dirt biking, or similar activities — Bob's Bicycles are not designed or intended for such purposes or usages.

The user assumes the risk of any personal injuries, damage to or failure of the bicycle, and any other losses if Bob's Bicycles are used in any competitive event.

It is the responsibility of the person who completes the assembly of the bicycle to install all parts included with it in the factory-sealed shipping carton and to make minor adjustments of functional parts such as brakes, steering assembly, etc., as is required for proper operation.

---

1 **Authorized** means "officially approved."

2 Here, **commercial** means "relating to business."

3 **Incurred in** means "resulting from."

Understand Technical Directions

People turn to technical writing to understand the steps of a process to reach an intended outcome or create an item. What text features in the following selection organize the information into logical parts?

How to Fix a Flat Tire on a Bicycle

If you ride a bicycle, you've probably had a flat tire at one time or another. Knowing how to fix a flat tire is a skill you may need someday.

Materials

- 2 tire levers (small tools used to pry the tire from the rim)
- 1 six-inch crescent wrench
- a tube repair kit
- an air pump

Directions

Different steps are taken to remove the rear wheel and the front wheel. Removing the rear wheel is more involved.

Removing the Rear Wheel

Most flat tires occur in the rear tire. First, you need to remove the brake cable. To remove the brake cable, press both brake pads toward the wheel. This gives you enough slack in the cable so you can easily lift the cable's loose end from its housing in the brake lever. Next, put the bike on its back. Flip the quick-release lever[1] or use the crescent wrench to loosen both axle nuts. Take the derailleur body[2] and pull it back toward you. Then, lift the chain and remove the wheel.

Removing the Front Wheel

First, remove the brake cable. Next, put the bike on its back. Then loosen the axle nuts or release lever. At this point, the wheel is off of the bike. Now it is time to take the tire off of the wheel.

Taking the Tire Off the Wheel

Start at a point opposite from the tire valve.[3] Work the spoon-like end of the tire lever under one edge of the tire,

Skim Quickly read through the document. What are the two major sections?

---

1 A **quick-release lever** is the lever that operates a mechanism that allows for the quick attachment or removal of the bicycle's wheels.

2 The **derailleur body** is the mechanism that moves the chain from sprocket to sprocket to change gears on a multi-speed bicycle.

3 A **tire valve** is the device attached to the inner tube of the bicycle tire through which the tire is inflated.

between the tire and metal rim. Then hook the slotted end of the tire lever onto a spoke. Now use the second lever to pry off more of the tire, working your way toward the tire valve. Soon you'll have one side of the tire off the rim. Use your tire levers to pry off the other side of the tire. Finally, remove the inner tube.

Locating and Repairing the Leak

Find the air leak. Pump air into the tube and listen for a *pssss* sound.

Prepare the area around the leak. Use the sandpaper or metal scraper that comes in your tire repair kit. Sand or scrape the area all around the hole in your tire. This is called "roughing" the area. This will help the patch stick better to the tire. Next, cover the rough area with glue. This will be in your repair kit as well. Now wait for the glue to dry. It's important to wait for the glue to dry *before* you put the patch on.

Put the patch on the tube. Press down the edges of the patch with your tire lever. Look and feel inside the tire for what might have caused the flat. Be sure the "rim tape" (the rubber or cloth strip covering the spoke ends) is in place. You don't want all of your hard work to be wasted by allowing a rock or nail to remain in the rim!

Pump a couple of strokes of air into the tube. This will prevent the tube from becoming twisted.

Putting Your Bike Back Together

Put the tube back into the tire. Push the valve stem into the valve hole in the rim. Use your fingers to tuck one side of the tire back onto the rim. Use the tire lever when there are six inches of tire left. DO NOT PINCH THE TUBE. Then tuck the other side of the tire into the rim. Check that the valve stem stands straight up when you are through. Pump up the tire. Next, replace the wheel by following the first step in reverse and refastening the brake cable.

Your flat tire is now repaired. It is always a good idea to check the pressure on both tires before riding again. Be extra careful to avoid any nails, screws, or sharp pebbles as you ride. But if you should get a flat again, now you know how to fix it! 🚲

Scan Review the directions. Then restate them in your own words.

After You Read

Respond and Think Critically

Read the questions about the functional documents on pages 200–206 and select the best answer.

Test Skills Practice

1. As described in the consumer choice article, which one of the following bicycle types does not have flat-resistant tires?
   A. mountain
   B. hybrid
   C. comfort
   D. recumbent

Test Skills Practice

2. The writer of the technical directions wants to help you
   F. learn about a product you'd like to purchase.
   G. get service on a product you've purchased.
   H. repair a product you've purchased.
   I. use a product you've just purchased.

Test Skills Practice

3. Which of the following best summarizes the consumer choice article?
   A. Buy the bike that you like.
   B. Mountain bikes are the best.
   C. Analysis is important.
   D. Buy the cheapest bike.

4. The final section of the warranty addresses "Exclusions." What wording in the section helps you understand the meaning of "Exclusions"?

5. The consumer choice article notes that "if you're surrounded by beautiful trails, an off-road bike might be a better choice." Which of the six bike types described in the article are considered to be off-road bikes?

Writing Tip

Write Technical Directions Think of a multi-step process or activity you know how to do well. Write technical directions explaining how to complete the process or create an item. Before you write, consider

- the tools or materials needed in the process

- the order of the steps in the process

- text features, like headings and charts, to make clear each part of the explanation

Literature Online

Selection Resources For Selection Quizzes, eFlashcards, and Reading-Writing Connection activities, go to glencoe.com and enter QuickPass code GL39770u2.

Media Workshop

Media Elements

The story of "Huge, Freed Pet Pythons Invade Florida Everglades" might appear on a TV news show. Here's how it might begin:

> News Anchor, behind a desk says:
>
> *"Huge pythons let loose in Everglades National Park have disrupted the habitat. Reports tell of battles between pythons and native alligators."*
>
> [Shift to video of a python and alligator grappling. Snake wraps itself around the alligator. Alligator rolls over and grabs snake between its teeth.]

Now think about the purposes of a TV news story—to present news, keep the viewer's attention, and make the viewer feel right in the middle of the action. What other purposes might a news story have?

The chart shows more things you will hear, see, and experience in this news report. These are **media elements**. How do these elements help news people achieve their purposes?

Media Element	What It Is	Example
Text and Content	**Text** is the words the audience hears and sees. All the text together makes up **content,** or the verbal information the story provides.	• News anchor: "And it's not just pythons—people release tarantulas and lizards, also." • Park biologist: "Please don't release your pet pythons into the wild."
Visuals	**Visuals** are what you see in a story, including **images, movement,** and **color.**	• Map of Florida Everglades • Photos of python and tarantula
Audio	**Audio** is what the viewers or listeners hear.	• Splashing, slapping sounds of the battle • Yells of surprise from tourists who see the battle

Hollywood's Rise to Fame

Connect to the Informational Text

What do you know about Hollywood? Consider what Hollywood is famous for and why people go there.

Partner Talk With a partner, talk about what you would like to do or see if you visited a movie studio in Hollywood. What would make a trip to Hollywood special for you?

Build Background

In "Hollywood's Rise to Fame," Robert D. San Souci describes how Hollywood became the moviemaking capital of the world.

- A common nickname for Hollywood is "Tinseltown" because of the glamour associated with movie stars.

- Many movies are now filmed "on location," which means they are filmed in the actual setting—a town, a forest, a desert—where the story takes place instead of in a studio. Most Hollywood lots and sound stages are now used to produce television shows.

Vocabulary

convey (kən vā′) v. to show or communicate by statement, gesture, or appearance (p. 212). *The crowd clapped and cheered to convey its enthusiasm for the singer's performance.*

influx (in′ fluks) n. a continual flow (p. 212). *States with warm, sunny weather receive an influx of tourists during the winter months.*

obscure (əb skyoor′) adj. not well known (p. 213). *Not many people had read the obscure book.*

rival (rī′ vəl) adj. describing two or more trying to achieve what only one can possess (p. 214). *The rival teams competed for the title of state champion.*

enterprise (en′ tər prīz′) n. a business organization (p. 214). *The mayor urged the town's citizens to support each local enterprise.*

Meet Robert D. San Souci

"I love it when a book lets me celebrate my home state."
—Robert D. San Souci

A Family Affair Robert D. San Souci was born in San Francisco, where he still resides. "Books were always important in my family," San Souci says. His parents read constantly. As a boy, he mowed lawns— at 25 cents an hour—so he could buy books and "build my own 'library.'"

Literary Works San Souci has won numerous awards for his works. Many of San Souci's books are illustrated by his brother Daniel.

Robert D. San Souci was born in 1946.

 Literature Online

Author Search For more about Robert D. San Souci, go to glencoe.com and enter QuickPass code GL39770u2.

Set Purposes for Reading

BQ BIG Question

Reading magazines and nonfiction books about a subject in which you are interested can be informative and enjoyable. Read to learn how Hollywood became the moviemaking capital of the world.

Literary Element Text Structure

Text structure is the way an author organizes information. One type of text structure is **chronological order,** or time order. When authors organize information in chronological order, they tell about events in the order in which they occurred. To recognize the order of events, look for time-order words and phrases such as *first, next, then, later,* and *finally.* Dates can also help you recognize chronological order.

Identifying the order of events is important because it helps you recognize how one event leads to another. It also helps you find and recall key ideas and events.

As you read, look for time-order words and dates to understand how one event in Hollywood's history relates to another.

Reading Skill Identify Cause-and-Effect Relationships

A **cause** is something that happens. An **effect** is what happens as a result of the cause. For example, Jason hit a baseball (cause) that broke a window (effect). Authors use a cause-and-effect approach to explore the reasons for something and to examine the results of actions or events.

It is important to identify cause-and-effect relationships to see how events are connected. To identify cause-and-effect relationships,

- ask yourself, "Why did this event happen?" Your answer will tell you the *cause.*
- ask yourself, "What will happen as a result of this event?" Your answer will tell you the *effect.*
- look for signal words such as *so, because,* and *as a result.*

As you read, identify the people and events that caused Hollywood to become a center for moviemaking. Use a graphic organizer like the one below to keep track of cause-and-effect relationships.

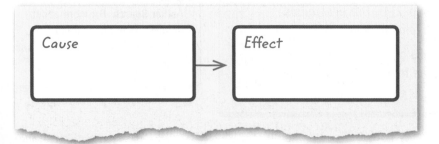

TRY IT

Identify Cause-and-Effect Relationships
Identify a possible effect of each of the causes below.

- Going to bed late
- Studying hard and participating in class
- Leaving the bathtub water running
- Doing something kind for a neighbor

HOLLYWOOD'S RISE TO FAME

Robert D. San Souci

Many cities or towns might have become *the* moviemaking capital of the world, but only Hollywood, California, can claim that title. This happened through a mix of luck, location, and business need.

The Hollywood story begins on the East Coast, with famed inventor Thomas Alva Edison and his associate William Kennedy Laurie Dickson. They were working in Edison's laboratories in West Orange, New Jersey. In 1891, they created a moving picture machine called a kinetoscope. Edison then began filming in and around

This early map of Hollywood advertises a quiet, orderly community. Today, the rise of motion pictures has made Hollywood a symbolic international movie capital.

Text Structure What happened after Edison invented the kinetoscope?

New York City. Other early movie companies made films in Philadelphia, Pennsylvania; Brooklyn, New York; and Jacksonville, Florida.

The bitterly cold winters of the East made year-round filming difficult. In addition, Edison tried to control the movie industry by applying for patents and establishing a monopoly on many of his filmmaking techniques. To avoid being under Edison's watchful eye, some people decided to head west.

Early film producers[1] who came to southern California found an ideal climate for making motion pictures. The clear, sunny weather enhanced shooting, which took place mostly outdoors. Within 200 miles was scenery that could be used to **convey** places as distinct as the Sahara Desert or the planet Mars. Land for production studios and labor for industry jobs—from building sets to playing extras— were available and inexpensive.

Historians believe that the movie business officially moved to Hollywood in 1911 when a group of producers rented a building at the corner of Gower Street and Sunset Boulevard and began shooting a film. Back then, no one would have guessed what a big business Hollywood filmmaking would become. After all, Hollywood was a small town and its citizens did not particularly welcome "movie people." Indeed, many local landlords took to hanging out signs exclaiming, "No Dogs or Actors Allowed!" And Hollywood locals had good reason to dislike the **influx** of people: One of the first filmmakers, Colonel William N. Selig, brought in cowboys who whooped and hollered and fired guns on and off the set. In addition, cameramen seldom bothered to build sets—they simply shot film anywhere they pleased. Stores, houses, parks, roads, and private properties were photographed, with accompanying stories

> **Identify Cause-and-Effect Relationships** What effect did the cold winters and Edison's behavior have on the early movie industry?

> **Text Structure** What part of this sentence tells you when the movie business officially began in Hollywood?

---

1 **Producers** are in charge of the finances, development, and presentation of a film.

Vocabulary ....

convey (kən vā´) v. to show or communicate by statement, gesture, or appearance

influx (in´fluks) n. a continual flow

made up along the way. Traffic constantly was snarled by camera crews shooting street scenes.

Early on, a future for the film industry in Hollywood was not guaranteed. Even the actors and directors lived simply in rented rooms or apartments—as if always at the ready to pack up and move back to New York or other filmmaking centers. It still is something of a mystery why Hollywood, described in the early 1900s as "an **obscure** and dusty suburb" of Los Angeles, became the moviemaking capital of the world.

Things began to change there in 1915 when director D. W. Griffith's film *The Birth of a Nation* was shown in Los Angeles. People began to gain some respect for motion pictures and the folks who made them. The rise of beloved

Mary Pickford, D. W. Griffith, Charlie Chaplin, and Douglas Fairbanks (above) used their star status to form their own film company, United Artists.

Text Structure What happened after *The Birth of a Nation* was shown in Los Angeles?

Vocabulary
....

obscure (əb skyoor′) *adj.* not well known

stars such as Mary Pickford, Douglas Fairbanks, and Charlie Chaplin, as well as great directors such as Cecil B. DeMille, helped ease matters, especially since they all had become citizens of Hollywood. And when the original Hollywood community saw how hard the motion picture industry worked to support the American effort during World War I (1914–1918), it began to accept the new people in its midst.

Hollywood also gained importance as it took control of film production *and* distribution. Movies made outside Hollywood could not reach as many theaters, be seen by as many people, or make as much money. Hollywood films gradually crowded out **rival** films and film companies.

Over the years, the film industry began to change. In the silent movie era, well-known actors and actresses could be spotted doing "real people" things like running errands around town. When movies with sound (talkies) came into being in 1927, soundproof studios were built, and the actual making of movies turned into a true business.

Writers also were drawn to Hollywood—some to write original pieces and others to see their stories or books come alive on the screen. In 1914, L. Frank Baum, author of *The Wonderful Wizard of Oz*, used the money that he received from the popular book to build a grand Hollywood home called Ozcot. Later, such literary greats as F. Scott Fitzgerald, William Faulkner, Nathaniel West, and Dorothy Parker came to Hollywood, all eager to write for—and about—the movies.

Eventually, studios needed room to produce more and bigger movies. Some moved nearby in southern California; others went elsewhere in the United States or the world. Filmmaking became an international **enterprise.** Today, only a small number of movies actually are filmed in Hollywood. But just the name itself still brings to mind images of excitement and magic, and the promise of dreams-come-true.

Vocabulary

rival (rī´vəl) *adj.* describing two or more trying to achieve what only one can possess

enterprise (en´tər prīz´) *n.* a business organization

BQ **BIG Question**

How do facts like these help you understand the ways in which a business can grow?

Identify Cause-and-Effect Relationships What led writers like F. Scott Fitzgerald to move to Hollywood?

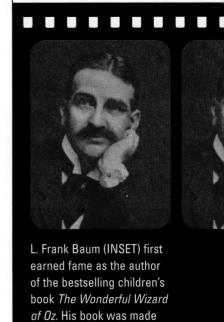

L. Frank Baum (INSET) first earned fame as the author of the bestselling children's book *The Wonderful Wizard of Oz*. His book was made into a popular movie in 1939—and was one of the first films to use color.

After You Read

Respond and Think Critically

1. What role did Thomas Edison play in the founding of the film industry? [Recall and Identify]

2. Compare the early days of filmmaking to its later development. Which aspects of this industry changed? [Compare and Contrast]

3. Do you agree with the writer that Hollywood still brings to mind "the promise of dreams-come-true"? Why or why not? [Conclude]

4. **Literary Element** Text Structure Review the article for its use of **chronological order**. How does this text structure help you understand the article's subject? [Analyze]

5. **Reading Skill** Identify Cause-and-Effect Relationships What has caused only a small number of today's movies to be filmed in Hollywood? Use your graphic organizer to help you. [Infer]

6. **BQ** BIG Question What is the most interesting thing about the film industry that you learned from reading this selection? [Evaluate]

Vocabulary Practice

On a separate sheet of paper, write the vocabulary word that correctly completes each sentence. If none of the words fits the sentence, write "none."

| convey | influx | obscure | rival | enterprise |

1. The sale attracted a/an _____ of visitors to the mall.

2. The _____ actors competed for the same role.

3. Everyone I know has seen the _____ movie.

4. A successful _____ usually provides goods and services that people want or need.

5. The _____ restaurant became popular after it received a positive review in the newspaper.

6. When the fire drill sounded, there was a/an _____ of students from the building.

7. Actors use facial expressions to _____ their emotions.

Writing

Write a Summary Write a summary of how Hollywood became the moviemaking capital of the world. Restate the most important events and details in your own words. For tips on writing a summary, see Respond Through Writing on page 185.

TIP

Analyzing
Here are some tips to help you analyze. Remember that, when you analyze, you look at separate parts of the selection to understand the whole selection.

- Skim the selection to identify the arrangement of ideas.

- Look for dates and words such as *first, next, then,* and *finally* to determine chronological order.

- Ask yourself how this text structure affects your understanding of the information presented.

FOLDABLES Keep track of **Study Organizer** your ideas about the **BIG Question** in your unit Foldable.

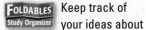

Learning Objectives

For page 216

In this workshop, you will focus on the following objectives:

Grammar: Recognizing sentence fragments.

Using sentence fragments to attain certain effects in writing.

Sentence Fragments

Robert D. San Souci avoids sentence fragments in "Hollywood's Rise to Fame." A **sentence fragment** is a group of words that doesn't express a complete thought. It may also be missing a subject, a predicate, or both.

Complete Sentences

A complete sentence has both a subject and a predicate and expresses a complete thought.

Gabrielle sees many Hollywood movies.

In this complete sentence:

- The subject is "Gabrielle." Readers know whom the sentence is about.
- The predicate "sees" tells readers what Gabrielle does. The predicate also can tell readers what a subject *has* or *is like.*

Correcting Sentence Fragments

In the examples below, notice the different ways in which you can turn fragments into complete sentences.

Problem 1 The fragment lacks a subject.

Liked Southern California's sunny weather.

Solution Add a subject to form a complete sentence.

Producers liked Southern California's sunny weather.

Problem 2 The fragment lacks a predicate.

Early Hollywood a small town.

Solution Add a predicate to form a complete sentence.

Early Hollywood was a small town.

Problem 3 The fragment lacks a subject and a predicate.

A kinetoscope in 1891.

Solution Add a subject and a predicate to form a complete sentence.

Edison's laboratory created a kinetoscope in 1891.

> ### Watch Out!
>
> Be sure to use complete sentences for all formal writing you do, such as school or business writing.

> ### Helpful Hint
>
> You can use fragments when talking with friends or in personal letters and journals. Sometimes a writer will even use a fragment to produce a certain effect. For example: *Elise has always wanted to visit Hollywood. Always.*

LOG ON ▶ **Literature** Online

Grammar For more grammar practice, go to glencoe.com and enter QuickPass code GL39770u2.

TRY IT: Sentence Fragments

Use the solutions above to turn these fragments into sentences.

1. To Hollywood.
2. Mary Pickford.
3. Hung signs saying, "No Dogs or Actors Allowed!"

Part 2

Reading for Enjoyment

The Oil Lamp, c. 1898–1900. Pierre Bonnard. Oil on canvas. Fitzwilliam Museum, University of Cambridge. ©DACS.

BQ BIG Question **Reading: What's in It for You?**

How does the painting *The Oil Lamp* show that the girl enjoys reading? Where are your favorite places to enjoy reading books?

Pretty Words and Introduction to Poetry

Learning Objectives

For pages 218–221

In studying these texts, you will focus on the following objective:

Literary Study: Analyzing simile.

Connect to the Poems

Poems often have words and images that speak to a reader's thoughts and feelings.

Make a List *Swish. Click. Swirl.* Do these words snag your attention, spark a feeling, or suggest interesting images? Make a list of some of your favorite words and phrases. Next to each, write what it makes you think of.

Build Background

Figures of speech, or figurative language, describe ordinary things in new ways. Poets rely on figures of speech to bring ideas and feelings to life.

- Poet Elinor Wylie uses playful, vivid descriptions to tell why she loves poems.
- Poet Billy Collins uses humor and exaggeration to describe what he believes is the best way to approach a poem.

Set Purposes for Reading

BQ BIG Question

Read "Pretty Words" and "Introduction to Poetry" to find out what the speakers enjoy about poetry.

Literary Element Simile

A **simile** is a figure of speech in which a writer uses *like* or *as* to compare seemingly unlike things: "The crowd drifted away like smoke." "The coat was as soft as a kitten." In "Pretty Words," Elinor Wylie compares words to various animals. In "Introduction to Poetry," Billy Collins uses comparisons to show how readers should—and shouldn't—approach a poem.

Literature Online

Author Search For more about Elinor Wylie and Billy Collins, go to glencoe.com and enter QuickPass code GL39770u2.

Meet the Authors

Elinor Wylie

Elinor Wylie was born in 1885 and died in 1928. She wrote four novels and many volumes of poetry. "Pretty Words" appeared in 1932.

Billy Collins

Known for his humorous poetry, Billy Collins was appointed Poet Laureate of the United States in 2001. Collins has published numerous volumes of poetry. He was born in 1941.

Goldfish. Lincoln Seligman.
Private Collection.

Pretty Words

Elinor Wylie

Poets make pets of pretty, docile° words:
I love smooth words, like gold-enameled fish
Which circle slowly with a silken swish,
And tender ones, like down-feathered birds;
5 Words shy and dappled, deep-eyed deer in herds,
Come to my hand, and playful if I wish,
Or purring softly at a silver dish,
Blue Persian kitten, fed on cream and curds.

I love bright words, words up and singing early;
10 Words that are luminous in the dark, and sing;
Warm lazy words, white cattle under trees;
I love words opalescent,° cool, and pearly,
Like midsummer moths, and honeyed words
   like bees,
Gilded and sticky, with a little sting.

Simile As described in the poem, words are "like" what living things?

BQ BIG Question
What feeling do lines 9–11 create in you?

---

1 ***Docile*** means "easily trained or taught."

12 Something that is ***opalescent*** has a milky shimmer like the mineral opal.

Introduction to **Poetry**

Typesetting. Kevin O'Shea.
View the Art Think about the colors and the arrangement of letters in this painting. What message about writing do they convey?

Billy Collins

I ask them to take a poem
and hold it up to the light
like a color slide

or press an ear against its hive.°

5   I say drop a mouse into a poem
and watch him probe his way out,

or walk inside the poem's room
and feel the walls for a light switch.

I want them to waterski
10   across the surface of a poem
waving at the author's name on the shore.

But all they want to do
is tie the poem to a chair with rope
and torture a confession out of it.

15   They begin beating it with a hose
to find out what it really means.

---

4 A *hive* is home to a colony of honeybees.

Simile What does the simile in lines 1–3 suggest about the way we should approach a poem?

BQ **BIG Question**
Based on the image in lines 9–11, how does the poet want you to feel when you read a poem?

After You Read

Respond and Think Critically

1. What season of the year do you associate with Elinor Wylie's poem? [Identify]

2. Based on lines 12–15 of "Pretty Words," how might the speaker respond to a sorrowful poem? A humorous poem? [Infer]

3. What feeling does Billy Collins create in these lines: "I say drop a mouse into a poem / and watch him probe his way out, / or walk inside the poem's room / and feel the walls for a light switch"? [Interpret]

4. Identify the recurring theme, or similar message, of these poems. Which poem is more successful at conveying the theme? [Draw Conclusions]

5. **Literary Element** Simile Identify three similes from the poems. What specific comparisons are made in each example? [Analyze]

6. BIG Question What qualities of these poems make them enjoyable to read? [Evaluate]

Spelling Link

Some spelling patterns are based on the **meaning** of a word. Think of the word *confession* in "Introduction to Poetry." How would you know not to spell this word *confessian*? The endings *-ian* and *-ion* sound alike, but a simple rule can help you determine which ending to use.

Rule:	Examples:
-cian always means a person ⟶	physician, musician
-tion and *-sion* are never used for people ⟶	nutrition, possession

Practice On a sheet of paper, list these words: *communication, electrician, discussion, politician, pollution,* and *mathematician.* Next to each word, write a short explanation of why it is spelled with *-cian, -tion,* or *-sion.*

Writing

Write a Journal Entry Think about the way these two poems make you feel about poetry. Write a paragraph in which you describe your feelings and identify the words and images in the poems that helped create those feelings.

TIP

Interpreting
Here are some tips to help you interpret. Remember, when you interpret, you use your own understanding of the world to decide what something means. For example, think about

- how a mouse in a maze might feel

- how you would feel in a dark room, searching for the light switch

FOLDABLES Study Organizer Keep track of your ideas about the **BIG Question** in your unit Foldable.

 Literature Online

Selection Resources
For Selection Quizzes, eFlashcards, and Reading-Writing Connection activities, go to glencoe.com and enter QuickPass code GL39770u2.

Casey at the Bat

Connect to the Poem

Think about a time when you felt pressure to give your best performance—at school, at home, on stage, or on the playing field.

Quickwrite Freewrite for a few minutes about how you felt when you had to perform under pressure. Did you feel nervous, confident, or a little of both? Write a brief answer.

Build Background

"Casey at the Bat" is a poem about a fictional baseball player whose team is depending on him for a game-winning hit.

- Abner Doubleday, an army officer from New York, was once credited with inventing baseball in Cooperstown, New York, in 1839. However, the National Baseball Hall of Fame recognizes 1845 as the year the modern sport of baseball was founded.

- In 1845, Alexander Cartwright and his Knickerbocker Base Ball Club of New York introduced baseball as we know it today. They established bases and the "three strikes, you're out" rule.

- Jacques Barzun, a modern writer, teacher, and baseball fan once said, "Whoever wants to know the heart and mind of America had better learn baseball."

Meet Ernest Lawrence Thayer

Poet and Columnist
Ernest Lawrence Thayer could have followed in his father's footsteps and run one of his family's woolen mills in Massachusetts. Instead, he surprised his family by taking a job as a humor columnist for the *San Francisco Examiner*. Thayer had a low opinion of his writing ability and once said, "I put out large quantities of nonsense . . . from advertisements to editorials." The ballad "Casey at the Bat" was one of Thayer's last contributions to the *Examiner*.

Literary Works Thayer wrote other poetry for the *Examiner*, but none as popular as "Casey at the Bat," which was published in 1888.

Ernest Lawrence Thayer was born in 1863 and died in 1940.

 Literature Online

Author Search For more about Ernest Lawrence Thayer, go to glencoe.com and enter QuickPass code GL39770u2.

Set Purposes for Reading

BQ BIG Question

When you watch any thrilling sport, contest, or competition, you probably feel excitement as you wait to see what will happen. As you read, see if you can enjoy a very tense moment for a group of baseball fans.

Literary Element Suspense

Suspense is a feeling of curiosity, uncertainty, or dread about what may happen next. Authors often add suspense to a narrative by **foreshadowing**— giving readers hints about what may happen later.

Paying close attention to the clues that Ernest Lawrence Thayer gives in his poem can help you make predictions about the plot. Your predictions may either ease or increase the tension or dread you feel.

As you read, notice the moments when Thayer builds suspense by slowing down the action. Also, look for hints he gives that create suspense. Do these hints help you predict the ending?

Reading Strategy Visualize

When you **visualize**, you picture in your mind what you are reading by using the descriptive details the author provides. Fiction writers and poets often use vivid words and phrases to bring the characters and setting of a story or poem to life. For example, a detail such as the image of a stadium packed with people can help you visualize what it's like to be at a baseball game.

Visualizing is important because it can help readers enjoy, understand, and remember the selections they read. It is also a useful strategy to help repair comprehension when a reader might be confused.

As you read, notice descriptive details and sensory words that help you picture what the author describes. You may find it helpful to use a visualization chart like the one below.

Description from Poem	Visualization
1. defiance gleamed in Casey's eye, a sneer curled Casey's lip	1. I picture a baseball player glaring at the other players and wearing a mean smile.
2.	2.
3.	3.

Learning Objectives

For pages 222–228

In studying this text, you will focus on the following objectives:

Literary Study: Analyzing suspense.

Reading: Visualizing.

TRY IT

Visualize *A man in a dark overcoat walks into an enormous old house. The house has cracked windows and doors hanging on hinges. He enters a dark and dusty living room. The furniture is old and worn. To his right, is a broken-down staircase. He looks toward the top of the stairs and sees a dusty shoe extending from behind the wall.*

What are the most memorable details that you visualized in this paragraph? Explain.

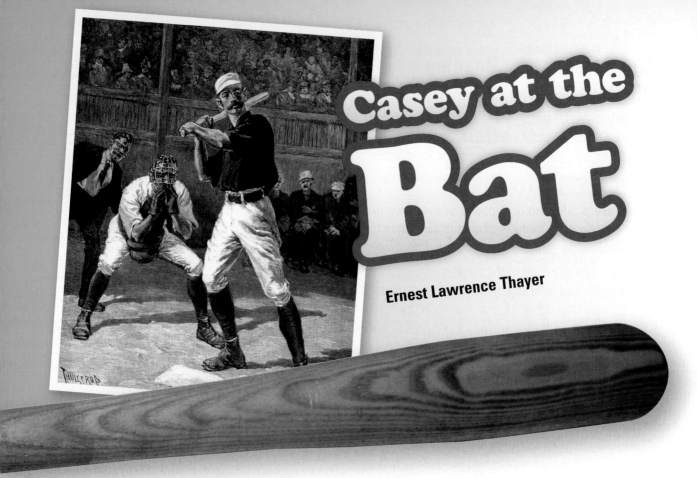

Casey at the Bat

Ernest Lawrence Thayer

The outlook wasn't brilliant
   for the Mudville nine that day:
The score stood four to two
   with but one inning more to play.

And then when Cooney died at first,
   and Barrows did the same,
A sickly silence fell
   upon the patrons of the game.

5 A straggling few got up
   to go in deep despair. The rest
Clung to that hope which springs eternal
   in the human breast;

They thought if only Casey
   could but get a whack at that—
We'd put up even money[1] now
   with Casey at the bat.

Suspense In what way do the words "with but one inning more to play" add suspense to the poem?

Suspense Based on these words, what might happen next in this poem?

---

1 ***Put up even money*** means fans recognize that the teams have an even chance of winning.

But Flynn preceded[2] Casey,
    as did also Jimmy Blake,

10 And the former[3] was a lulu
    and the latter was a cake;

So upon that stricken multitude
    grim melancholy[4] sat,
For there seemed but little chance
    of Casey's getting to the bat.

But Flynn let drive a single,
    to the wonderment of all,
And Blake, the much-despised,
    tore the cover off the ball;

15 And when the dust had lifted,
    and the men saw what had occurred,
There was Jimmy safe at second
    and Flynn a-hugging third.

Then from 5,000 throats and more
    there rose a lusty yell;
It rumbled through the valley,
    it rattled in the dell;

It knocked upon the mountain
    and recoiled upon the flat,
20 For Casey, mighty Casey,
    was advancing to the bat.

There was ease in Casey's manner
    as he stepped into his place;
There was pride in Casey's bearing
    and a smile on Casey's face.

And when, responding to the cheers,
    he lightly doffed his hat,
No stranger in the crowd could doubt
    'twas Casey at the bat.

Visualize Based on the speaker's description, how do you picture Casey in your mind? What words would you use to describe him?

---

2 **Preceded** means "came before."

3 **Former** refers to the first one mentioned, and **latter** to the last one mentioned. Both Flynn and Blake seem to be considered poor batters.

4 **Grim melancholy** describes the crowd's mood, which is serious and sadly thoughtful.

25 Ten thousand eyes were on him
        as he rubbed his hands with dirt;
    Five thousand tongues applauded
        when he wiped them on his shirt.

    Then while the writhing pitcher
        ground the ball into his hip,
    Defiance gleamed in Casey's eye,
        a sneer curled Casey's lip.

    And now the leather-covered sphere
        came hurtling through the air,
30 And Casey stood a-watching it
        in haughty grandeur there.

    Close by the sturdy batsman
        the ball unheeded sped—
    "That ain't my style," said Casey.
        "Strike one," the umpire said.

    From the benches, black with people,
        there went up a muffled roar,
    Like the beating of the storm-waves
        on a stern and distant shore.

35 "Kill him! Kill the umpire!"
        shouted someone on the stand;
    And it's likely they'd have killed him
        had not Casey raised his hand.

    With a smile of Christian charity
        great Casey's visage[5] shone;
    He stilled the rising tumult;[6]
        he bade the game go on;

    He signaled to the pitcher,
        and once more the spheroid[7] flew;
40 But Casey still ignored it,
        and the umpire said, "Strike two."

Suspense How does Casey's action in these lines help build suspense?

---

5 Casey's **visage** (viz′ ij) is his face.

6 **Tumult** (tōo′ məlt) means "noisy uproar."

7 A **spheroid** is a round three-dimensional object—in this case, a baseball.

Crowd at the Polo Ground, 1895. Jay Hambridge. Four-color proof, 18 7/8 x 14 in. Museum of the City of New York, NY.

View the Art In what ways is this scene similar to the one described in "Casey at the Bat"?

"Fraud!" cried the maddened thousands,
   and the echo answered fraud;
But one scornful look from Casey
   and the audience was awed.

They saw his face grow stern and cold,
   they saw his muscles strain,
And they knew that Casey
   wouldn't let that ball go by again.

45 The sneer is gone from Casey's lips,
   his teeth are clenched in hate;
He pounds with cruel violence
   his bat upon the plate.

And now the pitcher holds the ball,
   and now he lets it go,
And now the air is shattered
   by the force of Casey's blow.

Oh, somewhere in this favored land
   the sun is shining bright;
50 The band is playing somewhere,
   and somewhere hearts are light,

And somewhere men are laughing,
   and somewhere children shout;
But there is no joy in Mudville—
   mighty Casey has struck out.

Visualize Has your image of Casey changed? Explain.

Suspense What are your feelings at this point in the poem?

BQ **BIG Question**

What parts of the poem were the most entertaining? Include specific details in your answer.

After You Read

Respond and Think Critically

1. Why is Casey's turn at bat so important to the game? [Summarize]

2. What does Casey's behavior reveal about his personality? [Draw Conclusions]

3. Why do you think the poet portrays Casey striking out? [Analyze]

4. **Literary Element** Suspense Is Thayer successful in creating suspense in this poem? Use examples to support your answer. [Evaluate]

5. **Reading Strategy** Visualize Give an example of a description the poet uses to help readers visualize the crowd's anger. Use your visualization chart for help. Tell why you think the poet chose to describe the crowd in this way. [Interpret]

6. **BQ** BIG Question Do you think most students your age would enjoy this poem? Explain your thoughts. [Make Judgments]

Spelling Link

Words with _ie_ and _ei_ can cause spelling problems. Think of the word _receive_. Casey would receive applause. How would you know that _e_ comes before _i_ in _receive_? The following spelling rule should help you spell _ie_ and _ei_ words.

Rules for _ie_ or _ei_:

1. Usually, the letter combination is _ie_ and has the sound of long _e_.

   → retrieve, grieve

2. If the letters are right after _c_, then they are _ei_.

   → deceive, receipt

3. If the letters create a long _a_ sound, they are _ei_.

   → eighty, veil

Examples:

Here are some exceptions to this rule.

Exceptions weird, either, neither, seize, leisure, protein, height

Practice List the words _relieve, freight, perceive,_ and _achieve_. Next to each, explain why it is spelled with _ei_ or _ie_.

Writing

Write a Letter Pretend you are a fan of Casey. Write a letter to Casey about the game described in the poem. What did you think of the game? What was your reaction to Casey's performance? What else might you want to write? Refer to details from the poem in your letter.

TIP

Drawing Conclusions
The answer to question 2 is not stated directly. To answer it, find details about Casey's appearance and actions. Then ask yourself what this information tells you about him. Use this knowledge to describe Casey's personality.

 FOLDABLES **Study Organizer** Keep track of your ideas about the **BIG Question** in your unit Foldable.

 Literature Online

Selection Resources
For Selection Quizzes, eFlashcards, and Reading-Writing Connection activities, go to glencoe.com and enter QuickPass code GL39770u2.

Media Workshop

Media Ethics

Ethics are standards of behavior. When you act ethically, you are doing what is right, honest, and proper. Media ethics cover a wide range of conduct, but one area that matters a lot to you as a student is plagiarism. When you present a writer's words or ideas as your own, you are plagiarizing that person. Look at this passage from "Huge, Freed Pet Pythons Invade Florida Everglades":

"The Burmese python is just one of thousands of non-native animal and plant species that have invaded the United States in the last decades."

Now look at a version of this passage that a student may have written:

"Thousands of non-native animal and plant species have invaded the United States, including the Burmese python."

Did you notice the similarities? Because what the student wrote is nearly the same as the original version, the student must credit the source—indicate where the information came from. Even if the student changes the order or substitutes a word, he or she must credit the writer. If that doesn't happen, the student is committing plagiarism.

The chart below offers ways to avoid plagiarism in your own work.

Writing Strategy	What It Is	How to Do It
Cite It	Giving credit to the source—acknowledging where the information came from	Quote from, and clearly indicate, the source. When you reference the source, include author, title, publication, and date of publication. ***Example:*** According to Stefan Lovgren, "invasive species are a leading cause of species endangerment and extinction both in the United States and worldwide" ("Huge, Freed Pet Pythons Invade Florida Everglades," *National Geographic News,* June 3, 2004).
Rewrite It	Restating the passage in your own words	Think about how you can paraphrase the passage, or say it in your own way. ***Example:*** When a species enters a new area, it can threaten, and even lead to the extinction of, species that already live there.

Learning Objectives

For page 229
In this workshop, you will focus on the following objective:

Reading:
Recognizing and avoiding plagiarism.

TRY IT

Analyze Media Ethics
Select a passage from a nonfiction selection in this unit.

- Write a sentence in which you cite the passage.
- Rewrite the passage in your own words.

Next find a reliable source that supports a conclusion in the selection. Write a brief presentation that supports the author's point, using the source you found and making sure to properly cite it.

 Literature Online

Media Literacy For project ideas, templates, and media analysis guides, go to glencoe.com and enter QuickPass code GL39770u2.

Before You Read

The Tell-Tale Heart

Connect to the Short Story

Think about how other people think of you—at home, at school, or in another place.

Quickwrite Freewrite for a few minutes about why you may see yourself differently than others see you.

Build Background

Although Edgar Allan Poe spent much of his career creating poems, he is perhaps best known today for his tales of terror. Like other authors of Gothic literature, Poe often created an atmosphere, or mood, of chilling uncertainty in his fictional work.

- In stories such as "The Tell-Tale Heart," the plots focus on mysterious happenings or terrible outcomes. The characters are often mad, half-mad, or frightened to death. Also, they may exhibit strange behavior and odd physical traits.

- Additionally, Poe invented the modern detective story. His character C. Auguste Dupin is widely viewed as a forerunner of Sherlock Holmes and other beloved fictional detectives.

Vocabulary

acute (ə kūt´) *adj.* sharp; strong or intense (p. 232).
A rabbit's sense of hearing is very acute.

conceived (kən sēvd´) *v.* planned (p. 232). *The coach conceived the scheme that won the game for us.*

vexed (vekst) *adj.* annoyed or distressed (p. 233). *He was vexed by the dog's constant barking.*

profound (prə found´) *adj.* showing great understanding, knowledge, or insight (p. 233). *The philosopher impressed the audience with profound statements about life.*

stifled (stī´fəld) *adj.* held back; muffled (p. 234). *The lecture was interrupted by the speaker's stifled sneeze.*

refrained (ri frānd´) *v.* kept oneself from doing or saying something (p. 235). *She refrained from talking with her friends in the library.*

Meet Edgar Allan Poe

"To be thoroughly conversant with a man's heart, is to take our final lesson in the iron-clasped volume of despair."
—Edgar Allan Poe

Tales of Horror Poe is known for writing about mysterious forces, wicked crimes, and death. Unfortunately, his life was as sad as those of most of his characters. His mother died when he was two, and he was disowned by his foster father. Poe himself died young, but left behind classic works of horror and the first modern detective stories.

Literary Works Poe wrote many poems, essays, and short stories. "The Tell-Tale Heart" was first published in *Pioneer* magazine in 1843.

Edgar Allan Poe was born in 1809 and died in 1849.

 Literature Online

Author Search For more about Edgar Allan Poe, go to glencoe.com and enter Quickpass code GL39770u2.

Set Purposes for Reading

BQ BIG Question

With its suspense, twists, and chills, reading "The Tell-Tale Heart" is like watching a scary movie. As you read, think of what makes the story so entertaining and effective.

Literary Element Mood

Mood is the emotional effect that a story or poem has on a reader. The author creates a mood through the type of words and sentences he or she uses. For example, when a story is set during a dark and stormy night, the mood may be tense or suspenseful.

Mood is important in helping a reader become emotionally involved with the story. To identify the mood of a story, look for descriptive words and phrases. Here is the story's opening sentence: "True!— nervous—very, very dreadfully nervous I had been and am; but why *will* you say that I am mad?" What emotions do these words create?

As you read "The Tell-Tale Heart," consider how Poe uses word choice and sentence structure to craft a story with an unforgettable mood.

Reading Strategy Paraphrase

Reading older stories, such as "The Tell-Tale Heart," can be difficult because they often contain unfamiliar words and complicated sentences. One way that you can make sense of Poe's story is to **paraphrase** or restate information in your own words. A paraphrase is usually the same length as the original passage but contains simpler language.

Paraphrasing is important because it helps you understand—and communicate—descriptions. When you paraphrase, you

- identify words and phrases that are unclear
- look up the words you don't know in a dictionary
- explain what the sentence means by using your own words

As you read, ask yourself, how can I say this in my own way? You may find it helpful to use a graphic organizer like the one below.

Poe's Words	Paraphrase

Learning Objectives

For pages 230–241

In studying this text, you will focus on the following objectives:

Literary Study: Analyzing mood.

Reading: Paraphrasing.

TRY IT

Paraphrase In "The Tell-Tale Heart," the narrator tells of opening a door "until, at length, a single dim ray, like the thread of the spider, shot from out the crevice and fell upon the vulture eye." What would be another way to say this?

The Tell-Tale Heart

Edgar Allan Poe

True!—nervous—very, very dreadfully nervous I had been and am; but why *will* you say that I am mad? The disease had sharpened my senses—not destroyed—not dulled them. Above all was the sense of hearing **acute.** I heard all things in the heaven and in the earth. I heard many things in hell. How, then, am I mad? Hearken![1] and observe how healthily—how calmly I can tell you the whole story.

It is impossible to say how first the idea entered my brain; but once **conceived,** it haunted me day and night. Object there was none. Passion there was none. I loved the old man. He had never wronged me. He had never given me insult. For his gold I had no desire. I think it was his eye! yes, it was this! One of his eyes resembled that of a **vulture**—a pale blue eye, with a film over it. Whenever it fell upon me, my blood ran cold; and so by degrees—very gradually—I made up my mind to take the life of the old man, and thus rid myself of the eye for ever.

1 When the narrator says "*Hearken*," he is asking the reader to pay attention.

Visual Vocabulary

A **vulture** is a large, bald-headed bird that circles in the air in search of food.

Mood What mood is created by phrases like "blood ran cold," "take the life of the old man," and "rid myself of the eye"?

Vocabulary

acute (ə kūt´) *adj.* sharp; strong or intense
conceived (kən sēvd´) *v.* planned

Now this is the point. You fancy me mad. Madmen know nothing. But you should have seen *me*. You should have seen how wisely I proceeded—with what caution—with what foresight—with what dissimulation I went to work![2] I was never kinder to the old man than during the whole week before I killed him. And every night, about midnight, I turned the latch of his door and opened it— oh, so gently! And then, when I had made an opening sufficient for my head, I put in a dark lantern, all closed, closed, so that no light shone out, and then I thrust in my head. Oh, you would have laughed to see how cunningly[3] I thrust it in! I moved it slowly—very, very slowly, so that I might not disturb the old man's sleep. It took me an hour to place my whole head within the opening so far that I could see him as he lay upon his bed. Ha!—would a madman have been so wise as this? And then, when my head was well in the room, I undid the lantern cautiously—oh, so cautiously—cautiously (for the hinges creaked)—I undid it just so much that a single thin ray fell upon the vulture eye. And this I did for seven long nights—every night just at midnight—but I found the eye always closed; and so it was impossible to do the work; for it was not the old man who **vexed** me, but his Evil Eye. And every morning, when the day broke, I went boldly into the chamber, and spoke courageously to him, calling him by name in a hearty tone, and inquiring how he had passed the night. So you see he would have been a very **profound** old man, indeed, to suspect that every night, just at twelve, I looked in upon him while he slept.

Upon the eighth night I was more than usually cautious in opening the door. A watch's minute hand moves more quickly than did mine. Never before that night, had I *felt*

---

2 *Foresight* means "care or preparation for the future." *Dissimulation* means "the hiding or disguising of one's true feelings and intentions."

3 *Cunningly* means "cleverly."

Vocabulary ....

vexed (vekst) *adj.* annoyed or distressed

profound (prə found´) *adj.* showing great understanding, knowledge, or insight

the extent of my own powers—of my sagacity.[4] I could scarcely contain my feelings of triumph. To think that there I was, opening the door, little by little, and he not even to dream of my secret deeds or thoughts. I fairly chuckled at the idea; and perhaps he heard me; for he moved on the bed suddenly, as if startled. Now you may think that I drew back—but no. His room was as black as pitch with the thick darkness, (for the shutters were close fastened, through fear of robbers,) and so I knew that he could not see the opening of the door, and I kept pushing it on steadily, steadily.

I had my head in, and was about to open the **lantern,** when my thumb slipped upon the tin fastening, and the old man sprang up in the bed, crying out—"Who's there?"

I kept quite still and said nothing. For a whole hour I did not move a muscle, and in the meantime I did not hear him lie down. He was still sitting up in the bed, listening; —just as I have done, night after night, hearkening to the death watches[5] in the wall.

Presently I heard a slight groan, and I knew it was the groan of mortal terror. It was not a groan of pain or of grief—oh, no!—it was the low **stifled** sound that arises from the bottom of the soul when overcharged with awe. I knew the sound well. Many a night, just at midnight, when all the world slept, it has welled up from my own bosom, deepening, with its dreadful echo, the terrors that distracted me. I say I knew it well. I knew what the old man felt, and pitied him, although I chuckled at heart. I knew that he had been lying awake ever since the first slight noise, when he had turned in the bed. His fears had been ever since growing upon him. He had been trying to fancy them causeless, but could not. He had been saying to himself—"It is nothing but the wind in the chimney—it

Mood How does the length of this sentence help establish the mood?

Visual Vocabulary

A **lantern** is a transparent case that holds a light. Like a flashlight, a lantern can be carried by hand.

Paraphrase What is another way to state this sentence?

---

4 **Sagacity** (sə gas′ə tē) is wisdom and good judgment.

5 **Death watches** are beetles that bore into wood, especially of old houses and furniture. Some people believe that the insects' ticking sounds warn that death is approaching.

Vocabulary ....

stifled (stī′fəld) adj. held back; muffled

is only a mouse crossing the floor," or "it is merely a cricket which has made a single chirp." Yes, he has been trying to comfort himself with these suppositions: but he had found all in vain. *All in vain*; because Death, in approaching him, had stalked with his black shadow before him, and enveloped[6] the victim. And it was the mournful influence of the unperceived shadow that caused him to feel—although he neither saw nor heard—to *feel* the presence of my head within the room.

When I had waited a long time, very patiently, without hearing him lie down, I resolved to open a little—a very, very little crevice in the lantern. So I opened it—you cannot imagine how stealthily, stealthily—until, at length, a single dim ray, like the thread of the spider, shot from out the crevice and fell upon the vulture eye.

It was open—wide, wide open—and I grew furious as I gazed upon it. I saw it with perfect distinctness—all a dull blue, with a hideous veil over it that chilled the very marrow in my bones; but I could see nothing else of the old man's face or person: for I had directed the ray as if by instinct, precisely upon the damned spot.

And now have I not told you that what you mistake for madness is but overacuteness of the senses?—now, I say, there came to my ears a low, dull, quick sound, such as a watch makes when enveloped in cotton. I knew *that* sound well, too. It was the beating of the old man's heart. It increased my fury, as the beating of a drum stimulates the soldier into courage.

But even yet I **refrained** and kept still. I scarcely breathed. I held the lantern motionless. I tried how steadily I could maintain the ray upon the eye. Meantime the hellish tattoo[7] of the heart increased. It grew quicker and quicker, and louder and louder every instant. The old

---

6 Here, ***enveloped*** means "enclosed."

7 A ***tattoo*** is a drumming or rapping sound. (This tattoo comes from a Dutch word; the other tattoo, a design on the skin, comes from the language of Tahiti, a Pacific island.)

Vocabulary

refrained (ri frānd´) *v.* kept oneself from doing or saying something

man's terror *must* have been extreme! It grew louder, I say, louder every moment!—do you mark me well? I have told you that I am nervous: so I am. And now at the dead hour of the night, amid the dreadful silence of that old house, so strange a noise as this excited me to uncontrollable terror. Yet, for some minutes longer I refrained and stood still. But the beating grew louder, louder! I thought the heart must burst. And now a new anxiety seized me—the sound would be heard by a neighbor! The old man's hour had come! With a loud yell, I threw open the lantern and leaped into the room. He shrieked once—once only. In an instant I dragged him to the floor, and pulled the heavy bed over him. I then smiled gaily, to find the deed so far done. But, for many minutes, the heart beat on with a muffled sound. This, however, did not vex me; it would not be heard through the wall. At length it ceased. The old man was dead. I removed the bed and examined the corpse. Yes, he was stone, stone dead. I placed my hand upon the heart and held it there many minutes. There was no pulsation. He was stone dead. His eye would trouble me no more.

If still you think me mad, you will think so no longer when I describe the wise precautions I took for the concealment of the body. The night waned, and I worked hastily, but in silence. First of all I dismembered the corpse. I cut off the head and the arms and the legs.

I then took up three planks from the flooring of the chamber, and deposited all between the scantlings.[8] I then replaced the boards so cleverly, so cunningly, that no human eye—not even *his*—could have detected anything wrong. There was nothing to wash out—no stain of any kind—no blood-spot whatever. I had been too wary for that. A tub had caught all—ha! ha!

When I had made an end of these labors, it was four o'clock—still dark as midnight. As the bell sounded the hour, there came a knocking at the street door. I went down to open it with a light heart—for what had I *now* to fear? There entered three men, who introduced

---

8 The *scantlings* are the boards that hold up the floor planks.

Mood In what way does the time in which the story is set affect the mood?

BQ ⟩ **BIG Question**
Does the narrator's unusual sense of humor add to your enjoyment of the story? Explain your opinion.

themselves, with perfect suavity,[9] as officers of the police. A shriek had been heard by a neighbor during the night; suspicion of foul play had been aroused; information had been lodged at the police office, and they (the officers) had been deputed[10] to search the premises.

I smiled—for *what* had I to fear? I bade the gentlemen welcome. The shriek, I said, was my own in a dream. The old man, I mentioned, was absent in the country. I took my visitors all over the house. I bade them search—search *well*. I led them, at length, to *his* chamber. I showed them his treasures, secure, undisturbed. In the enthusiasm of my confidence, I brought chairs into the room, and desired them *here* to rest from their fatigues, while I myself, in the wild audacity of my perfect triumph, placed my own seat upon the very spot beneath which reposed the corpse of the victim.

The officers were satisfied. My *manner* had convinced them. I was singularly at ease. They sat, and while I answered cheerily, they chatted of familiar things. But, ere long, I felt myself getting pale and wished them gone. My head ached, and I fancied a ringing in my ears: but still they sat and still chatted. The ringing became more distinct—it continued and became more distinct: I talked

View the Art What details in this image help convey the mood of "The Tell-Tale Heart"?

Paraphrase How would you say this in your own words?

---

9 *Suavity* (swäv´ə tē) is a smooth, polite, gracious manner.

10 The officers were assigned a duty, or *deputed*, by a superior.

more freely to get rid of the feeling: but it continued and gained definitiveness—until, at length, I found that the noise was *not* within my ears.

No doubt I now grew *very* pale—but I talked more fluently,[11] and with a heightened voice. Yet the sound increased—and what could I do? It was *a low, dull, quick sound—much such a sound as a watch makes when enveloped in cotton.* I gasped for breath—and yet the officers heard it not. I talked more quickly—more vehemently; but the noise steadily increased. I arose and argued about trifles, in a high key and with violent gesticulations;[12] but the noise steadily increased. Why *would* they not be gone? I paced the floor to and fro with heavy strides, as if excited to fury by the observations of the men—but the noise steadily increased. Oh God! what *could* I do? I foamed—I raved—I swore! I swung the chair upon which I had been sitting, and grated it upon the boards, but the noise arose over all and continually increased. It grew louder—louder—*louder*! And still the men chatted pleasantly, and smiled. Was it possible they heard not? Almighty God!—no, no! They heard!—they suspected!—they *knew*!—they were making a mockery of my horror!—this I thought, and this I think. But anything was better than this agony! Anything was more tolerable than this derision![13] I could bear those hypocritical smiles no longer! I felt that I must scream or die!—and now—again!—hark! louder! louder! louder! *louder*!—

"Villains!" I shrieked, "dissemble[14] no more! I admit the deed!—tear up the planks!—here, here!—it is the beating of his hideous heart!"

---

11 To speak **fluently** is to do so smoothly and effortlessly.

12 **Trifles** are unimportant things. Bold, expressive hand movements are **gesticulations.**

13 To make a **mockery** of a thing is to make it seem stupid or worthless. **Derision** is ridicule.

14 Here, **dissemble** means "to disguise one's true thoughts or feelings; act in an insincere way."

After You Read

Respond and Think Critically

1. Summarize the narrator's reaction to the presence of the police officers. [Summarize]

2. Why does the narrator confess to the crime? [Interpret]

3. What is making the ticking noise at the end of the story? [Infer]

4. How does the mood change from the beginning to the end of the story? Support your answer with details from the story. [Analyze]

5 Review the paraphrases that you created as you read the story. What do these passages reveal about the narrator? [Draw Conclusions]

6. **BQ** BIG Question What do you think of "The Tell-Tale Heart"? Did you find the story to be frightening, unbelievable, amusing? What elements of the story made you feel that way? [Evaluate]

TIP

Drawing Conclusions
Here are some tips to help you draw conclusions. Remember when you draw conclusions, you use a number of pieces of information to see the "big picture."

• Note details about the narrator's thoughts and actions.

• Think about how the thoughts and the actions are connected to events.

• Make a general statement on the basis of these details.

 FOLDABLES **Study Organizer** Keep track of your ideas about the **BIG Question** in your unit Foldable.

You're the Critic

Poe's Tales of Terror

Poe is famous for his dark stories shrouded in an eerie, unsettling mood. Read these two excerpts from reviews of his stories.

"The degree of skill shown in the management of revolting or terrible circumstances makes the pieces that have such subjects more interesting than others."
—**Review of Poe's Tales**

"Mr. Poe is too fond of the wild, unnatural and horrible! Why will he not permit genius to soar into purer, brighter, and happier regions?" —**Richmond Compiler**

Group Activity Discuss the following questions with classmates. Refer to the excerpts and use evidence from the story to support your answers.

1. The first excerpt praises Poe's use of "terrible circumstances." Why do you think horror stories and movies appeal to people?

2. The second excerpt questions the value of Poe's horrible situations. Should we only have stories about "brighter" situations? Explain.

Literary Element Mood

Test Skills Practice

1. Read this sentence from the end of the story: "They heard!—they suspected!—they knew!—they were making a mockery of my horror!—this I thought, and this I think."

   The mood is best described as

   A sad.
   B happy.
   C exciting.
   D disturbing.

Review: Narrator and Point of View

As you learned on page 8, the **narrator** is the voice that tells the story. "The Tell-Tale Heart" is told from the first-person **point of view** by a character in the story who describes his own thoughts and experiences. You can tell that the story is told from the first-person point of view because the narrator uses the words *I* and *me.* We see the story through one character's eyes, which limits our knowledge of events to what the character reveals.

2. How might the story be different if it were told in the first-person point of view by one of the police officers?

Reading Strategy Paraphrase

3. Paraphrase the following sentences from "The Tell-Tale Heart": "It is impossible to say how first the idea entered my brain; but once conceived, it haunted me day and night. Object there was none. Passion there was none. I loved the old man. He had never wronged me. He had never given me insult. For his gold I had no desire. I think it was his eye! yes, it was this!"

Vocabulary Practice

Synonyms are words that have the same or nearly the same meaning. Match each vocabulary word in the left-hand column with its synonym in the right-hand column. (Two of the words in the right-hand column will not have matches.) Then write six sentences, each sentence using a different vocabulary word.

1. acute	**a.** smothered
2. conceived	**b.** excited
3. vexed	**c.** planned
4. profound	**d.** held back
5. stifled	**e.** began
6. refrained	**f.** sharp
	g. insightful
	h. annoyed

Example: vexed

Sentence: The cat's frequent scratching vexed its owner.

Academic Vocabulary

The narrator had **psychological** reasons for confessing to the murder.

In the preceding sentence, *psychological* means "related to the mind," such as a person's awareness, feelings, or motivation. Think about what thoughts the narrator in the story reveals before his confession, and then fill in the blank for this statement:

_____ was a psychological reason that led to the narrator's confession.

 Literature Online

Selection Resources For Selection Quizzes, eFlashcards, and Reading-Writing Connection activities, go to glencoe.com and enter QuickPass code GL39770u2.

Respond Through Writing

Expository Essay

Analyze Plot Poe builds suspense throughout "The Tell-Tale Heart." In a short essay, analyze the plot of the story, explaining how the order of events makes the story effective.

Understand the Task The **plot** is the series of events showing how a conflict or problem arises and is resolved. The conflict may be between characters; between a character and an idea (such as *right or wrong*); or between a character and a force, such as *nature.* Think about what the conflict is in "The Tell-Tale Heart."

Prewrite A plot usually unfolds in five steps: The **exposition** introduces the story's setting and characters and sets up the conflict. The **rising action** develops the story's conflict and builds suspense. The **climax** is the moment of greatest suspense, emotion, and interest. The **falling action** shows what happened to the characters after the climax and moves toward a conclusion. The **resolution** completes the falling action and reveals the final outcome of the conflict.

Keep track of your ideas using a chart like the one below. You can use words from the Word Bank to help you describe the plot.

1. Exposition	
2. Rising Action	
3. Climax	
4. Falling Action	
5. Resolution	

Draft As you draft, keep an overall plan in mind. For example, you may decide to write an introduction, a paragraph about each plot step, and then a conclusion. After you figure out your plan, write your thesis statement. This sentence frame might help you:

> In "The Tell-Tale Heart," the conflict revolves around _____.

Revise After you have written your first draft, read it to determine whether the paragraphs are in a logical order. Rearrange text as necessary so that your ideas are easy to follow.

Edit and Proofread Proofread your paper, correcting any errors in spelling, grammar, and punctuation.

Word Bank

These words may be helpful in describing the plot of "The Tell-Tale Heart."

wicked

desperate

crazed

suspenseful

tense

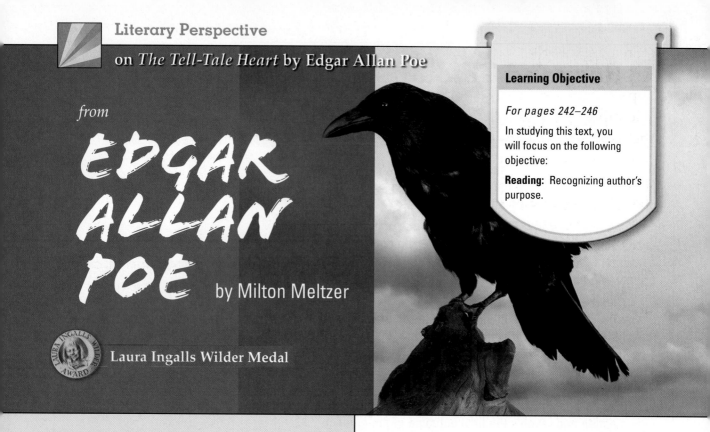

from

EDGAR ALLAN POE

by Milton Meltzer

Laura Ingalls Wilder Medal

Learning Objective

For pages 242–246

In studying this text, you will focus on the following objective:

Reading: Recognizing author's purpose.

Set a Purpose for Reading

Read to learn more about Edgar Allan Poe, the author of "The Tell-Tale Heart."

Build Background

What caused Poe to become a master of horror? Many believe that Poe's misfortunes colored his work. He grew up as an orphan. As an adult, he had severe money problems, and his beloved wife died when she was only 24.

Reading Skill Recognize Author's Purpose

The **author's purpose** is the intention of the writer. With a biography, a writer aims to provide information about a person's life. As you read the selection, ask yourself, what is Milton Meltzer's purpose for writing this text? Write down your ideas and details from the selection using a chart like the one shown.

Purpose	Details
to inform reader about Poe's detective fiction	Poe inspired the creator of Sherlock Holmes

In April 1841, *Graham's* [a literary magazine] published Poe's "The Murders in the Rue Morgue." It was the first detective story ever to see print, and it changed the course of world literature. It was the archetype[1] for the modern detective story. Sir Arthur Conan Doyle, who in 1887 created Sherlock Holmes, the most famous detective in fiction, said that Poe "was the father of the detective tale, and covered its limits so completely that I fail to see how his followers can find any fresh ground which they can confidently call their own."

At the heart of "Rue Morgue" is the detective Auguste Dupin, perhaps Poe's most interesting character. He is

---

1 An *archetype* (är′kə tīp) is a model or pattern that is widely copied.

a Frenchman with an analytical mind who loves to tackle problems with his superior intellect. He combines scientific logic with the artist's leap of the imagination. Dupin (like Poe) is raised in a rich family but has fallen on hard times. Dupin has a companion—like Sherlock Holmes's Watson—who is slow-witted and needs to have everything explained. This of course shows us how brilliant Dupin is. He observes facts, analyzes them, and deduces their meaning. It was a recognizable, repeatable method that gave the detective the central role in the solution of crime whether in real life or in the detective fiction to come.

The clues that puzzle the police Dupin sees in a new way, and he discloses[2] the solution to the mystery. The story had many of the elements that would come to delight fans of detective stories: the brilliant amateur detective, the clumsy cops, the naive pal. Poe's story and the several others like it he would write are examples of ratiocination, meaning the process of exact thinking. . . .

In 1842 the Poes were living in a small row house near Philadelphia's Fairmount Park. While Maria [Poe's mother-in-law] and Virginia [Poe's wife] did their best to keep the rooms clean and orderly, the family's poverty was plain to any visitor. They celebrated Poe's thirty-third birthday on January 19. The next evening,

disaster struck. Virginia was singing and playing the piano when a blood vessel burst in her lungs and she almost drowned in the blood pouring from her mouth. Miraculously, she recovered, but only partially. The ruinous effect of her TB[3] persisted; she would suffer continually in the five years left to her.

Virginia needed the greatest care as an invalid,[4] care almost impossible to provide in such cramped, close quarters and with little money to find better living conditions or meet Virginia's mounting medical expenses. Her long-drawn-out illness, a visitor noted, had a devastating effect on Poe, "who was so sensitive and irritable . . . he would not allow a word about the danger of her dying—the mention of it drove him wild." Increasingly, Poe would act wildly, go on drinking binges, and express murderous rage in his tales.

Yet somehow he managed to continue writing. Several of his best stories appeared in the early 1840s. Auguste Dupin figures again in "The Mystery of Marie Rogêt," which was based on an actual murder that occurred in 1841 in Manhattan. "The Gold Bug," using Poe's knowledge of cryptography, won a $100 prize from a newspaper, and down the years has proved to be his most popular story.

---

2 When Dupin *discloses* the solution, he reveals what the solution is.

3 *TB* (tuberculosis) is an infectious disease that causes swelling, especially in the lungs.

4 An *invalid* (in′ və lid) is a person disabled due to injury or illness.

VIRGINIA

EDGAR

In "The Pit and the Pendulum," the captive narrator is in a dark dungeon, nearly driven mad by thirst and hunger, and the fear of a razor-sharp pendulum that threatens to slice him to death.

"The Masque of the Red Death" deals with aristocrats fleeing to avoid a plague. Here Poe drew upon the cholera[5] epidemic he had observed in Baltimore in 1831 and on his wife's terrifying hemorrhage[6] to describe the symptoms and the swift ending of the victims:

There were sharp pains, and sudden dizziness, and then profuse bleeding at the pores, with dissolution. The scarlet stains upon the body and especially upon the face of the victim, were the pest ban which shut him out from the aid and from the sympathy of his fellow-men. And the whole seizure, progress and termination of the disease, were the incidents of half an hour. . . .

Early in 1843, Poe's work began to appear in a new Boston magazine, *Pioneer*. It was started by a young Harvard graduate, James Russell Lowell, whose poems Poe had published in *Graham's*, predicting

---

5 ***Cholera*** (kol′ər ə) is an infectious disease of the intestines.

6 A ***hemorrhage*** is a severe loss of blood.

Lowell would become one of America's best poets. Like Poe, Lowell wanted to avoid the trashy stuff that peppered the pages of the popular magazines. When Poe offered to write for him, Lowell promised to pay $10 for each piece. The first three issues carried Poe's story "The Tell-Tale Heart," his poem "Leonore," and an article on writing verse.

"The Tell-Tale Heart" is a chilling murder story. It is told from the killer's point of view, and illustrates the desire to exercise power over an adversary. It is not a whodunit. The reader knows from the start who the murderer is. The psychology of the killer is what Poe focuses on.

Bad luck hit both Lowell and Poe. The magazine, up against a host of new ones, failed after its third issue, leaving Lowell deep in debt and Poe with the loss of a promising outlet. But broke as he was, Poe generously wrote Lowell not to worry about paying him the $30 he was owed.

It was mostly the Philadelphia publications that carried Poe's work, and far more often his tales than his poems. In June 1843 his "The Gold Bug" won a $100 prize from a local paper, and shortly after a dramatization of it was presented at a local theater. The prize money was a godsend,[7] though not nearly enough to sustain the family.

In desperation, Poe decided to look into a new source of income—speaking to public audiences. This, though he had earlier put down what he termed "the present absurd rage for lecturing." The lyceum system, as it was called, arose out of the habit of American parents in the early 1800s to read aloud to the family from the works of authors. By the early 1830s this admirable custom had bloomed into the lyceum system. People wanted to be instructed or entertained by standing or sitting among many fellow listeners, concentrating on what some notable person had to say. This reliance on the spoken word arose long before people had easy access to newspapers, magazines, radio, television, movies. It soon became a source of income important to writers, thinkers, crusaders for social change— to anyone seeking self-improvement.

A lyceum would organize paid-in-advance lectures at regular intervals. Each time a different speaker would appear to talk on a different topic. By the mid-1830s there were about three thousand such lyceums, mostly in the North. The point was not only educational but social. In towns without the cultural or entertainment attractions we enjoy today, just getting together once a week—meeting old friends and making new ones—was a pleasure to look forward to. . . .

---

7 A **godsend** is the unexpected arrival of something desperately wanted or needed.

Poe of course was well aware of how profitable this might be for him, and he began writing to lyceum committees in the hope of setting up a series of lectures for himself. It worked: Within the next few months he would speak in Philadelphia, Newark, Wilmington, Baltimore, Reading. Popular interest in this odd author was so intense that hundreds couldn't get seats at the first lecture in Philadelphia.

Although he had sneered at lyceums, he worked hard to make a good showing, gathering good reviews everywhere. He was praised for his eloquence, graceful manner, and good voice. The title he used for his lectures was "The Poetry of America."

Even though he would speak for two hours, audiences didn't mind. (They were used to it. Later, political candidates like Abraham Lincoln and Stephen A. Douglas would debate the issue of slavery before audiences of 15,000 people standing outdoors for many long hours, reveling in the oratory.) Poe gossiped about infighting in the literary world, discussed the function of criticism, and recited some of his poems. Good show, the audience felt.

Now thirty-five, Poe got rid of his side-whiskers and grew the dashing mustache most remember him with. Conscious of personal appearance, he made fun of that concern with a sketch he published called "The Spectacles." It's about a man who is too vain to wear his eyeglasses, and with faulty vision is overwhelmed by the beauty of a woman—who turns out to be not only elderly but his own grandmother.

It seemed time to see if he could do better outside Philadelphia. He made a deal with a local paper called the *Columbia Spy* to write a series of pieces about life in the big city—New York. In April 1844, once again, the Poe family moved to New York. 🔖

Respond and Think Critically

1. What role did poet James Russell Lowell play in Poe's life? [Recall and Identify]

2. In what ways are Auguste Dupin and Sherlock Holmes alike? [Compare]

3. Would a lyceum be popular today? Explain why or why not. [Evaluate]

4. **Text-to-Text** In what ways does knowledge of Poe's life affect your understanding of "The Tell-Tale Heart"? [Interpret]

5. Reading Strategy Recognize Author's Purpose In this selection, is Meltzer trying to inform, explain a process, entertain, or persuade? Explain your thoughts. [Analyze]

6. BQ BIG Question Detective stories are popular in books, in movies, and on TV. Describe a detective story you've read or seen. [Connect]

The Monkey's Paw

Connect to the Story

Think about a time when you made an outrageous wish, such as wishing to win a million dollars or to travel back in time.

Partner Talk With a partner, talk about what you wished for. Discuss what might have happened if the wish had been granted. How might your life have changed?

Build Background

"The Monkey's Paw" is a classic horror story about a family who receives a magical monkey's paw that grants its possessor three wishes, but the wishes come with terrible consequences.

- The story was published in 1902. It takes place in London around the turn of the century.

- One of the main characters in the story is a sergeant who has returned from a tour of duty in India. India became a colony of Great Britain in the mid-1800s and did not gain independence until 1947. During this time, it was common for British soldiers to serve in India.

Vocabulary

amiably (ā′ mē ə blē) *adv.* in a friendly, good-natured way (p. 250). *After Joanna received help from her older sister with algebra, she amiably offered to wash her sister's car.*

intercept (in′ tər sept′) *v.* to stop the course or progress of (p. 250). *When I realized that my friend had left her backpack at my house, I rushed to intercept her before she got home.*

grimace (grim′ is) *n.* a twisted expression of the face (p. 252). *The grumpy woman always wore a grimace.*

sinister (sin′ is tər) *adj.* bad, evil, dishonest (p. 259). *The characters in the movie had a sinister plan to steal a car and rob a bank.*

inaudible (in ô′ də bəl) *adj.* not able to be heard (p. 259). *Alex's voice was inaudible over the roar of the crowd.*

oppressive (ə pres′ iv) *adj.* hard to bear; distressing (p. 262). *The heat today is oppressive.*

Meet W. W. Jacobs

From Humor to Horror
Although W. W. Jacobs wrote mostly comic stories, he is best known for his horrifying tale, "The Monkey's Paw." Jacobs grew up among sailors and dock-workers on the banks of the Thames River in London where he set many of his humorous stories. As an adult, he worked as a bank clerk, a job that bored him, and he wrote in his spare time. He worked at the bank for nearly twenty years before he was able to quit and earn his living as a full-time writer.

Literary Works Jacobs wrote dozens of short story collections and a number of plays. "The Monkey's Paw" was first published in 1902.

W. W. Jacobs was born in 1863 and died in 1943.

 Literature Online

Author Search For more about W. W. Jacobs, go to glencoe.com and enter QuickPass code GL39770u2.

Set Purposes for Reading

BQ BIG Question

As you read, identify the parts of the story that you enjoy most and think about why you enjoy them.

Literary Element Diction

Diction is a writer's choice of words and how those words are arranged in phrases, in sentences, or in lines of poetry. A writer uses diction to convey character traits and create different tones and moods throughout a story.

Studying diction is important because it helps you gain knowledge of the author's ideas about the characters, setting, and plot.

As you read, look closely at the writer's use of descriptive and figurative language. Think about what this evidence tells the reader about each character as well as what mood and tone it creates.

Reading Skill Analyze Plot

Plot is the sequence of events in a narrative text. Most plots begin with **exposition**, which introduces the characters, setting, and situation. Next, the **rising action** adds complications to the story's **conflicts**, or problems, leading to the **climax**, or point of greatest interest or suspense. The **falling action** is the result of the climax and leads to the **resolution**, which presents the final outcome.

When you analyze a plot, you look at its separate parts to understand the story.

To analyze plot,

- identify and think about each element of the plot.

- use what you've learned to identify the theme and author's purpose.

As you read, you can use a larger version of a graphic organizer like the one below to help you analyze the plot.

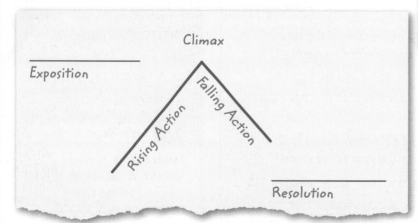

Learning Objectives

For pages 247–265

In studying this text, you will focus on the following objectives:

Literary Study: Analyzing diction.

Reading: Analyzing plot.

TRY IT

Analyze Plot *Isabelle ignored her mother's warnings and went outside without her shoes on. After playing on the slide in her backyard, she rode her bike along the sidewalk. Once she got up to speed, she took her feet off the pedals and let her legs fly out to each side. As she tried to return her feet to the pedals, she missed with her right foot and scraped it against the sidewalk, leaving her with a battered and bloodied big toe.*

What elements of plot do you see in this brief story? What message does the author provide?

The Monkey's Paw

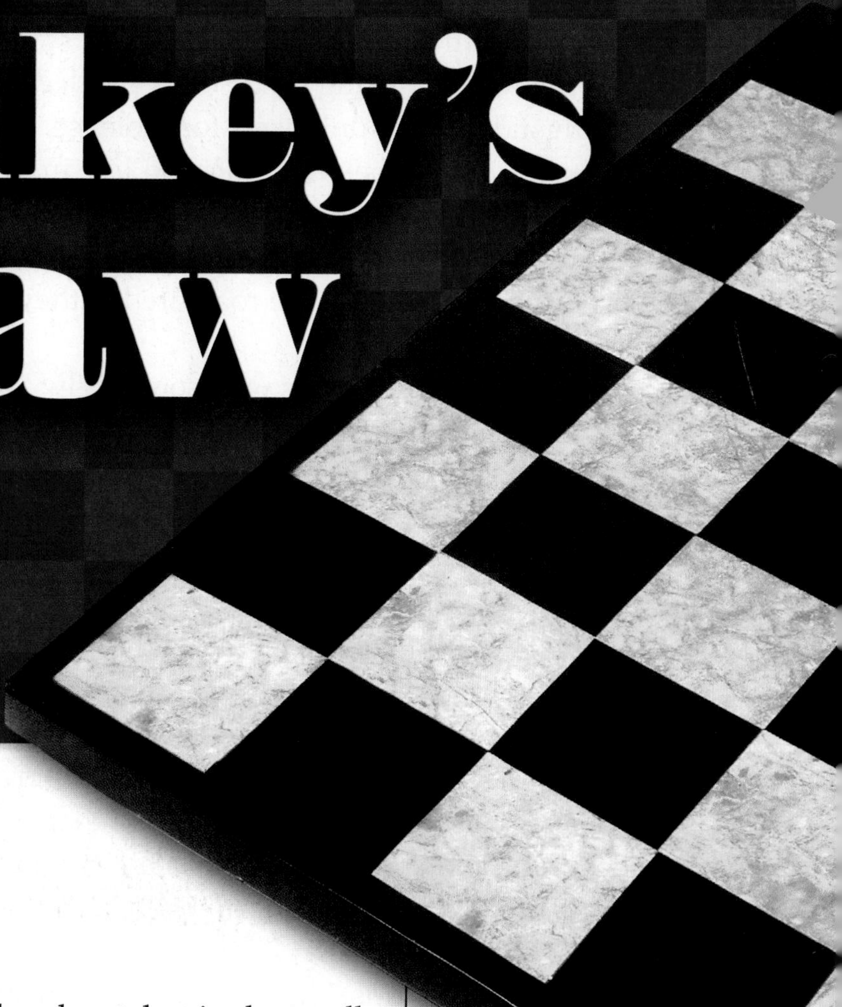

W. W. Jacobs

Without, the night was cold and wet, but in the small parlor of Laburnam Villa the blinds were drawn and the fire burned brightly. Father and son were at chess, the former, who possessed ideas about the game involving radical changes, putting his king into such sharp and unnecessary perils that it even provoked comment from the white-haired old lady knitting placidly[1] by the fire.

---

1 **Placidly** means "calmly and peacefully."

"Hark at the wind," said Mr. White, who, having seen a fatal mistake after it was too late, was **amiably** desirous of preventing his son from seeing it.

"I'm listening," said the latter, grimly surveying the board as he stretched out his hand. "Check."

"I should hardly think that he'd come tonight," said his father, with his hand poised over the board.

"Mate," replied the son.

"That's the worst of living so far out," bawled Mr. White, with sudden and unlooked-for violence; "of all the beastly, slushy, out-of-the-way places to live in, this is the worst. Pathway's a bog, and the road's a torrent. I don't know what people are thinking about. I suppose because only two houses on the road are let, they think it doesn't matter."

"Never mind, dear," said his wife soothingly; "perhaps you'll win the next one."

Mr. White looked up sharply, just in time to **intercept** a knowing glance between mother and son. The words died away on his lips, and he hid a guilty grin in his thin gray beard.

"There he is," said Herbert White, as the gate banged too loudly and heavy footsteps came toward the door.

The old man rose with hospitable haste, and, opening the door, was heard condoling[2] with the new arrival. The new arrival also condoled with himself, so that Mrs. White said, "Tut, tut!" and coughed gently as her husband entered the room, followed by a tall burly man, beady of eye and rubicund of visage.[3]

"Sergeant Major Morris," he said, introducing him.

The sergeant major shook hands, and, taking the

Analyze Plot At what part of the plot is the story at this point? Think about what you know about the characters and the setting.

Diction Think about the specific words the author uses to describe each member of the family. What does the author's description of the family members tell you about them?

---

2 *Condoling* is expressing sympathy.

3 *Rubicund of visage* means "reddish or rosy in the face."

Vocabulary . . . .

amiably (ā′ mē ə blē) *adv.* in a friendly, good-natured way

intercept (in′tər sept′) *v.* to stop the course or progress of

proffered seat by the fire, watched contentedly while his host got out whiskey and **tumblers** and stood a small copper kettle on the fire.

At the third glass his eyes got brighter, and he began to talk, the little family circle regarding with eager interest this visitor from distant parts, as he squared his broad shoulders in the chair and spoke of strange scenes and doughty[4] deeds, of wars and plagues and strange peoples.

"Twenty-one years of it," said Mr. White, nodding at his wife and son. "When he went away he was a slip of a youth in the warehouse. Now look at him."

"He don't look to have taken much harm," said Mrs. White politely.

"I'd like to go to India myself," said the old man, "just to look around a bit, you know."

"Better where you are," said the sergeant major, shaking his head. He put down the empty glass and, sighing softly, shook it again.

"I should like to see those old temples and fakirs[5] and jugglers," said the old man. "What was that you started telling me the other day about the monkey's paw or something, Morris?"

"Nothing," said the soldier hastily. "Leastways, nothing worth hearing."

"Monkey's paw?" said Mrs. White curiously.

"Well, it's just a bit of what you might call magic, perhaps," said the sergeant major offhandedly.

His three listeners leaned forward eagerly. The visitor absent-mindedly put his empty glass to his lips and then set it down again. His host filled it for him.

"To look at," said the sergeant major, fumbling in his pocket, "it's just an ordinary little paw, dried to a mummy."

He took something out of his pocket and proffered it.

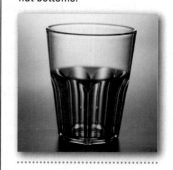
Analyze Plot Why does Morris hesitate to talk about the monkey's paw? Think about how this might be a sign of the developing conflict in the plot.

---

4 A **doughty** deed is a brave or valiant one.

5 A **fakir** (fə kēr') is a member of a Muslim or Hindu sect who takes a vow of poverty and lives by begging. Fakirs sometimes do extraordinary and dangerous tricks.

Mrs. White drew back with a **grimace,** but her son, taking it, examined it curiously.

"And what is there special about it?" inquired Mr. White as he took it from his son and, having examined it, placed it upon the table.

"It had a spell put on it by an old fakir," said the sergeant major, "a very holy man. He wanted to show that fate ruled people's lives, and that those who interfered with it did so to their sorrow. He put a spell on it so that three separate men could each have three wishes from it."

His manner was so impressive that his hearers were conscious that their light laughter jarred somewhat.

"Well, why don't you have three, sir?" said Herbert White cleverly.

The soldier regarded him in the way that middle age is wont[6] to regard presumptuous youth. "I have," he said quietly, and his blotchy face whitened.

"And did you really have the three wishes granted?" asked Mrs. White.

"I did," said the sergeant major, and his glass tapped against his strong teeth.

"And has anybody else wished?" inquired the old lady.

"The first man had his three wishes, yes," was the reply. "I don't know what the first two were, but the third was for death. That's how I got the paw."

His tones were so grave that a hush fell upon the group.

"If you've had your three wishes, it's no good to you now, then, Morris," said the old man at last. "What do you keep it for?"

The soldier shook his head. "Fancy, I suppose," he said slowly. "I did have some idea of selling it, but I don't think I will. It has caused enough mischief already. Besides, people won't buy. They think it's a fairy tale, some of

Analyze Plot What conflict does Morris describe? Think about how this conflict might help you understand the story better.

---

6 **Wont** means "accustomed, used."

....

grimace (grim´is) *n.* a twisted expression of the face

Frank John St. Jay, 1900. Thomas Eakins. Oil on canvas, 23 7/8 x 19 7/8 in. Fine Arts Museum of San Francisco, CA. Gift of Mr. and Mrs. John D. Rockefeller III. 1979.7.7.

View the Art What does the posture of the man in the painting reveal about his character? In what way is this man similar to Sergeant Major Morris?

them, and those who do think anything of it want to try it first and pay me afterward."

"If you could have another three wishes," said the old man, eyeing him keenly, "would you have them?"

"I don't know," said the other. "I don't know."

He took the paw, and dangling it between his front finger and thumb, suddenly threw it upon the fire. White, with a slight cry, stooped down and snatched it off.

"Better let it burn," said the soldier solemnly.

"If you don't want it, Morris," said the old man, "give it to me."

Diction What do the words *slight cry* tell about Mr. White at this point in the story?

"I won't," said his friend doggedly. "I threw it on the fire. If you keep it, don't blame me for what happens. Pitch it on the fire again, like a sensible man."

The other shook his head and examined his new possession closely. "How do you do it?" he inquired.

"Hold it up in your right hand and wish aloud," said the sergeant major, "but I warn you of the consequences."

"Sounds like the *Arabian Nights*," said Mrs. White, as she rose and began to set the supper. "Don't you think you might wish for four pairs of hands for me?"

Her husband drew the talisman[7] from his pocket and then all three burst into laughter as the sergeant major, with a look of alarm on his face, caught him by the arm. "If you must wish," he said gruffly, "wish for something sensible."

Mr. White dropped it back into his pocket, and placing chairs, motioned his friend to the table. In the business of supper the talisman was partly forgotten, and afterward the three sat listening in an enthralled fashion to a second installment of the soldier's adventures in India.

"If the tale about the monkey paw is not more truthful than those he has been telling us," said Herbert, as the door closed behind their guest, just in time for him to catch the last train, "we shan't make much out of it."

"Did you give him anything for it, Father?" inquired Mrs. White, regarding her husband closely.

"A trifle," said he, coloring slightly. "He didn't want it, but I made him take it. And he pressed me again to throw it away."

"Likely," said Herbert, with pretended horror. "Why, we're going to be rich, and famous, and happy. Wish to be an emperor, Father, to begin with: then you can't be bossed around."

He darted round the table, pursued by the maligned[8] Mrs. White armed with an **antimacassar.**

Analyze Plot Why is the soldier's attempt to destroy the monkey's paw important to the story? What does Mr. White's refusal to destroy the paw tell you about how the story is moving forward?

Visual Vocabulary

An **antimacassar** is a protective covering for the backs of chairs and sofas.

---

7 A **talisman** is a charm believed to have magical powers.

8 If you are **maligned,** someone has spoken ill of you or told harmful untruths about you.

Mr. White took the paw from his pocket and eyed it dubiously. "I don't know what to wish for, and that's a fact," he said slowly. "It seems to me I've got all I want."

"If you only cleared the house, you'd be quite happy, wouldn't you?" said Herbert, with his hand on his shoulder. "Well, wish for two hundred pounds, then; that'll just do it."

His father, smiling shamefacedly at his own credulity,[9] held up the talisman, as his son, with a solemn face somewhat marred by a wink at his mother, sat down at the piano and struck a few impressive chords.

"I wish for two hundred pounds," said the old man distinctly.

A fine crash from the piano greeted the words, interrupted by a shuddering cry from the old man. His wife and son ran toward him.

"It moved," he cried, with a glance of disgust at the object as it lay on the floor. "As I wished it twisted in my hands like a snake."

"Well, I don't see the money," said his son, as he picked it up and placed it on the table, "and I bet I never shall."

"It must have been your fancy, Father," said his wife, regarding him anxiously.

He shook his head. "Never mind, though; there's no harm done, but it gave me a shock all the same."

They sat down by the fire again while the two men finished their pipes. Outside, the wind was higher than ever, and the old man started nervously at the sound of a door banging upstairs. A silence unusual and depressing settled upon all three, which lasted until the old couple rose to retire for the night.

"I expect you'll find the cash tied up in a big bag in the middle of your bed," said Herbert, as he bade them good night, "and something horrible squatting up on top of the wardrobe watching you as you pocket your ill-gotten gains."

He sat alone in the darkness, gazing at the dying fire, and seeing faces in it. The last face was so horrible and so simian[10]

BQ BIG Question

Do you enjoy the idea of the monkey's paw granting three wishes? Explain what you find enjoyable about that or other events at this point in the story.

Analyze Plot What conflict begins to unfold with this event? Think about a theme this conflict might be pointing to.

---

9 **Credulity** (kri dōō ′li tē) is a tendency to believe too readily.

10 To be **simian** is to resemble a monkey.

that he gazed at it in amazement. It got so vivid that, with a little uneasy laugh, he felt on the table for a glass containing a little water to throw over it. His hand grasped the monkey's paw, and with a little shiver he wiped his hand on his coat and went up to bed.

In the brightness of the wintry sun next morning as it streamed over the breakfast table Herbert laughed at his fears. There was an air of prosaic[11] wholesomeness about the room which it had lacked on the previous night, and the dirty, shriveled little paw was pitched on the sideboard with a carelessness which betokened no great belief in its virtues.

"I suppose all old soldiers are the same," said Mrs. White. "The idea of our listening to such nonsense! How could wishes be granted in these days? And if they could, how could two hundred pounds hurt you, Father?"

"Might drop on his head from the sky," said the frivolous Herbert.

"Morris said the things happened so naturally," said his father, "that you might if you so wished attribute it to coincidence."

"Well, don't break into the money before I come back," said Herbert, as he rose from the table. "I'm afraid it'll turn you into a mean, avaricious[12] man, and we shall have to disown you."

His mother laughed, and following him to the door, watched him down the road, and, returning to the breakfast table, was very happy at the expense of her husband's credulity. All of which did not prevent her from scurrying to the door at the postman's knock, nor prevent her from referring somewhat shortly to retired sergeant majors of bibulous[13] habits when she found that the post brought a tailor's bill.

Diction How does the diction in this sentence convey the mood of the scene?

Analyze Plot What explains the changes in Mrs. White's behavior?

---

11 **Prosaic** means "ordinary or commonplace."

12 An **avaricious** (av ə rish´əs) person is greedy.

13 Anyone of **bibulous** (bib´yə ləs) habits is fond of alcoholic beverages and drinks them regularly.

"Herbert will have some more of his funny remarks, I expect, when he comes home," she said, as they sat at dinner.

"I dare say," said Mr. White, pouring himself out some beer; "but for all that, the thing moved in my hand; that I'll swear to."

"You thought it did," said the old lady soothingly.

"I say it did," replied the other. "There was no thought about it. I had just—What's the matter?"

His wife made no reply. She was watching the mysterious movements of a man outside, who, peering in an undecided fashion at the house, appeared to be trying to make up his mind to enter. In mental connection with the two hundred pounds, she noticed that the stranger was well dressed and wore a silk hat of glossy newness. Three times he paused at the gate, and then walked on again. The fourth time he stood with his hand upon it, and then with sudden resolution flung it open and walked up the path. Mrs. White at the same moment placed her hands behind her, and hurriedly unfastening the strings of her apron, put that useful article of apparel beneath the cushion of her chair.

She brought the stranger, who seemed ill at ease, into the room. He gazed furtively at Mrs. White, and listened in a preoccupied fashion as the old lady apologized for the appearance of the room, and her husband's coat, a garment which he usually reserved for the garden. She then waited patiently for him to broach[14] his business, but he was at first strangely silent.

"I—was asked to call," he said at last, and stooped and picked a piece of cotton from his trousers. "I came from Maw and Meggins."

The old lady started. "Is anything the matter?" she asked breathlessly. "Has anything happened to Herbert? What is it? What is it?"

Her husband interposed. "There, there, Mother," he said hastily. "Sit down and don't jump to conclusions.

Analyze Plot What might the man's behavior foreshadow, or hint at?

Diction How does Jacobs's word choice convey Mrs. White's emotions?

---

14 To *broach* a subject is to mention it for the first time.

The Old Version, 1881. Thomas Hovenden. Oil on canvas, 24 x 19 in. Fine Arts Museum of San Francisco, CA. Gift of Mr. and Mrs. John D. Rockefeller III. 1993.35.17.

View the Art At what point in the story might Mr. and Mrs. White have resembled the couple in the painting? Explain.

You've not brought bad news, I'm sure, sir," and he eyed the other wistfully.

"I'm sorry—" began the visitor.

"Is he hurt?" demanded the mother wildly.

The visitor bowed in assent. "Badly hurt," he said quietly, "but he is not in any pain."

"Oh, thank God!" said the old woman, clasping her hands. "Thank God for that! Thank—"

Analyze Plot Think about what he might mean by this statement. How does the event he describes contribute to the rising action?

She broke off suddenly as the **sinister** meaning of the assurance dawned upon her and she saw the awful confirmation of her fears in the other's averted face. She caught her breath, and turning to her husband, laid her trembling old hand upon his. There was a long silence.

"He was caught in the machinery," said the visitor at length, in a low voice.

"Caught in the machinery," repeated Mr. White, in a dazed fashion, "yes."

He sat staring blankly out at the window, and taking his wife's hand between his own, pressed it as he had been wont to do in their old courting days nearly forty years before.

"He was the only one left to us," he said, turning gently to the visitor. "It is hard."

The other coughed, and, rising, walked slowly to the window. "The firm wished me to convey their sincere sympathy with you in your great loss," he said, without looking around. "I beg that you will understand I am only their servant and merely obeying orders."

There was no reply; the old woman's face was white, her eyes staring, and her breath **inaudible;** on the husband's face was a look such as his friend the sergeant might have carried into his first action.

"I was to say that Maw and Meggins disclaim all responsibility," continued the other. "They admit no liability at all, but in consideration of your son's services they wish to present you with a certain sum as compensation."

Mr. White dropped his wife's hand, and rising to his feet, gazed with a look of horror at his visitor. His dry lips shaped the words, "How much?"

"Two hundred pounds," was the answer.

Unconscious of his wife's shriek, the old man smiled faintly, put out his hands like a sightless man, and dropped, a senseless heap, to the floor.

Diction How does Jacobs's word choice show the horror of the situation?

Vocabulary
. . . .

sinister (sin´is tər) *adj.* bad, evil, dishonest
inaudible (in ô´də bəl) *adj.* not able to be heard

♟♟♟

In the huge new cemetery, some two miles distant, the old people buried their dead, and came back to a house steeped in shadow and silence. It was all over so quickly that at first they could hardly realize it, and remained in a state of expectation as though of something else to happen—something else which was to lighten this load, too heavy for old hearts to bear.

But the days passed, and expectations gave place to resignation—the hopeless resignation of the old, sometimes miscalled apathy. Sometimes they hardly exchanged a word, for now they had nothing to talk about, and their days were long to weariness.

It was about a week after that the old man, waking suddenly in the night, stretched out his hand and found himself alone. The room was in darkness, and the sound of subdued weeping came from the window. He raised himself in bed and listened.

"Come back," he said tenderly. "You will be cold."

"It is colder for my son," said the old woman, and wept afresh.

The sound of her sobs died away on his ears. The bed was warm, and his eyes heavy with sleep. He dozed fitfully, and then slept until a sudden wild cry from his wife awoke him with a start.

"The *paw!*" she cried wildly. "The monkey's paw!"

He started up in alarm. "Where? Where is it? What's the matter?"

She came stumbling across the room toward him. "I want it," she said quietly. "You've not destroyed it?"

"It's in the parlor, on the bracket," he replied, marveling. "Why?"

She cried and laughed together, and bending over, kissed his cheek.

"I only just thought of it," she said hysterically. "Why didn't I think of it before? Why didn't *you* think of it?"

"Think of what?" he questioned.

"The other two wishes," she replied rapidly. "We've only had one."

Diction How does the author's word choice in this paragraph help you understand the sadness and loneliness that the Whites feel?

"Was not that enough?" he demanded fiercely.

"No," she cried triumphantly; "we'll have one more. Go down and get it quickly, and wish our boy alive again."

The man sat up in bed and flung the bedclothes from his quaking limbs. "You are mad!" he cried, aghast.

"Get it," she panted; "get it quickly, and wish—Oh, my boy, my boy!"

Her husband struck a match and lit the candle. "Get back to bed," he said unsteadily. "You don't know what you are saying."

"We had the first wish granted," said the old woman feverishly; "why not the second?"

"A coincidence," stammered the old man.

"Go and get it and wish," cried his wife, quivering with excitement.

The old man turned and regarded her, and his voice shook. "He has been dead ten days, and besides he—I would not tell you else, but—I could only recognize him by his clothing. If he was too terrible for you to see then, how now?"

"Bring him back," cried the old woman, and dragged him toward the door. "Do you think I fear the child I have nursed?"

He went down in the darkness, and felt his way to the parlor, and then to the mantelpiece. The talisman was in its place, and a horrible fear that the unspoken wish might bring his mutilated son before him ere he could escape from the room seized upon him, and he caught his breath as he found that he had lost the direction of the door. His brow cold with sweat, he felt his way round the table, and groped along the wall until he found himself in the small passage with the unwholesome thing in his hand.

Even his wife's face seemed changed as he entered the room. It was white and expectant, and to his fears seemed to have an unnatural look upon it. He was afraid of her.

"*Wish!*" she cried, in a strong voice.

"It is foolish and wicked," he faltered.

"*Wish!*" repeated his wife.

Analyze Plot What does Mrs. White believe will happen if Mr. White wishes Herbert alive again? Think about what message the author might be trying to convey.

He raised his hand. "I wish my son alive again."

The talisman fell to the floor, and he regarded it shudderingly. Then he sank trembling into a chair as the old woman, with burning eyes, walked to the window and raised the blind.

He sat until he was chilled with the cold, glancing occasionally at the figure of the old woman peering through the window. The candle end, which had burned below the rim of the china candlestick, was throwing pulsating shadows on the ceiling and walls, until, with a flicker larger than the rest, it expired. The old man, with an unspeakable sense of relief at the failure of the talisman, crept back to his bed, and a minute or two afterward the old woman came silently and apathetically beside him.

Neither spoke, but both lay silently listening to the ticking of the clock. A stair creaked, and a squeaky mouse scurried noisily through the wall. The darkness was **oppressive,** and after lying for some time screwing up his courage, he took the box of matches, and striking one, went downstairs for a candle.

At the foot of the stairs the match went out, and he paused to strike another, and at the same moment a knock, so quiet and stealthy as to be scarcely audible, sounded on the front door.

The matches fell from his hand and spilled in the passage. He stood motionless, his breath suspended until the knock was repeated. Then he turned and fled swiftly back to his room, and closed the door behind him. A third knock sounded through the house.

"What's that?" cried the old woman, starting up.

"A rat," said the old man, in shaking tones—"a rat. It passed me on the stairs."

His wife sat up in bed listening. A loud knock resounded through the house.

"It's Herbert!" she screamed. "It's Herbert!"

She ran to the door, but her husband was before her, and catching her by the arm, held her tightly.

Diction What mood does Jacobs create with his description of the knock on the door?

Vocabulary
. . . .

oppressive (ə pres´iv) *adj.* hard to bear; distressing

"What are you going to do?" he whispered hoarsely.

"It's my boy; it's Herbert!" she cried, struggling mechanically. "I forgot it was two miles away. What are you holding me for? Let's go. I must open the door."

"Don't let it in," cried the old man, trembling.

"You're afraid of your own son," she cried, struggling. "Let me go. I'm coming, Herbert; I'm coming."

There was another knock, and another. The old woman with a sudden wrench broke free and ran from the room. Her husband followed to the landing, and called after her appealingly as she hurried downstairs. He heard the chain rattle back and the bottom bolt drawn slowly and stiffly from the socket. Then the old woman's voice, strained and panting.

"The bolt," she cried loudly. "Come down. I can't reach it."

But her husband was on his hands and knees groping wildly on the floor in search of the paw. If he could only find it before the thing outside got in. A perfect fusillade[15] of knocks reverberated through the house, and he heard the scraping of a chair as his wife put it down in the passage against the door. He heard the creaking of the bolt as it came slowly back, and at the same moment he found the monkey's paw, and frantically breathed his third and last wish.

The knocking ceased suddenly, although the echoes of it were still in the house. He heard the chair drawn back and the door opened. A cold wind rushed up the staircase, and a long loud wail of disappointment and misery from his wife gave him courage to run down to her side, and then to the gate beyond. The street lamp flickering opposite shone on a quiet and deserted road. ❧

Diction Why does Jacobs use the word *it* instead of *him* to describe Herbert? Think about the effect this might have on readers.

Analyze Plot Think about what Mr. White's final wish might have been. How would this wish resolve the conflict?

---

15 A **fusillade** (fū´sə lād´) is the firing of many guns in rapid succession or anything that resembles such a sound, as the knocks do here.

After You Read

Respond and Think Critically

1. Restate Sergeant Major Morris's tale of the monkey's paw. [Summarize]

2. What purpose do Morris's warnings serve? [Infer]

3. What can you conclude about whether Mr. White's first wish was a sensible choice? Explain your answer. [Draw Conclusions]

4. Describe the story's theme. Does the author communicate the theme through plot developments? Explain your thoughts. [Analyze]

5. Think about whether the Whites wasted their last two wishes. What do you think they could have wished for that might have eased the pain of their great loss? Explain. [Synthesize]

6. **BQ** BIG Question Which events in "The Monkey's Paw" did you find most frightening? In what ways did these events add to your enjoyment of the story? [Evaluate]

Vocabulary

Respond to these questions.

1. Which activity would someone be more likely to do **amiably**—empty the trash or feed the dog?

2. Which of these could you **intercept**—a disapproving look or a puppy that is running away?

3. Who would be more likely to wear a **grimace**—someone who is in pain or someone who is asleep?

4. Which of these acts is **sinister**—helping a neighbor or intentionally damaging something valuable?

5. Which of these is more likely to be **inaudible**—a clap of thunder or a whispering child?

6. Which would you consider **oppressive**—extreme heat or a day of fun?

Academic Vocabulary

The man from Maw and Meggins presented Mr. and Mrs. White with a certain sum as **compensation** for their son's death. In the preceding sentence, *compensation* refers to a payment as an equivalent for a loss. Think about what the man gave to the Whites, and then fill in the blank for this statement: _____ was the compensation Maw and Meggins provided the Whites for the loss of their son.

TIP

Inferring
Here are some tips to help you infer. Remember when you infer, you use your reason and experience to guess at what an author does not come right out and say.

- Review Morris's comments about the monkey's paw.

- Review his actions in relation to the monkey's paw.

- Review the author's words about the object.

- Use these clues to figure out what the author wants readers to know about the monkey's paw.

 FOLDABLES Study Organizer Keep track of your ideas about the **BIG Question** in your unit Foldable.

 Literature Online

Selection Resources
For Selection Quizzes, eFlashcards, and Reading-Writing Connection activities, go to glencoe.com and enter QuickPass code GL39770u2.

1. Herbert White says about Morris, "If the tale about the monkey paw is not more truthful than those he has been telling us, we shan't make much out of it." What does Herbert mean, and what attitude is conveyed by his words?

2. When Mr. White hears a knock on the door after the second wish is made, the author describes him as standing "motionless" with "his breath suspended." How does the author's word choice help build tension in this scene?

Review: Character

Authors use diction to convey **characters' personalities** to readers. The words an author uses to describe a character as well as the character's own words and actions show what the character is like.

3. Consider Mr. White's words and actions while playing chess with Herbert. How would you describe Mr. White's personality?

4. Near the end of the story, the author describes Mrs. White as crying out "wildly" and speaking "hysterically" and "feverishly." How does his word choice help you understand Mrs. White's emotional state?

Reading Skill Analyze Plot

5. List the important events that occur in the story's climax and resolution. Explain how you know that each event is part of either the climax or the resolution. Support your answer with details from the story.

Grammar Link

The **present perfect tense** expresses an action or condition that occurred at some indefinite time in the past.

This tense also shows an action or condition that began in the past and continues in the present.

> (Sergeant Morris *has entered* the house. Mr. White *has lived* here for many years.)

The present perfect tense consists of the helping verb *have* or *has* and the past participle of the main verb.

The **past perfect tense** indicates that one past action or condition began and ended before another past action started.

> (Mr. White *had made* another wish before Mrs. White opened the door.)

The past perfect tense consists of the helping verb *had* and the past participle of the main verb.

Practice Look for a sentence in "The Monkey's Paw" that uses present perfect tense. Identify the time period that the sentence describes. Then look for another sentence that uses past perfect tense. Explain how the sentences are different from each other.

Write with Style

Apply Diction Think of an idea for an eerie or suspenseful short story. Write the opening paragraph for the story. Use figurative language that creates an eerie or suspenseful mood.

Comparing Literature

A Retrieved Reformation (short story)
and *A Retrieved Reformation* (graphic story)

BQ **BIG Question**

As you read these two versions of an O. Henry story, think about which version of "A Retrieved Reformation" you enjoy more, the short story or the graphic story.

Literary Elements **Setting and Mood**

Setting is the time and place in which the events of a short story, novel, or drama occur. The setting often helps create an atmosphere, or **mood**. As you read each selection, look for details that describe or illustrate the setting. Think about the atmosphere, or mood, that each setting creates.

Reading Skill **Compare and Contrast**

Most schools have basic things in common—for example, classrooms, lockers, and a playground. However, important details such as the location and the teachers make schools different. When you **compare** two or more things, such as schools, you look for ways they are alike. When you **contrast** them, you look for ways they are different.

You can understand literature better when you compare and contrast literary elements, such as setting. On the following pages, you'll compare and contrast two different ways of using setting in the same story. You may find it helpful to use a chart like the one below to record details about the setting in both versions of the story. Add any other parts of the setting that you think are important.

Setting	Description and mood in short story	Pictures and mood in graphic story
Prison		
Jimmy's apartment above Mike Dolan's café		
Elmore		

Learning Objectives

For pages 266–286

In studying these texts, you will focus on the following objectives:

Literary Study: Comparing settings.

Meet the Authors

O. Henry

O. Henry is the pen name of William Sydney Porter, a colorful character who began writing stories while serving a short prison sentence. He was born in 1862 and died in 1910.

Gary Gianni

Gary Gianni writes graphic novels and stories. He has also written and drawn for Dark Horse Comics and is the creator of the *Monsterman Mysteries*.

 Literature Online

Author Search For more about O. Henry and Gary Gianni, go to glencoe.com and enter QuickPass code GL39770u2.

A Retrieved
REFORMATION

O. Henry

A guard came to the prison shoe shop, where Jimmy Valentine was assiduously stitching uppers,[1] and escorted him to the front office. There the warden handed Jimmy his pardon, which had been signed that morning by the governor. Jimmy took it in a tired kind of way. He had served nearly ten months of a four-year sentence. He had expected to stay only about three months, at the longest. When a man with as many friends on the outside as Jimmy Valentine had is received in the "stir"[2] it is hardly worthwhile to cut his hair.

"Now, Valentine," said the warden, "you'll go out in the morning. Brace up, and make a man of yourself. You're not a bad fellow at heart. Stop cracking safes, and live straight."

"Me?" said Jimmy, in surprise. "Why, I never cracked a safe in my life."

"Oh, no," laughed the warden. "Of course not. Let's see, now. How was it you happened to get sent up on that Springfield job? Was it because you wouldn't prove an alibi for fear of compromising somebody in

Comparing Literature
Notice the important details in the setting of this first scene. What mood does this setting create? Write the details and mood on your comparison chart.

---

1 If you do something **assiduously**, you do it steadily and with care. Jimmy was busy sewing the **uppers**—the top part of shoes—onto the soles.

2 The **stir** is another name for prison.

extremely high-toned society? Or was it simply a case of a mean old jury that had it in for you? It's always one or the other with you innocent victims."

"Me?" said Jimmy, still blankly virtuous. "Why, warden, I never was in Springfield in my life!"

"Take him back, Cronin," smiled the warden, "and fix him up with outgoing clothes. Unlock him at seven in the morning, and let him come to the bull-pen. Better think over my advice, Valentine."

At a quarter past seven on the next morning Jimmy stood in the warden's outer office. He had on a suit of the villainously fitting, ready-made clothes and a pair of stiff, squeaky shoes that the state furnishes to its discharged compulsory[3] guests.

The clerk handed him a railroad ticket and the five-dollar bill with which the law expected him to rehabilitate himself into good citizenship and prosperity. The warden gave him a cigar, and shook hands. Valentine, 9762, was chronicled on the books "Pardoned by Governor," and Mr. James Valentine walked out into the sunshine.

Disregarding the song of the birds, the waving green trees, and the smell of the flowers, Jimmy headed straight for a restaurant. There he tasted the first sweet joys of liberty in the shape of a broiled chicken and a bottle of white wine—followed by a cigar a grade better than the one the warden had given him. From there he proceeded leisurely to the depot. He tossed a quarter into the hat of a blind man sitting by the door, and boarded his train. Three hours set him down in a little town near the state line. He went to the café of one Mike Dolan and shook hands with Mike, who was alone behind the bar.

"Sorry we couldn't make it sooner, Jimmy, me boy," said Mike. "But we had that protest from Springfield to buck against, and the governor nearly balked. Feeling all right?"

Comparing Literature
What new details about the setting has the narrator revealed at this point? In what ways has the mood changed?

---

3 A **compulsory** (kəm pul´sər ē´) guest is someone who is forced or required to be at a certain place.

"Fine," said Jimmy. "Got my key?"

He got his key and went upstairs, unlocking the door of a room at the rear. Everything was just as he had left it. There on the floor was still Ben Price's collar-button that had been torn from that eminent detective's shirt-band when they had overpowered Jimmy to arrest him.

Pulling out from the wall a folding-bed, Jimmy slid back a panel in the wall and dragged out a dust-covered suitcase. He opened this and gazed fondly at the finest set of burglar's tools in the East. It was a complete set, made of specially tempered steel, the latest designs in drills, punches, braces and bits, jimmies, clamps, and augers, with two or three novelties invented by Jimmy himself, in which he took pride. Over nine hundred dollars they had cost him to have made at _____, a place where they make such things for the profession.

In half an hour Jimmy went downstairs and through the café. He was now dressed in tasteful and well-fitting clothes, and carried his dusted and cleaned suitcase in his hand.

"Got anything on?" asked Mike Dolan, genially.

"Me?" said Jimmy, in a puzzled tone. "I don't understand. I'm representing the New York Amalgamated Short Snap Biscuit Cracker and Frazzled Wheat Company."

This statement delighted Mike to such an extent that Jimmy had to take a seltzer-and-milk on the spot. He never touched "hard" drinks.

A week after the release of Valentine, 9762, there was a neat job of safe-burglary done in Richmond, Indiana, with no clue to the author. A scant eight hundred dollars was all that was secured. Two weeks after that a patented, improved, burglar-proof safe in Logansport was opened like a cheese to the tune of fifteen hundred dollars, currency; securities and silver[4] untouched. That

<aside>
Comparing Literature
Notice the important details in Jimmy's room. What atmosphere does this setting create?
</aside>

---

4 *Currency* is paper money, *securities* are stocks and bonds, and *silver* is silver coins. Valentine is careful not to steal securities that could be difficult to sell or silver that could be heavy and attention-getting. He doesn't want to get caught.

began to interest the rogue catchers. Then an old-fashioned bank safe in Jefferson City became active and threw out of its crater an eruption of banknotes amounting to five thousand dollars. The losses were now high enough to bring the matter up into Ben Price's class of work. By comparing notes, a remarkable similarity in the methods of the burglaries was noticed. Ben Price investigated the scenes of the robberies, and was heard to remark: "That's Dandy Jim Valentine's autograph. He's resumed business. Look at that combination knob—jerked out as easy as pulling up a radish in wet weather. He's got the only clamps that can do it. And look how clean those tumblers were punched out! Jimmy never has to drill but one hole. Yes, I guess I want Mr. Valentine. He'll do his bit next time without any short-time or clemency foolishness."

Ben Price knew Jimmy's habits. He had learned them while working up the Springfield case. Long jumps, quick getaways, no confederates,[5] and a taste for good society—these ways had helped Mr. Valentine to become noted as a successful dodger of retribution.[6] It was given out that Ben Price had taken up the trail of the elusive cracksman, and other people with burglar-proof safes felt more at ease.

One afternoon Jimmy Valentine and his suitcase climbed out of the mailhack[7] in Elmore, a little town five miles off the railroad down in the blackjack country of Arkansas. Jimmy, looking like an athletic young senior just home from college, went down the board sidewalk toward the hotel.

A young lady crossed the street, passed him at the corner, and entered a door over which was the sign "The Elmore Bank." Jimmy Valentine looked into her

Comparing Literature
Describe the change in setting. Does the mood of the story change also?

---

5 **Confederates**, here, are friends or accomplices.

6 **Retribution** (ret´rə bū´shən) is punishment for past evil deeds.

7 The **mailhack** was a horse-drawn carriage that delivered mail and carried passengers.

eyes, forgot what he was, and became another man. She lowered her eyes and colored slightly. Young men of Jimmy's style and looks were scarce in Elmore.

Jimmy collared a boy that was loafing on the steps of the bank as if he were one of the stockholders, and began to ask him questions about the town, feeding him dimes at intervals. By and by the young lady came out, looking royally unconscious of the young man with the suitcase, and went her way.

"Isn't that young lady Miss Polly Simpson?" asked Jimmy, with specious guile.[8]

"Naw," said the boy. "She's Annabel Adams. Her pa owns this bank. What'd you come to Elmore for? Is that a gold watch-chain? I'm going to get a bulldog. Got any more dimes?"

Jimmy went to the Planters' Hotel, registered as Ralph D. Spencer, and engaged a room. He leaned on the desk and declared his platform to the clerk. He said he had come to Elmore to look for a location to go into business. How was the shoe business, now, in the town? He had thought of the shoe business. Was there an opening?

The clerk was impressed by the clothes and manner of Jimmy. He, himself, was something of a pattern of fashion to the thinly gilded youth of Elmore, but he now perceived his shortcomings. While trying to figure out Jimmy's manner of tying his four-in-hand[9] he cordially gave information.

Yes, there ought to be a good opening in the shoe line. There wasn't an exclusive shoe store in the place. The

---

8 If something is **specious** (spē′ shəs), it seems true but isn't. Someone who has **guile** (gīl) is sly and dishonest. Jimmy wants to look as if he's asking an innocent question, even though he's not.

9 A **four-in-hand** is a necktie.

dry-goods and general stores handled them. Business in all lines was fairly good. Hoped Mr. Spencer would decide to locate in Elmore. He would find it a pleasant town to live in, and the people very sociable.

Mr. Spencer thought he would stop over in the town a few days and look over the situation. No, the clerk needn't call the boy. He would carry up his suitcase, himself; it was rather heavy.

Mr. Ralph Spencer, the phoenix[10] that arose from Jimmy Valentine's ashes—ashes left by the flame of a sudden and alterative[11] attack of love—remained in Elmore, and prospered. He opened a shoe store and secured a good run of trade.

Socially he was also a success and made many friends. And he accomplished the wish of his heart. He met Miss Annabel Adams, and became more and more captivated by her charms.

At the end of a year the situation of Mr. Ralph Spencer was this: he had won the respect of the community, his shoe store was flourishing, and he and Annabel were engaged to be married in two weeks. Mr. Adams, the typical, plodding, country banker, approved of Spencer. Annabel's pride in him almost equaled her affection. He was as much at home in the family of Mr. Adams and that of Annabel's married sister as if he were already a member.

One day Jimmy sat down in his room and wrote this letter, which he mailed to the safe address of one of his old friends in St. Louis:

DEAR OLD PAL,
I want you to be at Sullivan's place, in Little Rock, next Wednesday night, at nine o'clock. I want you to wind up some little matters for me. And, also, I want to make you a present of my kit of tools. I know you'll be glad to get them—

Comparing Literature Think about the ways that Elmore is different from other places Jimmy has been. In what ways do you think the setting might change Jimmy's ways?

---

10 A *phoenix* (fē′nix) was a mythological bird with a lifespan of five hundred years. After that time it built a great fire and died in the flames, but a new phoenix came out of the fire. The author is comparing Jimmy in his new life to the phoenix arising from the ashes.

11 *Alterative* (ôl′tə rā′tiv) means "causing or capable of causing change."

you couldn't duplicate the lot for a thousand dollars. Say, Billy, I've quit the old business—a year ago. I've got a nice store. I'm making an honest living, and I'm going to marry the finest girl on earth two weeks from now. It's the only life, Billy—the straight one. I wouldn't touch a dollar of another man's money now for a million. After I get married I'm going to sell out and go West, where there won't be so much danger of having old scores brought up against me. I tell you, Billy, she's an angel. She believes in me; and I wouldn't do another crooked thing for the whole world. Be sure to be at Sully's, for I must see you. I'll bring along the tools with me.

Your old friend,
JIMMY

On the Monday night after Jimmy wrote this letter, Ben Price jogged unobtrusively into Elmore in a **livery buggy.** He lounged about town in his quiet way until he found out what he wanted to know. From the drugstore across the street from Spencer's shoe store he got a good look at Ralph D. Spencer.

"Going to marry the banker's daughter are you, Jimmy?" said Ben to himself, softly. "Well, I don't know!"

The next morning Jimmy took breakfast at the Adamses. He was going to Little Rock that day to order his wedding suit and buy something nice for Annabel. That would be the first time he had left town since he came to Elmore. It had been more than a year now since those last professional "jobs," and he thought he could safely venture out.

After breakfast quite a family party went down together—Mr. Adams, Annabel, Jimmy, and Annabel's married sister with her two little girls, aged five and nine. They came by the hotel where Jimmy still boarded, and he ran up to his room and brought along his suitcase. Then they went on to the bank. There stood Jimmy's horse and buggy and Dolph Gibson, who was going to drive him over to the railroad station.

All went well inside the high, carved oak railings into the banking room—Jimmy included, for Mr. Adams's

Comparing Literature What does this proposed change of setting mean to Jimmy?

Visual Vocabulary

A **livery buggy** is a hired horse-drawn carriage.

future son-in-law was welcome anywhere. The clerks were pleased to be greeted by the good-looking, agreeable young man who was going to marry Miss Annabel. Jimmy set his suitcase down. Annabel, whose heart was bubbling with happiness and lively youth, put on Jimmy's hat and picked up the suitcase. "Wouldn't I make a nice drummer?"[12] said Annabel. "My! Ralph, how heavy it is. Feels like it was full of gold bricks."

"Lot of nickel-plated shoehorns in there," said Jimmy, coolly, "that I'm going to return. Thought I'd save express charges by taking them up. I'm getting awfully economical."

The Elmore Bank had just put in a new safe and vault. Mr. Adams was very proud of it, and insisted on an inspection by everyone. The vault was a small one, but it had a new patented door. It fastened with three solid steel bolts thrown simultaneously[13] with a single handle, and had a time lock. Mr. Adams beamingly explained its workings to Mr. Spencer, who showed a courteous but not too intelligent interest. The two children, May and Agatha, were delighted by the shining metal and funny clock and knobs.

While they were thus engaged Ben Price sauntered in and leaned on his elbow, looking casually inside between the railings. He told the teller that he didn't want anything; he was just waiting for a man he knew.

Suddenly there was a scream or two from the women, and a commotion. Unperceived by the elders, May, the nine-year-old girl, in a spirit of play, had shut Agatha in the vault. She had then shot the bolts and turned the knob of the combination as she had seen Mr. Adams do.

The old banker sprang to the handle and tugged at it for a moment. "The door can't be opened," he groaned. "The clock hasn't been wound nor the combination set."

Agatha's mother screamed again, hysterically.

"Hush!" said Mr. Adams, raising his trembling hand.

---

12 A **drummer** is a traveling salesperson.

13 **Simultaneously** (sī′məl ta′nē əs lē) means "at the same time."

"All be quiet for a moment. Agatha!" he called as loudly as he could. "Listen to me." During the following silence they could just hear the faint sound of the child wildly shrieking in the dark vault in a panic of terror.

"My precious darling!" wailed the mother. "She will die of fright! Open the door! Oh, break it open! Can't you men do something?"

"There isn't a man nearer than Little Rock who can open that door," said Mr. Adams, in a shaky voice. "My God! Spencer, what shall we do? That child—she can't stand it long in there. There isn't enough air, and, besides, she'll go into convulsions from fright."

Agatha's mother, frantic now, beat the door of the vault with her hands. Somebody wildly suggested dynamite. Annabel turned to Jimmy, her large eyes full of anguish, but not yet despairing. To a woman nothing seems quite impossible to the powers of the man she worships.

"Can't you do something, Ralph—try, won't you?"

He looked at her with a queer, soft smile on his lips and in his keen eyes.

"Annabel," he said, "give me that rose you are wearing, will you?"

Hardly believing that she had heard him aright, she unpinned the bud from the bosom of her dress, and placed it in his hand. Jimmy stuffed it into his vest pocket, threw off his coat and pulled up his shirt sleeves. With that act Ralph D. Spencer passed away and Jimmy Valentine took his place.

"Get away from the door, all of you," he commanded, shortly.

He set his suitcase on the table, and opened it out flat. From that time on he seemed to be unconscious of the presence of anyone else. He laid out the shining, queer implements swiftly and orderly, whistling softly to himself as he always did when at work. In a deep silence and immovable, the others watched him as if under a spell.

Comparing Literature
In what way might the details of this setting help you predict what might happen next?

Comparing Literature In what ways have the setting and mood changed in the past few paragraphs?

In a minute Jimmy's pet drill was biting smoothly into the steel door. In ten minutes—breaking his own burglarious record—he threw back the bolts and opened the door.

Agatha, almost collapsed, but safe, was gathered into her mother's arms.

Jimmy Valentine put on his coat, and walked outside the railings toward the front door. As he went he thought he heard a faraway voice that he once knew call "Ralph!" But he never hesitated. At the door a big man stood somewhat in his way.

"Hello, Ben!" said Jimmy, still with his strange smile. "Got around at last, have you? Well, let's go. I don't know that it makes much difference, now."

And then Ben Price acted rather strangely.

"Guess you're mistaken, Mr. Spencer," he said. "Don't believe I recognize you. Your buggy's waiting for you, ain't it?"

And Ben Price turned and strolled down the street. ✍

BQ **BIG Question**

What important lessons did you learn from the story?

View the Art In what ways does this town remind you of Elmore? Support your answer with specific details from the art.

218977

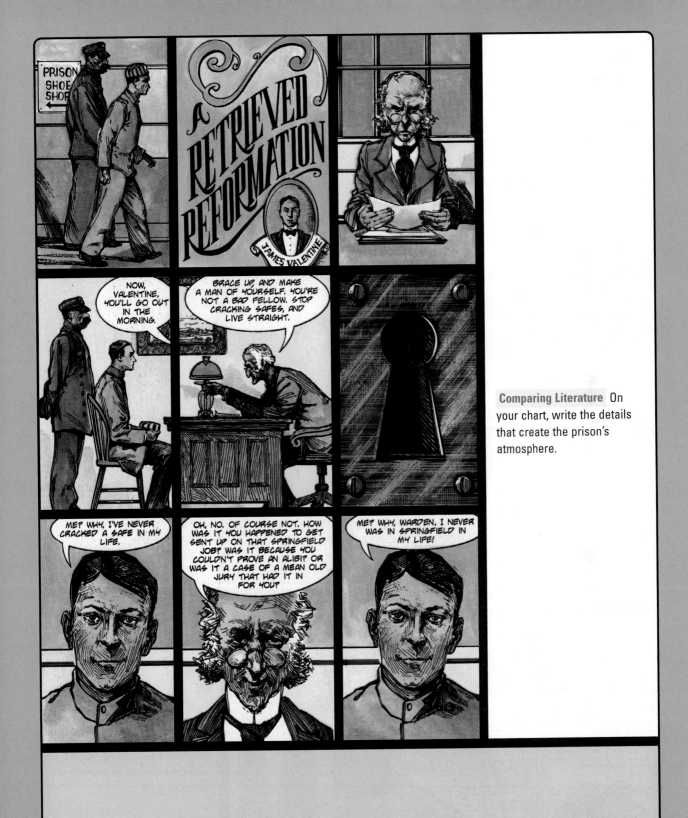

Comparing Literature On your chart, write the details that create the prison's atmosphere.

TAKE HIM BACK, CRONIN, AND FIX HIM UP WITH OUTGOING CLOTHES. UNLOCK HIM AT SEVEN IN THE MORNING.

BETTER THINK OVER MY ADVICE, VALENTINE.

THE NEXT MORNING, THE CLERK HANDED HIM A RAILROAD TICKET AND THE FIVE-DOLLAR BILL WITH WHICH THE LAW EXPECTED HIM TO REHABILITATE HIMSELF INTO GOOD CITIZENSHIP AND PROSPERITY. DISREGARDING THE SONG OF THE BIRDS, JIMMY HEADED STRAIGHT FOR A RESTAURANT. THERE HE TASTED THE FIRST JOYS OF LIBERTY IN THE SHAPE OF A BROILED CHICKEN AND A BOTTLE OF WINE.

FROM THERE HE PROCEEDED LEISURELY TO THE DEPOT. HE TOSSED A QUARTER INTO THE HAT OF A BLIND MAN, AND BOARDED HIS TRAIN.

THREE HOURS SET HIM DOWN IN A LITTLE TOWN WHERE HE WENT TO THE CAFÉ OF ONE MIKE DOLAN.

JIMMY GOT HIS KEY AND WENT UPSTAIRS.

SORRY WE COULDN'T MAKE IT SOONER, JIMMY, ME BOY. BUT WE HAD THAT PROTEST FROM SPRINGFIELD.

EVERYTHING WAS JUST AS HE HAD LEFT IT.

THERE ON THE FLOOR WAS STILL BEN PRICE'S COLLAR-BUTTON THAT HAD BEEN TORN FROM THAT EMINENT DETECTIVE'S SHIRT WHEN THEY HAD OVERPOWERED JIMMY TO ARREST HIM.

JIMMY SLID BACK A PANEL IN THE WALL AND DRAGGED OUT A SUITCASE. HE GAZED FONDLY AT THE FINEST SET OF BURGLAR'S TOOLS IN THE EAST. IT WAS A COMPLETE SET, MADE OF TEMPERED STEEL, THE LATEST DESIGNS IN DRILLS, PUNCHES, BRACES AND BITS, JIMMIES, CLAMPS AND AUGERS...

...WITH TWO OR THREE NOVELTIES INVENTED BY JIMMY HIMSELF.

In half an hour, Jimmy went downstairs.

Got anything on?

Me? I'm representing the New York Amalgamated Short Snap Biscuit Cracker and Frazzled Wheat Company.

A week after the release of Valentine, there was a neat job of safeburglary done in Richmond, Indiana, with no clue to the author.

Two weeks after that, a patented, improved, burglar-proof safe in Logansport was opened like a cheese.

Then a bank in Jefferson City threw out of its crater an eruption of bank-notes amounting to five thousand dollars.

The losses were now high enough to bring the matter up to Ben Price's class of work.

BEN PRICE

It had been given out that he had taken up the trail of the elusive cracksman, and people with burglar-proof safes felt more at ease.

That's dandy Jim's autograph. He's resumed business.

Look at that combination knob-- jerked out as easy as pulling up a radish in wet weather.

Yes, I guess I want Mister Valentine. He'll do his bit next time without any short-time or clemency foolishness.

Comparing Literature
Describe the settings you see on this page. How do the details and mood of these settings help develop the plot of this graphic story?

Comparing Literature Look at the street scene. On your chart, write the details that tell you about the town and the time period. Think about the ways that this setting contributes to the mood of the story.

Comparing Literature On this page, how does the artist show the story's time period? Think about the details he emphasizes.

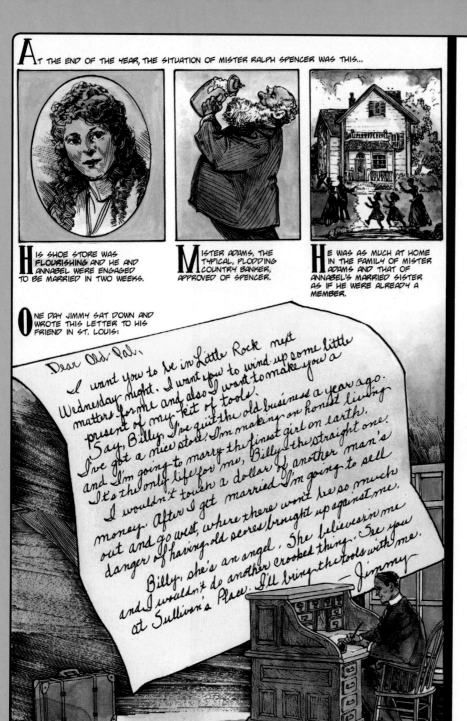

AT THE END OF THE YEAR, THE SITUATION OF MISTER RALPH SPENCER WAS THIS...

HIS SHOE STORE WAS FLOURISHING AND HE AND ANNABEL WERE ENGAGED TO BE MARRIED IN TWO WEEKS.

MISTER ADAMS, THE TYPICAL, PLODDING COUNTRY BANKER, APPROVED OF SPENCER.

HE WAS AS MUCH AT HOME IN THE FAMILY OF MISTER ADAMS AND THAT OF ANNABEL'S MARRIED SISTER AS IF HE WERE ALREADY A MEMBER.

ONE DAY JIMMY SAT DOWN AND WROTE THIS LETTER TO HIS FRIEND IN ST. LOUIS:

Dear Old Pal,

I want you to be in Little Rock next Wednesday night. I want you to wind up some little matters for me and also I want to make you a present of my kit of tools.

Say, Billy, I've quit the old business a year ago. I've got a nice store. I'm making an honest living and I'm going to marry the finest girl on earth. It's the only life for me, Billy, the straight one. I wouldn't touch a dollar of another man's money. After I get married I'm going to sell out and go west, where there won't be so much danger of having old scores brought up against me.

Billy, she's an angel. She believes in me and I wouldn't do another crooked thing. See you at Sullivan's Place. I'll bring the tools with me.

— Jimmy

Comparing Literature
Notice the main details of Jimmy's room. Why do you think the artist chose to include each of these details?

ONE MONDAY NIGHT AFTER JIMMY WROTE THIS LETTER, BEN PRICE JOGGED UNOBTRUSIVELY INTO ELMORE.

HE LOUNGED ABOUT THE TOWN IN HIS QUIET WAY UNTIL HE FOUND OUT WHAT HE WANTED TO KNOW.

GOING TO MARRY THE BANKER'S DAUGHTER ARE YOU, JIMMY? WELL, I DON'T KNOW.

JIMMY WAS GOING TO LITTLE ROCK THAT DAY TO ORDER HIS WEDDING-SUIT. QUITE A FAMILY PARTY WENT DOWNTOWN TOGETHER WHERE JIMMY'S HORSE AND BUGGY STOOD READY TO TAKE HIM TO THE RAILROAD STATION.

ALL WENT INSIDE THE BANK-- MISTER ADAMS, ANNABEL AND ANNABEL'S MARRIED SISTER WITH HER TWO LITTLE GIRLS. JIMMY WAS INCLUDED, FOR MISTER ADAMS' FUTURE SON-IN-LAW WAS WELCOME ANYWHERE.

MY! RALPH, HOW HEAVY THIS SUITCASE IS.

LOTS OF NICKEL-PLATED SHOE-HORNS IN THERE.

THE BANK HAD JUST PUT IN A NEW SAFE. MISTER ADAMS WAS VERY PROUD OF IT, AND INSISTED ON AN INSPECTION BY EVERYONE.

THIS VAULT IS A SMALL ONE, BUT IT HAS A NEW PATENTED DOOR. IT FASTENS WITH THREE SOLID STEEL BOLTS...

...AND IT HAS A TIME-LOCK.

Comparing Literature Look at the last frame in the bottom row. The vault is described as "a small one," but its opening appears to be twice as tall as the children. Why do you think the artist drew it this way?

Comparing Literature Think of ways that the scene in the fourth frame is similar to and different from the way you pictured the same scene in the original version of the story.

Comparing Literature

Now use the unit Big Question to compare and contrast the two versions of "A Retrieved Reformation." With a group of classmates discuss questions such as

- What do you get out of each version of "A Retrieved Reformation"?

- In what ways do the authors communicate the main message or theme in each story?

- Which version do you like better? Why?

Support each answer with evidence from the stories.

Literary Elements **Setting and Mood**

Use the details you wrote in your comparison chart to compare and contrast the settings in the two versions of "A Retrieved Reformation." With a partner, answer the following questions.

1. In what ways is the setting similar in the original story and in the graphic version? For example, you might think about the prison scenes or the bank robbery scenes. Choose two scenes that stand out for you. In what ways are the two scenes similar in the original and in the graphic version? Discuss similar details, feelings, or any other ways you think the presentations are similar.

2. In what ways are the same two scenes different in the original and in the graphic version? Discuss differences in details, feelings, or any other ways you think the presentations are different.

Write to Compare

In one or two paragraphs, compare the ways in which both O. Henry and Gianni present the setting in ways that show changes in Jimmy. You might focus on these ideas as you write:

- Choose one or two parts of the setting you feel contribute most to Jimmy's change.

- Explain the ways in which each writer uses these parts of the setting to show that changes that are occurring in the character of Jimmy.

- Explain whether reading the same story in two different forms, short story and graphic story, affected your feelings about Jimmy and the way his life changes.

 Writing Tip

An **adjective** is a word that modifies, or describes, a noun or a pronoun. Use precise, colorful adjectives as you describe O. Henry's written setting and Gianni's graphic setting. For example: *The picture of Jimmy's mysterious kit of complex tools made a powerful impression on me.*

 Literature Online

Selection Resources
For Selection Quizzes, eFlashcards, and Reading-Writing Connection activities, go to glencoe.com and enter QuickPass code GL39770u2.

Vocabulary Workshop

Word Parts

Learning Objectives

For page 287

In this workshop, you will focus on the following objective:

Vocabulary: Understanding prefixes, suffixes, and roots of words.

Connection to Literature

"There was no reply; the old woman's face was white, her eyes staring, and her breath inaudible."

—W. W. Jacobs, "The Monkey's Paw"

You can sometimes find clues to a word's meaning by looking at its parts. The **root** is the main part of a word. An **affix** is a part added at the beginning (**prefix**) or the end (**suffix**) of a word that changes its meaning. For example, the root of *audible* is *aud,* meaning "to hear." The prefix *in-* means "not," and the suffix *-ible* means "can be done." Thus *inaudible* means "cannot be heard."

Here are other words from "The Monkey's Paw."

Word	Word Parts	Meaning
intercept	*inter-:* between, among *cept:* take, receive	to take or seize something between one place and another
hospitable	*hospit:* host, guest *-able:* quality or state of	the quality of being friendly toward guests
sympathy	*sym-:* together *path:* feeling, disease *y:* quality or state of (used to form a noun)	the act of sharing the feelings of another person

TRY IT: Use the chart above to help you answer each question.

1. What prefix could you add to the word *hospitable* to form a word that means "unfriendly toward guests"?
2. If the suffix *-ology* means "study or science of," what does the word *pathology* mean?
3. What does the word *international* mean?

Tip

Vocabulary Terms The root is the main part of a word. If it's a complete word, it may be called the base word. You change the meaning of a root or base word when you add a prefix or a suffix.

Test-taking Tip When you come across a new word, check whether you recognize its root and note any affixes. Prefixes sometimes change a root word to its opposite. Suffixes can signal parts of speech.

 Literature Online

Vocabulary For more vocabulary practice, go to glencoe.com and enter QuickPass code GL39770u2.

Functional Document

Conferences are meetings that address the needs of a group of people through a schedule of activities. In this workshop, you will write a memo that includes a schedule and directions that will help you think about the Unit 2 Big Question: Reading: What's in It for You?

Review the writing prompt, or assignment, below. Then read the Writing Plan. It will tell you what you need to do to write your memo.

Writing Assignment

A functional document gives readers useful facts, instructions, and other types of information for a specific purpose. Write a memo announcing a day-long sales conference to introduce a new product. Include a schedule that lists the day's activities as well as travel directions to the conference location. The audience, those reading your document, should be the sales staff who will attend the conference.

Prewrite

When planning a conference, you must consider its purpose, the number of people who will attend, and the location. The scheduled activities and directions must be presented in a clear order.

Gather Ideas

Brainstorm a list of new products in a field that interests you. Then do research on the Internet to find out what other products are being developed in that field. Make another list of locations in or near your hometown for a sales conference to introduce your new product. Use the Internet to help you find suitable locations.

Choose a Product and Place

Select the product that interests you most and the place that would be best suited to presenting it.

Partner Talk With a partner, create a list of activities to introduce the product. Then work together to write two sentences: one that states why you chose the product and the location you did, and another that summarizes the activities planned for the sales conference.

I have selected _____ as the product to introduce and _____ as the location for a sales conference because _____.

A sales conference to introduce this product will include the following activities: _____.

> ## Writing Plan
>
> - Make the purpose of the document clear to the audience.
> - Present information in logical and effective organizational patterns.
> - Include supporting details to clarify information and interest the reader.
> - Use visual aids to clarify and add to the information.
> - Use text features to highlight and organize information.

 Prewriting Tip

As you conduct your research, be sure to think about what important details you should include that will be helpful to your audience.

Get Organized

Make an invitation chart that gives the 5Ws and H—the *who, what, where, when, why,* and *how*—of the sales meeting.

Now make a chart of directions to the location. Divide the directions into legs. Conduct research to get specific details for the chart.

Directions and Map Chart		
Details of Trip	**Leg 1**	**Leg 2**
Starting Point:	Baltimore, MD	York, PA
Ending Point:	York, PA	Lancaster, PA
Distance:	55 miles	
Cardinal/Ordinal Direction:		
Streets or Highways:		

Draft

Organize your ideas and add more details to your writing. Use the following skills to develop your draft.

Get It On Paper

- Review your notes on your product and conference location.
- Your meeting schedule should only cover the events for one day. Open with a statement to announce the conference. Follow with the planned activities relating to the 5Ws and H.
- Below the schedule, write your travel directions. Number each leg in sequential order.
- Draw the information in the directions on a rough sketch of a map.
- Don't worry about spelling, grammar, or punctuation right now.

Develop Your Draft

1. Keep the **purpose** and **audience** of your memo in mind as you write.

> **To:** Omega Office Products Sales Staff
>
> Mark your calendars now for the introduction of Omega Office Products' newest creation.

2. Use the type of **organization** that suits each part of your memo: for example, sequence for the directions.

> 1. From Baltimore, head north on I-83.
> 2. Follow I-83 N to Pennsylvania exit 19.

Literature Online

Writing and Research For prewriting, drafting, and revising tools, go to glencoe.com and enter QuickPass code GL39770u2.

Sequence As you write the directions to the conference center, make sure you are putting them in the order in which the steps will occur, and number each step.

TRY IT

Analyzing Cartoons
In this cartoon, which convention of language does Redondo ignore? With a partner, discuss what the man's reaction tells you about the importance of following those conventions.

©Zits Partnership. Reprint with Permission of King Features Syndicate, Inc.

3. Include **supporting details** that clarify information.

> At the third traffic light (car dealership on the corner), turn right onto US-30 E.

4. Make sure your **visual aids** help your audience understand the document. Match the map exactly with the directions and mark it clearly.

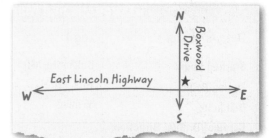

5. Use **text features** to make information clear. Add headings and map symbols such as a direction compass and distance scale.

> How to Get There.

Apply Good Writing Traits: Conventions

Conventions are the rules of language—grammar, usage, spelling, punctuation, capitalization, and paragraphing. Following the rules of language makes your writing easier for others to understand.

Read the following sentences from "How to Fix a Flat Tire." How do the conventions help you understand the directions?

> Use the sandpaper or metal scraper that comes in your tire repair kit.

> Sand or scrape the area all around the hole in your tire. This is called "roughing" the area.

> It's important to wait for the glue to dry *before* you put the patch on.

As you draft your memo, pay attention to the rules of language. After you finish, read your draft and ask yourself, "Did I properly use conventions to make my ideas easier to understand?"

Analyze a Student Model

MEMO

To: Omega Office Products Sales Staff

Mark your calendars now for the introduction of Omega Office Products' newest creation.

What: New-Product Sales Conference

Where: Boxwood Conference Center, Lancaster, PA

When: Saturday, November 22, 2008, 8AM–5PM

Why: Hear about the Omega X635-1 Digital 3-in-1 Scanner/Fax/Copier and discuss sales strategies for the product

Preliminary Schedule

8:00—Introduction of staff

8:30—Presentation of product features and technology

12:00—Lunch break

1:00—Sales strategies activities

3:00—Q & A, closing comments

How to Get There

1. From Baltimore, head north on I-83. After about 9 miles, you'll pass the intersection with I-695. Continue on I-83 toward Towson/York, PA.

2. Follow I-83 N to Pennsylvania exit 19 (Market Street/PA-462 E).

3. At the third traffic light (car dealership on the corner), turn right onto US-30 E.

4. Follow US-30 northeast for about 26 miles to Lancaster, PA.

5. After US-30 becomes East Lincoln Hwy, continue east for three more miles. Turn left onto Boxwood Drive.

6. Follow Boxwood Drive 1/4 mile, and you will see Boxwood Conference Center (blue star on the map) on the right.

Purpose and Audience
The audience for this memo is the sales staff and the purpose is to learn about the new copier.

Organizational Pattern
The schedule is organized chronologically.

Supporting Details
Be specific. Exact locations and ordinal directions help your audience follow directions.

Visual Aids
The map should provide a visual that supports the written directions.

Text Features
Map symbols help your audience read the map.

Reading-Writing Connections Think about the writing techniques that you have just learned and try them out in a memo of your own.

Revise

Now it's time to revise your draft so your ideas really shine. Revising is what makes good writing great, and great writing takes work!

Peer Review Trade drafts with a partner. Use the chart below to review your partner's draft by answering the questions in the *What to do* column. Talk about your peer review after you have glanced at each other's drafts and written down the answers to the questions. Next, follow the suggestions in the *How to do it* column to revise your draft.

Revising Plan

What to do	How to do it	Example
Are the purpose and audience of your document clear?	Include the 5Ws and H in your invitation.	‸To: Omega Office Products Sales Staff: **Mark your calendars now for the introduction of Omega Office Products' newest creation.**
Is the organization presented in a clear and logical way?	Organize the memo by considering the importance of the information, the chronological order of the schedule, and the spatial order of the map.	Why: Meet the Omega X635-1 Digital 3-in-1 Scanner/Fax/Copier and discuss marketing strategies What: New-Product Conference Where: Boxwood Conference Center, Lancaster, PA When: Saturday, November 22, 2008
Will your audience know where to go and what to expect?	Use precise words and include all important details.	4. Follow US-30 northeast ‸for about 26 miles to Lancaster, PA.
Does your visual aid agree with your written directions?	Read your written directions while following your map.	5. The Boxwood Conference Center is on the ~~left~~ ‸right.
Is it clear where one section ends and the next begins?	Separate the parts of your memo with headings.	‸Preliminary Schedule 8:00—Introduction of staff

Edit and Proofread

For your final draft, read your memo one sentence at a time. The **Editing and Proofreading Checklist** inside the back cover of this book can help you spot errors. Use this resource to help you make any necessary corrections.

Grammar Focus: Capitalization

Capitalize a proper noun, which is the name of a particular person, place, thing, or idea. Words that indicate particular sections of the country are proper nouns and should be capitalized. However, words that simply indicate direction are not proper nouns, so they should not be automatically capitalized.

Problem: It's not clear whether a word is a proper noun or a common noun.

Omega Office products

Solution: Capitalize the name of a particular thing, in this case, the company.

Omega Office Products

Problem: A particular place is not capitalized.

Follow I-83 to pennsylvania exit 19

Solution: Capitalize the name of a particular place.

Follow I-83 to Pennsylvania exit 19.

Problem: A direction is capitalized as if it were a geographic area.

Continue East for three miles.

Solution: Use a lowercase letter for a direction.

Continue east for three miles.

Present

It's almost time to share your writing with others. Write your memo neatly in print or cursive on a separate sheet of paper. If you have access to a computer, type your memo and check your spelling. Save your document to a disk and print it out. Finally, add your map.

Grammar Tip

Proper Names Double-check proper nouns to make sure you've spelled the names of people, places, and things correctly.

Presenting Tip

If you have prepared your document electronically, send it to friends by e-mail, as if they are the sales staff you are asking to attend the conference. Scan the map and send it as an attachment.

Literature Online

Writing and Research For editing and publishing tools, go to glencoe.com and enter QuickPass code GL39770u2.

Speaking, Listening, and Viewing Workshop

Informative Presentation

Activity

Connect to Your Writing Deliver an informative presentation to your classmates. You might want to adapt the schedule in the memo you wrote for the Writing Workshop on pages 288–293. Remember that you focused on the Unit 2 Big Question: Reading: What's in It for You?

Plan Your Presentation

Reread the schedule in your memo and highlight the sections you want to emphasize in your presentation. Just like your written memo, your informative presentation should be clear about the 5Ws and H of the schedule.

Rehearse Your Presentation

Practice your presentation several times. Try rehearsing in front of a mirror so you can watch your movements and facial expressions. Post an enlarged version of your schedule and an image of the new product to refer to as you deliver your presentation. Make sure to practice your informative presentation enough times so that you won't lose eye contact with your audience.

Deliver Your Presentation

- Speak clearly and precisely.
- Use visual aids to clarify your information.
- Change the tone or volume of your voice to communicate emotions or add emphasis.
- Change the pace of your speaking, slowing down to help clarify potentially confusing parts of the presentation.

Listen to Learn

Take notes as you listen to another student's presentation to make sure you understand the presentation. Use the following question frames to learn more about the information from the presenter:

- I was confused about one part. Can you please review _____?
- I was interested in _____. Can you tell me more about that?
- I think the purpose of this conference is _____. Is that correct?

Presentation Checklist

Answer the following questions to evaluate your presentation:

- ❏ Did you speak clearly and precisely?
- ❏ Did you use visual aids to help clarify information?
- ❏ Did you vary the tone, pace, and volume of your voice to add interest to and clarify points in the presentation?
- ❏ Did you make eye contact with your audience?

LOG ON ▶ **Literature** Online

Speaking, Listening, and Viewing For project ideas, templates, and presentation tips, go to glencoe.com and enter QuickPass code GL39770u2.

Answer the BIG Question

In Unit 2, you explored the Big Question through reading, writing, speaking, and listening. Now it's time for you to complete one of the Unit Challenges below with your answer to the Big Question.

READING:
What's in It for You?

Learning Objectives

For page 295

In this assignment, you will focus on the following objective:

Writing: Creating a reading chart or writing a reading plan.

Use the notes you took in your Unit 2 **Foldable** to complete the Unit Challenge you have chosen.

Before you present your Unit Challenge, be sure it meets the requirements below. Use this first plan if you choose to make a reading chart, describing what you like to read.

On Your Own Activity: Create a Reading Chart

❏ What do you enjoy reading? Books? Newspapers? Online magazines? Make a list of your preferences.

❏ Make a chart with the headings *What I Read, Why I Read It,* and *What I Learn from It.* Fill in the chart using your list.

❏ In a small group, take turns presenting your charts.

❏ Think about your hobbies, interests, and goals. With a partner, discuss what you want to read in the future.

Use this second plan if you choose to write a reading plan to help you develop your interests and reach your goals.

Group Activity: Write a Reading Plan

❏ Work with a small group to create a list of goals you share.

❏ Talk with your group members about what books, authors, or resources might help you reach your goals.

❏ Create a web diagram for one of your goals. Show your goal at the center and the different kinds of resources you would use in boxes around it.

❏ Present your group's web to the class.

Independent Reading

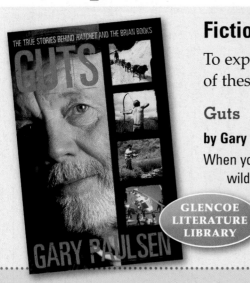

Fiction

To explore the Big Question in other works, choose one of these books from your school or local library.

Guts

by Gary Paulsen

When young Brian takes off in a plane to join his father in the Canadian wilderness for the summer, he has no idea that his life will be changed forever. While in flight, the pilot has a fatal heart attack, leaving Brian to think quickly, to draw upon all he has ever learned from books, movies, and TV, and to fight panic.

Letters from Rifka

by Karen Hesse

When young Rifka and her family flee Russia to immigrate to America, the journey is filled with obstacles. Rifka is left behind in Poland, prohibited from boarding the train with her family because she is ill. In letters to her friend, she describes her experiences. When she arrives on Ellis Island, she is prevented from entering the country. She then must use her wit and energy to reunite with her family.

Johnny Tremain

by Esther Forbes

Johnny Tremain is a story about a young boy who learns valuable lessons about developing pride and overcoming obstacles. The story is also a historical drama of the events leading up to the Declaration of Independence in 1776. History comes alive as the author weaves daily life and encounters with famous individuals into the story of a boy becoming a young man.

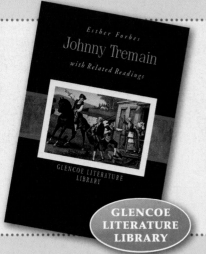
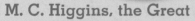

M. C. Higgins, the Great

by Virginia Hamilton

Sarah's Mountain has been home to fifteen-year-old M. C. Higgins's family since his great-grandmother settled there. Now their home is threatened. Strip-mining has left a giant pile of rubble, ready to crumble, above their house. When strangers offer a solution, M. C. learns about making choices.

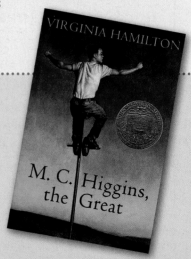

Nonfiction

Sitting Bull and His World

by Albert Marrin

This biography of the distinguished Native American leader describes his life and times as well as the customs and beliefs that made him who he was. Sitting Bull's youth, his development into a brave and wise man, and his tragic death are presented along with explanations of the culture of Plains Indians.

Guinea Pig Scientists: Bold Self-Experimenters in Science and Medicine

by Leslie Dendy and Mel Boring

Here are ten stories of real scientists who used themselves as their own test subjects, or guinea pigs. Their explorations of such things as digestion, deadly diseases, and safety gear are brave, often dangerous, and sometimes shocking. Each chapter ends with a description of what was learned from the scientist's work and what is now known about the subject.

His Promised Land: The Autobiography of John P. Parker, Former Slave and Conductor on the Underground Railroad

edited by Stuart Seely Sprague

John P. Parker is born enslaved, but he purchases his own freedom after teaching himself to read. As a freedman, Parker becomes an important member of the Underground Railroad. Read to learn how Parker risks his life time and again to help hundreds of people who were enslaved escape to freedom.

 Write an Interview

Write an interview with the author of the book you read. Questions and answers should be supported from your reading. Include questions about ideas, people, or events in the book. Present your interview to the class.

Assessment

Reading

Read the passage and answer the questions. Write your answers on a separate sheet of paper.

---

from "Kamau's Finish" by Muthoni Muchemi

1   "Wooyay, please with sugarcane juice," I silently pray. "Let me be one of the lucky ones today." Although Kenyatta Primary Academy in Nairobi has almost four hundred students, not many parents have showed up for Sports Day. I don't care about other parents so long as Baba is there for me.

2   While the headmistress screeches something or other on the squeaky microphone, I scan the group standing on the other side of the track. Baba is not among them. He's tall and big like Meja Rhino the champion wrestler, so you can't miss him.

3   My team is the Red House, and we're squashed between the Yellow and Blue House teams. Immediately across is the three-step winners' podium. I cross my eyes three times in its direction, shooting lucky *uganga*[1] rays.

4   But Chris and Daudi pull my T-shirt and break my concentration. I bat their hands away and crouch down. We're sitting on the ground right in front of the track. Mr. Juma, our sports master, let us sit here because we helped him mark the track into lanes with white chalk. Murram[2] dust will fly in our faces during the races, but we'll still have the best view.

5   Suddenly I see a tall figure approaching from a distance and shoot up again. But Baba is half bald, and this man has tight clumps that look like sleeping safari ants scattered about his head.

6   "Down, Kamau!" barks Mr. Juma.

---

1 *Uganga* is a Swahili word that means "magic" or "charms."

2 A *murram* road is made of hard soil and stones.

7   My race will start in a few minutes. I close my eyes and slowly mouth the secret word. *Ndigidigimazlpixkarumbeta!* Please let Baba be here by the end of this blink. But I open my eyes too soon, way too soon.

8   Still, I will not lose faith.

1. What unspoken question most contributes to a feeling of suspense in this passage?
   A. Will Baba show up?
   B. When will Kamau's race begin?
   C. Who will win the next race?
   D. Why is Kamau waiting for Baba?

2. Why does Kamau close his eyes in paragraph 7?
   A. It is part of his making a wish.
   B. It helps him remember the secret word.
   C. He wants to keep out murram dust.
   D. He doesn't want to get his hopes up again.

3. The phrases *uganga rays, sugarcane juice,* and *safari ants* all contribute to a reader's understanding of
   A. the author's purpose.
   B. the plot's rising action.
   C. the story's cultural context.
   D. the narrator's superstitious beliefs.

4. Which elements of plot does this excerpt from the story introduce?
   A. conflict, suspense, and resolution
   B. characters, conflict, and climax
   C. setting, situation, and falling action
   D. characters, setting, and situation

5. Which phrase would be *most* likely to appear in a summary of this passage?
   A. Meja Rhino
   B. Sports Day
   C. white chalk
   D. murram dust

Extended Answer

6. What is making Kamau nervous in this passage? Use details and evidence from the story to support your answer.

Literature Online

Assessment For additional test practice, go to glencoe.com and enter QuickPass code GL39770u2.

Study the advertisement and answer the questions. Write your answers on a separate sheet of paper.

New 1951 Packard Convertible–one of nine all-new models

Pride of Possession is Standard Equipment

How can we put a price tag on your neighbors' look of envy . . . or on your own feeling of well-being . . . as you drive your new 1951 Packard home for the first time?

We can't, of course. So— *Pride of Possession is Standard Equipment.*

Like the exclusiveness of Packard beauty—and the years–ahead superiority of Packard engineering—you can't buy a new 1951 Packard without it. And you never can match it—no matter how much you may be willing to pay—*in any other car!*

It's more than a car . . . it's a

PACKARD

ASK THE MAN WHO OWNS ONE

7. The setting in the photograph is meant to help create a sense of

  A. luxury.
  B. sincerity.
  C. adventure.
  D. practicality.

8. Which sentence *best* states the theme of this ad?

  A. Buying a new car is always a thrill.
  B. Everyone deserves a good, reliable car.
  C. Quality is more important than appearance.
  D. Packards are special cars for special people.

Vocabulary Skills

On a separate sheet of paper, write the numbers 1–14. Next to each number, write the letter of the word or phrase that means about the same as the underlined word.

1. <u>illiteracy</u> among adults
   A. inability to read
   B. income
   C. poverty
   D. unemployment

2. such <u>intolerant</u> remarks
   A. foolish
   B. soft-spoken
   C. misunderstood
   D. narrow-minded

3. the <u>rival</u> plans
   A. odd
   B. new
   C. secret
   D. opposing

4. talking <u>amiably</u>
   A. cheerfully
   B. sadly
   C. loudly
   D. angrily

5. <u>inaudible</u> cries
   A. too soft
   B. too loud
   C. frightening
   D. too late

6. to see a <u>horde</u>
   A. mob
   B. team
   C. display
   D. small group

7. the <u>oppressive</u> climate
   A. severe
   B. pleasant
   C. famous
   D. unchanging

8. a cheerful <u>outlook</u>
   A. smile
   B. appearance
   C. forecast
   D. memory

9. to worry about <u>endangerment</u>
   A. risk
   B errors
   C. criticism
   D. corrections

10. asking <u>persistently</u>
    A. quietly
    B. loudly
    C. happily
    D. constantly

11. a <u>sinister</u> person
    A. strange
    B. wicked
    C. phony
    D. ridiculous

12. to <u>convey</u> a feeling
    A. hide
    B. guess
    C. make fun of
    D. make known

13. playing <u>competently</u>
    A. rapidly
    B. happily
    C. noisily
    D. skillfully

14. if they <u>vexed</u> you
    A. chose
    B. irritated
    C. scolded
    D. surprised

Writing Strategies

The following is a rough draft of part of a student's report. It contains errors. Read the passage. Then answer the questions on a separate sheet of paper.

---

(1) There is a saying I have heard. (2) "Think globally; act locally." (3) It means we should think about world problems. (4) Should make ourselves aware of them. (5) However, we should act as well as think. (6) Actions have good results. (7) At least, some does. (8) We should take action locally. (9) Everyone are able to see local problems. (10) If I see one, I have a responsibility to try to solve it. (11) If I have a good idea, I should act on it.

1. Read this sentence from the report.

> **At least, some does.**

How could this sentence be corrected?

A. Change *does* to *do.*
B. Change *some* to *a few.*
C. Change *some* to *several.*
D. Change *does* to *have done.*

2. In which sentence is *have* used as a helping verb?

A. sentence 1   C. sentence 10
B. sentence 6   D. sentence 11

3. Which "sentence" in the report is actually a fragment?

A. sentence 2   C. sentence 7
B. sentence 4   D. sentence 8

4. Read this sentence from the report.

> **Everyone are able to see local problems.**

How could this sentence be corrected?

A. Change *are* to *is.*
B. Change *are* to *were.*
C. Change *everyone* to *anybody.*
D. Change *to see* to *while seeing.*

5. Which of the following verbs from the passage is a regular verb?

A. think   C. make
B. mean   D. solve

Writing Product

Read the prompt in the box below and follow the "Directions for Writing." Use one piece of paper to jot down ideas and organize your thoughts. Then neatly write your essay on another sheet. You may not use a dictionary or other reference materials.

Writing Situation:

Students in your school have formed a new club, the Ecology Club. The club will publish a weekly column in the school newspaper about environmental problems. Your turn to write a column is coming up.

Directions for Writing:

Think about an environmental problem that you think your fellow students and other local people could work toward solving. Now write an article in which you describe the problem and explain one or more ways in which the situation could be improved.

Keep these hints in mind when you write.

- Concentrate on what the prompt tells you to write.
- Organize the way you will present your ideas.
- Provide good, clear support for your ideas.
- Use different kinds of sentence structures.
- Use precise words that express your ideas clearly.
- Check your essay for mistakes in spelling, grammar, and punctuation.

WHAT'S More Important, the Journey or the Destination?

THE **BIG** Question

> " *No one can leave his character behind when he goes on a journey.* "
>
> —YORUBA WEST AFRICAN PROVERB

FOLDABLES®
Study Organizer

Unit 3
What's More Important,
the Journey or the Destination?

title	title
title	title
title	title
title	title
title	title

Throughout Unit 3, you will read, write, and talk about the **BIG** Question—"What's More Important, the Journey or the Destination?" Use your Unit 3 **Foldable**, shown here, to keep track of your ideas as you read. Turn to the back of this book for instructions on making this **Foldable.**

WHAT'S More Important, the Journey or the Destination?

Y ou have just learned a Yoruba West African proverb about a journey—that you can never leave your character behind when you go on a journey. Still, it's important to have a destination, or place you want to go on your journey. Sometimes, though, the experience you gain along the way is just as valuable as reaching your final destination. In fact, a journey may even change your character, or personality. In Unit 3, you will explore how the journey may be just as important as the destination.

Think about the importance of both journeys and destinations in your life and in the lives of others:

- Difficult Paths
- Memorable Places

What You'll Read

Reading about different people and their journeys can help you explore the importance of both the journey and the destination. In this unit, you will read **poetry**, a compact, expressive form of literature that uses language, images, sound, and rhythm to communicate emotions and ideas. You will also read short stories, myths, and other texts that can lead you to discover answers to the Big Question.

What You'll Write

As you explore the Big Question, you'll write notes in your Unit 3 **Foldable**. Later, you'll use these notes to complete two writing assignments related to the Big Question.

1. Write a Poem
2. Choose a Unit Challenge

   - On Your Own Activity: Write an Interview
   - Group Activity: Stage a Debate

What You'll Learn

Literary Elements

conflict
line and stanza
speaker
myth
rhyme and rhyme scheme
metaphor
characterization
rhythm and meter
assonance and consonance
onomatopoeia and alliteration
motivation
imagery
sonnet

Reading Skills and Strategies

analyze style
draw conclusions about plot
monitor comprehension
interpret author's meaning
analyze setting
analyze historical context
preview
identify cause-and-effect relationships
analyze theme
analyze characterization
paraphrase
compare and contrast motivation

Explore the BIG Question

TRAVEL

Edna St. Vincent Millay

The railroad track is miles away,
    And the day is loud with voices speaking,
Yet there isn't a train goes by all day
    But I hear its whistle shrieking.

5 All night there isn't a train goes by,
    Though the night is still for sleep and dreaming
But I see its cinders° red on the sky,
    And hear its engine steaming.

My heart is warm with the friends I make,
10   And better friends I'll not be knowing,
Yet there isn't a train I wouldn't take,
    No matter where it's going.

Set a Purpose for Reading

Read the poem "Travel" to decide which the poet thinks is more important— the journey or the destination.

BQ BIG Question

Think about the poet's imagery and what you know about trains. Why might a train ride be a difficult journey for some people?

BQ BIG Question

In what ways does the speaker let readers know whether she prefers the journey or the destination?

7 Here, **cinders** are the burning ashes the train's engine gives off.

After You Read

Respond and Think Critically

1. Using your own words, restate Millay's poem. **[Summarize]**
2. Why can the speaker hear the train from miles away, even at night when others are sleeping? **[Infer]**
3. Why do you think Millay has titled this poem "Travel"? **[Interpret]**
4. Does reading this poem make you want to ride a train? Explain your opinion. **[Evaluate]**

Writing

Write a Poem Write a four-line poem in which you tell about your favorite form of transportation, such as biking, flying, or riding in a car. You may want to begin your brief poem with a description of why you like this form of travel:

"Traveling by _____ is _____."

In "Travel," notice that, for every four lines, the last words of the first and third lines rhyme and the last words of the second and fourth lines rhyme. You might want to use the same rhyme scheme in your short poem.

Include a simile in your poem. You have already learned that a simile is a figure of speech in which a writer uses *like* or *as* to compare seemingly unlike things: " The train roared like caged lions." "The biscuit was as hard as a rock."

Learning Objectives

For page 308

In studying this text, you will focus on the following objectives:

Literary Study:
Analyzing literary genres.

Connecting to the literature.

Writing: Writing a poem.

 Literature Online

Unit Resources For additional skills practice, go to glencoe.com and enter Quickpass code GL39770u3.

Part 1

Difficult Paths

Central Station II, 1974–75. Jeffrey Smart. Synthetic polymer paint on canvas.
Art Gallery of New South Wales, Sydney.

BQ ⟩⟩ **BIG Question** **What's More Important, the Journey or the Destination?**

Why does the running man in the picture seem to be taking a difficult path? What
people do you know who have traveled difficult paths?

The Drummer Boy of Shiloh

Connect to the Short Story

Think about a time two armies faced each other during a war—in our country or elsewhere.

Quickwrite Freewrite for a few minutes from the point of view of an inexperienced soldier who is about to go into battle. What would you say to the soldier about what to expect from a battle?

Build Background

An important battle of the U.S. Civil War took place in April 1862 in Shiloh, Tennessee. The Union Army, led by General Ulysses S. Grant, won the battle, but at the cost of thousands of lives. With this battle began the legend of a drummer boy.

- Most drummers in the Civil War were boys, some as young as twelve.

- The drummer boy's beat and the blare of bugles heard above the cannon and rifle booms alerted soldiers to change formations during battle.

Vocabulary

riveted (riv′it id) *v.* fastened with threadless metal bolts (p. 313). *Factory workers riveted the tank's armor plates together.*

immortality (im′ôr tal′ə tē) *n.* the state of living or lasting forever (p. 313). *In the myth, a Greek god granted immortality to a worshipper.*

legitimately (li jit′ə mit lē) *adv.* in a way that follows the rules; legally (p. 315). *Susan won the contest legitimately by making sure she followed all the rules.*

resolute (rez′ə lo̅o̅ t′) *adj.* characterized by steady determination (p. 317). *The resolute runner continued the race, even though his knee was hurting.*

mutely (mūt′lē) *adv.* without speaking; silently (p. 318). *The baby mutely pointed to the teddy bear.*

tremor (trem′ər) *n.* a rapid shaking or vibrating movement (p. 318). *The earthquake caused a major tremor.*

Meet Ray Bradbury

"Everything's play. . . . Everything must be approached happily, for having a lot of fun—even the most serious thing."
—Ray Bradbury

A Need to Write
Ray Bradbury is often called the greatest living science fiction writer, but he has written about all sorts of subjects. The award-winning author wrote his first stories on a toy typewriter at age twelve. Since then, he has written hundreds of short stories, novels, poems, essays, plays, and films.

Literary Works Bradbury is the author of many science fiction works, including *The Martian Chronicles.* "The Drummer Boy of Shiloh" first appeared in the *Saturday Evening Post* in 1960.

Ray Bradbury was born in 1920.

 Literature Online

Author Search For more about Ray Bradbury, go to glencoe.com and enter QuickPass code GL39770u3.

Set Purposes for Reading

BQ BIG Question

As you read, think about the difficult paths the two characters take toward a dangerous battle. Why is each path so difficult?

Literary Element Conflict

Conflict is the central struggle between opposing forces in a story or play. An **external conflict** is the struggle of a character against an outside force, such as fate, nature, society, or another person. An **internal conflict** exists in the mind of a character. Many stories have both kinds of conflict.

Understanding conflict is important because it allows you to identify strongly with the main characters and the difficulties they face. A story can often be judged by the quality of its conflict.

As you read, analyze the internal and external conflicts that the characters face and evaluate how the conflicts are resolved.

Reading Skill Analyze Style

When you analyze an author's **style**, you look carefully at that author's word choice, sentences and paragraph structure, and use of figurative language and imagery.

Analyzing style is important because it helps you gain a greater understanding of the author's purpose and of the work itself. When you analyze style, think about how and why the author

- chooses and arranges words, phrases, and sentences to move the story along and to describe people, places, and things.
- uses figurative language, sensory images, and unusual expressions to create a mood or communicate a message.

As you read, ask yourself which words, figures of speech, images, and sentences are most effective. For each piece of interesting language you find you might use a graphic organizer like the one below.

> Interesting
> Language, page 312: "Blossoms fell from orchard trees and lit with rustling taps on the drumskin."

> How It Is Effective
> It is unexpected that a fragile blossom can tap a drum.

> How It Affects the Story
> It is such a small detail that it creates a focused, relaxed mood in the story.

Learning Objectives

For pages 310–319

In studying this text, you will focus on the following objectives:

Literary Study:
Analyzing conflict.

Analyzing style.

TRY IT

Analyze Style Read the passage from "The Tell-Tale Heart" by Edgar Allan Poe. Discuss with a partner the mood Poe's style creates and how his style helps reveal the narrator's character.

It is impossible to say how first the idea entered my brain; but once conceived, it haunted me day and night. Object there was none. Passion there was none. I loved the old man. He had never wronged me. He had never given me insult. For his gold I had no desire. I think it was his eye! yes, it was this! One of his eyes resembled that of a vulture—a pale blue eye, with a film over it.

The Drummer Boy of Shiloh

Ray Bradbury ★★★★★★★★

Union Drummer Boy at Shiloh

I n the April night, more than once, blossoms fell from the orchard trees and lit with rustling taps on the drumskin. At midnight a peach stone left miraculously on a branch through winter, flicked by a bird, fell swift and unseen, struck once, like panic, which jerked the boy upright. In silence he listened to his own heart ruffle away, away, at last gone from his ears and back in his chest again.

After that, he turned the drum on its side, where its great lunar face peered at him whenever he opened his eyes.

His face, alert or at rest, was solemn.[1] It was indeed a solemn time and a solemn night for a boy just turned fourteen in the peach field near the Owl Creek not far from the church at Shiloh.

"... thirty-one, thirty-two, thirty-three ..."

Unable to see, he stopped counting.

Beyond the thirty-three familiar shadows, forty thousand men, exhausted by nervous expectation, unable to sleep for romantic dreams of battles yet unfought, lay

Analyze Style What words, sentences, or images have made the greatest impact on you so far? Why?

---

1 **Solemn** means "serious."

crazily askew in their uniforms. A mile yet farther on, another army was strewn helter-skelter,[2] turning slow, basting themselves with the thought of what they would do when the time came: a leap, a yell, a blind plunge their strategy, raw youth their protection and benediction.[3]

Now and again the boy heard a vast wind come up, that gently stirred the air. But he knew what it was, the army here, the army there, whispering to itself in the dark. Some men talking to others, others murmuring to themselves, and all so quiet it was like a natural element arisen from south or north with the motion of the earth toward dawn.

What the men whispered the boy could only guess, and he guessed that it was: Me, I'm the one, I'm the one of all the rest won't die. I'll live through it. I'll go home. The band will play. And I'll be there to hear it.

Yes, thought the boy, that's all very well for them, they can give as good as they get!

For with the careless bones of the young men harvested by night and bindled[4] around campfires were the similarly strewn steel bones of their rifles, with **bayonets** fixed like eternal lightning lost in the orchard grass.

Me, thought the boy, I got only a drum, two sticks to beat it, and no shield.

There wasn't a man-boy on this ground tonight did not have a shield[5] he cast, **riveted** or carved himself on his way to his first attack, compounded of remote but nonetheless firm and fiery family devotion, flag-blown patriotism and cocksure **immortality** strengthened by the touchstone of very real gunpowder, ramrod,

---

2 Both armies were scattered *(strewn)* in a disorganized way *(helter-skelter)*.

3 A ***benediction*** (ben′ ə dik′ shən) is a divine blessing or the condition of being blessed.

4 ***Bindled*** means "bedded" or "bundled." A *bindle* is a bed roll.

5 Civil War soldiers didn't carry *shields* of armor. The narrator is referring to ways the men prepared themselves for battle mentally and emotionally.

Vocabulary

riveted (riv′ it id) *v.* fastened with threadless metal bolts

immortality (im′ ôr tal′ ə tē) *n.* the state of living or lasting forever

Conflict Based on this passage, what is the main external conflict of this story?

Visual Vocabulary

A **bayonet** is a knife attached to the end of the rifle and used in hand-to-hand combat.

minnieball and flint.[6] But without these last the boy felt his family move yet farther off away in the dark, as if one of those great prairie-burning trains had chanted them away never to return, leaving him with this drum which was worse than a toy in the game to be played tomorrow or some day much too soon.

The boy turned on his side. A moth brushed his face, but it was peach blossom. A peach blossom flicked him, but it was a moth. Nothing stayed put. Nothing had a name. Nothing was as it once was.

If he lay very still, when the dawn came up and the soldiers put on their bravery with their caps, perhaps they might go away, the war with them, and not notice him lying small here, no more than a toy himself. "Well, by God, now," said a voice.

The boy shut up his eyes, to hide inside himself, but it was too late. Someone, walking by in the night, stood over him.

Analyze Style Think about the ideas the *shield* represents. How does the author's use of this comparison help you understand the boy's circumstances?

Conflict Identify the story's external conflict. What internal conflict does it create for the boy? Explain.

General Ulysses Simpson Grant, commander of the Union forces at the Battle of Shiloh, 6-7th April, 1862. Color Lithograph.

6 A **touchstone** is anything used to test for quality or genuineness. In the mid-1800s, a rifle had to be loaded for each shot. The **ramrod** forced gunpowder down the rifle barrel. The **minnieball** was a kind of bullet. **Flint** ignited the powder that shot the bullet.

"Well," said the voice quietly, "here's a soldier crying *before* the fight. Good. Get it over. Won't be time once it all starts."

And the voice was about to move on when the boy, startled, touched the drum at his elbow. The man above, hearing this, stopped. The boy could feel his eyes, sense him slowly bending near. A hand must have come down out of the night, for there was a little rat-tat as the fingernails brushed and the man's breath fanned his face.

"Why, it's the drummer boy, isn't it?"

The boy nodded, not knowing if his nod was seen. "Sir, is that *you*?" he said.

"I assume it is." The man's knees cracked as he bent still closer.

He smelled as all fathers should smell, of salt sweat, ginger tobacco, horse and boot leather, and the earth he walked upon. He had many eyes. No, not eyes, brass buttons that watched the boy.

He could only be, and was, the General.

"What's your name, boy?" he asked.

"Joby," whispered the boy, starting to sit up.

"All right, Joby, don't stir." A hand pressed his chest gently, and the boy relaxed. "How long you been with us, Joby?"

"Three weeks, sir."

"Run off from home or joined **legitimately**, boy?"
Silence.

"Fool question," said the General. "Do you shave yet, boy? Even more of a fool. There's your cheek, fell right off the tree overhead. And the others here not much older. Raw, raw, the lot of you. You ready for tomorrow or the next day, Joby?"

"I think so, sir."

"You want to cry some more, go on ahead. I did the same last night."

"*You*, sir?"

"God's truth. Thinking of everything ahead. Both sides figuring the other side will just give up, and soon, and the war done in weeks, and us all home. Well, that's not how it's going to be. And maybe that's why I cried."

Analyze Style Notice the sentence structure and pacing of the General's speech. What impression does it make on you?

"Yes, sir," said Joby.

The General must have taken out a cigar now, for the dark was suddenly filled with the Indian smell of tobacco unlit as yet, but chewed as the man thought what next to say.

"It's going to be a crazy time," said the General. "Counting both sides, there's a hundred thousand men, give or take a few thousand out there tonight, not one as can spit a sparrow off a tree, or knows a horse clod from a minnieball. Stand up, bare the breast, ask to be a target, thank them and sit down, that's us, that's them. We should turn tail and train four months, they should do the same. But here we are, taken with spring fever and thinking it blood lust, taking our sulphur[7] with cannons instead of with molasses as it should be, going to be a hero, going to live forever. And I can see all of them over there nodding agreement, save the other way around. It's wrong, boy, it's wrong as a head put on hind side front and a man marching backward through life. It will be a double massacre if one of their itchy generals decides to picnic his lads on our grass. More innocents will get shot out of pure Cherokee enthusiasm than ever got shot before. Owl Creek was full of boys splashing around in the noonday sun just a few hours ago. I fear it will be full of boys again, just floating, at sundown tomorrow, not caring where the tide takes them."

The General stopped and made a little pile of winter leaves and twigs in the darkness, as if he might at any moment strike fire to them to see his way through the coming days when the sun might not show its face because of what was happening here and just beyond.

The boy watched the hand stirring the leaves and opened his lips to say something, but did not say it. The General heard the boy's breath and spoke himself.

"Why am I telling you this? That's what you want to ask, eh? Well, when you got a bunch of wild horses on a loose rein somewhere, somehow you got to bring order, rein them in. These lads, fresh out of the milkshed, don't know what I know, and I can't tell them: men actually die,

Analyze Style Describe the General's feelings about this battle. What specific aspects of style—such as word choice, imagery, and sentence length—contribute to your understanding of these feelings?

---

7 **Blood lust** means "a desire for bloodshed." **Sulphur** (now usually spelled *sulfur*) is a chemical once used as an ingredient of gunpowder; also, when combined with molasses, it was used as a medicine.

in war. So each is his own army. I got to make *one* army of them. And for that, boy, I need you."

"Me!" The boy's lips barely twitched.

"Now, boy," said the General quietly, "you are the heart of the army. Think of that. You're the heart of the army. Listen, now."

And, lying there, Joby listened.

And the General spoke on.

If he, Joby, beat slow tomorrow, the heart would beat slow in the men. They would lag by the wayside. They would drowse in the fields on their muskets. They would sleep forever, after that, in those same fields, their hearts slowed by a drummer boy and stopped by enemy lead.

But if he beat a sure, steady, ever faster rhythm, then, then their knees would come up in a long line down over that hill, one knee after the other, like a wave on the ocean shore! Had he seen the ocean ever? Seen the waves rolling in like a well-ordered cavalry charge to the sand? Well, that was it, that's what he wanted, that's what was needed! Joby was his right hand and his left. He gave the orders, but Joby set the pace!

So bring the right knee up and the right foot out and the left knee up and the left foot out. One following the other in good time, in brisk time. Move the blood up the body and make the head proud and the spine stiff and the jaw **resolute**. Focus the eye and set the teeth, flare the nostrils and tighten the hands, put steel armor all over the men, for blood moving fast in them does indeed make men feel as if they'd put on steel. He must keep at it, at it! Long and steady, steady and long! Then, even though shot or torn, those wounds got in hot blood—in blood he'd helped stir—would feel less pain. If their blood was cold, it would be more than slaughter, it would be murderous nightmare and pain best not told and no one to guess.

The General spoke and stopped, letting his breath slack off. Then, after a moment, he said, "So there you are, that's it. Will you do that, boy? Do you know now you're general of the army when the General's left behind?"

> **Conflict** What more do you learn here about the General's conflict? Try to predict how the drummer boy might help the General face the conflict.

> **Analyze Style** Think about the comparison the General is making here. What image of the soldiers do his words create in your mind?

Vocabulary

resolute (rez′ə loo t) *adj.* characterized by steady determination

The boy nodded **mutely**.

"You'll run them through for me then, boy?"

"Yes, sir."

"Good. And, God willing, many nights from tonight, many years from now, when you're as old or far much older than me, when they ask you what you did in this awful time, you will tell them—one part humble and one part proud— 'I was the drummer boy at the battle of Owl Creek,' or the Tennessee River, or maybe they'll just name it after the church there. 'I was the drummer boy at Shiloh.' Good grief, that has a beat and sound to it fitting for Mr. Longfellow.[8] 'I was the drummer boy at Shiloh.' Who will ever hear those words and not know you, boy, or what you thought this night, or what you'll think tomorrow or the next day when we must get up on our legs and *move!*"

The general stood up. "Well, then. God bless you, boy. Good night."

"Good night, sir."

And, tobacco, brass, boot polish, salt sweat and leather, the man moved away through the grass.

Joby lay for a moment, staring but unable to see where the man had gone.

He swallowed. He wiped his eyes. He cleared his throat. He settled himself. Then, at last, very slowly and firmly, he turned the drum so that it faced up toward the sky.

He lay next to it, his arm around it, feeling the **tremor**, the touch, the muted thunder as, all the rest of the April night in the year 1862, near the Tennessee River, not far from the Owl Creek, very close to the church named Shiloh, the peach blossoms fell on the drum. ❧

BQ **BIG Question**

In what way does the General encourage Joby to follow a difficult path toward his destination?

Analyze Style In what ways do the words in this closing paragraph affect the story?

---

8 Henry Wadsworth *Longfellow* (1807–1882), an American poet, was very popular and highly respected during his lifetime.

Vocabulary

. . . .

mutely (mūt′lē) *adv.* without speaking; silently

tremor (trem′ər) *n.* a rapid shaking or vibrating movement

After You Read

Respond and Think Critically

1. Explain what the General says to Joby. **[Summarize]**

2. How are Joby and the General alike in their conflicts? **[Compare]**

3. What does the General mean when he says that there "will be a double massacre if one of their itchy generals decides to picnic his lads on our grass"? **[Infer]**

4. **Literary Element** Conflict What effect do the General's words have on Joby and his internal conflict? **[Analyze]**

5. **Reading Skill** Analyze Style Review your graphic organizer. Which aspects of style—word choice, sentence structure, imagery, and figurative language—does Bradbury use most effectively? **[Evaluate]**

6. **BQ** BIG Question Which moments in the story best show the difficult path the characters must follow? **[Draw Conclusions]**

TIP

Comparing
Here are some tips to help you compare. Remember, when you compare, you find specific similarities and differences between two or more people, places, things, or ideas.

- Review Joby's actions, thoughts, and conflicts.

- Review the General's actions, thoughts, and conflicts.

- Think about ways in which each character's actions, thoughts, and conflicts are similar and how they are different.

- Make a general statement explaining how the characters' internal conflicts are similar and how they are different.

Vocabulary Practice

Identify whether the paired words have the same or the opposite meaning. Then write a sentence using each vocabulary word or draw a picture that represents the word.

riveted and loosened

immortality and short-lived

legitimately and legally

resolute and determined

mutely and soundlessly

tremor and vibration

Academic Vocabulary

The general made his point very **convincingly**.

In this sentence, *convincingly* means "in a way that causes someone to believe or feel certain." Think about the General's words, and then fill in the blank for this statement:

When the General explained that _____ it helped him make his point very convincingly.

Writing

Write a Persuasive Letter Suppose you are a fourteen-year-old in 1862. Write a persuasive letter to a friend who might run away to join the army. Explain why your friend should or should not join the army.

FOLDABLES Study Organizer Keep track of your ideas about the **BIG Question** in your unit Foldable.

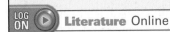

Selection Resources
For Selection Quizzes, eFlashcards, and Reading-Writing Connection activities, go to glencoe.com and enter QuickPass code GL39770u3.

The Dying Cowboy

Connect to the Poem

When you think of the Old West, what comes to mind? Cowboys? Horses? Canyons?

Partner Talk With a partner, talk about what you know about the Old West from books, pictures, and movies. Discuss positive and negative images you associate with the Old West.

Build Background

In the 1800s, the western part of the United States became known as the "Wild West." New towns sprang up in what had once been wilderness. With little law and order, people sometimes lived careless, criminal lives. This lifestyle—in a time and place where guns were widespread—could have deadly consequences.

- The ballad describes the life and death of one cowboy who died young as a result of his irresponsible behavior.

- Other versions of this ballad are known as "The Cowboy's Lament" and "The Streets of Laredo."

Set Purposes for Reading

BQ **BIG Question**

Read "The Dying Cowboy" to find out how the way a person behaves on the journey of life can lead to an unexpected—and unpleasant—destination.

Literary Element Stanza

"The Dying Cowboy" is a type of poem called a **ballad.** Ballads tell stories. Most ballads contain stanzas. A **stanza** is a grouping of lines. Like a paragraph, a stanza conveys a particular thought or describes one aspect of an incident. "The Dying Cowboy" has stanzas of equal length and a regular rhyme scheme. These qualities make ballads easy to remember—they are often passed from one generation to the next as songs. As you read "The Dying Cowboy," imagine it being sung beside a campfire.

The Cowboy, c. 1897. Frederic Remington. Watercolor on paper. Hogg Brothers Collection, Gift of Miss Ima Hogg, Museum of Fine Arts, Houston, TX.

The Dying Cowboy

traditional American ballad

As I rode out by Tom Sherman's barroom,
As I rode out so early one day,
'Twas there I espied a handsome young cowboy,
All dressed in white linen, all clothed for the grave.

5   "I see by your outfit that you are a cowboy,"
These words he did say as I boldly stepped by.
"Come sit down beside me and hear my sad story,
For I'm shot in the breast and I know I must die.

"Then beat your drum slowly and play your fife°
    lowly,
10 And play the dead march as you carry me along,
And take me to the graveyard and throw the sod
    o'er me,
For I'm a young cowboy and I know I've done
    wrong.

Stanza How do stanzas help make the poem easy to remember?

9 A **fife** is a musical instrument that is like a small flute.

"'Twas once in the saddle I used to go dashing,
'Twas once in the saddle I used to go gay,
15   But I first took to drinking and then to card playing,
Got shot in the body and I'm dying today.

"Let sixteen gamblers come handle my coffin,
Let sixteen young cowboys come sing me a song,
Take me to the green valley and lay the sod o'er me,
20   For I'm a poor cowboy and I know I've done wrong.

"Go bring me back a cup of cool water
To cool my parched lips," this cowboy then said.
Before I returned, his soul had departed
And gone to his Maker—the cowboy lay dead.

25   We swung our ropes slowly and rattled our spurs
       lowly,
And gave a wild whoop as we carried him on,
For we all loved our comrade, so brave, young and
       handsome,
We all loved our comrade, although he'd done wrong.

BQ ▸ BIG Question
Why does the young cowboy say he had "done wrong" in the path he had followed?

Noon Day Heat, 1921. Charles Ephraim Burchfield. Watercolor on paper.
Private Collection, James Goodman Gallery, NY.
View the Art How does the town in the picture compare to what you know of towns in the Old West?

After You Read

Respond and Think Critically

1. What led to the cowboy's downfall? [Summarize]

2. Who is telling the young cowboy's story? [Identify]

3. Why does the cowboy want other cowboys to bury him? [Interpret]

4. Besides thirst, why do you think the cowboy asks for water? [Infer]

5. **Literary Element** Stanza What overall effect is created by the poem's stanza structure? [Analyze]

6. **BQ** **BIG Question** How might the cowboy's death encourage those who buried him to follow a different path? [Draw Conclusions]

Spelling Link

Unstressed Vowels are vowels that are not pronounced as strongly as either short or long vowels. For example, the word *portable* has an unstressed *a*. Most vowels can be used to spell this sound, so you may not know which one to use.

Rule:

An unstressed vowel is usually pronounced as a schwa (ə) that sounds like /uh/ or like a very short *i* or *e* sound.

There is no one rule about how to spell words with unstressed vowels. The best way to spell these words correctly is to learn to spell them by practicing them. Some common English word groups that have an unstressed vowel include words ending in *-ent, -ence, -ant, -ance, -ible, -ibility, -able,* and *-ability.*

Examples:

resilient
evidence
tolerant
clearance
sensible
responsibility
charitable
amiability

Practice On a sheet of paper, correct each misspelled word below. Then use each in a written sentence.

importence, reliuble, incredeble, likible, compatability

 Writing

Write an Action Scene Write an action scene that might be in a movie western. Write both the dialogue between characters and the stage directions that the characters follow as they act out the scene. For example, COWBOY 1 (*angrily*): I don't want to argue.

Before You Read

the lesson of the moth and *Identity*

Connect to the Poems

Do you crave the thrill of new experiences, or do you prefer safe and predictable situations? Think about how important adventure is in your life.

List List some of the unusual or exciting things you hope to do in your life. Then describe the risks that are associated with these goals. Think about what your list reveals about the type of person you want to be.

Build Background

- Author Don Marquis created a character named Archy, a cockroach who wrote poetry by hurling himself at the keys of a typewriter. "After about an hour of this frightfully difficult literary labor he fell to the floor exhausted," Marquis said.

- Because Archy couldn't reach the shift key, his writing didn't include capitalization or punctuation.

Set a Purpose for Reading

BQ BIG Question

Read "the lesson of the moth" and "Identity" to find out how taking a difficult path through life can involve both risk and reward.

Literary Element Speaker

In a poem, the **speaker** is the voice that talks to the reader. Readers often assume that the speaker and the poet are the same, but this is not always the case. The speaker may be the poet or a fictional character. For example, the speaker in "the lesson of the moth" is Archy, a cockroach. As you read these poems, look for clues that will help you understand the speaker and his or her feelings about the subject of the poem. Think about each poet's purpose for choosing the speaker he chose.

LOG ON **Literature** Online

Author Search For more about Don Marquis and Julio Noboa Polanco, go to glencoe.com and enter QuickPass code GL39770u3.

Meet the Authors

Don Marquis

Don Marquis (mär′ kwĭs) was a newspaper columnist, poet, and playwright.

Don Marquis was born in 1878 and died in 1937.

Julio Noboa Polanco

Julio Noboa Polanco (hoo lē′ ō nä bō′ ä pō lön′ kō) focuses much of his work on Hispanic history, culture, and education.

Julio Noboa Polanco was born in 1949.

the lesson of the moth

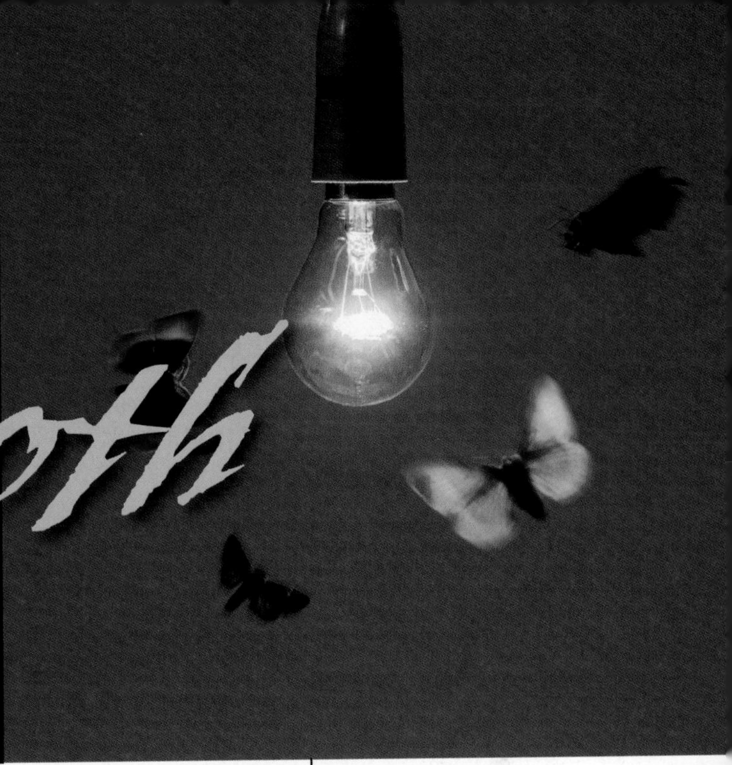

Don Marquis

i was talking to a moth
the other evening
he was trying to break into
an electric light bulb
and fry himself on the wires

why do you fellows
pull this stunt i asked him
because it is the conventional°
thing for moths or why
if that had been an uncovered
candle instead of an electric
light bulb you would
now be a small unsightly cinder
have you no sense

plenty of it he answered
but at times we get tired
of using it
we get bored with the routine
and crave beauty
and excitement

Speaker What details in lines 1–5 suggest that the speaker of the poem may be a fictional character?

8 ***Conventional*** describes what is usual, customary, or traditional.

fire is beautiful
and we know that if we get
too close it will kill us
but what does that matter
25 it is better to be happy
for a moment
and be burned up with beauty
than to live a long time
and be bored all the while

30 so we wad all our life up
into one little roll
and then we shoot the roll
that is what life is for
it is better to be a part of beauty
35 for one instant and then cease to
exist than to exist forever
and never be a part of beauty
our attitude toward life
is come easy go easy
40 we are like human beings
used to be before they became
too civilized to enjoy themselves

and before i could argue him
out of his philosophy°
45 he went and immolated° himself
on a patent cigar lighter
i do not agree with him
myself i would rather have
half the happiness and twice
50 the longevity°

but at the same time i wish
there was something i wanted
as badly as he wanted to fry himself
archy

BQ **BIG Question**

Why does the speaker
envy the moth for taking
a difficult path?

---

44 Here, **philosophy** refers to the personal beliefs and principles that guide one's life.

45 The most common meaning of **immolate** is "to destroy by fire," but it can also
mean "to offer in sacrifice."

50 **Longevity** (lon jev′ ə tē) means "long life."

Identity

Julio Noboa Polanco

Let them be as flowers,
always watered, fed, guarded, admired,
but harnessed to a pot of dirt.

I'd rather be a tall, ugly weed,
5   clinging on cliffs, like an eagle
wind-wavering above high, jagged rocks.

To have broken through the surface of stone
to live, to feel exposed to the madness
of the vast, eternal sky.
10   To be swayed by the breezes of an ancient sea,
carrying my soul, my seed beyond the mountains
   of time
or into the abyss of the bizarre.°

I'd rather be unseen, and if,

then shunned° by everyone
15   than to be a pleasant-smelling flower,
growing in clusters in the fertile valley
where they're praised, handled, and plucked
by greedy, human hands.

I'd rather smell of musty, green stench
20   than of sweet, fragrant lilac.
If I could stand alone, strong and free,
I'd rather be a tall, ugly weed.

Speaker Reread lines 1–6. Explain the comparison the speaker makes between people who are "as flowers" and himself or herself. What words or phrases would you use to describe the speaker?

BQ **BIG Question**

Why is the speaker willing to take a difficult path? Think about the rewards that this way of life offers.

---

12 An ***abyss*** is an immeasurably deep hole or vast emptiness. The ***bizarre*** (bi zär′) is something that is extremely strange.

14 A person who is being ***shunned*** is being avoided.

After You Read

Respond and Think Critically

1. In your own words, describe the events of "the lesson of the moth." [Summarize]

2. What lesson does the moth offer the speaker? [Interpret]

3. Why does the speaker of "Identity" wish to be a weed and not a flower? Support your answer with details from the poem. [Analyze]

4. Which image do you identify with the most: the moth, the flower, or the weed? Explain your response. [Connect]

5. **Literary Element** Speaker Compare the speakers' attitudes toward beauty and beautiful things. In what ways are they similar? In what ways are they different? [Compare]

6. **BQ** BIG Question Which speaker puts more emphasis on the journey of life, and which puts more emphasis on the destination or outcome? [Evaluate]

TIP

Connecting
Here are some tips to help you connect the poems to your own life.

- Write short descriptions of the moth, the flower, and the weed. Be sure to base your descriptions on evidence in the poems.

- Write a short list of things you value in your life.

- Decide which image you identify with the most.

 Keep track of your ideas about the **BIG Question** in your unit Foldable.

Spelling Link

Adding **suffixes to words with a silent *e*** may cause confusion. The following rule will help you know what to do.

Rule:
For most words with silent *e,* keep the *e* when adding a suffix. When you add the suffix *-ly* to a word that ends in *l* plus silent *e,* drop the *-le.* Also drop the silent *e* when you add a suffix beginning with a vowel or a *y.*

Examples:
time + ly = timely
gentle + ly = gently
skate + ing = skating

There are exceptions to this rule, including the following:
judge + ment = judgment, true + ly = truly, noise + ly = noisily

Practice On a sheet of paper, add the suggested suffixes to each of the following words:
fine + ly, wonderful + ly, sensible + ly, horrible + ly, mindful + ly, possible + ly

---

 Writing

Write a Journal Entry Describe your attitude about taking risks. Then compare your attitude with the ideas expressed by one of the speakers in the poems you read. In what ways is your outlook on life similar to and different from the speaker you chose? Explain your thoughts and feelings in a journal entry.

LOG ON **Literature** Online

Selection Resources
For Selection Quizzes, eFlashcards, and Reading-Writing Connection activities, go to glencoe.com and enter QuickPass code GL39770u3.

Icarus and Daedalus

Connect to the Myth

Think about something you really wanted to achieve and the thought and effort you dedicated toward this goal.

Partner Talk With a partner, talk about what you wanted. How did you try to achieve it? Were you successful? Do you think you can try too hard? Share your thoughts with the class.

Build Background

"Icarus and Daedalus" is a Greek myth that has been retold many times over the centuries. A **myth** is an ancient story about gods, goddesses, or other supernatural beings and their influence on people and nature.

- The story imagines a time when humans and gods lived on the island of Crete.

- When people in myths overstep their bounds and try to act like supernatural beings, they usually learn a lesson about the limitations of being human.

Vocabulary

cunning (kun′ing) *adj.* artfully shrewd or crafty; sly (p. 331).
The cunning mouse took the cheese from the trap.

imprisoned (im priz′ənd) *v.* put or kept in a prison (p. 331).
The criminal was imprisoned for robbing a bank.

wavered (wā′vərd) *v.* moved unsteadily up and down or from side to side; swayed (p. 332).
The calf wavered on her legs when she first stood.

rash (rash) *adj.* characterized by too great haste or lack of thought (p. 332).
His rash act put us all in danger.

vacancy (vā′kən sē) *n.* unoccupied or empty space (p. 333).
There was no vacancy at the hotel so we looked elsewhere.

quench (kwench) *v.* to satisfy (p. 333).
The marathon runners drank water to quench their thirst.

Meet Josephine Preston Peabody

"One never learns by success. Success is the plateau that one rests upon to take breath and look down from upon the straight and difficult path."

—Josephine Preston Peabody

Poet and Playwright
Josephine Preston Peabody published her first poem when she was only fourteen years old. She went on to achieve fame for her poetry and plays. Her play "The Piper" was produced at theaters in New York City and London.

Literary Works Peabody's poem collections include *The Book of the Little Past.* "Icarus and Daedalus" was published in *Old Greek Folk Stories Told Anew,* in 1897.

Peabody was born in 1874. She died in 1922.

 Literature Online

Author Search For more about Josephine Preston Peabody, go to glencoe.com and enter QuickPass code GL39770u3.

Set Purposes for Reading

BQ BIG Question

Read "Icarus and Daedalus" to learn what happens to a boy who attempts a dangerous journey.

Literary Element Myth

A **myth** is a traditional story of unknown origin that explains the beliefs and practices of a people. Myths may tell of extraordinary events from earlier times and may deal with gods, heroes, and supernatural events.

Myths are important because they often share the deepest beliefs not only of a group of people but of *all* people. Myths help us understand what it means to be human. For instance, "Icarus and Daedalus" is about an important human quality—our desire to "reach for the stars." But the myth cautions: there is a danger in reaching too high.

As you read "Icarus and Daedalus," ask yourself, what insights or lessons does this story offer about human strengths and weaknesses?

Reading Strategy Draw Conclusions About Plot

When you **draw conclusions,** you use different pieces of information to make a general statement about people, places, events, and ideas. For example, in many myths gods punish mortals who try to acquire what is only fit for the gods. From this, you may conclude that most gods aren't fond of humans who display too much ambition.

Drawing conclusions is important because, as you make connections among different elements of the story, you deepen your understanding of the entire work. When you draw conclusions, you

- notice details about characters, ideas, and events
- find connections among these elements
- form a general statement based on the details and what you know

As you read, ask yourself, what conclusions can be drawn about the plot from the characters and events? Use a graphic organizer like the one below to help you gather details from the story.

Learning Objectives

For pages 329–335

In studying this text, you will focus on the following objectives:

Literary Study:
Analyzing myth.

Reading:
Drawing conclusions.

TRY IT

Draw Conclusions You can draw conclusions about characters by looking at what they say, do, and think. For example, what might you conclude about a character who is always smiling, is eager to lend a hand, and only makes positive comments about others?

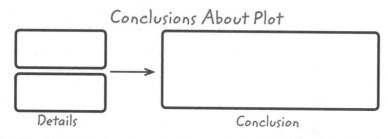

Conclusions About Plot

Details → Conclusion

Josephine Preston Peabody

Icarus and Daedalus

Joy. Lee Campbell. Oil on canvas, 86.3 x 91.4 cm. Private Collection.

Among all those mortals[1] who grew so wise that they learned the secrets of the gods, none was more **cunning** than Daedalus.[2]

He once built, for King Minos of Crete, a wonderful **Labyrinth** of winding ways so cunningly tangled up and twisted around that, once inside, you could never find your way out again without a magic clue. But the king's favor veered with the wind, and one day he had his master architect **imprisoned** in a tower. Daedalus managed to escape from his cell; but it seemed impossible to leave the island, since every ship that came or went was well guarded by order of the king.

---

1 Humans are *mortals,* which means that they eventually die. Greek gods were believed to be immortal.

2 *Daedalus* (dĕd′əl əs)

Vocabulary

cunning (kŭn′ing) *adj.* artfully shrewd or crafty; sly

imprisoned (im priz′ənd) *v.* put or kept in a prison

At length, watching the sea gulls in the air—the only creatures that were sure of liberty—he thought of a plan for himself and his young son Icarus,[3] who was captive with him.

Little by little, he gathered a store of feathers great and small. He fastened these together with thread, molded them in with wax, and so fashioned[4] two great wings like those of a bird. When they were done, Daedalus fitted them to his own shoulders, and after one or two efforts, he found that by waving his arms he could winnow the air and cleave[5] it, as a swimmer does the sea. He held himself aloft, **wavered** this way and that with the wind, and at last, like a great **fledgling,** he learned to fly.

Without delay, he fell to work on a pair of wings for the boy Icarus, and taught him carefully how to use them, bidding him beware of **rash** adventures among the stars. "Remember," said the father, "never to fly very low or very high, for the fogs about the earth would weigh you down, but the blaze of the sun will surely melt your feathers apart if you go too near."

For Icarus, these cautions went in at one ear and out by the other. Who could remember to be careful when he was to fly for the first time? Are birds careful? Not they! And not an idea remained in the boy's head but the one joy of escape.

The day came, and the fair wind that was to set them free. The father bird put on his wings, and, while the light urged them to be gone, he waited to see that all was well with Icarus, for the two could not fly hand in hand. Up they rose, the boy after his father. The hateful ground of Crete sank beneath them; and the country folk, who caught a glimpse of them when they were high above the treetops, took it for a vision of the gods—Apollo, perhaps, with Cupid[6] after him.

3 **Icarus** (ik′ ər əs)

4 Here, **fashioned** means "made or constructed."

5 **Winnow** and **cleave** both mean "to separate or divide."

6 In mythology, **Apollo** is the god of the sun, and **Cupid** is the god of love.

Vocabulary

wavered (wā′ vərd) v. moved unsteadily up and down or from side to side; swayed

rash (rash) adj. characterized by too great haste or lack of thought

Draw Conclusions About Plot What conclusion can you draw about Daedalus's plan from his belief that the gulls were "sure of liberty"?

Visual Vocabulary

A **fledgling** is a young bird that has recently grown the feathers it needs to fly.

Myth In what way is Daedalus's advice characteristic of a myth? Explain.

At first there was a terror in the joy. The wide **vacancy** of the air dazed them—a glance downward made their brains reel. But when a great wind filled their wings, and Icarus felt himself sustained, like a halcyon-bird[7] in the hollow of a wave, like a child uplifted by his mother, he forgot everything in the world but joy. He forgot Crete and the other islands that he had passed over: he saw but vaguely that winged thing in the distance before him that was his father Daedalus. He longed for one draft[8] of flight to **quench** the thirst of his captivity: he stretched out his arms to the sky and made toward the highest heavens.

Alas for him! Warmer and warmer grew the air. Those arms, that had seemed to uphold him, relaxed. His wings wavered, drooped. He fluttered his young hands vainly—he was falling—and in that terror he remembered. The heat of the sun had melted the wax from his wings; the feathers were falling, one by one, like snowflakes; and there was none to help.

He fell like a leaf tossed down the wind, down, down, with one cry that overtook Daedalus far away. When he returned, and sought high and low for the poor boy, he saw nothing but the bird-like feathers afloat on the water, and he knew that Icarus was drowned.

The nearest island he named Icaria, in memory of the child; but he, in heavy grief, went to the temple of Apollo in Sicily, and there hung up his wings as an offering. Never again did he attempt to fly. 🔊

The Fall of Icarus, 1975. Marc Chagall. ©ARS, NY. Private Collection.

View the Art How does this painting illustrate the author's description of Icarus's fall?

BQ **BIG Question**

What is the destination in this story? How does the specific journey relate to the destination?

Draw Conclusions About Plot What conclusion can you draw about the resolution to this plot?

---

7 Here, ***sustained*** means "to be kept from sinking or falling." The ***halcyon-bird,*** or kingfisher, glides slowly and smoothly near the water's surface as it hunts for fish.

8 Here, ***draft*** means "taste."

Vocabulary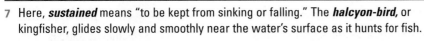

vacancy (vā′kən sē) *n.* unoccupied or empty space
quench (kwench) *v.* to satisfy

After You Read

Respond and Think Critically

1. Retell this myth in your own words. [Summarize]

2. Why do the people of Crete think that Daedalus and Icarus are gods when they see the father and son flying overhead? [Infer]

3. How wise was Daedalus's method of escape? [Draw Conclusions]

4. In what ways are King Minos and the gods alike in their treatment of Daedalus? Explain your thoughts. [Analyze]

5. How might the lesson of "Icarus and Daedalus" apply to life today? Provide an example. [Connect]

6. **BQ** BIG Question Which do you think was more important to Daedalus, the journey or the destination? Which do you think was more important to Icarus? Explain your answers. [Evaluate]

Vocabulary Practice

On a separate sheet of paper, write the vocabulary word that correctly completes each sentence. If none of the words fits the sentence, write "none."

cunning   imprisoned   wavered   rash   vacancy   quench

1. The child's _____ comment hurt her mother's feelings.

2. The _____ dictionary showed fifteen definitions for the word.

3. The clown _____ on the chair before falling over.

4. The hotel clerk informed us that there was only one _____ available.

5. The desert sun _____ the survivor's thirst.

6. I will _____ my desire for attention by publishing a book.

7. The _____ leader was unable to speak to his people.

8. The _____ art thief quietly waited for the museum to close.

Academic Vocabulary

The thrill of flying **exceeded** Icarus's expectations. In the preceding sentence, *exceeded* means "went beyond." Think about something that exceeded your expectations. What made it so special?

TIP

Inferring
Here are some tips to help you infer. Remember that when you infer, you use your reason and experience to guess at what an author does not come right out and say. To answer the question, ask yourself:

- What do I know about mythology?

- What are Daedalus and Icarus doing that is special or unusual?

- How do people today fly from one place to another?

FOLDABLES Study Organizer Keep track of your ideas about the **BIG Question** in your unit Foldable.

Literature Online

Selection Resources
For Selection Quizzes, eFlashcards, and Reading-Writing Connection activities, go to glencoe.com and enter QuickPass code GL39770u3.

Literary Element Myth

1. What do you think is the story's main purpose? Explain your thoughts.

Review: Narrator and Point of View

As you read on page 8, the **narrator** is the storyteller. The **point of view** is the relationship of the narrator to the story. There are various points of view. The narrator may be a character who participates in the story or a voice outside the story. The most common point of view found in mythology is **third-person omniscient.** Here, the narrator is outside the story and "knows all"—revealing events, thoughts, and actions as well as background information important to the story.

2. Which point of view is "Icarus and Daedalus" told from? How can you tell?

3. Give a specific example of how the story would have been different if it were told from a different point of view.

Reading Strategy

Draw Conclusions About Plot

Test Skills Practice

4. Which conclusion about the plot can readers draw from Icarus's internal conflict and his resulting actions?
   A   Children should never disagree with an adult.
   B   Children don't always listen to their parents.
   C   Children believe they will live forever.
   D   Children think they know everything.

Grammar Link

Common and Proper Nouns Nouns are words that name people, places, things, feelings, or ideas.

A **common noun** refers to *any* person, place, thing, feeling, or idea. A common noun is not capitalized unless it begins a sentence.

- Three students visited a museum.

  (The nouns *students* and *museum* do not refer to specific students or a specific museum. They are common nouns and are therefore not capitalized.)

A **proper noun** refers to a *specific* person, place, thing, or idea. Proper nouns are always capitalized.

- Ed, Alicia, and Al visited Harris Museum.

  (The nouns *Ed, Alicia,* and *Al* refer to specific students; the noun *Harris Museum* refers to a specific museum. The nouns are capitalized because they are proper nouns.)

Practice Find three examples each of common and proper nouns in "Icarus and Daedalus." Think about what makes each of these common or proper. Then write a sentence for each word you found. Make sure you use correct capitalization.

Listening and Speaking

Oral Report Imagine that you are on a news team reporting on what happened to Icarus. Write your report and present it to the class. Your report should include an introduction, a body, transitional phrases, and a conclusion.

As you write your report, make sure you answer the following questions:

- *What* happened?
- *Who* was involved?
- *When* did it happen?
- *Where* did it happen?
- *Why* did it happen?
- *How* did it happen?

Learning Objectives

For pages 336–337

On these pages, you will focus on the following objective:

Literary Study: Analyzing poetic structure, sound devices, imagery, and figurative language.

Genre Focus:
Poetry

Poetry is a type of literature in which words are chosen and arranged to create a specific effect. Poets often use imagery and figurative language to convey complex ideas in a small amount of space. Poetry is also meant to be read aloud and heard by an audience. Poets use sound devices, such as rhythm, meter, and rhyme, to help make their works musical and memorable.

Ballads, odes, sonnets, elegies, and epics are different forms of poetry.

Literary Elements

Structure and Sound Devices Poets usually arrange their works into **lines** and **stanzas** instead of sentences. Each line is part of a stanza, or group of lines, that conveys a particular thought or incident.

The following devices help poets create specific structures and sounds.

- **Rhyme** is the repetition of identical or similar sounds at the ends of nearby words. **Rhyme scheme** is the pattern formed by end rhymes.

- **Rhythm** is the pattern of stressed and unstressed syllables in a poem. A regular pattern of rhythm is called **meter.**

- **Repetition** is the use of a word, phrase, line or sound more than once in a poem.

- **Alliteration** is the repetition of consonant sounds, most often at the beginnings of nearby words and syllables.

- **Assonance** is the repetition of vowel sounds in nearby words.

- **Onomatopoeia** is a word or phrase that imitates the sound of what it describes, such as *buzz* for the sound bees make.

Imagery and Figurative Language Many poems have **imagery**, language that appeals to the five senses—sight, hearing, smell, taste, and touch. Poets may also choose to use **figurative language**, writing that conveys ideas beyond the literal meanings of words.

The following figures of speech help poets create imaginative expressions.

- A **simile** uses *like* or *as* to compare two unlike things. *The house was as still as a winter pond.*

- A **metaphor** describes one thing as if it were something else. *His mother's voice was a warm blanket, gently comforting him.*

- **Personification** gives a human quality to an animal, object, or idea. *The lonely saxophone sobbed until the early hours of morning.*

TRY IT

Using a web like the one on the next page, identify the literary elements of a poem in this unit.

Characteristics of the Genre

To gain a better understanding of the literary elements in poetry, study the web diagram below.

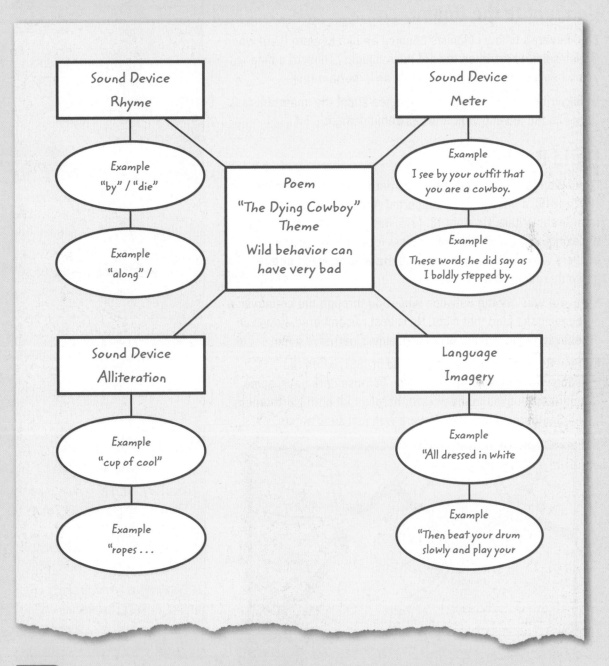

Sound Device
Rhyme

Example
"by" / "die"

Example
"along" /

Poem
"The Dying Cowboy"
Theme
Wild behavior can
have very bad

Sound Device
Meter

Example
I see by your outfit that
you are a cowboy.

Example
These words he did say as
I boldly stepped by.

Sound Device
Alliteration

Example
"cup of cool"

Example
"ropes . . .

Language
Imagery

Example
"All dressed in white

Example
"Then beat your drum
slowly and play your

Paul Revere's Ride

Connect to the Poem

Paul Revere's fellow colonists counted on him to warn them when British soldiers marched toward their villages. Think of a time when people depended on you to do an important task.

Quickwrite Freewrite for a few minutes about the important task. Describe the job and your feelings about doing it.

Build Background

"Paul Revere's Ride" celebrates the patriotism of Paul Revere (1735–1818), a colonist who supported American independence from Great Britain. On April 18, 1775, Revere rode from Boston to Lexington, Massachusetts, to warn local leaders that British soldiers were preparing to advance. He was arrested before he could reach his final destination.

- Revere was not the only one who rode through the countryside sounding the alert that night. He is best remembered, however, because of the popularity of Longfellow's narrative poem.

- "Paul Revere's Ride" was published in 1861, when the nation was beginning the Civil War. In those dark days, some Americans looked to the past for heroes that both Northerners and Southerners admired. Revere was just such a man.

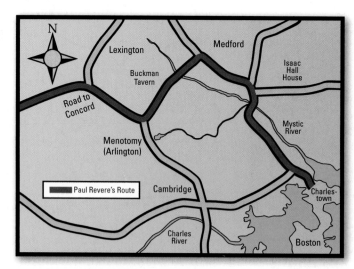

A map showing Paul Revere's historic ride.

Meet Henry Wadsworth Longfellow

"We judge ourselves by what we feel capable of doing, while others judge us by what we have already done."

—Henry Wadsworth Longfellow

A Popular Poet Using his knowledge of European writing traditions, Henry Wadsworth Longfellow created poems that are distinctly American. Many of his poems focused on people and events in American history. His gentle, romantic vision of the world made him the most popular American poet of his time.

Literary Works Longfellow's historical poems include *The Song of Hiawatha*. "Paul Revere's Ride" was published in *Tales of a Wayside Inn*, in 1863.

Henry Wadsworth Longfellow was born in 1807 and died in 1882.

Set Purposes for Reading

BQ BIG Question

As you read "Paul Revere's Ride," think about the journey Paul Revere takes. What makes his route a difficult path?

Literary Elements Rhyme and Rhyme Scheme

Rhyme is the repetition of the ending sounds in words that are near each other in a poem. The most common form of rhyme in poetry is **end rhyme,** where the rhyming words appear at the ends of lines.

The pattern of rhyme formed by the end rhyme is called **rhyme scheme.** A rhyme scheme can be shown by using letters to represent the end rhymes. Lines that rhyme share the same letter. For example, if you look at the first five lines of "Paul Revere's Ride," you will see that the rhyme scheme is *aabba.*

Rhyme and rhyme scheme are important because they make a poem pleasing to hear and easier to remember.

As you read, think about the rhyme and rhyme scheme of Longfellow's poem. Do rhyme and rhyme scheme make the poem more enjoyable for you to hear and easier for you to remember?

Reading Strategy Monitor Comprehension

When you monitor your **comprehension,** you check to see whether you understand what you are reading *as you are reading it.*

It's especially important to monitor your comprehension when you read poetry. Poems may present familiar ideas in new ways or use figurative language to tell a story.

When you monitor comprehension, you

- stop and summarize what you've read
- paraphrase difficult passages in simpler language
- ask yourself questions about the passage and try to answer them
- clarify, or go back and reread a confusing section more slowly

As you read the narrative poem "Paul Revere's Ride," monitor your comprehension by making sure that you can identify the main character and setting and that you can summarize the main plot events. You may find it helpful to use a graphic organizer like the one below to summarize each stanza.

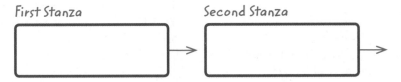

First Stanza → Second Stanza →

Learning Objectives

For pages 338–346

In studying this text, you will focus on the following objectives:

Literary Study: Analyzing rhyme and rhyme scheme.

Reading: Monitoring comprehension.

TRY IT

Monitor Comprehension
Read the excerpt from "The Drummer Boy of Shiloh." What questions might you ask to understand the text? What words would you look up? Try to paraphrase the paragraph.

[F]orty thousand men, exhausted by nervous expectation, unable to sleep for romantic dreams of battles yet unfought, lay crazily askew in their uniforms. A mile yet farther on, another army was strewn helter-skelter, turning slow, basting themselves with the thought of what they would do when the time came: a leap, a yell, a blind plunge their strategy, raw youth their protection and benediction.

PAUL REVERE'S RIDE

Henry Wadsworth Longfellow

Listen, my children, and you shall hear
Of the midnight ride of Paul Revere,
On the eighteenth of April, in Seventy-five;[1]
Hardly a man is now alive
5   Who remembers that famous day and year.
He said to his friend, "If the British march
By land or sea from the town to-night,
Hang a lantern aloft in the belfry arch
Of the North Church tower as a signal light,—
10 One, if by land, and two, if by sea;
And I on the opposite shore will be,
Ready to ride and spread the alarm
Through every Middlesex[2] village and farm,
For the country folk to be up and to arm."

15 Then he said, "Good night!" and with muffled oar
Silently rowed to the Charlestown shore,
Just as the moon rose over the bay,
Where swinging wide at her moorings[3] lay
The Somerset, British man-of-war;
20 A phantom ship, with each mast and spar
Across the moon like a prison bar,
And a huge black hulk, that was magnified
By its own reflection in the tide.

Meanwhile, his friend, through alley and street,
25 Wanders and watches with eager ears,
Till in the silence around him he hears

Rhyme and Rhyme Scheme
How would you show in letters the rhyme scheme for lines 6 to 14?

---

1   **Seventy-five** refers to 1775, the year of Paul Revere's ride.

2   The county of **Middlesex**, Massachusetts, includes the town of Concord, where the first shots of the Revolutionary War were fired on April 19, 1775.

3   The place where a ship is docked is called its **moorings**.

The muster of men at the barrack door,
The sound of arms, and the tramp of feet,
And the measured tread of the grenadiers,[4]
30 Marching down to their boats on the shore.

Then he climbed the tower of the Old North Church,
By the wooden stairs, with stealthy tread,
To the belfry-chamber overhead,
And startled the pigeons from their perch
35 On the somber[5] rafters, that round him made
Masses and moving shapes of shade,—
By the trembling ladder, steep and tall,
To the highest window in the wall,
Where he paused to listen and look down
40 A moment on the roofs of the town,
And the moonlight flowing over all.

Beneath, in the churchyard, lay the dead,
In their night-encampment on the hill,
Wrapped in silence so deep and still

Monitor Comprehension
How do you know whom this sentence is referring to—Paul Revere or his friend?

---

4 The ***measured tread*** is a steady march or walk. In the British army, ***grenadiers*** (gre′ nə dērs) were foot soldiers.

5 ***Somber*** (som′ bər) means "dark and gloomy."

45   That he could hear, like a sentinel's[6] tread,
The watchful night-wind, as it went
Creeping along from tent to tent,
And seeming to whisper, "All is well!"
A moment only he feels the spell
50   Of the place and the hour, and the secret dread
Of the lonely belfry and the dead;
For suddenly all his thoughts are bent
On a shadowy something far away,
Where the river widens to meet the bay,—
55   A line of black that bends and floats
On the rising tide, like a bridge of boats.

Meanwhile, impatient to mount and ride,
Booted and spurred, with a heavy stride
On the opposite shore walked Paul Revere.
60   Now he patted his horse's side,
Now gazed at the landscape far and near,
Then, impetuous, stamped the earth,
And turned and tightened his saddlegirth;[7]
But mostly he watched with eager search
65   The belfry-tower of the Old North Church,
As it rose above the graves on the hill,

Rhyme and Rhyme Scheme
Look at the rhymes for the word *ride*. What effect do you think those rhyming words might have on a reader?

---

6 A **sentinel** (sent′ ə nəl) is a guard.

7 Here **impetuous** means "acting suddenly." When Revere **tightened his saddlegirth,** he checked the belt that holds the saddle on a horse.

Lonely and spectral[8] and somber and still.
And lo! as he looks, on the belfry's height
A glimmer, and then a gleam of light!
70 He springs to the saddle, the bridle he turns,
But lingers and gazes, till full on his sight
A second lamp in the belfry burns!

A hurry of hoofs in a village street,
A shape in the moonlight, a bulk in the dark,
75 And beneath, from the pebbles, in passing, a spark
Struck out by a steed flying fearless and fleet:[9]
That was all! And yet, through the gloom and
    the light,
The fate of a nation was riding that night;
And the spark struck out by that steed, in his flight,
80 Kindled the land into flame with its heat.

He has left the village and mounted the steep,[10]
And beneath him, tranquil and broad and deep,
Is the Mystic,[11] meeting the ocean tides;
And under the alders[12] that skirt its edge,
85 Now soft on the sand, now loud on the ledge,
Is heard the tramp of his steed as he rides.

It was twelve by the village clock,
When he crossed the bridge into Medford town.
He heard the crowing of the cock,
90 And the barking of the farmer's dog,
And felt the damp of the river fog,
That rises after the sun goes down.

It was one by the village clock,
When he galloped into Lexington.
95 He saw the gilded[13] weathercock
Swim in the moonlight as he passed,

Monitor Comprehension
What idea is Longfellow trying to convey with "kindled the land into flame"? Think about the clues that help you understand this phrase.

---

8 Something *spectral* is ghost-like.

9 Here *fleet* means "very fast."

10 As a noun, *steep* means "a steep slope."

11 The *Mystic* is a short river that flows into Boston Harbor.

12 *Alders* are trees in the birch family.

13 A *gilded* object has, or seems to have, a thin coating of gold.

And the meeting-house windows, blank and bare,
Gaze at him with a spectral glare,
As if they already stood aghast
100   At the bloody work they would look upon.

It was two by the village clock,
When he came to the bridge in Concord town.
He heard the bleating of the flock,
And the twitter of birds among the trees,
105   And felt the breath of the morning breeze
Blowing over the meadows brown.
And one was safe and asleep in his bed
Who at the bridge would be first to fall,
Who that day would be lying dead,
110   Pierced by a British musket-ball.

You know the rest. In the books you have read,
How the British Regulars[14] fired and fled,—
How the farmers gave them ball for ball,
From behind each fence and farm-yard wall,
115   Chasing the red-coats down the lane,
Then crossing the fields to emerge again
Under the trees at the turn of the road,
And only pausing to fire and load.

So through the night rode Paul Revere;
120   And so through the night went his cry of alarm
To every Middlesex village and farm,—
A cry of defiance and not of fear,
A voice in the darkness, a knock at the door,
And a word that shall echo forevermore!
125   For, borne on the night-wind of the Past,
Through all our history, to the last,
In the hour of darkness and peril[15] and need,
The people will waken and listen to hear
The hurrying hoof-beats of that steed,
130   And the midnight message of Paul Revere.

---

14   **Regulars** are soldiers and officers belonging to a permanent professional army.
Irregulars are those who are drafted for a short time.

15   **Peril** means "danger."

Rhyme and Rhyme Scheme
Look ahead to the words that rhyme with *bed* and *fall.* How does this rhyme scheme affect the way the poem would sound if you read it aloud?

BQ BIG Question
Which do you think was more important: Paul Revere's destination or his journey? Give reasons for your answer.

After You Read

Respond and Think Critically

1. In a few sentences, sum up the story of Paul Revere's ride as it is described in the narrative poem. [Summarize]

2. What did hanging two lanterns in the church represent? Why do you think it mattered if the British came by land or by sea? [Recall and Interpret]

3. In line 78, what does the speaker mean by "the fate of a nation was riding that night"? [Infer]

4. If Paul Revere's ride had failed, in what way might our country be different today? [Draw Conclusions]

5. The poem says that Revere rode into Concord. In reality, he was arrested before he could get there. What might be the effect of a completely factual ending to the poem? [Synthesize]

6. **BQ** BIG Question Do you think that being alone while riding on his difficult path makes Paul Revere more or less heroic? Explain your opinion. [Evaluate]

Academic Vocabulary

"Paul Revere's Ride" describes how the people of Middlesex, Massachusetts, **coordinated** a plan of attack against the British on the night of April 18, 1775. In the preceding sentence, *coordinated* means "worked together in a common effort."

To become more familiar with the word *coordinated,* draw and fill out a graphic organizer like the one below. Use a dictionary or thesaurus if necessary.

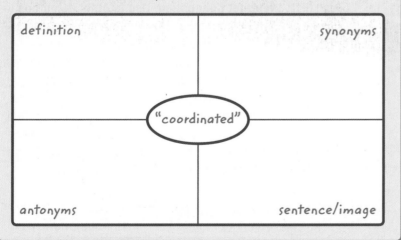

definition	synonyms
antonyms	sentence/image

TIP

Inferring
Here are some tips to help you infer. Remember that when you infer, you use your reason and experience to guess at what the author does not come right out and say.

- Skim the selection for clues that may help explain the meaning of the line.

- Identify what descriptions, events, or relationships might tell you something the author wants you to know.

- Check to see if your inference makes sense in the context of the selection.

- Compare the events to your own experiences and then think about what the author is really saying.

FOLDABLES Study Organizer Keep track of your ideas about the **BIG Question** in your unit Foldable.

 Literature Online

Selection Resources
For Selection Quizzes, eFlashcards, and Reading-Writing Connection activities, go to glencoe.com and enter QuickPass code GL39770u3.

1. Which end rhymes can you find in the third stanza?

2. What is the rhyme scheme of the second stanza of the poem? Assign a letter to name each rhyme in the sequence, such as *aabbaacc*.

3. Explain why rhyme and rhyme scheme are so important to this poem.

Review: Narrative Poetry

As you learned on page 101, **narrative poetry** is verse that tells a story. It has characters, a setting, and a plot with a conflict. Unlike prose stories, a narrative poem contains rhythm, rhyme, and other poetic sound devices.

4. The first stanza of the poem establishes the setting. Describe the setting in a few sentences, paying attention to the time, place, and mood. What mood does Longfellow create by beginning the poem this way?

Reading Strategy Monitor Comprehension

5. Think about the strategies you used to monitor your comprehension as you read "Paul Revere's Ride." In which two places in the poem were your strategies most helpful? Explain your experiences.

Grammar Link

Pronouns A **pronoun** is a word that takes the place of one or more nouns. The word or group of words that a pronoun refers to is called its **antecedent**.

Reflexive pronouns and **intensive pronouns** are formed by adding -*self* or -*selves* to certain personal and possessive pronouns.

Examples: *myself, ourselves*

Use a reflexive pronoun when a pronoun that is *not possessive* refers back to a noun or pronoun earlier in the sentence, showing that the same person or thing is involved.

Example: Paul Revere's friend lit the lanterns himself.

Use an intensive pronoun to add emphasis to another noun or pronoun. **Example:**

Paul Revere himself delivered the warning.

The intensive pronoun *himself* emphasizes that Paul Revere gave the warning.

Practice With a partner, write four sentences about "Paul Revere's Ride," two using reflexive pronouns and two using intensive pronouns.

Research and Report

Internet Connection Use Internet resources to learn about other Revolutionary War patriots. Be sure to use reliable resources, such as online encyclopedias and university Web sites. Try to find primary sources, such as letters from colonists, as well as historical accounts. In your report, provide the source of each fact you use. Make a list of three to five patriots, and explain why each one was important. Use a graphic organizer like the one below.

American Patriot	Contribution to Revolution

Exile

Connect to the Poem

Think about a time when you or someone you know had to make a difficult journey.

Quickwrite Freewrite for a few minutes about this journey. What was challenging about it? Looking back, was the journey worth taking? Write a brief answer.

Build Background

In the poem "Exile," the speaker, or the voice that talks to the reader, is fleeing the Dominican Republic with her family. This poem may reflect Alvarez's real-life experiences of exile. The word *exile* means "a forced absence from one's home country."

- The Dominican Republic is a Latin American country located in the middle of the Caribbean islands. It makes up the eastern two-thirds of the island of Hispaniola. The country of Haiti makes up the western third.

- From 1930 to 1961, the Dominican Republic was controlled by the violent dictator Rafael Trujillo. Trujillo was known to hurt or even kill people who disagreed with him.

- Some people who lived in the Dominican Republic tried to remove Trujillo from power. This was very dangerous, and many of the attempts were unsuccessful. Alvarez's family left the Dominican Republic because her father participated in one of these failed attempts.

Meet Julia Alvarez

"I had become a hybrid. . . . I was not a mainstream American girl and I wasn't a totally Dominican girl anymore."
—Julia Alvarez

Bridging Two Worlds
When Julia Alvarez was ten years old, her family was forced to flee the Dominican Republic for political reasons. Torn from her childhood home and culture, she felt out of place in New York City. Alvarez turned to writing stories and poems to bridge the gap between her two worlds.

Literary Works Alvarez is the author of many books, including *How the García Girls Lost Their Accents.* "Exile" was published in *The Other Side/El Otro Lado,* in 1995.

Julia Alvarez was born in 1950.

 Literature Online

Author Search For more about Julia Alvarez, go to glencoe.com and enter QuickPass code GL39770u3.

Set Purposes for Reading

BQ **BIG Question**

As you read, decide whether the speaker's journey ends when she reaches her destination.

Literary Element | Metaphor

A **metaphor** is a figure of speech that compares seemingly unlike things without using the words *like* or *as*. A metaphor often implies the comparison instead of stating it directly. An **extended metaphor** is a specific type of metaphor that is used throughout an entire poem or story.

Extended metaphors can add impact to an author's message. When an author develops the same metaphor throughout a work, readers have the opportunity to think deeply about the comparison being made.

To identify the extended metaphor in "Exile," note the images and ideas that the poet repeats, and ask yourself what two things are being compared throughout the poem.

Reading Strategy | Interpret Author's Meaning

When you interpret an **author's meaning,** you try to understand what an author is communicating. There can be many ways to interpret a work. Good interpretations are supported by details in the text.

To interpret an author's meaning,

- identify the literal, or directly stated, meaning of the poem. If the poem tells a story, determine the basic plot.

- look for the deeper, or implied, meaning. What message about life is the poet trying to communicate?

- think about the overall feeling the poem gives you. What specific words and phrases give you that feeling?

As you read "Exile," interpret the poem by looking for the literal and implied meanings and the overall feeling you get from the poem. You may find it helpful to use a graphic organizer like the one below.

	Interpretation	Evidence
Literal Meaning	The poet is leaving her homeland.	Papi drives the car to the airport.
Implied Meaning		
Overall Feeling		

Learning Objectives

For pages 347–353

In studying this text, you will focus on the following objectives:

Literary Study: Analyzing metaphor.

Reading: Interpreting author's meaning.

TRY IT

When a friend sends you an e-mail or a text message, he or she probably uses phrases and abbreviations that have a special meaning for the two of you. Write a brief message in an e-mail or text message style. Exchange it with a friend and interpret the message you receive.

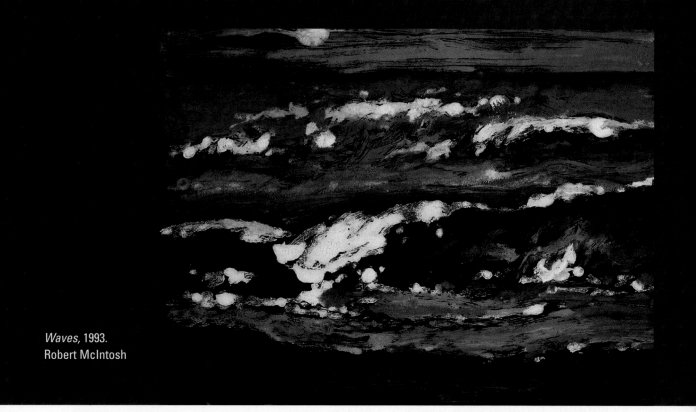

Waves, 1993.
Robert McIntosh

EXILE

Julia Alvarez
Ciudad Trujillo, New York City, 1960

The night we fled the country, Papi,
you told me we were going to the beach,
hurried me to get dressed along with the others,
while posted at a window, you looked out

5   at a curfew-darkened Ciudad Trujillo,°
speaking in worried whispers to your brothers,
which car to take, who'd be willing to drive it,
what explanation to give should we be discovered . . .

On the way to the beach, you added, eyeing me.
10 The uncles fell in, chuckling phony chuckles,
What a good time she'll have learning to swim!
Back in my sisters' room Mami was packing

Interpret Author's Meaning
Is the speaker really going
to the beach?
How do you know?

---

5 Santo Domingo is the capital of the Dominican Republic. In 1936, its
name was changed to **Ciudad Trujillo** (sē ōō däd´ trōō hē´yō) to honor the
dictator Rafael Trujillo.
The name Santo Domingo was restored after Trujillo's death in 1961.

a hurried bag, allowing one toy apiece,
her red eyes belying° her explanation:

15 *a week at the beach so Papi can get some rest.*
She dressed us in our best dresses,
    party shoes.

Something was off, I knew, but I was young
and didn't think adult things could go wrong.
So as we quietly filed out of the house
20 we wouldn't see again for another decade,

I let myself lie back in the deep waters,
my arms out like Jesus' on His cross,
and instead of sinking down as I'd always done,
magically, that night, I could stay up,

25 floating out, past the driveway, past the gates,
in the black Ford, Papi grim at the wheel,
winding through back roads, stroke by
    difficult stroke,
out on the highway, heading toward the coast.

Past the checkpoint, we raced towards the airport,
30 my sisters crying when we turned before
the family beach house, Mami consoling,°
there was a better surprise in store for us!

She couldn't tell, though, until . . .
    until we were there.
But I had already swum ahead and guessed
35 some loss much larger than I understood,
more danger than the deep end of the pool.

At the dark, deserted airport we waited.
All night in a fitful sleep, I swam.
At dawn the plane arrived, and as we boarded,
40 Papi, you turned, your eyes scanned the horizon

as if you were trying to sight a distant swimmer,
your hand frantically waving her back in,

Metaphor To what does the speaker compare her journey?

---

14 **Belying** is showing something to be false.

31 A **consoling** person comforts others.

for you knew as we stepped inside the cabin
that a part of both of us had been set adrift.

45 Weeks later, wandering our new city, hand in hand,
you tried to explain the wonders: escalators
as moving belts; elevators: pulleys and ropes;
blond hair and blue eyes: a genetic code.

We stopped before a summery display window
50 at Macy's,° *The World's Largest Department Store,*
to admire a family outfitted for the beach:
the handsome father, slim and sure of himself,

so unlike you, Papi, with your thick mustache,
your three-piece suit, your fedora hat, your accent.
55 And by his side a girl who looked like Heidi
in my storybook waded in colored plastic.

We stood awhile, marveling at America,
both of us trying hard to feel luckier
than we felt, both of us pointing out
60 the beach pails, the shovels, the sandcastles

no wave would ever topple, the red and blue boats.
And when we backed away, we saw our reflections
superimposed,° big-eyed, dressed too formally
with all due respect as visitors to this country.

65 Or like, Papi, two swimmers looking down
at the quiet surface of our island waters,
seeing their faces right before plunging in,
eager, afraid, not yet sure of the outcome.

Interpret Author's Meaning
What does the speaker mean when she says, "a part of both of us had been set adrift"?

BQ **BIG Question**
Do you think the speaker's journey ends when she reaches New York City? Explain why or why not.

---

50 The **Macy's** flagship store is located in New York City. The speaker's family has moved to New York City.

63 An image that is **superimposed** is placed on top of another image so that both images are seen at the same time.

After You Read

Respond and Think Critically

1. In your own words, describe the night the speaker left the Dominican Republic. [Summarize]

2. Why does the poet put the words about the trip to the beach in italics? [Interpret]

3. In what ways are the speaker and her father different from the family in the display window? [Compare]

4. In what ways is moving to a new country like plunging into the water? [Analyze]

5. Does the speaker feel at home in America? Explain your thoughts. [Infer]

6. **BIG Question** For the speaker, arriving at her destination safely is very important. However, she also learns about herself and her family along the way. Why do you think it is important to learn from a journey while not losing sight of your destination? [Make Judgments]

Academic Vocabulary

At the end of "Exile," the speaker makes an **assumption** that her father feels the same way she does. To become more familiar with the word *assumption,* fill out the graphic organizer below.

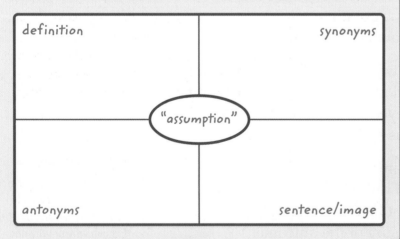

definition

synonyms

"assumption"

antonyms

sentence/image

TIP

Inferring
Here are some tips to help you make an inference. Remember that when a question asks you to infer, the answer is not directly stated.

- Pay attention to the speaker's reactions to the things she sees in her new home.

- Think about your own experiences with new places or situations.

- Combine information in the text with your own knowledge to answer the question.

FOLDABLES Keep track of **Study Organizer** your ideas about the **BIG Question** in your unit Foldable.

 Literature Online

Selection Resources
For Selection Quizzes, eFlashcards, and Reading-Writing Connection activities, go to glencoe.com and enter QuickPass code GL39770u3.

Literary Element Metaphor

1. The speaker compares her journey to America to swimming. What do these experiences have in common? Support your answer with details from the poem.

2. Do you think the metaphor the speaker uses for her journey is effective? Why or why not?

Review: Line and Stanza

Poems are made up of **lines.** A line of poetry may or may not be a complete sentence. Poets use line breaks to affect the rhythm, meaning, and look of a poem. A **stanza** is a group of lines that form a unit in a poem. Stanzas are like the paragraphs of poems.

Poems with lines that don't rhyme but that have a regular pattern of stressed and unstressed syllables are written in **blank verse.** Poems that have a rhythm but don't rhyme or follow a regular pattern of stressed and unstressed syllables are written in **free verse.** When read aloud, free verse sounds more like natural speech than blank verse.

3. How many lines are in each stanza of "Exile"?

4. Is "Exile" an example of blank verse or free verse? Why do you think the poet chose to write the poem in this form?

Reading Strategy
Interpret Author's Meaning

5. The speaker says that the night her family fled, she floated instead of sinking. What does this reaction suggest about her faith in her parents?

Grammar Link

Future Tense The **future tense** of a verb shows that the action will happen in a time yet to come.

To form the future tense of a verb, use the helping verb *will* with the present tense form of the verb. For example,

> Mami and Papi will move their family to America.

Practice Rewrite these sentences from "Exile" in the future tense. Then write two future tense sentences in which you tell what you think will happen next to the speaker.

1. She dressed us in our best dresses, party shoes.

2. At the dark, deserted airport, we waited.

Write with Style

Apply Figurative Language Write a short poem about a memorable journey you have taken. Include an extended metaphor to describe your experience. For example, the speaker in "Exile" compares her move to America to swimming. Review the poem to help you develop your own creative writing style. Use a graphic organizer like the one below to help you plan your poem.

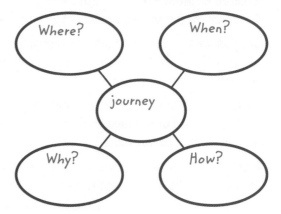

The Oxcart

Connect to the Folktale

Have you ever tried to take the easy way out of a situation only to discover that the path you chose wasn't so easy after all?

Quickwrite Write a few sentences about this situation and what you learned from the experience.

Build Background

"The Oxcart" is a folktale that was told for hundreds of years before it was written down. Everyone who told it gave a slightly different version. The person responsible for writing this version is Eric A. Kimmel.

- "The Oxcart" can be classified as a **cautionary tale**—a story in which people are punished for breaking society's rules or misbehaving. Though the punishment in cautionary tales is usually harsh and heavy-handed, the punishment in "The Oxcart" is definitely lighthearted.

- The story takes place in Japan when there were very strict rules about how people of different social classes should behave. No one had pity on those who broke the rules. If a noble disgraced himself, he could be thrown out of his house and have everything taken from him by the ruler.

Vocabulary

assured (ə shoord´) v. told with certainty (p. 358). *I assured my parents that I would be home on time.*

unforeseen (un´fôr sēn´) adj. not known beforehand; unexpected (p. 359). *He was late for class because of unforeseen traffic delays.*

stricken (strik´ən) adj. strongly affected or overwhelmed, as if by disease or sickness (p. 360). *She was suddenly stricken with a high fever.*

outskirts (out´skurts´) n. pl. a part or an area away from the center (p. 360). *I live on the outskirts of the city.*

Meet Eric A. Kimmel

"Stories aren't dead. . . . They change with each teller. They change as they move across continents and generations."

—Eric A. Kimmel

Teller of Tales Eric A. Kimmel knew that he would grow up to be a storyteller. His earliest memories are of listening to his grandmother tell him stories from her childhood in Eastern Europe. His New York neighborhood was home to people and stories from many cultures.

Literary Works Kimmel has shared his love of stories from around the world in more than fifty books. "The Oxcart" is included in *Sword of the Samurai: Adventure Stories from Japan,* published in 2000.

Eric Kimmel was born in 1946.

 Literature Online

Author Search For more about Eric A. Kimmel, go to glencoe.com and enter QuickPass code GL39770u3.

Set Purposes for Reading

BQ BIG Question

Read "The Oxcart" to find out what happens to three samurai on a journey and what lesson they learn in the end.

Literary Element Characterization

Characterization consists of the methods an author uses to develop a character. In **direct characterization,** the narrator makes statements about a character's personality. In **indirect characterization,** a character's personality is revealed through his or her words, thoughts, and actions or through what other characters think and say about him or her.

As you read "The Oxcart," ask yourself how the author develops the personalities of the three samurai.

Reading Skill Analyze Setting

Setting is the time and place in which the events of a story, novel, poem, or play occur.

It is important to analyze the setting because the setting often helps create an atmosphere, or mood. A setting can include a historical period, a geographical location, customs and traditions, and social classes.

As you read "The Oxcart," think about how the setting affects the mood of the story. You may find it helpful to use a graphic organizer like the one below.

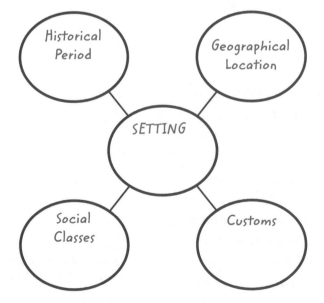

TRY IT

Analyze Setting Imagine a perfect setting for playing your favorite sport outdoors. How would you describe the setting? For example: Where would you play? What time of day would it be? What would the weather be like? What team would you be playing against if it's a team sport?

From the *Illustrations to 100 Poems by 100 Poets.* Katsushika Hokusai. Japan.

The Oxcart

Eric A. Kimmel

Old Japan had strict rules governing how people of all classes should behave. Highborn women were not allowed to have any contact with commoners. They could travel only in two-wheeled oxcarts. Small windows and heavy curtains hid the passengers from unwelcome stares. Although these carts were beautifully furnished and decorated, they were cramped, poorly ventilated, and extremely uncomfortable to ride in. The oxcarts were reserved for women. No male samurai could ride in one. If he did and was caught, he faced severe punishment, possibly even the loss of his samurai status. The three samurai in this story tried to cut corners. They learned a well-deserved lesson.

Analyze Setting What do you learn about the importance of rules in Old Japan?

The governor of Settsu had three outstanding samurai[1] in his service. Their names were Taira no Hidemichi, Taira no Suetake, and Sakata no Kintoki. Once in late fall, when the time of the Kamo festival was approaching, the three samurai wanted to go to Murasakino to watch the procession. They looked forward to seeing the beautiful shrines[2] pulled through the streets on wagons while the great *taiko* drums filled the air with their pounding rhythm.

"How will we get to Murasakino?" Hidemichi asked.

"We'll ride our horses," Suetake suggested.

"That's not a good idea," said Kintoki. "The streets in Murasakino are going to be crowded. Our horses are trained for war. Once they find themselves in the middle of those crowds, they'll think they're on a battlefield. They'll start kicking and plunging. Someone's bound to get hurt, and it will be our fault. The governor will be very angry with us."

"Then we'll walk," said Hidemichi.

"Three samurai walking along on foot, like common peasants? We'd be disgraced," Suetake replied.

"We could cover our faces so no one would know who we are," Kintoki suggested.

Hidemichi argued against that idea. "The city guards would take us for bandits. We'd end up in jail, and the governor would have to get us out. Even if we could go by foot, it's a long walk to Murasakino and back. I don't want to do it."

"Neither do we," Kintoki and Suetake agreed.

"If we can't walk or ride, how will we get there?" Suetake asked.

"I have an idea," Kintoki said. "We'll go in an oxcart."

"What? A farmer's wagon?"

"No! I mean the kind of closed oxcart that the wives and daughters of highborn nobles ride in."

Characterization What do Suetake's words tell you about how the samurai see themselves?

Analyze Setting What can you tell about the lives of upper-class women in Japan at that time?

---

1 **Samurai** were members of the Japanese military class, just below powerful nobles in importance. Samurai were expected to fight bravely and live perfect lives.

2 In this case, a **shrine** is a case or box for sacred objects.

"Is that a good idea?" Hidemichi asked. "Samurai are warriors. We aren't allowed to ride in carts or wagons. If anyone sees us, we'll be disgraced."

"Nobody will see us," Kintoki **assured** him. "These oxcarts are completely enclosed. The windows are covered with heavy curtains so no one can see inside."

"How will we get one?" Suetake asked. "Three samurai can't hire an oxcart without the whole town learning about it."

"I've thought of that already," said Kintoki. "My sister is lady-in-waiting[3] to the governor's wife. The governor has plenty of oxcarts. Some are hardly ever used. My sister can arrange for us to borrow one. We'll walk along beside it on the way through town, pretending we're an escort.[4] When no one is looking, we'll get in and ride all the way to Murasakino. Our servant, Akira, will lead the ox while we travel in comfort."

Characterization What does Kintoki's plan reveal about him?

Japanese samurai warriors, c.1880. R.P. Kingston.

3 A *lady-in-waiting* was a noblewoman who was a servant to an even more rich and powerful woman, often a queen.

4 An *escort* is one who accompanies another person on a journey to give protection.

Vocabulary

assured (ə shoord´) *v.* told with certainty

Ashida, from *"Stations on the Kisokaido Highway,"* c.1838. Ando or Utagawa Hiroshige. Woodblock color print. Brooklyn Museum of Fine Art, NY. Frank L. Babbott Fund.

<u>View the Art</u> What can you infer about what it would be like to travel on the road in this picture?

The plan worked perfectly—except for one **unforeseen** difficulty. The three samurai had never traveled in an oxcart. Although the vehicle looked elegant, it had no springs. Every bump in the road bounced them around like grains of rice pounded in a mortar. And there were many, many bumps, holes, and gullies along the way to Murasakino.

They had hardly gone a mile when Suetake turned pale. "I feel sick. I think I'm going to throw up," he said. "Hurry! Open the door! Let me out!"

Kintoki and Hidemichi grabbed him. "You can't go out! The road is full of people. If they see us riding in this oxcart, we'll be in trouble!"

"I can't help it!" Suetake moaned. "You have to let me out. I'm going to be—"

Vocabulary . . . .

unforeseen (un´fôr sēn´) *adj.* not known beforehand; unexpected

Poor Suetake threw up all over the oxcart. Like a seasick traveler, he couldn't stop vomiting, even when his stomach was empty. He lay helpless on the floor, moaning and coughing.

Hidemichi turned pale. "What a terrible stench! Open the curtains, Kintoki, or I'll be sick, too!"

"I can't open the curtains! No one must see us in here!" said Kintoki.

"Then I am going to be sick with Suetake!" Hidemichi clutched his stomach and threw up, too. Within minutes, Kintoki joined him. The three samurai lay in a heap, vomiting on each other, groaning in misery.

The people on the road to Murasakino heard terrible groans coming from the oxcart. "What is going on in there?" they asked Akira, the samurais' servant. "It sounds as if someone is dying. Open the door! The people inside need help."

"Don't touch that door!" Akira blurted out. He could not allow his masters to be discovered riding in a women's oxcart. "The governor's aunt is inside. She was suddenly **stricken** with a terrible disease. Oozing sores broke out all over her body. The doctors can't help her. She is going to the temple in Murasakino to pray for a cure. No one must go near that cart. She might have the plague."[5]

Needless to say, no one approached the cart again. The opposite happened. People on the road ran away when they saw the oxcart coming. It continued on to Murasakino, lurching back and forth on the bumpy road, with the three miserable samurai tumbling around inside it.

At last the cart stopped. "Masters, we are here. We've reached the **outskirts** of Murasakino," Akira whispered. He waited for a reply but heard nothing. Finally he said, "I'm going to find a pasture for the ox. Then I'm going to watch the procession. Come quickly. It will be starting soon."

Analyze Setting From the samurai's behavior, what can you tell about the importance of shame and honor in Japanese culture during that time?

Characterization What do Akira's actions tell you about his character?

---

5 The *plague* is an infectious, deadly disease.

Vocabulary . . . .

stricken (strik′ən) *adj.* strongly affected or overwhelmed, as if by disease or sickness
outskirts (out′skurts′) *n. pl.* a part or an area away from the center

Mount Fuji viewed from the province of Hara in Suruga, 1860. Hiroshige II. Color woodcut. Victoria and Albert Museum, London.

Akira unhitched the ox and led it away. When he returned hours later, he found the oxcart door still shut, with no sign that his masters had ever emerged. Fearing they might be dead, Akira opened the door and peeped inside.

He saw the three samurai lying in a heap, too weak to stand or even groan. Akira lifted them out of the cart, one by one. "Masters, I am so sorry. I did not know you were so ill. Have you been here the whole time? Didn't you go to the festival?"

"How could we?" Kintoki answered. "We were so sick we could hardly lift our heads."

"How stupid we were to ride in that cart!" Suetake exclaimed.

Characterization What does Suetake's comment reveal about the lesson the three samurai learn?

Hidemichi agreed. "We suffered for nothing. We missed the whole festival."

Akira ran to an inn down the road. He returned with hot water, new clothes, and a kettle of hot soup. The samurai felt better after cleaning themselves and eating.

"Let's go home," Kintoki said, disgusted.

"Not in that cart," said Hidemichi and Suetake. "We'll walk beside it. We'll pretend we're an escort."

The three samurai walked all the way back to Settsu. It took a long time to get there. They walked slowly, holding their stomachs, dragging their swords in the dust.

Kintoki's sister was waiting for them. "Where have you been? I was expecting you hours ago. Why do you look so pale? Why does the cart smell so bad?"

"You're lucky we brought it back at all. This cart should be burned!" Kintoki told her.

"The horrid vehicle nearly killed us!" Hidemichi added.

"I'd rather face slow death by torture than ride in an oxcart again!" said Suetake.

Kintoki's sister began to laugh. "You samurai are always telling your wives and sisters how tough you are! You only went to Murasakino. One short ride in an oxcart and you come back looking like corpses. We women are tougher than you! We ride in these carts all the time. Ha, ha, ha!"

Kintoki, Suetake, and Hidemichi slunk away without a word.

The three samurai had long, distinguished careers. Kintoki climbed the walls of an enemy castle and opened the gate, all by himself. Suetake stood alone in the middle of a bridge and fought off an attacking army. Hidemichi, after losing his sword, pulled an enemy general off his horse and captured him with his bare hands. But brave as they were, not one of the three ever went near an oxcart again.

"A samurai does not fear death," they would say. "But some things are worse than death. An oxcart is one of them." 🔖

BQ **BIG Question**

A familiar saying claims that you cannot understand another person until you walk a mile in that person's shoes. What do you think the samurai understand about Japanese women after traveling in the oxcart?

Characterization What method of characterization does the author use here—direct or indirect?

After You Read

Respond and Think Critically

1. List the three possible ways the samurai consider traveling to the festival. [Identify]

2. The three samurai couldn't hire an oxcart without the town finding out about it. What does this tell you about the town and the people in it? [Infer]

3. Do you think it's funny that the samurai get sick? Explain. [Respond]

4. What similar character traits do the three samurai share? [Compare]

5. How are the samurai punished for breaking the rules of their society? [Analyze]

6. **BQ** BIG Question What do you think the journey of the three samurai taught them about themselves? [Draw Conclusions]

TIP

Analyzing
Here are some tips to help you analyze.

- Skim the selection to look for both the physical and emotional suffering the samurai endured.

- Explain that the samurai endured these consequences because they broke their society's rules.

FOLDABLES Study Organizer Keep track of your ideas about the **BIG Question** in your unit Foldable.

View the Art

Japanese Samurai Warriors

The Japanese warriors known as **samurai** came to power in twelfth-century Japan. They were known for their military skills and prided themselves on their bravery and ability to tolerate physical stress. The ideal samurai was supposed to be a stoic warrior who followed an unwritten code of conduct, holding bravery, honor, and personal loyalty above life itself. The samurai class disappeared in the 1870s, when feudalism was abolished in Japan.

A Japanese samurai warrior.

Group Activity Discuss the following questions with classmates.

1. Review the photos on this page and on page 358. What does the armor worn by the samurai tell you about the way they fought?

2. What details about their armor and weapons suggest that the samurai had a high social status?

Literary Element Characterization

1. When the samurai slink away after Kintoki's sister teases them, what does the characters' body language tell you about how they feel? Is this an example of direct or indirect characterization? Explain.

2. How do the samurai's attitudes change from the beginning of the folktale to the end? Support your answer with examples of the characters' words and actions.

Review: Plot

Plot is the sequence of events in a story. The plot begins with the **exposition,** which introduces the story's characters, setting, and situation. **The rising action** adds complications to the story's **conflicts,** or problems, and leads to the **climax,** or the point of greatest interest or suspense in a story. The **falling action** is the logical result of the climax, and the **resolution** presents the final outcome of the plot.

3. Think back to the exposition of the story. In your own words, tell who the main characters are, what the setting is, and what situation the characters are facing.

4. What is the resolution of the plot? Explain what you learn about the outcome of the conflict the three samurai face.

Reading Skill Analyze Setting

5. Curtains hide noblewomen riding in oxcarts from public view. What does this custom tell you about the lives of noblewomen in Old Japan?

6. Describe what you think the procession at Murasakino would have been like.

Vocabulary Practice

Synonyms are words that have the same or nearly the same meaning. Match each vocabulary word with its synonym in the right-hand column. Two of the words in the right-hand column will not have matches. Then write a sentence using each vocabulary word or draw or find a picture that represents each word.

1. **assured**   a. unexpected
2. **unforeseen**   b. parades
3. **outskirts**   c. edges
4. **stricken**   d. promised
                     e. overwhelmed
                     g. argued

Example:

assured and *promised* = synonyms

Sentence: José assured the coach that he would be ready for the big game.

Academic Vocabulary

When the samurai rode in the oxcart, they **violated** the social rules during that time in Japan.

When they *violated* the rules, they didn't show proper respect for the rules. Think about a time someone you know violated a rule. What happened?

Literature Online

Selection Resources For Selection Quizzes, eFlashcards, and Reading-Writing Connection activities, go to glencoe.com and enter QuickPass code GL39770u3.

Respond Through Writing

Research Report

Investigate Japanese Folktales "The Oxcart" captures details about ancient Japanese culture. In a research report, discuss other Japanese folktales to compare their plots, themes, and characters.

Understand the Task In your research report, you will be comparing different Japanese folktales.

Prewrite Use research tools such as library books and the Internet to find Japanese folktales. Take note of plots, themes, and characters. Keep track of your research in a chart like the one below.

	folktale #1	folktale #2	folktale #3
plots			
themes			
characters			

Draft Sometimes it's helpful to use sentence frames as you draft a report. For instance, your introduction will include a thesis statement that might be stated as follows:

The Japanese folktales _____, _____, and _____ provide interesting details about ancient Japanese culture.

Your body paragraphs will discuss the topics you've introduced in your thesis, such as the following:

One folktale, _____, teaches its readers to avoid being excessively proud.

Revise After you have written your first draft, read it to determine whether you have accurately described each folktale. Revise sentences as necessary so that your ideas are clear.

Edit and Proofread Proofread your report, correcting any errors in spelling, grammar, and punctuation. Review the Grammar Tip in the side column for information on correct use of semicolons.

Learning Objectives

For page 365

In this assignment, you will focus on the following objective:

Writing: Writing a research report.

Grammar Tip

Semicolons
Use semicolons to join two independent clauses. Look at this sentence. It uses a semicolon to join two independent clauses.

The plan did not work perfectly; there was one unforeseen difficulty.

As you write, try using a semicolon to join two related sentences.

Harriet Tubman

Connect to the Poem

Think of someone you know or have heard about who helped rescue others from a dangerous situation.

Partner Talk With a partner, talk about what this person did. Would you have put yourself in such a difficult situation? Explain.

Build Background

This poem describes Harriet Tubman's courage and her hard work in helping others escape their enslaved condition.

- Born enslaved, Harriet Tubman worked at various jobs—a maid, a nurse, a field hand, a cook, and a woodcutter.

- In 1849, after hearing rumors that she was going to be sold, she fled North to escape slavery.

- She returned to the South nineteen times from 1850 to 1860 to help others take the path to freedom.

Set a Purpose for Reading

BQ BIG Question

Read the poem to understand Harriet Tubman's attitude toward her difficult path and her destination.

Literary Elements Rhythm and Meter

Rhythm refers to the pattern of sound created by the arrangement of stressed and unstressed syllables in a line of poetry. Stressed syllables of a line are marked with the symbol ´, while unstressed syllables are marked with the symbol ˘. A regular or predictable pattern of rhythm is called **meter.**

Har˘ri˘et Tub´man did˘n't take´ no˘ stuff´

Wasn't scared´ of noth´ing neit´her

Poems, like songs, depend on sound to help express thoughts and emotions. Rhythm gives poetry a musical quality and helps you understand its meaning.

As you read aloud "Harriet Tubman," ask yourself how Eloise Greenfield uses rhythm to convey information about Harriet Tubman and her journeys.

Learning Objectives

For pages 366–368

In studying this text, you will focus on the following objective:

Literary Study:
Analyzing rhythm and meter.

Meet Eloise Greenfield

"If we could know more about our ancestors . . . we would then know much more about what has shaped us and our world."

—Eloise Greenfield

African-American Life Eloise Greenfield's work often portrays strong, loving African-American families and communities. She has stated that her family and her efforts to fight racism are her most important concerns.

Eloise Greenfield was born in 1929.

 Literature Online

Author Search For more about Eloise Greenfield, go to glencoe.com and enter QuickPass code GL39770u3.

HARRIET TUBMAN

Eloise Greenfield

Harriet Tubman, 1945. William H. Johnson. Oil on paperboard, 29 3/8 x 23 3/8 in. National Museum of American Art; Washington, DC.

Harriet Tubman didn't take no stuff
Wasn't scared of nothing neither
Didn't come in this world to be no slave
And wasn't going to stay one either

5 "Farewell!" she sang to her friends one night
She was mighty sad to leave 'em
But she ran away that dark, hot night
Ran looking for her freedom
She ran to the woods and she ran through the woods
10 With the slave catchers right behind her
And she kept on going till she got to the North
Where those mean men couldn't find her

Nineteen times she went back South
To get three hundred others
15 She ran for her freedom nineteen times
To save Black sisters and brothers
Harriet Tubman didn't take no stuff
Wasn't scared of nothing neither
Didn't come in this world to be no slave
20 And didn't stay one either
And didn't stay one either

<u>View the Art</u> In what ways does this portrait reflect Harriet Tubman as described in the poem?

Rhythm and Meter Read lines 5–8 of the poem aloud. What syllables or words are stressed? Describe the musical quality they help to create.

BQ **BIG Question**
Why would Tubman risk her life after she had already reached safety?

After You Read

Respond and Think Critically

1. Use your own words to retell the events described in the poem. [Summarize]

2. What does the speaker mean when she writes, "Harriet Tubman didn't take no stuff"? [Interpret]

3. For what reason does the speaker repeat the first four lines of the poem as the closing lines of the poem? [Infer]

4. Do you think you would take a journey as risky as the ones Tubman took? Explain why or why not. [Connect]

5. **Literary Elements** Rhythm and Meter In your own words, describe the musical quality of the whole poem or its rhythm and meter. What feelings does the poem's sound create in you as a reader and listener? [Evaluate]

6. **BQ** BIG Question Which do you think is more important to Tubman—her journey or her destination? [Draw Conclusions]

Spelling Link

Rule for adding suffixes to words ending in y When you are adding a suffix to words ending in a vowel + y, keep the y.

For words ending with a consonant + y, change the y to i unless the suffix begins with i.

Examples: display + ed   displayed
                mighty + er   mightier

Alternative spellings: Some words can have more than one spelling.

Examples: sly + er   *slyer* or *slier*
                shy + est   *shyest* or *shiest*

Practice Generate a list of 5–10 more words that end with y. Exchange lists with a partner and add a suffix to each word on your partner's list. Then compare and correct both lists. Compose five sentences with five of the new words.

Writing

Write a Stanza Think of someone who took a difficult path. The person may be a historical figure, an athlete, a friend, or a family member. Write a stanza in which you describe the person's actions. Your stanza should have a strong rhythm and meter.

TIP

Summarizing
Here are some tips to help you summarize. Remember, when you summarize, you retell the main ideas or events in your own words and in a logical sequence.

- Skim the poem to identify Harriet Tubman's actions.

- Retell the events in the order in which they occurred.

- Use transition words such as *first, next, then,* and *finally.*

FOLDABLES Keep track of
Study Organizer your ideas about
the **BIG Question** in your unit Foldable.

 Literature Online

Selection Resources
For Selection Quizzes, eFlashcards, and Reading-Writing Connection activities, go to glencoe.com and enter QuickPass code GL39770u3.

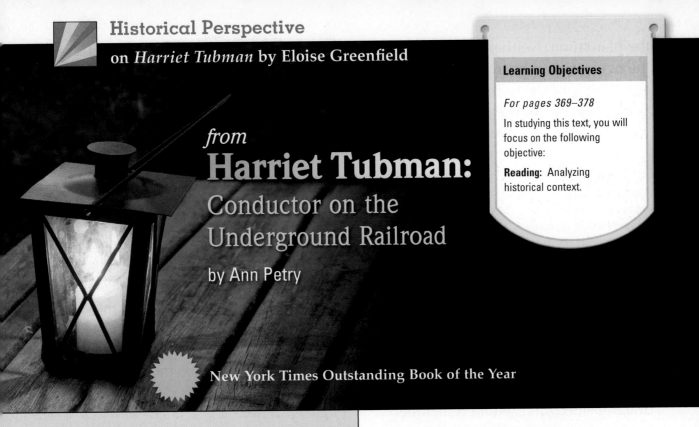

from

Harriet Tubman:
Conductor on the Underground Railroad

by Ann Petry

New York Times Outstanding Book of the Year

Set a Purpose for Reading
Read to understand Harriet Tubman's difficult path as she led others to freedom.

Build Background
In the period before and during the Civil War, the Underground Railroad was a series of secret travel routes and hiding places where people who opposed slavery hid enslaved people who were traveling North toward freedom. Harriet Tubman guided and aided runaways.

Reading Skill Analyze Historical Context

When you analyze the **historical context** of a biography, you examine how the people in the text were affected by what was taking place in the world around them. As you read, use a web diagram like the one below to note the obstacles runaways faced as they escaped slavery.

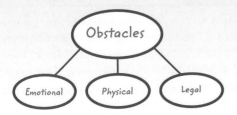

A long the Eastern Shore of Maryland, in Dorchester County, in Caroline County, the masters kept hearing whispers about the man named Moses,[1] who was running off slaves. At first they did not believe in his existence. The stories about him were fantastic, unbelievable. Yet they watched for him. They offered rewards for his capture.

They never saw him. Now and then they heard whispered rumors to the effect that he was in the neighborhood. The woods were searched. The roads were watched. There was never anything to indicate his whereabouts. But a few days afterward, a goodly number of slaves would be gone from

---

1 ***Moses*** was a Hebrew prophet who led his people out of slavery in Egypt. To enslaved persons, biblical figures like Moses represented the hope of freedom.

the plantation. Neither the master nor the overseer had heard or seen anything unusual in the quarter.[2] Sometimes one or the other would vaguely remember having heard a

whippoorwill call somewhere in the woods, close by, late at night. Though it was the wrong season for whippoorwills.

Sometimes the masters thought they had heard the cry of a hoot owl, repeated, and would remember having thought that the intervals between the low moaning cry were wrong, that it had been repeated four times in succession instead of three. There was never anything more than that to suggest that all was not well in the quarter. Yet when morning came, they invariably discovered that a group of the finest slaves had taken to their heels.

Unfortunately, the discovery was almost always made on a Sunday. Thus a whole day was lost before the machinery of pursuit could be set in motion. The posters offering rewards for the fugitives could not be printed until Monday. The men who made a living hunting for runaway slaves were out of reach, off in the woods with their dogs and their guns, in pursuit of four-footed game, or they were in camp meetings[3] saying their prayers with their wives and families beside them.

Harriet Tubman could have told them that there was far more involved in this matter of running off slaves than signaling the would-be runaways by imitating the call of a whippoorwill, or a hoot owl, far more involved than a matter of waiting for a clear night when the North Star was visible.

In December, 1851, when she started out with the band of fugitives that she planned to take to Canada, she had been in the vicinity of the plantation for days, planning the trip, carefully selecting the slaves that she would take with her.

She had announced her arrival in the quarter by singing the forbidden spiritual[4]—"Go down, Moses, 'way down to Egypt Land"—singing it softly outside the door of a slave cabin, late at night. The husky voice was beautiful even when it was barely more than a murmur borne[5] on the wind.

Once she had made her presence known, word of her coming spread from cabin to cabin. The slaves whispered to each other, ear to mouth, mouth to ear, "Moses is here." "Moses has come." "Get ready. Moses is back again." The ones who had agreed to go

---

2 Here, *quarter* refers to the area in which the enslaved people lived on a farm or plantation.

3 *Camp meetings* are religious meetings held in a tent or outdoors.

4 Many African-American *spirituals*, like "Go Down Moses," had secret references to the Underground Railroad. Certain songs were forbidden for fear that they might inspire enslaved people to escape or rebel.

5 *Borne* is the past participle of *to bear* and in this context means "carried."

North with her put **ashcake** and salt herring in an old bandanna, hastily tied it into a bundle, and then waited patiently for the signal that meant it was time to start.

There were eleven in this party, including one of her brothers and his wife. It was the largest group that she had ever conducted, but she was determined that more and more slaves should know what freedom was like.

She had to take them all the way to Canada. The Fugitive Slave Law[6] was no longer a great many incomprehensible words written down on the country's lawbooks. The new law had become a reality. It was Thomas Sims, a boy, picked up on the streets of Boston at night and shipped back to Georgia. It was Jerry and Shadrach, arrested and jailed with no warning.

She had never been in Canada. The route beyond Philadelphia was strange to her. But she could not let the runaways who accompanied her know this. As they walked along she told them stories of her own first flight, she kept painting vivid word pictures of what it would be like to be free.

But there were so many of them this time. She knew moments of doubt when she was half-afraid, and kept looking back over her shoulder, imagining that she heard the sound of pursuit. They would certainly be pursued. Eleven of them. Eleven thousand dollars' worth of flesh and bone and muscle that belonged to Maryland planters. If they were caught, the eleven runaways would be whipped and sold South, but she—she would probably be hanged.

They tried to sleep during the day but they never could wholly relax into sleep. She could tell by the positions they assumed, by their restless movements. And they walked at night. Their progress was slow. It took them three nights of walking to reach the first stop. She had told them about the place where they would stay, promising warmth and good food, holding these things out to them as an incentive to keep going.

When she knocked on the door of a farmhouse, a place where she and her parties of runaways had always been welcome, always been given shelter and plenty to eat, there was no answer. She knocked again, softly. A voice from within said, "Who is it?" There was fear in the voice.

She knew instantly from the sound of the voice that there was something wrong. She said, "A friend with friends," the password on the Underground Railroad.

---

6 The 1850 *Fugitive Slave Law* allowed slave owners to get back escaped slaves, even if the slaves had reached free states.

Fugitive Slaves, 1864. Artist unknown. Wood engraving.

The door opened, slowly. The man who stood in the doorway looked at her coldly, looked with unconcealed astonishment and fear at the eleven disheveled runaways who were standing near her. Then he shouted, "Too many, too many. It's not safe. My place was searched last week. It's not safe!" and slammed the door in her face.

She turned away from the house, frowning. She had promised her passengers food and rest and warmth, and instead of that, there would be hunger and cold and more walking over the frozen ground. Somehow she would have to instill courage into these eleven people, most of them strangers, would have to feed them on hope and bright dreams of freedom instead of the fried pork and corn bread and milk she had promised them.

They stumbled along behind her, half-dead for sleep, and she urged them on, though she was as tired and as discouraged as they were. She had never been in Canada but she kept painting wondrous word pictures of what it would be like. She managed to dispel[7] their fear of pursuit, so that they would not become hysterical, panic-stricken. Then she had to bring some of the fear back, so that they would stay awake and keep walking though they drooped with sleep.

Yet during the day, when they lay down deep in a thicket, they never really slept, because if a twig snapped or the wind sighed in the branches of a pine tree, they jumped to their feet, afraid of their own shadows, shivering

---

7 To **dispel** something is to make it go away or disappear.

and shaking. It was very cold, but they dared not make fires because someone would see the smoke and wonder about it.

She kept thinking, eleven of them. Eleven thousand dollars' worth of slaves. And she had to take them all the way to Canada. Sometimes she told them about Thomas Garrett, in Wilmington. She said he was their friend even though he did not know them. He was the friend of all fugitives. He called them God's poor. He was a Quaker and his speech was a little different from that of other people. His clothing was different, too. He wore the wide-brimmed hat that the Quakers wear.

She said that he had thick white hair, soft, almost like a baby's, and the kindest eyes she had ever seen. He was a big man and strong, but he had never used his strength to harm anyone, always to help people. He would give all of them a new pair of shoes. Everybody. He always did. Once they reached his house in Wilmington, they would be safe. He would see to it that they were.

She described the house where he lived, told them about the store where he sold shoes. She said he kept a pail of milk and a loaf of bread in the drawer of his desk so that he would have food ready at hand for any of God's poor who should suddenly appear before him, fainting with hunger. There was a hidden room in the store. A whole wall swung open, and behind it was a room where he could hide fugitives. On the wall there were shelves filled with small boxes—boxes of shoes—so that you would never guess that the wall actually opened.

While she talked, she kept watching them. They did not believe her. She could tell by their expressions. They were thinking, New shoes, Thomas Garrett, Quaker, Wilmington—what foolishness was this? Who knew if she told the truth? Where was she taking them anyway?

That night they reached the next stop—a farm that belonged to a German. She made the runaways take shelter behind trees at the edge of the fields before she knocked at the door. She hesitated before she approached the door, thinking, suppose that he, too, should refuse shelter, suppose— Then she thought, Lord, I'm going to hold steady on to You and You've got to see me through—and knocked softly.

She heard the familiar guttural[8] voice say, "Who's there?"

She answered quickly, "A friend with friends."

He opened the door and greeted her warmly. "How many this time?" he asked.

"Eleven," she said and waited, doubting, wondering.

He said, "Good. Bring them in."

He and his wife fed them in the lamp-lit kitchen, their faces glowing, as they offered food and more food, urging them to eat, saying there was plenty for everybody, have more milk, have more bread, have more meat.

---

8 A *guttural* voice has a rough, harsh sound.

They spent the night in the warm kitchen. They really slept, all that night and until dusk the next day. When they left, it was with reluctance. They had all been warm and safe and well-fed. It was hard to exchange the security offered by that clean warm kitchen for the darkness and the cold of a December night.

Harriet had found it hard to leave the warmth and friendliness, too. But she urged them on. For a while, as they walked, they seemed to carry in them a measure of contentment; some of the serenity and the cleanliness of that big warm kitchen lingered on inside them. But as they walked farther and farther away from the warmth and the light, the cold and the darkness entered into them. They fell silent, sullen, suspicious. She waited for the moment when some one of them would turn mutinous.[9] It did not happen that night.

Two nights later she was aware that the feet behind her were moving slower and slower. She heard the irritability in their voices, knew that soon someone would refuse to go on.

She started talking about William Still and the Philadelphia Vigilance Committee. No one commented. No one asked any questions. She told them the story of William and Ellen Craft and how they escaped from Georgia. Ellen was so fair that she looked as though she were white, and so she dressed up in a man's clothing and she looked like a wealthy young planter. Her husband, William, who was dark, played the role of her slave. Thus they traveled from Macon, Georgia, to Philadelphia, riding on the trains, staying at the finest hotels. Ellen pretended to be very ill—her right arm was in a sling, and her right hand was bandaged, because she was supposed to have rheumatism. Thus she avoided having to sign the register at the hotels for she could not read or write. They finally arrived safely in Philadelphia, and then went on to Boston.

No one said anything. Not one of them seemed to have heard her.

She told them about Frederick Douglass, the most famous of the escaped slaves, of his eloquence, of his magnificent appearance. Then she told them of her own first vain effort at running away, evoking[10] the memory of that miserable life she had led as a child, reliving it for a moment in the telling.

But they had been tired too long, hungry too long, afraid too long, footsore too long. One of them suddenly cried out in despair, "Let me go back. It is better to be a slave than to suffer like this in order to be free."

She carried a gun with her on these trips. She had never used it—except as a threat. Now as she aimed it, she experienced a feeling of guilt, remembering that time, years ago, when she had prayed for the death of Edward Brodas, the Master, and

---

9 To turn **mutinous** means "to become openly rebellious."

10 Tubman is **evoking**, or calling up, this memory.

then not too long afterward had heard that great wailing cry that came from the throats of the field hands, and knew from the sound that the Master was dead.

One of the runaways said, again, "Let me go back. Let me go back," and stood still, and then turned around and said, over his shoulder, "I am going back."

She lifted the gun, aimed it at the despairing slave. She said, "Go on with us or die." The husky low-pitched voice was grim.

He hesitated for a moment and then he joined the others. They started walking again. She tried to explain to them why none of them could go back to the plantation. If a runaway returned, he would turn traitor, the master and the overseer would force him to turn traitor. The returned slave would disclose the stopping places, the hiding places, the cornstacks they had used with the full knowledge of the owner of the farm, the name of the German farmer who had fed them and sheltered them. These people who had risked their own security to help runaways would be ruined, fined, imprisoned.

She said, "We got to go free or die. And freedom's not bought with dust."

This time she told them about the long agony of the Middle Passage[11] on the old slave ships, about the black horror of the holds, about the chains and the whips. They too knew these

Slaves escaping to the North through southern swamps.

stories. But she wanted to remind them of the long hard way they had come, about the long hard way they had yet to go. She told them about Thomas Sims, the boy picked up on the streets of Boston and sent back to Georgia. She said when they got him back to Savannah, got him in prison there, they whipped him until a doctor who was standing by watching said, "You will kill him if you strike him again!" His master said, "Let him die!"

Thus she forced them to go on. Sometimes she thought she had become nothing but a voice speaking in the darkness, cajoling, urging, threatening. Sometimes she told them things to make them laugh, sometimes she sang to them, and heard the eleven voices behind her blending softly with hers, and then she knew that for the moment all was well with them.

She gave the impression of being a short, muscular, indomitable[12] woman who could never be defeated. Yet at any moment she was liable to be

---

11 The **Middle Passage** was the sea route followed by slave traders between Africa and the Americas.

12 **Indomitable** means "cannot be conquered" or "unbeatable."

seized by one of those curious fits of sleep,[13] which might last for a few minutes or for hours.

Even on this trip, she suddenly fell asleep in the woods. The runaways, ragged, dirty, hungry, cold, did not steal the gun as they might have, and set off by themselves, or turn back. They sat on the ground near her and waited patiently until she awakened. They had come to trust her implicitly[14], totally. They, too, had come to believe her repeated statement, "We got to go free or die." She was leading them into freedom, and so they waited until she was ready to go on.

Finally, they reached Thomas Garrett's house in Wilmington, Delaware. Just as Harriet had promised, Garrett gave them all new shoes, and provided carriages to take them on to the next stop.

By slow stages they reached Philadelphia, where William Still hastily recorded their names, and the plantations whence they had come, and something of the life they had led in slavery. Then he carefully hid what he had written, for fear it might be discovered. In 1872 he published this record in book form and called it *The Underground Railroad*. In the foreword to his book he said: "While I knew the danger of keeping strict records, and while I did not then dream that in my day slavery would be blotted out, or

Slaves Escaping Through the Swamp, 1862. Thomas Moran. Oil on canvas. Philbrook Museum of Art, Tulsa,

that the time would come when I could publish these records, it used to afford me great satisfaction to take them down, fresh from the lips of fugitives on the way to freedom, and to preserve them as they had given them."

William Still, who was familiar with all the station stops on the Underground Railroad, supplied Harriet with money and sent her and her eleven fugitives on to Burlington, New Jersey.

Harriet felt safer now, though there were danger spots ahead. But the biggest part of her job was over. As they went farther and farther north, it grew colder; she was aware of the wind on the Jersey ferry and aware of the cold damp in New York. From New York they went on to Syracuse, where the temperature was even lower.

---

13 Tubman's ***curious fits of sleep*** were occasional, unexplained spells of dizziness or unconsciousness.

14 To trust ***implicitly*** is to have complete faith, with no question, doubt, or hesitation.

In Syracuse she met the Reverend J. W. Loguen, known as "Jarm" Loguen. This was the beginning of a lifelong friendship. Both Harriet and Jarm Loguen were to become friends and supporters of Old John Brown.

From Syracuse they went north again, into a colder, snowier city—Rochester. Here they almost certainly stayed with Frederick Douglass, for he wrote in his autobiography:

"On one occasion I had eleven fugitives at the same time under my roof, and it was necessary for them to remain with me until I could collect sufficient money to get them to Canada. It was the largest number I ever had at any one time, and I had some difficulty in providing so many with food and shelter, but, as may well be imagined, they were not very fastidious[15] in either direction, and were well content with very plain food, and a strip of carpet on the floor for a bed, or a place on the straw in the barnloft."

Late in December, 1851, Harriet arrived in St. Catharines, Canada West (now Ontario), with the eleven fugitives. It had taken almost a month to complete this journey; most of the time had been spent getting out of Maryland.

That first winter in St. Catharines was a terrible one. Canada was a strange frozen land, snow everywhere, ice everywhere, and a bone-biting cold the like of which none of them had ever experienced before. Harriet rented a small frame house in the town and set to work to make a home. The fugitives boarded with her. They worked in the forests, felling trees, and so did she. Sometimes she took other jobs, cooking or cleaning house for people in the town. She cheered on these newly arrived fugitives, working herself, finding work for them, finding food for them, praying for them, sometimes begging for them.

Often she found herself thinking of the beauty of Maryland, the mellowness of the soil, the richness of the plant life there. The climate itself made for an ease of living that could never be duplicated in this bleak, barren countryside.

In spite of the severe cold, the hard work, she came to love St. Catharines, and the other towns and cities in Canada where black men lived. She discovered that freedom meant more than the right to change jobs at will, more than the right to keep the money that one earned. It was the right to vote and to sit on juries. It was the right to be elected to office. In Canada there were black men who were county officials and members of school boards. St. Catharines had a large colony of ex-slaves, and they owned their own homes, kept them neat and clean and in good repair. They lived in whatever part of town they chose and sent their children to the schools.

When spring came she decided that she would make this small Canadian city her home—as much as any place

---

15 **Fastidious** means "having high standards" or "difficult to please." When Douglass said the fugitives were not very fastidious, he was not being serious, as they had no choice but to take what they were given.

could be said to be home to a woman who traveled from Canada to the Eastern Shore of Maryland as often as she did.

In the spring of 1852, she went back to Cape May, New Jersey. She spent the summer there, cooking in a hotel. That fall she returned, as usual, to Dorchester County, and brought out nine more slaves, conducting them all the way to St. Catharines, in Canada West, to the bone-biting cold, the snow-covered forests—and freedom.

She continued to live in this fashion, spending the winter in Canada, and the spring and summer working in Cape May, New Jersey, or in Philadelphia. She made two trips a year into slave territory, one in the fall and another in the spring. She now had a definite crystallized[16] purpose, and in carrying it out, her life fell into

a pattern which remained unchanged for the next six years.

Harriet Tubman. Photographed in 1895.

View the Art Review this historical photograph of Harriet Tubman. What can you infer about her personality based on her facial expression, posture, and clothing? Is this image of Tubman in keeping with Ann Petry's portrayal? Explain.

---

16 Here, ***crystallized*** means "having a clear, specific form."

Respond and Think Critically

1. Write a brief summary of the main events in this biography before you answer the following questions. For help on writing a summary, see page 185. [Summarize]

2. What is another way of saying "Freedom's not bought with dust"? [Interpret]

3. What were some effective methods that Tubman used to motivate the escapees? [Infer]

4. **Text-to-Text** In what ways does your knowledge of Tubman's journey with the eleven fugitives affect your understanding of Greenfield's poem "Harriet Tubman"? [Connect]

5. **Reading Skill** Analyze Historical Context What were some obstacles that the runaways faced on their journey? Use your web to help you answer the question. [Analyze]

6. **BQ** BIG Question What do you think were the most difficult things Tubman had to accept when she decided to devote her life to helping others escape slavery? [Evaluate]

Part 2
Memorable Places

Reverie, 2005. Lee Campbell. Oil on canvas. Private Collection.

BQ **BIG Question** **What's More Important, the Journey or the Destination?**

Imagine you could travel to the place shown in the painting. What would you remember most about this scene? What places have you visited that you will long remember?

TIME

On Top of the WORLD

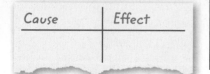
It has been more than 50 years since two adventurers first climbed Mount Everest.

By **MARTHA PICKERILL**

On May 29, 1953, Edmund Hillary and his mountain-climbing companion, Tenzing Norgay, got a glimpse of Asia that no other human had ever enjoyed. They became the first to look down from the dizzying height of the world's tallest mountain, Mount Everest, while standing upon its snowy top. But it wasn't a time for celebrating.

"I didn't leap or throw my hands in the air or something," Hillary recalled in an interview. "We were tired, of course." But finally in May 2003, the long-delayed celebration took place. Hillary, who lives in New Zealand, joined his friends and fans in Kathmandu, Nepal, to honor the 50th anniversary of his towering feat.

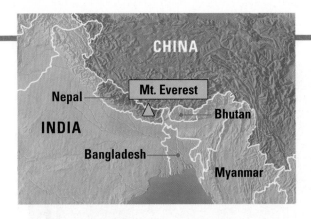

CHINA

Nepal

Mt. Everest

Bhutan

INDIA

Bangladesh

Myanmar

The Quest for the Top

Sir George Everest, a British surveyor who mapped India and part of the Himalayan range, probably never saw the big mountain. But his colleagues,[1] who measured the peak and declared it the world's tallest in 1852, wanted to honor Everest's work by naming it after him. The 29,035-foot-tall mountain straddles the border of Nepal and the Tibet region of China.

---

1 **Colleagues** are people who work in the same profession.

Climbing to Mount Everest's summit became an irresistible goal for many adventurers. But people risked their lives to get to the top. Has the challenge been worth the serious risk? When a reporter asked George Mallory, a British mountaineer, why he wanted to climb Everest, he famously replied, "Because it is there." Mallory's final attempt in 1924 to climb to the top of Mount Everest ended in his death. At least 175 climbers are known to have died on Everest since 1920. Nearly 1,200 others have made it to the top.

One Mean Mountain

Anyone who has climbed Everest can tell you that humans are not meant to hang around 5.5 miles above sea level. The ice, snow, freezing wind, deep ice cracks, called crevasses, and lack of

Sherpas carried tons of supplies for the 1953 climb.

Royal Geographic Society

Hillary and Norgay have tea after their triumph in 1953.

Climber Heidi Howkins uses a ladder to cross a crevasse in the Khumbu Ice Fall, a jumble of ice blocks on the path to the top.

View the Photograph How does the photo above help you appreciate the various dangers faced by those climbing Mount Everest?

oxygen are constant threats to climbers' safety and health. Because of the thin air, most climbers breathe from oxygen tanks. Some climbers have lost toes, ears, and fingers to frostbite.[2] All of these factors force climbers who do reach the top to turn around and scramble back down as quickly as possible.

---

2 **Frostbite** happens when a part of the body becomes so cold that the blood cannot circulate. Usually frostbite affects the fingers, toes, and ears.

"You cannot conquer Everest. It's not possible," says Norgay's son Jamling, who has climbed Everest with Hillary's son, Peter. "Everest will give you a chance to stand on the top for a few minutes, and that's it."

It's Still There

The mountain is much less a mystery now than when Hillary and Norgay reached its peak in 1953. People have approached climbing it from all sides and have succeeded in getting to its top by 15 different routes. Satellite phones and other equipment keep adventurers in touch with the world below. Special clothes made for climbing are now made of high-tech thermal fabrics. Hillary and Norgay had only layers of wool and cotton and a simple cotton tent to keep them warm. They didn't have any high-tech equipment as safety nets.

Some modern climbers who are inexperienced pay a lot of money to have professional guides take them to the top. But even with guides, the climb can be risky. In 1996, tragedy struck. On one of the mountain's busiest days, a storm blew in, and eight climbers died in a single night.

Hillary continued a life of achievement. After being knighted[3] by Queen Elizabeth II, Sir Edmund Hillary led a team across Antarctica to the South Pole and climbed many mountains. He has worked for decades to build desperately needed schools and hospitals for Norgay's people, the Sherpas of Nepal. "That's how I'd like to be remembered," says Hillary. "Not for Everest but for the work I did and the cooperation I had with my Sherpa friends."

---

3 When a person is **knighted**, he or she is honored by a king or queen for services to the country.

Respond and Think Critically

1. How would you summarize "On Top of the World"? Include only important details that readers need to know. [Summarize]

2. Sir Edmund Hillary said he wants to be remembered "[n]ot for Everest but for the work I did and the cooperation I had with my Sherpa friends." What does this tell you about Hillary as a person? [Infer]

3. Do you agree with the statement that climbers cannot conquer Everest? Explain. [Evaluate]

4. **Text-to-Self** Given the chance, would you try to climb Mount Everest? Explain. [Connect]

5. **Reading Skill** Identify Cause-and-Effect Relationships What are three cause-and-effect relationships you found in the article? Refer to the cause-and-effect chart you created for examples. [Analyze]

6. **BQ** BIG Question The article notes that Mount Everest is "much less a mystery now" than it was in 1953. Why do you think people still climb the mountain: because of the journey (the challenge of the climb) or the destination (the chance to stand on top of the world's tallest mountain)? Explain your ideas.

Stopping by Woods on a Snowy Evening

Connect to the Poem

Think about a time when you had to choose between something familiar and something unfamiliar.

Write a Journal Entry Write about the choice you made. What did you consider before you made your decision?

Build Background

"Stopping by Woods on a Snowy Evening" is a poem about a person traveling alone one winter's night. The speaker in the poem is drawn to the peaceful solitude of the dark woods but moves on toward the village because he or she has commitments there.

- You may have heard the saying "Stop and smell the roses." It means to live in this moment instead of always planning for the future. The speaker in this poem is torn: Should he or she stop to enjoy the beauty of nature or stick to the schedule and meet obligations to other people?

- This poem contrasts the woods with the village. Traditionally, this kind of distinction, often called wilderness versus civilization, is symbolic of the conflict between behaving as we want to (wilderness) and behaving as we ought to (civilization).

The New England States

Meet Robert Frost

"This is no prejudice against the city. I am fond of several great cities. It is merely an inclination to country things."

—Robert Frost

A Country Poet Robert Frost knew early that he wanted to be a poet. He graduated from high school as class poet. Fame didn't come quickly, though. He was in his early forties before his work won wide acceptance. Many of Frost's poems are set in the New England countryside he loved so much.

Literary Works "Stopping by Woods on a Snowy Evening" appeared in Frost's first Pulitzer Prize–winning book, *New Hampshire,* published in 1923.

Robert Frost was born in 1874 and died in 1963.

 Literature Online

Author Search For more about Robert Frost, go to glencoe.com and enter QuickPass code GL39770u3.

Set Purposes for Reading

BQ BIG Question

Read "Stopping by Woods on a Snowy Evening" to determine why the woods are a memorable place. As you read, decide which details of setting are most significant.

Literary Elements Assonance and Consonance

Assonance and **consonance** are sounds repeated within words. In assonance, the vowel sounds are repeated. In consonance, identical or similar consonant sounds repeat either at the ends of lines or within a line. For example, "steam-heated" has assonance. The words *buckle* and *tackle* have consonance.

Recognizing assonance and consonance is important because it can help readers appreciate the sound of a poem. The two literary devices help connect words within a line. As part of the poet's style, they add meaning and reveal the poet's purpose and attitude.

As you read "Stopping by Woods on a Snowy Evening," look for examples of assonance and consonance.

Reading Skill Analyze Theme

Theme is the central message or meaning of a poem or story. Some themes are directly stated; others are implied. Often a poem's theme can be stated as a simple sentence such as "Trust your instincts."

To analyze a poem's theme,

- read the whole poem to gain a first impression
- reread each line to find the speaker's thoughts and actions
- look for words with multiple meanings or images that may be symbolic of other ideas
- state the theme as a brief message

As you read, ask yourself what universal message Frost's poem conveys. Use a graphic organizer like the one shown to help you.

Details			
Speaker's Thoughts / Actions	Expected Behavior	Symbolic Images	Repetitions

Learning Objectives

For pages 384–388

In studying this text, you will focus on the following objectives:

Literary Study: Analyzing assonance and consonance.

Reading: Analyzing theme.

TRY IT

Analyze Theme Think of a refrain to a favorite song. Analyze the repeated words or phrases and the singer's tone, volume, and pace. Use these clues to state the song's theme in your own words.

Stopping by Woods on a Snowy Evening

Robert Frost

Whose woods these are I think I know.
His house is in the village though;
He will not see me stopping here
To watch his woods fill up with snow.

5   My little horse must think it queer°
To stop without a farmhouse near
Between the woods and frozen lake
The darkest evening of the year.

He gives his harness bells a shake
10 To ask if there is some mistake.
The only other sound's the sweep
Of easy wind and downy° flake.

The woods are lovely, dark and deep.
But I have promises to keep,
15 And miles to go before I sleep,
And miles to go before I sleep.

---

5 Here, **queer** means "unusual" or "not routine."

12 **Downy** describes something that is light, soft, and fluffy, like a chick's feathers.

Country Doctor or Night Call, 1935. Horace Pippin. Oil on fabric, 28 1/8 x 32 1/8 in. Museum of Fine Arts, Boston. Abraham Shuman Fund.

Analyze Theme What decision is the speaker facing at this point in his or her journey?

Assonance and Consonance How does the soft buzz of the *z* sound repeating throughout the poem affect its tone or mood? Remember that *s* can sound like *z* (for example, the *s* at the end of *woods* and the *s* in *easy*).

After You Read

Respond and Think Critically

1. In your own words, retell the story of "Stopping by Woods on a Snowy Evening." [Summarize]

2. What does the speaker stop to do? What does this tell you about the speaker's personality? [Recall and Draw Conclusions]

3. What is the speaker's conflict at the poem's end? How is that conflict resolved? [Analyze]

4. How effectively does Frost convey the speaker's attitude toward the woods and the snowy evening? Support your answer with specific references to the poem. [Evaluate]

5. How do assonance and consonance strengthen the poem? [Analyze]

6. **BQ** BIG Question Think about the memorable place the speaker encounters along his or her journey to a destination. What do you think are the qualities of a memorable place? Explain your answer with details from your own life or from your own reading. [Connect]

Academic Vocabulary

Robert Frost's poem "Stopping by Woods on a Snowy Evening" **transmits** numerous images through the use of vibrant descriptive details.

In the preceding sentence, *transmits* means "sends or causes to go from one person or place to another." To become more familiar with the word *transmits,* fill out a graphic organizer like the one below.

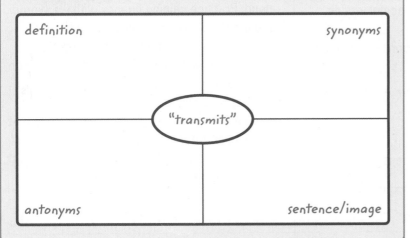

definition	synonyms
"transmits"	
antonyms	sentence/image

TIP

Evaluating
Here are some tips to help you evaluate. Remember when you evaluate, you judge whether the poem has unity, coherence, logic, and consistency. To evaluate how well the poet conveys the speaker's attitude, ask yourself

- Is the speaker's attitude clear?

- Which words reflect the speaker's attitude?

 FOLDABLES Study Organizer Keep track of your ideas about the **BIG Question** in your unit Foldable.

 Literature Online

Selection Resources
For Selection Quizzes, eFlashcards, and Reading-Writing Connection activities, go to glencoe.com and enter QuickPass code GL39770u3.

Literary Elements

Assonance and Consonance

1. In "Stopping by Woods on a Snowy Evening," find three instances of assonance in lines 7 and 8 by identifying the words that repeat the long sound of *e*. What is one other instance of assonance you can find in the poem?

2. List as many words ending in the soft, hissing *s* sound as you can find in the poem.

3. What is the effect of the soft *s* sound and *z* sound on the poem? How do these sounds help convey the speaker's attitude about his or her stop in the woods? How does this element of style help convey the poet's attitude toward nature?

Review: Speaker

As you learned on page 324, the **speaker** is the voice of the poem. The speaker's tone, word choice, and actions reveal his or her attitude about the theme.

4. The speaker's observations in "Stopping by Woods on a Snowy Evening" suggest a feeling of
   A. anger at the uncaring owner of the woods.
   B. panic at being alone in the woods in the dark.
   C. conflict between the peaceful woods and commitments.
   D. worry about the harsh consequences of winter.

Reading Skill Analyze Theme

Test Skills Practice

5. The poem's most likely theme is
   A. life is unfair.
   B. darkness fears the light.
   C. wilderness is more important than society.
   D. responsibility forces difficult choices.

Grammar Link

Adjectives and Adverbs Both adjectives and adverbs are modifiers. They modify, or describe, other words.

An **adjective** describes a person, place, or thing. An adjective answers questions like *How many?*, *What kind?*, *Which one?*, and *Whose?* For example:

> *Three tall oak* trees stood near *Jane's thick stone* wall.

An **adverb** describes a verb, an adjective, or another adverb. An adverb answers questions like *How?*, *When?*, *How often?*, and *How much?* For example:

> The wall is *very* thick, but it is *not* tall.

Practice Find two adjectives and two adverbs in the poem. Write a new sentence in your own words using at least one of the adjectives and one of the adverbs. Then write another sentence related to the first. This time use at least one original adjective and adverb.

Listening and Speaking

Performance With a partner, read the poem aloud. Practice gaining fluency with the words and the poem's rhythm. Next, test different speaking methods. How do they change the overall mood and tone? Try speaking quickly or slowly, dramatically or in a monotone. Which reading best suits the speaker and the theme? Write a few sentences describing the style that works best. After listening to all the versions of the poem, draw scales like the one below. Mark the point on each scale where the reading sounded most effective.

Before You Read

The Sound of Night

Learning Objectives

For pages 389–392

In studying this text, you will focus on the following objectives:

Literary Study:
Analyzing onomatopoeia.

Analyzing alliteration.

Connect to the Poem

Have you ever gone camping? If so, then you've probably listened to a strange and wonderful chorus of night sounds.

List Make a list of animals you've heard at night and the sounds they make.

Build Background

"The Sound of Night" is a poem that describes the noises certain animals make at night. Camping can be a strange or even scary experience for people who aren't used to the outdoors. Like the speaker, frequent campers may learn to identify the sounds made by animals they can't see.

• Although some of the descriptive words, such as *huggermugger,* might seem as if the poet invented them for their sound qualities, they are actual words that can be found in a dictionary.

Set a Purpose for Reading

BQ BIG Question

As you read "The Sound of Night," ask yourself how the poet creates a memorable place for her readers.

Literary Elements Onomatopoeia and Alliteration

Poets often use sound devices such as onomatopoeia and alliteration to make their poems more lively and enjoyable. **Onomatopoeia** is the use of a word or phrase that imitates or suggests the sound of what it describes. For example, *buzz* imitates the sound of a nearby insect, while *hiss* suggests an angry cat or worse, a snake. **Alliteration** is the repetition of the same consonant sound in writing, usually at the beginning of words and syllables. For example, "the sweet, simple song of the sparrow" is alliterative because of the repetition of the *s* sound at the beginning of the words.

 Literature Online

Author Search For more about Maxine Kumin, go to glencoe.com and enter QuickPass code GL39770u3.

Meet Maxine Kumin

"These New England upland pastures are like a secret garden, like a poem. Every dip and scrap is now engraved on my brain pan."

—Maxine Kumin

Observing Nature Poet and author Maxine Kumin lives on a farm in New Hampshire. Kumin says that she closely observes nature so that she can get every detail correct in her writing.

Literary Works Kumin is the author of many poetry books, including *Up Country: Poems of New England. Up Country* won the Pulitzer Prize in 1973.

Maxine Kumin was born in 1925.

The Sound of Night

Maxine Kumin

On the Edge of the Lagoon, 1997. Peter Davidson. Oil on paper. Private Collection.

And now the dark comes on, all full of chitter noise.
Birds huggermugger° crowd the trees,
the air thick with their vesper cries,
and bats, snub seven-pointed kites,
5 skitter across the lake, swing out,
squeak, chirp, dip, and skin on skates
of air, and the fat frogs wake and prink°
wide-lipped, noisy as ducks, drunk
on the boozy black, gloating chink-chunk.

10 And now on the narrow beach we defend
    ourselves from dark.
The cooking done, we build our firework
bright and hot and less for outlook
than for magic, and lie in our blankets
while night nickers° around us. Crickets
15 chorus hallelujahs; paws, quiet
and quick as raindrops, play on the stones
expertly soft, run past and are gone;
fish pulse in the lake; the frogs hoarsen.

Now every voice of the hour—the known, the
    supposed, the strange,
20 the mindless, the witted, the never seen—
sing, thrum, impinge,° and rearrange
endlessly; and debarred from sleep we wait
for the birds, importantly silent,
for the crease of first eye-licking light,
25 for the sun, lost long ago and sweet.
By the lake, locked black away and tight,
we lie, day creatures, overhearing night.

Alliteration Note the repeated consonant sound in lines 4–6. What effect does this sound device have on your reading of the poem?

Onomatopoeia What are three words the poet uses in the first stanza to represent the sounds that the night animals are making?

BQ BIG Question
Does the poet's unique and memorable use of language help you imagine a campsite? Explain why or why not.

---

2 *Huggermugger* means "confusedly" or "in a disorderly fashion."

7 *Prink* means "to dress in a showy manner."

14 The night neighs (*nickers*) like a horse.

21 *Impinge* means "to come into contact with" or "to border."

After You Read

Respond and Think Critically

1. What are three night animals the poet describes? [Identify]

2. What does the speaker mean in line 22 when she says she is "debarred from sleep"? [Interpret]

3. Does the speaker like, dislike, or have mixed feelings about camping outside all night? Note words and phrases that support your opinion. [Make Judgments]

4. **Literary Element** **Alliteration** With what alliterative phrase does the poet describe the early dawn? [Analyze]

5. **Literary Element** **Onomatopoeia** Identify three distinct examples of onomatopoeia in the poem. Which example do you think is the most lively and musical? Explain. [Evaluate]

6. **BQ** **BIG Question** What words or phrases in the poem lead you to conclude that the speaker appreciates the outdoor setting as a memorable place? [Draw Conclusions]

Spelling Link

When adding suffixes to words that end in a consonant, you must sometimes **double the final consonant.**

Rule: Double the final consonant when a word ends with a single consonant preceded by one vowel and the word is one syllable, or when the last syllable of the word is accented both before and after adding the suffix. For example, *sit + ing = sitting.*

Exceptions: Do not double the final consonant if the suffix begins with a consonant, if the accent is not on the last syllable, if the accent moves when the suffix is added, or if the word ends in two consonants. When adding *-ly* to a word that ends in *ll,* drop one *l.*

Practice On a sheet of paper, list these words: *running, submitted, stardom, finding, frilly.* Next to each word, explain why it does or does not have a doubled consonant.

Writing

Write a Stanza Think of a memorable place that you have visited. The place may be in nature or somewhere else. Write a one-stanza poem in which you show why the place is special to you. Describe the place using onomatopoeia and alliteration.

TIP

Evaluating
Here are some tips to help you evaluate. Remember, when you evaluate, you make a judgment or form an opinion about something in the text.

- Locate examples of onomatopoeia in the text. Review the definition of onomatopoeia, if necessary.

- Think about what you like or dislike about these descriptions.

- Decide which example adds to your enjoyment of the poem the most.

 FOLDABLES **Study Organizer** Keep track of your ideas about the **BIG Question** in your unit Foldable.

 Literature Online

Selection Resources
For Selection Quizzes, eFlashcards, and Reading-Writing Connection activities, go to glencoe.com and enter QuickPass code GL39770u3.

Checkouts

Connect to the Short Story

Think about a time when you hesitated and missed your chance to do something.

Partner Talk With a partner, talk about what you missed out on. Was it really important? Do you think it mattered that you missed this or, when you look back, does it not seem to matter that much? Share your thoughts with the class.

Build Background

In "Checkouts," the main character develops a crush on a boy she sees in the grocery store.

- A typical crush is a sudden intense fascination with someone, followed by a sudden loss of interest. Crushes are rarely long-lasting or meaningful.

- People often have crushes on people they'll never meet in real life, such as movie stars, musicians, or athletes.

Vocabulary

impulse (im´puls) *n.* a sudden urge to do something (p. 395). *On an impulse, I bought a second pair of shoes.*

lapse (laps) *v.* to slip or fall (p. 396). *My mother would lapse into a dreamlike state when she listened to music.*

meditation (med´ə tā´shən) *n.* the act of thinking or reflecting deeply (p. 396). *Some say meditation makes a mind healthier.*

brazen (brā´zən) *adj.* shameless, defiant (p. 397). *The brazen child tossed his dinner onto the floor after being scolded about throwing food.*

deftly (deft´lē) *adv.* skillfully (p. 397). *My mother deftly knitted a scarf.*

tedious (tēd´ē əs) *adj.* causing boredom or weariness (p. 398). *Picking up litter can be a tedious task.*

Meet Cynthia Rylant

"Without a doubt [West Virginia was] a small, sparkling universe that gave me a lifetime's worth of material for my writing."
—Cynthia Rylant

Life in the Mountains
Cynthia Rylant grew up in the mountains of West Virginia. Like many of her neighbors, she lived in a house with no running water or electricity. Although poor, Rylant remembers joys as well as hardships. Many of her novels, stories, and poems draw on her childhood experiences.

Literary Works Rylant's novels include the award-winning *A Fine White Dust* and *Missing May.* "Checkouts" was published in *A Couple of Kooks: And Other Stories about Love* in 1990.

Rylant was born in 1954.

 Literature Online

Author Search For more about Cynthia Rylant, go to glencoe.com and enter QuickPass code GL39770u3.

Set Purposes for Reading

BQ BIG Question

Read "Checkouts" to learn about the journey two teens make on their way to finding happiness.

Literary Element Motivation

Motivation is the reason characters do certain things. A character's beliefs and perspective or the preceding plot events can be motivations in a story. For example, parents may motivate children to do chores at home by offering rewards.

Motivation is important because it helps reveal characterization or plot events. To understand a character's motivation, think about the reasons for his or her thoughts, actions, and words.

As you read, think about why the main characters act the way they do.

Reading Skill Analyze Characterization

When you analyze **characterization,** you look at the techniques the author uses to show what a character is like. In direct characterization, the story's narrator makes statements about a character's personality. In indirect characterization, a character's personality is revealed through what the character says and does and what others say and think about the character. These techniques are often combined.

Analyzing characterization is important because it helps you understand the story's characters and appreciate the author's skill in presenting them.

When you analyze characterization, you draw conclusions

- from what the narrator says about characters' personalities
- about characters from their own words and actions
- about characters from what other characters say and think

As you read, ask yourself what motivates the characters' thoughts and actions. You may want to use a graphic organizer like the one below.

Character	Character Trait	Story Detail
The main girl	impulsive	She falls in love when the bag boy drops the mayonnaise.

Learning Objectives

For pages 393–401

In studying this text, you will focus on the following objectives:

Literary Study: Analyzing motivation.

Analyzing characterization.

Analyzing style.

TRY IT

Analyze Characterization
Your best friend, who usually doesn't spend a lot of time on her appearance, starts putting on makeup before math class every day. She also starts spending more time on her math homework. You notice that she's talking a lot about Jerry, a boy in that math class. What do these details tell you about her character (and about what is motivating her to do well and look good in math class)?

CHECKOUTS

Cynthia Rylant

Her parents had moved her to Cincinnati, to a large house with **beveled glass** windows and several porches and the *history* her mother liked to emphasize. You'll love the house, they said. You'll be lonely at first, they admitted, but you're so nice you'll make friends fast. And as an **impulse** tore at her to lie on the floor, to hold to their ankles and tell them she felt she was dying, to offer anything, anything at all, so they might allow her to finish growing up in the town of her childhood, they firmed their mouths and spoke from their chests and they said, It's decided.

They moved her to Cincinnati, where for a month she spent the greater part of every day in a room full of beveled glass windows, sifting through photographs of the life she'd lived and left behind. But it is difficult work, suffering, and in its own way a kind of art, and finally she didn't have the energy for it anymore, so she emerged from the beautiful house and fell in love with a bag boy at the supermarket. Of course, this didn't happen all at once, just like that, but in the sequence of things that's exactly

Analyze Characterization
What do you learn about the girl from the description here?

Vocabulary

impulse (im´ puls) *n.* a sudden urge to do something

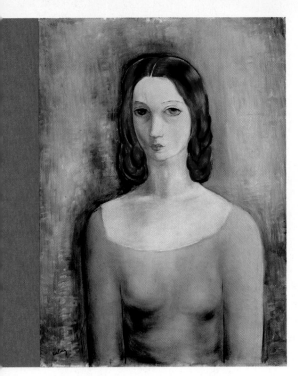

Young Woman. Moise Kisling. Oil on canvas, 73 x 54.5 cm. Private Collection. VAGA, NY.

View the Art Does this painting capture the mood of the story? Explain, with evidence from the story and the painting.

the way it happened.

She liked to grocery shop. She loved it in the way some people love to drive long country roads, because doing it she could think and relax and wander. Her parents wrote up the list and handed it to her and off she went without complaint to perform what they regarded as a great sacrifice of her time and a sign that she was indeed a very nice girl. She had never told them how much she loved grocery shopping, only that she was "willing" to do it. She had an intuition which told her that her parents were not safe for sharing such strong, important facts about herself. Let them think they knew her.

Once inside the supermarket, her hands firmly around the handle of the cart, she would **lapse** into a kind of reverie and wheel toward the produce. Like a Tibetan monk in a solitary **meditation,** she calmed to a point of deep, deep happiness; this feeling came to her, reliably, if strangely, only in the supermarket.

Then one day the bag boy dropped her jar of mayonnaise and that is how she fell in love.

He was nervous—first day on the job—and along had come this fascinating girl, standing in the checkout line with the unfocused stare one often sees in young children, her face turned enough away that he might take several full looks at her as he packed sturdy bags full of food and

Motivation What is her motivation for not wanting her parents to know she enjoys grocery shopping?

Vocabulary

lapse (laps) *v.* to slip or fall

meditation (med′ ə tā′shən) *n.* the act of thinking or reflecting deeply

the goods of modern life. She interested him because her hair was red and thick, and in it she had placed a huge orange bow, nearly the size of a small hat. That was enough to distract him, and when finally it was her groceries he was packing, she looked at him and smiled and he could respond only by busting her jar of mayonnaise on the floor, shards of glass and oozing cream decorating the area around his feet.

She loved him at exactly that moment, and if he'd known this perhaps he wouldn't have fallen into the brown depression he fell into, which lasted the rest of his shift. He believed he must have looked the fool in her eyes, and he envied the sureness of everyone around him: the cocky cashier at the register, the grim and harried store manager, the bland butcher, and the **brazen** bag boys who smoked in the warehouse on their breaks. He wanted a second chance. Another chance to be confident and say witty things to her as he threw tin cans into her bags, persuading her to allow him to help her to her car so he might learn just a little about her, check out the floor of the car for signs of hobbies or fetishes[1] and the bumpers for clues as to beliefs and loyalties.

But he busted her jar of mayonnaise and nothing else worked out for the rest of the day.

Strange, how attractive clumsiness can be. She left the supermarket with stars in her eyes, for she had loved the way his long nervous fingers moved from the **conveyor belt** to the bags, how **deftly** (until the mayonnaise) they had picked up her items and placed them into her bags. She had loved the way the hair kept falling into his eyes as he leaned over to grab a box or a tin. And the tattered

Glyn, Welsh Guards, 1960. Peter Samuelson. Oil on board. Private Collection.

Analyze Characterization
What do you learn about the boy's self-confidence from reading this paragraph?

Visual Vocabulary

A **conveyor belt** is a belt that runs over a set of rollers. It is used to carry materials either short or long distances.

---

1 Here, *fetishes* are obsessions.

Vocabulary

brazen (brā′zən) *adj.* shameless, defiant
deftly (deft′lē) *adv.* skillfully

brown shoes he wore with no socks. And the left side of his collar turned in rather than out.

The bag boy seemed a wonderful contrast to the perfectly beautiful house she had been forced to accept as her home, to the *history* she hated, to the loneliness she had become used to, and she couldn't wait to come back for more of his awkwardness and dishevelment.[2]

Incredibly, it was another four weeks before they saw each other again. As fate would have it, her visits to the supermarket never coincided with his schedule to bag. Each time she went to the store, her eyes scanned the checkouts at once, her heart in her mouth. And each hour he worked, the bag boy kept one eye on the door, watching for the red-haired girl with the big orange bow.

Yet in their disappointment these weeks there was a kind of ecstasy. It is reason enough to be alive, the hope you may see again some face which has meant something to you. The anticipation of meeting the bag boy eased the girl's painful transition into her new and jarring life in Cincinnati. It provided for her an anchor amid all that was impersonal and unfamiliar, and she spent less time on thoughts of what she had left behind as she concentrated on what might lie ahead. And for the boy, the long and often **tedious** hours at the supermarket which provided no challenge other than that of showing up the following workday . . . these hours became possibilities of mystery and romance for him as he watched the electric doors for the girl in the orange bow.

And when finally they did meet up again, neither offered a clue to the other that he, or she, had been the object of obsessive thought for weeks. She spotted him as soon as she came into the store, but she kept her eyes strictly in front of her as she pulled out a cart and wheeled it toward the produce. And he, too, knew the instant she came

Motivation What is the girl's main motivation for falling in love with the bag boy?

September 2005: 'Hurricane Rita has hit the Florida Keys and is believed to be strengthening,' 2005. Ben McLaughlin. Oil on panel. Private Collection.

---

2 **Dishevelment** is the condition of being messy, as applied to clothing or hair.

Vocabulary
....

tedious (tēd´ē əs) *adj.* causing boredom or weariness

through the door—though the orange bow was gone, replaced by a small but bright yellow flower instead—and he never once turned his head in her direction but watched her from the corner of his vision as he tried to swallow back the fear in his throat.

It is odd how we sometimes deny ourselves the very pleasure we have longed for and which is finally within our reach. For some perverse reason she would not have been able to articulate,[3] the girl did not bring her cart up to the bag boy's checkout when her shopping was done. And the bag boy let her leave the store, pretending no notice of her.

This is often the way of children, when they truly want a thing, to pretend that they don't. And then they grow angry when no one tries harder to give them this thing they so casually rejected, and they soon find themselves in a rage simply because they cannot say yes when they mean yes. Humans are very complicated. (And perhaps cats, who have been known to react in the same way, though the resulting rage can only be guessed at.)

The girl hated herself for not checking out at the boy's line, and the boy hated himself for not catching her eye and saying hello, and they most sincerely hated each other without having ever exchanged even two minutes of conversation.

Eventually—in fact, within the week—a kind and intelligent boy who lived very near her beautiful house asked the girl to a movie and she gave up her fancy for the bag boy at the supermarket. And the bag boy himself grew so bored with his job that he made a desperate search for something better and ended up in a bookstore where scores of fascinating girls lingered like honeybees about a hive. Some months later the bag boy and the girl with the orange bow again crossed paths, standing in line with their dates at a movie theater, and, glancing toward the other, each smiled slightly, then looked away, as strangers on public buses often do, when one is moving off the bus and the other is moving on. 🐾

---

3 To *articulate* is to put into words.

Analyze Characterization What does the boy's inability to act on his feelings show about his character?

Motivation What is her motivation for not going to the boy's checkout line?

Motivation What is the girl's motivation for moving on to another boy?

BQ **BIG Question**
How are the two main characters' destinations different from what they expected?

After You Read

Respond and Think Critically

1. In your own words, tell what happens in the story. [Summarize]

2. What motivation might the boy need to say something to the girl the second time he sees her? [Analyze]

3. How do the boy and girl feel after they ignore each other on their second meeting? Why do they feel that way? [Recall and Interpret]

4. How do the boy and the girl feel at story's end? Explain. [Interpret]

5. What is the main technique the author uses to characterize the orange-bow girl and the bag boy? Refer to story details in your explanation. [Analyze]

6. **BQ** BIG Question How are the boy and the girl each part of the other's journey through life? [Connect]

Vocabulary Practice

On a sheet of paper, write the vocabulary word that completes each sentence. If none of the words fits, write "none."

impulse, lapse, meditation, brazen, deftly, tedious

1. He _____ moved out of the way of the hard-hit ball.

2. She turned _____ and knocked over the stack of cans.

3. The _____ lecture seemed to go on for hours.

4. The couple would _____ into silence in the woods.

5. I was nervous, and my mind was in a state of _____.

6. A moment of _____ before the test helped keep him calm.

7. She felt an _____ to laugh during the speech but restrained herself.

8. The _____ robbers attacked the man in broad daylight.

Academic Vocabulary

Although bothered by her brother's taunts, the girl showed **restraint** by not responding.

In the preceding sentence, *restraint* means "the act of holding back or keeping in check." Think about a time you showed restraint. What effect did your restraint have on the situation?

TIP

Analyzing
Here are some tips to help you analyze. Remember, when you analyze, you look at separate parts of a selection to understand the entire selection.

- Think about what motivates the characters to feel or behave in a certain way.

- Think about what the characters do and don't do as a result of their motivations.

- Put these details together to compose a general statement about the author's characterization.

FOLDABLES Keep track of
Study Organizer your ideas about
the **BIG Question** in your
unit Foldable.

 **Literature** Online

Selection Resources
For Selection Quizzes, eFlashcards, and Reading-Writing Connection activities, go to glencoe.com and enter QuickPass code GL39770u3.

Literary Element Motivation

Test Skills Practice

1. What is the boy's motivation for leaving his job at the grocery store? How might his motivation have changed if he had made contact with the girl that second day? Support your answer with details and information from the story.

Review: Style

As you learned on page 311, **style** is the author's choice and arrangement of words and sentences in a literary work.

2. How would you describe the author's style in the second paragraph of this story? What effects do you think that style would have on a reader?

3. How would you describe the overall style of this selection? What effect do you think this overall style would have on the reader? Support your answer with details from the text.

4. Based on Rylant's writing style, how would you describe her purpose for writing and her attitude toward her subjects? Explain your answer with details and evidence from the story.

Reading Skill Analyze Characterization

Test Skills Practice

5. Which of the following sentences best sums up the character of the girl in "Checkouts"?
   A. "[She sifted] through photographs of the life she'd lived and left behind."
   B. "She would lapse into a kind of reverie and wheel toward the produce."
   C. "Her hair was red and thick, and in it she had placed a huge orange bow . . ."
   D. "An impulse tore at her to lie on the floor, to hold their ankles and tell them she was dying."

Grammar Link

Modifying Phrases and Clauses A **modifying phrase or clause** is a group of words that describes another word. A clause has a subject and a predicate; a phrase does not. The phrase or clause works the same way as a one-word adjective or adverb, making writing more interesting and specific.

An **adjective** phrase or clause is a group of words that modifies a noun or pronoun. For example:

> The girl *with the orange bow in her hair* stood quietly.

An **adverb** phrase or clause may modify an action verb, an adjective, or another adverb. For example:

> They didn't see each other *for almost four weeks.*

Practice Look for examples of modifying phrases and clauses in "Checkouts." Note whether they are adjectives or adverbs. Then write an original sentence with an adjective phrase or clause and an original sentence with an adverb phrase or clause.

Research and Report

Visual/Media Presentation Create a presentation that evokes the sights and sounds and feelings of a store like the one in this story. Evaluate the best tools to use for your presentation. Use photos, video, or any digital or multimedia tools to depict the grocery store. Use a graphic organizer like the one below to keep track of your ideas.

Sights	Sounds

Vocabulary Workshop

Multiple-Meaning Words

Connection to Literature

"She spotted him as soon as she came into the store, but she kept her eyes strictly in front of her as she pulled out a cart and wheeled it toward the produce."

—Cynthia Rylant, "Checkouts"

Tip

Vocabulary Terms When you look up a multiple-meaning word in a dictionary, you will see various definitions within a single entry.

Test-taking Tip To figure out the intended use of a multiple-meaning word, look for context clues in the words that surround it.

Many English words are **multiple-meaning words.** A multiple-meaning word has more than one definition. The word *spotted* is a multiple-meaning word. In the passage above, Rylant uses *spotted* as a verb to mean "identified or recognized." Other related meanings include "marked with a spot or spots," "stained," and "disgraced."

Here are other multiple-meaning words from "Checkouts."

Word	Meanings	Example Sentences
admitted *(v.)*	acknowledged	The girl's parents *admitted* that she would feel lonely at first.
	confessed	She never *admitted* her interest in the boy.
	allowed entry	She *admitted* romantic thoughts into her mind.
vision *(n.)*	a range of sight	The boy watched the girl from the corner of his *vision*.
	someone or something of great beauty	With her red hair and orange bow, the girl was a *vision* to the boy across the room.

TRY IT: Using the chart above, write the correct meaning of the underlined word.

1. Rosa <u>admitted</u> to her parents that she had forgotten to walk their dog.
2. Dust caused Josh's <u>vision</u> to become blurry.
3. The waterfall was an absolute <u>vision</u>.
4. The coach <u>admitted</u> to his team that the next game would be difficult.
5. Mrs. King <u>admitted</u> the repairman into her home.

Literature Online

Vocabulary For more vocabulary practice, go to glencoe.com and enter the QuickPass code GL39770u3.

Knoxville, Tennessee
and *Los New Yorks*

Connect to the Poems

Think about your hometown. What makes it special? How is it different from other places that you have visited or read about?

List Make a list of things you like about your hometown. You might want to list adjectives describing the town or list favorite traditions, people, and places that make it unique.

Build Background

In "Knoxville, Tennessee" and "Los New Yorks," two poets reflect on important places and moments from their childhood.

- In her poem "Knoxville, Tennessee," Nikki Giovanni describes some of her most vivid memories of summers spent with her grandparents in Knoxville.

- Victor Hernández Cruz moved from Puerto Rico to New York when he was only five years old, yet his memories of Puerto Rico remained vivid. In his poem "Los New Yorks," he applies images of his island home to his new urban one.

Set a Purpose for Reading

BQ **BIG Question**

As you read "Knoxville, Tennessee" and "Los New Yorks," consider what makes these places memorable to the poets.

Literary Element Imagery

Imagery is the use of words and phrases that appeal to readers' five senses. Poets who effectively use imagery can bring their writing to life by helping readers form mental pictures of the people, places, or things described. As you read the poems, note words and phrases that help you imagine how things look, feel, sound, smell, or taste.

Learning Objectives

For pages 403–409

In studying these texts, you will focus on the following objective:

Literary Study: Analyzing imagery.

Meet the Authors

Meet Nikki Giovanni

In addition to being a poet, Nikki Giovanni is a professor, a recording artist, and an activist.

Giovanni was born in 1943.

Meet Victor Hernández Cruz

Victor Hernández Cruz writes many of his poems in a mix of Spanish and English.

Cruz was born in 1949.

Hot July Wind, 1955–60. Charles Ephraim Burchfield. Watercolor on paper. Private collection, Photo ©Christie's Images.

<u>View the Art</u> What details about the home in this painting suggest that it's a happy place?

Knoxville, Tennessee

Nikki Giovanni

I always like summer
best
you can eat fresh corn
from daddy's garden
5 and okra
and greens
and cabbage°
and lots of
barbecue
10 and buttermilk
and homemade ice-cream
at the church picnic
and listen to
gospel music
15 outside
at the church
homecoming
and go to the mountains with
your grandmother
20 and go barefooted
and be warm
all the time
not only when you go to bed
and sleep

Imagery Which two senses do the details in lines 1–17 appeal to the most?

BQ **BIG Question**

What experiences in Knoxville make it a memorable place for the speaker?

7 ***Okra, greens,*** and ***cabbage*** are all vegetables commonly eaten in the South.

Wind on Washington Square, New York City, 1988.
Charlotte Johnson Wahl. Oil on canvas. Private Collection.

Los New Yorks

Victor Hernández Cruz

In the news that sails through the air
Like the shaking seeds of maracas°
I find you out

Suena°

5 You don't have to move here
Just stand on the corner

---

2 **Maracas** (mə ra´ kəs) are dried gourd-like rattles that contain seeds.

4 **Suena** (swā´ nä) means "it echoes."

Everything will pass you by
Like a merry-go-round the red
bricks will swing past your eyes
10 They will melt
So   old
will move out by themselves

Suena

I present you the tall skyscrapers
15 as merely huge palm trees with lights
Suena

The roaring of the trains is a fast guaguanco°
dance of the ages
Suena
20 Snow falls
Coconut chips galore
Take the train to Caguas and the bus is only ten cents
to Aguas Buenas°

Suena

25 A tropical wave settled here
And it is pulling the sun
with a romp
No one knows what to do

Suena

30 I am going home now
I am settled there with my fruits
Everything tastes good today
Even the ones that are grown here
Taste like they're from outer space
35 Walk y Suena
Do it strange
Los New Yorks.

---

17 The *guaguanco* (gwä gwäng kō′) is a complex, rhythmic dance.

23 *Caguas* (kä′gwäs) and *Aguas Buenas* (ä′gwäs bwä′näs) are locations in Puerto Rico.

After You Read

Respond and Think Critically

1. In "Knoxville, Tennessee," what does the speaker enjoy about summer? [Summarize]

2. What might the speaker in "Knoxville, Tennessee" mean when she says that summer is a time to "be warm / all the time / not only when you go to bed / and sleep"? [Interpret]

3. Why do you think the speaker in "Los New Yorks" repeats the word *suena*? Think about the meaning of this word and the effect it has on your reading of the poem. [Analyze]

4. Identify three examples in which the speaker in "Los New Yorks" describes New York City using sights and sounds that are common in Puerto Rico. Which description do you find most interesting? Explain. [Make Judgments]

5. Note the poets' use of imagery in "Knoxville, Tennessee" and "Los New Yorks." Which poem gives you a stronger sense of place through the sensory details it includes? Provide reasons for your choice. [Evaluate]

6. **BQ** BIG Question What do both poems suggest are the things that make a place memorable? [Draw Conclusions]

Academic Vocabulary

In "Los New Yorks," Victor Hernández Cruz uses **analogies** to compare his home in Puerto Rico to his home in New York. An analogy is a comparison between two things that are alike in some ways. Using analogies can make something unfamiliar easier to understand. How might using analogies help you understand different places and cultures?

TIP

Analyzing
Here are some tips to help you analyze. Remember, when you analyze, you look at separate parts of the poem to create an understanding of the entire text.

- Review what *suena* means by looking at the footnote.
- Look for appearances of *suena* in the poem. Does there seem to be a pattern to where the word is used?
- Determine the effect the placement of the word has on the overall poem and write a general statement based on the details.

FOLDABLES Keep track of
Study Organizer your ideas about the **BIG Question** in your unit Foldable.

 Literature Online

Selection Resources
For Selection Quizzes, eFlashcards, and Reading-Writing Connection activities, go to glencoe.com and enter QuickPass code GL39770u3.

Test Skills Practice

1. In "Los New Yorks," what image does the author use to help the reader understand the busy pace of New York?

   A a sailing boat

   B a falling coconut

   C a shaking maraca

   D a spinning merry-go-round

Review: Diction

As you learned on page 248, diction is an author's choice of words. Depending on his or her audience, an author can choose different words to mean the same thing.

2. What does the diction in "Knoxville, Tennessee" tell you about the author's feelings about spending the summer in Knoxville?

3. Why might the author of "Los New Yorks" use Spanish words?

4. Which poem is easier for you to interpret? Think about how the poem's diction influences your understanding. Use a graphic organizer like the one shown to help you organize your thoughts.

Diction	Interpretation

Grammar Link

Comparative and Superlative Writers use the **comparative** form of adjectives and adverbs to compare one person, place, thing, or action with another. To form the comparative of most one-syllable words and some two-syllable words, add -er to the end. In the following example, one person's age is compared to another:

Carrie is older than Heba.

Writers use the **superlative** form to compare one person, place, thing, or action with more than one other. To form the superlative of many one- or two-syllable words, add -est. In the following example, one person's age is compared to several others:

Lou is the oldest of the eight children.

Use the words *more* or *less* to form the comparative of most multi-syllabic adjectives or adverbs (*more sensitive, less patient*). Use *most* or *least* to form the superlative (*most courageous, least tired*).

Practice On a separate piece of paper, write the comparative and superlative forms of each of these words: *loud, big, popular,* and *talented.*

Write with Style

Apply Imagery Look back at the poems to see how the poets' use of imagery creates a strong impression of important places in their lives. Refer to the list about your hometown that you made at the beginning of the lesson. Use the list to help you write one or two stanzas for a poem about this place. Include sensory language in your poem that will help your readers see, hear, smell, taste, and feel what it's like to live there. Creating poems can help you develop your own personal writing style.

The New Colossus and *Childhood*

Connect to the Poems

Think about a place that evokes vivid memories or creates strong emotions in you. It could be your old neighborhood, a relative's house, or a special place you have visited.

Quickwrite Freewrite for a few minutes about the place you selected. Briefly describe it and tell why it makes you feel the way it does.

Build Background

In the late nineteenth and early twentieth centuries, people from around the world immigrated to the United States. Many came with nothing but the clothes on their backs and the dream of a better life. Life during this time was often difficult. Many people had to work long hours in sickening conditions, and equal rights for all people had not yet been established.

- "The New Colossus" by Emma Lazarus is the poem engraved on the pedestal on which the Statue of Liberty stands. The Statue of Liberty was a gift given to the United States by France in 1885. It stands in New York Harbor and has become one of the most well-known and beloved symbols of freedom in the United States.

- "Childhood" is set in the segregated South of the 1920s. Many formerly enslaved families had become sharecroppers. Sharecroppers had to pay landowners a large portion of the crops they grew for the use of their land. Many sharecroppers worked long hours under harsh conditions and received little in return.

Meet the Authors

Emma Lazarus

When Jews began fleeing Russia in 1881, Lazarus urged her fellow Americans to open their country to immigrants.

"The New Colossus" was written to help raise money for a base for the Statue of Liberty.

Emma Lazarus was born in 1849 and died in 1887.

Margaret Walker

Margaret Walker was a poet, novelist, essayist, and educator. Walker's writings focus on African-American history and culture, and civil rights.

Walker wrote many books, including the 1942 poetry collection *For My People*, which contains "Childhood."

Margaret Walker was born in 1915 and died in 1998.

 Literature Online

Author Search For more about Emma Lazarus and Margaret Walker, go to glencoe.com and enter QuickPass code GL39770u3.

Set Purposes for Reading

BQ ▶ BIG Question

Read the two poems to identify where they are set and to determine which is more important: the journey to these places or the arrival.

Literary Element | Sonnet

A **sonnet** is a poem of fourteen lines. Sonnets usually have strict rhyme patterns and deal with a single theme, idea, or emotion. For example, many of William Shakespeare's sonnets address the topic of love.

Sonnets are an important and challenging form of poetry. To identify a sonnet, determine the rhyme pattern at the ends of the lines. Also, look for **iambic pentameter.** An **iamb** is a pair of syllables whose first syllable is unstressed and whose second syllable is stressed (like the word *today*). **Pentameter** means the line has five such pairs of syllables.

As you read the poems, identify the traits that make them sonnets: Softly tap the rhythm, listen for the end rhymes, and identify the theme.

Reading Strategy | Paraphrase

When you **paraphrase,** you retell the information and details in a story, poem, or text in your own words. You include more details than you would in a summary. A paraphrase is about as long as the original text.

Paraphrasing is an important strategy because it confirms your understanding of a text. If you can put the information in your own words, you probably understood what you read.

When you paraphrase a sentence, you

- replace key words with synonyms (words that mean almost the same thing)
- rearrange the order of the words in a way that still makes sense
- take care not to change the author's meaning

As you read, ask yourself how you can write the parts of the poems in your own way. You may find it helpful to use a graphic organizer like the one below to help you paraphrase each line.

Line	My Paraphrase
"Not like the brazen giant of Greek fame, . . ."	Unlike the giant statue that was famous in Greece

Learning Objectives

For pages 410–415

In studying these texts, you will focus on the following objectives:

Literary Study: Analyzing sonnets.

Reading: Paraphrasing.

TRY IT

Paraphrase Think of a line from one of your favorite songs. Paraphrase it by putting it in your own words. Why do you think the singer wrote the lyrics the way he or she did?

The New Colossus

Emma Lazarus

Not like the brazen giant of Greek fame,°
With conquering limbs astride from land to land;
Here at our sea-washed, sunset gates shall stand
A mighty woman with a torch, whose flame
5   Is the imprisoned lightning, and her name
Mother of Exiles.° From her beacon-hand
Glows world-wide welcome; her mild eyes command
The air-bridged harbor that twin cities frame,
"Keep, ancient lands, your storied pomp!"° cries she
10 With silent lips. "Give me your tired, your poor,
Your huddled masses yearning to breathe free,
The wretched refuse° of your teeming shore,
Send these, the homeless, tempest-tossed° to me,
I lift my lamp beside the golden door!"

 BQ **BIG Question**
Why do you think the Statue of Liberty is a memorable place for many people?

Sonnet How are the first eight lines (the octet) different from the final six lines (the sestet)?

---

1 The **Colossus** was a giant statue said to have stood with one foot on each side of the harbor entrance at the Greek island of Rhodes.

6 **Mother of Exiles** means that the Statue of Liberty is a symbolic caretaker of immigrants to the United States.

9 **Storied pomp** refers to the displays of wealth of royalty and upper-class families of Europe.

12 **Refuse** (ref´ūs) means "waste" or "rubbish."

13 **Tempest-tossed** means "knocked around by storms and fate."

Childhood

Margaret Walker

At the Coalface, 1942.
Henry Spencer Moore.
Pencil, chalk, pen and ink,
watercolour and bodycolour
on paper. Whitworth Art
Gallery, The University of
Manchester, UK.

When I was a child I knew red miners
dressed raggedly and wearing carbide lamps.
I saw them come down red hills to their camps
dyed with red dust from old Ishkooda mines.°
5 Night after night I met them on the roads,
or on the streets in town I caught their glance;
the swing of dinner buckets in their hands,
and grumbling undermining all their words.

I also lived in low cotton country
10 where moonlight hovered over ripe haystacks,
or stumps of trees, and croppers' rotting shacks
with famine, terror, flood, and plague near by;
where sentiment and hatred still held sway°
and only bitter land was washed away.

Paraphrase How would
you paraphrase the
last four lines of the
first stanza?

Sonnet How does the poet
create a sense of rhythm?

---

4 ***Ishkooda mines*** refers to a mining company in Birmingham, Alabama.

13 ***Still held sway*** means "still had power."

After You Read

Respond and Think Critically

1. In "The New Colossus," how does Emma Lazarus describe the Statue of Liberty? [Recall and Identify]

2. In "The New Colossus," to what does "the golden door" refer? [Interpret]

3. Imagine you are a newly arrived immigrant to the United States. How would you feel if you saw the Statue of Liberty for the first time? Explain why you think you would feel that way? [Connect]

4. In "Childhood," what can you conclude about the feelings of the miners returning from work? [Draw Conclusions]

5. How are the two sonnets alike and different? [Compare]

6. **BQ** BIG Question Which would be more memorable to you: a visit to a historic national monument, such as the Statue of Liberty, or to a famous person's childhood home? Why? [Evaluate]

TIP

Comparing
Consider what defines a sonnet and determine how the poems are alike and different.

- Find the rhyme pattern by giving each new ending sound a new letter to form a pattern, such as *abba*.

- Speak the lines to look for iambic pentameter.

- Decide how the structure affects sound, theme, and description.

FOLDABLES
Study Organizer Keep track of your ideas about the **BIG Question** in your unit Foldable.

Just 10 years ago, Duom Deng, David Ayiik, and James Biar were refugees too. During Sudan's civil war, the three boys had seen their parents killed and their villages destroyed. Then they and thousands of other orphaned children

Examine Media

The Power of Symbols

Companies have long used symbols to sell their products and services. In advertising, a symbol is a visual image that represents some idea or thing. Patriotic symbols like the Statue of Liberty can have a very powerful effect on consumers.

For example, in 2003 a credit card company began using the Statue of Liberty to promote its card. A carmaker has also used the statue to sell its products. Even a video game maker has added the statue to one of its most popular games.

Group Activity

Discuss the following questions in a small group.

1. Why do you think companies use patriotic symbols in their advertising? What effect do they hope the symbols will have on viewers?

2. The Statue of Liberty has been called "a beacon of freedom and hope to the world." Do you think it's a good idea to use such a meaningful symbol to sell credit cards or cars or video games? Why or why not?

Literary Element Sonnet

1. What is the rhyme scheme of "The New Colossus"? (Remember, you label the first end rhyme *a*, the second end rhyme *b*, and so on.) How many lines' last words rhyme with *fame?* How many lines' last words rhyme with *land?*

2. Why do you think Margaret Walker created a sonnet in two stanzas instead of the traditional one stanza?

Review: Setting

As you learned on page 92, the **setting** is where and when a poem or story takes place. The setting can affect the overall mood of the text.

3. Many of the details in "The New Colossus" describe where the Statue of Liberty is instead of really describing what the statue is like. List two of these details that describe the statue's setting.

4. What are the two settings in "Childhood"? How might the mood of the poem change if the poet had grown up in a busy city or in a prosperous suburban neighborhood?

5. How are the settings for the two poems alike and different? Create a graphic organizer like the one below to help you compare and contrast the poems' settings.

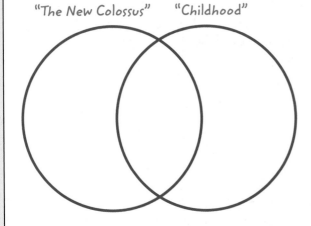

"The New Colossus"   "Childhood"

Reading Strategy Paraphrase

6. Paraphrase what the Statue of Liberty cries "With silent lips" at the end of "The New Colossus."

7. Paraphrase the following lines from "Childhood": "where sentiment and hatred still held sway / and only bitter land was washed away." Use a graphic organizer like the one below to help you.

Lines from Poem	My Paraphrase

Academic Vocabulary

In "The New Colossus," when immigrants come to the United States, they are making a **transition** to a new country.

In the preceding sentence, *transition* means "passage from one state, position, condition, or activity to another." Think about the differences between junior high/middle school and high school. What sorts of changes do you expect from your transition to high school?

Literature Online

Selection Resources For Selection Quizzes, eFlashcards, and Reading-Writing Connection activities, go to glencoe.com and enter QuickPass code GL39770u3.

Respond Through Writing

Expository Essay

Compare and Contrast Mood In "The New Colossus" and "Childhood," the poets choose their words carefully to describe special places and evoke a mood for the reader. In an expository essay, compare and contrast the moods in these two poems.

Understand the Task The **mood** is the emotional quality or atmosphere in a story or poem. **Setting** can affect the mood. For example, a poem about a sunny beach will create a different mood from one about a stormy sea. Think about how the feelings created by these two poems are alike and different.

Prewrite Think about places in each poem where the mood is most apparent. To help you organize your essay, fill out a Venn diagram like the one below. List differences in mood in the outer circles and similarities in the center section. In parentheses next to each point, write the line numbers in the poem that create this mood.

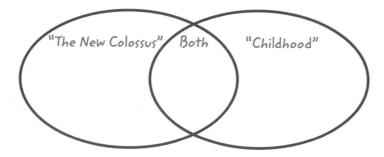

Draft Before you begin drafting, make a plan. Begin with an introduction that states your thesis. In the body, you may choose to write about similarities between the poems in one paragraph and differences in the next. Restate your thesis in the conclusion. This sentence frame might help you move from similarities to differences:

Both "The New Colossus" and "Childhood" share a mood of _____.
However, _____.

Revise After you have written your first draft, read it to make sure it is organized in a logical way and the distinctions between similarities and differences are clear. Add phrases such as *similar to* to signal comparisons and phrases such as *in contrast to* to signal contrasts.

Edit and Proofread Proofread your expository essay, correcting any errors in spelling, grammar, and punctuation. Review the Grammar Tip in the side column for information on using colons.

Learning Objectives

For page 416

In this assignment, you will focus on the following objective:

Writing: Writing an expository essay that compares and contrasts mood.

> ## Grammar Tip

Colons
A **colon** is often used to introduce a list of items. For example:

The Statue of Liberty welcomes these people: the tired, the poor, and the homeless.

A colon can also be used to introduce an explanation or definition. For example:

Walker does not fondly remember her childhood home in cotton country: it was a place of famine, terror, flood, and plague.

Remember to use a colon to introduce an explanation or definition.

Comparing Literature

from *Beowulf* and *Racing the Great Bear*

BQ BIG Question

As you read the paired selections, think about the journey each of the main characters in *Beowulf* and "Racing the Great Bear" undertakes. In what ways are the characters changed by their journeys? How do their destinations differ?

Literary Element Motivation

A character's **motivation** is the reason he or she acts in a certain way. A character is motivated by needs or desires such as fame, greed, and love. As you read each selection, think about the main character's motivation for acting the way he does.

Reading Skill Compare and Contrast

How did you choose which shirt to wear today? You may have considered two or three shirts. To decide on one over another, you **compare and contrast** the shirts. You think about how the shirts are alike and different.

You can understand literature better when you compare and contrast literary elements such as character motivation. On the following pages, you'll compare and contrast the motivations of the main characters of *Beowulf* and "Racing the Great Bear."

You can use a graphic organizer like the Venn diagram below to help you compare and contrast the two characters. In the left circle, write motivations that are only true of Beowulf. In the right circle, add motivations that are only true of Swift Runner. In the middle, where the circles cross, enter motivations that are common to both characters.

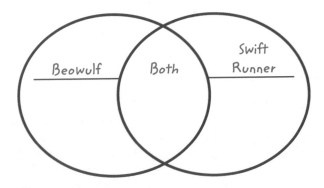

Beowulf | Both | Swift Runner

Learning Objectives

For pages 417–433

In studying these texts, you will focus on the following objectives:

Literary Study: Analyzing motivation.

Reading: Comparing and contrasting.

Meet the Authors

The *Beowulf* Poet

Beowulf is the oldest surviving epic poem in the English language. Its unknown author is referred to as the *Beowulf* poet.

Joseph Bruchac

Joseph Bruchac has written many works based on Native American myths. He was born in 1942.

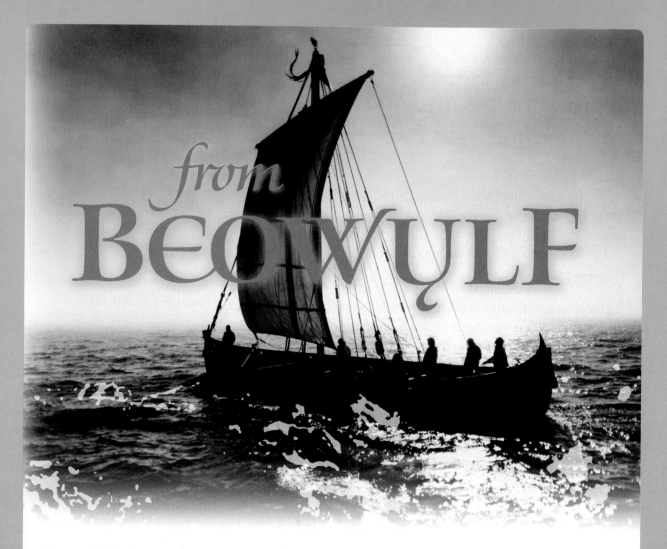

from BEOWULF

Denmark's King Hrothgar builds a huge banquet hall for his people. Their noisy celebrations anger a monster named Grendel, who terrorizes and attacks them, killing many. In nearby Geatland, a young hero named Beowulf hears of the Danes' suffering.

TRANSLATED BY BURTON RAFFEL

the COMING of BEOWULF

In his far-off home Beowulf, Higlac's
Follower and the strongest of the Geats—greater
And stronger than anyone anywhere in
   this world—
Heard how Grendel [the monster] filled nights
   with horror

Comparing Literature In this section of the poem, Beowulf immediately sets out to fight against Grendel. What is Beowulf's motivation?

5   And quickly commanded a boat fitted out,
     Proclaiming that he'd go to that famous king,
     Would sail across the sea to Hrothgar,
     Now when help was needed. None
     Of the wise ones regretted his going, much
10 As he was loved by the Geats: the omens
       were good,
     And they urged the adventure on. So Beowulf
     Chose the mightiest men he could find,
     The bravest and best of the Geats, fourteen
     In all, and led them down to their boat;
15 He knew the sea, would point the prow[1]
     Straight to that distant Danish shore.
       Then they sailed, set their ship
     Out on the waves, under the cliffs.
     Ready for what came they wound through
       the currents,
20 The seas beating at the sand, and were borne
     In the lap of their shining ship, lined
     With gleaming armor, going safely
     In that oak-hard boat to where their hearts
       took them.
     The wind hurried them over the waves,
25 The ship foamed through the sea like a bird
     Until, in the time they had known it would take,
     Standing in the round-curled prow they could see
     Sparkling hills, high and green,
     Jutting up over the shore, and rejoicing
30 In those rock-steep cliffs they quietly ended
     Their voyage. Jumping to the ground, the Geats
     Pushed their boat to the sand and tied it
     In place, mail shirts and armor rattling
     As they swiftly moored their ship. And then
35 They gave thanks to God for their easy crossing . . .

Comparing Literature In what ways do the words of the wise ones support and increase Beowulf's motivation to make this journey?

---

1 The *prow* is the forward part of a ship.

Beowulf arrives at Herot, where he addresses King Hrothgar. Beowulf describes his feats of heroism and vows to slay the monster.

the BATTLE WITH GRENDEL

    Out from the marsh, from the foot of misty
Hills and bogs, bearing God's hatred,
Grendel came, hoping to kill
Anyone he could trap on this trip to high Herot.[2]
40 He moved quickly through the cloudy night,
Up from his swampland, sliding silently
Toward that gold-shining hall. He had visited
    Hrothgar's
Home before, knew the way—
But never, before nor after that night,
45 Found Herot defended so firmly, his reception
So harsh. He journeyed, forever joyless,
Straight to the door, then snapped it open,
Tore its iron fasteners with a touch
And rushed angrily over the threshold.
50 He strode quickly across the inlaid
Floor, snarling and fierce: his eyes
Gleamed in the darkness, burned with a gruesome
Light. Then he stopped, seeing the hall
Crowded with sleeping warriors, stuffed
55 With rows of young soldiers resting together.
And his heart laughed, he relished the sight,
Intended to tear the life from those bodies
By morning; the monster's mind was hot
With the thought of food and the feasting his belly
60 Would soon know. But fate, that night, intended
Grendel to gnaw the broken bones
Of his last human supper. Human
Eyes were watching his evil steps;
Waiting to see his swift hard claws.
65 Grendel snatched at the first Geat
He came to, ripped him apart, cut

---

2 **Herot** is the banquet hall built by King Hrothgar as a place to house his men and show off his riches.

Performance photographs are from a 2007 adaptation of *Beowulf*.

His body to bits with powerful jaws.
Drank the blood from his veins and bolted
Him down, hands and feet; death
70 And Grendel's great teeth came together,
Snapping life shut. Then he stepped to another
Still body, clutched at Beowulf with his claws,
Grasped at a strong-hearted wakeful sleeper
—And was instantly seized himself, claws
75 Bent back as Beowulf leaned up on one arm.
    That shepherd of evil, guardian of crime,
Knew at once that nowhere on earth
Had he met a man whose hands were harder;
His mind was flooded with fear—but nothing
80 Could take his talons[3] and himself from that tight
Hard grip. Grendel's one thought was to run
From Beowulf, flee back to his marsh and
    hide there:
This was a different Herot than the hall he
    had emptied.
But Higlac's follower remembered his final
85 Boast and, standing erect, stopped
The monster's flight, fastened those claws
In his fists till they cracked, clutched Grendel
Closer. The infamous[4] killer fought

Comparing Literature
Why doesn't Beowulf let Grendel leave?

---

3 **Talons** are claws.
4 Here, **infamous** (in´fə məs) means "evil and wicked."

For his freedom, wanting no flesh but retreat,
90 Desiring nothing but escape; his claws
Had been caught, he was trapped. That trip
  to Herot
Was a miserable journey for the writhing[5] monster!
  The high hall rang, its roof boards swayed,
And Danes shook with terror. Down
95 The aisles the battle swept, angry
And wild. Herot trembled, wonderfully
Built to withstand the blows, the struggling
Great bodies beating at its beautiful walls;
Shaped and fastened with iron, inside
100 And out, artfully worked, the building
Stood firm. Its benches rattled, fell
To the floor, gold-covered boards grating
As Grendel and Beowulf battled across them.
Hrothgar's wise men had fashioned Herot
105 To stand forever; only fire,
They had planned, could shatter what such skill
  had put
Together, swallow in hot flames such splendor
Of ivory and iron and wood. Suddenly
The sounds changed, the Danes started
110 In new terror, cowering in their beds as the terrible
Screams of the Almighty's enemy sang

Comparing Literature
How would you describe Beowulf's motivation at this point? Think about how it is different than it was before.

---

5 Something that is **writhing** is twisting and rolling wildly.

In the darkness, the horrible shrieks of pain
And defeat, the tears torn out of Grendel's
Taut throat, hell's captive caught in the arms
115 Of him who of all the men on earth
Was the strongest.

                That mighty protector of men
Meant to hold the monster till its life
Leaped out, knowing the fiend was no use
120 To anyone in Denmark. . . .
                   Grendel
Saw that his strength was deserting him, his claws
Bound fast, Higlac's brave follower tearing at
His hands. The monster's hatred rose higher,
But his power had gone. He twisted in pain,
125 And the bleeding sinews[6] deep in his shoulder
Snapped, muscle and bone split
And broke. The battle was over, Beowulf
Had been granted new glory: Grendel escaped,
But wounded as he was could flee to his den,
130 His miserable hole at the bottom of the marsh,
Only to die, to wait for the end
Of all his days. And after that bloody
Combat the Danes laughed with delight.
He who had come to them from across the sea,
135 Bold and strong-minded, had driven affliction
Off, purged Herot clean. He was happy,
Now, with that night's fierce work; the Danes
Had been served as he'd boasted he'd serve them;
    Beowulf,
A prince of the Geats, had killed Grendel,
140 Ended the grief, the sorrow, the suffering
Forced on Hrothgar's helpless people
By a bloodthirsty fiend. No Dane doubted
The victory, for the proof, hanging high
From the rafters where Beowulf had hung it, was
    the monster's
145 Arm, claw and shoulder and all. ✿

---

6 **Sinews** are tendons, or bands of tissue connecting muscles to bones.

Comparing Literature
Why is Beowulf happy?
Think about how his
motivation has changed at
this point in the story.

Racing the Great Bear

Retold by Joseph Bruchac

*N*e ONENDJI. Hear my story, which happened long ago. For many generations, the five nations of the Haudenosaunee, the People of the Longhouse, had been at war with one another. No one could say how the wars began, but each time a man of one nation was killed, his relatives sought revenge in the blood feud,[1] and so the fighting continued. Then the Creator took pity on his people and sent a messenger of peace.

The Peacemaker traveled from nation to nation, convincing the people of the Five Nations—the Mohawk, the Oneida, the Onondaga, the Cayuga, and the Seneca[2]—that it was wrong for brothers to kill one another. It was not easy, but finally the nations agreed and the Great Peace began. Most welcomed that peace, though there were some beings with bad hearts who wished to see the return of war.

One day, not long after the Great Peace had been established, some young men in a Seneca village decided they would pay a visit to the Onondaga people.

"It is safe now to walk the trail between our nations," the young men said. "We will return after the sun has risen and set seven times."

Comparing Literature What motivations caused the people of the Five Nations to begin the Great Peace?

---

1 A *feud* is a long, bitter quarrel between two individuals or groups.

2 *Oneida* (ō nī′ də), *Onondaga* (on′ ən dô′ ga), *Cayuga* (kā u′ gə), and *Seneca* (sen′ ə kə) are northeastern Native American groups.

Then they set out. They walked toward the east until they were lost from sight in the hills. But many more than seven days passed, and those young men never returned. Now another group of young men left, wanting to find out where their friends had gone. They, too, did not return.

The people grew worried. Parties were sent out to look for the vanished young men, but no sign was found. And the searchers who went too far into the hills did not return, either.

The old chief of the village thought long and hard. He asked the clan[3] mothers, those wise women whose job it was to choose the chiefs and give them good advice, what should be done.

Comparing Literature What is the chief's motivation for finding out what has happened to his people?

"We must find someone brave enough to face whatever danger is out there," the clan mothers said.

So the old chief called the whole village to a council meeting. He held up a white strand of wampum beads made from quahog[4] clamshells as he spoke.

"Hear me," he said. "I am of two minds about what has happened to our people. It may be that the Onondaga have broken the peace and captured them. It may be there is something with an evil mind that wishes to destroy this new peace and so has killed our people. Now someone must go and find out. Who is brave enough? Who will come and take this wampum[5] from my hand?"

Many men were gathered in that council. Some were known to speak of themselves as brave warriors. Still, though they muttered to one another, no man stepped forward to take the strand of wampum. The old chief began to walk about the circle, holding the wampum in front of each man in

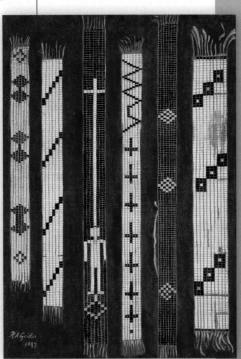

Iroquois Wampum Belts. Rufus Grider. Newberry Library, Chicago, IL.

---

3 A *clan* is a group of families who descended from a common ancestor.

4 The *quahog* (kwô´hôg´) is a type of clam found on the Atlantic coast of North America.

5 *Wampum* (wom´pəm) is a string of shell beads. Some Native Americans used wampum as a form of money, but it was also used in tribal rituals and to record history.

turn. But each man only lowered his eyes to the ground. No man lifted his hand to take the wampum.

Just outside the circle stood a boy who had not yet become a man. His parents were dead, and he lived with his grandmother in her old lodge at the edge of the village. His clothing was always torn and his face dirty because his grandmother was too old to care for him as a mother would. The other young men made fun of him, and as a joke they called him Swift Runner—even though no one had ever seen him run and it was thought that he was weak and lazy. All he ever seemed to do was play with his little dog or sit by the fire and listen when the old people were talking.

"Our chief has forgotten our greatest warrior," one of the young men said to another, tilting his head toward Swift Runner.

"*Nyoh*," the other young man said, laughing. "Yes. Why does he not offer the wampum to Swift Runner?"

The chief looked around the circle of men, and the laughing stopped. He walked out of the circle to the place where the small boy in torn clothes stood. He held out the wampum and Swift Runner took it without hesitating.

"I accept this," Swift Runner said. "It is right that I be the one to face the danger.

"In the eyes of the people I am worthless, so if I do not return, it will not matter. I will leave when the sun rises tomorrow."

When Swift Runner arrived home at his grandmother's lodge, the old woman was waiting for him.

"Grandson," she said, "I know what you have done. The people of this village no longer remember, but your father was a great warrior. Our family is a family that has power."

Then she reached up into the rafters and took down a heavy bow. It was blackened with smoke and seemed so thick that no man could bend it.

Comparing Literature
In what way does the opinion of the villagers affect Swift Runner?

"If you can string this bow, Grandson," the old woman said, "you are ready to face whatever waits for you on the trail."

Swift Runner took the bow. It was as thick as a man's wrist, but he bent it with ease and strung it.

"Wah-hah!" said his grandmother. "You are the one I knew you would grow up to be. Now you must sleep. At dawn we will make you ready for your journey."

It was not easy for Swift Runner to sleep, but when he woke the next morning, he felt strong and clearheaded. His grandmother was sitting by the fire with a cap in her hand.

"This was your grandfather's cap," she said. "I have sewed four hummingbird feathers on it. It will make your feet more swift."

Swift Runner took the cap and placed it on his head.

His grandmother held up four pairs of moccasins.

"Carry these tied to your waist. When one pair wears out, throw them aside and put on the next pair."

Swift Runner took the moccasins and tied them to his belt.

Next his grandmother picked up a small pouch. "In this pouch is cornmeal mixed with maple sugar," she said. "It is the only food you will need as you travel. It will give you strength when you eat it each evening."

Swift Runner took the pouch and hung it from his belt by the moccasins.

"The last thing I must give you," said the old woman, "is this advice. Pay close attention to your little dog. You have treated him well and so he is your great friend. He is small, but his eyes and nose are keen.[6] Keep him always in front of you. He will warn you of danger before it can strike you."

Easter Woodlands Moccasins. Iroquois. Hide, dyed quills, beads. Length: 10 in. Private Collection.

---

6 Something that is **keen** is highly sensitive or sharp.

Then Swift Runner set out on his journey. His little dog stayed ahead of him, sniffing the air and sniffing the ground. By the time the sun was in the middle of the sky, they were far from the village. The trail passed through deep woods, and it seemed to the boy as if something was following them among the trees. But he could see nothing in the thick brush.

The trail curved toward the left, and the boy felt even more the presence of something watching. Suddenly his little dog ran into the brush at the side of the trail, barking loudly. There were the sounds of tree limbs breaking and heavy feet running. Then out of the forest came a Nyagwahe, a monster bear. Its great teeth were as long as a man's arm. It was twice as tall as a moose. Close at its heels was Swift Runner's little dog.

"I see you," Swift Runner shouted. "I am after you. You cannot escape me."

Swift Runner had learned those words by listening to the stories the old people told. They were the very words a monster bear speaks when it attacks, words that terrify anyone who hears them. On hearing those words, the great bear turned and fled from the boy.

"You cannot escape me," Swift Runner shouted again. Then he ran after the bear.

The Nyagwahe turned toward the east, with Swift Runner and his dog close behind. It left the trail and plowed through the thick forest, breaking down great trees and leaving a path of destruction like that of a whirlwind. It ran up the tallest hills and down through the swamps, but the boy and the dog stayed at its heels. They ran past a great cave in the rocks. All around the cave were the bones of people the bear had caught and eaten.

"My relatives," Swift Runner called as he passed the cave, "I will not forget you. I am after the one who killed you. He will not escape me."

Throughout the day, the boy and his dog chased the great bear, growing closer bit by bit. At last, as the sun

Comparing Literature
What motivates the great bear to flee from the boy?

Comparing Literature Why does Swift Runner continue chasing the great bear?

began to set, Swift Runner stopped at the head of a small valley and called his small dog to him.

"We will rest here for the night," the boy said. He took off his first pair of moccasins, whose soles were worn away to nothing. He threw them aside and put on a new pair. Swift Runner made a fire and sat beside it with his dog. Then he took out the pouch of cornmeal and maple sugar, sharing his food with his dog.

"Nothing will harm us," Swift Runner said. "Nothing can come close to our fire." He lay down and slept.

In the middle of the night, he was awakened by the growling of his dog. He sat up with his back to the fire and looked into the darkness. There, just outside the circle of light made by the flames, stood a dark figure that looked like a tall man. Its eyes glowed green.

"I am Nyagwahe," said the figure. "This is my human shape. Why do you pursue[7] me?"

"You cannot escape me," Swift Runner said. "I chase you because you killed my people. I will not stop until I catch you and kill you."

The figure faded back into the darkness.

"You cannot escape me," Swift Runner said again. Then he patted his small dog and went to sleep.

As soon as the first light of the new day appeared, Swift Runner rose. He and his small dog took the trail. It was easy to follow the monster's path, for trees were uprooted and the earth torn by its great paws. They ran all through the morning. When the sun was in the middle of the sky, they reached the head of another valley. At the other end they saw the great bear running toward the east. Swift Runner pulled off his second pair of moccasins, whose soles were worn away to nothing. He put on his third pair and began to run again.

All through that day, they kept the Nyagwahe in sight, drawing closer bit by bit. When the sun began to

Beaded Pouch. Iroquois. Velvet, metal, beads, cloth. Length: 6 1/2 in. Private Collection.

---

7 **Pursue** means to chase after.

set, Swift Runner stopped to make camp. He took off the third pair of moccasins, whose soles were worn away to nothing, and put on the last pair.

"Tomorrow," he said to his small dog, "we will catch the monster and kill it." He reached for his pouch of cornmeal and maple sugar, but when he opened it, he found it filled with worms. The magic of the Nyagwahe had done this. Swift Runner poured out the pouch and said in a loud voice, "You have spoiled our food, but it will not stop me. I am on your trail. You cannot escape me."

That night, once again, he was awakened by the growling of his dog. A dark figure stood just outside the circle of light.

It looked smaller than the night before, and the glow of its eyes was weak.

"I am Nyagwahe," the dark figure said. "Why do you pursue me?"

"You cannot escape me," Swift Runner said. "I am on your trail. You killed my people. You threatened the Great Peace. I will not rest until I catch you."

"Hear me," said the Nyagwahe. "I see your power is greater than mine. Do not kill me. When you catch me, take my great teeth. They are my power, and you can use them for healing. Spare my life and I will go far to the north and never again bother the People of the Longhouse."

"You cannot escape me," Swift Runner said. "I am on your trail."

The dark figure faded back into the darkness, and Swift Runner sat for a long time, looking into the night.

At the first light of day, the boy and his dog took the trail. They had not gone far when they saw the Nyagwahe ahead of them. Its sides puffed in and out as it ran. The trail was beside a big lake with many alder trees close to the water. As the great bear ran past, the leaves were torn from the trees. Fast as the bear went, the boy and his dog came closer, bit by bit. At last, when the sun was in the middle of the sky, the giant

Comparing Literature What effect does the spoiled food have on Swift Runner?

Northeast Woodlands Pottery Vessel. Iroquois. 27 cm. Canadian Museum of Civilization, Quebec, Canada.

bear could run no longer. It fell heavily to the earth, panting so hard that it stirred up clouds of dust.

Swift Runner unslung his grandfather's bow and notched an arrow to the sinewy[8] string.

"Shoot for my heart," said the Nyagwahe. "Aim well. If you cannot kill me with one arrow, I will take your life."

"No," Swift Runner said. "I have listened to the stories of my elders. Your only weak spot is the sole of your foot. Hold up your foot and I will kill you."

The great bear shook with fear. "You have defeated me," it pleaded. "Spare my life and I will leave forever."

"You must give me your great teeth," Swift Runner said. "Then you must leave and never bother the People of the Longhouse again."

"I shall do as you say," said the Nyagwahe. "Take my great teeth."

Swift Runner lowered his bow. He stepped forward and pulled out the great bear's teeth. It rose to its feet and walked to the north, growing smaller as it went. It went over the hill and was gone.

Carrying the teeth of the Nyagwahe over his shoulder, Swift Runner turned back to the west, his dog at his side. He walked for three moons before he reached the place where the bones of his people were piled in front of the monster's empty cave. He collected those bones and walked around them four times. "Now," he said, "I must do something to make my people wake up." He went to a big hickory tree and began to push it over so that it would fall on the pile of bones.

"My people," he shouted, "get up quickly or this tree will land on you."

The bones of the people who had been killed all came together and jumped up, alive again and covered with flesh. They were filled with joy and gathered around Swift Runner.

"Great one," they said, "who are you?"

Comparing Literature Why does Swift Runner take the bear's teeth instead of killing the creature?

---

8 Something that is **sinewy** is tough and strong.

Bear Claw Necklace. Native American.
Bear claws, metal beads, otter or fisher tail.
Length: 57 1/2 in. Private Collection.

"I am Swift Runner," he said.

"How can that be?" one of the men said. "Swift Runner is a skinny little boy. You are a tall, strong man."

Swift Runner looked at himself and saw that it was so. He was taller than the tallest man, and his little dog was bigger than a wolf.

"I am Swift Runner," he said. "I was that boy and I am the man you see before you."

Then Swift Runner led his people back to the village. He carried with him the teeth of the Nyagwahe, and those who saw what he carried rejoiced. The trails were safe again, and the Great Peace would not be broken. Swift Runner went to his grandmother's lodge and embraced her.

"Grandson," she said, "you are now the man I knew you would grow up to be. Remember to use your power to help the people."

So it was that Swift Runner ran with the great bear and won the race. Throughout his long life, he used the teeth of the Nyagwahe to heal the sick, and he worked always to keep the Great Peace.

Da neho.[9] I am finished. 🐾

Comparing Literature
What do you think motivated Swift Runner the most on his journey? Support your answer with details from the text.

---

9 *Da neho* is a common ending for Iroquois stories. It means "That is all."

Comparing Literature

BQ BIG Question

Now use the unit Big Question to compare and contrast *Beowulf* and "Racing the Great Bear." With a group of classmates discuss questions such as

- What is each character's main goal?
- What challenges do Beowulf and Swift Runner face on their journeys?
- In each story, is the journey or the final destination more important? Explain.

Support each answer with evidence from the readings.

Literary Element Motivation

Use the details you wrote in your Venn diagram to think about the characters in *Beowulf* and "Racing the Great Bear." With a partner, answer the following questions.

1. In what ways are the motivations of Beowulf and Swift Runner similar? What do they both seek?

2. In what ways are the motivations of Beowulf and Swift Runner different? For example, what does each character gain from his efforts?

Write to Compare

In one or two paragraphs, explain how the *Beowulf* poet and Joseph Bruchac reveal the motivations of their main characters. You might focus on these ideas as you write.

- Think about how each character is described. How does the description help readers understand the character's motivations?
- Explain how the major events in each story reveal the character's motivations.
- Examine how similarities and differences between the characters' motivations affect your feelings about each character.
- Explain how each character's motivations lead to his success.

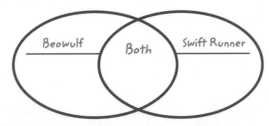

Writing Tip

Word Choice As you write, use clear, concise words to convey the exact meaning you want to express. For example, instead of writing "Beowulf *put* Grendel's arm on the wall," write "Beowulf *displayed* Grendel's arm on the wall," to show the purpose behind Beowulf's act.

 Literature Online

Selection Resources
For Selection Quizzes, eFlashcards, and Reading-Writing Connection activities, go to glencoe.com and enter QuickPass code GL39770u3.

Response to Literature

In this workshop, you will write a response to literature that will help you think about the Unit 3 Big Question: What's More Important, the Journey or the Destination?

Review the writing prompt, or assignment, below. Then read the Writing Plan. It will tell you what to do to write your response to literature.

Writing Assignment

A response to literature is an expository essay in which you interpret aspects of a literary selection. Write an interpretation of how the Big Question "What's More Important, the Journey or the Destination?" is addressed in one of the poems you have read in this unit. The audience, those reading your document, should be your classmates and teacher.

Prewrite

Which poem in this unit do you find most interesting? How does this poem address the Big Question?

Gather Ideas

Review the poems in the unit, determining what each says about whether the journey or the destination is more important. Note any lines that address the Big Question especially well.

Choose a Poem

Choose one of the poems you reviewed. To get started, talk about the poem with a partner.

Partner Talk With a partner, do the following:

1. In your own words, explain the main idea of the poem. Then discuss how that idea relates to the importance of the journey or the destination.

2. With help from your partner, write a sentence, or thesis statement, explaining how th\e poem addresses the Big Question.

The poem _____ by _____ shows _____ about the importance of the journey or the destination.

Writing Plan

- Present the thesis, or main idea, of the essay in the introduction.

- Organize the essay around several clear, insightful ideas.

- Include text evidence from the literary selection, reference to other works, or personal experience to support each idea and to show understanding of the text and the impact of the writer's technique on readers.

- Use precise and vivid language to help the reader understand the interpretation.

- Conclude by linking back to the thesis of the essay.

Get Organized

Use your notes to create a web of text evidence.

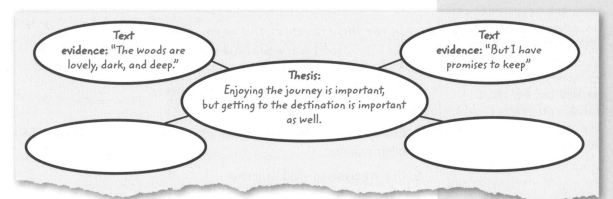

Next, create an outline of your essay.

Thesis: In Robert Frost's "Stopping by Woods on a Snowy Evening," the journey and the destination are both important.

A. The journey

   1. Man riding a horse through the woods

   2. Enjoys journey through beautiful, quiet night

B. The destination

Draft

Get It On Paper

- Review your web, notes, and thesis statement about the poem.
- Begin by writing several sentences connecting the poem to the Big Question. Add your thesis statement.
- For each body paragraph, write a topic sentence that explains how the text evidence addresses the Big Question.
- End your essay by restating your thesis in a different way.

Develop Your Draft

1. Include your **thesis** in the introduction of your draft.

> In Robert Frost's poem, "Stopping by Woods on a Snowy Evening," the journey and the destination are both important.

2. Begin each paragraph with a **clear idea.**

 Writing Tip

Remember that a thesis statement expresses the main idea of an essay. It makes a point that can be supported with examples or evidence.

LOG ON **Literature** Online

Writing and Research
For prewriting, drafting, and revising tools, go to glencoe.com and enter QuickPass code GL39770u3.

3. Support your thesis statement with examples from the text, other works, or personal experience.

> In the last stanza of the poem, the speaker reluctantly admits "But I have promises to keep, / And miles to go before I sleep" (14–15).

4. Explain the effects the poem had on you or effects it might have on other readers.

5. Use precise and vivid language.

> I wanted to just stand there under that twinkling dome and never go back into the house.

6. Link your **conclusion** to your thesis.

> In Frost's poem, the speaker says that people should take time to enjoy the journey but still realize they need to get to their destination.

Apply Good Writing Traits: Word Choice

Precise, vivid words can make writing clearer and help it live for years in readers' memories.

A word's **denotation** is its dictionary definition. However, a word's **connotation** implies a special attitude or emotion. For example, flowers have a *fragrance* but garbage has a *stench*. Both words mean "smell," but the connotations are different.

> *They became the first to look down from the dizzying height of the world's tallest mountain, Mount Everest.*

> *All of these factors force climbers who do reach the top to turn around and scramble back down as quickly as possible.*

Read these sentences from "On Top of the World" by Martha Pickerill. Which words create a clear picture and make her description memorable? Notice the word *scramble.* What is its denotation? What is its connotation in this selection?

Analyze a Student Model

What's more important, the journey or the destination? The message of Robert Frost's poem "Stopping by Woods on a Snowy Evening" is that they're both important. The poem describes the speaker's conflict between enjoying traveling through a snowy forest and having to get to his destination. Instead of resolving the conflict, the speaker suggests that both the journey and the destination are necessary.

The journey is the main focus of the poem. Frost describes a person traveling alone on a horse-drawn wagon on a dark, snowy night. The speaker is in uninhabited land "between the woods and frozen lake" (7) and is amazed by the stillness. It's so quiet he can hear "the sweep / Of easy wind and downy flake" (11–12). The moment is magical, and the speaker stops, wanting it to continue. I had a similar experience looking up at the stars on my grandfather's farm. I wanted to just stand there under that twinkling dome and never go back into the house.

I did go inside, though, and the poem expresses the speaker's need move on as well. In the last stanza of the poem, he reluctantly admits, "But I have promises to keep, / And miles to go before I sleep" (14–15). The speaker then repeats the last line. This represents a definite change in the focus of the poem. The destination has become as important in the speaker's mind as appreciating the journey.

In "Stopping by Woods on a Snowy Evening," the speaker wants to both stay in the woods and get to his destination. The speaker of the poem means that the journey and the destination are equally important, because there can be no journey without a destination and no destination without a journey.

Thesis Statement
The writer begins by clearly stating the main idea of the essay.

Main Idea
Each paragraph includes a topic sentence.

Support
Examples from the text and the writer's personal experience support the main idea.

Vivid Language
Sensory words like *twinkling dome* paint a clear picture of the scene for readers.

Conclusion
The essay ends by referring back to the thesis of the essay.

Reading-Writing Connection Think about the writing techniques that you have just learned and try them out in an essay of your own.

Revise

Now it's time to revise your draft so your ideas really shine. Revising is what makes good writing great, and great writing takes work!

Peer Review Trade drafts with a partner. Use the chart below to review your partner's draft by answering the questions in the *What to do* column. Talk about your peer review after you have glanced at each other's drafts and written down the answers to the questions. Next, follow the suggestions in the *How to do it* column to revise your draft.

Revising Plan

What to do	How to do it	Example
Will readers know immediately what your thesis is?	State the thesis in your introduction.	What's more important, the journey or the destination? The message of Robert Frost's poem "Stopping by Woods on a Snowy Evening" is ~~an answer to that question~~ ∧that they're both important .
Is the main idea of each paragraph clear?	Make sure there is a topic sentence in each paragraph.	Frost describes a person traveling alone on a horse-drawn wagon on a dark, snowy night. ∧The journey is the main focus of the poem.
Do you include evidence to support your main ideas?	Include one or more examples to support each main idea.	The speaker is in uninhabited land ∧"between the woods and frozen lake" (7) and is amazed by the stillness.
Are the words you use clear and vivid?	Include strong, specific nouns, verbs, and modifiers.	The moment is ~~great,~~ ∧magical and the speaker stops, wanting it to continue.
Does your conclusion refer back to the thesis of your essay?	Restate your thesis in the last paragraph.	The speaker of the poem means that ∧the journey and the destination are equally important, because there can be no journey without a destination and no destination without a journey.

 Revising Tip

Emphasize the completeness of your essay by using your conclusion to remind readers of your thesis statement.

Edit and Proofread

For your final draft, read your essay one sentence at a time. The **Editing and Proofreading Checklist** inside the back cover of this book can help you spot errors. Use this resource to help you make any necessary changes.

Grammar Focus: Quotations from Poetry

When you use direct quotations from the poem, copy the words exactly and put them in quotation marks. Put commas or periods inside, not outside, the end quotation mark. If you are quoting more than one line, show the end of a line by inserting a slash (/). Indicate the line the words come from in parentheses after the quote. Below are examples of problems with poetry quotations from the Workshop Model and their solutions.

Problem: It's not clear which words are quoted and which are the writer's.

It's so quiet he can hear the sweep / Of easy wind and downy flake (11–12).

Solution: Enclose exact words from the poem in quotation marks.

It's so quiet he can hear "the sweep / Of easy wind and downy flake" (11–12).

Problem: Readers might have trouble locating the quoted lines in the original poem.

In the last stanza of the poem, he reluctantly admits, "I have promises to keep, / And miles to go before I sleep."

Solution: Add line numbers in parentheses after the quotation.

In the last stanza of the poem, he reluctantly admits, "I have promises to keep, / And miles to go before I sleep" (14–15).

Present

It's almost time to share your writing with others. Write your essay neatly in print or cursive on a separate sheet of paper. If you have access to a computer, type your essay on the computer and check your spelling. Save your document to a disk and print it out. Then share your essay with your teacher and classmates.

Grammar Tip

Exact Wording Double-check the exact wording of your quotations to make sure they match the original.

Presenting Tip

Include a copy of the poem you interpreted with your essay. Write it on a separate piece of paper, citing the author and source of the poem.

 Literature Online

Writing and Research For editing and publishing tools, go to glencoe.com and enter QuickPass code GL39770u3.

Speaking, Listening, and Viewing Workshop

Oral Response to Literature

Activity

Connect to Your Writing Deliver an oral response to literature to your classmates. You might want to adapt the response to literature you wrote for the Writing Workshop on pages 434–439. Remember that you focused on the Unit 3 Big Question: What's More Important, the Journey or the Destination?

Plan Your Presentation

Reread your response. Highlight parts to present. As in your written response, your oral response should be organized around clear, well-supported ideas that help the audience understand your interpretation. Be sure to include your inferences about the effects of the literary work on its audience. In addition to references to the poem, you can include references to other authors' works or to personal knowledge.

Rehearse Your Presentation

Practice several times. Rehearse in front of a mirror to watch your movements and expressions. You may use note cards to remind you of your main points and supporting evidence, but practice enough times so that you can maintain eye contact with your audience.

Deliver Your Presentation

- Review the Presentation Checklist on this page before you begin.
- Make eye contact with your audience to help them feel involved in what you are saying.
- Stop for a moment after each important point. This emphasizes the point and allows listeners to think about what you've said.
- Use gestures if you have practiced them.

Listen to Understand

Take notes as you listen to another student's presentation. Use these question frames to learn more about the interpretation:

- It seems to me that the tone of this interpretation is _____. Do others agree or disagree?
- To summarize your interpretation: _____. Is that correct?

▶ Presentation Checklist

Answer the following questions to evaluate your presentation:

- ❑ Did you speak clearly and precisely?
- ❑ Did you speak with a style that distinguished your ideas from the literary text?
- ❑ Did you vary the tone, pace, and volume of your speaking to add emphasis?
- ❑ Did you use gestures to draw attention to specific points?

LOG ON ▶ **Literature** Online

Speaking, Listening, and Viewing For project ideas, templates, and presentation tips, go to glencoe.com and enter QuickPass code GL39770u3.

Unit Challenge

Answer the BIG Question

In Unit 3, you explored the Big Question through reading, writing, speaking, and listening. Now it's time for you to complete one of the Unit Challenges below with your answer to the Big Question.

WHAT'S More Important, the Journey or the Destination?

Use the notes you took in your Unit 3 **Foldable** to complete the Unit Challenge you have chosen. Before you present your Unit Challenge, be sure it meets the requirements below. Use this first plan if you choose to interview someone who has taken a major journey.

On Your Own Activity: Write an Interview

❑ Choose someone to interview.

❑ Prepare a list of questions related to the Big Question.

❑ Ask your questions and record the answers.

❑ Write an essay on what you've learned from the interview. Relate at least one event as a narrative with precise details.

❑ Be sure that your essay has a thesis statement, an introduction, at least one body paragraph, and a conclusion that presents your answer to the Big Question.

Use this second plan if you choose to stage a debate of the Big Question.

Group Activity: Stage a Debate

❑ Form two debate teams, one representing "Journey" and the other "Destination."

❑ Choose Unit 3 selections to support your side of the debate.

❑ Each member will be an "expert" on a particular selection.

❑ As a team, use a brief written statement to help engage in the debate. The statement should contain a clear thesis, details from selections, and a well-reasoned conclusion.

❑ Stage a second round of the debate. Treat your opponent's positions with respect, but try to uncover bias or faulty logic.

❑ After the debate, the class will vote on the winner.

Learning Objectives

For page 441

In this assignment, you will focus on the following objectives:

Writing: Writing an informational essay.

Listening: Conducting an interview.

Speaking: Delivering a speech.

Independent Reading

Fiction

To explore the Big Question in other works, choose one of these books from your school or local library.

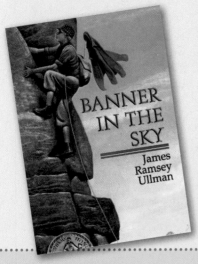

Banner in the Sky

by James Ramsey Ullman

When Rudi's father dies in his attempt to scale a mountain in the Alps, Rudi decides that he must conquer the peak that killed his father. Read to find out more about Rudi's courageous journey in this tense tale written by an experienced climber.

Sounder

by William H. Armstrong

The difficult lives of an African American sharecropper family become even harder when the father is jailed for stealing food. Then, the family's hunting dog, Sounder, is hurt while trying to protect his master. The eldest son takes on the responsibility of providing for the family. During a journey to find his father, the boy discovers inner strength and learns that the compassion of one person can bring hope to those around him.

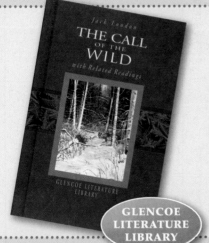

The Call of the Wild

by Jack London

This classic tale follows the life of a dog, Buck, who is stolen from his California home and taken to the harsh wilds of Alaska to work as a sled dog during the gold rush of 1897. Told from a dog's perspective, this story represents the journey undertaken by anyone who has left the predictable and safe for adventure and danger.

Where the Red Fern Grows

by Wilson Rawls

Young Billy Colman is pleased to be free to roam the Ozark hills of Oklahoma with his cherished dogs. A tragedy leaves Billy grieving, but he learns important lessons about life from a culture very different from his own.

Nonfiction

I Know Why the Caged Bird Sings

by Maya Angelou

Maya Angelou is a well-known and highly respected writer and poet. In this autobiography Angelou tells about her childhood in the Deep South. She writes about her real experiences, even though many of them were painful. She also describes some of the people who helped her along her journey.

Open Your Eyes: Extraordinary Experiences in Faraway Places

edited by Jill Davis

This collection of autobiographical stories reveals how being exposed to other cultures can change a young person's life. Ten writers describe their experiences in places ranging from a boarding school in England to a small shop in Tokyo.

Escape from Saigon: How a Vietnam War Orphan Became an American Boy

by Andrea Warren

Living in an orphanage in Saigon at the end of the Vietnam War, the young Amerasian boy Hoang Van Long did not know what his future would hold. Read to learn about his dangerous journey to find a new life and join a new family in the United States.

Write a Review

Write a book review for your classmates. Be sure to explain what you found interesting, unusual, exciting, or even annoying in the book. Include specific examples and descriptive details to support your ideas.

Assessment

Reading

Read the poems and answer the questions that follow each. Write your answers on a separate sheet of paper.

"Jenny Kissed Me" by Leigh Hunt

Jenny kissed me when we met,
Jumping from the chair she sat in;
Time, you thief, who love to get
Sweets into your list, put that in!
Say I'm weary, say I'm sad,
Say that health and wealth have missed me,
Say I'm growing old, but add,
Jenny kissed me.

---

1. What is personified in this poem?

  A. age
  B. time
  C. a kiss
  D. health and wealth

2. Which line from the poem demonstrates the use of alliteration?

  A. Say I'm weary, say I'm sad,
  B. Say I'm growing old, but add,
  C. Time, you thief, who love to get
  D. Jumping from the chair she sat in;

3. Which line from the poem best demonstrates the use of consonance?

  A. Jenny kissed me when we met,
  B. Jumping from the chair she sat in;
  C. Time, you thief, who love to get
  D. Sweets into your list, put that in!

4. In which line are the accented syllables correctly underlined?

  A. <u>Say</u> that <u>health</u> and <u>wealth</u> have <u>missed</u> me
  B. Say <u>that</u> health <u>and</u> wealth <u>have</u> missed <u>me</u>
  C. Say that <u>health</u> and wealth <u>have</u> missed me
  D. <u>Say</u> that health <u>and</u> wealth have <u>missed</u> me

5. What is the basic message of this poem?

  A. Time affects everything.
  B. Age changes joy to misery.
  C. Health and wealth are really unimportant.
  D. An affectionate gesture can change a person's outlook.

"The Cloud-Mobile"
by May Swenson

Above my face is a map
where continents form and fade.
Blue countries, made
on a white sea, are erased;
white countries are traced
on a blue sea.

It is a map that moves
faster than real
but so slow;
only my watching proves
that island has being,
or that bay.

It is a model of time;
mountains are wearing away,
coasts cracking, the ocean
spills over, then new
hills heap into view
with river-cuts of blue
  between them.

It is a map of change:
this is the way things are
with a stone or a star.
This is the way things go,
hard or soft,
swift or slow.

6. What is the extended metaphor in this poem?
   A. Maps are models.
   B. The sky is a map of Earth.
   C. Sometimes the clouds are seas.
   D. Sometimes the clouds are continents.

7. Which word best describes the tone of the poem?
   A. sad
   B. angry
   C. humorous
   D. thoughtful

8. What is the main message of this poem?
   A. All things change.
   B. Change happens very quickly.
   C. The world is an unhappy place.
   D. The sky is a miraculous work of art.

9. What is the rhyme scheme of the final stanza?
   A. abbcdc
   B. ababab
   C. aaaabb
   D. abcdef

LOG ON **Literature** Online

Assessment For additional test practice, go to glencoe.com and enter QuickPass code GL39770u3.

"Fog"
by Carl Sandburg

The fog comes
on little cat feet.

It sits looking
over harbor and city
on silent haunches
and then moves on.

---

10. What makes this poem an example of
free verse?

   A. It is only six lines long.
   B. It has no regular rhyme or meter.
   C. It describes a scene with imagery.
   D. The stanzas have different lengths.

11. The author's main purpose in this
poem is to

   A. express a deep emotion.
   B. provide information about fog.
   C. create an image of fog in the city.
   D. show the similarities between
cats and fog.

12. What quality of fog does this
poem emphasize?

   A. how quiet it is
   B. how damp it is
   C. how beautiful it is
   D. how quickly it comes and goes

Extended Answer

13. Do you think the central metaphor of
describing fog as if it were a cat is a
good one? Why or why not? Use details
from the poem to support your answer.

Vocabulary Skills

On a separate sheet of paper, write the numbers 1–14. Next to each number, write the letter of the word or phrase that means about the same as the underlined word.

1. a <u>tedious</u> journey
  A. satisfying   **C.** costly
  B. necessary   **D.** tiring

2. <u>rash</u> behavior
  A. boring   **C.** foolish
  B. annoying   **D.** cautious

3. <u>unforeseen</u> repairs
  A. complicated   **C.** unnecessary
  B. unpredicted   **D.** expensive

4. <u>resolute</u> when facing danger
  A. determined   **C.** fearful
  B. careless   **D.** worried

5. <u>mutely</u> standing by
  A. confidently   **C.** wordlessly
  B. smilingly   **D.** thoughtlessly

6. the <u>outskirts</u> of town
  A. edges   **C.** center
  B. rundown areas   **D.** main part

7. a <u>vacancy</u> in his life
  A. problem   **C.** recklessness
  B. hope   **D.** blankness

8. their <u>cunning</u> plan
  A. evil   **C.** clumsy
  B. smart   **D.** successful

9. an hour of <u>meditation</u>
  A. practice   **C.** exercise
  B. brain work   **D.** conversation

10. to sign <u>legitimately</u>
  A. clearly   **C.** rightfully
  B. falsely   **D.** hopefully

11. <u>deftly</u> throwing the ball
  A. clumsily   **C.** rapidly
  B. silently   **D.** expertly

12. longing for <u>immortality</u>
  A. endless life   **C.** excellent health
  B. a good meal   **D.** a painless death

13. a brief <u>tremor</u>
  A. warm-up   **C.** urge
  B. quake   **D.** thought

14. the <u>impulse</u> to leave
  A. right time   **C.** strong wish
  B. willingness   **D.** preparations

Writing Strategies

The following is a paragraph from a student's report. It contains errors. Read the passage. Then answer the questions on a separate sheet of paper.

___

(1) Carl Sandburg is best known as a poet, but he was a successful biographer as well. (2) After several years of writing poetry, he changed to prose and wrote biographies of Abraham Lincoln. (3) The Pulitzer Prize was awarded to him for a book about Lincoln's life during the civil war. (4) Many of Sandburg's poems have to do with Chicago. (5) Others show what life is like for people who have to work at low-paying jobs to support theirselves. (6) Sandburg had done such work himself as a boy and remembered it well.

1. Read this sentence.

> **Carl Sandburg is best known as a poet, but he was a successful biographer as well.**

The adverb in this sentence is

- A. best.
- B. known.
- C. successful.
- D. biographer.

2. What kind of phrase is *of Abraham Lincoln* in sentence 2?

- A. an adverb phrase modifying *wrote*
- B. an adjective phrase modifying *biographies*
- C. an adverb phrase modifying *changed*
- D. an adjective phrase modifying *prose*

3. Which pronoun in the report is incorrect?

- A. *he* in sentence 2
- B. *him* in sentence 3
- C. *theirselves* in sentence 5
- D. *himself* in sentence 7

4. Which word or words in the report is a proper noun and needs to be capitalized?

- A. poet
- B. life
- C. civil war
- D. biographies

Writing Product

Read the assignment in the box below and follow the directions. Use one piece of paper to jot down ideas and organize your thoughts. Then neatly write your essay on another sheet. You may not use a dictionary or other reference materials.

Writing Situation:

At the end of every semester, your English teacher shows a movie during class. The movie can be on any subject, but it must include a lesson or a moral that makes it worth watching. This semester, she has asked each student in your class to suggest a suitable movie to watch.

Directions for Writing:

Think about a movie that you feel is worthwhile and would like to share with your classmates. Now write a short persuasive essay to convince your teacher that your choice is the most appropriate.

Keep these hints in mind when you write.

- Focus on what the prompt tells you to write.
- Organize the way you will present your ideas.
- Provide good, clear support for your ideas.
- Use different kinds of sentence structures.
- Use precise words that express your ideas clearly.
- Check your essay for mistakes in spelling, grammar, and punctuation.

WHAT'S Worth Fighting For?

THE BIG Question

> "*You must be the change you wish to see in the world.*"
>
> —MOHANDAS GANDHI

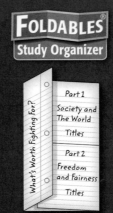

FOLDABLES®
Study Organizer

Throughout Unit 4, you will read, write, and talk about the **BIG Question**—"What's Worth Fighting For?" Use your Unit 4 **Foldable,** shown here, to keep track of your ideas as you read. Turn to the back of this book for instructions on making this **Foldable.**

What's Worth Fighting For?

Part 1
Society and The World
Titles

Part 2
Freedom and Fairness
Titles

WHAT'S Worth Fighting For?

What are some issues that need change in your neighborhood or school? Homelessness, poverty, and crime are examples of important community issues. How can you decide which issues matter most to you and are worth fighting for? You can start by exploring causes that others have fought for.

Think about causes worth fighting for:

○ Society and the World

○ Freedom and Fairness

What You'll Read

It's important to get the support of other people when you are fighting for something. Using **persuasive writing** is one good way to get someone to help your cause or to decide whether you want to support a certain cause. In this unit you will read **persuasive essays**, as well as short stories, poems, and other texts, to help you decide what's worth fighting for.

What You'll Write

As you explore the Big Question, you'll write notes in your Unit **Foldable**. Later, you'll use these notes to complete two writing assignments related to the Big Question.

1. **Write a Persuasive Essay**

2. **Choose a Unit Challenge**

   ○ **On Your Own Activity: Propose a Change**

   ○ **Group Activity: Make a Mural**

What You'll Learn

Literary Elements

argument
thesis
style
author's perspective
parallelism
text structure
ode
argument and persuasion
tone
theme
symbol
dialogue

Reading Skills and Strategies

distinguish fact and opinion
evaluate argument
make predictions about plot
monitor comprehension
paraphrase
synthesize
analyze evidence
compare and contrast
analyze cause-and-effect
   relationships
preview
recognize bias
analyze conflict

HOMELESS

Anna Quindlen

Her name was Ann, and we met in the Port Authority[1] Bus Terminal several Januarys ago. I was doing a story on homeless people. She said I was wasting my time talking to her; she was just passing through, although she'd been passing through for more than two weeks. To prove to me that this was true, she rummaged through a tote bag and a manila envelope and finally unfolded a sheet of typing paper and brought out her photographs.

They were not pictures of family, or friends, or even a dog or cat, its eyes brown-red in the flashbulb's light. They were pictures of a house. It was like a thousand houses in a hundred towns, not suburb, not city, but somewhere in between, with aluminum siding and a chain-link fence, a narrow driveway running up to a one-car garage and a patch of backyard. The house was yellow. I looked on the back for a date or a name, but neither was there. There was no need for discussion. I knew what she was trying to tell me, for it was something I had often felt. She was not adrift, alone, anonymous,[2] although her bags and her raincoat with the grime shadowing its creases had made me believe she was. She had a house, or at least once upon a time

---

1 In the New York City area, the **Port Authority** operates all of the major bus and train terminals, airports, harbors, bridges, and tunnels.

2 An **anonymous** (ə non′ə m əs) person is someone with no known name or origin.

had had one. Inside were curtains, a couch, a stove, potholders. You are where you live. She was somebody.

I've never been very good at looking at the big picture, taking the global view, and I've always been a person with an overactive sense of place, the legacy[3] of an Irish grandfather. So it is natural that the thing that seems most wrong with the world to me right now is that there are so many people with no homes. I'm not simply talking about shelter from the elements,[4] or three square meals a day or a mailing address to which the welfare people can send the check—although I know that all these are important for survival. I'm talking about a home, about precisely those kinds of feelings that have wound up in cross-stitch and French knots on samplers over the years.

Home is where the heart is. There's no place like it. I love my home with a ferocity totally out of proportion to its appearance or location. I love dumb things about it: the hot-water heater, the plastic rack you drain dishes in, the roof over my head, which occasionally leaks. And yet it is precisely those dumb things that make it what it is—a place of certainty, stability, predictability, privacy, for me and for my family. It is where I live. What more can you say about a place than that? That is everything.

Yet it is something that we have been edging away from gradually during my lifetime and the lifetimes of my parents and grandparents. There was a time when where you lived often was where you worked and where you grew the food you ate and even where you were buried. . . .

And so we have come to something else again, to children who do not understand what it means to go to their rooms because they have never had a room, to men and women whose fantasy is a wall they can paint a color of their own choosing, to old people reduced to sitting on molded plastic chairs, their skin blue-white in the lights of a bus station, who pull pictures of houses

---

3 A *legacy* (leg′ə sē) is anything handed down from an ancestor or a relative.

4 Here, *elements* means "the forces of nature; weather."

BQ BIG Question

What does Quindlen say is unfair in the world? Think about the words in this sentence that show that Quindlen has found a cause worth fighting for.

BQ BIG Question

In what ways does Quindlen support her point that homelessness is unfair and is a cause worth fighting for?

out of their bags. Homes have stopped being homes. Now they are real estate.

People find it curious that those without homes would rather sleep sitting up on benches or huddled in doorways than go to shelters. Certainly some prefer to do so because they are emotionally ill, because they have been locked in before and they are damned if they will be locked in again. Others are afraid of the violence and trouble they may find there. But some seem to want something that is not available in shelters, and they will not compromise, not for a cot, or oatmeal, or a shower with special soap that kills the bugs. "One room," a woman with a baby who was sleeping on her sister's floor, once told me, "painted blue." That was the crux[5] of it; not size or location, but pride of ownership. Painted blue.

This is a difficult problem, and some wise and compassionate[6] people are working hard at it. But in the main I think we work around it, just as we walk around it when it is lying on the sidewalk or sitting in the bus terminal—the problem, that is. It has been customary to take people's pain and lessen our own participation in it by turning it into an issue, not a collection of human beings. We turn an adjective into a noun: the poor, not poor people; the homeless, not Ann or the man who lives in the box or the woman who sleeps on the subway grate.

Sometimes I think we would be better off if we forgot about the broad strokes and concentrated on the details. Here is a woman without a bureau. There is a man with no mirror, no wall to hang it on. They are not the homeless. They are people who have no homes. No drawer that holds the spoons. No window to look out upon the world. My God. That is everything.

BQ ⟩ **BIG Question**

What simple freedom and fairness do homeless people desire, according to Quindlen?

BQ ⟩ **BIG Question**

What do you think Quindlen is saying about the best ways to fight homelessness in our society and in the world?

---

5 The ***crux*** (kruks) of an issue is its most important point or part.

6 A ***compassionate*** person sympathizes with the misfortune of others.

After You Read

Respond and Think Critically

1. Use your own words to restate briefly the most important points of Anna Quindlen's essay. [Summarize]

2. Explain who Ann is in the essay. Why does she show Quindlen a picture of a house? [Interpret]

3. Quindlen says that we "lessen our own participation" when we refer to "the homeless, not Ann or the man who lives in the box or the woman who sleeps on the subway grate." What can you infer from this statement? [Infer]

4. Are you persuaded by Quindlen's argument about the homeless and the importance of home? Explain your thoughts. [Evaluate]

⚡ Writing

Write a Letter Write a short informal letter to Anna Quindlen, telling her your thoughts and feelings about her essay "Homeless."

You may want to use this topic sentence to get you started:

Your essay "Homeless" made me feel that _____.

As you plan what you will write, think about whether you found the essay persuasive. Did it move you to want to fight for a solution to homelessness in your city or community? Explain. Do you think Quindlen's essay would persuade others to act? Support your opinions with details from the essay.

Be sure your letter includes the date, a salutation (such as *Dear Anna Quindlen)*, an introduction, at least one body paragraph, a conclusion, a closing (such as *Yours truly*), and your signature.

Learning Objectives

For page 456

In this assignment, you will focus on the following objectives:

Reading:
Analyzing and evaluating arguments.

Connecting to contemporary issues.

Writing:
Writing a letter.

LOG ON ▶ **Literature** Online

Unit Resources For additional skills practice, go to glencoe.com and enter QuickPass code GL39770u4.

Society and the World

People Holding Peace. Artist Unknown.

BQ BIG Question **What's Worth Fighting For?**

In the picture, eight people stand on a globe and share or hold peace signs. What message does the image convey about the relationships among different societies around the globe? What issues about society and the world most concern you?

Saving Water

Connect to the Essay

When you look at the world around you, you probably notice that there are many problems that need to be addressed. Think about a time when you felt strongly about an issue and took steps—big or small—to bring about change.

Partner Talk With a partner, talk about the change you tried to make. Did you succeed? Was it difficult? Share your experience with the class.

Build Background

Not everyone takes water for granted. For many people around the world, finding safe, clean water is a struggle every day.

- Roughly one-sixth of the world's people do not have enough drinking water.

- In some African and Asian countries, people walk nearly four miles to get water.

- Many people around the world drink untreated water, which can put them at risk for sickness.

Meet Marjorie Lamb

"It starts to get pretty scary, what we are doing to the planet. It becomes a very personal responsibility to look after the earth."

—Marjorie Lamb

Waste Not, Pollute Not
Marjorie Lamb's parents taught her to be kind to the planet. Lamb says that everyone can do things that do not take a lot of time but that can help the environment. Small activities, such as turning off the faucet when brushing your teeth, can make a difference.

Literary Works Lamb is the author of several books. "Saving Water" is from *2 Minutes a Day for a Greener Planet*, published in 1990.

 Literature Online

Author Search For more about Marjorie Lamb, go to glencoe.com and enter QuickPass code GL39770u4.

Set Purposes for Reading

BQ BIG Question

As you read this essay, think about why the author believes that saving water is a cause worth fighting for.

Literary Element Argument

In literature, an **argument** refers to a writer's opinion on an issue or a problem. An argument is sometimes referred to as a **proposition.** A writer must provide **support,** such as reasons and evidence, for his or her argument. Writers often use persuasive techniques, or appeals, to win the reader's favor. The following are common types of appeals:

Appeal to reason: appeal to the "head" rather than the "heart" through the use of logic, facts, and other types of hard evidence

Ethical appeal: appeal to the reader's sense of right and wrong; the writer's claim to be a good and moral person who can be trusted

Emotional appeal: appeal to the reader's heart, or emotions, in an effort to get the reader to care about a problem or an issue

As you read "Saving Water," examine whether the writer supports her argument by using appeals to reason, ethics, or emotion.

Reading Skill Distinguish Fact and Opinion

When deciding whether to agree with a writer's argument, you need to be able to distinguish fact and opinion. A **fact** is a statement that can be proved with supporting information. An **opinion,** on the other hand, is what a writer believes. It is his or her personal viewpoint.

Distinguishing facts and opinions is important because it can help you evaluate the strength of a writer's argument. An argument that is supported by facts is likely to be more believable than one that only appeals to the reader's emotions.

As you read, use a chart like the one below to keep track of facts and opinions in the essay.

Fact	Opinion
Each of us consumes nearly 53 gallons of water a day at home.	We could all use less water than we do.

Learning Objectives

For pages 458–467

In studying this text, you will focus on the following objectives:

Literary Study:
Analyzing argument.

Analyzing appeals to logic, emotion, and ethics.

Reading:
Distinguishing fact and opinion.

TRY IT

Write a brief review of a movie you saw recently. Identify actors and actresses in the movie and describe how believable they were in portraying their roles. Which of the statements you made are facts and which are opinions?

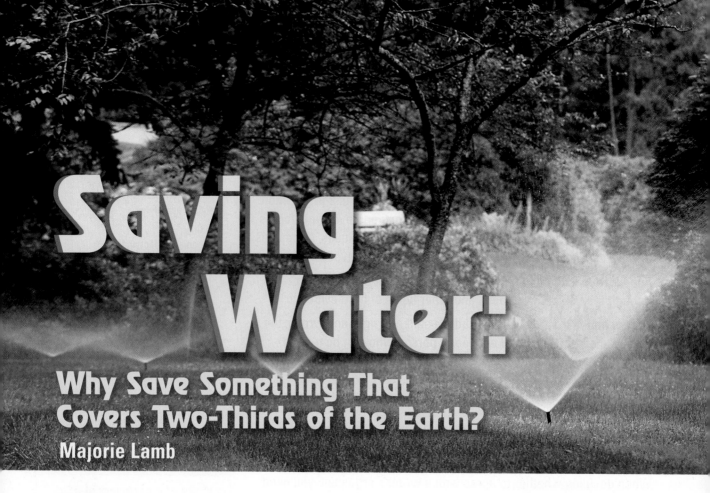

Saving Water:

Why Save Something That Covers Two-Thirds of the Earth?

Majorie Lamb

All life on this planet is supported by a fixed quantity of water. We use the same water over and over again, the same water which our grandparents used for brickmaking, the same water in which Shakespeare washed his feet, the same water in which Moses floated in a basket through the bullrushes, the same water the ancient Romans transported through their **aqueducts** to support life in their city. In fact, the water that you used to brush your teeth this morning is over four billion years old. So have a little respect.

Of all water on our planet Earth, 97% is salt water. Only 3% is fresh water, and most of that is frozen in the polar ice caps. Less than 1% of Earth's water is available for our use.

We can't make new water, any more than we can make new land. If we misuse the water we have, we can't send out for some fresh stuff. Water comes out of the tap in unlimited quantities whenever we want it. We generally assume that we have vast reserves of water available.

And we generally assume that it's free, or almost free. But before clean water comes out of our taps, several things have to happen. We have to find a source of water, build machinery to pump it, piping to carry it, plants to treat it. Thanks to our treatment of water, chlorine[1] has become an acquired taste in millions of households. We have to elect politicians who will run our municipal affairs, and look after our water treatment, and do the paperwork involved in supplying us with water. Once we get the water to our houses, we have to install pipes and valves and shut-offs and vents. We have to put in a separate line and a heater to heat some of the water.

Once we've got water, what do we do with it? We put it through our washing machines, toilets, sinks, dishwashers, car washes and pesticide-filled lawns. We use it to wash our windows, our sidewalks and streets. We spray it in the air for pretty fountains. We put out fires with it. We clean wounds with it. We make concrete with it. We use it in the production of plastics, steel and paper. We hose down chemical spills and industrial work sites with it. We clean paintbrushes in it. And we drink it.

What if we had water meters beside our kitchen sink? What if they read dollars and cents instead of gallons or liters?

Then we have to deal with getting rid of it. We need to build another whole network of drains to carry away our dirty water and sewage. We need to build treatment plants, and hire people to run them. And we need to elect politicians who will vow to "do something" to clean up the water that we've polluted.

---

1 *Chlorine* (klôr´ ēn´), a green-yellow gas, is an element used to disinfect water.

Distinguish Fact and Opinion Is this information fact or opinion? Explain how you know.

The process costs billions of dollars worldwide, and still people suffer and die in many parts of the world for want of clean water, while we blithely open our taps and let our most precious resource pour down the drain.

There's not much we can do at home about the unequal distribution of water in the world. But the other major problems, contamination and waste, we can do something about. Although most of the advice in this chapter has to do with waste (we'll deal with contamination in other chapters), these two problems are connected in ways that might not be obvious.

The more we process our water, the more chance it has to become contaminated. That's because we have one sewage system for all purposes. We put our drinking water, our toilet waste and commercially contaminated waters all down the same system. We do our best to clean it up, then we pour it all out into the same river, lake or stream, and then we drink it again.

Argument Here Lamb appeals to readers' emotions. How does she make readers feel?

And of course, the more water we have to process, the more bleach we have to produce (which isn't a terrific thing to have around—it is, after all, a poison), and, naturally, the more we have to pay our governments for looking after all this stuff for us. So it's not so easy to keep cleaning our water.

Yes, we could be drinking Shakespeare's bathwater, but more to the point, will our great grandchildren be able to drink the water we used to hose down the dog? Will there be any clean water left?

Does it make any sense for us to save water at home? Isn't our home usage just a drop in the bucket, compared to what agriculture and industry uses?

Household usage is about 5% to 10% of total fresh water used worldwide. Most of that is used in North America.

On average each of us consumes nearly 53 gallons of water a day at home. Some citizens of water-poor countries survive on as little as 4 gallons a day. We've grown used to seeing water flow out of our taps and down the drains. What if we had an automatic shut-off on our household water that limited us to, say, 13 gallons of water a day?

What to Do

1. **Turn the tap on briefly to wet your toothbrush, and turn it off until it's time to rinse.**

In our house, the average toothbrushing time is about a minute and 20 seconds. If we turn on the tap at the beginning of that time and don't turn it off until we're finished, we will have put down the drain approximately 2 gallons of water. In our little household of three people, we could waste over 4000 gallons of water per year just in toothbrushing.

Take the test in your household. How long does it take you to brush your teeth? Multiply that by the number of times you brush your teeth each day, then multiply that by

Distinguish Fact and Opinion Note Lamb's opinion about processing water. How does she support her opinion?

Argument The writer makes an appeal to reason by including facts about how water is needlessly wasted. Does this information persuade you to change your habits?

the number of people in your household, and you'll soon see that you could have a terrific amount of water rushing uselessly down the drains.

My sister, Elizabeth, spent a great deal of time traveling the earth's oceans on sailboats, where she learned to brush her teeth with ¼ cup of water. The captain brushed without any water at all. We don't need to go that far, but we could all use less water than we do.

2. Keep a bottle of water in the fridge.

We use bottled water—from the tap. Have you ever let the tap run for a minute to get an ice cold drink? About 15 years ago, I filled an empty soft drink bottle with tap water and stuck it in the fridge. That same bottle is still in our fridge today. Of course it has different water in it.

Our water bottle has its own spot, in one of those bottle hangers that goes under the fridge shelf (it's been in the same place for years, even when we've moved houses and changed fridges), so that we never have to run the tap for a drink of water. It's always cold and handy. If you're just starting this system, be sure to label the bottle "Drinking Water." Once, years ago, when my Dad was visiting, he took a big swig from the bottle in our fridge, only to discover that someone had put a bottle of white rum in to cool.

3. Take a five minute shower instead of bathing.

Abandon the bathtub, and hit the showers. Sometimes it just feels great to soak in the tub, but that tub holds between nine and 33 gallons (40 to 150 liters) of water, depending on how full we fill it. We'd have to shower for 15 minutes before we used up the quantity of water it takes to fill the tub. When we were kids, we used to share a bath. We thought it was fun, but little did we know that our smart parents were saving on water heating. My daughter Caroline still enjoys a bath with her little cousin, Lisa.

4. Learn the cold water hand wash.

If every time you wash your hands, you turn on the hot tap and wait for the water to get warm, you could run anywhere from a few cups to a gallon or

Argument Here Lamb shows that she follows her own advice, which helps her appear trustworthy. What kind of persuasive appeal is she using?

Distinguish Fact and Opinion What is the fact in this sentence? What is the opinion? Consider why the writer might include both types of information.

more of water down the drain. There are two problems with that.

First, it's water that has gone through the entire system of our waterworks for nothing. It's been pumped from the lake or river, using energy, it's been bleached, it's been pushed through miles of pipes, and then it just goes back down the drain to be processed all over again with our sewage, having done nothing.

Second, it's water that's already been heated in your home water heater, but has cooled before it gets to you. The energy that was used to heat it, which you pay for, has been wasted.

I even wash my face in cold water every morning and night. I'm trying to convince myself that cold water is kinder to my skin than hot, but frankly, I know of no studies that would back me up on this one. However, my partner, Barry, tells me he once read that Paul Newman soaks his face in ice water to stay young looking, so maybe I'm on to something here. Masochistic[2] as it may sound, I find it refreshing to start my day with a cold splash. I confess that so far I've made very few converts to this theory, but I still swear by it.

Do you get as clean with cold water as with warm? The answer is yes, although there are exceptions. If your hands are greasy or oily, warm water will help to dissolve the grease or oil more quickly than cold water. But for ordinary, garden-variety dirt or stickiness, cold water works just as well as warm.

What about germs? Ordinarily hand soap will take care of whatever germs are washable. If you wanted to be totally antiseptic, you would have to use boiling water, probably for several minutes. I think most of us would opt for just plain clean, thanks anyway.

Think of saving water this way: what if you had to carry home all the water you needed every day—in jars on your head?

2 Lamb is making a little joke here. If someone is **masochistic** (mas′ ə kis′ tik), he or she doesn't mind pain or suffering.

BQ BIG Question

Why does the author believe that conserving water is worth fighting for?

After You Read

Respond and Think Critically

1. In your own words, describe Marjorie Lamb's argument. [Summarize]

2. What did you find surprising or disturbing about how water gets processed? Explain. [Respond]

3. Read the following sentences: "What if we had water meters beside our kitchen sink? What if they read dollars and cents instead of gallons or liters?" What does the writer suggest about what motivates people to take action? [Interpret]

4. What type of persuasive appeal do you think Lamb uses most effectively in her wessay? Explain. [Evaluate]

5. Does Lamb rely more on facts or on opinions to make her argument? Think about the purpose each type of information serves in the essay. [Draw Conclusions]

6. **BQ** BIG Question Do you believe water conservation is something worth fighting for? Why or why not? [Connect]

Academic Vocabulary

In "Saving Water," Marjorie Lamb gives information about how much water humans **consume.** To become more familiar with the word *consume,* complete a graphic organizer like the one below.

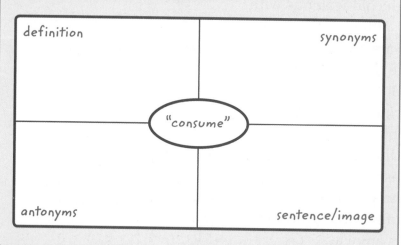

TIP

Drawing Conclusions
Here are some tips to help you draw a conclusion. Remember, when you draw a conclusion, you combine information in the text with your own knowledge.

- Skim the essay and review your chart of facts and opinions.

- Think about which type of information persuaded you more as you read.

 FOLDABLES Study Organizer Keep track of your ideas about the **BIG Question** in your unit Foldable.

 Literature Online

Selection Resources
For Selection Quizzes, eFlashcards, and Reading-Writing Connection activities, go to glencoe.com and enter QuickPass code GL39770u4.

Literary Element Argument

1. Read the sentence: "On average each of us consumes nearly 53 gallons of water a day at home. Some citizens of water-poor countries survive on as little as 4 gallons a day." What kind of appeal is this? Why?

Review: Text Features

Text features are visual clues that highlight information for readers. Common text features are titles, headings, photographs/illustrations, captions, tables, charts, diagrams, and numbered or bulleted lists. Writers use text features to show what they think is important. For example, bold or italic fonts are used to signal important words or phrases.

2. Read through the numbered list that follows the heading "What to Do." Why do you think the writer ended the essay with such a list? Consider whether this section of the essay affected your attitude about water conservation.

Reading Skill Distinguish Fact and Opinion

3. Read each statement and decide if it is a fact or an opinion. Then explain why.

- "In our house, the average toothbrushing time is about a minute and 20 seconds."

- "The energy that was used to heat it, which you pay for, has been wasted."

- "Ordinarily hand soap will take care of whatever germs are washable."

- "I think most of us would opt for just plain clean, thanks anyway."

Grammar Tip

Double Negatives

Negative words express the idea of "no." Negative words include *not, never, nobody, none, nothing,* and *nowhere.* Two negative words used together in a sentence create an error called a *double negative.* Avoid using two negative words together in the same sentence.

Correct: People in some parts of the world never have enough water.

Correct: People in some parts of the world don't ever have enough water.

Double negatives can make your writing awkward and confusing. Only one negative word is necessary to convey a negative meaning. Correct a sentence that has a double negative by removing one of the negative words or by replacing one of the negative words with an affirmative one such as *always, anybody, all, any, someone, something,* and *some.*

Practice Look in "Saving Water" for examples of correctly used negative words. Think about how double negatives would affect the meaning of the sentences.

Listening and Speaking

Persuasive Speech Prepare a persuasive speech that explains why people should conserve natural resources. Make sure you support your opinions with facts. Practice delivering your speech to a partner. Discuss how your tone of voice and body language can affect the persuasiveness of your argument.

The Trouble with Television

Connect to the Essay

How much time do you spend watching television? Do you spend as many hours doing more important activities, like homework?

List Make a list of your favorite activities and calculate how much time you spent on each one during the last week. What did you spend the most time doing? What did you spend the least time doing? Is there anything you would like to spend more time on? If so, how will you find the time?

Build Background

In 1950, only 9 percent of U.S. households owned a TV. Today, more than 98 percent of U.S. households have at least one TV.

- Viewers with cable or satellite TV often have access to more than 200 channels.

- In the United States, one hour of network television usually contains between fifteen and twenty minutes of commercials that try to sell you products and services.

Vocabulary

enhances (en hans´ iz) v. makes greater or heightens; intensifies (p. 471). *Adding cinnamon to the pie enhances its flavor.*

coherence (kō hîr´ əns) n. logical connection; consistency (p. 472). *The scribbled directions to the stadium lacked any coherence.*

unattainable (un´ ə tān´ ə bəl) adj. not able to be achieved or gained (p. 473). *She realized too late that the goals she had set for herself were unattainable.*

resolutions (rez´ ə lōō´ shənz) n. results of settling, explaining, or solving (p. 473). *The students got together to discuss resolutions to the town's pollution problem.*

Meet Robert MacNeil

"People . . . contend that you have sixty seconds to make a point before viewers begin to lose interest . . . We have proved, at least, that in-depth journalism has its place on TV."
—Robert MacNeil

Covering the News Robert MacNeil is best known as a television news journalist. For twenty years, he co-hosted an award-winning news program with Jim Lehrer. Unlike most news programs, "The MacNeil/Lehrer News Hour" discussed one issue each night.

Literary Works MacNeil has written many books, including *The People Machine: The Influence of Television on American Politics.*

Robert MacNeil was born in 1931.

 Literature Online

Author Search For more about Robert MacNeil, go to glencoe.com and enter QuickPass code GL39770u4.

Set Purposes for Reading

BQ BIG Question

As you read "The Trouble with Television," note why Robert MacNeil thinks Americans should spend less time watching television.

Literary Element Thesis

A **thesis** is the main idea of an essay or other work of nonfiction. It is briefly stated in one or two sentences known as the **thesis statement.** The thesis statement is usually located in the essay's introduction. Often, the thesis is restated in the conclusion as well.

Identifying the thesis can help you better understand a work as a whole. When you keep the thesis in mind as you read, you will increase your comprehension of the text. You will recognize the author's purpose for writing, and you will see how the body of the text relates back to the thesis.

As you read, look for clues that help you determine the thesis.

Reading Strategy Evaluate an Argument

Evaluating an **argument** requires you to make a judgment about an author's opinion and how well it is supported. In this essay, MacNeil uses **proposition-and-support** text structure. Consider his argument (proposition) as well as his evidence and reasoning (support).

Evaluating arguments helps you become a wise reader. When you carefully consider the merit of an argument, you can avoid being misled by illogical or false statements.

When you evaluate an argument, you identify its main idea and

- evaluate the unity and consistency of the argument—whether all the paragraphs work together to support the argument
- determine what evidence the author uses to support the argument
- decide whether or not the argument is coherent, persuasive, logical, and fully supported by evidence

As you read, take notes on MacNeil's opinions and the support he provides for them. You may find it helpful to use a graphic organizer like the one below.

Opinions	Supporting Details

Learning Objectives

For pages 468–474

In studying this text, you will focus on the following objectives:

Literary Study:
Analyzing a thesis.

Reading:
Evaluating an argument.

TRY IT

Evaluate Argument Choose a column from your local newspaper about a controversial subject. Identify the columnist's argument. What support does the columnist provide for the argument? Is the support strong enough to convince you to share the writer's opinion?

the trouble with
TELEVISION

Robert MacNeil

It is difficult to escape the influence of television. If you fit the statistical averages,[1] by the age of 20 you will have been exposed to at least 20,000 hours of television. You can add 10,000 hours for each decade you have lived after the age of 20. The only things Americans do more than watch television are work and sleep.

Calculate for a moment what could be done with even a part of those hours. Five thousand hours, I am told, are what a typical college undergraduate spends working on a bachelor's degree.[2] In 10,000 hours you could have learned enough to become an astronomer or engineer. You could have learned several languages fluently. If it appealed to you, you could be reading Homer in the original Greek or Dostoyevski[3] in Russian. If it didn't, you could have walked around the world and written a book about it.

---

1 **Statistical averages** tell you about a typical person's behavior.

2 **Undergraduates** are students at a college or university who do not yet have a degree. A **bachelor's degree** is awarded to undergraduates who complete a four-year program of study.

3 **Homer** was a Greek poet who is believed to have lived around 800 B.C. Fyodor **Dostoyevski** was a Russian novelist who lived from 1821 to 1881.

The trouble with television is that it discourages concentration. Almost anything interesting and rewarding in life requires some constructive, consistently applied effort. The dullest, the least gifted of us can achieve things that seem miraculous to those who never concentrate on anything. But television encourages us to apply no effort. It sells us instant gratification. It diverts[4] us only to divert, to make the time pass without pain.

Television's variety becomes a narcotic, not a stimulus. Its serial, kaleidoscopic exposures[5] force us to follow its lead. The viewer is on a perpetual guided tour: thirty minutes at the museum, thirty at the cathedral, then back on the bus to the next attraction—except on television, typically, the spans allotted are on the order of minutes or seconds, and the chosen delights are more often car crashes and people killing one another. In short, a lot of television usurps[6] one of the most precious of all human gifts, the ability to focus your attention yourself, rather than just passively surrender it.

Capturing your attention—and holding it—is the prime motive of most television programming and **enhances** its role as a profitable advertising vehicle.[7] Programmers live in constant fear of losing anyone's attention—anyone's. The surest way to avoid doing so is to keep everything brief, not to strain the attention of anyone but instead to provide constant stimulation through variety, novelty, action and movement. Quite simply, television operates on the appeal to the short attention span.

It is simply the easiest way out. But it has come to be regarded as a given, as inherent in the medium itself; as an imperative, as though General Sarnoff, or one of the other august pioneers of video, had bequeathed[8] to us tablets of

Thesis This is the thesis statement. What is the purpose of this statement?

Thesis Compare this statement to the thesis statement. In what way do you think this sentence supports the thesis?

---

4 *Instant gratification* is immediate satisfaction. *Diverts* means "distracts."

5 A *narcotic* is a substance that soothes. *Serial, kaleidoscopic exposures* (sēr′ ē əl kə lī′ də skōp′ik iks pō′ zhərs) are continuous and constantly changing images.

6 *Usurps* (ū surps′) means "takes by force or without right."

7 The author writes that the *prime motive* (goal) of television is to enhance its role as a *profitable advertising vehicle* (a moneymaker for companies that broadcast ads).

8 Here, *august* (ô gust′) means "honored." *Bequeathed* (bi kwēthd′) means "handed down."

Vocabulary ....

enhances (en hans′iz) *v.* makes great or heightens; intensifies

stone commanding that nothing in television shall ever require more than a few moments' concentration.

In its place that is fine. Who can quarrel with a medium that so brilliantly packages escapist entertainment as a mass-marketing tool? But I see its values now pervading[9] this nation and its life. It has become fashionable to think that, like fast food, fast ideas are the way to get to a fast-moving, impatient public.

In the case of news, this practice, in my view, results in inefficient communication. I question how much of television's nightly news effort is really absorbable and understandable. Much of it is what has been aptly described as "machine gunning with scraps." I think the technique fights coherence. I think it tends to make things ultimately boring and dismissible[10] (unless they are accompanied by horrifying pictures) because almost anything is boring and dismissible if you know almost nothing about it.

I believe that TV's appeal to the short attention span is not only inefficient communication but decivilizing as well. Consider the casual assumptions that television tends to cultivate: that complexity must be avoided, that visual stimulation is a substitute for thought, that verbal precision is an anachronism.[11] It may be old-fashioned, but I was taught that thought is words, arranged in grammatically precise ways.

There is a crisis of literacy in this country. One study estimates that some 30 million adult Americans are "functionally illiterate" and cannot read or write well enough to answer a want ad or understand the instructions on a medicine bottle.

Literacy may not be an inalienable human right,[12] but it

Evaluate Argument In what ways does using a negative word like "boring" support or detract from the author's argument?

Evaluate Argument What does literacy have to do with the author's argument? Think about the evidence he gives to support a link between TV and illiteracy.

---

9 The author compares TV to a *mass-marketing tool,* a device used to sell products to large numbers of people. *Pervading* means "spreading through all parts of."

10 *Aptly* means "correctly and accurately." Something that is *dismissible* is easily put out of one's mind.

11 *Decivilizing* is getting rid of knowledge, good taste, and social skills. *Assumptions* are beliefs that have not been proved true. To *cultivate* something is to encourage it to grow. An *anachronism* is something that is out of place in the present time.

12 An *inalienable human right* is a basic right that cannot be taken away.

Vocabulary
....

coherence (kō hîr′əns) *n.* logical connection; consistency

is one that the highly literate Founding Fathers might not have found unreasonable or even **unattainable**. We are not only not attaining it as a nation, statistically speaking, but we are falling further and further short of attaining it. And, while I would not be so simplistic as to suggest that television is the cause, I believe it contributes and is an influence.

Everything about this nation—the structure of the society, its forms of family organization, its economy, its place in the world—has become more complex, not less. Yet its dominating[13] communications instrument, its principal form of national linkage, is one that sells neat **resolutions** to human problems that usually have no neat resolutions. It is all symbolized in my mind by the hugely successful art form that television has made central to the culture, the thirty-second commercial: the tiny drama of the earnest housewife who finds happiness in choosing the right toothpaste.

When before in human history has so much humanity collectively surrendered so much of its leisure to one toy, one mass diversion? When before has virtually an entire nation surrendered itself wholesale[14] to a medium for selling?

Some years ago Yale University law professor Charles L. Black, Jr., wrote: ". . . forced feeding on trivial fare is not itself a trivial matter." I think this society is being force-fed with trivial fare, and I fear that the effects on our habits of mind, our language, our tolerance for effort, and our appetite for complexity are only dimly perceived. If I am wrong, we will have done no harm to look at the issue skeptically and critically, to consider how we should be resisting it. I hope you will join with me in doing so.

---

13 **Dominating** means "commanding the most attention."

14 In this paragraph, the author asks if there has been another time when **humanity** (the entire human race) has **collectively** (together as one) given up so much of its free time to one **mass diversion** (source of amusement and distraction), or **surrendered itself wholesale**—given itself up completely to a medium for selling.

Vocabulary ....

unattainable (un´ ə tān´ ə bəl) *adj.* not able to be achieved or gained

resolutions (rez´ ə lōō´ shənz) *n.* results of settling, explaining, or solving

Thesis How well does the author restate his thesis in the conclusion? Do you think this essay would convince most people of that thesis?

BQ **BIG Question**
What cause is Robert MacNeil asking you to join him in fighting for?

After You Read

Respond and Think Critically

1. In your own words, restate MacNeil's argument, or proposition. In what ways does he support his argument? [Summarize]

2. According to MacNeil, what are two negative effects of television? Why do you think he considers these negative? [Recall and Interpret]

3. Why do you think MacNeil starts his article with statistics about the number of hours people spend watching television? Use details from the selection to support your answer. [Analyze]

4. **Literary Element** Thesis Why do you think MacNeil chose the proposition that he presented? Does he identify other troubles with television? [Draw Conclusions]

5. **Reading Strategy** Evaluate Argument Do you think MacNeil argues his proposition well? Why or why not? Use your "Opinion and Support" graphic organizer to help answer this question. [Evaluate]

6. **BQ** BIG Question Do you agree with the author that television is harmful? Think of an aspect of society that you consider harmful. How would you suggest changing this harmful element? [Synthesize]

Vocabulary Practice

Synonyms are words that have the same or nearly the same meaning. **Antonyms** are words that have the opposite meaning. Identify whether the paired words in each set are synonyms or antonyms. Then write a sentence using the first word of each pair or draw or find a picture that represents the word.

enhances and refines   **coherence** and disorder
unattainable and reachable   **resolutions** and conclusions

Example:
enhances and refines = synonyms

Sentence: Listening to a variety of music enhances her songwriting ability.

  Writing

Write a Blurb Write a blurb to be posted on a Web site in response to Robert MacNeil's argument, or proposition. You may agree or disagree with him. Make a persuasive argument of your own about whether or not you feel MacNeil's proposition is valid.

Media Workshop

Propaganda

In this unit, you have learned how persuasive essays and speeches can influence people's opinions. Another tool for influencing opinions is known as **propaganda.** Propaganda uses media to shape ideas or opinions, often through the use of stereotypes, faulty generalizations, logical fallacies, or emotional language.

Think about the purpose of propaganda. What idea is this poster trying to get you to support?

The chart below describes common techniques used in propaganda. Think about how these techniques work to persuade people. Understanding these techniques will help you think critically about propaganda. Which techniques are used in the example above?

Propaganda Technique	What It Is	Example
Name-calling	Using negative words to turn opinions against a subject	Referring to a political opponent as a "traitor" or a "terrorist"
Glittering generalities	Using vague, positive words to support a subject	Telling people you stand for "liberty" and "justice"
Transfer	Linking the qualities of one subject to another	Standing in front of a flag to appear more patriotic
Testimonial	Using a famous or respected person to support or detract from a subject	Having Tiger Woods endorse a product
Bandwagon	Convincing an audience that "everyone else is doing it, so you should, too"	An ad telling you not to be the last kid on your block to own something
Fear	Scaring an audience to get them to act a certain way	Showing pictures of car accidents to stop drunk driving

Learning Objectives

For page 475

In this workshop, you will focus on the following objective:

Reading: Analyzing propaganda and persuasive techniques in different media.

TRY IT

Analyze Propaganda Political advertisements are a form of propaganda. Watch a political ad and then answer the following questions:

- Was the ad trying to get you to support or oppose its subject?

- What visual images were presented? Explain how they affected your impressions and opinions.

- What techniques did the ad use to shape your opinion?

 Literature Online

Media Literacy For project ideas, templates, and media analysis guides, go to glencoe.com and enter QuickPass code GL39770u4.

The Treasure of Lemon Brown

Connect to the Short Story

Think about your most valuable possession. What is it? How did you get it?

Quickwrite Freewrite for a few minutes describing the possession and telling why it is so important to you. What do you do to keep this possession safe?

Build Background

"The Treasure of Lemon Brown" is set mostly in an abandoned building in the New York City neighborhood known as Harlem.

- Harlem was founded by the Dutch and once was a Revolutionary War battle site. It is now a northern district of New York City with a large African American population.

- Harlem is known for its blues artists. The blues is a style of music that evolved from the experiences of African Americans over the last three centuries. Blues songs often express sorrow and hardship.

Vocabulary

vaulted (vôl′tid) v. jumped or leaped (p. 480). *The rabbit vaulted over the garden into its hole.*

musty (mus′tē) adj. smelling of damp or mold (p. 480). *The basement often becomes quite musty after a heavy thunderstorm.*

gnarled (närld) adj. rough, knotted, and twisted, as if from old age or from work (p. 484). *After years of hard work, the carpenter's gnarled hands caused him great pain.*

banister (ban′is tər) n. a handrail and its upright supports along the edge of a staircase (p. 485). *You should always hold on to the banister as you walk down a steep staircase.*

scoundrels (skoun′drəlz) n. dishonest people, villains (p. 486). *The scoundrels stole money from the church collection.*

Meet Walter Dean Myers

"I write to give hope to those kids who are like the ones I knew—poor, troubled, treated indifferently by society."
—Walter Dean Myers

Connecting with Readers

Walter Dean Myers grew up loving stories—the ones his family told him and the ones he read. Many of his stories come from his own life. Myers also writes historical books that feature African Americans. He says he wants his readers to identify with the protagonist and come away with a sense of being valued.

Literary Works Myers is the author of many books, including *Scorpions* and *Fallen Angel*.

Walter Dean Myers was born in 1937.

 Literature Online

Author Search For more about Walter Dean Myers, go to glencoe.com and enter QuickPass code GL39770u4.

Set Purposes for Reading

BQ BIG Question

Read "The Treasure of Lemon Brown" to learn about Lemon Brown's unusual treasure. Why does he think the treasure is worth fighting for?

Literary Element Style

Style is the distinctive way an author writes. One element of an author's style is the use of dialect. A **dialect** is a special form of language spoken by a particular group. Dialect influences not only how a person pronounces words but also what words he or she uses. Conversations between characters, or dialogue, can reveal a character's dialect.

An author uses style to reveal information about characters. The way an author has a character speak can tell you about the character's personality, where the character comes from, what social group he or she belongs to, and what kind of education he or she has had.

As you read "The Treasure of Lemon Brown," think about how the author's writing style gives the characters distinct voices.

Reading Strategy Make Predictions About Plot

Predicting is making an educated guess about what will happen. When you make predictions about plot, you use clues from the text to anticipate what happens next in a story.

Making predictions about plot is an important element in being an active reader. Predicting gives you a reason to read because you will want to keep reading to find out if your predictions are right.

When you make predictions about plot, you

- look for clues in a selection that can tell you what will happen next
- combine those clues with what you know about plot structure
- make a guess about what will happen next by applying your knowledge to hints you have from the text

As you read, look for story details that will help you make predictions about plot. You may find it helpful to use a graphic organizer like the one below.

Story Detail	Prediction	What Happens

Learning Objectives

For pages 476–491

In studying this text, you will focus on the following objectives:

Literary Study: Analyzing style.

Reading: Making predictions about plot.

TRY IT

Make Predictions About Plot
Take a look at the comics section of your local newspaper. Most comic strips are three panels long. The first two panels set up the premise of the comic and the last delivers the resolution. Read a few comic strips to get a better understanding of their structure. Then look at the rest of the comics and try to make predictions about how the last panels will resolve the stories.

THE TREASURE OF
LEMON BROWN

Walter Dean Myers

Downtown View. Anthony Springer. Oil on canvas, 55.9 x 45.7 cm. Private Collection.

The dark sky, filled with angry swirling clouds, reflected Greg Ridley's mood as he sat on the stoop[1] of his building. His father's voice came to him again, first reading the letter the principal had sent to the house, then lecturing endlessly about his poor efforts in math.

"I had to leave school when I was 13," his father had said, "that's a year younger than you are now. If I'd had half the chances that you have, I'd. . . ."

Greg had sat in the small, pale green kitchen listening, knowing the lecture would end with his father saying he couldn't play ball with the Scorpions. He had asked his father the week before, and his father had said it depended on his next report card. It wasn't often the Scorpions took on new players, especially 14-year-olds, and this was a chance of a lifetime for Greg. He hadn't been allowed to play high school ball, which he had really wanted to do, but playing for the Community Center team was the next best thing. Report cards were due in a week, and Greg had been hoping for the best. But the principal had ended the suspense early when she sent that letter saying Greg would probably fail math if he didn't spend more time studying.

"And you want to play *basketball?*" His father's brows knitted over deep brown eyes. "That must be some kind of a joke. Now you just get into your room and hit those books."

That had been two nights before. His father's words, like the distant thunder that now echoed through the streets of Harlem, still rumbled softly in his ears.

It was beginning to cool. Gusts of wind made bits of paper dance between the parked cars. There was a flash of nearby lightning, and soon large drops of rain splashed onto his jeans. He stood to go upstairs, thought of the lecture that probably awaited him if he did anything except shut himself in his room with his math book, and started walking down the street instead. Down the block there was

Make Predictions About Plot What prediction can you make about the story after reading the first sentence?

Style In what way does the author's style help you "hear" Greg's father's voice?

---

1 A *stoop* is one or more steps at the entrance of a building that lead up to a raised platform or porch.

an old tenement that had been abandoned for some months. Some of the guys had held an impromptu[2] checker tournament there the week before, and Greg had noticed that the door, once boarded over, had been slightly ajar.

Pulling his collar up as high as he could, he checked for traffic and made a dash across the street. He reached the house just as another flash of lightning changed the night to day for an instant, then returned the graffiti-scarred building to the grim shadows. He **vaulted** over the outer stairs and pushed tentatively on the door. It was open, and he let himself in.

The inside of the building was dark except for the dim light that filtered through the dirty windows from the streetlamps. There was a room a few feet from the door, and from where he stood at the entrance, Greg could see a squarish patch of light on the floor. He entered the room, frowning at the **musty** smell. It was a large room that might have been someone's parlor at one time. Squinting, Greg could see an old table on its side against one wall, what looked like a pile of rags or a torn mattress in the corner, and a couch, with one side broken, in front of the window.

He went to the couch. The side that wasn't broken was comfortable enough, though a little creaky. From this spot he could see the blinking neon sign over the bodega[3] on the corner. He sat awhile, watching the sign blink first green then red, allowing his mind to drift to the Scorpions, then to his father. His father had been a postal worker for all Greg's life, and was proud of it, often telling Greg how hard he had worked to pass the test. Greg had heard the story too many times to be interested now.

---

2 *Impromptu* (im promp´ tōo) means "made or done on the spur of the moment, without preparation."

3 The Spanish word *bodega* (bō dā´ gə) can refer to a bar, a restaurant, a shop, or a pantry.

Vocabulary
....

vaulted (vôl´ tid) *v.* jumped or leaped

musty (mus´ tē) *adj.* smelling of damp or mold

For a moment Greg thought he heard something that sounded like a scraping against the wall. He listened carefully, but it was gone.

Outside the wind had picked up, sending the rain against the window with a force that shook the glass in its frame. A car passed, its tires hissing over the wet street and its red tail lights glowing in the darkness.

Greg thought he heard the noise again. His stomach tightened as he held himself still and listened intently.[4] There weren't any more scraping noises, but he was sure he had heard something in the darkness—something breathing!

He tried to figure out just where the breathing was coming from; he knew it was in the room with him. Slowly he stood, tensing. As he turned, a flash of lightning lit up the room, frightening him with its sudden brilliance. He saw nothing, just the overturned table, the pile of rags and an old newspaper on the floor. Could he have been imagining the sounds? He continued listening, but heard nothing and thought that it might have just been rats. Still, he thought, as soon as the rain let up he would leave. He went to the window and was about to look out when he heard a voice behind him.

"Don't try nothin' 'cause I got a razor here sharp enough to cut a week into nine days!"

Greg, except for an involuntary tremor in his knees, stood stock still. The voice was high and brittle, like dry twigs being broken, surely not one he had ever heard before. There was a shuffling sound as the person who had been speaking moved a step closer. Greg turned, holding his breath, his eyes straining to see in the dark room.

The upper part of the figure before him was still in darkness. The lower half was in the dim rectangle of light that fell unevenly from the window. There were two feet, in cracked, dirty shoes from which rose legs that were wrapped in rags.

"Who are you?" Greg hardly recognized his own voice.

"I'm Lemon Brown," came the answer. "Who're you?"

"Greg Ridley."

---

4 **Intently** means "with concentration."

Make Predictions About Plot What do you predict will happen? Think about how the "scraping against the wall" influences your prediction.

Make Predictions About Plot In what way can statements that establish mood help you make a prediction about the plot?

Style In what way does the author represent Lemon Brown's dialect in his first line of dialogue?

"What you doing here?" The figure shuffled forward again, and Greg took a small step backward.

"It's raining," Greg said.

"I can see that," the figure said.

The person who called himself Lemon Brown peered forward, and Greg could see him clearly. He was an old man. His black, heavily wrinkled face was surrounded by a halo of crinkly white hair and whiskers that seemed to separate his head from the layers of dirty coats piled on his smallish frame. His pants were bagged to the knee, where they were met with rags that went down to the old shoes. The rags were held on with strings, and there was a rope around his middle. Greg relaxed. He had seen the man before, picking through the trash on the corner and pulling clothes out of a Salvation Army box. There was no sign of the razor that could "cut a week into nine days."

"What are you doing here?" Greg asked.

"This is where I'm staying," Lemon Brown said. "What you here for?"

"Told you it was raining out," Greg said, leaning against the back of the couch until he felt it give slightly.

"Ain't you got no home?"

"I got a home," Greg answered.

"You ain't one of them bad boys looking for my treasure, is you?" Lemon Brown cocked his head to one side and squinted one eye. "Because I told you I got me a razor."

"I'm not looking for your treasure," Greg answered, smiling. "*If* you have one."

"What you mean, *if* I have one," Lemon Brown said. "Every man got a treasure. You don't know that, you must be a fool!"

"Sure," Greg said as he sat on the sofa and put one leg over the back. "What do you have, gold coins?"

"Don't worry none about what I got," Lemon Brown said. "You know who I am?"

"You told me your name was orange or lemon or something like that."

Make Predictions About Plot What prediction can you make from Lemon Brown's question to Greg?

Style Why do you think the author chose to make Greg's dialect different from Lemon Brown's?

"Lemon Brown," the old man said, pulling back his shoulders as he did so, "they used to call me Sweet Lemon Brown."

"Sweet Lemon?" Greg asked.

"Yessir. Sweet Lemon Brown. They used to say I sung the blues so sweet that if I sang at a funeral, the dead would commence to rocking with the beat. Used to travel all over Mississippi and as far as Monroe, Louisiana, and east on over to Macon, Georgia. You mean you ain't never heard of Sweet Lemon Brown?"

"Afraid not," Greg said. "What . . . what happened to you?"

"Hard times, boy. Hard times always after a poor man. One day I got tired, sat down to rest a spell and felt a tap on my shoulder. Hard times caught up with me."

"Sorry about that."

"What you doing here? How come you didn't go home when the rain come. Rain don't bother you young folks none."

"Just didn't," Greg looked away.

"I used to have a knotty-headed boy just like you." Lemon Brown had half walked, half shuffled back to the corner and sat down against the wall. "Had them big eyes like you got. I used to call them moon eyes. Look into them moon eyes and see anything you want."

"How come you gave up singing the blues?" Greg asked.

"Didn't give it up," Lemon Brown said. "You don't give up the blues; they give you up. After a while you do good for yourself, and it ain't nothing but foolishness singing about how hard you got it. Ain't that right?"

"I guess so."

"What's that noise?" Lemon Brown asked, suddenly sitting upright.

Greg listened, and he heard a noise outside. He looked at Lemon Brown and saw the old man was pointing toward the window.

Make Predictions About Plot Note how the mood changes abruptly here. What do you predict will happen?

Greg went to the window and saw three n̲e̲ighborhood thugs, on the stoop. One was carrying a length of pipe. Greg looked back toward Lemon Brown, who moved quietly across the room to the window. The old man looked out, then beckoned frantically for Greg to follow him. For a moment Greg couldn't move. Then he found himself following Lemon Brown into the hallway and up darkened stairs. Greg followed as closely as he could. They reached the top of the stairs, and Greg felt Lemon Brown's hand first lying on his shoulder, then probing down his arm until he finally took Greg's hand into his own as they crouched in the darkness.

"They's bad men," Lemon Brown whispered. His breath was warm against Greg's skin.

"Hey! Rag man!" A voice called. "We know you in here. What you got up under them rags? You got any money?"

Silence.

"We don't want to have to come in and hurt you, old man, but we don't mind if we have to."

Lemon Brown squeezed Greg's hand in his own hard, **gnarled** fist.

There was a banging downstairs and a light as the men entered. They banged around noisily, calling for the rag man.

"We heard you talking about your treasure," the voice was slurred. "We just want to see it, that's all."

"You sure he's here?" One voice seemed to come from the room with the sofa.

"Yeah, he stays here every night."

"There's another room over there; I'm going to take a look. You got that flashlight?"

"Yeah, here, take the pipe too."

Greg opened his mouth to quiet the sound of his breath as he sucked it in uneasily. A beam of light hit the wall a few feet opposite him, then went out.

"Ain't nobody in that room," a voice said. "You think he's gone or something?"

> **Make Predictions About Plot** What do you think the thugs are going to do to Greg and Lemon? In what way does guessing what will happen next heighten suspense and motivate you to read further?

Vocabulary

gnarled (närld) *adj.* rough, knotted, and twisted, as if from old age or from work

"I don't know," came the answer. "All I know is that I heard him talking about some kind of treasure. You know they found that shopping bag lady with that money in her bags."

"Yeah. You think he's upstairs?"

"HEY, OLD MAN, ARE YOU UP THERE?"

Silence.

"Watch my back, I'm going up."

There was a footstep on the stairs, and the beam from the flashlight danced crazily along the peeling wallpaper. Greg held his breath. There was another step and a loud crashing noise as the man banged the pipe against the wooden **banister.** Greg could feel his temples throb as the man slowly neared them. Greg thought about the pipe, wondering what he would do when the man reached them—what he *could* do.

Then Lemon Brown released his hand and moved toward the top of the stairs. Greg looked around and saw stairs going up to the next floor. He tried waving to Lemon Brown, hoping the old man would see him in the dim light and follow him to the next floor. Maybe, Greg thought, the man wouldn't follow them up there. Suddenly, though, Lemon Brown stood at the top of the stairs, both arms raised high above his head.

"There he is!" A voice cried from below.

"Throw down your money, old man, so I won't have to bash your head in!"

Lemon Brown didn't move. Greg felt himself near panic. The steps came closer, and still Lemon Brown didn't move. He was an eerie sight, a bundle of rags standing at the top of the stairs, his shadow on the wall looming over him. Maybe, the thought came to Greg, the scene could be even eerier.

Greg wet his lips, put his hands to his mouth and tried to make a sound. Nothing came out. He swallowed hard, wet his lips once more and howled as evenly as he could.

Style What is the author trying to convey by capitalizing this line of dialogue?

Vocabulary

banister (ban′is tər) *n.* a handrail and its upright supports along the edge of a staircase

"What's that?"

As Greg howled, the light moved away from Lemon Brown, but not before Greg saw him hurl his body down the stairs at the men who had come to take his treasure. There was a crashing noise, and then footsteps. A rush of warm air came in as the downstairs door opened, then there was only an ominous[5] silence.

Greg stood on the landing. He listened, and after a while there was another sound on the staircase.

"Mr. Brown?" he called.

"Yeah, it's me," came the answer. "I got their flashlight."

Greg exhaled in relief as Lemon Brown made his way slowly back up the stairs.

"You O.K.?"

"Few bumps and bruises," Lemon Brown said.

"I think I'd better be going," Greg said, his breath returning to normal. "You'd better leave, too, before they come back."

"They may hang around outside for a while," Lemon Brown said, "but they ain't getting their nerve up to come in here again. Not with crazy old rag men and howling spooks. Best you stay awhile till the coast is clear. I'm heading out West tomorrow, out to East St. Louis."

"They were talking about treasures," Greg said. "You *really* have a treasure?"

"What I tell you? Didn't I tell you every man got a treasure?" Lemon Brown said. "You want to see mine?"

"If you want to show it to me," Greg shrugged.

"Let's look out the window first, see what them **scoundrels** be doing," Lemon Brown said.

They followed the oval beam of the flashlight into one of the rooms and looked out the window. They saw the men who had tried to take the treasure sitting on the curb near the corner. One of them had his pants leg up, looking at his knee.

"You sure you're not hurt?" Greg asked Lemon Brown.

Make Predictions About Plot What do you think Lemon Brown's treasure will (or will not) be? What hints from the story led you to make your guess?

---

5 **Ominous** (om'ə nəs) means "threatening harm or evil."

Vocabulary

scoundrels (skoun'drəlz) *n.* dishonest people, villains

"Nothing that ain't been hurt before," Lemon Brown said. "When you get as old as me all you say when something hurts is, 'Howdy, Mr. Pain, sees you back again.' Then when Mr. Pain see he can't worry you none, he go on mess with somebody else."

Greg smiled.

"Here, you hold this." Lemon Brown gave Greg the flashlight.

He sat on the floor near Greg and carefully untied the strings that held the rags on his right leg. When he took the rags away, Greg saw a piece of plastic. The old man carefully took off the plastic and unfolded it. He revealed some yellowed newspaper clippings and a battered harmonica.

"There it be," he said, nodding his head. "There it be."

Greg looked at the old man, saw the distant look in his eye, then turned to the clippings. They told of Sweet Lemon Brown, a blues singer and harmonica player who was appearing at different theaters in the South. One of the clippings said he had been the hit of the show, although not the headliner. All of the clippings were reviews of shows Lemon Brown had been in more than 50 years ago. Greg looked at the harmonica. It was dented badly on one side, with the reed holes on one end nearly closed.

"I used to travel around and make money for to feed my wife and Jesse—that's my boy's name. Used to feed them good, too. Then his mama died, and he stayed with his mama's sister. He growed up to be a man, and when the war come he saw fit to go off and fight in it. I didn't have nothing to give him except these things that told him who I was, and what he come from. If you know your pappy did something, you know you can do something too.

"Anyway, he went off to war, and I went off still playing and singing. 'Course by then I wasn't as much as I used to

Style Why do you think the author has Lemon Brown refer to pain as "Mr. Pain"?

be, not without somebody to make it worth the while. You know what I mean?"

"Yeah," Greg nodded, not quite really knowing.

"I traveled around, and one time I come home, and there was this letter saying Jesse got killed in the war. Broke my heart, it truly did.

"They sent back what he had with him over there, and what it was is this old mouth fiddle and these clippings. Him carrying it around with him like that told me it meant something to him. That was my treasure, and when I give it to him he treated it just like that, a treasure. Ain't that something?"

"Yeah, I guess so," Greg said.

"You *guess* so?" Lemon Brown's voice rose an octave as he started to put his treasure back into the plastic. "Well, you got to guess 'cause you sure don't know nothing. Don't know enough to get home when it's raining."

"I guess . . . I mean, you're right."

"You O.K. for a youngster," the old man said as he tied the strings around his leg, "better than those scalawags what come here looking for my treasure. That's for sure."

"You really think that treasure of yours was worth fighting for?" Greg asked. "Against a pipe?"

"What else a man got 'cepting what he can pass on to his son, or his daughter, if she be his oldest?" Lemon Brown said. "For a big-headed boy you sure do ask the foolishest questions."

Lemon Brown got up after patting his rags in place and looked out the window again.

"Looks like they're gone. You get on out of here and get yourself home. I'll be watching from the window so you'll be all right."

Lemon Brown went down the stairs behind Greg. When they reached the front door the old man looked out first, saw the street was clear and told Greg to scoot on home.

"You sure you'll be O.K.?" Greg asked.

"Now didn't I tell you I was going to East St. Louis in the morning?" Lemon Brown asked. "Don't that sound O.K. to you?

BQ ⟩ **BIG Question**
Why do you think Lemon's treasure is worth fighting for? Give reasons from the story?

Jazz Harmonica, 2002. Jay Russell Leach. Oil on silicone caulking on canvas.
Private Collection.

"Sure it does," Greg said. "Sure it does. And you take care of that treasure of yours."

"That I'll do," Lemon said, the wrinkles about his eyes suggesting a smile. "That I'll do."

The night had warmed and the rain had stopped, leaving puddles at the curbs. Greg didn't even want to think how late it was. He thought ahead of what his father would say and wondered if he should tell him about Lemon Brown. He thought about it until he reached his stoop, and decided against it. Lemon Brown would be O.K., Greg thought, with his memories and his treasure.

Greg pushed the button over the bell marked Ridley, thought of the lecture he knew his father would give him, and smiled.

Style In what way does the author's style help change the mood, or overall feeling, of the story?

After You Read

Respond and Think Critically

1. Explain where, when, and how Greg met Lemon and what they did together. [Summarize]

2. Why does Greg relax when he recognizes Lemon Brown? [Recall]

3. How was Lemon's actual treasure different from that envisioned by Greg and the thugs? [Compare]

4. Why does Greg's father lecture him so often about studying? [Interpret]

5. Review the details from your organizer notes. Were your predictions about the story events accurate? Explain how the story events may or may not have surprised you. [Analyze]

6. **BQ** **BIG Question** Think about the treasure you described before you read about Lemon Brown's treasure. What is a possible general statement regarding what makes a treasure worth fighting for? [Draw Conclusions]

TIP

Interpreting
Here are some tips to help you interpret. Remember when you interpret, you construct meaning on the basis of your understanding of the world.

- Skim the selection to find out what Greg's father says to Greg in his lectures.

- What do you already know about the traits shared by most father figures?

- What large idea might these lectures be about?

FOLDABLES Keep track of
Study Organizer your ideas about
the **BIG Question** in your
unit foldable.

Daily Life and Culture

The Origin and Influence of Blues Music

Blues music is a style of music created after the Civil War by African Americans in the South. Blues songs have several characteristics. Blues address the problems of ordinary, working class people. They are meant to express feelings—especially sadness—rather than tell stories. Musicians who accompany the blues singer with an electric guitar or harmonica create a great rhythmic and emotional intensity. When African Americans moved north as a result of the economic hardship caused by the Great Depression, they spread blues music to northern cities.

Blues music has had a significant impact on later music. Important jazz artists such as Louis Armstrong used blues elements in their music. Soul music and rhythm and blues also borrowed from the blues. Songs from rock singers such as Elvis Presley and the Rolling Stones have shown the influence of blues.

Group Activity Discuss the following questions with classmates.

1. How suitable a topic for blues songs are the lives of Greg Ridley and Lemon Brown based on the facts given here? Find details in the story to support your opinion.

2. Discuss this comment from Lemon Brown: "Every man got a treasure." What does this reveal about people in general?

Literary Element Style

Test Skills Practice

1. In paragraph 14, "Don't try nothin' 'cause I got a razor here sharp enough to cut a week into nine days," which is characteristic of Lemon Brown's dialect?

   A He avoids use of double negatives.

   B He speaks in imperative sentences.

   C He doesn't match subject with verb.

   D He doesn't say the ending letter of every word.

Review: Characterization

As you learned on page 355, **characterization** consists of the methods a writer uses to develop the personality of a character. In direct characterization, the story's narrator makes statements about a character's personality. In indirect characterization, a character's personality is gradually revealed through his or her words, thoughts, and actions.

Test Skills Practice

2. From what you know of Greg Ridley's father, how would you describe his personality?

   A He longs for the days when he was Greg's age.

   B He dislikes sports, especially Community Center basketball.

   C He loves Greg and wants him to have many opportunities.

   D He is contemptuous of school but has respect for mathematics.

Reading Strategy
Make Predictions About Plot

3. Greg thinks he knows how his father will react to his late arrival home. How do you predict Greg will respond to his father's lecture? What clues from the story helped you make your prediction?

Vocabulary Practice

Respond to these questions.

1. Which is the purpose of a **banister**—to support the stairs or assist people on the stairs?

2. What kind of behavior would you expect from people you knew to be **scoundrels**?

3. Which item are you likely to consider **musty**—a pair of sunglasses or a beach towel?

4. What can make a person's hands **gnarled**?

5. What animal do you think has **vaulted** more than the others—a turtle, a bear, or a deer?

Academic Vocabulary

My **perception** of colors grew worse with age.

In the preceding sentence, *perception* means "the act of becoming aware of through the senses." To become more familiar with the word *perception,* create and fill out a graphic organizer like the one below.

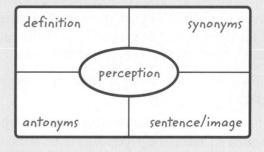

definition	synonyms
	perception
antonyms	sentence/image

Respond Through Writing

Expository Essay

Interpret Theme In "The Treasure of Lemon Brown," Lemon Brown protects his treasure against those who want to take it from him. In an expository essay, interpret the theme that the author is stating about treasure in this story.

Understand the Task The **theme** of a story is its central message or meaning. For example, in the story "The Monkey's Paw," W. W. Jacobs conveys the theme "be careful what you wish for."

Prewrite Think of at least three different ways that characters in the story viewed Lemon Brown's treasure. Keep track of your ideas in an organizer like the one below.

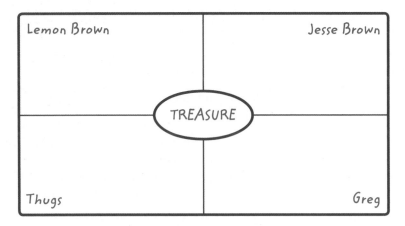

Draft Before you begin drafting, make an overall plan. For example, you may decide to write an introduction, a paragraph about each view of the treasure, and then a conclusion. After you figure out your plan, write a coherent thesis statement. This sentence frame might help:

In "The Treasure of Lemon Brown," the author's implied theme is that a person's treasure is _____.

Revise Reread your first draft to determine whether the paragraphs present an overall main idea, are in logical order, and are connected by transitions. Have you interpreted the theme in a way that the audience—your teacher—will find acceptable? Does your evidence support your conclusion?

Edit and Proofread Proofread your paper, correcting any errors in spelling, grammar, and punctuation. Review the Grammar Tip in the side column for information on commas.

Learning Objectives

For page 492

In this assignment, you will focus on the following objective:

Writing: Writing an expository essay.

▶ Grammar Tip

Commas
Use commas after introductory words, phrases, and clauses.

An **introductory word** may be an interjection, an adverb, or a present participle:

Yes, Lemon Brown has a treasure.

Fortunately, Lemon was kind to Greg.

Frightened, Greg could hardly move.

An **introductory phrase** begins with a preposition or a participle:

During the storm, Greg went to the tenement to get dry.

Running quickly, he could feel the raindrops hitting his face.

An **introductory clause** is a dependent clause that answers the questions *How? When? Where?*

After the thugs left, Greg began to relax.

When he went home, Greg talked to his father.

Vocabulary Workshop

Idioms

Connection to Literature

"'Now you [Greg] just get into your room and hit those books.'"

—Walter Dean Myers, "The Treasure of Lemon Brown"

You may know individual words within a phrase or sentence but the meaning may still be confusing. In fact, there are many expressions in English that cannot be understood literally. This kind of phrase or sentence is called an **idiom**. In the passage above, Greg's father tells him to "hit those books." He does not mean that Greg should strike the books. Instead, he wants Greg to study hard. To understand an idiom, follow these steps:

- Think about the words in the expression and their usual meanings.
- Use context clues to figure out a meaning that fits the entire expression.

Here are other idioms from "The Treasure of Lemon Brown."

Idioms	Meanings
Lemon Brown's razor could *cut a week into nine days.*	His razor was very sharp.
The thug tells his friends to *watch his back.*	He wants his companions to protect him.
Lemon Brown doesn't think the thugs will *get their nerve up* to return.	He doesn't think that they will be brave enough to return.

TRY IT: Use your prior knowledge of words and context clues to figure out the meaning of each underlined idiom. Then write a short definition of each idiom.

1. Although Lemon Brown <u>puts on an act</u> with Greg, he later reveals his real-life story to the boy.
2. Lemon Brown's raggedy appearance and shabby home suggest that he is living <u>out of the mainstream</u>.
3. His harmonica and newspaper clippings <u>mean the world to</u> Lemon Brown. They are his treasure.

Learning Objectives

For page 493

In this workshop, you will focus on the following objective:

Vocabulary: Understanding idioms.

Tip

Vocabulary Terms Idioms are groups of words that, when taken together, mean something different from the literal, or ordinary, meanings of the individual words.

Test-taking Tip If you read a phrase that doesn't seem to make sense, it may be an idiom. Look for clues within the text, such as examples, definitions, and restatements, to help you understand the meaning of the entire expression.

 Literature Online

Vocabulary For more vocabulary practice, go to glencoe.com and enter QuickPass code GL39770u4.

from *Civil War Journal*

Connect to the Journal

Think about a time when you have kept a journal or recorded your experiences.

Partner Talk With a partner, talk about what it was like to write down your feelings and experiences. Did you write regularly? Did you write as though you were addressing a person? Did you find it helpful or enjoyable?

Build Background

Louisa May Alcott, like many women, wanted to participate in the Civil War. Officially, women could not become soldiers (although a few women did so in disguise). One way for women to contribute to the war effort was to become nurses and tend to wounded and sick soldiers.

- At first, men thought the appalling conditions inside a military hospital should not be seen by women. However, doctors dropped their opposition to female nurses when the number of wounded and dying soldiers increased drastically.

- More than 3,000 Union women became unpaid nurses during the war. In the South, women ran the largest, most efficient hospital in Richmond, Virginia. Women improved standards of cleanliness on both sides of the conflict.

Vocabulary

dramatic (drə mat′ik) *adj.* exciting, vivid, striking (p. 496). *The hero's dramatic entrance caused quite a stir.*

bide (bīd) *v.* to wait patiently for a good opportunity (p. 497). *While waiting for a reply to my job application, I bide my time practicing my interview skills.*

patriotism (pā′trē ə tiz′əm) *n.* love for and enthusiastic support of one's country (p. 498). *During wartime, people's patriotism is more noticeable.*

vile (vīl) *adj.* extremely bad; repulsive (p. 499). *The rotting vegetables in the refrigerator had a vile smell.*

Meet Louisa May Alcott

"Resolve to take fate by the throat and shake a living out of her."

—Louisa May Alcott

A Courageous Writer As a teacher, writer, and editor, Louisa May Alcott worked hard to raise her family from poverty. She showed her passionate nature when she served as a nurse during the Civil War and, later, when she fought for women's voting rights.

Literary Works Alcott is best known for her semi-autobiographical novel *Little Women*, but she also wrote many other works. The letters she wrote while she was a Civil War nurse were published in the book *Hospital Sketches*.

Louisa May Alcott lived from 1832 to 1888.

 Literature Online

Author Search For more about Louisa May Alcott, go to glencoe.com and enter QuickPass code GL39770u4.

Set Purposes for Reading

BQ BIG Question

Read the excerpts from *Civil War Journal* to determine why Alcott decided that it was worth it to risk her life as a volunteer nurse.

Literary Element Author's Perspective

An **author's perspective** is an author's attitude toward, or way of looking at, an issue. An author's background and experience help create his or her perspective. Author's perspective should not be confused with bias. Every author has a perspective, but not every author has a one-sided outlook.

Understanding an author's perspective can give you clues to his or her purpose for writing and to his or her beliefs. To identify an author's perspective, look for examples of the author's thoughts and feelings.

As you read, note words or phrases that give you clues about the author's perspective about her experience as a Civil War nurse.

Reading Strategy Monitor Comprehension

When you **monitor comprehension,** you check your understanding of the text that you are reading. If you are confused, you try to fix your understanding. For example, you may get stuck on a word or concept when you read. If this happens, you should pause to think about what you have read and ask questions about what you don't understand.

Monitoring comprehension is important because it can help you keep up with ideas in a text so you can get the most out of what you read.

To monitor comprehension,

- skim earlier paragraphs to see if you skipped over important details
- write notes about what you *do* know; it may help fill in the gaps in your understanding
- read ahead to look for a main idea or to get an overview of a selection
- reread slowly to clarify if you still find something confusing

As you read, you may find it helpful to use a chart like the one below. In the left column, write questions about parts that confuse you. In the right column, write answers to your questions.

Question	Answer

TRY IT

Monitor Comprehension
List your favorite monitoring strategies when you realize you don't understand what you are reading.

from Civil War Journal

Louisa May Alcott

Armory Square Hospital during the United States Civil War.

1861

April—War declared with the South, and our Concord[1] company went to Washington. A busy time getting them ready, and a sad day seeing them off; for in a little town like this we all seem like one family in times like these. At the station the scene was very **dramatic**, as the brave boys went away perhaps never to come back again.

I've often longed to see a war, and now I have my wish. I long to be a man; but as I can't fight, I will content myself with working for those who can. . . .

1862

September, October—War news bad. Anxious faces, beating hearts, and busy minds.

I like the stir in the air, and long for battle like a warhorse when he smells powder. The blood of the Mays is up![2]

Author's Perspective What does this comment reveal about Alcott's perspective on the war?

---

1 Alcott lived in *Concord*, Massachusetts. A *company*, here, is a military unit, forming part of a battalion.

2 *May* was a family name, derived from Alcott's mother's side.

Vocabulary

dramatic (drə mat´ik) *adj.* exciting, vivid, striking

November—Thirty years old. Decided to go to Washington as a nurse if I could find a place. Help needed, and I love nursing, and *must* let out my pent up energy in some new way. Winter is always a hard and a dull time, and if I am away there is one less to feed and warm and worry over.

I want new experiences, and am sure to get 'em if I go. So I've sent in my name, and **bide** my time writing tales, to leave all snug behind me, and mending up my old clothes,—for nurses don't need nice things, thank Heaven!

December—On the 11th I received a note from Miss H[annah] M. Stevenson telling me to start for Georgetown next day to fill a place in the Union Hotel Hospital. Mrs. Ropes of Boston was matron, and Miss Kendall of Plymouth was a nurse there, and though a hard place, help was needed. I was ready, and when my commander said "March!" I marched. Packed my trunk, and reported in B[oston] that same evening.

We had all been full of courage till the last moment came; then we all broke down. I realized that I had taken my life in my hand, and might never see them all again. I said, "Shall I stay, Mother?" as I hugged her close. "No, go! and the Lord be with you!" answered the Spartan[3] woman; and till I turned the corner she bravely smiled and waved her wet handkerchief on the doorstep. Shall I ever see that dear old face again?

So I set forth in the December twilight, with May and Julian Hawthorne as an escort, feeling as if I was the son of the house going to war.

Friday, the 12th, was a very memorable day, spent in running all over Boston to get my pass, etc., calling for **parcels,** getting a tooth filled, and buying a veil,[4] my only purchase. A. C. gave me some old clothes, the dear Sewalls

Monitor Comprehension In this analogy, who is Alcott's "commander"?

Visual Vocabulary

Parcels are packages.

---

3 Here, **Spartan** means "courageous." It is derived from the name of an ancient Greek people known for their discipline.

4 The **pass** Alcott needed was probably a train ticket. She may have worn a **veil** as part of her uniform for nursing.

Vocabulary

bide (bīd) *v.* to wait patiently for a good opportunity

money for myself and boys, lots of love and help; and at 5 P.M., saying "good-by" to a group of tearful faces at the station, I started on my long journey, full of hope and sorrow, courage and plans.

A most interesting journey into a new world full of stirring sights and sounds, new adventures, and an evergrowing sense of the great task I had undertaken.

I said my prayers as I went rushing through the country white with tents, all alive with **patriotism,** and already red with blood.

A solemn time, but I'm glad to live in it; and am sure it will do me good whether I come out alive or dead.

Monitor Comprehension
What is a good strategy to determine what "it" refers to here? Explain.

All went well, and I got to Georgetown one evening very tired. Was kindly welcomed, slept in my narrow bed with two other roommates, and on the morrow[5] began my new life by seeing a poor man die at dawn, and sitting all day between a boy with pneumonia and a man shot through the lungs. A strange day, but I did my best; and when I put mother's little black shawl round the boy while he sat up panting for breath, he smiled and said, "You are real motherly, ma'am." I felt as if I was getting on. The man only lay and stared with his big black eyes, and made me very nervous. But all were well behaved; and I sat looking at the twenty strong faces as they looked back at me,—hoping that I looked "motherly" to them; for my thirty years made me feel old, and the suffering round me made me long to comfort every one. . . .

Author's Perspective What does Alcott see as her role at the hospital?

1863

January—I never began the year in a stranger place than this; five hundred miles from home, alone among strangers, doing painful duties all day long, & leading a life of constant excitement in this greathouse surrounded by 3 or 4 hundred men in all stages of suffering, disease & death. Though often home sick, heart sick & worn out, I

---

5 *"On the morrow"* means "the next day."

Vocabulary

patriotism (pā′trē ə tiz′əm) *n.* love for and enthusiastic support of one's country

like it—find real pleasure in comforting, tending & cheering these poor souls who seem to love me, to feel my sympathy though unspoken, & acknowledge my hearty good will in spite of the ignorance, awkwardness, & bashfulness which I cannot help showing in so new & trying a situation. The men are docile, respectful & affectionate, with but few exceptions; truly lovable & manly many of them. John Suhre, a Virginia **blacksmith** is the prince of patients, & though what we call a common man, in education & condition, to me is all that I could expect or ask from the first gentleman in the land. Under his plain speech & unpolished manner I seem to see a noble character, a heart as warm & tender as a woman's, a nature fresh & frank as any child's. He is about thirty, I think, tall & handsome, mortally wounded & dying royally, without reproach, repining, or remorse.[6] Mrs. Ropes & myself love him & feel indignant that such a man should be so early lost, for though he might never distinguish himself before the world, his influence and example cannot be without effect, for real goodness is never wasted.

Mon 4th—I shall record the events of a day as a sample of the days I spend—

Up at six, dress by gas light,[7] run through my ward & fling up the windows though the men grumble and shiver; but the air is bad enough to breed a pestilence & as no notice is taken of our frequent appeals for better ventilation I must do what I can. Poke up the fire, add blankets, joke, coax, & command; but continue to open doors & windows as if life depended on it; mine does, & doubtless many another, for a more perfect pestilence-box than this house I never saw—cold, damp, dirty, full of **vile** odors from wounds, kitchens, wash rooms, &

BQ **BIG Question**
What does Alcott believe is worth fighting for? Explain.

---

6 If a person is dying **"without reproach, repining, or remorse,"** he or she is dying bravely, without blame or regret.

7 A **gas light** was a type of lamp used before electricity that burned a type of oil or gas.

Vocabulary

vile (vīl) *adj.* extremely bad; repulsive

stables. No competent head, male or female, to right matters, & a jumble of good, bad, & indifferent nurses, surgeons & attendants to complicate the Chaos still more.

After this unwelcome progress through my stifling ward I go to breakfast with what appetite I may; find the inevitable fried beef, salt butter, husky bread & washy coffee; listen to the clack of eight women & a dozen men; the first silly, stupid or possessed of but one idea, the last absorbed in their breakfast & themselves to a degree that is both ludicrous and provoking, for all the dishes are ordered down the table *full* & returned *empty*; the conversation is entirely among themselves & each announces his opinion with an air of importance that frequently causes me to choke up in my cup or bolt my meals with undignified speed lest a laugh betray to these pompous beings that a "child's among them takin notes." Till noon I trot, trot, giving out rations, cutting up food for

A nurse caring for wounded soldiers during the U.S. Civil War

helpless "boys," washing faces, teaching my attendants how beds are made or floors swept, dressing wounds, taking Dr. Fitz Patrick's orders, (privately wishing all the time that he would be more gentle with my big babies,) dusting tables, sewing bandages, keeping my tray tidy, rushing up & down after pillows, bed linen, sponges, books & directions, till it seems as if I would joyfully pay down all I possess for fifteen minutes rest.

At twelve the big bell rings & up comes dinner for the boys who are always ready for it & never entirely satisfied. Soup, meat, potatoes & bread is the bill of fare. Charley Thayer the attendant travels up & down the room serving out the rations, saving little for himself yet always thoughtful of his mates & patient as a woman with their helplessness. When dinner is over some sleep, many read, & others want letters written. This I like to do for they put in such odd things & express their ideas so comically I have great fun interiorly while as grave as possible exteriorly. A few of the men word their paragraphs well & make excellent letters. John's was the best of all I wrote. The answering of letters from friends after some one has died is the saddest & hardest duty a nurse has to do.

Supper at five sets every one to running that can run & when that flurry is over all settle down for the evening amusements which consist of newspapers, gossip, Drs last round, & for such as need them the final doses for the night. At nine the bell rings, gas is turned down & day nurses go to bed.

Night nurses go on duty, & sleep & death have the house all to themselves. . . .

My work is changed to night watching or half night & half day, from twelve to twelve. I like it as it leaves me time for a morning run which is what I need to keep well, for bad air, food, water, work & watching are getting to be too much for me. I trot up & down the streets in all directions, some times to the Heights, then half way to Washington, again to the hill over which the long trains of army wagons are constantly vanishing & ambulances appearing. That way the fighting lies, & I long to follow.

Author's Perspective
What do you learn about Alcott's attitude toward her patients?

After You Read

1. What is Alcott's motivation for volunteering as a nurse? **[Recall and Identify]**

2. In your own words, retell the events of Alcott's journal entry from December 1862. **[Summarize]**

3. What does Alcott mean when she states that she opens doors and windows "as if life depended on it"? **[Interpret]**

4. In what ways does her experience as a nurse tending to sick and wounded soldiers affect Louisa May Alcott's perspective of the war? **[Draw Conclusions]**

5. What aspects of being a nurse does Alcott enjoy? Look back at the text to help you answer the question. **[Analyze]**

6. **BQ** BIG Question Do you think Alcott was fighting more for the men's lives—because she valued them as individuals—or for her side's war effort? Explain. **[Evaluate]**

Vocabulary Practice

Respond to these questions.

1. What situation would you describe as **dramatic**—solving a puzzle or winning a championship?

2. If you lost a student election, which would be the more productive way to **bide** your time until the next one—create a student survey or complain bitterly?

3. Which situation is more likely to cause you to feel **patriotism**—taking a nap or singing the national anthem? Explain.

4. How would you respond if a restaurant smells **vile**—order a meal or find another place to eat?

Academic Vocabulary

Louisa May Alcott **voluntarily** became a nurse during the Civil War. To do something *voluntarily* means to do it by choice. To become more familiar with the word *voluntarily,* fill out the graphic organizer below.

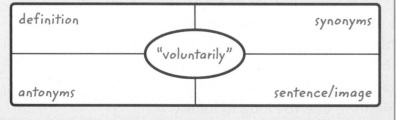

definition	synonyms
	"voluntarily"
antonyms	sentence/image

TIP

Drawing Conclusions
Here are some tips to help you conclude. Remember, when you conclude, you use details in the text and your own knowledge to make a general statement.

- Skim the selection for clues about how Alcott regarded the war before becoming a nurse.

- Look for details about her tending to specific soldiers.

- Make a general statement about how you think her experiences affected her opinion about the war.

 FOLDABLES Study Organizer Keep track of your ideas about the **BIG Question** in your unit Foldable.

 Literature Online

Selection Resources
For Selection Quizzes, eFlashcards, and Reading-Writing Connection activities, go to glencoe.com and enter QuickPass code GL39770u4.

Literary Element Author's Perspective

1. In what way does Alcott reveal her perspective about her job? Give examples of language from the text that are clues to her attitude.

2. In what way did being a nurse influence Alcott's perspective on the war? Explain. Think about how her perspective might have been different as a soldier or as someone who didn't participate in the war effort at all.

3. Why do you think Alcott decided to keep a journal?

Review: Text Structure

As you learned on page 210, **text structure** is the way an author organizes information in a text. One way a text might be structured is in **chronological order,** or time order. In chronological order, events are described in the order in which they actually happened. Journals are typically arranged in chronological order. Some words or phrases that can help you determine the order of events are *first, next, then, later,* and *finally.* Dates can also help you recognize chronological order.

4. In what way does the text structure of the journal help you to understand Alcott's volunteer experience? Think about how the text structure draws attention to her changing ideas about the war.

Reading Strategy Monitor Comprehension

5. Note the strategies you used to monitor comprehension as you read *Civil War Journal.* Which strategy was most helpful to you? Explain your thoughts.

Grammar Link

Capitalization of Sentences Always capitalize the first letter of the first word of every sentence and the first letter of the first word of every direct quotation. For example:

There were only four cars in the town.

Looking out, Mama said, "Corn's knee high by the Fourth of July."

When a quoted sentence is interrupted by explanatory words, such as *he said,* do NOT begin the second part of the quotation with a capital letter. For example:

"I'd go for a ride again," she said, "if I could."

Even if a quotation is just a single word or phrase, capitalize the first word. For example:

"That child!" Aunt Elvera said.

Practice Rewrite the following paragraph, correcting the three capitalization errors.

Louisa May Alcott served as a nurse in the Union Hotel Hospital. One soldier said to her, "you are real motherly, ma'am." she hoped she was motherly. "Thank you," she said to the soldier, "For making me feel like a good nurse."

Listening and Speaking

Persuasive Speech Prepare a persuasive speech about the importance of helping people during a time of need or a national crisis, such as a war or a natural disaster. Convince the audience that helping is important, and give examples from the selection. Practice reading your speech aloud to a partner. Discuss how your tone of voice and body language can affect the persuasiveness of the argument.

The Gettysburg Address

Connect to the Speech

Think about a time when you were moved by a public speaker—it could have been by a speech you heard live or recorded.

Quickwrite Write a few sentences about the speech and how the speaker's words and manner of speaking affected you.

Build Background

One of the bloodiest and most significant battles of the Civil War was fought near Gettysburg, Pennsylvania, July 1–3, 1863. The number of killed and wounded was estimated at more than 40,000 soldiers.

- President Lincoln was invited to give "a few appropriate remarks" at the dedication of the military cemetery in Gettysburg, where the Union soldiers were buried after the battle. He delivered the address on November 19, 1863.

- Lincoln's presentation of the Gettysburg Address, which lasted only two minutes, was not praised at first. Now it is considered Lincoln's most famous speech and is frequently quoted.

- Modern-day presidents have speech writers, but Lincoln wrote the Gettysburg Address himself. His ability to state an important truth in a few memorable words kept his message alive in the minds of his audience—and keeps it alive in the minds of readers today.

Vocabulary

endure (en door´) *v.* to continue to be; last (p. 507). *Her memory will endure long after she is gone.*

nobly (no´ blē) *adv.* in a worthy manner (p. 507). *He walked nobly into battle.*

resolve (ri zolv´) *v.* to decide (to do something); determine (p. 507). *I resolve to keep this house clean from now on.*

perish (per´ ish) *v.* to pass from existence; disappear (p. 507). *Whenever the sailors spot land, all their worries perish.*

Meet Abraham Lincoln

"Let us strive on to finish the work we are in; . . . to do all which may achieve and cherish a just and lasting peace among ourselves, and with all nations."
—Abraham Lincoln

Saving the Union Abraham Lincoln was elected president of the United States in 1860. He served as president during the Civil War, and one of the main things he is remembered for is saving the Union.

Freedom for All Lincoln declared slaves to be free in the Emancipation Proclamation. This led to the Thirteenth Amendment, which ended slavery in the United States.

Abraham Lincoln was born in 1809. He was assassinated by John Wilkes Booth in 1865 while he was still president.

Set Purposes for Reading

BQ BIG Question

Throughout history, people have waged wars. As you read, identify the beliefs and philosophies that Abraham Lincoln believed were worth fighting for.

Literary Element Parallelism

Parallelism is the use of a series of words, phrases, or sentences that have a similar grammatical form. An example of parallelism is the sentence, "I came, I saw, I conquered."

The use of parallelism is important because it shows the relationship between ideas and helps emphasize thoughts.

As you read the Gettysburg Address, look for examples of parallelism and their effect on the meaning of the speech.

Reading Strategy Paraphrase

When you **paraphrase**, you use your own words to restate specific information. Unlike a summary, a paraphrase is usually about the same length as the original passage.

It is important to paraphrase when you want to remember specific details or understand difficult passages.

To paraphrase, think about

- difficult sentences, or parts of sentences, you want to understand
- specific details you want to remember
- how you might say the passages in your own words

As you read the Gettysburg Address, you may want to use a graphic organizer like the one below to help you paraphrase the speech.

Author's Words	My Paraphrase

Learning Objectives

For pages 504–509

In studying this text, you will focus on the following objectives:

Literary Study: Analyzing parallelism.

Reading: Paraphrasing.

TRY IT

Paraphrase the paragraph below.

All students will follow these procedures during the lunch period. No students will be allowed in the hallways or classrooms. All students must be present in the cafeteria for the entire lunch period. Hot lunches and snacks must be purchased during the first fifteen minutes of the lunch period. Tables must be cleaned appropriately.

The Gettysburg Address

ABRAHAM LINCOLN

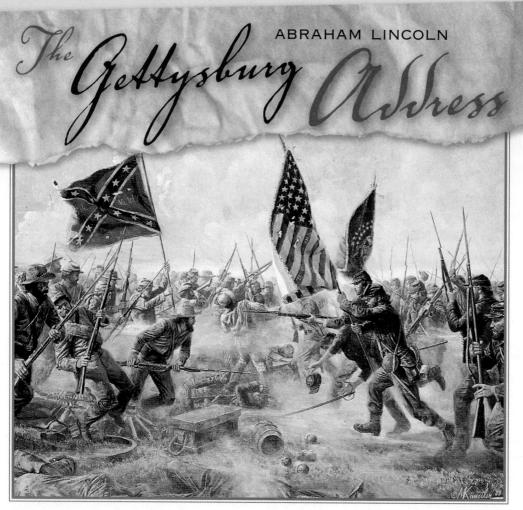

The Angle, Gettysburg, Pennsylvania, July 3, 1863, 1988. Mort Kuntsler. Oil on canvas, 18 x 24 in. Collection of Mr. and Mrs. Robert L. Sharpe.

View the Art What words or ideas in the Gettysburg Address does this painting illustrate?

Four score and seven[1] years ago our fathers[2] brought forth on this continent a new nation, conceived[3] in Liberty, and dedicated[4] to the proposition that all men are created equal.

Paraphrase Restate the first sentence of Lincoln's speech in your own words.

1 ***Four score and seven*** is 87. Lincoln was using the language of the St. James version of the Bible.

2 Lincoln refers to the "founding ***fathers,***" the men who wrote and adopted the Declaration of Independence and the U.S. Constitution.

3 Here, ***conceived*** means "formed" or "imagined."

4 Here ***dedicated*** means "given completely."

Now we are engaged in a great civil war, testing whether that nation, or any nation so conceived and so dedicated, can long **endure**. We are met on a great battlefield of that war. We have come to dedicate a portion of that field, as a final resting place for those who here gave their lives that that nation might live. It is altogether fitting and proper that we should do this.

But, in a larger sense, we can not dedicate[5]—we can not consecrate—we can not hallow[6]—this ground. The brave men, living and dead, who struggled here, have consecrated it, far above our poor power to add or detract. The world will little note, nor long remember what we say here, but it can never forget what they did here. It is for us the living, rather, to be dedicated here to the unfinished work which they who fought here have thus far so **nobly** advanced. It is rather for us to be here dedicated to the great task remaining before us—that from these honored dead we take increased devotion to that cause for which they gave the last full measure of devotion—that we here highly **resolve** that these dead shall not have died in vain[7] —that this nation, under God, shall have a new birth of freedom—and that government of the people, by the people, for the people, shall not **perish** from the earth.

Parallelism Find the parallelism in this sentence. What effect does this parallelism create?

BQ **BIG Question**
Do you think the listeners at the cemetery felt the soldiers had died for a worthy purpose? Why or why not? Consider who the listeners might be.

5 Here **dedicate** means "set aside for a certain purpose."

6 Both **consecrate** and **hallow** mean "make or honor as holy."

7 The phrase **in vain** means "for no good purpose; uselessly."

Vocabulary

endure (en door´) v. to continue to be; last

nobly (nō´blē) adv. in a worthy manner

resolve (ri zolv´) v. to decide (to do something); determine

perish (per´ish) v. to pass from existence; disappear

After You Read

Respond and Think Critically

1. What are the main ideas in Lincoln's speech? State the main ideas in your own words and in a logical order. [Summarize]

2. What does Lincoln mean when he states, "The brave men, living and dead, who struggled here, have consecrated [this ground] far above our poor power to add or detract"? [Infer]

3. Explain which passage in the speech was the most difficult to paraphrase. Refer to the graphic organizer you created. [Paraphrase]

4. What effect does Lincoln's use of parallelism help to create in his speech? [Analyze]

5. In your opinion, does "The Gettysburg Address" deserve the praise it has gotten as being one of the most important American speeches ever given? Explain. [Evaluate]

6. **BQ** **BIG Question** Do you think Lincoln's beliefs are worth fighting for today? [Draw Conclusions]

Vocabulary Practice

Choose the sentence that uses the vocabulary word correctly.

1. **A.** They **endure** when they don't study for the test.

   B. Plants can only **endure** so much dry weather.

2. **A. Nobly,** the child stole the cookies cooling on the counter.

   B. Nobly, she embraced the challenge ahead of her.

3. **A.** I **resolve** to complete my homework on time.

   B. I will **resolve** my studies in May.

4. **A.** Elephants **perish** well in zoos.

   B. Many animals will **perish** if global warming continues.

Academic Vocabulary

President Lincoln wanted the Union to remain a **federation.**

In the preceding sentence, *federation* means "a central-governing union formed by agreement between the states." Think about some of the common goals of the United States as a federation, and then fill in the blank for this statement:

_____ is a common goal of the United States as a federation.

Literature Online

Parallelism

1. Does Lincoln's use of parallelism make his speech more memorable? Why or why not?

2. In what way does Lincoln's use of parallelism tie his speech together?

Review: **Argument**

As you learned on page 459, **argument** is a type of persuasive writing in which logic or reason is used to try to influence a reader's or listener's ideas or actions. An argument includes reasons, examples, or references in support of the major points.

3. In what ways does Lincoln argue that the Civil War risks more than the destruction of the Union? Explain.

4. How persuasive do you find Lincoln's argument that the living should dedicate themselves to completing "the unfinished work"? Explain.

Reading Strategy **Paraphrase**

Test Skills Practice

5. How would you paraphrase the following: "It is altogether fitting and proper that we should do this"?

6. In your own words, restate the following lines from the speech: "that we here highly resolve that these dead shall not have died in vain—that this nation, under God, shall have a new birth of freedom."

Grammar Link

Misplaced/Dangling Modifiers
Adjectives and adverbs should connect clearly to the words they modify. A **misplaced modifier** connects to the wrong word or group of words. A **dangling modifier** makes it unclear *who* is doing *what* in a sentence. Misplaced or dangling modifiers can cause readers to misunderstand the meaning of a sentence. For example:

> Eric went home to eat on his bicycle.
> (*It sounds as if Eric ate on his bicycle.*)

> Running away, I saw my dog.
> (*It sounds like I was running away.*)

To fix these modifiers, bring each modifier closer to the word it describes. For example:

> Eric went home on his bicycle to eat.

> I saw my dog running away.

Practice On a piece of paper, write one sentence about Abraham Lincoln that has a misplaced or dangling modifier. Then write a second sentence that corrects the misplaced or dangling modifier.

Write with Style

Apply Parallelism Think about a person in your life you would like to honor. Write a short speech about why you think it is important to honor this person. To help get your point across, use parallelism at least twice. Use a graphic organizer like the one below to keep track of your use of parallelism.

Reasons	Parallelism

from

Lincoln:
A Photobiography

by Russell Freedman

Newbery Award Medal

Learning Objectives

For pages 510–515

In studying this text, you will focus on the following objective:

Reading: Synthesizing.

Set a Purpose for Reading

Read to learn about President Lincoln's role during the Civil War.

Build Background

During the election of 1860, Abraham Lincoln became unpopular in the South for stating that slavery should be banned from new territories. In March 1861, several southern states seceded from the Union and formed the Confederate States of America. The Civil War began six weeks later and continued for four years.

Reading Strategy Synthesize

Synthesizing is combining what you learn from various sources with what you already know to create new ideas, perspectives, and opinions. As you read this selection, ask yourself if your understanding of the ideas goes beyond the main ideas presented in the text. See if you can make some new connections based on what you now know after reading the selection.

L incoln wanted to believe that the Union could be saved without bloodshed. But that hope was about to vanish. Less than two weeks after his inauguration,[1] he faced his first crisis. Fort Sumter, at the entrance to Charleston harbor in South Carolina, still flew the Union flag. The state's governor was demanding that the fort be given up.

On March 15, Lincoln learned that Sumter was running out of supplies. While the fort was not of great military value, the president had pledged to defend federal property in the South. Sumter had become a symbol of Northern determination, and Lincoln had to make a decision. If he sent

---

1 Abraham Lincoln was *inaugurated* as the 16th president of the United States on Monday, March 4, 1861.

supplies, he risked an armed attack and war. If he didn't, the fort could not hold out for long.

He consulted with his military staff and members of his cabinet, but they could not agree on what should be done. Lincoln himself was uncertain. . . .

Finally the president acted. On April 6 he notified the South Carolina governor that a supply fleet was about to sail for Charleston. As the Union ships approached the city on the morning of April 12, rebel cannons ringing the harbor opened fire on Fort Sumter.

The American Civil War had begun.

On April 14, Lincoln heard that the fort had surrendered after a blistering thirty-six-hour bombardment. That day he issued a proclamation calling for 75,000 volunteers for enlistments[2] of ninety days, which seemed long enough. Surely the rebellion[3] would be put down by then. . . .

The North mobilized. Troops poured into Washington, ready to defend the capital. Across the Potomac River, Virginia had joined the Confederacy. From his office windows, Lincoln could see rebel flags flying over buildings in Alexandria, Virginia. . . .

By early summer, both sides were training large armies of volunteers, many of them inexperienced boys who could barely handle a rifle. Northern newspapers were calling for a massive drive against the Confederate capital in Richmond, Virginia. "On to Richmond!" became the popular rallying cry.

In July, Union forces under General Irwin McDowell marched into Virginia. McDowell had been ordered to capture the crucial railroad junction at Manassas, about twenty-five miles southwest of Washington. From there, he would sweep down to Richmond and crush the rebellion.

Word spread through Washington that McDowell would begin his attack on Sunday, July 21. That morning dozens of politicians and their wives, newspapermen, and other spectators drove down from Washington in buggies and carriages to watch their army defeat the rebels. None of these people had ever seen a battle, and they had little idea what to expect. They brought along picnic baskets, champagne, and opera glasses, camped on a hillside, and waited for the action to begin.

Lincoln waited anxiously in the White House. The first reports to reach him were confusing—the two armies had met at a muddy little creek called Bull Run. They were advancing and retreating in turn. Several hours later, Lincoln received word of a disaster. Union troops had broken ranks. McDowell's army had been routed.[4] . . .

---

2 **Enlistment** is the act of voluntarily signing up for military service.

3 **Rebellion** is an organized, armed resistance against a legal government.

4 **Broken ranks** means "abandoned their positions." **Routed** means "driven or forced out."

The picture depicts Pickett's Charge (named after the Confederate general George Pickett), the assault that many consider a major turning point in the war.

After Bull Run, Lincoln resolved to tighten the naval blockade,[5] call up more troops for longer enlistments, and launch three offensives at once— into Virginia, into Tennessee, and down the Mississippi.

He gave command of the Eastern armies to General George B. McClellan, a thirty-five-year-old veteran of the Mexican War. . . .

McClellan trained his growing army with meticulous[6] care, but as the months passed, he showed no signs of moving against the rebel forces massed in Virginia. . . . On the western front, it was the same story. Union commanders built up their forces and drilled their men, but they weren't ready to fight.

Congress and the public were losing patience. Why weren't the generals fighting? . . .

Lincoln, too, was tired of the delays. But he wasn't a military man himself, and he was reluctant to overrule his commanders. . . . Attorney General Edward Bates had told Lincoln that it was his presidential duty to "command the commanders. . . . The nation requires it, and history will hold you responsible." Lincoln began to play an active role in the day-to-day

---

5 A **blockade** is the shutting off of an area, such as a port, harbor, or city, by troops or ships to prevent the movement of people and supplies. The idea was that when supplies were exhausted, the people would surrender.

6 **Meticulous** means "extremely concerned about details."

conduct of the war, planning strategy and sometimes directing tactical maneuvers[7] in the field. . . .

Lee[8] was determined to carry the war into the North. In June, his troops pushed northwards from Virginia, marched across Maryland, and invaded Pennsylvania, throwing the North into a panic. Lincoln had replaced Hooker[9] with a new commander, General George Gordon Meade, who rushed his forces to Pennsylvania to stop the rebels. The two armies met on July 1 at the little country town of Gettysburg, where 170,000 troops clashed in the most spectacular battle of the war.

On July 4, after three days of fierce fighting, with more than fifty thousand casualties on both sides, Lee's broken and defeated army started back to Virginia. When news of the victory reached Lincoln, he ordered Meade to go after Lee and destroy his army once and for all. "Do not let the enemy escape," Lincoln cabled.[10] But Meade hesitated, allowing Lee to move his retreating troops safely across the Potomac. "We had them within our grasp," the president wailed. "We had only to stretch forth our hands and they were ours."

Lincoln had not yet found the commander he needed. He feared now that the war would go on indefinitely.[11] "What can I do with such generals as we have?" he asked. "What among them is any better than Meade?"

Four months later, a ceremony was held at Gettysburg to dedicate a national cemetery for the soldiers who had died there. The main speaker was to be Edward Everett of Massachusetts, the most celebrated orator[12] of the day. The president was asked to deliver "a few appropriate remarks" after Everett had finished.

Lincoln wanted to make a brief statement about the larger meaning of the war, which was now well into its third year. He started work on his speech in Washington, but it was not

---

11 **Indefinitely** means "without a specified end."

12 An **orator** is a public speaker.

Loss of life was heavy for both sides at Gettysburg.

Incidents of the War.

---

7 **Tactical maneuvers** are planned combat exercises.

8 **General Robert E. Lee** was then commander of the Army of Northern Virginia.

9 **Joseph Hooker**, known as "Fighting Joe," was a general in the Union Army.

10 Here, **cabled** means "sent by telegraph line."

Executive Mansion,

Washington, _____, 186_.

Four score and seven years ago our fathers brought forth, upon this continent, a new nation, conceived in liberty, and dedicated to the proposition that "all men are created equal"

Now we are engaged in a great civil war, testing whether that nation, or any nation so conceived, and so dedicated, can long endure. We are met on a great battle field of that war. We have come to dedicate a portion of it, as a final resting place for those who died here, that the nation might live. This we may, in all propriety do. But, in a larger sense, we can not dedicate— we can not consecrate— we can not hallow, this ground— The brave men, living and dead, who struggled here, have hallowed it, far above our poor power to add or detract. The world will little note, nor long remember what we say here; while it can never forget what they did here.

It is rather for us, the living, to stand here, ~~we here be dedica~~

---

yet finished when he rode a special train to Gettysburg the day before the ceremony. After dinner that evening, he retired[13] to his room to work on the speech again. He added the final touches after breakfast the next morning. He had written it out on two pieces of lined paper. There were about 270 words. "It is what I would call a short, short speech," he said.

That morning, wearing his familiar black suit and silk stove-pipe hat, Lincoln rode on horseback to the cemetery on the outskirts of Gettysburg. . . .

---

13 Here, **retired** means "withdrew to a place of privacy."

Edward Everett spoke for two hours. . . .

Lincoln spoke for two minutes. Some of his listeners were disappointed. Opposition[14] newspapers criticized the address as unworthy of the occasion, and some papers didn't mention it at all. Lincoln himself felt that the speech was a failure. He certainly didn't realize that the words he spoke at Gettysburg on the afternoon of November 19, 1863, would be remembered all over the world as an American classic more than a hundred years later.

The war was being fought, Lincoln had said, to preserve America's bold experiment in democracy. A new kind of government had been created by the Founding Fathers in 1776. It was based on the idea that all men have an equal right to liberty, that they can govern themselves by free elections.

---

14 Here, **opposition** refers to Confederacy.

BATTLE OF BULL RUN V.ª JULY 21ST 1861.

This cartoon shows General George McClellan (center) trying to mediate between President Abraham Lincoln (left) and Jefferson Davis (right), the President of the Confederate States of America during the Civil War.

View the Art How does the cartoon illustrate the threat of the Union being destroyed?

The war was a test to determine if such a government could endure. Thousands of men had fought and died at Gettysburg so that the nation and its idea of democracy might survive. Now it was up to the living to complete their unfinished work, to make sure that "those dead shall not have died in vain—that this nation under God shall have a new birth of freedom—and that the government of the people, by the people, for the people, shall not perish from the earth."

Respond and Think Critically

1. Using your own words, retell the main events in this selection in a logical order. [Summarize]

2. Why do you think the Union commanders were not in a hurry to lead their armies into battle? [Infer]

3. Consider some of the original responses to Lincoln's speech at Gettysburg. How do those responses differ from beliefs today about the speech? [Compare]

4. **Text-to-Text** Why do you think President Lincoln considered his Gettysburg speech a failure? [Connect]

5. Reading Strategy Synthesize Think about what Lincoln says in "The Gettysburg Address." Then consider his actions described in this selection. Using this information and what you already know, what can you say about Lincoln's beliefs about the importance of the Union? [Draw Conclusions]

6. **BQ** BIG Question What actions did President Lincoln take to show that he felt the Union was worth fighting for? [Identify]

Going, Going Green

Connect to the Persuasive Essay

Persuasive writing tries to convince readers to think, feel, or act in a certain way. Whenever you read an ad or watch a TV commercial, you're seeing persuasive writing at work.

Partner Talk With a partner, talk about the last time you tried to persuade someone. How did you support your position? Did you change the other person's mind? Why or why not?

Build Background

"Going, Going Green" is a persuasive essay about the effects of climate change on the sports world. In the recent past, alarming changes in weather patterns have been observed.

- Cities that traditionally had long, snowy winters have started having shorter, warmer winters.

- Glaciers have been melting, causing the water levels of oceans to rise.

Vocabulary

innovative (in´no vā tiv) *adj.* new; original; ground-breaking (p. 518).
The restaurant's innovative menu won praise for its unique flavor combinations.

avert (ə vurt´) *v.* to prevent or avoid (p. 520).
The tourists will avert danger if they leave the coastal town before the hurricane arrives.

exemption (ig zemp´shən) *n.* freedom from some obligation, especially a legal one (p. 521).
The new law has stricter rules on exemptions from paying property taxes.

galvanize (gal´və nīz´) *v.* to rouse suddenly into action (p. 522). *The charity run will galvanize support to find a cure for the disease.*

Meet Alexander Wolff

"Global warming is not coming; it is here. . . . All of which is changing the way we play and the sports we watch."
—Alexander Wolff

A Passion for Basketball Alexander Wolff played professional basketball before earning a degree in history. He has been a staff member of *Sports Illustrated* since 1980. He writes mostly about basketball, but also covers other sports.

Literary Works Wolff has written several books, including *Big Game, Small World.* "Going, Going Green" appeared in the March 6, 2007, issue of *Sports Illustrated.*

Alexander Wolff was born in 1957.

 Literature Online

Author Search For more about Alexander Wolff, go to glencoe.com and enter QuickPass code GL39770u4.

Set Purposes for Reading

BQ BIG Question

As you read, note the sports figures, teams, and organizations involved in fighting climate change. Ask yourself, "Is this cause worth fighting for?"

Literary Element Text Structure

Text structure is the pattern of organization a writer uses. In persuasive essays, the text is often structured around an **argument**—the writer's opinion on an issue or a problem. An argument may also be called a **proposition**. The writer usually offers an argument at the beginning of the essay and then provides **support** for his or her claim—details that back up the writer's stand.

Identifying text structure is important because it can help you locate and understand a writer's ideas.

As you read, ask yourself, what is the writer's argument? In what ways does the writer support his position?

Reading Skill Analyze Evidence

Your friend claims that the Cardinals are better than the Yankees. In response, you tell him to prove it. Whenever you tell someone to "prove it," you're asking for evidence. Evidence is detailed information showing that an idea is reasonable or well-founded. When you analyze **evidence,** you look closely at the facts and reasons that a writer presents to support his or her claim.

To analyze evidence in this essay, ask,

- Does the information truly support the writer's position?

- Does the writer provide enough information to prove his point?

You may find it helpful to use a chart like the one below. In one column, list evidence that the writer provides. In the other column, note reasons why the evidence may or may not support his argument.

Evidence	Analysis
p. 519: "searing heat" causes Texas high schools to have fewer practices	This supports the writer's claim that climate change is affecting the sports people play and watch.

Learning Objectives

For pages 516–524

In studying this text, you will focus on the following objectives:

Literary Study:
Analyzing text structure.

Reading:
Analyzing evidence.

TRY IT

Analyze Evidence A friend tells you that students in year-round schools are happier going to school twelve months a year instead of nine. Her opinion is based on student accounts she's read on different blog postings. Is the evidence believable? Does she have enough evidence to prove her point?

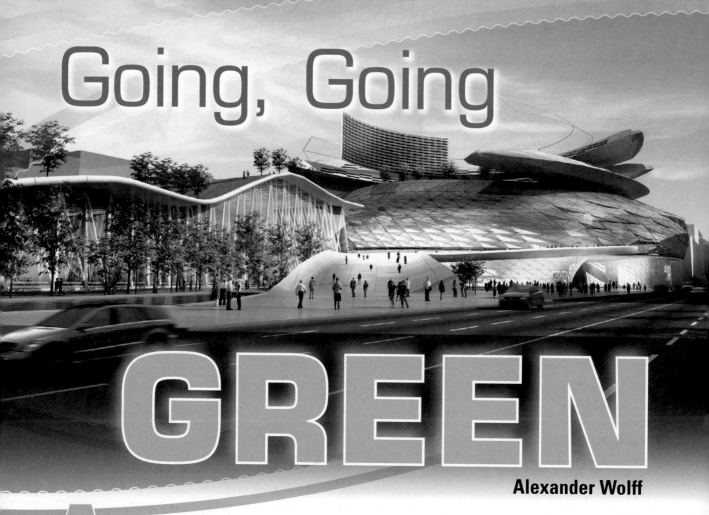

Going, Going GREEN

Alexander Wolff

As global warming changes the planet, it is changing the sports world. To counter the looming environmental crisis, surprising and **innovative** ideas are already helping sports adapt.

The next time a ball game gets rained out during the September stretch run, you can curse the momentary worthlessness of those tickets in your pocket. Or you can wonder why it got rained out—and ask yourself why practice had to be called off last summer on a day when there wasn't a cloud in the sky.

Global warming is not coming; it is here. Greenhouse gases—most notably carbon dioxide produced by burning coal, oil and gas—are trapping solar heat that once escaped from the Earth's atmosphere. As temperatures

View the Art Someday sports arenas might be self-sustaining and carbon neutral. Look at the design for an environmentally friendly sports area. What aspects of the design stand out to you the most?

Text Structure How does the writer support his argument that global warming is here?

Vocabulary

innovative (in′nō vā′tiv) *adj.* new; original; ground-breaking

around the globe increase, oceans are warming, fields are drying up, snow is melting, more rain is falling, and sea levels are rising.

All of which is changing the way we play and the sports we watch. Evidence is everywhere of a future hurtling toward us faster than scientists forecasted even a few years ago. Searing heat is turning that rite of passage of Texas high school football, the August two-a-day, into a one-at-night, while at the game's highest level the Miami Dolphins, once famous for sweating players into shape, have thrown in the soggy towel and built a climate-controlled practice bubble.

Sports condition us to notice first those things that happen at scatback speed, and until recently climate change took place in world-historical fashion, the way a soccer match unfolds. But that perception[1] is changing fast, especially for skiers, whose season has endured a whipsaw of extremes: One day in November enough snow fell at Colorado's Beaver Creek to cause the cancellation of practice for the men's downhill at a World Cup event. A day later on the other side of the globe, officials at the French resort of Val d'Isère called off another World Cup event on account of too little snow, as well as a forecast of prolonged warm temperatures—one of seven World Cup events in Europe this season to have all races canceled for the same reason.

The U.S. Nordic ski team returned home early from the European circuit after a December race was rescheduled four times in one week.

Indeed, the world's signature dogsled race, Alaska's Iditarod, hasn't begun at its traditional starting point in Wasilla since 2002 because of too little snow there. The Elfstedentocht, an 11-city skating marathon that the Dutch stage whenever the canals freeze over, has been run only once in the past two decades. The highest ski slope on the planet, Bolivia's Chacaltaya (altitude 17,388 feet), will soon be unskiable for lack of snow. Meanwhile backcountry skiing in North America and ice fishing in the upper Midwest are in jeopardy.

Analyze Evidence
Compare this detail with the rest of the evidence the writer includes about the effect of climate change on sports. Does this information surprise you?

---

1 A *perception* is how an issue is viewed or understood.

Humans are accelerating global warming, and we can at least minimize its damage, if not reverse it. By acting quickly, the two countries that emit most of the world's carbon dioxide, the U.S. and China, might be able to **avert** that forecasted five-degree temperature increase, slowing the rise of the seas enough to allow for the development of new technologies to redress the problem. What would it mean to act? Decrease the burning of fossil fuels, improve fuel efficiency and conserve energy in our daily lives.

The good news is that stadiums and arenas, if built with green aforethought, can remind us that we're all in this together. Site one near a public-transit line, and there's less need to build that most Earth-hostile of features, the vast parking lot. (The greenest ballpark in the country may be Fenway Park, because only an idiot would try driving and parking there.)

Turbines mounted on upper decks would catch the same wind that plays whimsically with pop flies, turning it into the source of power to offset at least some of the energy demands of a ball game.

Meantime, an eco-consciousness[2] is leaching ever so slowly into sports. You'd expect environmental awareness among extreme-sport athletes like the snowboarders and BMX riders who belong to the Action Sports Environmental Coalition, or from surfers whose vocation and avocation depend on the health of the seas. But less likely candidates are thinking globally and acting locally.

- NASCAR driver Ward Burton's foundation is pledged to habitat management, land conservation and environmental education in his home of Halifax County, Va.

- The Philadelphia Eagles may have some of the most discourteous followers in sports, but their management is a leader, having launched an environmental initiative replete with catchy slogans like Go Green and Time for Some Serious Trash Talk.

---

2 **Eco-consciousness** refers to the awareness and concern people have for ecology and the environment.

- The Natural Resources Defense Council (NRDC) is working with the NBA and Major League Baseball to help their teams get greener. Scientists told the NFL that Super Bowl XLI would put one million pounds of carbon dioxide into the air—not counting air travel to Miami—so the league planted 3,000 trees around Florida in an attempt to pull at least that much of the greenhouse gas out of the atmosphere.

By going green, motor sports could have the quickest impact on public awareness of the planet's fate. The Formula One circuit has already discovered hybrids and biofuels, and Indy cars are mixing ethanol into their fuel. NASCAR is poised to phase out leaded gasoline, a neurotoxin. (The Clean Air Act of 1970 included an **exemption** for race cars even as the public was barred from buying cars that ran on leaded gas.) It's only a short jump from a NASCAR driver with a raised consciousness to a NASCAR fan with the same.

Text Structure This statement supports what argument?

Vocabulary

exemption (ig zemp´shən) *n.* freedom from some obligation, especially a legal one

The stadium in the design below draws its power from the sun and the wind.

From his home in Ripton, Vt., Bill McKibben, writer, activist, and passionate cross-country skier, surveys this disfigurement of the world as we've known it with as much melancholy as indignation.[3] "If I were a deeply moral person, I should be kept awake at night by the thought of hundreds of millions of Bangladeshis fleeing rising waters and dengue and famine,"[4] says McKibben, who's helping to organize a nationwide call to action on climate change for April 14 that will include iconic outdoor and sporting sites Mount Hood and the Key West coral reefs. "But at some level I feel this most acutely in the winter, when I realize I've had fewer and fewer chances to put on my skis."

And therein may lie the great value of sports. What happens in an arena so familiar and beloved may sound an alarm we will hear and heed. At a time when so much in our lives is linear and digital, from the economy to technology, sports still run in graceful cycles, marking time in rhythm with the seasons.

McKibben says, "We're still so used to the idea that we can deal with the forces of nature that we think nothing of naming our teams Hurricanes and Cyclones. In 10 years, that will be like calling a team the Plagues."[5]

Ten years. That's two-and-a-half Olympiads—enough time for our teams and athletes to take the lead, **galvanize** attention and influence behavior. When they do, per usual, may we cheer and may we follow. But as we watch, let us remember that this game is different. We don't have the luxury of looking on from the sidelines. We must become players too.

BQ BIG Question

Do you agree with the writer that this is a cause worth fighting for? Why or why not?

---

3 McKibben is observing the world with *melancholy* because he is saddened and with *indignation* because he is angered.

4 In 2005, a tidal wave hit the coast of Bangladesh. Experts believe the tidal wave was caused by stormy weather out at sea.

5 McKibben believes that, with weather conditions worsening, "hurricanes" and "cyclones" will bring to mind images of death and suffering, much like the results of a plague.

Vocabulary
. . . .

galvanize (gal′və nīz′) *v.* to rouse suddenly into action

After You Read

Respond and Think Critically

1. What are greenhouse gases and how do they affect Earth's atmosphere? [Recall and Summarize]

2. Tell in your own words what could happen if the United States and China act quickly to fight global warming. [Paraphrase]

3. How do you think the Miami Dolphins football players will benefit from practicing in a "climate-controlled" building rather than outdoors? [Infer]

4. The writer argues that climate change is a real threat that is changing the sports people play and watch. Does the writer include enough support to convince you that his argument is valid? [Evaluate]

5. The writer describes the actions various sports organizations are taking to be "greener." Do you think the sports world, in general, is doing enough to combat the effects of climate change? [Make Judgments]

6. **BQ** BIG Question The writer of "Going, Going Green" believes that preventing global warming is a cause worth fighting for. What causes do you support? [Connect]

TIP

Evaluating
Here are some tips to help you evaluate.

- Read the writer's explanation for what causes global warming.

- Scan the selection for information about how recent changes in climate have affected sporting events.

- Decide if these changes are significant and threatening.

 FOLDABLES **Study Organizer** Keep track of your ideas about the **BIG Question** in your unit Foldable.

Connect to Science

People all over the world are making changes in their lives to slow global warming. This effort is called "reducing your carbon footprint." The "carbon" being referred to is carbon dioxide, the gas that contributes the most to global warming. Carbon dioxide is a heat-trapping gas found in the atmosphere, the blanket of air surrounding the Earth.

Life on our planet depends on the atmosphere. This protective layer regulates the temperature on Earth's surface. The more carbon dioxide in our atmosphere, the hotter the planet becomes.

How can you help reduce your carbon footprint? Electricity, heat, gas—these all create carbon dioxide. Try turning off unused lights. Organize carpools to get to school. Small changes can make a big difference.

On Your Own Answer the following questions on a separate sheet of paper.

1. What is a "carbon footprint"?

2. What could happen to temperatures on Earth if carbon dioxide continues to increase in the atmosphere?

3. How can you reduce your carbon footprint?

Literary Element Text Structure

Test Skills Practice

1. Which of the following sentences from the essay best summarizes the writer's position?

   A. "Humans are accelerating global warming, and we can at least minimize its damage, if not reverse it."

   B. "An eco-consciousness is leaching ever so slowly into sports."

   C. "By going green, motor sports could have the quickest impact on public awareness of the planet's fate."

   D. "At a time when so much in our lives is linear and digital, from the economy to technology, sports still run in graceful cycles, marking time in rhythm with the seasons."

Review: Diction

Diction is a writer's choice of words and how those words are arranged in phrases and sentences. In a persuasive essay, the writer uses diction to make you think or feel a certain way.

2. In "Going, Going Green," the writer states that "Evidence is everywhere of a future hurtling toward us faster than scientists forecasted even a few years ago." What feeling do you get from the writer's sentence? Explain.

Reading Skill Analyze Evidence

Test Skills Practice

3. Which one of the following is evidence for the claim that global warming is here?

   A. Sports players are sweating too much.

   B. Motor vehicles burn fossil fuel.

   C. Rising temperatures are causing fields to dry up.

   D. There is a rising awareness of the environment in the sports world.

Vocabulary Practice

Respond to these questions.

1. Which type of leader is **innovative**—a person who follows someone else's example or a person who comes up with bold new ideas?

2. What would you do if you wanted to **avert** the risk of a bicycle injury—wear a helmet or ride on the wrong side of the road?

3. How would you respond if you had an **exemption** from doing chores—protest to your parents or spend the time doing something fun?

4. If you wanted to **galvanize** support for a candidate—would you help the candidate get elected or would you spread rumors about him or her?

Academic Vocabulary

Alexander Wolff suggests ways that important figures in the sports world can stop being **contributors** to the problem of global warming. To become more familiar with the word *contributors*, fill out an organizer like the one below.

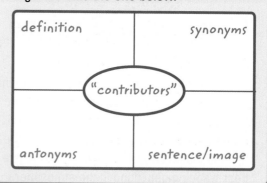

Respond Through Writing

Persuasive Essay

Argue a Position In "Going, Going Green," the writer provides evidence to support his argument that people in the sports world need to do what they can to fight global warming. Write a persuasive essay to the people of your community about the role you think local organizations and businesses should take in protecting the environment. Present your ideas in such a way that you inspire readers to take action.

Understand the Task You will need to provide reasons and evidence to support your argument that organizations and businesses have a special responsibility to the environment. Your word choice should reflect your belief that this is a cause worth fighting for. Use repetition of words, phrases, or grammatical structures to emphasize your ideas.

Prewrite Make a list of your thoughts on the topic. Then conduct research to find out what various organizations and businesses have done to be eco-conscious. What do these organizations and businesses say about why they're environmentally friendly?

Draft Organize your persuasive essay into the following four sections. Use the sentence frames for ideas on how to phrase your thoughts:

State your position
I believe that _____ because _____.

Support your position
The belief that _____ is supported by _____, _____, and _____.

Introduce and address a counterargument (contrasting position)
Of course, some might disagree with my position and say that _____.

Sum up your position
In conclusion, I believe _____.

Revise After writing your first draft, read it slowly and carefully to ensure that your paragraphs follow a logical order. You may need to rearrange and rewrite your text to make your ideas flow. Each idea should lead to, and help the reader understand, the next idea.

Edit and Proofread Proofread your paper, correcting any errors in spelling, grammar, and punctuation. Review the Grammar Tip in the side column for information on parallelism.

Learning Objectives

For page 525

In this assignment, you will focus on the following objective:

Writing:
Writing a persuasive essay.

> ### Grammar Tip
>
> **Parallelism** is the use of a series of words, phrases, or sentences in a similar grammatical structure. Writers use parallelism for emphasis. For example, Wolff writes:
> *As temperatures around the globe increase, oceans are warming, fields are drying up, snow is melting, more rain is falling, and sea levels are rising.*
>
> Notice how the sentence is arranged. One phrase builds on another to emphasize the extent and urgency of these global changes. When you use parallelism, remember to separate each item—word, phrase, or clause—in the series with a comma.

Ode to Thanks and Ode to Rain

Connect to the Poems

Think about an everyday object or event that is meaningful to you. What kind of poem might you write to celebrate it?

Graphic Organizer Draw and fill in a web like the one below with things that you might celebrate in a poem.

Things I Celebrated

Build Background

Poets sometimes celebrate everyday events or objects. By writing about such common things, poets give readers a new, or heightened, appreciation of ordinary life.

- Pablo Neruda writes a light and playful poem in praise of a simple, everyday word.

- Pat Mora writes a lyrical poem that celebrates a common event.

Set Purposes for Reading

BQ BIG Question

Read "Ode to Thanks" and "Ode to Rain" to find out why the poets value the subjects of these poems so highly.

Literary Element Ode

These two poems are **odes**—poems that are full of feeling and generally praise or celebrate something, often something famous or notable. Sometimes, though, an ode celebrates an everyday event or object. As you read, decide whether each ode helps you see the simple object or event in a new way.

LOG ON ▶ **Literature** Online

Author Search For more information about Pablo Neruda and Pat Mora, go to glencoe.com and enter QuickPass code GL39770u4.

Learning Objectives

For pages 526–532

In studying these texts, you will focus on the following objective:

Literary Study:
Analyzing poetic form and structure—ode.

Meet the Authors

Pablo Neruda

Born in Chile in 1904, Pablo Neruda described grand ideas as well as everyday objects and events in his poetry. In 1971 he won the Nobel Prize in Literature. Neruda died in 1973.

Pat Mora

Pat Mora writes poetry, children's books, and nonfiction. Mora often writes about Mexican Americans and their rich cultural traditions. She was born in 1942.

Ode to Thanks

Pablo Neruda

*Fruits of the Earth (Los frutos de la tierra), detail,
1926. Court of Fiestas, Level 3, North Wall. Diego
Rivera. Secretaria de Educacion Publica, Mexico
City, D.F., Mexico. ©Banco de Mexico Trust.
©ARS, NY.*

Thanks to the word
that says *thanks!*
Thanks to *thanks,*
word
5   that melts
iron and snow!

The world is a threatening place
until
thanks
10 makes the rounds
from one pair of lips to another,
soft as a bright
feather
and sweet as a petal of sugar,
15 filling the mouth with its sound
or else a mumbled
whisper.
Life becomes human again:
it's no longer an open window.
20 A bit of brightness
strikes into the forest,
and we can sing again beneath the leaves.
Thanks, you're the medicine we take
to save us from
25 the bite of scorn.
Your light brightens the altar of harshness.

Ode Think about the
way the speaker describes
the effect of the word
thanks. In what way is the
speaker celebrating that
simple word?

BQ BIG Question

According to the speaker,
how does *thanks* improve
society and the world?

Or maybe
a tapestry
known
30   to far distant peoples.
Travelers
fan out
into the wilds,
and in that jungle
35   of strangers,
merci°
rings out
while the hustling train
changes countries,
40   sweeping away borders,
then *spasibo*°
clinging to pointy
volcanoes, to fire and freezing cold,
or *danke*, yes! and *gracias*,° and
45   the world turns into a table:
a single word has wiped it clean,
plates and glasses gleam,
silverware tinkles,
and the tablecloth is as broad as a plain.

50   Thank you, *thanks*,
for going out and returning,
for rising up
and setting down.
We know, *thanks*,
55   that you don't fill every space—
you're only a word—
but
where your little petal
appears
60   the daggers of pride take cover,
and there's a penny's worth of smiles.

Ode What are some of the
images the speaker uses to
celebrate the word *thanks*?

---

36 *Merci* is the French word for "thanks."

41 *Spasibo* is the Russian word for "thanks."

44 *Danke* is the German word for "thanks," and *gracias* is the Spanish word for "thanks."

The Warm Rain, 1989. Rose Warnock. Oil on canvas. Private Collection.

Ode to Rain

Pat Mora

Earth blessing,
vertical river of memories,
    impetuous° refreshment,
you grace us
5   with your pine and aspen harmony.

---

3 Here, ***impetuous*** (im pech′ o͞o əs) means "rushing energetically and impulsively."

Ode What details in the first stanza express the speaker's feelings about and praise of rain?

Like a cascade of coins,
   you dance
staccato° on tin rooftops,
   cry on the windowpane
10   with a man staring
   at a fading photograph,
whisper a lullaby
   to a woman dreaming
herself, a child again
15   strutting
through a desert shower
   festooned° in damp diamonds.

   Liquid caress,
you wake hollyhocks°
20   from their parched, dusty sleep,
into the tangle of fertility.

   Silver language,
you slide and rise,
   gather and release,
25   instruct us in your circular practice
   of abundance, greening the earth.

BQ **BIG Question**

How does the speaker describe the importance of rain to the world?

---

8 **Staccato** (stə kä′ tō) describes sound that is made up of short, clear, separate tones.

17 **Festooned** means "decorated by a string of flowers, leaves, ribbons, or other decorative elements."

19 **Hollyhocks** are tall plants bearing stalks of large showy flowers and large, wrinkled, heart-shaped leaves.

After You Read

Respond and Think Critically

1. In each poem, summarize in one or two sentences the speaker's main points about ordinary acts or events such as saying "thanks" or a sudden rainstorm. [Summarize]

2. What words and phrases does Neruda use to describe the world without the word *thanks*? What is he really saying about the world and why saying *thanks* is important? [Infer]

3. Why do you think Neruda included the word *thanks* in a number of different languages? [Interpret]

4. What do you expect poems to be about? Compare and contrast your expectations of the subjects of poems with the subjects of these two poems. [Compare and Contrast]

5. Does each speaker convince you of the importance of the word or event being celebrated? Explain. [Evaluate]

6. **BQ** **BIG Question** Do you think ordinary acts and events are worth fighting for? Explain. [Synthesize]

Academic Vocabulary

Both speakers think of their subjects as being **crucial** (krōō′shəl) to society and to the world. In the preceding sentence, *crucial* means "extremely, or vitally, important." On a separate sheet of paper, use a graphic organizer like the one below to identify crucial things or ideas in your life.

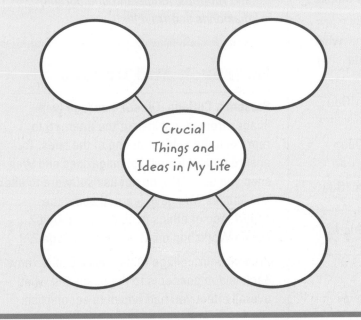

Crucial Things and Ideas in My Life

TIP

Comparing and Contrasting
Here are some tips to help you compare and contrast. Remember, when you compare and contrast, you identify similarities and differences between things. To answer the question, think about

- the subjects you expect to read about in poems and why you have these expectations

- the subjects of these two poems

- how the poems' subjects are similar to and different from the subjects you might expect

- what you might learn from examining these similarities and differences

FOLDABLES Keep track of
Study Organizer your ideas about the **BIG Question** in your unit Foldable.

 **Literature** Online

Selection Resources
For Selection Quizzes, eFlashcards, and Reading-Writing Connection activities, go to glencoe.com and enter QuickPass code GL39770u4.

1. In which ways does the first stanza of "Ode to Thanks" support the definition of ode?

2. What are some characteristics of rain celebrated by the speaker in "Ode to Rain"?

Review: Figurative Language

Figurative language is language that communicates ideas beyond the literal, or exact, meanings of words. Figurative language includes similes, metaphors, and personification. Although it appears in all kinds of writing, figurative language is especially prominent in poetry.

Similes are creative comparisons of unlike things or ideas using the words *like* or *as*. A simile points out the similarity between the two unlike things.

Metaphors are also creative comparisons of unlike things, but they do not use the clues *like* or *as.*

Personification is figurative language in which a human quality is given to an animal, object, or idea. The wind, for example, might be described as a person banging on a window.

3. In what way does the poet personify *thanks* in "Ode to Thanks"?

4. In the second stanza of "Ode to Rain," what human actions does the poet attribute to rain?

5. What are some similes for *thanks* in "Ode to Thanks"?

6. What is a simile relating to rain in "Ode to Rain"?

7. What metaphors does Neruda use in "Ode to Thanks"?

8. Does Mora use any metaphors in "Ode to Rain"? Explain.

Grammar Link

Demonstrative Adjectives
A **demonstrative adjective** describes a noun by answering the question "which one?" or "which ones?"

The demonstrative adjectives *this* and *that* are singular and describe a single object or person. For example,

> This is the book I want to read.
> That boy is smart.

The demonstrative adjectives *these* and *those* are plural and refer to more than one object or person. For example,

> Those girls play soccer.
> These socks have holes.

The demonstrative adjectives *that* and *those* refer to people, places, and objects that are at a distance. The demonstrative adjectives *this* and *these* refer to objects, places, and people that are nearby.

Practice Copy the words below. Add a demonstrative adjective in front of each word, using a different demonstrative adjective for each. Then write one sentence using each pair of words: *rain* and *rooftops, jungle* and *photograph, diamonds* and *traveler.*

Research and Report

Present a Collage Create a collage (with images from magazines or the Internet) to represent the subject of one of the odes. To ensure ethical usage, list magazines and Web sites you use. Also, do not use software to alter any images. You have learned about the importance of ethics in media in the Unit 2 Media Workshop on Media Ethics, page 229.

Present your collage to the class. Explain how each image connects to the poem and what overall effect you had hoped to accomplish.

Functional Documents

Connect to the Functional Documents

A cause or institution you strongly believe in is in need of money. What can you do to help raise funds? How about organizing a benefit concert?

Class Discussion With the rest of your class, talk about the challenges involved in staging a concert. Who would you need to talk to and what would you need to do to organize a charity concert event? What kinds of documents would you need to create or read in relation to the charity concert?

Build Background

You've read about functional documents in Unit 2, pages 199–207. On the following pages you will read four functional documents. These documents are all related to solving a problem—collecting money for a community center.

- As you read, pay special attention to text features.

- Try to understand the situation that is involved. Is the event the best way to solve the community's problem? Would you buy a ticket and attend the concert? Would you help organize the event?

Set a Purpose for Reading

Reading Skill Compare and Contrast Information

Skilled readers might **compare** and **contrast** functional or consumer documents to gain a better understanding of their purposes and the best ways to use them. As you read the four functional documents, follow these tips:

- Set a purpose. Think about what you must find out.

- Scan text features to locate the specific information that you are searching for.

- Clarify and review when you come across a question, statement, or symbol you don't understand, especially if you are filling out a form or application.

- Note the similarities and differences among these four documents in text structure, text features, purpose, and techniques for accomplishing that purpose.

Learning Objectives

For pages 533–538

In studying this text, you will focus on the following objectives:

Reading: Comparing and contrasting information.

Understanding functional documents.

Writing: Creating a poster.

Understand Event Posters

Posters, like ads, are meant to grab the attention of the audience and then persuade them of something. As you read a poster or an ad, be on the lookout for emotional appeals, such as:

- Coming to this concert will make you a happier person!
- Buying this product will make your neighbors jealous!
- Reading this magazine will make you a cool person!

EVENT POSTER

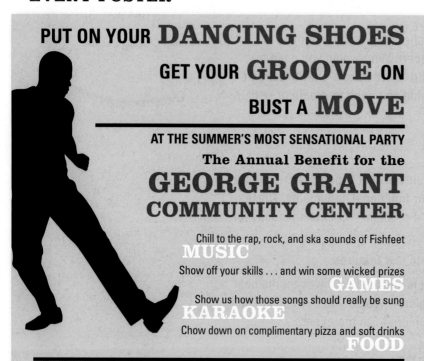

PUT ON YOUR **DANCING SHOES**

GET YOUR **GROOVE** ON

BUST A **MOVE**

AT THE SUMMER'S MOST SENSATIONAL PARTY

The Annual Benefit for the

GEORGE GRANT COMMUNITY CENTER

Chill to the rap, rock, and ska sounds of Fishfeet
MUSIC

Show off your skills . . . and win some wicked prizes
GAMES

Show us how those songs should really be sung
KARAOKE

Chow down on complimentary pizza and soft drinks
FOOD

When: Saturday, July 12 – 7:00 P.M.

Where: Quiroga Park Pavilion, 4th Street and College Drive

Why: Support the Center . . . and have a ton of fun

Admission: $10 adults, $5 students, Kids under 6 free

The George Grant Community Center serves more than 400 students a year. Students and their parents rave about our after-school activities (sports, tutoring, field trips), art and drama classes, and summer camp.

Our Annual Benefit is a vital source of revenue for the Center. When you buy a ticket, you not only help keep our programs going . . . you help hundreds in our community.

Tickets can be purchased at the George Grant Community Center, 1207 West Avery Street. Just visit the front office anytime Monday – Friday, 9:00 A.M. – 5:00 P.M. For more information, call Karen at (338) 476-1234.

DON'T MISS THE MOST KICKIN' EVENT OF THE SUMMER.

Compare and Contrast
Pay close attention to the use of text features in this poster—how headings, subheadings, art, boldface type, and lists are used. Which elements do you think are most effective?

BQ ⟩ **BIG Question**
Does this poster persuade you that the George Grant Community Center is a cause worth fighting for? Explain.

Understand Contracts

Contracts are legally binding documents that record an agreement between two parties. Contracts need to be very specific to avoid any confusion as to what precisely was promised. Anyone who signs a contract must read it very closely and be sure he or she understands everything the contract says.

BAND CONTRACT

FISHFEET
Booking Agreement

This contract, entered into on this 4th day of June, 2008, is for the musical services of "Fishfeet" (Musicians). It is for the performance described below. The Employer and the Musicians agree to the following:

1. The band "Fishfeet" will perform at the Quiroga Park Pavilion, 4th Street and College Drive.
2. There will be four Musicians in the band.
3. The performance will be at 7:00 P.M. on Saturday, July 12. The Musicians will arrive at the Quiroga Park Pavilion one hour before the performance.
4. The George Grant Community Center (Employer) agrees to pay the Musicians a total of $200. On the signing of this contract, the Employer will pay the Musicians a deposit of $50. The Employer will pay the rest of the fee at the end of the performance. Payment will be made by check.
5. The Musicians and their manager will be admitted without charge. The Musicians will also receive four free passes to the performance.
6. This contract is a complete and binding agreement between the Employer and the Musicians.

For Employer:_____ Date:_____

For Musicians:_____ Date:_____

Compare and Contrast

Contrast this document with the event poster. Are both documents intended for the same audience? How do they differ in terms of structure and features? What do you think are the most important features in each?

Understand Regulations

Why do we need regulations? Regulations, like laws, are meant to provide limits on what people can do. For example, the speed limit helps ensure that drivers don't travel at unsafe speeds, endangering themselves and others. The following document outlines what behavior is considered acceptable at the Quiroga Park Pavilion.

PAVILION REGULATIONS

QUIROGA PARK  4th Street and College Drive

Fax (338) 475-8810

Rules and Regulations

1. Reservations made on a first-come, first-served basis. A non-refundable rental fee of $50.00 and a refundable security/cleaning deposit of $50.00, payable in separate checks, are required to confirm the reservation. To make reservations, contact Darlene Royale, Village Hall, Room 105, (338) 475-8808.
2. The pavilion must be cleaned up by reserving party immediately after function is over.
3. No glass containers.
4. No loud or abusive language.
5. No alcohol allowed in park or pavilion.
6. No driving in areas other than those designated to parking. No motor vehicles in park.
7. All pets must be on a leash.
8. No fires except in barbecue pits.
9. No camping except by special permission.
10. Campers are responsible for cleaning up their camp sites before leaving park.
11. No littering.
12. No loud music (with exception of approved musical/theatrical performance).
13. Park closes at 10 P.M. unless previous arrangements are made.
14. Keys to the interior of the park are available, but are to be used for temporary access to set up or clean up.

Compare and Contrast
Which document on these pages is this one most similar to? Think about the ways in which they are similar and the ways in which they are different.

Compare and Contrast
The text structure of this document can be described as a list. Which other document has a similar text structure? In what ways does this particular text structure help you understand the park's rules and regulations?

Understand Forms and Applications

You have probably filled out forms—to get a library card or to sign up for summer camp, for example. To read this reservation form, first glance at the whole form to get an idea of which blanks you need to fill out and which you don't. Then read the form more closely. When you fill out a form you need to be careful to write all words and numbers correctly. How would you describe the function of this form?

RESERVATION FORM

QUIROGA PARK

4th Street and College Drive

Fax (338) 475-8810

Reservation Form

Date Needed: _____ Time: _____
How Many People Expected: _____
Organization: _____
Contact Person: _____
Business Phone: _____ Home Phone: _____ Cell: _____
Home Address:

_____

I have read the park rules and regulations and understand that I am responsible for cleanup. If the park is not cleaned up, I will be subject to any cost incurred by the Village to clean up the park. I am also responsible for making certain that all rules and regulations are followed. I am aware that violation of the rules and regulations could disallow future applications for reservations by me or by the organization I am representing.

Signature: _____ Date: _____

- -

Confirmation of Park
Village of Overby: _____ Date: _____

KEEP THIS FORM WITH YOU AT THE PARK.

Compare and Contrast
Which document on these pages is this one most similar to? Think about the ways in which they are similar and the ways in which they are different.

Respond and Think Critically

Read the questions about the functional documents on pages 534–537 and select the best answer.

Test Skills Practice

1. What is the main purpose of the event described on the poster?
   A. listen and dance to music
   B. eat as much as you like
   C. support the community center
   D. test your skill at various games

Test Skills Practice

2. Which condition is required of the band "Fishfeet," according to the terms of the contract?
   A. The band must have at least three members.
   B. The musicians must arrive two hours before their performance.
   C. The band must perform before it gets any fee.
   D. The band must complete its performance to receive full payment.

Test Skills Practice

3. The items in the regulations and contract are numbered
   A. because the items are placed in chronological (time) order.
   B. to organize them so the documents can be quickly and easily read.
   C. to extend the documents' overall length.
   D. to help the reader remember the items in the correct order.

4. In what ways do text features on these documents help people know what to expect at the concert? Discuss at least one text feature from each document.

5. Why is it important for the people involved to provide signatures on the contract and regulations?

6. From reading these documents, how would you explain the situation of the concert? How would you justify the presentation of the concert to collect funds?

Writing

Create a Poster Now that you've seen an example of an event poster, try creating a poster for the charity event you thought about at the beginning of the selection.

Before you create your poster, consider the following:

- Who is the audience for this particular poster?
- How do you get their attention?
- How do you persuade them to attend the event?

Literature Online

Selection Resources For Selection Quizzes, eFlashcards, and Reading-Writing Connection activities, go to glencoe.com and enter QuickPass code GL39770u4.

Part 2

Freedom and Fairness

Albert Einstein Among Other Immigrants. Ben Shahn. Community Center,
Jersey Homestead Roosevelt, NJ. Art ©Ben Shahn/Licensed by VAGA, New York, NY.

BQ ❯ **BIG Question** **What's Worth Fighting For?**

The panel from a 1930s mural features a group of immigrants, including Albert Einstein,
as they arrive in the United States. What does the mural suggest about freedom and
fairness? What sacrifices will people make to gain these ideals?

Genre Focus:
Argument and Persuasion

One purpose of informational texts can be **persuasion.** When a writer persuades, he or she tries to influence the audience to feel, think, or act in a certain way. **Argument** is a type of persuasive writing in which a writer uses logic and reason to influence the reader's ideas or actions.

Newspaper editorials as well as some essays and speeches are examples of argument and persuasion.

Literary Elements

Essay An essay is a short, formal piece of writing on a single topic. The purpose of an essay is to convey an idea or opinion. Many essays are persuasive and present arguments that are supported by reasons and facts.

Thesis The overall point the writer wants to make is the **thesis.** The writer supports the thesis with **evidence,** such as **examples, facts** (details that can be proved), and **opinions** (personal beliefs). The thesis of a persuasive piece may be written out as a statement or it may be implied—left for the reader to figure out.

Persuasive Appeals When stating a thesis, a writer may use a variety of persuasive appeals:

- **Appeal to Logic** The writer appeals to the reader's "head" through the use of reasons, facts, or other evidence that can be proved.

- **Appeal to Emotion** The writer appeals to the reader's "heart," or **emotions,** in an effort to get the reader to care about a problem.

- **Appeal to Ethics** The writer appeals to the reader's sense of justice or presents himself or herself as a person who can be trusted.

- **Appeal to Authority** The writer uses an expert's opinion to support a thesis. By doing this, the writer tries to convince the audience that if an expert agrees with the writer's opinion, the writer's opinion must be correct.

Repetition Repetition helps the audience learn and remember the information and can add a sense of rhythm to the text.

Parallelism Like repetition, **parallelism** has an impact on the audience. Parallelism is the use of a series of words, phrases, or sentences that have similar grammatical form.

TRY IT

Using graphic organizers like the ones on the next page, identify the characteristics of the essays and speeches in this unit.

Characteristics of the Genre

To gain a better understanding of argument and persuasion, study the information in the graphic organizers below.

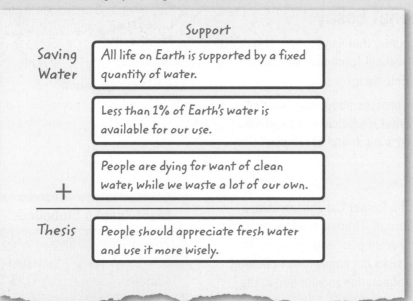

Support

Saving Water

All life on Earth is supported by a fixed quantity of water.

Less than 1% of Earth's water is available for our use.

People are dying for want of clean water, while we waste a lot of our own.

+

Thesis

People should appreciate fresh water and use it more wisely.

To evaluate the writer's argument, you may want to use a graphic organizer like the one below.

<u>Thesis:</u> People should appreciate fresh water and use it more wisely.

Supporting Evidence	Analysis
All life on Earth is supported by a fixed quantity of water.	☑ Persuasive: somewhat / very? ☑ Fully supports the thesis?
Less than 1% of Earth's water is available for our use.	☑ Persuasive: somewhat / very? ☑ Fully supports the thesis?
People are dying for want of clean water, while we waste a lot of our own.	☑ Persuasive: somewhat / very? ☑ Fully supports the thesis?

<u>Analysis of argument coherence:</u> The argument is fully supported by facts, as well as by appeals to logic and ethics to make the point that people should appreciate water and use it more wisely.

 Literature Online

Literature and Reading For more selections in this genre, go to glencoe.com and enter QuickPass code GL39770u4.

Before You Read

Escaping

Connect to the Personal Essay

The family in this essay left a country that limited their freedoms. Suppose you lived in a country without freedoms. What risks would you be willing to take to gain them?

Quickwrite Freewrite for a few minutes about why freedom is important to you. How would your life be different without freedoms such as the freedom of speech and of religion?

Build Background

Zdenko Slobodnik was born in the former Czechoslovakia, a communist country in central Europe. There were few good jobs available, and many people were poor and unhappy. In his essay, Slobodnik tells of the risks his family took in fleeing Czechoslovakia and of their determination to succeed in the United States.

- Under communism, economic conditions were poor and people had few rights. Many longed for the freedom of democracy offered by the United States.

- In 1993 Czechoslovakia split into two countries: the Czech Republic and Slovakia. Today, citizens of the Czech Republic are governed by a democratic government.

Set Purposes for Reading

BQ BIG Question

As you read "Escaping," consider why Slobodnik's family was willing to risk so much to gain freedom.

Literary Element Tone

Tone is an author's attitude toward his or her subject matter. In essays, tone can be conveyed through such elements as word choice, sentence structure, and figures of speech. *Serious, sad, bitter, gentle,* and *humorous* can describe different tones. As you read, note the author's tone at different points in his narrative.

Learning Objectives

For pages 542–546

In studying this text, you will focus on the following objective:

Literary Study:
Analyzing tone.

Meet Zdenko Slobodnik

"I remain thankful for the chance to live a wonderful life in which I have boundless opportunities."
—Zdenko Slobodnik

Living Life to the Fullest
Zdenko Slobodnik immigrated to the United States from Czechoslovakia as a child. After graduating college in 2006, he apprenticed at the Actors Theatre of Louisville. Slobodnik enjoys singing and playing the guitar. He also has a third degree black belt and is a certified instructor in Tae Kwon Do, a martial art.

Award Winner "Escaping" won an essay contest in which young people write about their values. The essay was published in *Teen Ink: What Matters* in 2002.

 Literature Online

Author Search For more about Zdenko Slobodnik, go to glencoe.com and enter QuickPass code GL39770u4.

ESCAPING

Zdenko Slobodnik

I learned about perseverance[1] when my parents decided that they wanted a better life for their children, their three-year-old son and their six-year-old daughter. We had been living in communist Czechoslovakia and were tired of the life we were living and the system.[2] At first they had doubts, as anyone might, but they would not let their children grow up as prisoners.

Leaving Czechoslovakia at that point was very difficult, however. They had to figure out a way to get to Austria, which was a free country. At first the plan was simple: They would claim I needed to see a doctor there for my ear infection. Their spirits were crushed when a border guard[3] gave their request a stern "No." As we approached a second border crossing, they hoped for a different response. However, as we sat in our car, the guard reached in, yanked out the keys and ordered my parents to turn themselves in to the police.

Feeling hopeless, they decided to take one last chance, which would be difficult. We would hike across the Alps into Austria, leaving behind everything we could not carry. It was extremely dangerous, and getting caught meant prison or even death. Yet we marched on because the freedom of America glistened[4] in our souls. As my parents saw the sign welcoming us to Austria, they knew they had succeeded.

---

1 **Perseverance** (pur´se vēr əns) means "steady determination."

2 The **system** refers to all the rules, punishments, and hardships connected to living under communist rule.

3 A **border guard** is a soldier or other official who prevents people from illegally crossing a country's border.

4 **Glistened** (glis´ənd) means "shone brightly."

> **BQ** **BIG Question**
> What does the word *prisoners* tell you about why the author's parents decided to seek freedom elsewhere?

> **Tone** Based on the phrases "Feeling hopeless" and "last chance," what is the author's attitude toward his circumstances?

A sign indicates the direction toward Austria.

Once in Austria, they found a refugee center[5] and then a hotel. We lived in this overcrowded, infested, dirty hotel for over a year. They often wondered if they had made the right decision leaving their homeland. However, once their time came to go to America and begin new, free lives, their question was answered.

Even in America, life was very hard at first. We lived in slums in Boston where my parents had to fight with the landlord to give us heat, and waking up every day was a hard realization. My parents' perseverance was strong, though, and within a few years my father had gained recertification[6] of his medical degree and my mother, foreign accent and all, finished first in her dental-assistant school.

Perseverance is a valuable law of life, imperative to reaching one's dreams. My parents had little when we lived under Communism, yet they were willing to live with nothing. Realizing that I cannot fully appreciate my parents' perseverance and indomitable[7] spirit that brought us here, I remain thankful for the chance to live a wonderful life, in which I had boundless[8] opportunities. In my parents' case, "Perseverance [made] the difference between success and defeat," and I am glad it did. ✍

Tone What tone does the list of adjectives—"overcrowded, infested, dirty"—help communicate to the reader?

BQ BIG Question
In what ways did perseverance help the Slobodniks in their struggle for freedom?

---

5 A **refugee center** offers a temporary place to stay for people who have left or been forced to leave their homes or countries.

6 The writer's father had been a doctor in Czechoslovakia. To gain **recertification** (rē sur′tə fi kā′shən), he had to pass tests to prove that he met certain standards and requirements for being a doctor in the United States.

7 **Indomitable** (in dom′ət ə bəl) means "unable to be conquered or overcome."

8 **Boundless** means "without limits."

After You Read

Respond and Think Critically

1. Explain why the author's parents wanted to leave Czechoslovakia. **[Summarize]**

2. Explain what happens the first time the family tries to escape into Austria. Why do you think they refuse to give up? **[Recall and Infer]**

3. In what way is the family's final plan for leaving the country different from their first plan? **[Compare]**

4. What challenges do the family members face on the way to the United States and during their early days there? What message do you think the author is trying to convey by recounting these challenges? **[Analyze]**

5. The author says, "Perseverance is . . . imperative to reaching one's dreams." What does this comment suggest about his attitude about his family's move to the United States? **[Interpret]**

6. **BIG Question** In your opinion, did the Slobodniks make a wise decision in risking their lives and their children's lives to gain freedom in the United States? **[Evaluate]**

Academic Vocabulary

Hoping to improve their living conditions, the Slobodniks lived **economical** lives during their first months in the United States. In the preceding sentence, *economical* means "careful in the use of money; thrifty." To become more familiar with the word *economical,* complete a graphic organizer like the one below.

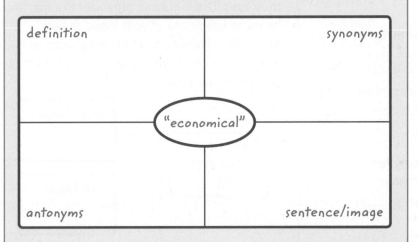

definition | synonyms

"economical"

antonyms | sentence/image

TIP

Evaluating
Here are some tips to help you evaluate. Remember that evaluating is making a judgment or forming an opinion about something you read. To evaluate,

- ask yourself what the author wants you to believe.

- look for evidence the author gives to support his or her argument.

- determine whether you think the Slobodniks made a wise decision.

FOLDABLES **Study Organizer** Keep track of your ideas about the **BIG Question** in your unit Foldable.

 Literature Online

Selection Resources
For Selection Quizzes, eFlashcards, and Reading-Writing Connection activities, go to glencoe.com and enter QuickPass code GL39770u4.

Literary Element Tone

1. Do you think the author's overall tone is appropriate to his subject matter? Explain.
2. Reread the final paragraph in the essay. How would you describe the author's tone at this point?
3. There is more than one tone present in this essay. Find two examples of tone, and use words or phrases from the text to show how the author has created each tone. Creating a graphic organizer like the one below can help you answer this question. An example has been done for you.

Tone	Examples from Text
hopeless	"spirits were crushed"

Review: **Author's Purpose**

As you learned on page 166, the **author's purpose** is why an author writes a selection. Reasons an author writes may include to entertain, persuade, inform, or describe.

Test Skills Practice

4. What are two purposes the author was trying to achieve when he wrote this selection?
   A. to entertain and amuse
   B. to persuade and inform
   C. to explain and frighten
   D. to celebrate and amuse

Grammar Link

Direct Object A **direct object** is the noun or pronoun in a sentence that receives the action of a verb. The direct object is located *after* the action verb. You can usually find it by asking *what?* or *whom?*

> The author's mother completed school in the United States.

The verb is *completed.* Then ask the question *"What* did the author's mother complete?" The answer is *school. School* is the direct object.

Practice On a separate sheet of paper, write three sentences from the selection that have direct objects. Circle each action verb and underline each direct object. Remember that some sentences may have two direct objects following a verb.

Listening and Speaking

Literature Group With a small group, discuss whether it is necessary to have difficulties in order to truly appreciate freedom and reaching one's dreams. Think of the positive and negative consequences people like Zdenko Slobodnik experience by facing obstacles in their lives. Use a graphic organizer like the one below to keep track of your ideas. In your discussion, practice good listening skills by asking each other questions and respecting each other's viewpoints.

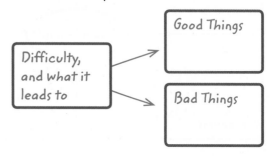

A Giant Step

Connect to the Essay

Think about a time when you made assumptions about someone based on his or her appearance and you turned out to be wrong.

Quickwrite Freewrite for a few minutes about the situation. What led you to form your assumptions? What did you learn from this experience?

Build Background

"A Giant Step" is an essay written by Henry Louis Gates Jr. that depicts a life-changing experience he had when he was 14. The experience affected Gates in more than one way.

- The major event in this essay takes place in 1964, the year in which the Civil Rights Act was passed. The act made it illegal in public places to discriminate against people based their race, color, religion, or national origin.

- Although the Civil Rights Act changed the law, it did not change many people's attitudes about race. Prejudice continued to be a problem in American society in the 1960s, and it even continues today.

Vocabulary

gait (gāt) *n.* a particular manner of walking or stepping (p. 549). *We all stopped to admire the graceful gait of the ballerina as she entered the room.*

agony (ag′ə nē) *n.* intense physical or emotional suffering (p. 550). *The pain from the accident was nothing compared with the agony of reliving that moment in his dreams.*

delinquent (di ling′kwənt) *n.* a person who repeatedly breaks laws or social codes (p. 550). *The delinquent ruined our community's mural by covering it with spray paint.*

abate (ə bāt′) *v.* to reduce in amount, degree, or intensity; to lessen (p. 551). *In a few hours, the storm will abate, and it will be safe to go outside.*

Meet Henry Louis Gates Jr.

"The society we have made simply won't survive without the values of tolerance. And cultural tolerance comes to nothing without cultural understanding."
—Henry Louis Gates Jr.

Understanding Culture Henry Louis Gates Jr. has long served as the director of the W. E. B. Du Bois Institute for African and African-American Research at Harvard University. His work explores the contributions of Africans and African Americans to literature, history, and culture.

Literary Works Gates has written many essays and books, including *Loose Canons: Notes on the Culture Wars.* "A Giant Step" was published in the *New York Times* in 1990.

Gates was born in 1950.

 Literature Online

Author Search For more about Henry Louis Gates Jr., go to glencoe.com and enter QuickPass code GL39770u4.

Purposes for Reading

[BQ] BIG Question

As you read, note the obstacles Gates overcomes that allow him to experience a greater sense of freedom.

Literary Element Theme

Theme is the main message in a literary work. It is a perception about life or human nature that the writer conveys to the reader. Sometimes themes are stated directly, but more often works have implied themes. Readers must examine a work carefully to see how its theme is revealed through important people, events, or symbols described in the text.

Theme is important because it reveals the writer's message for the reader. Often, the message suggests the way the writer views life or the way he or she thinks life should be.

As you read "A Giant Step," ask yourself how Gates's personal story helps reveal the theme of his essay.

Reading Skill Analyze Cause-and-Effect Relationships

In literature and in life, you often have to analyze **cause-and-effect relationships.** A cause is the reason behind a thought, action, or event. An effect is the result of a thought, action, or event.

Analyzing cause-and-effect relationships is important because it allows readers to understand how one event relates to another.

To analyze cause-and-effect-relationships,

- identify significant people and events in the essay
- determine the motivation for people's actions or the reasons behind events
- evaluate the consequences of people's actions or events described in the essay

As you read, ask yourself about the causes and effects of events described in the essay. You may find it helpful to use a graphic organizer like the one below to organize your thoughts. Remember that a cause may have more than one effect and an effect may have more than one cause.

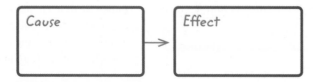

> ### TRY IT
>
> **Analyze Cause-and-Effect Relationships** Think of a game you've played or watched. Who won? What were the causes of the victory or loss?

a Giant Step

Henry Louis Gates Jr.

Man. Artist Unknown.
Oil on board.

"What's this?" the hospital janitor said to me as he stumbled over my right shoe.

"My shoes," I said.

"That's not a shoe, brother," he replied, holding it to the light.

"That's a brick."

It *did* look like a brick, sort of.

"Well, we can throw these in the trash now," he said.

"I guess so."

We had been together since 1975, those shoes and I. They were orthopedic shoes built around molds of my feet, and they had a 2¼-inch lift. I had mixed feelings about them. On the one hand, they had given me a more or less even **gait** for the first time in 10 years. On the other hand, they had marked me as a "handicapped person," complete with cane and special license plates. I went through a pair a year, but it was always the same shoe, black, wide, weighing about four pounds.

Analyze Cause-and-Effect Relationships What causes Gates's mixed feelings about his shoes?

> **Vocabulary**
>
> **gait** (gāt) *n.* a particular manner of walking or stepping

It all started 26 years ago in Piedmont, W. Va., a backwoods town of 2,000 people. While playing a game of touch football at a Methodist summer camp, I incurred a hairline fracture. Thing is, I didn't know it yet. I was 14 and had finally lost the chubbiness of my youth. I was just learning tennis and beginning to date, and who knew where that might lead?

Not too far. A few weeks later, I was returning to school from lunch when, out of the blue, the ball-and-socket joint of my hip sheared apart. It was instant **agony,** and from that time on nothing in my life would be quite the same.

I propped myself against the brick wall of the schoolhouse, where the school **delinquent** found me. He was black as slate, twice my size, mean as the day was long and beat up kids just because he could. But the look on my face told him something was seriously wrong, and—bless him—he stayed by my side for the two hours it took to get me into a taxi.

"It's a torn ligament in your knee," the surgeon said. (One of the signs of what I had—a "slipped epithysis"—is intense knee pain, I later learned.) So he scheduled me for a walking cast.

I was wheeled into surgery and placed on the operating table. As the doctor wrapped my leg with wet plaster strips, he asked about my schoolwork.

"Boy," he said, "I understand you want to be a doctor."

I said, "Yessir." Where I came from, you always said "sir" to white people, unless you were trying to make a statement.

Had I taken a lot of science courses?

"Yessir. I enjoy science."

"Are you good at it?"

"Yessir, I believe so."

"Tell me, who was the father of sterilization?"[1]

Theme Based on this event, what theme about life or human nature do you think Gates will share in this essay?

---

1 **Sterilization** is the process of removing bacteria or microorganisms.

Vocabulary

agony (ag′ə nē) *n.* intense physical or emotional suffering

delinquent (di ling′kwənt) *n.* a person who repeatedly breaks laws or social codes

"Oh, that's easy, Joseph Lister."

Then he asked who discovered penicillin.[2]

Alexander Fleming.

And what about DNA?[3]

Watson and Crick.

The interview went on like this, and I thought my answers might get me a pat on the head. Actually, they just confirmed the diagnosis he'd come to.

He stood me on my feet and insisted that I walked. When I tried, the joint ripped apart and I fell on the floor. It hurt like nothing I'd ever known.

The doctor shook his head. "Pauline," he said to my mother, his voice kindly but amused, "there's not a thing wrong with that child. The problem's psychosomatic.[4] Your son's an overachiever."

Back then, the term didn't mean what it usually means today. In Appalachia, in 1964, "overachiever" designated a sort of pathology: the overstraining of your natural capacity. A colored kid who thought he could be a doctor—just for instance—was headed for a breakdown.

What made the pain **abate** was my mother's reaction. I'd never ever heard her talk back to a white person before. And doctors, well, their words were scripture.

Not this time. Pauline Gates stared at him for a moment. "Get his clothes, pack his bags—we're going to the University Medical Center," which was 60 miles away.

Not great news: the one thing I knew was that they only moved you to the University Medical Center when you were going to die. I had three operations that year. I gave my tennis racket to the delinquent, which he probably used to club little kids with. So I wasn't going to make it to Wimbledon.[5] But at least I wasn't going to die, though

BQ ▶ **BIG Question**

Why does Mrs. Gates choose this moment to "talk back"? Think about what she is willing to fight for.

Analyze Cause-and-Effect Relationships What causes Gates to seek treatment at a different hospital? Think about the desired effect for this decision.

---

2 ***Penicillin*** is a powerful antibiotic made from mold.

3 ***DNA*** (deoxyribo nucleic acid) is an acid found in all living cells. It contains all the hereditary information that is passed from parent to child.

4 A pain that is ***psychosomatic*** is the result of emotional or mental conditions.

5 ***Wimbledon,*** England, is the site of an important annual tennis tournament.

Vocabulary ....

abate (ə bāt) *v.* to reduce in amount, degree, or intensity; to lessen

sometimes I wanted to. Following the last operation, which fitted me for a metal ball, I was confined to bed, flat on my back, immobilized by a complex system of weights and pulleys. It was six weeks of bondage—and bedpans. I spent my time reading James Baldwin,[6] learning to play chess and quarreling daily with my mother, who had rented a small room which we could ill afford—in a motel just down the hill from the hospital.

I think we both came to realize that our quarreling was a sort of ritual. We'd argue about everything—what time of day it was—but the arguments kept me from thinking about that traction system.

I limped through the next decade—through Yale and Cambridge[7] . . . as far away from Piedmont as I could get. But I couldn't escape the pain, which increased as the joint calcified and began to fuse over the next 15 years. My leg grew shorter, as the muscles atrophied and the ball of the ball-and-socket joint migrated into my pelvis. Aspirin, then Motrin, heating pads and massages, became my traveling companions.

Most frustrating was passing store windows full of fine shoes. I used to dream about walking into one of those stores and buying a pair of shoes. "Give me two pairs, one black, one cordovan," I'd say. "Wrap 'em up." No six-week wait as with the orthotics in which I was confined. These would be real shoes. Not bricks.

In the meantime, hip-joint technology progressed dramatically. But no surgeon wanted to operate on me until I was significantly older, or until the pain was so great that surgery was unavoidable. After all, a new hip would last only for 15 years, and I'd already lost too much bone. It wasn't a procedure they were sure they'd be able to repeat.

This year, my 40th, the doctors decided the time had come.

I increased my life insurance and made the plunge.

The nights before my operations are the longest nights of my life—but never long enough. Jerking awake,

Analyze Cause-and-Effect Relationships What are the short-term and long-term effects of the first doctor's wrong diagnosis?

---

6 *James Baldwin* (1924–1987) was an African-American essayist, novelist, and playwright.

7 *Yale* University is in Connecticut, and the University of *Cambridge* is in England.

grabbing for my watch, I experience a delicious sense of relief as I discover that only a minute or two have passed. You never want 6 A.M. to come.

And then the door swings open. "Good morning, Mr. Gates," the nurse says. "It's time."

The last thing I remember, just vaguely, was wondering where amnesiac[8] minutes go in one's consciousness, wondering if I experienced the pain and sounds, then forgot them, or if these were somehow blocked out, dividing the self on the operating table from the conscious self in the recovery room. I didn't like that idea very much. I was about to protest when I blinked.

"It's over, Mr. Gates," says a voice. But how could it be over? I had merely *blinked*. "You talked to us several times," the surgeon has told me, and that was the scariest part of all.

Twenty-four hours later, they get me out of bed and help me into a "walker." As they stand me on my feet, my wife bursts into tears. "Your foot is touching the ground!" I am afraid to look, but it is true: the surgeon has lengthened my leg with that gleaming titanium and chrome-cobalt alloy ball-and-socket-joint.

"You'll need new shoes," the surgeon says. "Get a pair of Dock-Sides; they have a secure grip. You'll need a ¾-inch lift in the heel, which can be as discreet as you want."

I can't help thinking about those window displays of shoes, those elegant shoes that, suddenly, I will be able to wear. Dock-Sides and sneakers, boots and loafers, sandals and **brogues.** I felt, at last, a furtive sympathy for Imelda Marcos, the queen of soles.

The next day, I walk over to the trash can, and take a long look at the brick. I don't want to seem ungracious or unappreciative. We have walked long miles together. I feel disloyal, as if I am abandoning an old friend. I take a second look.

Maybe I'll have them bronzed.[9]

Theme Many essays focus on people who overcome obstacles in their lives. What message about life is Gates sharing with readers when he says he might get his shoes bronzed?

---

8 **Amnesiac** refers to amnesia, the loss of memory.

9 When an object is **bronzed**, it is preserved by a layer of brownish-red metal made from copper and tin.

After You Read

Respond and Think Critically

1. Describe the events that led to Gates's first surgery. [Summarize]

2. Gates's injury was a defining moment in his life. Compare his life before the injury with how it changed after the injury. [Compare]

3. What does the doctor's misdiagnosis reveal about his racial attitudes? [Infer]

4. **Literary Element** Theme What is Gates's overall message about life or human nature in this essay? [Draw Conclusions]

5. **Reading Skill** Analyze Cause-and-Effect Relationships The selection begins with Gates's desire to throw out his old shoes but ends with his desire to bronze them. Given Gates's experiences, which is the more appropriate action? Why? [Make Judgments]

6. **BQ** BIG Question Gates was able to set aside the first doctor's comments and become very successful. Have you ever let someone else's criticism stop you from doing something? Explain. [Connect]

Vocabulary Practice

Choose the sentence that uses the vocabulary word correctly.

1. **A.** The horse's unusual **gait** led Martin to call the veterinarian.

   B. The coach won't be satisfied until we **gait** around the track fifty times.

2. **A.** Claire was filled with **agony** when she realized the cafeteria had run out of ranch dressing.

   B. Only sleep could relieve my **agony** after the operation.

3. **A.** The **delinquent** stole both of the twins' new bikes.

   B. My room was **delinquent**; it never stayed clean.

4. **A.** After my parents' bad moods **abate**, I'll ask them if I can spend the night at your house.

   B. When your brother teases you, he is just trying to **abate** you!

Writing

Write a Scene Imagine a situation in which a person is unfairly treated. Realistically, how might that person react? Write a scene in which you describe the setting, situation, character, and outcome.

TIP

Making Judgments
Here are some tips to help you make a judgment. Remember, when you make a judgment, you form an opinion about something you read. To answer the question, you must

- identify the important events in the essay.

- ask yourself what Gates might think of when he sees the shoes.

- make a statement based on the opinion you've formed from these details.

FOLDABLES Study Organizer Keep track of your ideas about the **BIG Question** in your unit Foldable.

 Literature Online

Selection Resources
For Selection Quizzes, eFlashcards, and Reading-Writing Connection activities, go to glencoe.com and enter QuickPass code GL39770u4.

Napa, California and Working Hands

Connect to the Poems

Think about a time when you had to do a difficult job. Did you do it because you wanted to or because it was absolutely necessary?

List With a partner, make a list of 5–10 difficult jobs. Discuss what makes each job challenging and rank the jobs from easiest to hardest.

Build Background

"Napa, California" and "Working Hands" are poems that describe jobs that are both physically demanding and low-paying.

- Sometimes, the people who do this difficult work in the United States are migrant workers from countries such as Mexico.

- Poet Ana Castillo writes about workers who harvest grapes for wine. Poet Francisco X. Alarcón writes about household help.

Set Purposes for Reading

BQ BIG Question

Read "Napa, California" and "Working Hands" to determine why many laborers feel they receive unfair treatment from the people who depend on them.

Literary Element Symbol

A **symbol** is an object, person, place, or experience that stands for something beyond itself. For example, the Statue of Liberty is not just a statue—it is a symbol of freedom and hope to many Americans and people around the world.

It is important to look for symbols in literature. Poets often use symbols to intensify the feeling or message they want to convey in their poems.

As you read, identify symbols and ask yourself what they might represent.

 Literature Online

Author Search For more about Ana Castillo and Francisco X. Alarcón, go to glencoe.com and enter QuickPass code GL39770u4.

Learning Objectives

For pages 555–560

In studying these texts, you will focus on the following objective:

Literary Study: Analyzing symbols.

Meet the Authors

Ana Castillo

Ana Castillo (kəs tē′ ō) is a poet, novelist, and educator. She says that the rich storytelling tradition of her Mexican heritage forms the basis of her writing.

Ana Castillo was born in 1953.

Francisco X. Alarcón

Poet Francisco X. Alarcón grew up in California and Mexico. He writes many of his poems in both Spanish and English.

Alarcón was born in 1954.

Napa, California

Ana Castillo

We pick
the bittersweet grapes
at harvest
one
5   by
        one
with leather worn hands
   as they pick
     at our dignity
10   and wipe our pride
      away
      like the sweat we wipe
      from our sun-beaten brows
      at midday

15 In fields
so vast
   that our youth seems
   to pass before us
   and we have grown
20   very
     very
       old
          by dusk° . . .

Symbol In what ways are "leather worn hands" symbolic of the workers' lives?

BQ BIG Question

What does the speaker think is unfair about the workers' hard labor?

---

23 **Dusk** means "twilight or evening; the end of the day as the sun is setting."

(*bueno pues, ¿qué vamos a hacer, Ambrosio?*
25 *¡bueno pues, seguirle, compadre, seguirle!*
¡Ay, Mama!
Si pues, ¿qué vamos a hacer, compadre?
¡Seguirle, Ambrosio, seguirle!)°

We pick
30 with a desire
that only survival
inspires
While the end
of each day only brings
35 a tired night
that waits for the sun
and the land
that in turn waits
for us . . .

---

28 The Spanish words mean: Well, what are we going to do, Ambrosio? / Well,
continue, my friend, continue! / Oh, Mother! / Yes, well, what else can we do,
friend? / Continue, Ambrosio, continue.

Working Hands

Francisco X. Alarcón

we clean
your room

we do
your dishes

5   a footnote
for you

but hands
like these

one day
10 will write

the main text
of this land

Symbol Hands are also used as a symbol in this poem. What struggles and hopes do hands represent to the speaker?

BQ **BIG Question**
What does the speaker suggest is a way to overcome unfair treatment?

After You Read

Respond and Think Critically

1. Describe the workday of the laborers depicted in "Napa, California." [**Summarize**]

2. Why have the workers in "Napa, California" grown "very very old" by the end of one day? [**Interpret**]

3. The speaker in "Working Hands" uses the words *we* and *you* to refer to two different groups of people. According to the speaker, how do the two groups perceive each other? [**Analyze**]

4. What can you infer about how the speaker in "Working Hands" sees the future of his or her people? [**Infer**]

5. Which of the poems do you think more powerfully uses the symbol of working hands to express the lives of laborers? Explain your answer. [**Evaluate**]

6. **BQ** **BIG Question** What makes people feel like they are being treated fairly on a job? Think of some things employers can do to make workers feel valued. [**Make Judgments**]

Academic Vocabulary

In "Napa, California" Ana Castillo describes the lives of **migrant** workers. To become more familiar with the word *migrant,* complete a graphic organizer like the one below.

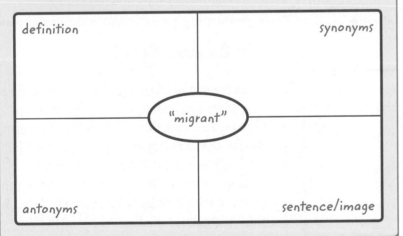

definition | synonyms

"migrant"

antonyms | sentence/image

Literary Element | Symbol

1. In what way does the symbol of the "leather worn hands" contribute to the meaning of "Napa, California"?

2. What do you think is the "main text" mentioned in "Working Hands"?

Review: Line and Stanza

As you learned on page 320, poems are often organized into **lines** (a word or series of words forming a single verse of poetry) and **stanzas** (groups of lines that form units in poetry). Lines and stanzas make the overall appearance of a poem distinctly different from most prose. Also, the use of lines and stanzas can contribute to the poem's meaning, such as when a poem whose lines appear broken or scattered resembles a hurricane's impact on a town.

3. In what ways do the couplets (short, two-line stanzas) in "Working Hands" give the poem force and feeling?

4. In "Napa, California," why do you think Castillo gives the second stanza such a distinct shape? Think about how the shape of this stanza—or the arrangement of the words on the page—increases the power of what she is writing here. Record your ideas in a chart like the one below.

Shape of Stanza	Meaning

Grammar Link

Indirect Objects An **indirect object** answers the question *to whom, for whom, to what,* or *for what,* after an action verb. In order for there to be an indirect object, there must be a direct object. For example, in the sentence "I bought a book," the word *book* is the direct object of the verb. In the sentence "I bought Ellie a book," *Ellie* is the indirect object because she is the recipient of the direct object, the book.

A common mistake in identifying the indirect object is selecting the object of a preposition. For example, in the following sentence, the pronoun *her* serves as an object of a preposition: "Bruce bought the book for her."

Practice On a sheet of paper, write two sentences that contain a main verb and a prepositional phrase starting with *for* or *to*. Then, rewrite the sentences to include an indirect object. For example, "I gave the grapes to my bosses" becomes "I gave my bosses the grapes."

Write with Style

Apply Figurative Language Think about a topic for a poem that relates to a struggle that you have experienced. Before you write your poem, choose a symbol that you can use to stand for the struggle. The symbol should make the message of the poem more powerful. Once you have chosen a symbol, write your poem. Use a graphic organizer like the one below to keep track of your ideas.

Subject:

Symbol:

Details About the Symbol:

Learning Objectives

For pages 561–563

In studying this text, you will focus on the following objectives:

Reading:
Previewing.

Recognizing bias.

Set a Purpose for Reading

Read to discover what the writer reveals about protesting something thought to be unfair.

Preview the Article

1. Read the **deck**, or text just below the title. What do you predict the answer to this question will be?

2. Look at the picture's **caption**, or words with an image. What does it tell you about the writer's conclusions?

Reading Strategy

Recognize Bias

A writer shows **bias** when he or she shows a strong personal, and sometimes unreasonable, opinion. To evaluate an article for bias, decide if the writer favors one side of a story over another. Then think about the reasons for the writer's slant as well as what information the writer may have left out because it didn't agree with his or her point of view.

TIME

TEEN CURFEWS

Are teens unfairly targeted?

By J. TODD FOSTER

When Katelyn Kimmons was 6 years old, the precocious youngster[1] announced to her family that she was "The Woman in Black" and that from then on she planned to wear nothing but black. Later, in high school, she aced chemistry but failed physical education for refusing to wear the required white socks.

With strong convictions[2] like these, Katelyn surprised no one when, at 16, she took her city to court—and brought a controversial[3] youth curfew program to a grinding halt for more than a year.

---

1 A ***precocious youngster*** is a child who displays maturity at an unusually early age.

2 Here, ***convictions*** are strong beliefs or opinions.

3 ***Controversial*** means "causing disagreement."

"Parents should bring up their kids," says Katelyn Kimmons, "not the establishment. I was brought up to stand up for myself."

Katelyn was a junior at George Washington High School in Charleston, West Virginia, when the city council passed the Youth Protection Ordinance[4] in December 1997. The ordinance stated that individuals under 18 could not be in public places after 10 P.M. on weekdays or after midnight on weekends. Officially, there were exceptions, such as for emergencies and after-school jobs—but police officers could stop anyone they thought might be violating[5] the ordinance.

Katelyn and classmates Anna Sale, then 18, and Lealah Pollock, then 15, agreed that the curfew violated their constitutional rights. With assistance from the West Virginia American Civil Liberties Union (ACLU), in March 1998 they filed a lawsuit to overturn the city ordinance, claiming it discriminates against[6] teenagers because of their age. "Kids are being unfairly targeted, scapegoated,"[7] says Lealah. "If someone commits a crime, then arrest them for that."

As the protest got under way, it churned up controversy in Charleston. Anna's parents got calls from friends and neighbors who complained about how much money the city was spending to defend itself against Anna's lawsuit. And many believed the curfew was necessary and important to make Charleston a better place by curbing delinquent behavior by juveniles.[8] "Parents tell me they can use this law to get their kids to come in at night," says Frederick Snuffer, the city council member who introduced the ordinance.

---

4 An ***ordinance*** is a law.

5 Here, ***violating*** is breaking or disregarding a law or rule.

6 Here, ***discriminates against*** means "shows prejudice against."

7 To be ***scapegoated*** is to be blamed for what someone else has done.

8 ***Curbing delinquent behavior by juveniles*** means "limiting illegal behavior by teenagers." ***Curbing*** is holding back or controlling. ***Delinquent***, as an adjective, refers to breaking the law or not following the rules. ***Juveniles***, in its general meaning, refers to all children and young people. Most states define *juveniles* as being people under 18, but the age varies from state to state.

However, Katelyn, Anna, and Lealah stood their ground,[9] and the city of Charleston decided to put the curfew on hold until a judge could rule on it. On July 15, 1998, the three teenagers walked past a crowd of reporters, supporters, and protesters to testify before the county circuit court about their lawsuit and the discriminatory effect of the city curfew ordinance. Mike Carey, a lawyer on the opposing side, grilled each of them for several minutes. "I was fired up and excited," recalls Katelyn. "It bothers me when people in authority positions treat me as if I'm not worth as much because I'm younger."

But Katelyn's enthusiasm was short-lived: Less than a year later, the court ruled against the girls and upheld the curfew law. Since then, more than 50 Charleston kids have been arrested or were issued warnings and sent home to their parents. "Why does the city have the right to overrule parents?" asks Lealah.

The girls appealed to the West Virginia Supreme Court of Appeals. In July 2000, the West Virginia Supreme Court voted 4–1 to uphold the law.

"This [perspective] bothers me," Anna says. "There's this thinking that kids are predators,[10] that we are to be feared. Of course, I want to cure society's ills, but not by creating a law that says if you're under 18, then we don't trust you."

---

9 **Stood their ground** means "kept their position and did not retreat."

10 Here, **predators** get what they want by stealing from or harming others.

Respond and Think Critically

1. Retell in your own words the teens' arguments against the curfew. [Summarize]

2. What does Lealah mean when she says that the city shouldn't have the right to "overrule" parents? [Interpret]

3. What can you infer about the city council's beliefs about how the curfew would affect disruptive behavior in Charleston's public places? [Infer]

4. **Text-to-World** What other examples can you think of in which people publicly protested something they considered unfair? [Connect]

5. Reading Strategy Recognize Bias Do you think the writer of this article shows a bias toward the teens or the adults? Explain. [Evaluate]

6. BQ BIG Question Compare those who supported Katelyn and those who opposed her. Use details from the text to explain whether each side seemed passionate about its beliefs. [Compare]

Gentleman of Río en Medio

Connect to the Short Story

Think about a time when someone was generous toward you.

Quickwrite Freewrite for a few minutes about how that person's generosity affected you and how you responded to his or her generosity.

Build Background

"Gentleman of Río en Medio" takes place in New Mexico in the early 1900s, before New Mexico became the 47th U.S. state in 1912. Río en Medio is in the mountains north of Sante Fe, the capital of New Mexico.

- Spanish colonists were the first Europeans to settle New Mexico. It was a part of New Spain and the United Mexican States until the end of the Mexican-American War in 1848.

- *Río en Medio* means "river in the middle" in Spanish.

Vocabulary

surveyor (sər vā′ ər) *n.* one whose work is to determine the shape, area, and boundaries of a region (p. 567).
The surveyor took measurements of the unexplored land.

overrunning (ō ′ vər run′ ing) *v.* swarming or spreading over or throughout (p. 568).
The weeds are overrunning the yard.

preliminary (pri lim′ ə ner′ ē) *adj.* preceding and leading up to the main event, subject, or action (p. 568).
The lawyer made a preliminary statement before beginning his closing arguments.

descendants (di sen′ dənts) *n.* people who come from a particular ancestor or group of ancestors (p. 569).
Many people claim to be descendants of royalty.

Meet Juan A. A. Sedillo

A Person of Many Roles

Juan A. A. Sedillo was born in New Mexico. His ancestors were early Spanish colonists to the Southwest. Sedillo had several careers—lawyer, judge, writer, and even actor. When he was in law school, a movie executive discovered him. In 1929, Sedillo played a Cuban detective in a movie called *The Girl from Havana.*

Turning Life Into Art

"Gentleman of Río en Medio" is based on an actual legal case. Sedillo published the short story in the *New Mexico Quarterly* in 1930.

Juan A. A. Sedillo was born in 1902 and died in 1982.

 Literature Online

Author Search For more about Juan A. A. Sedillo, go to glencoe.com and enter QuickPass code GL39770u4.

Set Purposes for Reading

BQ ▸ BIG Question

As you read, identify the major conflicts in the story and consider whether you think they were resolved fairly.

Literary Element ▸ Dialogue

In literature, **dialogue** is the conversation between characters. Dialogue is generally set off with quotation marks and dialogue tags (for example, *I said* or *He said).* In a story like "Gentleman of Río en Medio" with a first-person narrator, you need to pay special attention to these indicators. Be careful not to confuse the spoken dialogue with the narrator's internal monologue—his private thoughts and feelings.

Dialogue helps you understand the characters in a story. It reveals their personalities by conveying their spoken thoughts and feelings. Dialogue can also create a mood, advance the plot, and develop the theme.

As you read, think about how the dialogue reveals the thoughts and beliefs of the characters.

Reading Skill ▸ Analyze Conflict

You probably remember that **conflict** in a story refers to the struggle between opposing forces. An **external conflict** exists when a character fights against some outside force, such as another person, nature, or society. An **internal conflict** refers to a struggle within a character's mind.

Analyzing conflict is important because it helps you understand the relationships among the characters and the forces at work in a story. It also helps you understand the author's purpose for writing.

When you analyze conflict, you

- identify the main problem(s) faced by the character(s) in a story
- determine what types of conflict are suggested by the problem
- identify the outcome of each conflict and its importance to the story

As you read, ask yourself what the main character's internal conflict tells you about him. To determine the internal conflict, it helps to identify all the external conflicts in the story. You may find it helpful to use a graphic organizer like the one below.

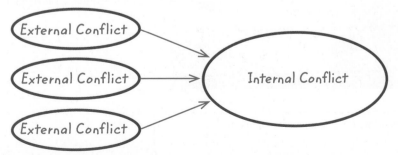

Learning Objectives

For pages 564–570

In studying this text, you will focus on the following objectives:

Literary Study: Analyzing dialogue.

Reading: Analyzing conflict.

TRY IT

Analyze Conflict With a classmate, talk about a movie you have both seen. What conflicts can you recall? Did they reflect a character's internal conflict? How were the conflicts resolved?

Gentleman of Río en Medio

Juan A. A. Sedillo

It took months of negotiation to come to an understanding with the old man. He was in no hurry. What he had the most of was time. He lived up in Río en Medio, where his people had been for hundreds of years. He tilled the same land they had tilled. His house was small and wretched, but quaint. The little creek ran through his land. His orchard was gnarled and beautiful.

The day of the sale he came into the office. His coat was old, green and faded. I thought of Senator Catron,[1] who

Farmhouse, 1914. Diego Rivera. Oil on canvas, 70 x 80 cm. Museo Dolores Olmedo Patino, Mexico City.

Analyze Conflict Who is one person involved in the conflict mentioned here? Does it sound like this conflict has been resolved? How do you know?

---

1 Thomas Benton *Catron* helped establish New Mexico as a state and later represented it in the U.S. Senate.

had been such a power with these people up there in the mountains. Perhaps it was one of his old Prince Alberts. He also wore gloves. They were old and torn and his fingertips showed through them. He carried a cane, but it was only the skeleton of a worn-out umbrella. Behind him walked one of his innumerable kin—a dark young man with eyes like a gazelle.[2]

The old man bowed to all of us in the room. Then he removed his hat and gloves, slowly and carefully. Chaplin[3] once did that in a picture, in a bank—he was the janitor. Then he handed his things to the boy, who stood obediently behind the old man's chair.

There was a great deal of conversation, about rain and about his family. He was very proud of his large family. Finally we got down to business. Yes, he would sell, as he had agreed, for twelve hundred dollars, in cash. We would buy, and the money was ready. "Don[4] Anselmo," I said to him in Spanish, "we have made a discovery. You remember that we sent that **surveyor,** that engineer, up there to survey your land so as to make the deed. Well, he finds that you own more than eight acres. He tells us that your land extends across the river and that you own almost twice as much as you thought." He didn't know that. "And now, Don Anselmo," I added, "these Americans are *buena gente,* they are good people, and they are willing to pay you for the additional land as well, at the same rate per acre, so that instead of twelve hundred dollars you will get almost twice as much, and the money is here for you."

The old man hung his head for a moment in thought. Then he stood up and stared at me. "Friend," he said, "I do

Dialogue How can you tell that the narrator's inner thoughts have stopped and his dialogue with Don Anselmo has begun?

---

2 A *gazelle* is a graceful antelope.

3 Charlie **Chaplin** was a famous English comedian. He often played characters who had no money but great dignity.

4 *Don* is the Spanish form of respectful address for a man, usually used before the first name only.

Vocabulary

surveyor (sər vā′ ər) *n.* one whose work is to determine the shape, area, and boundaries of a region

not like to have you speak to me in that manner." I kept still and let him have his say. "I know these Americans are good people, and that is why I have agreed to sell to them. But I do not care to be insulted. I have agreed to sell my house and land for twelve hundred dollars and that is the price."

I argued with him but it was useless. Finally he signed the deed and took the money but refused to take more than the amount agreed upon. Then he shook hands all around, put on his ragged gloves, took his stick and walked out with the boy behind him.

A month later my friends had moved into Río en Medio. They had replastered the old adobe[5] house, pruned the trees, patched the fence, and moved in for the summer. One day they came back to the office to complain. The children of the village were **overrunning** their property. They came every day and played under the trees, built little play fences around them, and took blossoms. When they were spoken to they only laughed and talked back good-naturedly in Spanish.

I sent a messenger up to the mountains for Don Anselmo. It took a week to arrange another meeting. When he arrived he repeated his previous **preliminary** performance. He wore the same faded cutaway, carried the same stick and was accompanied by the boy again. He shook hands all around, sat down with the boy behind his chair, and talked about the weather. Finally I broached the subject. "Don Anselmo, about the ranch you sold to these people. They are good people and want to be your friends and neighbors always. When you sold to them you signed a document, a deed, and in that deed you agreed to several things. One thing was that

Analyze Conflict What is the conflict here? How does this compare to the conflict mentioned at the start of the story?

Clovis Sagot, 1909. Pablo Picasso. Oil on canvas, 82 x 66 cm. Inv. 2986. Hamburger Kunsthalle, Hamburg. ©ARS, NY.

View the Art Does the old man in the painting resemble the image of Don Anselmo you have in your mind? Explain why or why not.

---

5 An *adobe* house is made of sun-dried bricks.

Vocabulary

overrunning (ō´vər run´ing) *v.* swarming or spreading over or throughout

preliminary (pri lim´ə ner´ē) *adj.* preceding and leading up to the main event, subject, or action

they were to have the complete possession of the property. Now, Don Anselmo, it seems that every day the children of the village overrun the orchard and spend most of their time there. We would like to know if you, as the most respected man in the village, could not stop them from doing so in order that these people may enjoy their new home more in peace."

Don Anselmo stood up. "We have all learned to love these Americans," he said, "because they are good people and good neighbors. I sold them my property because I knew they were good people, but I did not sell them the trees in the orchard."

This was bad. "Don Anselmo," I pleaded, "when one signs a deed and sells real property one sells also everything that grows on the land, and those trees, every one of them, are on the land and inside the boundaries of what you sold."

"Yes, I admit that," he said. "You know," he added, "I am the oldest man in the village. Almost everyone there is my relative and all the children of Río en Medio are my *sobrinos* and *nietos*,[6] my **descendants.** Every time a child has been born in Río en Medio since I took possession of that house from my mother I have planted a tree for that child. The trees in that orchard are not mine, *Señor*,[7] they belong to the children of the village. Every person in Río en Medio born since the railroad came to Santa Fe owns a tree in that orchard. I did not sell the trees because I could not. They are not mine."

There was nothing we could do. Legally we owned the trees but the old man had been so generous, refusing what amounted to a fortune for him. It took most of the following winter to buy the trees, individually, from the descendants of Don Anselmo in the valley of Río en Medio. 🌿

Dialogue How does Don Anselmo's answer move the plot in a new direction?

BQ **BIG Question**

Why does the narrator decide that it was not worth fighting Don Anselmo for the orchard trees?

---

6 **Sobrinos** is Spanish for "nephews and nieces." **Nietos** is Spanish for "grandchildren."

7 **Señor** means "sir" and is a polite way to address a man in Spanish.

Vocabulary

descendants (di sen′dənts) *n.* people who come from a particular ancestor or group of ancestors

After You Read

Respond and Think Critically

1. In your own words, retell the events of the first meeting between Don Anselmo and the narrator. [Paraphrase]

2. Why does Don Anselmo feel insulted by the narrator's offer of more money for his land? [Infer]

3. Early on, the narrator mentions that Don Anselmo is very proud of his large family. How does that detail hint at the story's ending? [Predict]

4. **Literary Element** Dialogue How successful do you think the dialogue is in conveying Don Anselmo's motivations? Give examples from the story. [Evaluate]

5. **Reading Skill** Analyze Conflict What conflict is caused by the trees on Don Anselmo's land? How is this conflict resolved? [Analyze]

6. **BQ** BIG Question Think about the resolution of the story's internal and external conflicts. Were the conflicts resolved fairly and to your satisfaction? Give reasons for your answer. [Connect]

Vocabulary Practice

Choose the sentence that uses the vocabulary word correctly.

1. **A.** Jackie called on a **surveyor** to keep track of her money.

   B. Jonah called on a **surveyor** to measure his property.

2. **A.** Pigeons are **overrunning** the park.

   B. Henry lost the race because he was **overrunning**.

3. **A.** The top-ranked tennis player was eliminated in a **preliminary** match.

   B. The main event is the **preliminary** one after the opening act.

4. **A.** People who explore caves are called **descendants**.

   B. My grandchildren are my **descendants**.

🖊 Writing

Write a Summary Write a summary of how the Americans ended up having to buy every tree on the land Don Anselmo sold to them. Be sure to retell the most important events and details in your own words and in a logical order. For tips on writing a summary, see page 54.

TIP

Inferring
Here are some tips to help you infer. When you infer, you use clues in the story plus your reason and experience to guess at what the author means but does not come right out and say.

- Think about the things Don Anselmo says and does.

- Look for clues about the old man in the descriptions given by the narrator.

- Use the text details and your own knowledge to guess at Don Anselmo's motivation.

FOLDABLES
Study Organizer Keep track of your ideas about the **BIG Question** in your unit Foldable.

Literature Online

Selection Resources
For Selection Quizzes, eFlashcards, and Reading-Writing Connection activities, go to glencoe.com and enter QuickPass code GL39770u4.

Comparing Literature

Harlem and *I Have a Dream*

BQ BIG Question

As you read the paired selections, ask yourself what makes something worth fighting for.

Literary Element Theme

Theme is the main message of a speech, story, poem, or play often expressed as a general statement about life. Some works have a **stated theme,** which is expressed directly. More commonly, works have an **implied theme,** which is revealed gradually through other elements such as plot, character, setting, point of view, and symbol. **Recurring themes** appear over generations in many works of literature.

Reading Skill Compare and Contrast

When you compare, you look for similarities; when you contrast, you look for differences. By comparing and contrasting a recurring theme in two pieces of writing, you deepen your understanding of both works. You also see how different writers treat a similar theme. On the following pages, you'll compare and contrast the themes of "Harlem" and "I Have a Dream."

As you read, use a graphic organizer like the one below to help make your comparison. If your answer to a question in column one is "yes," place a check mark in the column next to it. Briefly explain your answer in the "Notes" column.

Does the writer...	Harlem	I Have a Dream	Notes
repeat certain words?			
ask the reader questions?			
tell the reader to do something?			
offer a solution to a problem?			

Learning Objectives

For pages 571–581

In studying these texts, you will focus on the following objectives:

Literary Study: Analyzing theme.

Reading: Comparing and contrasting texts.

Meet the Authors

Langston Hughes

Langston Hughes is best known for his poetry. Hughes was born in 1902 and died in 1967.

Martin Luther King Jr.

Martin Luther King Jr. won the Nobel Peace Prize in 1964. King was born in 1929 and died in 1968.

 Literature Online

Author Search For more about Langston Hughes and Martin Luther King Jr., go to glencoe.com and enter QuickPass code GL39770u4.

Langston Hughes. Winold Reiss. Pastel on artist board, 76.3 x 54.9 cm. National Portrait Gallery, Washington DC.

View the Art In what ways can you compare the mood of this painting to the mood of the poem? Support your answer with details from both.

Harlem

Langston Hughes

What happens to a dream deferred?°

Does it dry up
like a raisin in the sun?
Or fester° like a sore—
5   And then run?
Does it stink like rotten meat?
Or crust and sugar over—
like a syrupy sweet?

Maybe it just sags
10   like a heavy load.

Or does it explode?

Comparing Literature What main message about dreams does this poem offer?

BQ **BIG Question**

What does Hughes suggest are the consequences of "a dream deferred"?

---

1 **Deferred** (di furd′) means "set aside or put off until a later time."

4 **Fester** (fes′ tər) means "to rot or decay."

I Have a Dream

Martin Luther King Jr.

I am happy to join with you today in what will go down in history as the greatest demonstration for freedom in the history of our nation.[1]

Fivescore years ago, a great American, in whose symbolic shadow we stand today, signed the

---

1 King gave this speech at the March for Jobs and Freedom in Washington, D.C., on August 28, 1963. The crowd was estimated at between 250,000 and 400,000 people.

Martin Luther King Jr. as he offered his "I Have a Dream" speech to onlookers at the Lincoln Memorial in Washington, D.C., on August 28, 1963.

Emancipation Proclamation. This momentous[2] decree came as a great beacon light of hope to millions of Negro slaves who had been seared in the flames of withering injustice. It came as a joyous daybreak to end the long night of their captivity.

But one hundred years later, the Negro still is not free; one hundred years later, the life of the Negro is still sadly crippled by the manacles of segregation and the chains of discrimination;[3] one hundred years later, the Negro lives on a lonely island of poverty in the midst of a vast ocean of material prosperity; one hundred years later, the Negro is still languished[4] in the corners of American society and finds himself in exile in his own land.

So we've come here today to dramatize a shameful condition. In a sense we've come to our nation's capital to cash a check. When the architects of our republic wrote the magnificent words of the Constitution and the Declaration of Independence, they were signing a promissory note[5] to which every American was to fall heir. This note was the promise that all men, yes, black men as well as white men, would be guaranteed the unalienable rights[6] of life, liberty, and the pursuit of happiness.

It is obvious today that America has defaulted[7] on this promissory note in so far as her citizens of color are concerned. Instead of honoring this sacred obligation,

Comparing Literature What is the most important word in this sentence? Explain what it tells you about the theme of this speech.

---

2 One score is twenty, so **fivescore** is one hundred. King is echoing Abraham Lincoln's Gettysburg Address, which begins with "fourscore and seven years ago." **Momentous** (mō men′təs) means "extremely important."

3 **Manacles** (man′ə kəls) are handcuffs. **Segregation** is the practice of separating people because of their race or skin color. **Discrimination** is unfair treatment, especially because of people's race or skin color.

4 King uses **languished** (lang′gwishd) to mean "suffering from neglect."

5 A **promissory note** is a written promise to pay a certain amount of money to someone at a future date.

6 **Unalienable rights,** according to the Declaration of Independence, are rights that may not be taken away.

7 **Defaulted** means "failed to do what was required."

America has given the Negro people a bad check; a check which has come back marked "insufficient funds." We refuse to believe that there are insufficient funds in the great vaults of opportunity of this nation. And so we've come to cash this check, a check that will give us upon demand the riches of freedom and the security of justice.

We have also come to this hallowed[8] spot to remind America of the fierce urgency of now. This is no time to engage in the luxury of cooling off or to take the tranquilizing drug of gradualism.[9] Now is the time to make real the promises of democracy; now is the time to rise from the dark and desolate[10] valley of segregation to the sunlit path of racial justice; now is the time to lift our nation from the quicksands of racial injustice to the solid rock of brotherhood; now is the time to make justice a reality for all God's children. It would be fatal for the nation to overlook the urgency of the moment. This sweltering summer of the Negro's legitimate discontent will not pass until there is an invigorating[11] autumn of freedom and equality.

Nineteen sixty-three is not an end, but a beginning. And those who hope that the Negro needed to blow off steam and will now be content, will have a rude awakening if the nation returns to business as usual. There will be neither rest nor tranquility in America until the Negro is granted his citizenship rights. The whirlwinds of the revolt will continue to shake the foundations of our nation until the bright day of justice emerges.

But there is something that I must say to my people, who stand on the warm threshold which leads into the

Comparing Literature
Identify the phrase that is repeated in this sentence. What does it tell you about the theme of this paragraph?

---

8   King spoke from the steps of the Lincoln Memorial, a place many people consider holy **(hallowed).**

9   **Gradualism** is the process of trying to bring about social change gradually or slowly.

10 Here **desolate** (des′ə lit) means "without joy or comfort."

11 **Sweltering** means "very hot and humid," and **invigorating** means "bringing new life and energy." King is talking about more than just seasonal changes.

palace of justice. In the process of gaining our rightful place, we must not be guilty of wrongful deeds. Let us not seek to satisfy our thirst for freedom by drinking from the cup of bitterness and hatred. We must forever conduct our struggle on the high plain of dignity and discipline. We must not allow our creative protest to generate into physical violence. Again and again we must rise to the majestic heights of meeting physical force with soul force; and the marvelous new militancy,[12] which has engulfed the Negro community, must not lead us to a distrust of all white people. For many of our white brothers, as evidenced by their presence here today, have come to realize that their

Comparing Literature What does this sentence tell you about the theme of King's speech?

---

12 **Militancy** (mil′ə tən sē) refers to being ready to fight for a cause.

At the Lincoln Memorial, the crowd listens as TV cameras capture King's speech.

destiny is tied up with our destiny. And they have come to realize that their freedom is inextricably[13] bound to our freedom. We cannot walk alone. And as we talk, we must make the pledge that we shall always march ahead. We cannot turn back.

There are those who are asking the devotees of Civil Rights, "When will you be satisfied?" We can never be satisfied as long as the Negro is the victim of the unspeakable horrors of police brutality; we can never be satisfied as long as our bodies, heavy with the fatigue of travel, cannot gain lodging in the motels of the highways and the hotels of the cities; we cannot be satisfied as long as the Negro's basic mobility is from a smaller ghetto to a larger one; we can never be satisfied as long as our children are stripped of their selfhood and robbed of their dignity by signs stating "For Whites Only"; we cannot be satisfied as long as the Negro in Mississippi cannot vote and a Negro in New York believes he has nothing for which to vote. No! no, we are not satisfied, and we will not be satisfied until "justice rolls down like waters and righteousness like a mighty stream."[14]

I am not unmindful that some of you have come here out of great trials and tribulations.[15] Some of you have come fresh from narrow jail cells. Some of you have come from areas where your quest for freedom left you battered by the storms of persecution and staggered by the winds of police brutality. You have been the veterans of creative suffering. Continue to work with the faith that unearned suffering is redemptive.[16] Go back to Mississippi. Go back to Alabama. Go back to South Carolina. Go back to Georgia. Go back to Louisiana. Go back to the slums and ghettos of our Northern cities, knowing that somehow this situation

> **Comparing Literature**
> How can you use this question to find the theme in the paragraph?

---

13 **Inextricably** (in eks′tri kə blē) means "in a way that cannot be separated."

14 This line is from the Old Testament's book of Amos.

15 A **tribulation** (trib yə lā′shən) is a great misery or distress.

16 If something is **redemptive** (ri demp′tiv), it brings rescue or freedom.

I Have a Dream. Kathleen Ritz. Watercolor.

can and will be changed. Let us not wallow[17] in the valley of despair.

I say to you today, my friends, so even though we face the difficulties of today and tomorrow, I still have a dream. It is a dream deeply rooted in the American dream. I have a dream that one day this nation will rise up and live out the true meaning of its creed, "We hold these truths to be self-evident, that all men are created equal." I have a dream that one day on the red hills of Georgia, sons of former slaves and the sons of former slave owners will be able to sit down together at the

Comparing Literature How does King's "dream" build upon points made earlier in the speech?

---

17 In this context, to *wallow* is to become or remain helpless

table of brotherhood. I have a dream that one day even the state of Mississippi, a state sweltering with the heat of injustice, sweltering with the heat of oppression, will be transformed into an oasis of freedom and justice. I have a dream that my four little children will one day live in a nation where they will not be judged by the color of their skin, but by the content of their character.

I have a dream today!

I have a dream that one day down in Alabama—with its vicious racists, with its Governor having his lips dripping with the words of interposition and nullification[18]—one day right there in Alabama, little black boys and black girls will be able to join hands with little white boys and white girls as sisters and brothers.

I have a dream today!

I have a dream that one day "every valley shall be exalted[19] and every hill and mountain shall be made low. The rough places will be made plain and the crooked places will be made straight, and the glory of the Lord shall be revealed, and all flesh shall see it together."[20]

This is our hope. This is the faith that I go back to the South with. With this faith we shall be able to transform the jangling discords[21] of our nation into a beautiful symphony of brotherhood. With this faith we will be able to work together, to pray together, to struggle together, to go to jail together, to stand up for freedom together, knowing that we will be free one day. And this will be the day. This will be the day when all of God's children will be able to sing with new meaning, "My country 'tis of thee, sweet land of liberty, of thee I sing. Land where my fathers died, land of the pilgrim's pride, from every

Comparing Literature
Review the sentence you have just read. What word or words in this sentence tell you about the overall theme of this speech?

---

18 George Wallace, Alabama's then-governor, opposed all efforts to end official segregation in his state. **Interposition** and **nullification** are legal arguments regarding a state's right to reject or refuse to enforce federal laws.

19 Something that is **exalted** is raised in status, dignity, power, or glory.

20 This passage is taken from the Old Testament's book of Isaiah.

21 **Discords** are disagreements or conflicts.

mountain side, let freedom ring." And if America is to be a great nation, this must become true.

So let freedom ring from the prodigious[22] hilltops of New Hampshire; let freedom ring from the mighty mountains of New York; let freedom ring from the heightening Alleghenies of Pennsylvania; let freedom ring from the snowcapped Rockies of Colorado; let freedom ring from the curvaceous slopes of California. But not only that. Let freedom ring from Stone Mountain of Georgia; let freedom ring from Lookout Mountain of Tennessee; let freedom ring from every hill and molehill of Mississippi. From every mountainside, let freedom ring.

And when this happens, and when we allow freedom to ring, when we let it ring from every village and every hamlet, from every state and every city; we will be able to speed up that day when all God's children, black men and white men, Jews and gentiles,[23] Protestants and Catholics, will be able to join hands and sing in the words of the old Negro spiritual: "Free at last. Free at last. Thank God Almighty, we are free at last." 🔊

---

22 Here, **prodigious** (prə dij′ əs) means "enormous."

23 People who are not Jews are referrred to as **gentiles** (jen′ tīls).

Comparing Literature

BQ BIG Question

Now use the unit Big Question to compare and contrast "Harlem"and "I Have a Dream." With a group of classmates discuss questions such as,

- What does Langston Hughes think is worth fighting for? Explain how you know.

- What does Martin Luther King Jr. think is worth fighting for? How do you know?

- In what ways does each author show a problem and a solution?

- Which work do you prefer? Provide at least three reasons for your preference. Your reasons should also show what you think is worth fighting for.

Support each answer with evidence from the readings.

Literary Element Theme

Use the details you wrote in your comparison chart to think about the recurring theme in "Harlem" by Langston Hughes and "I Have a Dream" by Martin Luther King Jr.

With a partner, answer the following questions.

1. In what ways are the themes of "Harlem"and "I Have a Dream" similar?

2. Are the themes of "Harlem"and "I Have a Dream" different in any ways? Explain.

3. What literary techniques do Langston Hughes and Martin Luther King Jr. use to make their themes memorable and clear to a listening audience?

Write to Compare

In one or two paragraphs, explain how the theme of each selection affected you personally.

- Which was a more effective form for the theme or themes—a poem or a speech?

- Describe any differences in tone and style between the two selections. In what ways did these differences affect your reaction to the theme or themes?

- Has the theme of each selection changed ways you might think, feel, or act? Explain your thoughts.

 Writing Tip

Direct Quotation As you write, use quotations, or actual words from each selection (enclosed in quotation marks), to help make your point about the themes in each work.

 Literature Online

Selection Resources
For Selection Quizzes, eFlashcards, and Reading-Writing Connection activities, go to glencoe.com and enter QuickPass code GL39770u4.

Persuasive Essay

People have always fought for freedom. What else is worth fighting for? In this workshop, you will write a persuasive essay that will help you think about the Unit 4 Big Question: What's Worth Fighting For?

Review the writing prompt, or assignment, below. Then read the Writing Plan. It will tell you what you need to do to write your essay.

Writing Assignment

In a persuasive essay you usually argue for or against something and often ask your readers to take action. Write a persuasive essay about a problem you think is worth fighting for, present your argument, and recommend specific actions your readers should take to address the problem. The audience should be your classmates and teacher.

Prewrite

What issues affecting society are tackled in this unit? What solutions are offered? For example, what problem and solution does Robert MacNeil describe in "The Trouble with Television"? What facts and opinions does he present to support his argument?

Gather Ideas

To decide on a topic, ask yourself these questions:

- What are some issues, ideas, or people that matter to me?
- What stories in the news have made me want to take a stand?
- What changes would I like to see made in my community?

Use the library or the Internet to research some of the issues you are considering. Look for both primary and secondary sources. As you take notes, separate them into facts and opinions.

Choose a Topic

Once you choose a topic, write your **thesis.** A good thesis statement should define the problem, summarize your argument, and state your solution. Use this sentence frame to help you write your thesis.

_____ is a problem because _____; and _____ is the best solution.

Group Discussion Once you have written your thesis, read it to a small group of your classmates. Ask the group for their comments.

 Prewriting Tip

Audience When you select a topic, think about its impact on your audience. Will the topic seem relevant and important to your readers? Will it affect them as much as it affects you?

Get Organized

Think about the problem you selected and its possible solutions. Using the chart below as a guide, create a list of arguments **pro** (for) and **con** (against) your solution. A strong essay will consider both sides of an argument, giving reasons and evidence supporting your position and refuting counterarguments, or objections. Next to each pro or con, write **F** if it's a fact and **O** if it's an opinion.

PROS		CONS	
Test scores increased in year-round schools.	F	Students enjoy outdoor activities more in summer.	O

Draft

Now begin writing. Use the following strategies to develop your draft.

Get It On Paper

- Using your notes and your chart, create an outline for your essay.
- Write a thesis statement that clearly explains your argument.
- Write topic sentences that support your argument. Each topic sentence will represent a paragraph in your essay. Add a sentence to address counterarguments.
- Determine how you will summarize your argument in your conclusion and what specific action you would like readers to take.
- Don't worry about spelling, grammar, or punctuation right now.
- When you're finished, look over your outline. Is your argument thorough and persuasive? Add more information if you need to.

Develop Your Draft

1. Clearly state your **argument** in the introduction to your essay.

> I believe that having school year-round will improve students' learning and make the United States more competitive with other countries.

2. Organize your evidence in order of importance.

> Year-round school would give students a chance to digest and remember what they learn more effectively than they do in the current system.

Writing and Research
For prewriting, drafting, and revising tools, go to glencoe.com and enter QuickPass code GL39770u4.

3. Address reader concerns and **counterarguments**.

> Some students might object to attending classes all year. However, there are many reasons for having year-round school.

4. Use strong, specific **language** to create a persuasive voice.

> These shorter breaks would help students to retain what they learned in one term and connect it to what they learn in the next term.

5. Conclude by **summarizing** your argument for action.

> Please write your local representatives and urge them to make year-round school a reality.

Apply Good Writing Traits: Voice

Like a person's speaking voice, an author's writing voice expresses his or her distinctive personality. The words a writer uses and how they're arranged contribute to this individual style. Read the sentences below from "The Trouble with Television" by Robert MacNeil. What does MacNeil's writing tell you about his personality and beliefs?

> Television's variety becomes a narcotic, not a stimulus.

> When before in human history has so much humanity collectively surrendered so much of its leisure to one toy, one mass diversion?

As you draft your essay, use the words you would use if you were speaking. Read your sentences aloud, asking yourself if they sound the way you do when you're speaking.

Analyze a Student Model

Students in the United States are falling behind students in the rest of the world, especially in math and science. This is a big problem because it affects the ability of the United States to compete with other countries in business, research, and technology. We need to improve our educational system. I believe that having school year-round will help students learn better and help our country compete with the rest of the world.

Year-round school would give students a chance to remember what they learn more effectively than they do in the current system. Over the summer, students forget much of what they learned, so teachers spend class time reviewing old material in the fall. With a year-round system, there would be several short breaks throughout the year, rather than a long summer break. These shorter breaks would help students to retain what they learned in one term and connect it to what they learn in the next.

Some scientists argue that students will forget as much over a short break as they do over a long one. Studies show that this isn't true. In one California school district that has been on a year-round schedule since 1976, students' test scores have increased significantly.

Students might object that they spend more than enough days in school already and don't want to give up their summers. In fact, though, year-round school wouldn't involve any additional class time. The time would just be evenly spread out over the year. The several short breaks would allow students to enjoy outdoor activities in all seasons—not just summer.

In conclusion, attending school year-round will equip students with the knowledge and skills to keep the United States competitive in our changing world. Please write your local representatives and urge them to make year-round school a reality.

Argument
Clearly state your argument in the introduction.

Organization
Begin with the most important point—in this case, year-round school will help students learn better.

Counterarguments
Anticipate and respond to counterarguments.

Precise Language
Give specific details that help readers understand the argument clearly.

Summary
Restate your argument and tell readers exactly what to do.

Reading-Writing Conventions Think about the writing techniques that you have just learned and try them out in a persuasive essay of your own.

Revise

Now it's time to revise your draft so your ideas really shine. Revising is what makes good writing great, and great writing takes work!

Peer Review Trade drafts with a partner. Use the chart below to review your partner's draft by answering the questions in the *What to do* column. Talk about your peer review after you have glanced at each other's drafts and written down the answers to the questions. Next, follow the suggestions in the *How to do it* column to revise your draft.

Revising Tip

To improve the persuasiveness of your argument, repeat or rephrase it throughout your essay. Restate your position as strongly as possible in the conclusion.

Revising Plan

What to do	How to do it	Example
Do readers learn about the issue and your position on it right away?	State your thesis clearly in the introduction.	Because students in other countries do better than U.S. students ^, I believe that having school year-round is necessary to improve our students and our country.
Does all your evidence support your main points?	Delete information that doesn't relate to your argument.	Students would be able to enjoy outdoor activities in all seasons—not just summer. ~~I particularly enjoy swimming.~~
Have you identified and answered counterarguments?	Explain why you disagree with counterarguments and give supporting evidence.	Some scientists say that students will forget as much over a short break as they do over a long one. Studies show that this isn't true. ^In one California school district that has been on a year-round schedule since 1976, students' test scores have increased significantly.
Are any words vague or unclear?	Replace weak language with specific descriptions and terms.	In fact, year-round school wouldn't ~~be any different~~ ^involve any additional class time.
Do readers know what you want them to do?	Include a clear call for action in your conclusion.	~~I hope you agree with me.~~ ^Please write your local representatives and urge them to make year-round school a reality.

Edit and Proofread

For your final draft, read your narrative one sentence at a time. The **Editing and Proofreading Checklist** inside the back cover of this book can help you spot errors. Use this resource to help you make any necessary corrections.

Grammar Focus: Parallelism

Parallelism is the use of a series of words, phrases, or sentences that have similar grammatical form. Parallel structures help create unity in writing, emphasize certain ideas, and give rhythm to the words. Below are examples of problems with parallelism and solutions from the Workshop Model.

> **Problem:** It's not clear that ideas are similar.
>
> *This affects the ability of the United States to compete with other countries in business, doing research, and technologically.*
>
> **Solution:** Use similar grammatical structures for items in a list.
>
> *This affects the ability of the United States to compete with other countries in business, research, and technology.*
>
> **Problem:** Sentences stating similar ideas are disconnected and do not flow smoothly.
>
> *These shorter breaks would help students to retain what they learned in one term. Connecting it to what they learn in the next term would be easier, too.*
>
> **Solution:** Follow the same grammatical structure to create rhythm and add emphasis.
>
> *These shorter breaks would help students to retain what they learned in one term and connect it to what they learn in the next.*

Present

It's almost time to share your writing with others. Write your essay neatly in print or cursive on a separate sheet of paper. If you have access to a computer, type your essay on the computer and check your spelling. Save your document to a disk and print it out.

Speaking, Listening, and Viewing Workshop

Persuasive Speech

Activity

Connect to Your Writing Deliver a persuasive speech to your classmates. You might want to adapt the persuasive essay you wrote for the Writing Workshop on pages 582–587. Remember that you focused on the Unit 4 Big Question: What's Worth Fighting For?

Plan Your Speech

Reread your persuasive essay and highlight the sections you want to include in your speech. Just like your persuasive essay, your speech should present a clear, well-supported argument about a problem and offer a solution, or an action you'd like the audience to take.

Rehearse Your Speech

Practice your speech several times. Try rehearsing in front of a mirror so you can watch your movements and facial expressions. You may use note cards to remind you of your main points and persuasive evidence, but practice your speech enough times so that you can maintain eye contact with your audience.

Deliver Your Speech

○ Use precise detailed language and active voice instead of passive.

○ Adjust your speaking style to help your audience distinguish between your arguments and counterarguments.

○ Change the tone and pace of your speaking to help emphasize important ideas and differentiate fact from opinion.

○ Use gestures and visual aids to direct the audience's attention to specific points and clarify your arguments.

Listen to Learn

Take notes as you listen to make sure you understand the speech. Use the following question frames to learn more about the speech from the speaker and to provide constructive feedback.

○ I suspect you may be biased in your point about _____ because _____. Can you offer more balanced evidence for that point?

○ To paraphrase the point about _____ in your speech: _____. Is that correct?

Unit Challenge

Answer the BIG Question

In Unit 4, you explored the Big Question through reading, writing, speaking, and listening. Now it's time for you to complete one of the Unit Challenges below with your answer to the Big Question.

WHAT'S Worth Fighting For?

Learning Objectives

For page 589

In this assignment, you will focus on the following objectives:

Writing:
Writing persuasive texts.

Evaluating information in text.

Use the notes you took in your Unit 4 **Foldable** to complete the Unit Challenge you have chosen.

Before you present your Unit Challenge, be sure it meets the requirements below. Use this first plan if you choose to write a proposal for a change.

On Your Own Activity: Propose a Change

❏ Brainstorm ideas for a change you'd like to make in your school or community.

❏ Choose a change that's worth fighting for. Think about what steps you and others can take to make the change happen, as well as what obstacles you may face.

❏ Make a brief outline of your ideas.

❏ Use your outline to write a proposal for this change. Be sure to explain why the change is worth making.

❏ Revise your proposal and present it to your classmates.

Use this second plan if you choose to create a mural that honors people who have fought for important causes.

Group Activity: Make a Mural

❏ With a few classmates, discuss people who took a stand for what they believed in.

❏ Make a list of the people you discussed.

❏ Conduct searches about the people on your list using both print and online materials. Make sure to compare several sources of information, including primary and secondary sources.

❏ Work together to make a mural that honors people on your list.

Independent Reading

Fiction

To explore the Big Question in other works, choose one of these books from your school or local library.

Nightjohn
by Gary Paulsen

Sarny, an enslaved girl living on the Waller plantation, tells the story of how she learned to read. Even after she is caught and severely punished, Sarny continues to pursue her studies. Her inspiration is Nightjohn, a young man who gives up his freedom and risks torture to teach other enslaved people to read. Based on true events.

Across Five Aprils
by Irene Hunt

The conflict of the Civil War reaches the Creightons' farming community. Jethro Creighton, too young to enlist, must face the tensions within his family, his community, and his own soul as his brothers choose opposing sides in the war.

GLENCOE LITERATURE LIBRARY

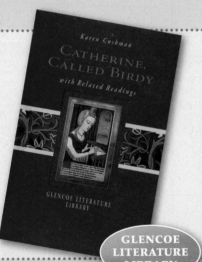

Catherine, Called Birdy
by Karen Cushman

Written in diary form, this book tells the story of Catherine, a rebellious young girl living in thirteenth-century England. Her father is determined to marry off his free-spirited daughter to any wealthy suitor who will have her, but Catherine wants nothing to do with any of them. Using her wit and sharp tongue, she manages to keep her suitors at bay, while sharing with readers the details of life in England in 1290.

GLENCOE LITERATURE LIBRARY

Animal Farm
by George Orwell

In *Animal Farm,* animals work to set up a free society, only to be oppressed by a select group of animals. Read to see how deception can make you confused about what is worth fighting for.

Nonfiction

The Great Hispanic Heritage: César Chávez

by Hal Marcovitz

The Great Depression affected many farm families in the Southwest. César Chávez was ten when his family lost their farm in Arizona and left to find jobs in California. As migrant workers, the family moved often from farm to farm across the state. Chávez's experience in the fields led to a lifetime of fighting for the fair treatment of migrant workers.

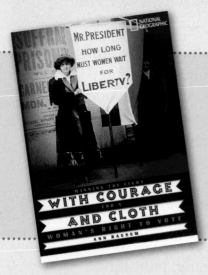

With Courage and Cloth: Winning the Fight for a Woman's Right to Vote

by Ann Bausum

From 1906 to 1920, a new and contentious group of suffragists emerged. Ann Bausum takes a close look at the women of the National Woman's Party and at others who shaped the fight for women's right to vote. Read Bausum's book to learn more about the people—passionate, determined, and utterly fearless—who paid a high price for equality.

Remember: The Journey to School Integration

by Toni Morrison

This powerful blend of photography and narrative tells about the fight of African Americans for integrated schooling. Packed with facts and photos, Morrison's book is also a tribute to those who risked, and lost, so that others could enjoy a more equal society. Read to learn more about those individuals—and about the courage and conviction that won the fight for integration.

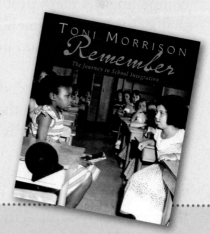

Write a Review

Write a book review for your classmates. Be sure to explain what you found interesting, unusual, exciting, or even annoying in the book. Include specific examples and descriptive details to support your ideas.

Assessment

Reading

Read the passage and answer the questions. Write your answers on a separate sheet of paper.

from **"I Chose Schooling"** by Jacqueline Nwaiwu

The author was born in Nigeria and came to the United States as a teenager. Here she describes an incident that occurred during her freshman year in high school.

Over the course of the year, every student in my homeroom chose either to take school seriously or to slack off. In homeroom, cliques started to form. The slackers sat on one side of the room, while the studious, grade-conscious students sat on the other side. Students on the slacker side of the room constantly yelled and were rowdy, while the students on the grade-conscious side of the room were busy trying to study or complete homework.

One day, I came into homeroom and sat in my designated spot: the studious, grade-conscious side of the room. The morning announcements were blaring while I frantically tried to complete my homework. I was completing my math problems when suddenly the bell rang, indicating that it was time for first hour. I ignored it and continued to finish the problems due that hour. Before I knew it, the second bell rang and I was late for math class.

I quickly jammed my books in my bag and ran out of my fourth-floor homeroom. I ran down the hall and up the stairs to the fifth floor. When I got to the fifth floor, I was blocked by a group of African American girls. The five rowdy girls stood in the entrance of the stairwell. I was so agitated. I wanted to push the girls out of my way so I could get to class. But instead, I maneuvered through the crowd. As I was doing that, one of the girls loudly said, "Who do she think she is anyway, huh?" The group of girls roared with laughter. Another girl said, "Ya'll leave her alone. She trying to get her an edgamacation." And with that, everyone laughed even more. I turned around and looked at them, but said nothing. I simply walked to my math class humiliated.

At that moment, I strongly regretted running down the halls like some geek. I strongly regretted not saying something to them. I strongly regretted having the intense desire to go to my math class and do well in school. It was as if the girls were saying, "Who do she think she is, huh? A black girl trying to be white. An oreo black on the outside but white on the inside. Do she think she betta than us? She betta not, 'cause she ain't. School ain't that important for her to be running like that to some class. Some black girls don't know their race. Education ain't all that important. I'd rather clown wit my homies than run to class actin' like I'm white tryin' ta git an education."

"Who she think she is anyway, huh?" I was furious. What exactly did she mean by that! I was only trying to get to class. Excuse me if school means a little more to me than "hangin' out wit da homies." I couldn't believe I gave those girls so much power that they were able to ruin my day.

The next day, I went to homeroom. I mentioned the story to Meg, the girl with spiky, blue hair. Meg said, "Forget them. School is more important than trying to fit into some popular clique. Look at me. I have blue hair. I try not to fit into groups who don't accept me for me. School is much more important. Don't waste your energy on ignorant people."

Right as she said that, everything was clear. I didn't have to waste my energy on them. I chose schooling over socializing. I chose to study for tests instead of "gossiping over someone's baby's mamma." I selected education over ignorance. I am not any less black; I am just being me. I preferred work over play, homework instead of fitting into a crowd where I don't belong. I chose schooling. I wish those girls would know that we **all** can strive for greatness. That doing well in school isn't just for some races of people, or for nerds, but for **everyone.** Getting an education is the key that unlocks many opportunities.

When looking back at the experience I had with those girls, I thank God every day. That particular experience reaffirmed my goal, which was to attain a sound education. I thank God for giving me the initiative to select the right path, despite all odds.

LOG ON ▶ **Literature** Online

Assessment For additional test practice, go to glencoe.com and enter QuickPass code GL39770u4.

1. Which statement best identifies the thesis of this essay?

   A. People can be cruel to each other.
   B. Race is the cause of many conflicts.
   C. The high school years can be very difficult.
   D. Education is more important than popularity.

2. The author's tone can best be described as

   A. sad.
   B. serious.
   C. sarcastic.
   D. humorous.

3. Which quotation from the essay is a statement of opinion?

   A. "School is much more important."
   B. "The next day, I went to homeroom."
   C. "The group of girls roared with laughter."
   D. "But instead, I maneuvered through the crowd."

4. Read these sentences.

   At that moment, I strongly regretted running down the halls like some geek. I strongly regretted not saying something to them.

   In these sentences, the author uses

   A. evidence.
   B. metaphor.
   C. parallelism.
   D. symbolism.

5. In this essay, Meg's spiky, blue hair can be seen as a symbol of

   A. helpfulness.
   B. intelligence.
   C. individuality.
   D. dislike of school.

6. The passage suggests that the most important similarity between Meg and the author is a similarity in their

   A. clothes.
   B. goals.
   C. appearance.
   D. backgrounds.

7. How does the author organize this essay?

   A. She presents the steps involved in a process.
   B. She presents a situation and then describes its causes and effects.
   C. She describes a situation, giving details from least important to most important.
   D. She describes a problem and then describes how her realizations and choices solved it.

Extended Answer

8. How do you think the author's experiences in school will affect her life in the future? Base your response on evidence from the text and your own knowledge.

Vocabulary Skills

On a separate sheet of paper, write the numbers 1–14. Next to each number, write the letter of the word or phrase that is closest in meaning to the underlined word.

1. bide a while
   - A. sleep
   - B. wander
   - C. stay
   - D. forget

2. a young delinquent
   - A. lawbreaker
   - B. honor student
   - C. police officer
   - D. athlete

3. a king's descendants
   - A. jewels
   - B. duties
   - C. guards
   - D. offspring

4. to endure hard times
   - A. hate
   - B. describe
   - C. enjoy
   - D. live through

5. known to be a scoundrel
   - A. specialist
   - B. scholar
   - C. bad person
   - D. foolish person

6. an unusual gait
   - A. age
   - B. height
   - C. color
   - D. way of moving

7. overrunning the country
   - A. visiting
   - B. ruining
   - C. invading
   - D. managing

8. to behave nobly
   - A. like a coward
   - B. like a crook
   - C. like a hero
   - D. like a baby

9. a vile taste
   - A. sweet
   - B. disgusting
   - C. spicy
   - D. satisfying

10. to abate the noise
    - A. listen to
    - B. object to
    - C. increase
    - D. decrease

11. some preliminary thoughts
    - A. introductory
    - B. interesting
    - C. final
    - D. unhappy

12. to perish in the snow
    - A. play
    - B. die
    - C. search
    - D. tunnel

13. the agony of the family members
    - A. joy
    - B. confusion
    - C. pain
    - D. relief

14. to resolve to be good
    - A. desire
    - B. try
    - C. fail
    - D. decide

Writing Strategies

The following is part of a student's personal essay. It contains errors. Read the passage. Then answer the questions on a separate sheet of paper.

---

(1) I hated this school at first. (2) To begin with, I didn't know nobody. (3) Arriving that first day, nothing was familiar. (4) I walked all over, looking for the principal in my dumb uniform. (5) Then, some kids gave me directions to the gym instead of the cafeteria. (6) I'd like to see them kids try to do that to me again! (7) I'm not worried about being tricked by other students these days. (8) It isn't never a problem for me anymore.

1. Read sentence 2.

   To begin with, I didn't know nobody.

   Which revision of this sentence corrects a double negative?

   A. To begin with, I didn't know no one.
   B. To begin with, I never knew nobody.
   C. To begin with, I didn't know anybody.
   D. To begin with, nobody didn't know me.

2. Read sentence 4.

   I walked all over, looking for the principal in my dumb uniform.

   Which is the best revision of this sentence?

   A. Walking all over, I looked for the principal in my dumb uniform.
   B. I walked all over in my dumb uniform, looking for the principal.
   C. I walked all over and looked for the principal in my dumb uniform.
   D. Looking for the principal in my dumb uniform, I walked all over.

3. Which sentence contains a dangling modifier?

   A. sentence 2
   B. sentence 3
   C. sentence 5
   D. sentence 6

4. Which phrase from the essay contains an incorrect demonstrative article?

   A. this school
   B. that first day
   C. them kids
   D. these days

5. Read sentence 8 from the essay.

   It isn't never a problem for me anymore.

   Which revision of this sentence fails to correct a double negative?

   A. It isn't a problem for me anymore.
   B. It is never a problem for me anymore.
   C. It isn't ever no problem for me anymore.
   D. It is not ever a problem for me anymore.

Writing Product

Read the assignment in the box below and follow the directions. Use one piece of paper to jot down ideas and organize your thoughts. Then neatly write your essay on another sheet. You may not use a dictionary or other reference materials.

Writing Situation:

The principal of your school has asked for suggestions about ways to improve the atmosphere at your school.

Directions for Writing:

Think about a change that would improve the quality of your school experience. Now write to persuade your principal that the change you propose is worth considering.

Keep these hints in mind when you write.

- Focus on what the directions tell you to write.
- Organize the way you will present your ideas.
- Provide good, clear support for your ideas.
- Use different kinds of sentence structures.
- Use precise words that express your ideas clearly.
- Check your essay for mistakes in spelling, grammar, and punctuation.

WHAT
Really Matters?

THE **BIG** Question

> "*Let us be grateful to people who make us happy.*"
>
> —MARCEL PROUST

FOLDABLES®
Study Organizer

Unit 5: Big Question
What Really Matters?

Reading Selection
Title

Throughout Unit 5, you will read, write, and talk about the **BIG** Question— "What Really Matters?" Use your Unit 5 **Foldable**, shown here, to keep track of your ideas as you read. Turn to the back of this book for instructions on making this **Foldable**.

WHAT
Really Matters?

How can you decide what really matters in life? Are personal connections, like family, most important to you, or are you more concerned with an important issue or cause? The quotation on page 599 reminds you to be grateful to people who make you happy. Is that what matters most to you? How do you decide what's important? Explore what really matters to you.

Think about what really matters through three perspectives:

- Personal Connections
- Social Issues
- Scientific Matters

What You'll Read

Reading about other people's lives can help you explore what really matters to you. In this unit, **biographies** and **autobiographies**—stories of real people's lives—are excellent sources for learning about what really matters to people. You will also read short stories, poetry, and other texts that can lead you to discover answers to the Big Question.

What You'll Write

As you explore the Big Question, you'll write notes in your Unit **Foldable**. Later, you'll use these notes to complete two writing assignments related to the Big Question.

1. **Write a Research Report**
2. **Choose a Unit Challenge**
   - **On Your Own Activity: Choose a Spokesperson**
   - **Group Activity: Create a Newsletter**

What You'll Learn

Literary Elements

voice

elegy

free verse

biography and autobiography

description

simile and metaphor

repetition

irony

foreshadowing

tone

Reading Skills and Strategies

analyze mood

preview

analyze cultural context

interpret author's meaning

connect to personal experience

activate prior knowledge

analyze tone

evaluate argument

interpret figurative language

analyze text structure

make inferences about characters

compare and contrast

from

The Book Of
ROCK STARS

Kathleen Krull

Bob Marley (b. 1945–d. 1981)

Few rock stars have national holidays in their honor. On the beautiful but poor Caribbean island of Jamaica, February 6 is National Bob Marley Day.

> **Set a Purpose for Reading**
>
> Read this excerpt from *The Book of Rock Stars* to discover what really mattered to Bob Marley.

He was born into rural poverty and left home at fourteen to pursue music in the big city of Kingston. Three years later, he recorded his first single, called "Judge Not." With a catchy Jamaican rock beat—reggae—his fierce songs gave voice to the day-to-day struggles of oppressed[1] people.

He teamed up with childhood friends and fellow singers to form a dynamic new reggae band, the Wailers. Members included Bunny Livingstone and Peter Tosh, as well as Rita Anderson, whom he later married. Marley was the hypnotic[2] lead singer, and audiences couldn't stop dancing. The music was infused[3] with devout spirituality, social commentary, and encouragement to rebel. Plus it was pure fun. With tunes like "Stir It Up" and "No Woman, No Cry," Bob Marley and the Wailers could do no wrong in Jamaica.

When their song "I Shot the Sheriff" became a hit for Eric Clapton, reggae went global. As the first Third World[4] superstar, Marley introduced Jamaican music to the world and laid the groundwork for much to follow.

Pulsing hits flowed—"Jamming," "Waiting in Vain," "One Love/People Get Ready," and "Is This Love?" They were wildly popular, not just in Jamaica, but also Africa, Great Britain, and Scandinavia. Yet the band made so little in royalties[5] that Marley once worked in a factory for a year to support his family.

His last haircut was in 1968. After that his hair stayed in dreadlocks, as part of the Rastafari faith, the Jamaican religion that was the keystone of his life.

As famous a rock star as Marley was outside Jamaica, those at home saw him as almost godlike. On political and religious issues, ordinary Jamaicans hung on his

BQ BIG Question

Bob Marley was born into rural poverty. In what ways do you think this might have affected the topics of his music?

BQ BIG Question

Besides the welfare of the Jamaican poor, what other things mattered to Bob Marley? How can you tell?

---

1 People who are **oppressed** are controlled or governed by the cruel and unjust use of force or authority.

2 A **hypnotic** singer is one who holds the complete attention of the audience.

3 Here, **infused** means "filled."

4 The **Third World** consists of relatively poor, developing countries.

5 Many artists and writers are paid **royalties.** These are fees paid to the artist each time his or her work is sold or used.

every word. He became such a national hero that some in power even took him as a threat. In 1976 he was wounded in an assassination attempt and had to leave Jamaica for his safety.

Five years later, while jogging in New York's Central Park, he collapsed. Doctors discovered that he had advanced cancer. He released his final album, *Uprising*, and died at age thirty-six. Fans went into shock at the premature[6] loss of the freedom-fighting entertainer.

---

6 A **premature** loss is one that occurs unexpectedly and too soon.

After You Read

Respond and Think Critically

1. Use your own words to briefly restate the most important events of Bob Marley's life. [Summarize]

2. Why do you think Bob Marley's music became so popular? [Interpret]

3. Think about why Bob Marley left Jamaica. What does this suggest about the effects of fame for Marley? [Infer]

4. What can you conclude about Bob Marley's character after reading this short biography? [Conclude]

Writing

Write a Letter Write a one-page letter that you could send to a music magazine in tribute to Bob Marley. What would you say? Think about what mattered to Marley and how he showed it. Think about what you learned in this short biography and also about what the readers of the music magazine would find interesting. If you enjoyed the way Kathleen Krull wrote about Marley, try to write in a style similar to hers. You may want to begin your letter with this sentence:

"I admire Bob Marley because the things that really mattered to him were _____."

Before you write, think about what matters to you. Did reading about Bob Marley's life influence your thinking about what really matters? Express your thoughts in your letter.

Be sure your letter includes the following:
- the date
- a salutation, such as "Dear Publisher of _____ magazine,"
- an introductory paragraph
- a body paragraph or paragraphs
- a concluding paragraph
- a closing, such as "Yours truly,"
- your signature

Learning Objectives

For page 604

In studying this text, you will focus on the following objectives:

Literary Study:
Analyzing and evaluating biography.

Connecting to contemporary issues.

Writing:
Writing a letter.

 Literature Online

Unit Resources For additional skills practice, go to glencoe.com and enter QuickPass code GL39770u5.

Personal Connections

Summer Party. Anna Mary Robertson Moses (Grandma Moses). Oil on masonite, 65.4 x 45.4 cm.
Museum of Fine Arts, Houston, TX. Wintermann Collection, Gift of Mr. & Mrs. D. R. Wintermann.

BQ **BIG Question** **What Really Matters?**

Why do you think the people in the painting *Summer Party* link arms to form a chain?
How does having fun with your friends or family help build personal connections?

Clean Sweep

Connect to the Short Story

Think about how organized you are—your room, your desk, your backpack.

Partner Talk With a partner, discuss ways to organize your life more effectively by getting rid of clutter. Where would you start? What would you keep and what would you throw away? How might these changes affect your life?

Build Background

"Clean Sweep" features one character who may suffer from hypochondria (hī´pə kon´drē ə)—a condition characterized by worrying too much about one's health.

- A hypochondriac may be convinced that he or she is ill even without any physical signs of illness, or he or she may exaggerate the minor aches and pains.

- In Greek, *hypo* means "under" and *chondros* means "cartilage or breastbone." This refers to an ancient belief that the abdomen was the seat of deep sadness.

Vocabulary

eliminating (i lim´ə nā´ting) *v.* getting rid of, disposing of (p. 609). *Tanya is eliminating her bad habits, such as interrupting people.*

dingy (din´jē) *adj.* not bright and fresh; discolored, dull (p. 611). *The room looked dingy even after we scrubbed the walls.*

inhumane (in´hū mān´) *adj.* not feeling or showing kindness, pity, or compassion for other human beings or animals (p. 613). *Gerard has lost friends because of his recent inhumane behavior.*

turmoil (tur´moil) *n.* state or condition of confused agitation or commotion (p. 616). *The classroom was in a turmoil until the principal walked in.*

Meet Joan Bauer

"Laughter is a gift we've been given as human beings, not just to make us feel good, but to empower us to overcome dark times."

—Joan Bauer

Drawing on Loss The divorce of her parents and resulting loss of her father pained eight-year-old Joan Bauer deeply. When she began writing fiction, Bauer drew upon these experiences in exploring serious issues with a humorous touch.

Literary Works Bauer has won many awards for her young adult novels, including the Newbery Honor Award for *Hope Was Here.*

Joan Bauer was born in 1951.

 Literature Online

Author Search For more about Joan Bauer, go to glencoe.com and enter QuickPass code GL39770u5.

Set Purposes for Reading

BQ BIG Question

As you read, ask yourself, what really matters to the main characters in this story?

Literary Element Flashback

A **flashback** is an interruption in a chronological narrative. It presents readers with scenes from events that occurred before that point in the story or before the story began.

Flashbacks are important because they can provide background reasons for plot developments or reveal elements of a character's personality. Flashbacks often increase the reader's interest and motivate the reader to continue reading the story.

As you read "Clean Sweep," identify the flashbacks and think about their effects on the story.

Reading Skill Analyze Diction

Diction is an author's choice of words and how those words are arranged in phrases or sentences. The diction in a story can convey character traits and create different moods.

Analyzing a story's diction is important because it helps the reader understand how the author's word choice creates distinct impressions of the characters' personalities, feelings, and experiences.

To analyze diction in a story,

- look for words that form a clear impression in your mind about what the characters are like
- think about the particular feeling or meaning the words convey and why
- draw conclusions based on the words and the meanings they convey

As you read, jot down revealing words or phrases, who said them, and a conclusion you can draw from each of those words or phrases. You may find it helpful to use a chart like the one below.

Word or Phrase	Who Said It?	Conclusion
ten gazillion times its size	Katie	Katie sounds young, and she exaggerates.

Learning Objectives

For pages 606–621

In studying this text, you will focus on the following objectives:

Literary Study: Analyzing flashback.

Reading: Analyzing diction.

TRY IT

Analyze Diction How is the description of a character as "thin" and "ugly" different than a description of the same character as "slender" and "plain"? Explain.

Clean Sweep

Joan Bauer

"Have you ever seen a **dust mite**?"

My mother always lowers her voice when she asks this; it adds to the emotional impact. Never in the five years since she's had the cleaning business has anyone ever said they've seen one. That's because the only people who have seen dust mites are scientists who put dust balls on slides and look at them under microscopes. Personally I have better things to do than look at minuscule[1] animals who cause great torture among the allergic, but my mother has a photo of a dust mite blown up to ten gazillion times its size—she is holding it up now, as she always does in this part of her presentation—and the two women who sit on the floral couch before her gasp appropriately and shut their eyes, because dust mites, trust me, are ugly. Think *Invasion of the Body Snatchers* meets *The Hunchback of Notre Dame*, and you're just beginning to enter into the vileness[2] of this creature.

"They're everywhere," Mom says to the women. "Under the bed, on the sheets, clinging to the blinds; hiding, waiting. And at Clean Sweep," she offers quietly, but dramatically, "we *kill* them for you. We hate them even more than you do. *This* is why we're in business."

The two women look at each other and say *yes*, they want the cleaning service to start immediately.

Mom tells them our price. One woman, as expected, says, "That sounds a little high." People are so cheap. Everyone wants quality, no one wants to pay for it. Here's

1 **Minuscule** (min'ə skūl) means "very small."

2 In the movie *Invasion of the Body Snatchers*, pod-like aliens use long tendrils to clone people. In *The Hunchback of Notre Dame*, the main character has a large hump on his back. Here, **vileness** means "disgusting quality."

Visual Vocabulary

A **dust mite** is a tiny insect that causes or irritates allergies and other respiratory illnesses.

Analyze Diction

What words in this passage help you understand the mother's sales strategy?

the suburban dream—to hire great workers who are so meek that they don't have the guts to ask for a living wage.

This is not my mother's problem. She holds up the dust mite enlargement to make the point. "We cost more because we know where he and his army are hiding."

She used to say "we know where he and his friends are hiding," but "army" sounds more fierce, and when you are serious about **eliminating** dust, you'd better let everyone know it's war.

"Well . . . ," the other woman says, unsure.

Mom presses in. "We suggest two cleanings per week for one month to achieve total elimination. Then weekly cleanings should do, unless you have special needs."

Special needs in the cleaning world range from cleaning out attics to detoxification[3] of teenage bedrooms. I am a specialist in cleaning rooms of kids who have just gone off to college. It takes nerves of steel. And I have them.

My brother Benjamin doesn't. To begin with, he's allergic to dust— bad news when the family business is dedicated to eliminating it. To end with, he's a devoted underachiever, in stark contrast to myself. And Benjamin knows how to get out of work—he could give seminars on this. He gets the perfect look of abject[4] pain over his face, says he's not feeling too well, he's sorry, he doesn't want to be a *burden*. He talks about the pain moving across his back, down his leg, and into his ankle.

---

3 **Detoxification** (dē tok′sə fi kā′shən) is the process of removing a poison.

4 **Abject** means "utterly miserable."

Vocabulary

eliminating (i lim′ə nā′ting) *v.* getting rid of, disposing of

Auntie. Bernard Fleetwood-Walker. Royal Academy of Arts, London.

Then he gets dizzy and has to sit down; lying down comes moments later after his face gets a little pale (I don't know how he does this) and his hand touches his forehead which, I swear, has small drops of sweat on it. Then he'll try to get up and help, but by this time, you feel like such a snake that a sick person is going to get sicker because of your insensitive demands that you say, no, you rest, I'll do it.

This is what he's done to me today, and I'm not in the mood for the game. He tells me, groaning, he'll *try* to make it to Mrs. Leonardo's today to help her pack up her attic, but he's not sure he can even sit. He's lying on the couch in misery saying if he can sit, he will try to stand, and if he attempts standing, he will attempt actual walking—Mrs. Leonardo's house being four houses down the street. I throw my book bag at him. Suggest he *crawl* to Mrs. Leonardo's house and he says, "Thanks, Katie. Just thanks." To which I reply, "Look, Benny Boy, I'm getting sick of carrying your weight around here. If you think I'm going to do your job and mine until I die, think again." Benjamin groans deep, turns off the light, closes his eyes and says his headache is cosmic and could I please go get him some aspirin.

I don't get the aspirin. It's a big bad world out there and he needs to find it out now, at fourteen. This is what big sisters are for.

So I'm basically crabby and bitter all day; taking it out on random people. After school I have mounds of homework. You wonder what teachers are thinking—I have three hundred pages of reading in three textbooks plus a paper due on Friday. Have you ever noticed that it takes a textbook dozens of pages to say what normal people can cover fast?

Example:

What was the full impact of World War II?

Clear-cut teenage answer: We won.

So I'm close to dying young from excessive homework, and I have to help Mrs. Leonardo clean out her attic. She is paying big bucks for this, and, believe me, my family needs the money.

Mrs. Leonardo wants people there on time and working like ants. Ants carry their weight on their backs and are thrilled as anything to be abused. But that is the insect world; I am not one of them. I'm not in the mood to sit with her in her **dingy** attic and lug tons of garbage down the stairs and listen to her stories of how her family deserted her. I know that sounds mean, but Mrs. Leonardo is a mean person. It's easy to see why she's alone. The big joke is that when her husband died, he had a big smile on his face in the casket that he'd never had in real life. The

Analyze Diction What do Katie's words reveal about her personality?

Flashback In what way does this reference to the past support Katie's opinion about Mrs. Leonardo?

Vocabulary
....

dingy (din′ jē) *adj.* not bright and fresh; discolored, dull

funeral director said they tried to wipe that grin off his face, but they couldn't do it.

So I'm on my knees in the dust, putting things in bags, while Mrs. Leonardo tells me about her selfish brother Horace who deserted her, and her uncaring, money-grubbing cousin Cynthia who backed out of the driveway eight years ago and never came back. She tells me how she helped them and loaned them money which they never paid back. She's going on and on about how the world is a dark, dark place. I clear my throat: "Boy, Mrs. Leonardo, you've got a lot of stuff up here. Are you sure you want to keep it all?"

This is the wrong thing to say. Mrs. Leonardo's gray eyes get spitting mad and she says, *well*, she's seventy-six years old and she's had a *very* interesting life and she doesn't want to throw out anything of value. I look in a box with IRS tax forms dating back to 1955.

"Mrs. Leonardo, the IRS says you only need to keep tax records from the last three years. We could dump this whole box . . ." My mother told me this.

She lunges as much as a seventy-six-year-old person can and says she isn't giving her tax records to anyone so they can steal her secrets. Like tons of thieves are out there ready to pounce on this.

But at twenty-five dollars per hour, you learn to be patient. "Think of the money," my mother always says, "and the graciousness will come." So I'm taping the box and writing IMPORTANT PAPERS 1955–1963. Maybe she could turn this attic into a museum and people could walk through and learn all the things you should never hold on to.

Benjamin would have cracked under this pressure. Mrs. Leonardo is kneeling by a huge trunk, saying how the younger generation (mine) doesn't understand about manners, propriety, or simple human decency. Her grandniece, Veronica, walks around half naked with her belly button showing. She pulls old clothes out of the trunk and yanks this old lace tablecloth out and just looks at it. Finally, she says she got it when she was married and she's only used it once. She waited for a special occasion and only one came—her twentieth anniversary. No other

What words emphasize Katie's impression of Mrs. Leonardo's emotional state?

occasion was special enough, and then her husband died right before their twenty-fifth anniversary and the tablecloth has been in this trunk ever since—only used once, she keeps saying—beautiful Egyptian linen. She looks kind of sad, though stiff. I say, "You could start using it now, Mrs. Leonardo," which is the wrong thing to say. She shuts that trunk and asks me just who do I think she's going to invite to dinner since everyone she's ever done anything for has either deserted her or died.

I don't know how to answer a question like this. My mother didn't cover it during Clean Sweep boot camp training where I learned how to scour a bathtub that a toddler spilled ink in, how to clean pet stains from any carpet known to man, how to wash windows and not leave streaks, how to open a refrigerator with year-old meat and not gag in front of the client. I pledged that the customer was always right and I, the lowly dust eliminator, was always, always wrong.

But I'm not sure what to do. If I agree with her, I'm not helping, and if I listen, I won't get the job done. The truth is, I don't like Mrs. Leonardo—so there's a big part of me that doesn't care—even though I know this is probably **inhumane** because she's a sad person, really. Kneeling there in the dust, surrounded by the boxes of her so-called interesting life, going on and on about people who are gone. I'm thinking about the next stage of the job—the actual cleaning of the attic which is going to take two people, and I know Benjamin will be hurled into monumental physical aberrations[5] up here.

I'm tired, too, and my paper is late on King Lear who, in my opinion, thought too much and couldn't deliver. I'm thinking about my personal life—yes, dust eliminators have them. We have feelings; we have needs, dreams. I'm feeling that I work too much and I wish my mom had another business because what I do all day at school is

Analyze Diction What do Mrs. Leonardo's words reveal about her outlook on life?

---

5 **Aberrations** are differences from normal behavior.

Vocabulary ....

inhumane (in´ hū mān´) *adj.* not feeling or showing kindness, pity, or compassion for other human beings or animals

exhausting enough without having to do heavy lifting after school and on the weekends. I think about when my dad died four years ago, and because of disorganization—that is, getting behind on paying his life insurance premiums—his insurance policy was cancelled and we got no insurance money when he died. He never meant to hurt us, but it was so scary not knowing if we could keep the house mixed with all the pain of losing him. We never got a regular time of mourning because we were fighting to stay afloat. Mom was trying to sort through Dad's huge piles of papers. We loved him so much, but he could never get rid of what Mom called his "clutter demons."

It took several months, but we got his papers sorted. We learned firsthand how you get organized, clean up, and obliterate dust. We became total aces at it; learned how widespread the problem truly is. We knew then we needed to share what we'd learned with others who were suffering, and felt that twenty-five dollars an hour was reasonable.

I'm not sure if Mrs. Leonardo wants someone to help or someone to complain to. Between you and me, I feel that listening to complaining *and* busting dust should earn thirty-five dollars per hour. But, I'm remembering being in our attic after my dad died; trying to go through his things. He had a trunk that his grandfather had given him—inside were all his photos and papers from school. I remember reading some of his essays from high school and just crying. I couldn't throw those out. Mom said going through all that was therapeutic[6] for me because it was like being with him, kind of. He was forty-one years old when he died. Had a heart attack at work and was dead by the time the ambulance came.

Just thinking about the day makes me shaky. Over the years I've dissected every last thing I remember about the last morning I saw him. I should have made him breakfast—I knew how much he liked it when I did. I should have hugged him when he went out the door, but I was on the phone with Roger Rugsby who was my biology partner who needed me to go over my lab notes or

Analyze Diction What impression of Katie's father do you get from the term "clutter demons"? Explain.

Flashback In what way does this flashback change your understanding of Katie and her family? Explain.

6 Here, *therapeutic* (ther´ ə pū´ tik) means healing.

he would fail. I missed the bus and Dad missed his train and he took me to school. I was late, so I hurled myself out of the car and he said, "Go get 'em, kiddo." That's the last thing he ever said to me. But I did better than Benjamin who overslept and didn't even see Dad that morning.

Mrs. Leonardo leans over a trunk like the one my father had. I want to say something encouraging to her, like, "Gee, Mrs. Leonardo, I know how hard it must be going through all these memories," or, "I hope sorting through all this is helping you the way it helped me." Memories are the only things we have left sometimes. You can hold a photo of a person you loved who's gone, but it isn't alive. Memories—the best ones—are filled with sights, smells, love, and happiness. I try to hold some of those in my heart for my dad each day.

She goes through the trunk, stony-faced. I can't tell what she's found, can't tell if she's going to torch the contents or hold them to her heart. I lug a big bag over and throw old newspapers inside. Mrs. Leonardo stops going through the trunk. She's holding something in her hands, not moving. I look at her stiff face and for a moment in the weird light of the attic, she looks like she's going to cry. But that's impossible. Then I hear a sniff and she says softly, "My mother read this book to my sister and me every night before bed."

I look at the book—a well-worn brown leather cover. Doesn't look like much.

"I thought she had it," Mrs. Leonardo says sadly.

"Who had it?"

"My sister, Helen. I thought she had the book. She always wanted it."

In these situations it's best to say, "Oh."

"I thought . . . I thought I'd sent it to her after Mother died." She looks down.

I say, "It's hard to remember what you've done after someone important dies."

"But, she'd asked me for it. It was the one thing she'd wanted."

"Well . . ."

Analyze Diction What words or phrases in this paragraph make the greatest impression on you? Think about what these words or phrases tell you about the characters.

"I haven't talked to her since Mother died. I thought she . . ."

I'm not sure how to ask this. Is Helen still alive?

I dance around it. "What do you think you should do with the book, Mrs. Leonardo?" She doesn't answer.

I try again. "Why did Helen want it so bad?"

She hands me the book. "She said these stories were her best memories of childhood." I look through it. "The Naughty Frog," "The Little Lost Tulip," "Spanky, the Black Sheep." It's amazing what we put up with as children. But then I remember my favorite bedtime story—"Rupert, the Church Mouse"—about this little mouse who lives in a church and polishes all the **stained glass** windows every night before he goes to sleep so the light can come forth every morning.

"I know she lives in Vermont," Mrs. Leonardo offers. "I heard from a cousin a while ago . . ." Her voice trails off.

"I think you should call her, Mrs. Leonardo."

She shakes her old head. No—she couldn't possibly.

"I think you should call her and tell her you've got the book."

She glares at me. "I believe we're done for today." She grabs the book from my hands, puts it back in the trunk.

"Sorry, ma'am. I didn't mean . . ."

She heads down the attic stairs.

I tell Benjamin that I don't want to hear about his problems, that his back looks strong to me, the shooting pain in his leg will go away eventually, and his headache is just a reflection of his deep, inner **turmoil**. I say this as we're walking to Mrs. Leonardo's house.

"I think my whole left side is going numb," he whispers pitifully as we walk up her steps.

"Deal with it."

Mrs. Leonardo is waiting for us. We're late. I don't mention that having to drag a hypochondriac four doors down the street takes time. Great food smells swirl from her kitchen.

Mrs. Leonardo looks Benjamin up and down, not impressed. "You've not been here before," she says. Benjamin half smiles and rubs his tennis elbow, which makes me nuts because he doesn't play tennis.

I introduce them. Tell her Benjamin is here to help with dust elimination and heavy lifting, at which point Benjamin leans painfully against the wall and closes his eyes.

"He's a very dedicated worker once he gets started, Mrs. Leonardo."

I jam my elbow into his side.

Okay, so we're cleaning this cavernous attic like there's no tomorrow. We've got all the trunks and boxes wiped down and pushed to the far side. We're running the turbo-charged Clean Sweep Frankenstein portable vacuum that is so powerful it can suck up pets and small children if they get too close. Benjamin is wearing a dust mask over his nose and mouth—he wrote *The Terminator* over it. This boy is appropriately miserable, pulling down spiders' webs, sucking up dust mites. I can almost hear their little screams of terror. Almost, but not quite. My mother claims she can hear dust mites shrieking for mercy and uses this in her presentation if she thinks potential clients can handle it.

"Get the lace tablecloth from the trunk!" Mrs. Leonardo shouts from downstairs.

What's she want with that?

"And bring the book, too," she hollers impatiently.

I don't mention that we've shoved everything in the corner like she said to, that I'll have to move it all to get to the trunk, and, by the way, I'm going as fast as I can. I get the book and the lace tablecloth that's been folded in very old plastic. I look at the book—reddish brown leather— *Aunt Goody's Good Night Stories*, it's called. Benjamin comes over looking like some kind of cosmic alien with his mask, takes the book, starts laughing.

"The Naughty Little Frog," he says reading. "Once upon a time there was a naughty little frog named Edmond. Edmond was so naughty that he never, ever cleaned his

Analyze Diction In what way does Katie's description of cleaning the attic affect your understanding of her attitude and behavior?

Guests are Expected, 1981.
Olga N. Ludevig. Private Collection,
Photo ©Bonhams, London.

lily pad. It got so dirty that his mother had to make him
stay on that lily pad several times each day to—"

"You're going to have to wait for the end." I yank the
book from his hands and head down the creaky attic stairs
with the tablecloth. Mrs. Leonardo is in the kitchen
wearing a frilly[7] apron, stirring a pot of something that
smells beyond great.

She turns to look at me, puts her wooden spoon down.

"Help me put it on the table," she orders.

I'm smiling a little now because I know this tablecloth's
history. I'm wondering who's coming to dinner.

"Looks like you're having a party," I offer as we get the
tablecloth squared perfectly on the table.

Mrs. Leonardo says nothing, sets the table for two with
what looks like the good silverware, the good napkins.

Analyze Diction What is
the effect of the word
beyond in this description?

---

7 A *frilly* apron would have a strip of ribbon, lace, or border attached on one side.

Then she puts the storybook in front of one of the place settings.

"My sister, you see . . ." She pauses emotionally. "Well, she's . . . coming to dinner."

"You mean the one you haven't seen for a long time?"

"I only have *one* sister."

I'm just grinning now and I tell her I hope they have the best dinner in the world.

"Well, I do too." She looks nervously out the window and says whatever work we haven't finished can be done tomorrow. "You were right about . . . calling her, Katie."

I smile brightly, wondering if she's going to offer me some of her great-smelling food to show her gratitude. She doesn't. I head up the attic stairs and drag Benjamin to safety. He's sneezing like he's going to die. I take off his Terminator dust mask and lean him against a wall. Half of me wants to give Mrs. Leonardo a little hug of encouragement, but the other half warns, *Don't touch clients because they can turn on you.*

"Whatever you're cooking, Mrs. Leonardo, it sure smells good," I shout. "Your sister's going to love it." I'm not sure she hears all of that. Benjamin is into his fifth sneezing attack.

She nods from the kitchen; I push Benjamin out on the street.

"I could have died up there," he shouts, blowing his nose.

"But you didn't."

And I remember the book my dad would read to us when we were little about the baby animals and their parents and how each mother and father animal kissed their babies good night. That book was chewed to death, ripped, stained, and missing the last two pages, but I wouldn't give it up for anything.

We walk back home almost silently, except for Benjamin's sniffs, sneezes, and groans. People just don't understand what important things can be hiding in the dust.

Mom says that all the time in her presentation. 🐾

BQ **BIG Question**

What do Katie's feelings about the book reveal about what really matters to her?

After You Read

Respond and Think Critically

1. Use your own words to summarize the story from Katie's point of view. [Summarize]

2. In what ways is Mrs. Leonardo's reason for keeping the tablecloth similar to and different from Katie's reason for keeping the book her father read to her? [Compare]

3. Besides "removing dirt," what is another possible meaning for the title "Clean Sweep"? [Interpret]

4. The story includes a flashback of Katie's last morning with her father. In what way do you think Katie's memories of this day affect her advice to Mrs. Leonardo? Explain. [Infer]

5. Think about Katie's thoughts, words, and actions throughout the story. Do you think the author is successful in making Katie a believable teenage character? Cite examples to support your opinion. [Evaluate]

6. **BQ** BIG Question What really matters to Katie? Support your answers with details from the story. [Draw Conclusions]

TIP

Evaluating
Here are some tips to help you evaluate. Remember, when you evaluate, you make a judgment or form an opinion about something you have read.

- Skim the selection to review Katie's words, thoughts, and actions.

- Think about what you know about how teenagers talk and behave.

- Decide if Katie is a believable teenager.

 FOLDABLES Study Organizer Keep track of your ideas about the **BIG Question** in your unit Foldable.

View the Art

Memories and Keepsakes

The French artist Pierre-Auguste Renoir painted this picture of two girls at a piano.

Young Girls at the Piano, 1892. Pierre-Auguste Renoir. Oil on canvas. 116 x 90 cm. Musée d'Orsay, Paris.

Group Activity Discuss the following questions with classmates.

1. The painting depicts a happy childhood moment. In what ways are Katie's and Mrs. Leonardo's childhood memories similar to the scene pictured?

2. Both Katie and Mrs. Leonardo have sentimental objects, or keepsakes, from their past. What might be a keepsake for either girl in the painting when she becomes an adult? Explain.

3. In what ways does Katie seem different from the girls in the painting?

Literary Element Flashback

1. What important information do Katie's flashbacks provide the reader?

2. In what ways would the story be different without the information from these flashbacks? Explain.

Review: Characterization

As you learned on page 355, **characterization** is made up of the methods a writer uses to develop the personality of a character. In **direct characterization,** the story's narrator makes statements about a character's personality. In **indirect characterization,** a character's personality is gradually revealed through his or her words, thoughts, and actions and through what others think and say about the character.

3. Katie is the narrator in the story. Though she makes some direct comments about her own personality, readers mainly learn about her through indirect characterization. How would you describe Katie's personality? Support your answer with details from the story. Note whether the details are revealed through Katie's words, thoughts, actions, or other people's reactions to her.

4. Find three examples of direct characterization that the narrator uses to describe Mrs. Leonardo's personality.

Reading Skill Analyze Diction

5. What words or phrases in the story make Benjamin seem like a hypochondriac? Cite at least two examples.

6. Write down a word or phrase from the story that made a powerful impression on you. Then use that word in a sentence about your own life.

Vocabulary Practice

Match each vocabulary word in the left column with a word from the right column that has the same meaning. Two of the words in the right column will not have matches. Then write a sentence using each vocabulary word or draw or find a picture that represents each word.

1. eliminating
2. dingy
3. inhumane
4. turmoil

a. cruel
b. requiring
c. confusion
d. unsuspecting
e. erasing
f. dull

Academic Vocabulary

Katie's mother helps her clients **visualize** dust mites. In the preceding sentence, *visualize* means "to form a mental image of." Choose a place that you could help someone visualize. Think about details that make the place unique. What words would you use to help people visualize the place you chose?

Place	Details

Respond Through Writing

Autobiographical Narrative

Apply Characterization In "Clean Sweep," Katie reminisces about her father and characterizes him both directly and indirectly. Write an essay about an important person in your life. Use both direct and indirect methods of characterization to describe this person, a happy memory you had with him or her, and the role this person has played in your life.

Understand the Task Characterization can be direct or indirect. For example, when Katie describes her father as being disorganized, it is direct characterization because she comments directly on his personality. An example of indirect characterization is when Katie says that her father's last words to her were, "Go get 'em, kiddo." Readers must infer from these words that he was a supportive father.

Prewrite Keep track of your ideas about the important person in your life in an outline like the one below. The memory you describe should be an incident or event that reveals the person's traits that you admire most. Use direct and indirect methods of characterization to describe this person's words, actions, and influence on you.

> I. Introduction
>   A. Important person and his/her role in my life
> II. Happy Memory with Person
>   A. Direct Characterization
>   1.
>   2.
>   B. Indirect Characterization
>   1.
>   2.
> III. Conclusion

Draft As you draft, keep an overall plan in mind. For example, you may decide to write an introduction, a paragraph about the happy memory using each type of characterization, and then a conclusion.

Revise After you have written your first draft, read it to determine whether the paragraphs are in logical order. Rearrange text as necessary so that your ideas are easy to follow. Then exchange your essay with a peer and offer each other suggestions for improvement.

Edit and Proofread Proofread your paper, correcting any errors in spelling, grammar, and punctuation. Review the Grammar Tip and look for opportunities to add dashes to your essay.

Learning Objectives

For page 622

In this assignment, you will focus on the following objective:

Writing: Writing an autobiographical narrative, using the writing process.

> **Grammar Tip**
>
> **Dashes**
> Notice the use of dashes in the sentence below. Why are they used?
>
> *[T]hen her husband died right before their twenty-fifth anniversary and the tablecloth has been in this trunk ever since—only used once, she keeps saying—beautiful Egyptian linen.*
>
> "Only used once, she keeps saying" interrupts the sentence with information that is not essential to the sentence's meaning. When a long explanatory phrase or sudden break in thought occurs, writers can use dashes before and after the interruption for greater clarity.

Before You Read

The Night Ghost

Connect to the Autobiography

"The Night Ghost" recounts a scary episode in Gary Paulsen's life. Think about a time when you were frightened by something strange or mysterious.

Partner Talk With a partner, talk about when you were frightened. What scared you? How did you deal with your fear?

Build Background

"The Night Ghost" is a passage from Gary Paulsen's autobiography, *Woodsong*. Most of the book is an account of Paulsen's experience running the Iditarod, a challenging dogsled race held every year in Alaska.

- The course is more than a thousand miles from Anchorage to Nome. Portions of it follow the old Iditarod Trail dogsled mail route used in the early 1900s.

- It takes a team of 12 to 16 dogs and a musher, or sled driver, who is capable of overcoming all the obstacles and unexpected problems that present themselves along the course.

- Usually the teams finish the race in ten days or less. Most of the participants endure the hardships of the race because of the beauty of the harsh landscape experienced with just a team of dogs for company.

Vocabulary

sustain (sə stān′) *v.* keep going; keep in existence (p. 625).
There are not enough customers to sustain Mrs. Olsen's business.

internal (in turn′əl) *adj.* of, relating to, or existing on the inside (p. 626).
Internal organs include the heart, lungs, and liver.

ebbed (ebd) *v.* became less or weaker; declined (p. 627).
The boxer's strength ebbed in the final round.

diffused (di fūzd′) *v.* spread widely; dispersed (p. 628).
The breadcrumbs she threw on the water diffused and then disappeared.

Meet Gary Paulsen

"I want my . . . years on this ball of earth to mean something. Writing furnishes me a way for that to happen."

—Gary Paulsen

Writer and Adventurer

Despite a difficult childhood, Paulsen developed a passion for reading after a librarian gave him a book to read and his own library card. As an adult, Paulsen had many jobs before he discovered his love of writing. Paulsen weaves his life adventures into exciting books about survival.

Literary Works Paulsen has written more than 175 books and more than 200 articles and stories for children and adults, including *Dogsong* and *Hatchet*. "The Night Ghost" was first published in *Woodsong* in 1990.

Gary Paulsen was born in 1939.

 Literature Online

Author Search For more about Gary Paulsen, go to glencoe.com and enter QuickPass code GL39770u5.

Set Purposes for Reading

BQ **BIG Question**

Read "The Night Ghost" to find out what really matters to Gary Paulsen when he takes his dog team on a spooky, late-night ride.

Literary Element Voice

Voice is the distinctive use of language that conveys the author's or narrator's personality to the reader. Voice is determined by elements of style, such as word choice and tone.

Voice is important because it grabs the reader's attention and helps the reader connect to the text.

As you read "The Night Ghost," think about the effect Paulsen's voice has on you.

Reading Skill Analyze Mood

Mood is the emotional effect a text has on its reader. An author's choice of subject matter and setting contributes to mood. When you analyze mood, you look carefully at these elements to see how they work together to create the atmosphere of the text.

Analyzing the mood of a text is important because it will help you identify the emotions and atmosphere the text evokes and gain better insight into the author's purpose for writing.

As you read, here are some clues to help you analyze mood:

- Pause to think about how the text makes you feel.

- Identify the author's choice of subject matter, words, and setting (when and where the story takes place).

- Determine how those elements work together to create the atmosphere of the autobiography.

As you read, use these clues to analyze mood in the story. You may find it helpful to use a graphic organizer like the one below to organize your thoughts.

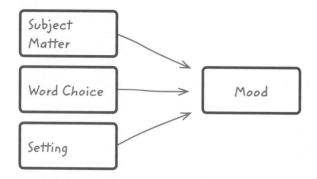

Learning Objectives

For pages 623–629

In studying this text, you will focus on the following objectives:

Literary Study:
Analyzing voice.

Reading:
Analyzing mood.

TRY IT

Analyze Mood Write a short journal entry about an experience you had watching a movie or television show that was especially funny, scary, or dramatic. When you have finished writing, look at the elements you used to convey the emotions you experienced. Were you successful in creating a specific mood?

Bäume Trees, 1883. Erich Heckel. Watercolor. Stadel Institute of Arts, Frankfurt.

The Night Ghost

Gary Paulsen

There are night ghosts.

Some people say that we can understand all things if we can know them, but there came a dark night in the fall when I thought that was wrong, and so did the dogs.

We had been running all morning and were tired; some of the dogs were young and could not **sustain** a long run. So we stopped in the middle of the afternoon when they seemed to want to rest. I made a fire, set up a gentle, peaceful camp, and went to sleep for four hours.

It hadn't snowed yet so we had been running with a three-wheel cart, which meant we had to run on logging roads and open areas. I had been hard pressed to find new country to run in to keep the young dogs from becoming bored and this logging trail was one we hadn't

Vocabulary

sustain (sə stān´) v. keep going; keep in existence

run. It had been rough going, with a lot of **ruts** and mud and the cart was a mess so I spent some time fixing it after I awakened, carving off the dried mud. The end result was we didn't get going again until close to one in the morning. This did not pose a problem except that as soon as I hooked the dogs up and got them lined out—I was running an eight-dog team—my head lamp went out. I replaced the bulb and tried a new battery, but that didn't help—the **internal** wiring was bad. I thought briefly of sleeping again until daylight but the dogs were slamming into the harnesses, screaming to run, so I shrugged and jumped on the rig[1] and untied it. Certainly, I thought, running without a head lamp would not be the worst thing I had ever done.

Immediately we blew into the darkness and the ride was madness. Without a lamp I could not tell when the rig was going to hit a rut or a puddle. It was cloudy and fairly warm—close to fifty—and had rained the night before. Without the moon or even starlight I had no idea where the puddles were until they splashed me—largely in the face—so I was soon dripping wet. Coupled with that, tree limbs I couldn't see hit at me as we passed, almost tearing me off the back of the rig. Inside an hour I wasn't sure if I was up, down, or sideways.

And the dogs stopped.

They weren't tired, not even a little, judging by the way they had been ripping through the night, but they stopped dead.

I had just taken a limb in the face and was temporarily blinded. All I knew was that they had stopped suddenly and that I had to jam down on the brakes to keep from running over them. It took me a couple of seconds to clear my eyes and when I did, I saw the light.

In the first seconds I thought it was another person coming toward me. The light had an eerie green-yellow glow. It was quite bright and filled a whole part of the

---

1 Here, *rig* is used informally and refers to the cart with its dogs.

Visual Vocabulary

A **rut** is a groove or track in the ground made by a wheel or by continuous wear.

Analyze Mood Identify the mood expressed in this paragraph. In what way does Paulsen's choice of words help create this mood?

Voice Compare Paulsen's voice, or personality, in this paragraph and the previous paragraph. In what way is it different?

dark night ahead, down the trail. It seemed to be moving. I was in deep woods, and couldn't think what a person would be doing there—there are no other teams where I train—but I was glad to see the light.

At first.

Then I realized the light was strange. It glowed and **ebbed** and seemed to fill too much space to be a regular light source. It was low to the ground, and wide.

I was still not frightened, and would probably not have become frightened except that the dogs suddenly started to sing.

I have already talked about some of their songs. Rain songs and first-snow songs and meat songs and come-back-and-stay-with-us songs and even puppy-training songs, but I had heard this song only once, when an old dog had died in the kennel. It was a death song.

And that frightened me.

They all sat. I could see them quite well in the glow from the light—the soft glow, the green glow, the ghost glow. It crept into my thinking without my knowing it: the ghost glow. Against my wishes I started thinking of all the things in my life that had scared me.

Ghosts and goblins and dark nights and snakes under the bed and sounds I didn't know and bodies I had found and graveyards under covered pale moons and death, death, death . . .

And they sang and sang. The cold song in the strange light. For a time I could do nothing but stand on the back of the wheeled rig and stare at the light with old, dusty terror.

But curiosity was stronger. My legs moved without my wanting them to move and my body followed them, alongside the team in the dark, holding to each dog like a security blanket until I reached the next one, moving closer to the light until I was at the front and there were no more dogs to hold.

The light had gotten brighter, seemed to pulse and flood

Voice In what ways does the author's voice here relate to the songs of the dogs that he has just mentioned?

back and forth, but I still could not see the source. I took another step, then another, trying to look around the corner, deeply feeling the distance from the dogs, the aloneness.

Two more steps, then one more, leaning to see around the corner and at last I saw it and when I did it was worse.

It was a form. Not human. A large, standing form glowing in the dark. The light came from within it, a cold-glowing green light with yellow edges that **diffused** the shape, making it change and grow as I watched.

I felt my heart slam up into my throat.

I couldn't move. I stared at the upright form and was sure it was a ghost, a being from the dead sent for me. I could not move and might not have ever moved except that the dogs had followed me, pulling the rig quietly until they were around my legs, peering ahead, and I looked down at them and had to laugh.

They were caught in the green light, curved around my legs staring at the standing form, ears cocked and heads turned sideways while they studied it. I took another short step forward and they all followed me, then another, and they stayed with me until we were right next to the form.

It was a stump.

A six-foot-tall, old rotten stump with the bark knocked off, glowing in the dark with a bright green glow. Impossible. I stood there with the dogs around my legs, smelling the stump and touching it with their noses. I found out later that it glowed because it had sucked phosphorus[2] from the ground up into the wood and held the light from day all night.

But that was later. There in the night I did not know this. Touching the stump, and feeling the cold light, I could not quite get rid of the fear until a black-and-white dog named Fonzie came up, smelled the stump, snorted, and peed on it.

So much for ghosts.

BQ ⟩ **BIG Question**
What details does Paulsen give that tell you his dogs really matter to him?

Analyze Mood In what way do details about setting alter the mood of Paulsen's story? Consider why the author might want a different mood at the conclusion.

---

2 **Phosphorus** is a poisonous, waxy substance that glows in the dark.

Vocabulary . . . .

diffused (di fūzd´) v. spread widely; dispersed

After You Read

Respond and Think Critically

1. In your own words, retell the events of Paulsen's strange encounter. [Summarize]

2. Why does Paulsen risk driving his cart in the dark? [Interpret]

3. After reading "The Night Ghost," do you think that the author believes in ghosts? Give reasons why or why not. [Infer]

4. **Literary Element** Voice Is Paulsen's voice effective? In your answer, explain whether or not you think the author's voice helps you to connect to the events of "The Night Ghost." [Evaluate]

5. **Reading Skill** Analyze Mood Consider how the natural setting contributes to the overall mood of the text. What conclusions can you draw about Paulsen's purpose for writing it? [Draw Conclusions]

6. **BQ** BIG Question In what ways can the things that really matter to you help you out in stressful circumstances? Give examples from Paulsen's autobiography. [Connect]

Vocabulary Practice

Match each boldfaced vocabulary word with a word from the right column that has the same meaning. Two of the words in the right column will not have matches. Then write a sentence for each vocabulary word.

1. **sustain**
2. **internal**
3. **ebbed**
4. **diffused**

a. scattered
b. receded
c. cease
d. maintain
e. inside
f. expanded

 Writing

Write a Journal Entry Think about an incident in your life that seemed scary at first but had a funny twist at the end. If you can't think of one, then make one up. Write a journal entry about this event. Include descriptive details and try to convey the mood of the incident to a reader unfamiliar with the incident.

TIP

Interpreting
When a question asks you to interpret, it is asking you to use your own knowledge and understanding to decide what the events or ideas of a selection mean.

- Think about what you already know that relates to what you are reading.

- Ask yourself what meaning the author is trying to convey.

- Determine what larger idea the selection is concerned with.

FOLDABLES Keep track of **Study Organizer** your ideas about the **BIG Question** in your unit Foldable.

 Literature Online

Selection Resources
For Selection Quizzes, eFlashcards, and Reading-Writing Connection activities, go to glencoe.com and enter QuickPass code GL39770u5.

Set a Purpose for Reading

As you read, think about what really matters to one father and his young daughter.

Preview the Article

1. Read the **title** and the **deck**, or the sentence below the title. What do you predict the article will be about?

2. Look at the **photographs** and read the **captions.** What do you learn about the place where the article is set?

Reading Skill

Analyze Cultural Context
When you analyze **cultural context,** you pay attention to the details that reveal the setting, values, and behaviors characteristic of a particular culture at a particular time in history. As you read, note details you learn about life in the towns of Lhasa and Dharmsala.

TIME

A Father's DARING TREK

A Tibetan man takes his 6-year-old daughter on a dangerous journey through the world's highest, harshest, mountains to give her a better life.

By JULIE K. L. DAM

After a weeklong march in the bitter, piercing cold and thin air of the Himalayan Mountains, the Tibetan father Kelsang and his daughter, Yangdol (not their real names), thought they had reached freedom. From the top of Nangapa La, a pass on the southern border of Chinese-occupied Tibet, a peaceful life in exile[1] seemed only steps away. Their perilous journey was only half over, though, because the trip down the pass would be just as difficult as the way up. Still the courageous father and daughter struggled on, determined to reach their goal.

---

1 People in **exile** (eg′zīl) live away from their home country.

Before heading into the mountains, Kelsang spreads butter on Yangdol's face to protect it from the sun and cold.

<u>View the Photograph</u> How does this photograph help you better understand the dangers Kelsang and Yangdol were preparing to face on their trek?

For Tibetans, the trek[2] to freedom is filled with hardships, both physical and emotional. Many make the heart-wrenching decision to become refugees, people who are forced to leave their country of birth because of political or religious persecution[3] or war. In 1951, Tibet lost its independence when Chinese troops invaded Lhasa, the Tibetan capital. The Chinese government claimed the region as part of its territory. During the 1950s, Tibetans protested Chinese rule and fought for independence. In 1959, the Dalai Lama, the Tibetan spiritual leader, set up a government-in-exile in Dharmsala, a hill town in northern India, and the Tibetans who could escape began to gather to him.

To this day, Tibet's culture has suffered under Chinese rule. China doesn't allow Tibetans to practice their religion, Tibetan Buddhism, and much of Tibetan culture has been lost. Many Tibetans have been imprisoned, tortured, or killed for standing up for their beliefs. Each year, thousands of Tibetan families choose to escape to Dharmsala. Once Tibetans like Kelsang and Yangdol decide that life as a refugee in India would be better than life under Chinese rule, they begin the demanding journey across the Himalayan Mountains, into neighboring Nepal, and—finally—to Dharmsala.

---

2 A **trek** is a long, often difficult journey.

3 People who suffer **religious persecution** (pur´sə kū´shən) receive cruel or harmful treatment because of their beliefs.

When Swiss photographer Manuel Bauer first met Kelsang, the 46-year-old father had decided to take his daughter to live in Dharmsala. The father knew the trek across the mountains would be challenging, but he believed life in Dharmsala—even as an exile far from home—would be better for him and his child.

The photographer persuaded Kelsang to let him join the father and daughter on their trip across the mountains. The three arranged a ride on the back of a truck and quietly left Lhasa one winter morning. However, their journey was soon delayed by snowstorms. Six days later, they got a lift to Tingri, Tibet, and began the achingly long march on foot across the Himalayas.

The mountain wind is so strong that Kelsang and Yangdol have to lie flat on the ground until it dies down.

Manuel Bauer/Lookat

The determined threesome hiked higher and higher up the mountains, battling frostbite,[4] dehydration,[5] frigid temperatures, and fierce winds. They traveled over the icy ground in silence, sometimes 14 hours a day, and were often too tired to even stop and eat. "They kept me going," says Bauer, "their story, sacrifice, and destiny."[6]

After 12 stressful days, the group crossed Nangapa La and wearily made their way down to Namche Bazaar, a Nepalese village near Mount Everest. At last the worst was over. They flew by helicopter to Kathmandu, Nepal's capital, where officials at the Tibetan

Reception Center greeted them and arranged a bus ride—a luxury after the long mountain trek—to their journey's end in Dharmsala.

Three days later, the father and daughter reached their destination, where they celebrated the journey's end with 50 other newly arrived refugees, many of whom had made much the same trek. Three long weeks after leaving Lhasa, Yangdol finally met the Dalai Lama and, with his blessing, began a new life—at home in exile.

---

4 **Frostbite** is a serious condition that occurs when a part of the body becomes too cold.

5 People often suffer **dehydration** when they do not have enough water.

6 A person's **destiny** (des′ tə nē) is his or her fate or fortune.

Respond and Think Critically

1. Summarize the events that happened in Tibet that caused people to want to leave. [Summarize]

2. Why do you think photographer Manuel Bauer joins Kelsang and Yangdol on their journey? [Infer]

3. **Text-to-Text** What kind of dangers do the father and daughter encounter on their trek? Think of other texts you've read about people who faced similar dangers. How are the experiences similar and different? [Recall and Connect]

4. In what ways do the photos affect your reaction to the article? Support your answer with details from the text. [Evaluate]

5. **Reading Skill** Analyze Cultural Context What do you learn about the Tibetan culture from the details in the article? [Analyze]

6. **BQ** BIG Question What conclusion can you draw about what really matters to the father and daughter in this article? Think about what would inspire you to take a dangerous journey. [Draw Conclusions]

My Father's Song and
I Ask My Mother to Sing

Connect to the Poems

Think about a memorable time when you were with a parent or another adult. It might have been a special event or just a quiet personal moment. What made this time unforgettable?

List Make a list of details that help you remember this time so clearly. Think about how things looked, sounded, and felt.

Build Background

Sometimes people share special moments with parents, relatives, or friends that they remember for a long time.

- In "My Father's Song," the speaker cherishes a childhood memory of his father. Ortiz's poetry grows out of his experience with New Mexico's landscape and his Native American culture.

- In "I Ask My Mother to Sing," the speaker remembers how it felt to hear his mother and grandmother sing. Lee's poetry stresses the joys and sorrows of family, home, loss, and love.

Set Purposes for Reading

BQ BIG Question

Read "My Father's Song" and "I Ask My Mother to Sing" to discover the speakers' views of what is truly important in life and in one's relationships with others.

Literary Element Free Verse

Poetry that has no fixed pattern of meter, rhyme, line length, or stanza arrangement is called **free verse**. Free verse lines often flow more easily than do rhymed lines. Free verse often imitates speech and gives the impression of spontaneous thought. Most modern poets write in free verse because it lets readers focus on the meaning of words more easily than in traditional forms.

LOG ON ▶ **Literature** Online

Author Search For more about Simon J. Ortiz and Li-Young Lee, go to glencoe.com and enter QuickPass code GL39770u5.

Learning Objectives

For pages 634–638

In studying these texts, you will focus on the following objective:

Literary Study: Analyzing free verse.

Meet the Authors

Simon J. Ortiz

Simon J. Ortiz is a Native American from New Mexico. He believes Native American culture survives through memory and storytelling.

Simon J. Ortiz was born in 1941.

Li-Young Lee

Li-Young Lee was born in Indonesia of Chinese parents. Many of his works explore his family history and cultural background.

Li-Young Lee was born in 1957.

Cornfield. Anthony Amies. Oil on canvas. Private Collection.

My Father's Song

Simon J. Ortiz

Wanting to say things,
I miss my father tonight.
His voice, the slight catch,
the depth, from his thin chest,
5   the tremble of emotion
in something he has just said
to his Son, his song:

    We planted corn one Spring at Aacqu°—
    we planted several times
10   but this one particular time
    I remember the soft damp sand
    in my hand.

    My father had stopped at one point
    to show me an overturned furrow;°
15   the plowshare° had unearthed
    the burrow nest of a mouse
    in the soft moist sand.

    Very gently, he scooped tiny pink animals
    into the palm of his hand
20   and told me to touch them.
    We took them to the edge
    of the field and put them in the shade
    of a sand moist clod.

    I remember the very softness
25   of cool and warm sand and tiny alive
    mice and my father saying things.

Free Verse In what ways does this poem reflect natural forms of speech?

BQ **BIG Question**

What important qualities of his father does the speaker reveal when he describes the incident with the baby mice?

---

8   **Aacqu**, or Acoma, is a Native American settlement outside of Albuquerque, New Mexico.

14 A **furrow** is a long, narrow groove or channel made in the ground by a plow.

15 A **plowshare** is the sharp edge or blade of a plow that cuts into the soil.

I Ask My Mother to Sing

Li-Young Lee

She begins, and my grandmother joins her.
Mother and daughter sing like young girls.
If my father were alive, he would play
his accordion° and sway like a boat.

5 I've never been in Peking, or the Summer Palace,°
nor stood on the great Stone Boat to watch
the rain begin on Kuen Ming Lake,° the picnickers
running away in the grass.

But I love to hear it sung;
10 how the waterlilies fill with rain until
they overturn, spilling water into water,
then rock back, and fill with more.

Both women have begun to cry.
But neither stops her song.

White Lotuses. Shi Dan.
View the Art Which lines in the poem best fit with this painting?

Free Verse How does the focus of each of the stanzas reflect spontaneous thought?

BQ **BIG Question**

In what ways is the connection the speaker has to his mother's and grandmother's song important to him?

---

4 An **accordion** is a portable musical instrument that has a keyboard and a hand-operated bellows that moves air through it to generate sound.

5 The **Summer Palace** is a large park with beautiful architecture in Beijing (formerly **Peking**), the capital of the People's Republic of China. It was originally the summer residence of China's imperial rulers.

7 **Kuen Ming Lake** is in the Summer Palace and features a two-story tall marble boat (referred to as the **Stone Boat** in the poem).

After You Read

Respond and Think Critically

1. Where did the parent come from in each poem? [Identify]

2. Why does the speaker in the Li-Young Lee poem suggest that his father would "sway like a boat" if he were there? [Interpret]

3. How does the speaker in the Ortiz poem show his love and respect for his father? [Infer]

4. How are the songs in the poems similar and different? [Compare]

5. **Literary Element** Free Verse Explain how the structure of each poem helps each poet communicate his ideas about family. [Analyze]

6. **BQ** BIG Question In your opinion, which of the poems best conveys what really matters in life? Explain your answer using examples from the poem you choose. [Evaluate]

Spelling Link

Forming Plurals of Nouns

For most nouns, you can form a plural by adding an -s to the end of the word. Some words, however, require you to change a letter before adding -s.

If the word ends in:	Rule	Example:
a consonant + *y*	change *y* to *i* and add -*es*	lily, lilies
a vowel + *o* or *y*	add only -*s*	rodeo, rodeos key, keys
a consonant + *o* common exceptions	generally add -*es* sometimes add only -*s*	potato, potatoes photo, photos
f or *ff* common exceptions	add -*s* change *f* to *v* and add -*es*	cliff, cliffs hoof, hooves
lf	change *f* to *v* and add -*es*	calf, calves

Practice On a sheet of paper, write the plural of each noun listed below. Then write a sentence for each word.

play, tomato, half, cameo, worry, party, puff

 Writing

Write a Letter Write a letter to a parent, other adult, or a friend about an important lesson you learned while spending time together. Explain why that time means a lot to you, and thank the person for helping you learn the important lesson.

TIP

Interpreting
Here are some tips to help you interpret. Remember when you interpret, you use your own understanding of the world to decide what the language in a poem means.

- Skim the Li-Young Lee poem to find the phrase "sway like a boat."

- Think about other images in the poem that might relate to "sway like a boat."

- Explain how the reference relates to these other images in the poem.

FOLDABLES Study Organizer Keep track of your ideas about the **BIG Question** in your unit Foldable.

 Literature Online

Selection Resources
For Selection Quizzes, eFlashcards, and Reading-Writing Connection activities, go to glencoe.com and enter QuickPass code GL39770u5.

Part 2

Social Issues

The Match Seller. Otto Dix. Staedtische Kunsthalle, Mannheim, Germany. ©ARS, NY.

BQ ▶ **BIG Question** **What Really Matters?**

How does the boy in the painting *The Match Seller* represent the problems of poverty? What social issues matter most to you?

O Captain! My Captain!

Connect to the Poem

Sometimes, the death of a public person can affect us almost as deeply as the death of a relative or friend. Do you know of a famous leader or other public person who has died? If this was someone you admired or liked, how did you feel when you heard about his or her death?

Partner Talk With a partner, talk about reasons why a person you have never met can still have a deep impact on your feelings.

Build Background

Poet Walt Whitman was deeply affected by the brutality of the Civil War. During the war, he spent a lot of time in hospitals, offering comfort to the wounded and dying Union and Confederate soldiers. Whitman had tremendous respect for President Abraham Lincoln, who guided the Union during those dark years. Just as the Union won the Civil War in 1865, Lincoln was shot and killed as he sat watching a play in a theater in Washington, D.C. Whitman wrote this poem after learning of Lincoln's death.

- The "Captain" in the title of this poem is President Lincoln.

- Throughout the poem, Whitman compares the nation after the war to a ship returning from a difficult journey.

Funeral Procession in Memory of President Abraham Lincoln, 1865. Charles Magnus. Color lithograph. Museum of the City of New York, NY.

Meet Walt Whitman

"Each of us limitless—each of us with his or her right upon the earth."

—Walt Whitman

A Poet of Democracy Poet, journalist, and essayist Walt Whitman loved the United States. Many of his poems celebrate democracy. Whitman greatly admired Abraham Lincoln, and "O Captain! My Captain!" is one of several poems he wrote about Lincoln.

Literary Works Whitman's poem collections include nine editions of *Leaves of Grass.* "O Captain! My Captain!" first appeared in *Sequel to Drum Taps,* published in 1865–1866.

Walt Whitman was born in 1819 and died in 1892.

 Literature Online

Author Search For more about Walt Whitman, go to glencoe.com and enter QuickPass code GL39770u5.

Set Purposes for Reading

BQ BIG Question

Read "O Captain! My Captain!" to learn more about the personal connection the poet Walt Whitman felt with President Lincoln, the subject of his poem.

Literary Element Elegy

An **elegy** is a mournful or melancholy poem that honors someone who is dead. Elegies often express both joy and sorrow. They proudly honor their subject's extraordinary achievements and also express sorrow related to losing this exceptional person.

Some elegies play an important role in expressing not only the emotions of the poet writing the piece, but the emotions of a larger group, such as an entire nation, as well.

As you read "O Captain! My Captain!" think about how the contrast between sorrow and joy makes this elegy emotionally powerful.

Reading Strategy Interpret Author's Meaning

When you interpret an **author's meaning,** you use your own understanding of the world to decide what the author intends to communicate in his or her descriptions of ideas or events.

Interpreting the author's meaning is important because it will help you better understand the thoughts and feelings the author is trying to share.

To interpret an author's meaning, ask yourself,

- why has the author chosen to describe these events in this way?
- what larger idea might these events be about?
- what is the author really trying to say?

In this poem, think of how to interpret the meaning of the ship the poet writes about. You may find it helpful to use a graphic organizer like the one below.

What Author Says	What I Already Know	What Author Means

TRY IT

Interpret Author's Meaning
Think of a song or poem that uses symbolism. For example, the song might use a living thing, such as a tree, to stand for something else, such as growth or life. Explain how you use the context of the song or poem to understand the meaning of the symbol. Write a few sentences to describe how you are able to interpret the song so that you know what it means.

O Captain! My Captain!

Walt Whitman

O Captain! my Captain! our fearful trip
    is done;
The ship has weather'd every rack,° the prize we
    sought is won;
The port is near, the bells I hear, the people all
    exulting,°
While follow eyes the steady keel, the vessel grim°
    and daring:
5   But O heart! heart! heart!
      O the bleeding drops of red,
         Where on the deck my Captain lies,
            Fallen cold and dead.

Elegy What words and phrases in these lines tell you that this poem is an elegy?

---

2 Here, **rack** means "storm" or "jolt."

3 People who are **exulting** are filled with joy.

4 The keel is the main timber that runs beneath a ship, so a **steady keel** is a straight, even course. A **grim** vessel is a ship that is gloomy or somber.

O Captain! my Captain! rise up and hear the
   bells;
10 Rise up—for you the flag is flung—for you the
   bugle trills;
For you bouquets and ribbon'd wreaths—for you
   the shores a-crowding;
For you they call, the swaying mass, their eager
   faces turning:
   Here, Captain! dear father!
     This arm beneath your head;
15   It is some dream that on the deck,
       You've fallen cold and dead.

My Captain does not answer, his lips are pale
   and still;
My father does not feel my arm, he has no pulse
   nor will;
The ship is anchor'd safe and sound, its voyage
   closed and done;
20 From fearful trip, the victor ship° comes in with
   object won:
   Exult, O shores, and ring, O bells!
    But I, with mournful tread,°
     Walk the deck my Captain lies,
      Fallen cold and dead.

Interpret Author's Meaning
What is the "fearful trip"
the author describes in
this line?

 **BIG Question**

From the speaker's
descriptions of himself
with the Captain, how would
you describe his personal
connection to the Captain?

---

20 A *victor ship* is one that has won in battle.

22 A *mournful tread* is slowed by sadness and grief.

After You Read

Respond and Think Critically

1. Think about the role of a ship's captain. How is comparing a ship's captain to President Lincoln an effective comparison? **[Compare]**

2. Why does the poet repeatedly refer to the trip the ship has completed as "fearful"? **[Analyze]**

3. What can you infer about why the crowds of people mentioned in the poem are celebrating? **[Infer]**

4. Why do you think the poet refers to himself as being with the Captain as he dies? **[Interpret]**

5. Based on the last lines of the poem, do you think the speaker has gotten over his grief? **[Draw Conclusions]**

6. **BQ** ❭ **BIG Question** Think about the contrast of feelings described in the poem. Do you think the poet places greater value on the grief of personal loss or on the collective joy of success? Or does he value both equally? Explain. **[Evaluate]**

Academic Vocabulary

"O Captain! My Captain!" portrays the fatal journey Lincoln took to fight for a **constitutional** change.

In the preceding sentence, *constitutional* refers to an amendment to the U.S. Constitution abolishing slavery. *Constitutional* also has other meanings. For instance:

The doctors think Jamal's shin splints are a **constitutional** weakness.

What do you think *constitutional* means in the preceding sentence? What is the difference between the two meanings?

TIP

Analyzing
Here are some tips to help you analyze. Remember when you analyze, you look at separate parts of a selection in order to understand the entire selection.

- Read the relevant parts of the poem.
- Determine what the ship in the poem has been through.
- Think about how these experiences might be fearful, or dreadful.

 FOLDABLES Keep track of **Study Organizer** your ideas about the **BIG Question** in your unit Foldable.

 Literature Online

Selection Resources
For Selection Quizzes, eFlashcards, and Reading-Writing Connection activities, go to glencoe.com and enter QuickPass code GL39770u5.

1. Find two examples of how deeply the poet mourns Lincoln's death. What words, phrases, and images does he use to convey his grief?

2. Elegies are often as much about celebrating a person's accomplishments in life as they are about mourning his or her death. Explain how Whitman's elegy praises the life of President Lincoln.

Review: **Rhyme and Rhyme Scheme**

As you learned on page 339, **rhyme** is the repetition of identical or similar sounds at the ends of words that appear close to one another.

3. What rhyme scheme appears in the last three lines of each stanza? Explain the effect this rhyme scheme has on the purpose of the poem. Use a graphic organizer like the one below to help you determine the rhyme scheme.

End Rhyme Word	Letter To Represent Word
red	a

Interpret Author's Meaning

4. When the poet writes "the prize we sought is won," what is the prize he is referring to?

5. How does the last stanza reveal the intensity of the poet's sadness?

6. A metaphor compares seemingly unlike things. What does the ship represent in this poem? Explain why the author may have chosen to use a metaphor of a ship.

Subject-Verb Agreement

Subject-verb agreement means using the verb form that agrees with the subject. There are two basic rules for writing the present tense of a verb.

1. If a sentence's subject is the pronoun *he, she,* or *it,* the verb must end in *-s.*

   • He <u>reads</u> well. • She <u>works</u> fast.

   • It <u>looks</u> beautiful.

2. If a sentence's subject is the pronoun *I, you, we,* or *they,* the verb does not end in *-s.*

   • I <u>bike</u> home. • You <u>run</u> fast.

   • We <u>bake</u> cakes. • They <u>eat</u> pears.

Practice In the following sentences, the subjects and verbs do not agree. Revise each sentence by fixing the verb.

1. He turn his head.

2. They rings the doorbell.

3. It sway in the wind.

4. We seeks a prize.

Listening and Speaking

Oral Report Make a list of qualities that you think a great leader should have. Then organize your ideas into an oral report. Include an introduction that states your thesis. In the body, group similar ideas together. Use transitions to show how each idea builds on the one before it. End with a conclusion that restates your thesis. As you deliver your report, adjust your tone and expression to match your message. Use a graphic organizer like the one below to keep track of the sequence of your ideas.

Beginning	Middle	End

Learning Objectives

For pages 646–647

On these pages, you will focus on the following objective:

Literary Study: Analyzing plot, setting, theme, author's perspective, and voice in biography and autobiography.

Genre Focus:
Biography and Autobiography

A **biography** is the story of a real person, written by another person. An **autobiography** is the story of a person written by the person himself or herself. Biography and autobiography are types of nonfiction—writing that is based on fact, history, or personal opinion. However, like fiction, they often have a plot, setting, and theme. Like characters in fiction, the people in these works have memorable traits and personalities.

Diaries, travel journals, memoirs, and anecdotes are shorter forms of biographical and autobiographical writing.

Elements of Biography and Autobiography

Plot Biographies and autobiographies are an account of part or all of a person's life. The **plot** is the series of events in the work—what happens to the person. In addition to learning what occurs, we usually learn how the individual, and other people in the narrative, respond to a conflict or problem.

Setting The **setting** is the time and place in which the events occur. Setting includes not only the physical surroundings but also the ideas, customs, values, and beliefs of a particular time and place.

Theme The theme is the main message of a story. Writers may state the theme directly (**stated theme**) or reveal the theme gradually through elements such as plot, character, setting, point of view, symbolism, and irony (**implied theme**).

Narrator The narrator is the person who tells the story. The relationship of the narrator to the story is the **point of view**. An autobiography is always written from a **first-person point of view**, using the pronoun *I*, because a person is

writing about his or her own life. A biography is written from a **third-person point of view**, using the pronoun *he* or *she*, because the writer is describing the life of someone else.

Author's Purpose The **author's purpose** is the reason a piece of literature was written—to entertain, inform, persuade, or explain. A biography or autobiography may be written with one, or several, of these purposes in mind.

Author's Perspective Sometimes an author has mixed feelings about the person he or she is writing about. The **author's perspective** is the author's attitude toward his or her subject. Does the author find much to admire or to criticize? What details or reasons does the author give to support his or her perspective?

TRY IT

Using graphic organizers like the ones on the next page, identify the characteristics of a biographical or autobiographical selection in this unit.

Characteristics of the Genre

To better understand elements of biography and autobiography, look at the Trait Web and Story Chain below. Both provide examples from "The March of the Mill Children."

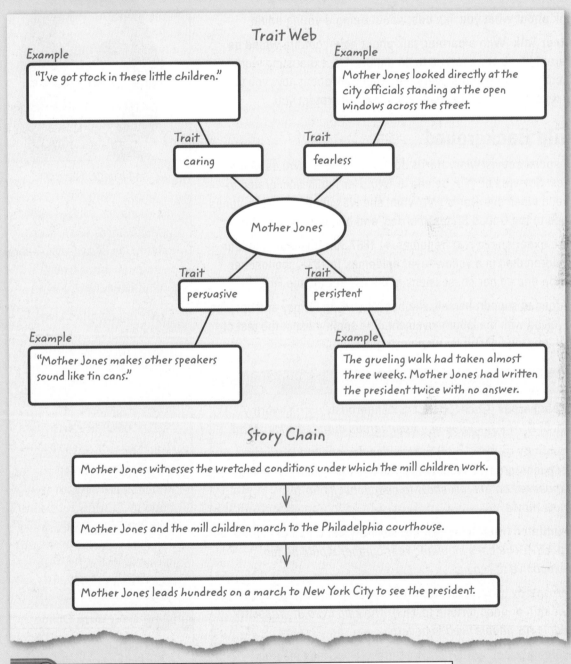

Trait Web

Example
"I've got stock in these little children."

Trait
caring

Example
Mother Jones looked directly at the city officials standing at the open windows across the street.

Trait
fearless

Mother Jones

Trait
persuasive

Trait
persistent

Example
"Mother Jones makes other speakers sound like tin cans."

Example
The grueling walk had taken almost three weeks. Mother Jones had written the president twice with no answer.

Story Chain

Mother Jones witnesses the wretched conditions under which the mill children work.

↓

Mother Jones and the mill children march to the Philadelphia courthouse.

↓

Mother Jones leads hundreds on a march to New York City to see the president.

LOG ON ▶ **Literature** Online

Literature and Reading For more selections in this genre, go to glencoe.com and enter QuickPass code GL39970u5.

The March of the Mill Children

Connect to the Historical Biography

Think about what you like best about being a young adult.

Partner Talk With a partner, talk about how your life would be different if you were forced to do dangerous, exhausting work in a factory for long hours every day. Then talk about how you would feel if someone tried to change the laws to protect you.

Build Background

The social activist Mary Harris Jones is better known as Mother Jones. She was born in Ireland in 1837. Her family immigrated to Canada when she was a girl. When she was in her twenties, Jones moved to the United States, married, and began raising a family.

- She experienced two tragedies. In 1867, her husband and four children died in a yellow fever epidemic. In 1871, she lost her home and all her possessions in the Great Chicago Fire.

- Forced to support herself, she began working for pay and became involved with the labor movement. She spent most of the rest of her long life fighting for workers' rights.

Vocabulary

treacherous (trech′ər əs) *adj.* dangerously untrustworthy (p. 651). *The road became treacherous during the ice storm.*

publicity (pu blis′ə tē) *n.* activities designed to increase public interest in something or somebody (p. 651). *The actor appeared on the talk show to gain publicity for his new movie.*

mutilated (mūt′əl āt′ ed) *adj.* severely deformed or injured (p. 651). *The car's mutilated rear bumper would be too expensive to repair.*

prosperity (pro sper′ə tē) *n.* the condition of having success, wealth, or good fortune (p. 653). *The king lived in prosperity, while his people lived in poverty.*

solemnly (sol′əm lē) *adv.* in a grave or serious manner (p. 656). *The accused walked solemnly into the courtroom.*

Meet Judith Pinkerton Josephson

"Writing biographies and childhood history books has drawn me into the past—the worlds of those I write about come to life through their letters, . . . diaries, and pictures."

—Judith Pinkerton Josephson

Exploring People's Lives Judith Pinkerton Josephson was inspired by her children to write poetry. This led to a career in writing. In addition to children's books, biographies, and history books, Josephson has coauthored two grammar books.

Literary Works Josephson has written several biographies, including *Jesse Owens: Track and Field Legend* and *Nikki Giovanni: Poet of the People.* "The March of the Mill Children" is from *Mother Jones*, published in 1997.

 Literature Online

Author Search For more about Judith Pinkerton Josephson, go to glencoe.com and enter QuickPass code GL39770u5.

Set Purposes for Reading

BQ BIG Question

As you read, think about what life was like for the children who worked in the mills. Consider how Mother Jones helped to bring this social injustice to the nation's attention.

Literary Element Description

Description is writing that creates an impression of a setting, person, animal, object, or event by appealing to one or more of the five senses.

Description is important in helping readers imagine what the people in a narrative see, hear, smell, taste, or touch. That imagining can help readers connect with the people being described. Descriptive language can also bring a setting to life.

As you read, notice the vivid details that help you imagine the working conditions in the factories and the children's journey.

Reading Strategy Activate Prior Knowledge

Because of your own life experiences, you know certain things and understand the meanings of certain words and ideas. This information, called **prior knowledge,** can help you understand what you read. When you activate prior knowledge, you think about what you already know about a topic and combine it with what you read to create meaning.

When you activate prior knowledge, ask yourself,

- what facts do I know about this topic?
- have I been to places similar to the setting described?
- what experiences have I had that compare with what I am reading?
- what people remind me of the people in the selection?

You may find it helpful to use a web like the one below. Start filling out the web before you read with any information you might already know about child labor in 1900. Then add to the web as you read, noting how your prior knowledge helps you understand the text.

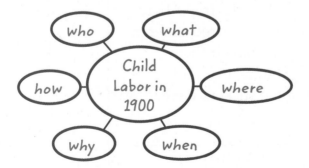

Learning Objectives

For pages 648–659

In studying this text, you will focus on the following objectives:

Literary Study:
Analyzing description.

Reading:
Activating prior knowledge

TRY IT

Activate Prior Knowledge
Before you read "The March of the Mill Children," think about rules and laws that make workplaces fair and safe for everyone, especially young people. Ask yourself how jobs would be different if these rules were not in place.

The March of the Mill Children

Judith Pinkerton Josephson

Mother Jones and a mining family.

"**I love children,**" Mother Jones once told a reporter.

In countless shacks and shanties across the country, she had tied the shoes of children, wiped their noses, hugged them when they cried, scrambled to find food for them, fought for their rights. By the turn of the century, almost two million children under the age of sixteen worked in mills, factories, and mines. Images of the child workers Mother Jones had seen stayed with her—the torn, bleeding fingers of the breaker boys, the mill children living on coffee and stale bread.

In June 1903, Mother Jones went to Philadelphia, Pennsylvania—the heart of a vast textile industry.[1] About one hundred thousand workers from six hundred different mills were on strike[2] there. The strikers wanted their workweek cut from sixty to fifty-five hours, even if it meant lower wages. About a sixth of the strikers were children under sixteen.

Activating Prior Knowledge
In what ways did your discussion of child labor help prepare you for the introduction to this selection?

---

1 The ***textile industry*** includes all the businesses that make and use yarn and fabrics.

2 When workers go on ***strike,*** they stop working to protest unfair working conditions.

Nationwide, eighty thousand children worked in the textile industry. In the South, Mother Jones had seen how dangerous their jobs were. Barefooted little girls and boys reached their tiny hands into the **treacherous** machinery to repair snapped threads or crawled underneath the machinery to oil it. At textile union headquarters, Mother Jones met more of these mill children. Their bodies were bone-thin, with hollow chests. Their shoulders were rounded from long hours spent hunched over the workbenches. Even worse, she saw "some with their hands off, some with the thumb missing, some with their fingers off at the knuckles"—victims of mill accidents.

Pennsylvania, like many other states, had laws that said children under thirteen could not work. But parents often lied about a child's age. Poor families either put their children to work in the mills or starved. Mill owners looked the other way, because child labor was cheap.

Mother Jones asked various newspaper publishers why they didn't write about child labor in Pennsylvania. The publishers told her they couldn't, since owners of the mills also owned stock in their newspapers.[3] "Well, I've got stock in these little children," she said, "and I'll arrange a little **publicity**."

Mother Jones, now seventy-three, gathered a large group of mill children and their parents. She led them on a one-mile march from Philadelphia's Independence Square to its courthouse lawn. Mother Jones and a few children climbed up on a platform in front of a huge crowd. She held one boy's arm up high so the crowd could see his **mutilated** hand. "Philadelphia's mansions were built on

Description How is the author's description of the children effective in showing why child labor is wrong?

BQ ⟩ **BIG Question**

What matters more to the parents than the law? What matters more to the mill owners?

---

3 People who own **stock** in a company own part of the company. Because the mill owners were part owners of the newspapers, they could tell the papers what to print.

Vocabulary ....

treacherous (trech′ər əs) *adj.* dangerously untrustworthy

publicity (pu blis′ə tē) *n.* activities designed to increase public interest in something or somebody

mutilated (mūt′əl āt′ed) *adj.* severely deformed or injured

the broken bones, the quivering hearts,[4] and drooping heads of these children," she said. She lifted another child in her arms so the crowd could see how thin he was.

Mother Jones looked directly at the city officials standing at the open windows across the street. "Some day the workers will take possession of your city hall, and when we do, no child will be sacrificed on the altar of profit."[5] Unmoved, the officials quickly closed their windows.

Local newspapers and some New York newspapers covered the event. How, Mother Jones wondered, could she draw national attention to the evils of child labor? Philadelphia's famous Liberty Bell, currently on a national tour and drawing huge crowds, gave her an idea. She and the textile union leaders would stage their own tour. They would march the mill children all the way to the president of the United States—Theodore Roosevelt. Mother Jones wanted the president to get Congress to pass a law that would take children out of the mills, mines, and factories, and put them in school.

When Mother Jones asked parents for permission to take their children with her, many hesitated. The march from Philadelphia to Sagamore Hill—the president's seaside mansion on Long Island near New York City—would cover 125 miles. It would be a difficult journey. But finally, the parents agreed. Many decided to come along on the march. Other striking men and women offered their help, too.

Small boys and men working in the spinning room of a South Carolina cotton mill in 1903. *View the Photograph* What does this picture reveal about the working conditions of cotton mills around the begining of the 20th century?

Activating Prior Knowledge
Think about protest marches you've seen in movies or on TV. How does your knowledge of them help you understand the march described here?

---

4 When something is ***quivering***, it is shaking. Mother Jones is describing the children as being really scared.

5 In a religious ***sacrifice***, an animal is killed on an ***altar***. Mother Jones is saying that she will not allow children to be harmed, or sacrificed, just so rich people can make more money.

On July 7, 1903, nearly three hundred men, women, and children—followed by four wagons with supplies—began the long march. Newspapers carried daily reports of the march, calling the group "Mother Jones's Industrial Army," or "Mother Jones's Crusaders." The army was led by a fife-and-drum corps[6] of three children dressed in Revolutionary War uniforms. Mother Jones wore her familiar, lace-fringed black dress. The marchers sang and carried flags, banners, and **placards** that read "We Want to Go to School!" "We Want Time to Play." "**Prosperity** Is Here, Where Is Ours?" "55 Hours or Nothing." "We Only Ask for Justice." "More School, Less Hospitals."

The temperature rose into the nineties. The roads were dusty, the children's shoes full of holes. Many of the young girls returned home. Some of the marchers walked only as far as the outskirts of Philadelphia. For the hundred or so marchers who remained, this trip was an adventure in spite of the heat. They bathed and swam in brooks and rivers. Each of them carried a knapsack with a knife, fork, tin cup, and plate inside. Mother Jones took a huge pot for cooking meals on the way. Mother Jones also took along costumes, makeup, and jewelry so the children could stop in towns along the route and put on plays about the struggles of textile workers. The fife-and-drum corps gave concerts and passed the hat. People listened and donated money. Farmers met the marchers with wagonloads of fruits, vegetables, and clothes. Railroad engineers stopped their trains and gave them free rides. Hotel owners served free meals.

On July 10, the marchers camped across the Delaware River from Trenton, New Jersey. They had traveled about forty miles in three days. At first, police told the group they couldn't enter the city. Trenton mill owners didn't want any trouble. But Mother Jones invited the policemen to stay for lunch. The children gathered around the cooking pot with their tin plates and cups. The policemen

Visual Vocabulary

A **placard** is a large, usually printed paper or cardboard sign to be displayed in a public place.

Description Based on this description, how is the march an adventure for some marchers?

---

6 This *fife-and-drum corps* was a small marching band that played drums and flutes.

Vocabulary

prosperity (pro sper′ə tē) *n.* the condition of having success, wealth, or good fortune

smiled, talked kindly to them, then allowed them to cross the bridge into Trenton. There Mother Jones spoke to a crowd of five thousand people. That night, the policemen's wives took the children into their homes, fed them, and packed them lunches for the next day's march.

By now, many of the children were growing weak. More returned home. Some adults on the march grumbled that Mother Jones just wanted people to notice *her*. They complained to reporters that Mother Jones often stayed in hotels while the marchers camped in hot, soggy tents filled with whining mosquitoes. Sometimes Mother Jones did stay in hotels, because she went ahead of the marchers to arrange for lodging and food in upcoming towns and to get publicity for the march.

As the remaining marchers pushed on to Princeton, New Jersey, a thunderstorm struck. Mother Jones and her army camped on the grounds of former President Grover Cleveland's estate. The Clevelands were away, and the caretaker let Mother Jones use the big, cool barn for a dormitory.

Mother Jones got permission from the mayor of Princeton to speak opposite the campus of Princeton University. Her topic: higher education. She spoke to a large crowd of professors, students, and residents. Pointing to one ten-year-old boy, James Ashworth, she said, "Here's a textbook on economics." The boy's body was stooped from carrying seventy-five-pound bundles of yarn. "He gets three dollars a week and his sister, who is fourteen, gets six dollars. They work in a carpet factory ten hours a day while the children of the rich are getting their higher education." Her piercing glance swept over the students in the crowd.

Mother Jones talked about children who could not read or write because they spent ten hours a day in Pennsylvania's silk mills. Those who hired these child workers used "the hands and feet of little children so they might buy automobiles for their wives and police dogs for their daughters to talk French to." She accused the mill owners of taking "babies almost from the cradle."

The next night, the marchers slept on the banks of the Delaware River. In every town, Mother Jones drew on

Activating Prior Knowledge
Based on your knowledge about making assumptions, how accurate do you think this assumption is?

Description What does Mother Jones say are the mill owners' real reasons for hiring young children?

Spindle boys in a Georgia cotton mill.

View the Photograph Not tall enough to operate these looms from the ground, two young boys climb the machines to do their jobs. What do you notice about the boy in the foreground? Why might this job be particularly risky for him?

what she did best—speaking—to gather support for her cause. One reporter wrote, "Mother Jones makes other speakers sound like tin cans."

Battling heat, rain, and swarms of mosquitoes at night, the marchers arrived in Elizabeth. Socialist party members helped house and feed the weary adults and children. The next morning, two businessmen gave Mother Jones her first car ride. She was delighted with this new "contraption."[7]

On July 15, Mother Jones wrote a letter to President Roosevelt. She told him how these poor mill children lived, appealed to him as a father, and asked him to meet with her and the children. President Roosevelt did not answer Mother Jones's letter. Instead, he assigned secret service officers to watch her. They thought she might be a

Activating Prior Knowledge
Why do you think Mother Jones becomes so angry that the Secret Service shadows her on the march?

---

7 A *contraption* is a mechanical device.

threat to the president. That made her furious.

On July 24, after more than two weeks on the road, the marchers reached New York City. By now, just twenty marchers remained. One of them was Eddie Dunphy, a child whose job was to sit on a high stool eleven hours a day handing thread to another worker. For this he was paid three dollars a week. Mother Jones talked about Eddie and about Gussie Rangnew, a child who packed stockings in a factory. She too worked eleven hours a day for pennies.

At one meeting, a crowd of thirty thousand gathered. "We are quietly marching toward the president's home," she told the people. "I believe he can do something for these children, although the press declares he cannot."

One man wanted the children to have some fun while they were in New York City. Frank Bostick owned the wild animal show at Coney Island, an amusement park and resort. He invited the mill children to spend a dayat the park. The children swam in the ocean and played along the beach.

When Frank Bostick's wild animal show ended that night, he let Mother Jones speak to the crowd that had attended. To add drama, she had some of the children crawl inside the empty cages. The smells of sawdust and animals hung in the air. But instead of lions and tigers, the cages held children. The children gripped the iron bars and **solemnly** stared out at the crowd while Mother Jones spoke.

"We want President Roosevelt to hear the wail of the children who never have a chance to go to school, but work eleven and twelve hours a day in the textile mills of Pennsylvania," she said, "who weave the carpets that he and you walk upon; and the lace curtains in your windows, and the clothes of the people."

She continued, "In Georgia where children work day and night in the cotton mills they have just passed a bill to protect songbirds. What about the little children from whom all song is gone?" After Mother Jones finished

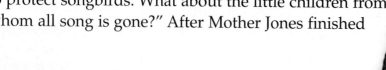

Mother Jones circa 1903.

Activating Prior Knowledge
What effect do you think Mother Jones intends by showing the children in cages? Explain.

Vocabulary

solemnly (sol´əm lē) *adv.* in a grave or serious manner

speaking, the crowd sat in stunned silence. In the distance, a lone lion roared.

The grueling walk had taken almost three weeks. Mother Jones had written the president twice with no answer. On July 29, she took three young boys to Sagamore Hill, where the president was staying. But the secret service stopped them at the mansion's gates. The president would not see them.

The group returned to New York City. Discouraged, Mother Jones reported her failure to the newspapers. Most of the marchers decided to return home. She stayed on briefly with the three children. Once more, she wrote President Roosevelt: "The child of today is the man or woman of tomorrow. . . . I have with me three children who have walked one hundred miles. . . . If you decide to see these children, I will bring them before you at any time you may set."

The president's secretary replied that the president felt that child labor was a problem for individual states to solve. "He is a brave guy when he wants to take a gun out and fight other grown people," said Mother Jones in disgust, "but when those children went to him, he could not see them."

In early August, Mother Jones finally took the last three children home. Soon after, the textile workers gave up and ended their strike. Adults and children went back to work, their working conditions unchanged.

Though she had not met with the president, Mother Jones had drawn the attention of the nation to the problem of child labor. She became even more of a national figure. Within a few years, Pennsylvania, New York, New Jersey, and other states did pass tougher child labor laws. The federal government finally passed a child labor law (part of the Fair Labor Standards Act) in 1938—thirty-five years after the march of the mill children.

BQ **BIG Question**

What does this selection teach about being committed to working to solve important social problems?

After You Read

Respond and Think Critically

1. What are the main points in Mother Jones's argument against child labor? [Summarize]

2. What message does Mother Jones suggest about the people in Georgia's government when she refers to its law about songbirds? [Infer]

3. In what ways is Mother Jones an effective leader? [Analyze]

4. Review the description of Mother Jones's behavior during the march. Which of her words or actions do you find most inspiring? Explain. [Evaluate]

5. Do you think there are places around the world where children still work in conditions like those described in the biography? Explain your answer. [Connect]

6. **BQ** BIG Question To Mother Jones and many parents, what matters more than the children's wages? Explain. [Analyze]

TIP

Evaluating
Here are some tips to help you evaluate.

- Reread selection parts that describe Mother Jones's behavior.

- Think about the obstacles she overcomes and the people she motivates.

- Decide which of her words and actions inspire you the most.

FOLDABLES Keep track of
Study Organizer your ideas about
the **BIG Question** in your
unit Foldable.

Just 10 years ago, Duom Deng, David Ayiik, and James Biar were refugees too. During Sudan's civil war, the three boys had seen their parents killed and their villages destroyed. Then they and thousands of other orphaned children walked 1,000 miles east to...

Examine Media

The Power of Photographs

There is a saying, "A picture is worth a thousand words." An image can evoke powerful emotions in viewers. Analyze the photograph below.

A child works in a factory or mill circa 1900.

On Your Own Think about the following questions and write your ideas on a separate sheet of paper.

1. Why were photos like this an important tool in ending child labor in the United States?

2. Today, how do newspapers influence readers with the photos they choose to show of newsworthy events and people?

Literary Element Description

1. What is the effect of the writer's description of the child laborers' physical features?

2. Why does Mother Jones refer to Philadelphia's mansions as being built on "the broken bones, the quivering hearts, and drooping heads" of the marching children?

Review: **Style**

As you learned on page 477, **style** refers to a writer's choice and arrangement of words and sentences in a literary work. One way a writer can create a unique style is by including anecdotes as part of the description of people and events. An **anecdote** is a brief story based on an interesting incident or event. Anecdotes are frequently biographical and reveal some aspect of a person's character. A writer may include an anecdote to help readers connect to the selection.

3. The writer of "The March of the Mill Children" includes an anecdote about Mother Jones calling a child worker a "textbook on economics" in a speech at Princeton University. What impression of Mother Jones do you think the writer is hoping to create in readers by including this story? What effect do you think Mother Jones herself hoped to have on her audience by using these words?

Reading Strategy
Activate Prior Knowledge

4. How did your prior knowledge help you understand the setting and major events? Support your response with details.

Vocabulary Practice

Choose the sentence that uses the vocabulary word correctly.

1. **A.** The sharp turn in the road is a **treacherous** place to stop and change a tire.

   B. People from around the world came to look for the hidden **treacherous.**

2. **A.** We were shocked when she announced her retirement to the **publicity.**

   B. The rock star staged an appearance for **publicity.**

3. **A.** The germ **mutilated** many times, growing more powerful.

   B. One **mutilated** pillow was all that remained after the pillow fight.

4. **A.** Ms. Erickson obtained her **prosperity** through hard work.

   B. The children trespassed on their neighbor's **prosperity.**

5. **A.** Jo laughed **solemnly** at the stand-up comic's routine.

   B. The girl **solemnly** apologized to her brother for breaking his guitar.

Academic Vocabulary

In the early 1900s, Pennsylvania and other states had laws that **prohibited** child labor.

Using context clues, try to figure out the meaning of the word *prohibited*. Check your guess in a dictionary.

 Literature Online

Selection Resources For Selection Quizzes, eFlashcards, and Reading-Writing Connection activities, go to glencoe.com and enter QuickPass code GL39770u5.

Respond Through Writing

Biographical Narrative

Apply Description "The March of the Mill Children" gives biographical information about Mother Jones. In a short essay, describe another important figure from U.S. history. Use descriptive details to tell about the person's life and accomplishments.

Understand the Task When writers use **description**, they help readers use their senses to picture people, settings, and events.

Prewrite Choose a famous person from U.S. history. The person should be someone whom you admire. Use a web like the one below to record information that you learn while conducting research about the person. Under each trait, list facts that show the trait in action.

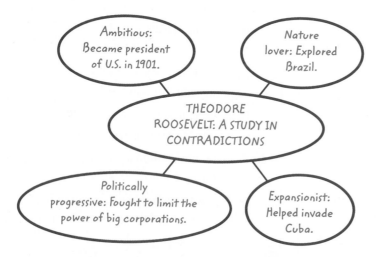

Draft As you draft, keep an overall plan in mind. For example, you may decide to write an introduction; paragraphs about the person's early life, later life, and accomplishments; and a conclusion. Be sure to explain why you admire the person.

Revise After you have written your first draft, read it to determine whether the paragraphs are arranged in a logical order. Rearrange text as necessary so that your ideas are easy to follow. Check to make sure you've included vivid descriptions of your subject, settings, and events. Then exchange your essay with a peer and offer each other suggestions for improvement.

Edit and Proofread Proofread your paper, correcting any errors in spelling, grammar, and punctuation. See the Word Bank in the side column for words you might use in your biographical narrative.

Learning Objectives

For page 660

In this assignment, you will focus on the following objective:

Writing: Writing a biographical narrative.

> ## Word Bank

admirably
achievement
contributor
courageous
dedicated
determined
energetic
influential
legislation
motivate
recognition

Vocabulary Workshop

Dictionary Skills

Connection to Literature

"The marchers sang and carried flags, banners, and placards . . ."

—Judith Pinkerton Josephson,
"The March of the Mill Children"

Learning Objectives

For page 661

In this workshop, you will focus on the following objective:

Vocabulary: Understanding language resources.

If you didn't know the meaning of the word *placard* or wanted to use another word in its place, you could refer to a **dictionary** or a **thesaurus** for help.

- A dictionary provides the pronunciation, part of speech, definition, and sometimes the origin of a word.

- A thesaurus lists synonyms, or words that have similar meanings. Both tools are available in book form, online, and in word-processing programs.

Study the dictionary and thesaurus entries for *placard*.

Word	Dictionary Entry	Thesaurus Entry
placard	(plak′ärd, -ərd) *n.* large, usually printed paper or cardboard sign or notice to be displayed in a public place; *v.t.* 1. to display placards on or in: *to placard the wall of a building.* 2. to make known by means of placards [French *placard* poster, from *plaquer,* to stick on, plaster, from Middle Dutch *placken* to patch, plaster]	*n.* sign, notice, poster, advertisement, billboard

TRY IT: Use the chart above to help you answer these questions.

1. In its first, or preferred, pronunciation does *placard* rhyme with *card* or *curd*?
2. Which thesaurus word would best replace *placard* in the following sentence? *The marchers carried placards protesting the mill.*
3. Which meaning of *placard* is the writer of the following sentence using? *Protestors sometimes placard windows of neighborhood shops.*
4. From what languages did the English language get the word *placard*?

from *Elegy on the Death of César Chávez*

Connect to the Poem

Think about a time in history when one person was willing to stand up against the *status quo* (the way life is right now).

List List historic figures you can think of who stood up to a system they believed was unfair in order to make life better for others.

Build Background

Rudolfo Anaya's work is an **elegy**, or a poem of mourning. The subject of his poem is the death of César Chávez, a farm worker of Mexican American descent. Chávez founded the National Farm Workers Association to fight against the dire conditions they experienced. It later became the United Farm Workers of America.

- The members were eventually able to gain better working conditions, minimum wage standards, child labor reform, and many other economic rights.

- The organization used a variety of nonviolent tactics modeled after the practices used by the civil rights movement, such as rallies, strikes, boycotts, and fasts.

Set Purposes for Reading

BQ BIG Question

Read this excerpt from "Elegy on the Death of César Chávez" to find out how one person made a difference to many.

Literary Elements Simile and Metaphor

Similes and **metaphors** are figures of speech that compare seemingly unlike things. A simile uses the words *like* or *as* to make the comparison. A metaphor, however, suggests the comparison instead of stating it directly. As a reader, you use your own prior knowledge to help you uncover the more complex meanings of these words and phrases. As you read this poem, write down the similes and metaphors that you find and what you think they mean.

Meet Rudolfo Anaya

Cultural Inspiration Born in New Mexico, Rudolfo Anaya finds much of the inspiration for his writing in his native landscape as well as *cuentos*, or folktales, he heard as a child.

Literary Works Mainly considered a novelist, Anaya has also written short stories, plays, children's books, and poems. He is perhaps best known for his first novel, now considered a classic, *Bless Me, Ultima*.

Rudolfo Anaya was born in 1937.

LOG ON ▶ **Literature** Online

Author Search For more about Rudolfo Anaya, go to glencoe.com and enter QuickPass code GL39770u5.

from
Elegy on the Death of César Chávez

Rudolfo Anaya

César is dead,
 And we have wept for him until our eyes are dry,
 Dry as the fields of California that
  He loved so well and now lie fallow.
5 Dry as the orchards of Yakima,° where dark buds
  Hang on trees and do not blossom.
 Dry as el Valle de Tejas° where people cross
  Their Foreheads and pray for rain.

This earth he loved so well is dry and mourning
10 For César has fallen, our morning star has fallen.

He was a wind of change that swept over our land.
  From the San Joaquín Valle° north to
   Sacramento
 From northwest Yakima to el Valle de Tejas
 From el Valle de San Luis° to Midwest fields of
  corn
15 He loved the land, he loved la gente.°

His name was a soft breeze to cool the campesino's°
 sweat
  A scourge° on the oppressors of the poor.

---

5 *Yakima* is a county in Washington State that uses migrant laborers in its apple orchards.

7 *El Valle de Tejas* is a dry area in Texas along the Mexican border (*Tejas* is the Spanish word for Texas).

12 *San Joaquin Valle* is Spanish for the San Joaquin Valley, a region of California.

14 *El Valle de San Luis* is the San Luis Valley, located in Colorado and New Mexico.

15 *La gente* is Spanish for "the people."

16 *Campesino* is Spanish for "farm worker."

17 A *scourge* is a person or thing that delivers punishment.

I hear César calling for us to gather.
    I hear the call to a new Huelga,°
20   I hear the sound of marching feet
    The guitarra strums of the New Movimiento
    The old and young, rich and poor, all move
    To build the House of Justice of César's dream!

Our César has not died!
25   He is the light of the new day.
    He is the rain that renews parched fields.
    He is the hope that builds the House of Justice.
    He is with us! Here! Today!
    Listen to his voice in the wind.
30   He is the spirit of Hope,
    A movement building to sweep away
        oppression!
    His spirit guides us in the struggle.
    Let us join his spirit to ours!
    Sing with me. Sing all over this land!

35   "Rise, mi gente, rise!°
       Rise, mi gente, rise!"

BQ BIG Question

How does the poem show that Chávez considered social issues as something that really matters?

---

19 *Huelga* is Spanish for "strike" or "walk out."

35 *"Rise, mi gente, rise!"* is a phrase Chávez used that means "Rise, my people, rise!"

After You Read

Respond and Think Critically

1. Think of a person who has inspired you. Explain what he or she did that you found so encouraging. **[Connect]**

2. How did the work of César Chávez affect the daily struggle of farm workers? **[Infer]**

3. Do you think the poem does a good job both mourning Chávez's death and celebrating his life? Explain. **[Evaluate]**

4. What does the phrase "The old and young, rich and poor, all move / To build the House of Justice of César's dream!" mean? **[Interpret]**

5. **Literary Elements** **Simile and Metaphor** In the poem, Chávez is called "the light of the new day" and "the rain that renews parched fields." How do these metaphors help you understand the impact Chávez had on the workers' lives? **[Analyze]**

6. **BQ** **BIG Question** What can you conclude about the speaker's feelings about whether or not Chávez will still have an impact on social issues after his death? Use details from the text to explain your conclusion. **[Draw Conclusions]**

Vocabulary

Each of the successes of the United Farm Workers resulted from **cooperative** work. In the preceding sentence, *cooperative* is an adjective meaning "characterized by working with others for a common purpose." *Cooperative* also has other meanings. For instance: Many families in the neighborhood were members of the local health food **cooperative**. What do you think *cooperative* means in this sentence? What is the difference between the two meanings?

Writing

Write an Informative Blurb Rudolfo Anaya's poem describes how César Chávez was an inspiration to workers. Review the poem to recall details about Chávez's effect on people. Then write a blurb, or short informative writing, that promotes Chávez. What type of man was he? Why was he an effective leader?

TIP

Interpreting
When you interpret, you apply your own ideas to the information that has been presented. There is often more than one interpretation of a selection.

- Look at the information the author has provided.
- Think about your own experiences or convictions as they relate to the selection.
- Decide for yourself what meaning can be gotten from the statement.

FOLDABLES **Study Organizer** Keep track of your ideas about the **BIG Question** in your unit Foldable.

 Literature Online

Selection Resources
For Selection Quizzes, eFlashcards, and Reading-Writing Connection activities, go to glencoe.com and enter QuickPass code GL39770u5.

Social Perspective

on *Elegy on the Death of César Chávez* by Rudolfo Anaya

Learning Objectives

For pages 667–668

In studying this text, you will focus on the following objective:

Reading: Analyzing tone.

from Remembering César

Coretta Scott King

Set a Purpose for Reading

Read to find out about people who devote their lives to what really matters to them.

Build Background

Martin Luther King Jr., the husband of Coretta Scott King, was a firm believer in the power of civil disobedience, a way of peacefully protesting unjust laws and practices. César Chávez used these same nonviolent methods to great success in his struggle to achieve rights for migrant farm workers.

Reading Skill Analyze Tone

Tone is the writer's attitude toward a subject shown in the language he or she uses. When you analyze tone, you try to determine how a writer feels about his or her subject. It is important to analyze tone because the author does not always state his or her feelings directly. Ask yourself if the words the author uses describe emotions. Look for details the author includes and determine whether they influence the way you feel about the topic.

I first met César Chávez in the early 1970s, and I have many warm memories of the time I was able to spend with him. I had a clear understanding from the beginning of our relationship that he was a rare and special kind of leader, completely devoid of ego, uninterested in the limelight[1] and devoted to the cause of oppressed farmworkers. In 1974, I presented The King Center's[2] highest award, the Martin Luther King, Jr. Nonviolent Peace Prize, to him in recognition of his uncompromising dedication to nonviolent social change in the spirit of Martin's teachings.

---

1 *Limelight* means the focus of public attention.

2 After her husband was assassinated, Coretta Scott King founded the *Martin Luther King, Jr. Center* for Nonviolent Social Change in Atlanta, Georgia.

We proudly supported César and the UFW during their organizing campaigns in California and Florida and their boycotts of lettuce and grapes. I marched with César and his followers in California, New York and Atlanta.

When I visited his office in La Paz, I was struck by the simplicity of the surroundings and how humble the material resources were.

César considered himself a disciple of Martin, just as my husband was a disciple of Gandhi.[3] César told me that the United Farm Workers modeled many of their campaigns on the nonviolent principles and strategies we employed in the Civil Rights Movement.

On another occasion, I was invited to deliver the keynote address at a rally in front of the jail in Salinas, where César was incarcerated for civil disobedience in a protest for better wages and working conditions for the farmworkers. I remember that a priest read from Martin's writings at the Salinas rally. I also visited César in Arizona during one of his many fasts[4] for justice for the farmworkers. Although he was weak from fasting, he sat through a press conference and rally.

César embodied a powerful humility and a great sense of dignity and decency. He had such a gentle spirit, quiet courage and radiant integrity,[5] I always left our meeting feeling renewed and inspired. ⌘

---

3 Mohandas Karamchand **Gandhi** was one of the people mainly responsible for India's independence from Great Britain and became well known for his practice of nonviolent resistance. Martin Luther King Jr. was a **disciple**, or follower, of his teachings.

4 Here, **fasts** are times spent without food; Chávez was refusing to eat until changes were made to improve conditions for farm workers.

5 **Radiant** means "shining brightly." **Integrity** is moral uprightness.

Respond and Think Critically

1. Write a brief summary of the main ideas in this essay. For help on writing a summary, see page 185. [Summarize]

2. In the essay, which people are mentioned as being associated with nonviolent protest? [Recall and Identify]

3. What does it mean when Coretta Scott King says that Chávez "embodied a powerful humility"? Explain. [Interpret]

4. **Text-to-Text** Think about the perception you formed of César Chávez after reading Rudolfo Anaya's poem "Elegy on the Death of César

Chávez." How was this perception of Chávez affected after you read King's essay? [Connect]

5. **Reading Skill** Analyze Tone How would you describe the tone King uses in remembering Chávez? Explain your thoughts. [Analyze]

6. **BQ** BIG Question Think about the prize King presented to Chávez and what Chávez did to earn the award. What can you conclude about King's and Chávez's feelings about whether the methods used to achieve goals matter as much as the goals themselves? [Draw Conclusions]

Part 3
Scientific Matters

The Rimfall. Jonathan Barry. Oil on canvas. Private Collection.

BQ ⟩⟩ **BIG Question** **What Really Matters?**

In the painting *The Rimfall,* two astronauts explore a fantasy world. How does this scene spark your imagination about space travel? What scientific matters do you wonder about?

Flowers for Algernon, Part 1

Connect to the Story

Think about a way you would like to improve yourself. What might happen if you were successful in achieving that improvement?

Quickwrite Freewrite for a few minutes about the improvement you would make. How and why would you make the improvement? How would it affect your life?

Build Background

"Flowers for Algernon" is a science fiction story about an experiment a man undergoes to improve his intelligence. The characters and situations are fictional, but the tests the psychologists use are real tests.

- Psychologists study how people behave, think, learn, and feel.

- There are many tests to measure human intelligence. The Intelligence Quotient, or IQ, is one measure.

- In recent years, scientists have come to think that people have "multiple intelligences"—special abilities in language, music, art, and physical coordination, for example.

Vocabulary

subconscious (sub kon′shəs) *n.* the part of a person's mind that stores thoughts, feelings, and experiences of which the person is not aware (p. 681). *Painful memories are sometimes buried in the subconscious.*

conscious (kon′shəs) *n.* the part of the mind that stores thoughts, feelings, and experiences of which the mind is aware (p. 681). *Memories you thought were lost can sometimes return to your conscious mind.*

laboratory (lab′rə tôr′ē) *n.* a room, building, or workshop for doing scientific experiments and tests (p. 683). *Javier studied a model of the human brain in the biology laboratory.*

plateau (pla tō′) *n.* a period of time or a stage where relatively little happens (p. 685). *After Geena finished her exams, her life reached a plateau.*

Meet Daniel Keyes

"I think of experiences and images . . . as being stored in the root cellar of my mind, hibernating in the dark until they are ready for stories."

—Daniel Keyes

Exploring the Mind Daniel Keyes has worked as an editor, photographer, English teacher, and merchant seaman. In college he studied psychology. He has said that he "loves to explore the complexities of the human mind." His books and stories show his interest in personality and intelligence.

Award-Winning Story Keyes first published the award-winning "Flowers for Algernon" as a short story in 1959. He later expanded the story into a novel, which he published in 1966.

Daniel Keyes was born in 1927.

 Literature Online

Author Search For more about Daniel Keyes, go to glencoe.com and enter QuickPass code GL39770u5.

Set Purposes for Reading

BQ BIG Question

Read the first part of "Flowers for Algernon" to see the scientific processes involved in testing and improving Charlie's intelligence.

Literary Element Irony

Irony is the contrast between the way things seem and the way they really are. In **situational irony**, a character expects one outcome but the opposite occurs. In **dramatic irony,** the reader or audience has important information that the character does not have.

Irony is an important part of an author's style. Authors use irony to make important points about characters and situations and to make stories interesting, humorous, and dramatic.

As you read, notice the situational and dramatic irony in the story.

Reading Skill Analyze Text Structure

Using **text structures,** authors organize their writing in specific ways for specific purposes. Some text structures are cause and effect, problem and solution, and listing. "Flowers for Algernon" is written as a journal, which is typically in **chronological order**, or time order.

Analyzing text structure is important because it helps you understand the organization of a text, making it easier to find and connect important ideas. Analyzing text structure helps you see the text's unity and coherence. A text has unity when all the paragraphs work together to express one main idea. Coherence refers to the logical connections between those paragraphs.

When you analyze text structure, you

- look for signal words and phrases, such as *first*, *then*, *as a result*, and *most importantly*
- determine what type of text structure the signal words indicate
- think about how text structure works to give meaning to the story

As you read "Flowers for Algernon," find clues to the chronological text structure. You may want to use a graphic organizer like the one below. Link important events with signal words that show time order, such as *next*, *later*, *before*, *after*, *first*, *finally*, and *in the meantime*.

Learning Objectives

For pages 670–688

In studying this text, you will focus on the following objectives:

Literary Study: Analyzing irony.

Reading Skill: Analyzing text structure.

TRY IT

Analyze Text Structure Write a short paragraph telling about the events that happened to you yesterday. Relate the events in chronological order. What words do you use to signal chronological order? In what ways does the chronological structure make your paragraph interesting and easy to read?

Charlie takes a Rorschach test and thinks he has failed. → Later → Charlie gets another test but can't make up stories about the pictures. →

Flowers for Algernon

part 1

Daniel Keyes

progris riport 1—martch 5 1965

Dr. Strauss says I shud rite down what I think and evrey thing that happins to me from now on. I dont know why but he says its importint so they will see if they will use me. I hope they use me. Miss Kinnian says maybe they can make me smart. I want to be smart. My name is Charlie Gordon. I am 37 years old and 2 weeks ago was my birthday. I have nuthing more to rite now so I will close for today.

progris riport 2—martch 6

I had a test today. I think I faled it. and I think that maybe now they wont use me. What happind is a nice young man was in the room and he had some white cards with ink spilled all over them. He sed Charlie what do you see on this card. I was very skared even tho I had my rabits foot in my pockit because when I was a kid I always faled tests in school and I spilled ink to.

I told him I saw a **inkblot**. He said yes and it made me feel good. I thot that was all but when I got up to go he stopped me. He said now sit down Charlie we are not thru yet. Then I dont remember so good but he wantid me to say

Visual Vocabulary

In this story, an **inkblot** is an ink mark made by spilling ink on a piece of paper and then folding the paper in half to make an interesting picture. It is used in a psychological test, called a Rorschach test, to see how a person interprets the shapes he or she sees.

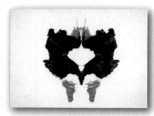

what was in the ink. I dint see nuthing in the ink but he said there was picturs there other pepul saw some picturs. I coudnt see any picturs. I reely tryed to see. I held the card close up and then far away. Then I said if I had my glases I coud see better I usally only ware my glases in the movies or TV but I said they are in the closit in the hall. I got them. Then I said let me see that card agen I bet Ill find it now.

I tryed hard but I still coudnt find the picturs I only saw the ink. I told him maybe I need new glases. He rote somthing down on a paper and I got skared of faling the test. I told him it was a very nice inkblot with littel points al around the eges. He looked very sad so that wasnt it. I said please let me try agen. Ill get it in a few minits becaus Im not so fast somtimes. Im a slow reeder too in Miss Kinnians class for slow adults but I'm trying very hard.

He gave me a chance with another card that had 2 kinds of ink spillled on it red and blue.

He was very nice and talked slow like Miss Kinnian does and he explained it to me that it was a ***raw shok.***[1] He said pepul see things in the ink. I said show me where. He said think. I told him I think a inkblot but that wasnt rite eather. He said what does it remind you—pretend something. I closd my eyes for a long time to pretend. I told him I pretned a fowntan pen with ink leeking all over a table cloth. Then he got up and went out.

I dont think I passd the *raw shok* test.

progris report 3—martch 7

Dr Strauss and Dr Nemur say it dont matter about the inkblots. I told them I dint spill the ink on the cards and I coudnt see anything in the ink. They said that maybe they will still use me. I said Miss Kinnian never gave me tests like that one only spelling and reading. They said Miss Kinnian told that I was her bestist pupil in the adult nite scool becaus I tryed the hardist and I reely wantid to lern. They said how come you went to the adult nite scool all by yourself Charlie. How did you find it. I said I askd pepul and sumbody told me where I shud go to lern to read and spell good. They said

Analyze Text Structure
What does the repetition of *then* in this paragraph tell you about the text structure of the selection? Think about how the text structure helps you follow the story's events.

Irony Review Charlie's reactions to the inkblot tests. In what way are his responses ironic?

---

1 When Charlie says ***raw shok***, he is talking about the **Rorschach** (rôr´ shäk) test, which is used to gather information about personality and intelligence.

why did you want to. I told them becaus all my life I wantid to be smart and not dumb. But its very hard to be smart. They said you know it will probly be tempirery. I said yes. Miss Kinnian told me. I dont care if it herts.

Later I had more crazy tests today. The nice lady who gave it me told me the name and I asked her how do you spellit so I can rite it in my progris riport. THEMATIC APPERCEPTION TEST.[2] I dont know the frist 2 words but I know what *test* means. You got to pass it or you get bad marks. This test lookd easy becaus I coud see the picturs. Only this time she dint want me to tell her the picturs. That mixd me up. I said the man yesterday said I shoud tell him what I saw in the ink she said that dont make no difrence. She said make up storys about the pepul in the picturs.

I told her how can you tell storys about pepul you never met. I said why shud I make up lies. I never tell lies any more becaus I always get caut.

She told me this test and the other one the raw-shok was for getting personalty. I laffed so hard. I said how can you get that thing from inkblots and fotos. She got sore and put her picturs away. I dont care. It was sily. I gess I faled that test too.

Later some men in white coats took me to a difernt part of the hospitil and gave me a game to play. It was like a race with a white mouse. They called the mouse Algernon. Algernon was in a box with a lot of twists and turns like all kinds of walls and they gave me a pencil and a paper with lines and lots of boxes. On one side it said START and on the other end it said FINISH. They said it was *amazed*[3] and that Algernon and me had the same *amazed* to do. I dint see how we could have the same *amazed* if Algernon had a box and I had a paper but I dint say nothing. Anyway there wasnt time because the race started.

One of the men had a watch he was trying to hide so I woudnt see it so I tryed not to look and that made me nervus.

Anyway that test made me feel worser than all the

Irony In what way does the March 7th progress report contain dramatic irony? Think about how the irony affects your reading of the story.

---

2 A ***Thematic Apperception*** (thē mat´ik ap´ər sep´shən) ***Test*** asks people to look at a few pictures and then make up a story about the pictures.

3 Charlie says ***amazed***, but he means "a maze," which is a confusing set of paths that are easy to get lost in.

others because they did it over 10 times with differnt *amazeds* and Algernon won every time. I dint know that mice were so smart. Maybe thats because Algernon is a white mouse. Maybe white mice are smarter then other mice.

progris riport 4—Mar 8

Their going to use me! Im so exited I can hardly write. Dr Nemur and Dr Strauss had a argament about it first. Dr Nemur was in the office when Dr Strauss brot me in. Dr Nemur was worryed about using me but Dr Strauss told him Miss Kinnian rekemmended me the best from all the people who she was teaching. I like Miss Kinnian becaus shes a very smart teacher. And she said Charlie your going to have a second chance. If you volenteer for this experament you mite get smart. They dont know if it will be perminint but theirs a chance. Thats why I said ok even when I was scared because she said it was an operashun. She said dont be scared Charlie you done so much with so little I think you deserv it most of all.

So I got scaird when Dr Nemur and Dr Strauss argud about it. Dr Strauss said I had something that was very good. He said I had a good *motor-vation.*[4] I never even knew I had that. I felt proud when he said that not every body with an eye-q[5] of 68 had that thing. I dont know what it is or where I got it but he said Algernon had it too. Algernons *motor-vation* is the cheese they put in his box. But it cant be that because I didnt eat any cheese this week.

Then he told Dr Nemur something I dint understand so while they were talking I wrote down some of the words.

He said Dr Nemur I know Charlie is not what you had in mind as the first of your new brede of intelek** (coudnt get the word) superman. But most people of his low ment** are host** and uncoop** they are usualy dull apath** and hard to reach. He has a good natcher hes intristed and eager to please.

BQ ⟩⟩ **BIG Question**

You know that the experiment involves an operation, most likely on Charlie's brain. What really matters here—the scientific experiment or Charlie's safety? Think about the reasons for your answer.

---

4 Charlie means *motivation* (mō′ tə vā′ shən). When people have motivation to do something, they feel that they want very much to do it.

5 When Charlie says *eye-q* he means IQ, which stands for "intelligence quotient" (kwō′ shənt). An IQ is the score a person gets on an intelligence test, which is supposed to measure a person's ability to learn.

Dr Nemur said remember he will be the first human beeng ever to have his intelijence trippled by surgicle meens.

Dr Strauss said exakly. Look at how well hes lerned to read and write for his low mentel age its as grate an acheve** as you and I lerning einstines therey of **vity[6] without help. That shows the intenss motorvation. Its comparat** a tremen** achev** I say we use Charlie.

I dint get all the words and they were talking to fast but it sounded like Dr Strauss was on my side and like the other one wasnt.

Then Dr Nemur nodded he said all right maybe your right. We will use Charlie. When he said that I got so exited I jumped up and shook his hand for being so good to me. I told him thank you doc you wont be sorry for giving me a second chance. And I mean it like I told him. After the operashun Im gonna try to be smart. Im gonna try awful hard.

progris ript 5—Mar 10

Im skared. Lots of people who work here and the nurses and the people who gave me the tests came to bring me candy and wish me luck. I hope I have luck. I got my rabits foot and my lucky penny and my horse shoe. Only a black cat crossed me when I was comming to the hospitil. Dr Strauss says dont be supersitis Charlie this is sience. Anyway Im keeping my rabits foot with me.

I asked Dr Strauss if Ill beat Algernon in the race after the operashun and he said maybe. If the operashun works Ill show that mouse I can be as smart as he is. Maybe smarter. Then Ill be abel to read better and spell the words good and know lots of things and be like other people. I want to be smart like other people. If it works perminint they will make everybody smart all over the wurld.

They dint give me anything to eat this morning. I dont know what that eating has to do with getting smart. Im very hungry and Dr Nemur took away my box of candy. That Dr Nemur is a grouch. Dr Strauss says I can have it back after the operashun. You cant eat befor a operashun . . .

Irony Charlie writes down the words the doctors are saying, but he does not understand them. Think about the kind of irony the author creates with these events. What words would describe your reaction to this irony?

Analyze Text Structure What event is about to happen? Think about how you know and think about how knowing this makes you feel.

---

6 When Charlie says *einstines therey of **vity*, he is talking about the theory of relativity developed by the scientist Albert Einstein, which changed the way people understand the world.

Progress Report 6—Mar 15

The operashun dint hurt. He did it while I was sleeping. They took off the bandijis from my eyes and my head today so I can make a PROGRESS REPORT. Dr Nemur who looked at some of my other ones says I spell PROGRESS wrong and he told me how to spell it and REPORT too. I got to try and remember that.

I have a very bad memary for spelling. Dr Strauss says its ok to tell about all the things that happin to me but he says I shoud tell more about what I feel and what I think. When I told him I dont know how to think he said try. All the time when the bandijis were on my eyes I tryed to think. Nothing happened. I dont know what to think about. Maybe if I ask him he will tell me how I can think now that Im suppose to get smart. What do smart people think about. Fancy things I suppose. I wish I knew some fancy things alredy.

Progress Report 7—mar 19

Nothing is happining. I had lots of tests and different kinds of races with Algernon. I hate that mouse. He always beats me. Dr Strauss said I got to play those games. And he said some time I got to take those tests over again. Thse inkblots are stupid. And those pictures are stupid too. I like to draw a picture of a man and a woman but I wont make up lies about people.

I got a headache from trying to think so much. I thot Dr Strauss was my frend but he dont help me. He dont tell me what to think or when Ill get smart. Miss Kinnian dint come to see me. I think writing these progress reports are stupid too.

Irony In what ways does this sentence show both dramatic irony and situational irony? Consider what this irony tells you about Charlie at this point in the experiment.

I tryed hard but I still coudnt find the picturs I only saw the ink.

Progress Report 8—Mar 23

Im going back to work at the factery. They said it was better I shud go back to work but I cant tell anyone what the operashun was for and I have to come to the hospitil for an hour evry night after work. They are gonna pay me mony every month for lerning to be smart.

Im glad Im going back to work because I miss my job and all my frends and all the fun we have there.

Dr Strauss says I shud keep writing things down but I dont have to do it every day just when I think of something or something speshul happins. He says dont get discoridged because it takes time and it happins slow. He says it took a long time with Algernon before he got 3 times smarter than he was before. Thats why Algernon beats me all the time because he had that operashun too. That makes me feel better. I coud probly do that *amazed* faster than a reglar mouse. Maybe some day Ill beat Algernon. Boy that would be something. So far Algernon looks like he mite be smart perminent.

Mar 25 (I dont have to write PROGRESS REPORT on top any more just when I hand it in once a week for Dr Nemur to read. I just have to put the date on. That saves time)

We had a lot of fun at the factery today. Joe Carp said hey look where Charlie had his operashun what did they do Charlie put some brains in. I was going to tell him but I remembered Dr Strauss said no. Then Frank Reilly said what did you do Charlie forget your key and open your door the hard way. That made me laff. Their really my friends and they like me.

Sometimes somebody will say hey look at Joe or Frank or George he really pulled a Charlie Gordon. I dont know why they say that but they always laff. This morning Amos Borg who is the 4 man at Donnegans used my name when he shouted at Ernie the office boy. Ernie lost a packige. He said Ernie for godsake what are you trying to be a Charlie Gordon. I dont understand why he said that. I never lost any packiges.

Mar 28 Dr Strauss came to my room tonight to see why I dint come in like I was suppose to. I told him I dont like to race with Algernon any more. He said I dont have to for a while but I shud come in. He had a present for me only it wasnt a present but just for lend. I thot it was a little television but it wasnt. He said I got to turn it on when I go to sleep. I said your kidding why shud I turn it on when Im going to sleep. Who ever herd of a thing like that. But he said if I want to get smart I got to do what he says. I told him I dint think I was going to get smart and he put his

Analyze Text Structure
Think about how this sentence helps you understand the chronological order of events in this story. Does it change what you expect to happen? Why or why not?

Irony In what way is this statement ironic?

hand on my sholder and said Charlie you dont know it yet but your getting smarter all the time. You wont notice for a while. I think he was just being nice to make me feel good because I dont look any smarter.

Oh yes I almost forgot. I asked him when I can go back to the class at Miss Kinnians school. He said I wont go their. He said that soon Miss Kinnian will come to the hospitil to start and teach me speshul. I was mad at her for not comming to see me when I got the operashun but I like her so maybe we will be frends again.

Mar 29   That crazy TV kept me up all night. How can I sleep with something yelling crazy things all night in my

View the Art Do you think that this image illustrates what is happening to Charlie? Explain.

ears. And the nutty pictures. Wow. I dont know what it says when Im up so how am I going to know when Im sleeping.

Dr Strauss says its ok. He says my brains are lerning when I sleep and that will help me when Miss Kinnian starts my lessons in the hospitl (only I found out it isnt a hospitil its a labatory). I think its all crazy. If you can get smart when your sleeping why do people go to school. That thing I dont think will work. I use to watch the late show and the late late show on TV all the time and it never made me smart. Maybe you have to sleep while you watch it.

Progress Report 9—April 3

Dr Strauss showed me how to keep the TV turned low so now I can sleep. I dont hear a thing. And I still dont understand what it says. A few times I play it over in the morning to find out what I lerned when I was sleeping and I dont think so. Miss Kinnian says Maybe its another langwidge or something. But most times it sounds american. It talks so fast faster then even Miss Gold who was my teacher in 6 grade and I remember she talked so fast I coudnt understand her.

I told Dr Strauss what good is it to get smart in my sleep. I want to be smart when Im awake. He says its the same thing and I have two minds. Theres the **subconscious** and the **conscious** (thats how you spell it). And one dont tell the other one what its doing. They dont even talk to each other. Thats why I dream. And boy have I been having crazy dreams. Wow. Ever since that night TV. The late late late late late show.

I forgot to ask him if it was only me or if everybody had those two minds.

(I just looked up the word in the dictionary Dr Strauss gave me. The word is *subconscious. adj. Of the nature of mental operations yet not present in consciousness; as,*

Irony In what way is Charlie's confusion over Dr. Strauss's device an example of situational irony?

Irony Think about the dramatic irony in this sentence. How does it make you feel about Charlie and about his progress?

Vocabulary

subconscious (sub kon′shəs) *n.* the part of a person's mind that stores thoughts, feelings, and experiences of which the person is not aware

conscious (kon′shəs) *n.* the part of the mind that stores thoughts, feelings, and experiences of which the mind is aware.

subconscious conflict of desires.) Theres more but I still don't know what it means. This isnt a very good dictionary for dumb people like me.

Anyway the headache is from the party. My frends from the factery Joe Carp and Frank Reilly invited me to go with them to Muggsys Saloon for some drinks. I dont like to drink but they said we will have lots of fun. I had a good time.

Joe Carp said I shoud show the girls how I mop out the toilet in the factory and he got me a mop. I showed them and everyone laffed when I told that Mr Donnegan said I was the best janiter he ever had because I like my job and do it good and never come late or miss a day except for my operashun.

I said Miss Kinnian always said Charlie be proud of your job because you do it good.

Everybody laffed and we had a good time and they gave me lots of drinks and Joe said Charlie is a card when hes potted.[7] I dont know what that means but everybody likes me and we have fun. I cant wait to be smart like my best frends Joe Carp and Frank Reilly.

I dont remember how the party was over but I think I went out to buy a newspaper and coffe for Joe and Frank and when I came back there was no one their. I looked for them all over till late. Then I dont remember so good but I think I got sleepy or sick. A nice cop brot me back home. Thats what my landlady Mrs Flynn says.

But I got a headache and a big lump on my head and black and blue all over. I think maybe I fell but Joe Carp says it was the cop they beat up drunks some times. I don't think so. Miss Kinnian says cops are to help people. Anyway I got a bad headache and Im sick and hurt all over. I dont think Ill drink anymore.

April 6   I beat Algernon! I dint even know I beat him until Burt the tester told me. Then the second time I lost because I got so exited I fell off the chair before I finished. But after that I beat him 8 more times. I must be getting smart to beat a smart mouse like Algernon. But I dont *feel* smarter.

Irony What do you know about this statement that Charlie doesn't? Think about how this dramatic irony makes you feel about Charlie and his situation.

---

7 ***Charlie is a card when he's potted*** is a slang way of saying that Charlie is funny when he drinks too much alcohol.

I wanted to race Algernon some more but Burt said thats enough for one day. They let me hold him for a minit. Hes not so bad. Hes soft like a ball of cotton. He blinks and when he opens his eyes their black and pink on the eges.

I said can I feed him because I felt bad to beat him and I wanted to be nice and make frends. Burt said no Algernon is a very specshul mouse with an operashun like mine, and he was the first of all the animals to stay smart so long. He told me Algernon is so smart that every day he has to solve a test to get his food. Its a thing like a lock on a door that changes every time Algernon goes in to eat so he has to lern something new to get his food. That made me sad because if he coudnt lern he woud be hungry.

I dont think its right to make you pass a test to eat. How woud Dr Nemur like it to have to pass a test every time he wants to eat. I think Ill be frends with Algernon.

April 9 Tonight after work Miss Kinnian was at the **laboratory**. She looked like she was glad to see me but scared. I told her dont worry Miss Kinnian Im not smart yet and she laffed. She said I have confidence in you Charlie the way you struggled so hard to read and right better than all the others. At werst you will have it for a littel wile and your doing somthing for sience.

We are reading a very hard book. I never read such a hard book before. Its called *Robinson Crusoe* about a man who gets merooned on a dessert Iland. Hes smart and figers out all kinds of things so he can have a house and food and hes a good swimmer. Only I feel sorry because hes all alone and has no frends. But I think their must be somebody else on the iland because theres a picture with his funny umbrella looking at footprints. I hope he gets a frend and not be lonly.

April 10 Miss Kinnian teaches me to spell better. She says look at a word and close your eyes and say it over and

> *I think Iu be frends with Algernon.*

Analyze Text Structure
Charlie's journal entry for *April 6* reveals the events leading up to Charlie's thought that he wants to be friends with Algernon. Reread the entry and list the events.

Vocabulary

laboratory (lab′rə tôr′ē) *n.* a room, building, or workshop for doing scientific experiments and tests

over until you remember. I have lots of truble with *through* that you say *threw* and *enough* and *tough* that you dont say *enew* and *tew*. You got to say *enuff* and *tuff*. Thats how I use to write it before I started to get smart. Im confused but Miss Kinnian says theres no reason in spelling.

April 14   Finished *Robinson Crusoe*. I want to find out more about what happens to him but Miss Kinnian says thats all there is. *Why*

April 15   Miss Kinnian says Im lerning fast. She read some of the Progress Reports and she looked at me kind of funny. She says Im a fine person and Ill show them all. I asked her why. She said never mind but I shoudnt feel bad if I find out that everybody isnt nice like I think. She said for a person who god gave so little to you done more then a lot of people with brains they never even used. I said all my frends are smart people but there good. They like me and they never did anything that wasnt nice. Then she got something in her eye and she had to run out to the ladys room.

April 16   Today, I lerned, the *comma*, this is a comma (,) a period, with a tail, Miss Kinnian, says its importent, because, it makes writing, better, she said, sombeody, could lose, a lot of money, if a comma, isnt, in the, right place, I dont have, any money, and I dont see, how a comma, keeps you, from losing it,

But she says, everybody, uses commas, so Ill use, them too,

April 17   I used the comma wrong. Its punctuation. Miss Kinnian told me to look up long words in the dictionary to lern to spell them. I said whats the difference if you can read it anyway. She said its part of your education so now on Ill look up all the words Im not sure how to spell. It takes a long time to write that way but I think Im remembering. I only have to look up once and after that I get it right. Anyway thats how come I got the word *punctuation* right. (Its that way in the dictionary). Miss Kinnian says a period is punctuation too, and there are lots of other marks to lern. I told her I thot all the periods had to have tails but she said no.

Irony Think about the real reason Miss Kinnian has to run out of the room. How does the dramatic irony here make you feel about Miss Kinnian?

You got to mix them up, she showed? me" how. to mix! them(up,. and now; I can! mix up all kinds" of punctuation, in! my writing? There, are lots! of rules? to lern; but Im gettin'g them in my head.

One thing I? like about, Dear Miss Kinnian: (thats the way it goes in a business letter if I ever go into business) is she, always gives me' a reason" when—I ask. She's a gen'ius! I wish! I cou'd be smart" like, her;

(Punctuation, is; fun!)

April 18   What a dope I am! I didn't even understand what she was talking about. I read the grammar book last night and it explanes the whole thing. Then I saw it was the same way as Miss Kinnian was trying to tell me, but I didn't get it. I got up in the middle of the night, and the whole thing straightened out in my mind.

Miss Kinnian said that the TV working in my sleep helped out. She said I reached a **plateau**. Thats like the flat top of a hill.

After I figgered out how punctuation worked, I read over all my old Progress Reports from the beginning. Boy, did I have crazy spelling and punctuation! I told Miss Kinnian I ought to go over the pages and fix all the mistakes but she said, "No, Charlie, Dr. Nemur wants them just as they are. That's why he let you keep them after they were photostated,[8] to see your own progress. You're coming along fast, Charlie."

That made me feel good. After the lesson I went down and played with Algernon. We don't race any more.

April 20   I feel sick inside. Not sick like for a doctor, but inside my chest it feels empty like getting punched and a heartburn at the same time.

I wasn't going to write about it, but I guess I got to, because it's important. Today was the first time I ever stayed home from work.

Analyze Text Structure
How does the chronological structure of the text help you see that Charlie's intelligence is increasing?

---

8   Something that is **photostated** has been copied onto specially treated paper.

Vocabulary ....

plateau   (pla tō´) *n.* a period of time or a stage where relatively little happens

Last night Joe Carp and Frank Reilly invited me to a party. There were lots of girls and some men from the factory. I remembered how sick I got last time I drank too much, so I told Joe I didn't want anything to drink. He gave me a plain Coke instead. It tasted funny, but I thought it was just a bad taste in my mouth.

We had a lot of fun for a while. Joe said I should dance with Ellen and she would teach me the steps. I fell a few times and I couldn't understand why because no one else was dancing besides Ellen and me. And all the time I was tripping because somebody's foot was always sticking out.

Then when I got up I saw the look on Joe's face and it gave me a funny feeling in my stomach. "He's a scream," one of the girls said. Everybody was laughing.

Frank said, "I ain't laughed so much since we sent him off for the newspaper that night at Muggsy's and ditched him."

"Look at him. His face is red."

"He's blushing. Charlie is blushing."

"Hey, Ellen, what'd you do to Charlie? I never saw him act like that before."

I didn't know what to do or where to turn. Everyone was looking at me and laughing and I felt naked. I wanted to hide myself. I ran out into the street and I threw up. Then I walked home. It's a funny thing I never knew that Joe and Frank and the others liked to have me around all the time to make fun of me.

Now I know what it means when they say "to pull a Charlie Gordon."

I'm ashamed.

Analyze Text Structure
What chronological signal words does Charlie use in the first four paragraphs of this entry? Think about the ways Charlie's use of signal words has improved since the beginning of the story.

BQ ⟩ **BIG Question**
What really matters to Charlie Gordon? Predict how he will change after his experience at his coworkers' party.

After You Read

Respond and Think Critically

1. Write a summary of the major events in the first part of "Flowers for Algernon." **[Summarize]**

2. Think about why the doctors have chosen Charlie for this experiment. Why do they have doubts about testing him? **[Infer]**

3. According to Charlie, why is he unable to interpret the inkblots and pictures? What do you think the real reasons are? **[Interpret]**

4. Charlie ends his April 14 Progress Report with the word *Why*. How does this word show that Charlie's thinking has changed? **[Analyze]**

5. Why is Charlie ashamed at the end of this part of the story? **[Conclude]**

6. **BQ** **BIG Question** What is your opinion of the experiment? Explain your thoughts. **[Evaluate]**

Vocabulary Practice

On a separate sheet of paper, write the vocabulary word that correctly completes the sentence. If none of the words fits the sentence, write "none."

subconscious   conscious   laboratory   plateau

1. After a summer of activities, Huan's life finally reached a _____.

2. Alfonso read the story and thought it was very _____.

3. I forget your name, but I'm sure it's somewhere in my _____.

4. The scientist entered the _____ to complete his experiment.

5. The long-forgotten memory appeared in my _____ mind.

6. In biology class, Tanya is studying _____.

Academic Vocabulary

The choice of Charlie for the operation causes **controversy.** In this sentence, *controversy* means "a dispute, debate, or disagreement." To become more familiar with the word *controversy,* fill in a graphic organizer like the one below.

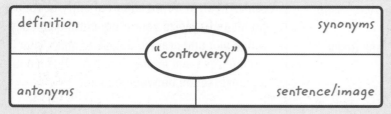

TIP

Drawing Conclusions
Here are some tips to help you draw conclusions. Remember when you draw a conclusion, you use a number of pieces of information to make a general statement about people, places, and events.

- Notice the details about characters.

- Think about the events that occur and the ideas the author is trying to communicate.

- Make a general statement based on all these details.

FOLDABLES Keep track of
Study Organizer your ideas about the **BIG Question** in your unit Foldable.

LOG ON **Literature** Online

Selection Resources
For Selection Quizzes, eFlashcards, and Reading-Writing Connection activities, go to glencoe.com and enter QuickPass code GL37541u5.

Literary Element Irony

1. In what ways could irony be connected to humor? Consider the two types of irony mentioned in the lesson and refer to story details.

2. How does the author's use of dramatic irony reveal Charlie's perspective and intelligence? Explain with story details.

Review: Point of View

Remember that **point of view** is the relationship of the narrator to the story. In the **first-person point of view**, the narrator is a character in the story, referred to as "I," who is telling the story. First-person point of view gives you excellent insight into the narrator's thoughts and feelings. In **limited third-person point of view**, the narrator is outside the story and reveals the thoughts of only one character. In a story with **omniscient third-person point of view**, the narrator can reveal events, thoughts, and actions of all the characters.

3. From what point of view is "Flowers for Algernon" written? Why do you think the author chose this point of view? Explain your answer with details from the story.

4. In what ways does Charlie's language show the effects of the operation on his mind?

Reading Skill Analyze Text Structures

Test Skills Practice

5. Which sentence best shows the story's chronological order?
   A. Dr Strauss and Dr Nemur say it dont matter about the inkblots.
   B. I have a very bad memary for spelling.
   C. Miss Kinnian said that the TV working in my sleep helped out.
   D. Last night Joe Carp and Frank Reilly invited me to a party.

Grammar Link

Commas with Appositives An **appositive** is a noun or pronoun next to another noun to identify it or add information.

- A **nonessential appositive** renames the noun or adds more information. The meaning of the sentence won't change without the appositive. Set off a nonessential appositive with commas.

  Charlie's teacher, **Miss Kinnian**, *recommended him for the procedure.*

  (*Miss Kinnian* identifies the noun *teacher.* She is Charlie's only teacher.)

- An **essential appositive** identifies another noun or adds information that is necessary to the meaning of the sentence. Don't set it off with commas.

  The lab mouse **Algernon** *was the most successful test subject.*

  (*Algernon* specifies which one of the lab's mice was the most successful.)

- Appositives can be phrases as well. Always set off an appositive phrase with commas.

  Dr. Nemur, *an accomplished neurosurgeon*, argued with Dr. Strauss.

  (The appositive phrase *an accomplished neurosurgeon* describes *Dr. Nemur.*)

Practice On a sheet of paper, write one sentence with a nonessential appositive, another with an essential appositive, and a third with an appositive phrase.

Writing

Apply Irony Think of an ironic situation that you've been in. Write a journal entry about the situation. Organize your entry chronologically with a plot and precise details to make your writing fresh and interesting. Include dialogue, or conversation between people.

Flowers for Algernon, Part 2

Connect to the Short Story

Charlie Gordon undergoes an operation to make him three times smarter, giving him an IQ higher than 200 and turning him into a genius. What would you do if you woke up three times smarter than you are now? How would your life be different?

Partner Talk With a partner, talk about the changes you would make in your life if you became three times smarter. Would you try to make the world a better place? Would you think of ways to make millions of dollars? What does your decision say about what's really important to you?

Build Background

In the second part of "Flowers for Algernon," Charlie becomes a genius, or a person with a very high intelligence quotient.

- Psychologists rate someone who scores 140 or above on an IQ test a genius.

- Some geniuses can see connections between things that are not obvious to most people.

- Scientists debate whether people are born geniuses, become geniuses because of their environment and experience, or both.

Vocabulary

technique (tek nēk´) *n.* a method used to perform an operation or achieve a goal (p. 694). *The surgeons used a new technique to repair the athlete's knee.*

petition (pə tish´ ən) *n.* a formal request to a superior for some favor, privilege, or compensation for a loss or wrong (p. 696). *The mayor received a petition to save the city park.*

tangible (tan´ jə bəl) *adj.* capable of being grasped or understood; definite; real (p. 698). *Keesha didn't understand the art lesson until the teacher showed a tangible example.*

cowered (kou´ ərd) *v.* moved away in fear or shame (p. 700). *The dog cowered in the corner during the thunderstorm.*

obscure (əb skyoor´) *v.* to hide (p. 704). *Complex words can obscure the meaning of a sentence.*

Set Purposes for Reading

BQ BIG Question

Read the second part of "Flowers for Algernon" to find out what matters most to Charlie Gordon.

Literary Element Foreshadowing

Foreshadowing is the use of clues by an author to prepare readers for events that will happen later in a narrative. Foreshadowing creates feelings of suspense, dread, or anticipation that involve the reader more fully in a story.

Foreshadowing is important because it helps readers predict what will happen in a story. Authors use this technique so readers will be motivated to keep reading to see if their predictions are right.

As you read "Flowers for Algernon," look for any clues that the author gives as to what might happen to Charlie. In what way do these clues make you want to keep reading?

Reading Strategy Make Inferences About Characters

Authors rarely state directly why characters act the way they do. However, you can use your reason and experience together with clues from a text to **make inferences**, or educated guesses.

Making inferences about characters is an important part of gaining understanding about the characters and the role that they play in the text. By making inferences, you look more deeply at characters.

When you make inferences about characters, you

- look at the descriptions, dialogue, events, and relationships that might tell you something the author wants to convey about the character

- apply your knowledge and experience to the story

- guess at what the author does not come right out and say

As you read the second part of "Flowers for Algernon," look for details to help you make inferences about the characters. You may find it helpful to use a graphic organizer like the one below for each character.

Story Details	Inferences About Character

Learning Objectives

For pages 689–713

In studying this text, you will focus on the following objectives:

Reading: Analyzing foreshadowing.

Making inferences about characters.

TRY IT

Make Inferences About Characters Read the following description and make an inference about why the character behaves in this manner.

Mr. Tiptoe walked slowly along the sidewalk. He took care not to step on cracks, walk under ladders, or go near black cats.

Flowers for Algernon
part 2

Daniel Keyes

PROGRESS REPORT 11

April 21   Still didn't go into the factory. I told Mrs. Flynn my landlady to call and tell Mr. Donnegan I was sick. Mrs. Flynn looks at me very funny lately like she's scared of me.

I think it's a good thing about finding out how everybody laughs at me. I thought about it a lot. It's because I'm so dumb and I don't even know when I'm doing something dumb. People think it's funny when a dumb person can't do things the same way they can.

Anyway, now I know I'm getting smarter every day. I know punctuation and I can spell good. I like to look up all the hard words in the dictionary and I remember them. I'm reading a lot now, and Miss Kinnian says I read very fast. Sometimes I even understand what I'm reading about, and it stays in my mind. There are times when I can close my eyes and think of a page and it all comes back like a picture.

Besides history, geography, and arithmetic, Miss Kinnian said I should start to learn a few foreign languages. Dr. Strauss gave me some more tapes to play while I sleep. I still don't understand how that conscious and unconscious mind works, but Dr. Strauss says not to worry yet. He asked me to promise that when I start learning college subjects next week I wouldn't read any books on psychology—that is, until he gives me permission.

Make Inferences About Characters Charlie thinks his landlady is afraid of him. What do his suspicions tell you about the changes he is experiencing? What clues can you find in the next paragraph that show Charlie's mental growth?

I feel a lot better today, but I guess I'm still a little angry that all the time people were laughing and making fun of me because I wasn't so smart. When I become intelligent like Dr. Strauss says, with three times my I.Q. of 68, then maybe I'll be like everyone else and people will like me and be friendly.

I'm not sure what an I.Q. is. Dr. Nemur said it was something that measured how intelligent you were—like a scale in the drugstore weighs pounds. But Dr. Strauss had a big argument with him and said an I.Q. didn't weigh intelligence at all. He said an I.Q. showed how much intelligence you could get, like the numbers on the outside of a measuring cup. You still had to fill the cup up with stuff.

Then when I asked Burt, who gives me my intelligence tests and works with Algernon, he said that both of them were wrong (only I had to promise not to tell them he said so). Burt says that the I.Q. measures a lot of different things including some of the things you learned already, and it really isn't any good at all.

So I still don't know what I.Q. is except that mine is going to be over 200 soon. I didn't want to say anything, but I don't see how if they don't know *what* it is, or *where* it is—I don't see how they know *how much* of it you've got.

Dr. Nemur says I have to take a *Rorshach Test* tomorrow. I wonder what *that* is.

April 22   I found out what a *Rorshach* is. It's the test I took before the operation—the one with the inkblots on the pieces of cardboard. The man who gave me the test was the same one.

I was scared to death of those inkblots. I knew he was going to ask me to find the pictures and I knew I wouldn't be able to. I was thinking to myself, if only there was some way of knowing what kind of pictures were hidden there. Maybe there weren't any pictures at all. Maybe it was just a trick to see if I was dumb enough to look for something that wasn't there. Just thinking about that made me sore at him.

"All right, Charlie," he said, "you've seen these cards before, remember?"

> **Foreshadowing** What do you think the author is trying to hint at by mentioning Charlie's hopes? Do you think Charlie's hopes will be fulfilled? Why or why not?

"Of course I remember."

The way I said it, he knew I was angry, and he looked surprised. "Yes, of course. Now I want you to look at this one. What might this be? What do you see on this card? People see all sorts of things in these inkblots. Tell me what it might be for you—what it makes you think of."

I was shocked. That wasn't what I had expected him to say at all. "You mean there are no pictures hidden in those inkblots?"

He frowned and took off his glasses. "What?"

"Pictures. Hidden in the inkblots. Last time you told me that everyone could see them and you wanted me to find them too."

He explained to me that the last time he had used almost the exact same words he was using now. I didn't believe it, and I still have the suspicion that he misled me at the time just for the fun of it. Unless—I don't know any more—could I have been *that* feeble-minded?[1]

We went through the cards slowly. One of them looked like a pair of bats tugging at something. Another one looked like two men fencing with swords. I imagined all sorts of things. I guess I got carried away. But I didn't trust him any more, and I kept turning them around and even looking on the back to see if there was anything there I was supposed to catch. While he was making his notes, I peeked out of the corner of my eye to read it. But it was all in code that looked like this:

WF+A DdF-Ad orig. WF-A SF+obj

The test still doesn't make sense to me. It seems to me that anyone could make up lies about things that they didn't really see. How could he know I wasn't making a fool of him by mentioning things that I didn't really imagine? Maybe I'll understand it when Dr. Strauss lets me read up on psychology.

> *The test still doesn't make sense to me. It seems to me that anyone could make up lies about things that they didn't really see.*

Make Inferences About Characters What does this incident tell you about the ways in which Charlie is changing?

---

1 Learning and understanding can be very difficult for a **feeble-minded** person.

April 25   I figured out a new way to line up the machines in the factory, and Mr. Donnegan says it will save him ten thousand dollars a year in labor and increased production. He gave me a twenty-five-dollar bonus.

I wanted to take Joe Carp and Frank Reilly out to lunch to celebrate, but Joe said he had to buy some things for his wife, and Frank said he was meeting his cousin for lunch. I guess it'll take a little time for them to get used to the changes in me. Everybody seems to be frightened of me. When I went over to Amos Borg and tapped him on the shoulder, he jumped up in the air.

People don't talk to me much any more or kid around the way they used to. It makes the job kind of lonely.

April 27   I got up the nerve today to ask Miss Kinnian to have dinner with me tomorrow night to celebrate my bonus.

At first she wasn't sure it was right, but I asked Dr. Strauss and he said it was okay. Dr. Strauss and Dr. Nemur don't seem to be getting along so well. They're arguing all the time. This evening when I came in to ask Dr. Strauss about having dinner with Miss Kinnian, I heard them shouting. Dr. Nemur was saying that it was *his* experiment and *his* research, and Dr. Strauss was shouting back that he contributed just as much, because he found me through Miss Kinnian and he performed the operation. Dr. Strauss said that someday thousands of neurosurgeons² might be using his **technique** all over the world.

Dr. Nemur wanted to publish the results of the experiment at the end of this month. Dr. Strauss wanted to wait a while longer to be sure. Dr. Strauss said that Dr. Nemur was more interested in the Chair of Psychology at Princeton³ than he was in the experiment. Dr. Nemur

Foreshadowing Think about the way Charlie acts differently at work now. What does this foreshadow about Charlie's work life?

Foreshadowing In what way might Dr. Strauss's caution be an example of foreshadowing?

---

2 **Neurosurgeons** are doctors who study and operate on the brain.

3 The **Chair of Psychology** is the head of the psychology department at a college or university. **Princeton** is a famous university in New Jersey.

Vocabulary ....

technique (tek nēk´) *n.* a method used to perform an operation or achieve a goal

said that Dr. Strauss was nothing but an opportunist[4] who was trying to ride to glory on *his* **coattails.**

When I left afterwards, I found myself trembling. I don't know why for sure, but it was as if I'd seen both men clearly for the first time. I remember hearing Burt say that Dr. Nemur had a shrew[5] of a wife who was pushing him all the time to get things published so that he could become famous. Burt said that the dream of her life was to have a big-shot husband.

Was Dr. Strauss really trying to ride on his coattails?

April 28 I don't understand why I never noticed how beautiful Miss Kinnian really is. She has brown eyes and feathery brown hair that comes to the top of her neck. She's only thirty-four! I think from the beginning I had the feeling that she was an unreachable genius—and very, very old. Now, every time I see her she grows younger and more lovely.

We had dinner and a long talk. When she said that I was coming along so fast that soon I'd be leaving her behind, I laughed.

"It's true, Charlie. You're already a better reader than I am. You can read a whole page at a glance while I can take in only a few lines at a time. And you remember every single thing you read. I'm lucky if I can recall the main thoughts and the general meaning."

"I don't feel intelligent. There are so many things I don't understand."

She took out a cigarette and I lit it for her. "You've got to be a *little* patient. You're accomplishing in days and weeks what it takes normal people to do in half a lifetime. That's what makes it so amazing. You're like a giant sponge now, soaking things in. Facts, figures, general knowledge. And soon you'll begin to connect them, too. You'll see how the different branches of learning are related. There are many levels, Charlie, like steps on a giant ladder that take you up higher and higher to see more and more of the world around you.

Make Inferences About Characters Why do you think Charlie is seeing Miss Kinnian in a new way?

Visual Vocabulary

Coattails are the back flaps of a man's dress coat. (They are also called simply "tails.") If you "ride on someone's coattails," you use, or take advantage of, that person's power in order to gain power for yourself.

---

4 An **opportunist** is someone who takes advantage of every opportunity, regardless of consequences.

5 Here, **shrew** means "a bad-tempered, nagging woman."

"I can see only a little bit of that, Charlie, and I won't go much higher than I am now, but you'll keep climbing up and up, and see more and more, and each step will open new worlds that you never even knew existed." She frowned. "I hope . . . I just hope to God—"

"What?"

"Never mind, Charles. I just hope I wasn't wrong to advise you to go into this in the first place."

I laughed. "How could that be? It worked, didn't it? Even Algernon is still smart."

We sat there silently for a while and I knew what she was thinking about as she watched me toying with the chain of my rabbit's foot and my keys. I didn't want to think of that possibility any more than elderly people want to think of death. I *knew* that this was only the beginning. I knew what she meant about levels because I'd seen some of them already. The thought of leaving her behind made me sad.

I'm in love with Miss Kinnian.

PROGRESS REPORT 12

April 30   I've quit my job with Donnegan's Plastic Box Company. Mr. Donnegan insisted that it would be better for all concerned if I left. What did I do to make them hate me so?

The first I knew of it was when Mr. Donnegan showed me the **petition.** Eight hundred and forty names, everyone connected with the factory, except Fanny Girden. Scanning the list quickly, I saw at once that hers was the only missing name. All the rest demanded that I be fired.

Joe Carp and Frank Reilly wouldn't talk to me about it. No one else would either, except Fanny. She was one of the few people I'd known who set her mind to something and believed it no matter what the rest of the world proved, said, or did—and Fanny did not believe that I should have been fired. She had been against the petition on principle and despite the pressure and threats she'd held out.

Foreshadowing Consider what Charlie is worried about. In what way might his concerns foreshadow upcoming events?

Make Inferences About Characters Why do you think Charlie's coworkers petitioned to have him fired?

Vocabulary
....

petition (pə tish′ ən) *n.* a formal request to a superior for some favor, privilege, or compensation for a loss or wrong

"Which don't mean to say," she remarked, "that I don't think there's something mighty strange about you, Charlie. Them changes. I don't know. You used to be a good, dependable, ordinary man—not too bright maybe, but honest. Who knows what you done to yourself to get so smart all of a sudden. Like everybody around here's been saying, Charlie, it's not right."

"But how can you say that, Fanny? What's wrong with a man becoming intelligent and wanting to acquire knowledge and understanding of the world around him?"

She stared down at her work and I turned to leave. Without looking at me, she said: "It was evil when Eve listened to the snake and ate from the tree of knowledge. It was evil when she saw that she was naked. If not for that none of us would ever have to grow old and sick, and die."

Once again now I have the feeling of shame burning inside me. This intelligence has driven a wedge between me and all the people I once knew and loved. Before, they laughed at me and despised me for my ignorance and dullness; now, they hate me for my knowledge and understanding. What in God's name do they want of me?

They've driven me out of the factory. Now I'm more alone than ever before . . .

May 15 Dr. Strauss is very angry at me for not having written any progress reports in two weeks. He's justified because the lab is now paying me a regular salary. I told him I was too busy thinking and reading. When I pointed out that writing was such a slow process that it made me impatient with my poor handwriting, he suggested that I learn to type. It's much easier to write now because I can type nearly seventy-five words a minute. Dr. Strauss continually reminds me of the need to speak and write simply so that people will be able to understand me.

I'll try to review all the things that happened to me during the last two weeks. Algernon and I were presented to the American Psychological Association sitting in convention with the World Psychological Association last Tuesday. We created quite a sensation. Dr. Nemur and Dr. Strauss were proud of us.

Make Inferences About Characters What can you tell about Charlie's writing and speaking from Dr. Strauss's reminder?

I suspect that Dr. Nemur, who is sixty—ten years older than Dr. Strauss—finds it necessary to see **tangible** results of his work. Undoubtedly the result of pressure by Mrs. Nemur.

Contrary to my earlier impressions of him, I realize that Dr. Nemur is not at all a genius. He has a very good mind, but it struggles under the spectre[6] of self-doubt. He wants people to take him for a genius. Therefore, it is important for him to feel that his work is accepted by the world. I believe that Dr. Nemur was afraid of further delay because he worried that someone else might make a discovery along these lines and take the credit from him.

Dr. Strauss on the other hand might be called a genius, although I feel that his areas of knowledge are too limited. He was educated in the tradition of narrow specialization;[7] the broader aspects of background were neglected far more than necessary—even for a neurosurgeon.

I was shocked to learn that the only ancient languages he could read were Latin, Greek, and Hebrew, and that he knows almost nothing of mathematics beyond the elementary levels of the calculus of variations.[8] When he admitted this to me, I found myself almost annoyed. It was as if he'd hidden this part of himself in order to deceive me, pretending—as do many people I've discovered—to be what he is not. No one I've ever known is what he appears to be on the surface.

Make Inferences About Characters What do Charlie's comments about Dr. Nemur and Dr. Strauss tell you about his intellectual growth?

Make Inferences About Characters What does this comment tell you about the ways in which Charlie has changed?

---

6 A *spectre* is something that haunts or troubles your mind a lot.

7 Here, *in the tradition of narrow specialization* refers to the fact that Dr. Strauss is an expert in only one subject.

8 *Calculus* is a branch of advanced mathematics. The *calculus of variations* is even more complicated than simple calculus.

Vocabulary ....

tangible (tan´jə bəl) *adj.* capable of being grasped or understood; definite; real

Dr. Nemur appears to be uncomfortable around me. Sometimes when I try to talk to him, he just looks at me strangely and turns away. I was angry at first when Dr. Strauss told me I was giving Dr. Nemur an inferiority complex.[9] I thought he was mocking me and I'm oversensitive at being made fun of.

How was I to know that a highly respected psychoexperimentalist like Nemur was unacquainted with Hindustani[10] and Chinese? It's absurd when you consider the work that is being done in India and China today in the very field of this study.

I asked Dr. Strauss how Nemur could refute[11] Rahajamati's attack on his method and results if Nemur couldn't even read them in the first place. That strange look on Dr. Strauss' face can mean only one of two things. Either he doesn't want to tell Nemur what they're saying in India, or else—and this worries me—Dr. Strauss doesn't know either. I must be careful to speak and write clearly and simply so that people won't laugh.

May 18   I am very disturbed. I saw Miss Kinnian last night for the first time in over a week. I tried to avoid all discussions of intellectual concepts[12] and to keep the conversation on a simple, everyday level, but she just stared at me blankly and asked me what I meant about the mathematical variance equivalent in Dorbermann's *Fifth Concerto.*

When I tried to explain she stopped me and laughed. I guess I got angry, but I suspect I'm approaching her on the wrong level. No matter what I try to discuss with her, I am unable to communicate. I must review Vrostadt's equations on *Levels of Semantic Progression.* I find that I don't communicate with people much any more. Thank God for books and music and things I can think about. I am alone in my apartment at Mrs. Flynn's boardinghouse most of the time and seldom speak to anyone.

Foreshadowing What could Charlie's struggle to communicate with Miss Kinnian foreshadow about the future of Charlie's relationships?

---

9 Someone with an **inferiority complex** feels less worthy or valuable than others.

10 **Hindustani** (hin´ doo stä´ nē) is a dialect spoken in India.

11 To **refute** the attack would be to prove that the criticism is false or incorrect.

12 **Intellectual concepts** are ideas that relate to learning and thinking.

May 20 I would not have noticed the new dishwasher, a boy of about sixteen, at the corner diner where I take my evening meals if not for the incident of the broken dishes.

They crashed to the floor, shattering and sending bits of white china under the tables. The boy stood there, dazed and frightened, holding the empty tray in his hand. The whistles and catcalls from the customers (the cries of "hey, there go the profits!" . . ."*Mazeltov!*"[13] . . . and "well, *he* didn't work here very long . . ." which invariably[14] seem to follow the breaking of glass or dishware in a public restaurant) all seemed to confuse him.

When the owner came to see what the excitement was about, the boy **cowered** as if he expected to be struck and threw up his arms as if to ward off the blow.

"All right! All right, you dope," shouted the owner, "don't just stand there! Get the broom and sweep that mess up. A broom . . . a broom, you idiot! It's in the kitchen. Sweep up all the pieces."

The boy saw that he was not going to be punished. His frightened expression disappeared and he smiled and hummed as he came back with the broom to sweep the floor. A few of the rowdier customers kept up the remarks, amusing themselves at his expense.

"Here, sonny, over here there's a nice piece behind you . . ."

"C'mon, do it again . . ."

"He's not so dumb. It's easier to break 'em than to wash 'em . . ."

As his vacant eyes moved across the crowd of amused onlookers, he slowly mirrored their smiles and finally broke into an uncertain grin at the joke which he obviously did not understand.

I felt sick inside as I looked at his dull, vacuous smile,

---

13 *Mazeltov* or *mazel tov* (mä′zəl təv′) means "good luck" or "congratulations" in the Hebrew language.

14 *Invariably* (in vār′ē ə blē) means constantly or always.

Vocabulary ....

cowered (kou′ərd) *v.* moved away in fear or shame

the wide, bright eyes of a child, uncertain but eager to please. They were laughing at him because he was mentally retarded.

And I had been laughing at him too.

Suddenly, I was furious at myself and all those who were smirking at him. I jumped up and shouted, "Shut up! Leave him alone! It's not his fault he can't understand! He can't help what he is! But for God's sake . . . he's still a human being!"

The room grew silent. I cursed myself for losing control and creating a scene. I tried not to look at the boy as I paid my check and walked out without touching my food. I felt ashamed for both of us.

How strange it is that people of honest feelings and sensibility, who would not take advantage of a man born without arms or legs or eyes—how such people think nothing of abusing a man born with low intelligence. It infuriated me to think that not too long ago I, like this boy, had foolishly played the clown.

And I had almost forgotten.

I'd hidden the picture of the old Charlie Gordon from myself because now that I was intelligent it was something that had to be pushed out of my mind. But today in looking at that boy, for the first time I saw what I had been. *I was just like him!*

Only a short time ago, I learned that people laughed at me. Now I can see that unknowingly I joined with them in laughing at myself. That hurts most of all.

I have often reread my progress reports and seen the illiteracy, the childish naiveté,[15] the mind of low intelligence peering from a dark room, through the keyhole, at the dazzling light outside. I see that even in my dullness I knew that I was inferior, and that other people had something I lacked—something denied me. In my mental blindness, I thought that it was somehow connected with the ability to read and write, and I was sure that if I could get those skills I would automatically have intelligence too.

Make Inferences About Characters Why does Charlie get so angry? Think about ways in which he might see his former self in the boy who dropped the dishes.

---

15 *Naiveté* (nä ēv´ tē) is innocence, or lack of worldly knowledge and experience.

Even a feeble-minded man wants to be like other men.

A child may not know how to feed itself, or what to eat, yet it knows of hunger.

This then is what I was like, I never knew. Even with my gift of intellectual awareness, I never really knew.

This day was good for me. Seeing the past more clearly, I have decided to use my knowledge and skills to work in the field of increasing human intelligence levels. Who is better equipped for this work? Who else has lived in both worlds? These are my people. Let me use my gift to do something for them.

Tomorrow, I will discuss with Dr. Strauss the manner in which I can work in this area. I may be able to help him work out the problems of widespread use of the technique which was used on me. I have several good ideas of my own.

There is so much that might be done with this technique. If I could be made into a genius, what about thousands of others like myself? What fantastic levels might be achieved by using this technique on normal people? On *geniuses*?

There are so many doors to open.

I am impatient to begin.

BQ BIG Question
Think about what really matters to Charlie now. In what ways, if any, has this changed since the first part of this story?

PROGRESS REPORT 13

May 23 It happened today. Algernon bit me. I visited the lab to see him as I do occasionally, and when I took him out of his cage, he snapped at my hand. I put him back and watched him for a while. He was unusually disturbed and vicious.

Foreshadowing What might this incident foreshadow? Remember, the scientists performed the same operation on both Charlie and Algernon.

May 24   Burt, who is in charge of the experimental animals, tells me that Algernon is changing. He is less cooperative; he refuses to run the maze any more; general motivation has decreased. And he hasn't been eating. Everyone is upset about what this may mean.

May 25   They've been feeding Algernon, who now refuses to work the shifting-lock problem. Everyone identifies me with Algernon. In a way we're both the first of our kind. They're all pretending that Algernon's behavior is not necessarily significant for me. But it's hard to hide the fact that some of the other animals who were used in this experiment are showing strange behavior.

Dr. Strauss and Dr. Nemur have asked me not to come to the lab any more. I know what they're thinking but I can't accept it. I am going ahead with my plans to carry their research forward. With all due respect to both of these fine scientists, I am well aware of their limitations. If there is an answer, I'll have to find it out for myself. Suddenly, time has become very important to me.

May 29   I have been given a lab of my own and permission to go ahead with the research. I'm on to something. Working day and night. I've had a cot moved into the lab. Most of my writing time is spent on the notes which I keep in a separate folder, but from time to time I feel it necessary to put down my moods and my thoughts out of sheer habit.

I find the *calculus of intelligence* to be a fascinating study. Here is the place for the application of all the knowledge I have acquired. In a sense it's the problem I've been concerned with all my life.

May 31   Dr. Strauss thinks I'm working too hard. Dr. Nemur says I'm trying to cram a lifetime of research and thought into a few weeks. I know I should rest, but I'm driven on by something inside that won't let me stop. I've got to find the reason for the sharp regression[16] in Algernon. I've got to know *if* and *when* it will happen to me.

Make Inferences About Characters Why has time become such a priority to Charlie?

Foreshadowing What do you think will happen to Charlie now that you know what has happened to Algernon? On what clues do you base your prediction?

---

16 When something returns to an earlier stage, it shows *regression* (ri gresh´ən).

LETTER TO DR. STRAUSS (*copy*)

Dear Dr. Strauss:

Under separate cover I am sending you a copy of my report entitled, "The Algernon-Gordon Effect: A Study of Structure and Function of Increased Intelligence," which I would like to have you read and have published.

As you see, my experiments are completed. I have included in my report all of my formulae, as well as mathematical analysis in the appendix. Of course, these should be verified.

Because of its importance to both you and Dr. Nemur (and need I say to myself, too?) I have checked and rechecked my results a dozen times in the hope of finding an error. I am sorry to say the results must stand. Yet for the sake of science, I am grateful for the little bit that I here add to the knowledge of the function of the human mind and of the laws governing the artificial increase of human intelligence.

I recall your once saying to me that an experimental *failure* or the *disproving* of a theory was as important to the advancement of learning as a success would be. I know now that this is true. I am sorry, however, that my own contribution to the field must rest upon the ashes of the work of two men I regard so highly.

Yours truly,

Charles Gordon

encl.: rept.

Foreshadowing In what ways do these words continue the foreshadowing of what is to come?

June 5 I must not become emotional. The facts and the results of my experiments are clear, and the more sensational aspects of my own rapid climb cannot **obscure** the fact that the tripling of intelligence by the surgical technique developed by Drs. Strauss and Nemur must be

Make Inferences About Characters Think about what Charlie might be feeling. Why do you think he uses such complex, scientific language in this paragraph?

Vocabulary ....

obscure (əb skyoor´) *v.* to hide

viewed as having little or no practical applicability (at the present time) to the increase of human intelligence.

As I review the records and data on Algernon, I see that although he is still in his physical infancy, he has regressed mentally. Motor activity is impaired; there is a general reduction of glandular activity; there is an accelerated loss of co-ordination.

There are also strong indications of progressive amnesia.[17]

As will be seen by my report, these and other physical and mental deterioration syndromes[18] can be predicted with statistically significant results by the application of my formula.

The surgical stimulus[19] to which we were both subjected has resulted in an intensification and acceleration of all mental processes. The unforeseen development, which I have taken the liberty of calling the *Algernon-Gordon Effect,* is the logical extension of the entire intelligence speed-up. The hypothesis[20] here proven may be described simply in the following terms: Artificially increased intelligence deteriorates at a rate of time directly proportional to the quantity of the increase.

I feel that this, in itself, is an important discovery.

As long as I am able to write, I will continue to record my thoughts in these progress reports. It is one of my few pleasures. However, by all indications, my own mental deterioration will be very rapid.

I have already begun to notice signs of emotional instability and forgetfulness, the first symptoms of the burnout.

Conversion. Diana Ong.
View the Art In what ways might the face in this painting show what Charlie is going through?

---

17 **Progressive amnesia** is a loss of memory that is getting worse.

18 **Deterioration** is a worsening, and **syndromes** are groups of symptoms that, together, indicate disease. The combined term refers to conditions that result in the lessening of some ability or strength.

19 A **stimulus** (stim´yə ləs) is something that causes a response.

20 A **hypothesis** is an unproven theory or idea.

June 10   Deterioration progressing. I have become absentminded. Algernon died two days ago. **Dissection** shows my predictions were right. His brain had decreased in weight and there was a general smoothing out of cerebral **convolutions** as well as a deepening and broadening of brain **fissures.**

I guess the same thing is or will soon be happening to me. Now that it's definite, I don't want it to happen.

I put Algernon's body in a cheese box and buried him in the back yard. I cried.

June 15   Dr. Strauss came to see me again. I wouldn't open the door and I told him to go away. I want to be left to myself. I have become touchy and irritable. I feel the darkness closing in. It's hard to throw off thoughts of suicide. I keep telling myself how important this introspective[21] journal will be.

It's a strange sensation to pick up a book that you've read and enjoyed just a few months ago and discover that you don't remember it. I remembered how great I thought John Milton was, but when I picked up *Paradise Lost* I couldn't understand it at all. I got so angry I threw the book across the room.

I've got to try to hold on to some of it. Some of the things I've learned. Oh, God, please don't take it all away.

June 19   Sometimes, at night, I go out for a walk. Last night I couldn't remember where I lived. A policeman took me home. I have the strange feeling that this has all happened to me before—a long time ago. I keep telling myself I'm the only person in the world who can describe what's happening to me.

June 21   Why can't I remember? I've got to fight. I lie in bed for days and I don't know who or where I am. Then it all comes back to me in a flash. Fugues of amnesia. Symptoms of senility[22]—second childhood. I can watch them coming on. It's so cruelly logical. I learned so much

Foreshadowing What possibility does Algernon's death foreshadow for Charlie?

Make Inferences About Characters Why do you think Charlie reacts the way he does to Algernon's death?

Visual Vocabulary

Charlie cuts up Algernon's brain to study it **(dissection)**. A healthy brain surface would have many irregular folds **(convolutions)** and cracks **(fissures)** that are long, narrow, and shallow.

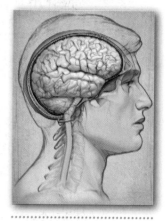

---

21 *Introspective* means "looking into or examining your own feelings and thoughts."

22 *Fugues* (fūgz) of *amnesia* (am nē′zhə) are times when a person seems to be aware of his or her actions but can't recall them later. *Senility* (si nil′ə tē) refers to the loss of physical and mental abilities that can accompany old age.

and so fast. Now my mind is deteriorating rapidly. I won't let it happen. I'll fight it. I can't help thinking of the boy in the restaurant, the blank expression, the silly smile, the people laughing at him. No—please—not that again . . .

June 22 I'm forgetting things that I learned recently. It seems to be following the classic pattern—the last things learned are the first things forgotten. Or is that the pattern? I'd better look it up again . . .

I reread my paper on the *Algernon-Gordon Effect* and I get the strange feeling that it was written by someone else. There are parts I don't even understand.

Motor activity impaired. I keep tripping over things, and it becomes increasingly difficult to type.

June 23 I've given up using the **typewriter** completely. My coordination is bad. I feel that I'm moving slower and slower. Had a terrible shock today. I picked up a copy of an article I used in my research, Krueger's *Uber psychische Ganzheit,* to see if it would help me understand what I had done. First I thought there was something wrong with my eyes. Then I realized I could no longer read German. I tested myself in other languages. All gone.

June 30 A week since I dared to write again. It's slipping away like sand through my fingers. Most of the books I have are too hard for me now. I get angry with them because I know that I read and understood them just a few weeks ago.

I keep telling myself I must keep writing these reports so that somebody will know what is happening to me. But it gets harder to form the words and remember spellings. I have to look up even simple words in the dictionary now and it makes me impatient with myself.

Dr. Strauss comes around almost every day, but I told him I wouldn't see or speak to anybody. He feels guilty. They all do. But I don't blame anyone. I knew what might happen. But how it hurts.

July 7 I don't know where the week went. Todays Sunday I know because I can see through my window people going to church. I think I stayed in bed all week but I remember Mrs. Flynn bringing food to me a few

Make Inferences About Characters What is Charlie dreading? Why does he want to avoid it?

Visual Vocabulary

This is an old-style manual **typewriter**. People used typewriters before computers were invented.

times. I keep saying over and over Ive got to do something but then I forget or maybe its just easier not to do what I say Im going to do.

I think of my mother and father a lot these days. I found a picture of them with me taken at a beach. My father has a big ball under his arm and my mother is holding me by the hand. I dont remember them the way they are in the picture. All I remember is my father drunk most of the time and arguing with mom about money.

He never shaved much and he used to scratch my face when he hugged me. My mother said he died but Cousin Miltie said he heard his mom and dad say that my father ran away with another woman. When I asked my mother she slapped my face and said my father was dead. I dont think I ever found out which was true but I don't care much. (He said he was going to take me to see cows on a farm once but he never did. He never kept his promises . . .)

July 10 My landlady Mrs Flynn is very worried about me. She says the way I lay around all day and dont do anything I remind her of her son before she threw him out of the house. She said she doesnt like loafers. If Im sick its one thing, but if Im a loafer thats another thing and she wont have it. I told her I think Im sick.

I try to read a little bit every day, mostly stories, but sometimes I have to read the same thing over and over again because I dont know what it means. And its hard to write. I know I should look up all the words in the dictionary but its so hard and Im so tired all the time.

Then I got the idea that I would only use the easy words instead of the long hard ones. That saves time. I put flowers on Algernons grave about once a week. Mrs Flynn thinks Im crazy to put flowers on a mouses grave but I told her that Algernon was special.

Daybed in the Afternoon, 2000. Elizabeth Solomon. Oil on panel, 25.4 x 20.3 cm. Private Collection, David Findlay Jr. Fine Art, NY.

Foreshadowing Study Charlie's writing. What clues do you see that his intelligence is decreasing?

July 14   Its sunday again. I dont have anything to do to keep me busy now because my television set is broke and I dont have any money to get it fixed. (I think I lost this months check from the lab. I dont remember)

I get awful headaches and asperin doesnt help me much. Mrs Flynn knows Im really sick and she feels very sorry for me. Shes a wonderful woman whenever someone is sick.

July 22   Mrs Flynn called a strange doctor to see me. She was afraid I was going to die. I told the doctor I wasnt too sick and that I only forget sometimes. He asked me did I have any friends or relatives and I said no I dont have any. I told him I had a friend called Algernon once but he was a mouse and we used to run races together. He looked at me kind of funny like he thought I was crazy.

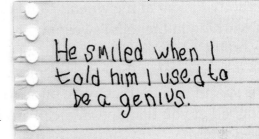

He smiled when I told him I used to be a genius.

He smiled when I told him I used to be a genius. He talked to me like I was a baby and he winked at Mrs Flynn. I got mad and chased him out because he was making fun of me the way they all used to.

July 24   I have no more money and Mrs Flynn says I got to go to work somewhere and pay the rent because I havent paid for over two months. I dont know any work but the job I used to have at Donnegans Plastic Box Company. I dont want to go back there because they all knew me when I was smart and maybe theyll laugh at me. But I dont know what else to do to get money.

July 25   I was looking at some of my old progress reports and its very funny but I cant read what I wrote. I can make out some of the words but they dont make sense.

Miss Kinnian came to the door but I said go away I dont want to see you. She cried and I cried too but I wouldnt let her in because I didnt want her to laugh at me. I told her I didn't like her any more. I told her I didnt want to be smart any more. Thats not true. I still love her and I still want to be smart but I had to say that so shed go away.

Make Inferences About Characters Why do you think Charlie tells Miss Kinnian that he doesn't like her anymore?

She gave Mrs Flynn money to pay the rent. I dont want that. I got to get a job.

Please . . . please let me not forget how to read and write . . .

July 27   Mr Donnegan was very nice when I came back and asked him for my old job of janitor. First he was very suspicious but I told him what happened to me then he looked very sad and put his hand on my shoulder and said Charlie Gordon you got guts.

Everybody looked at me when I came downstairs and started working in the toilet sweeping it out like I used to. I told myself Charlie if they make fun of you dont get sore because you remember their not so smart as you once thot they were. And besides they were once your friends and if they laughed at you that doesnt mean anything because they liked you too.

One of the new men who came to work there after I went away made a nasty crack he said hey Charlie I hear your a very smart fella a real quiz kid. Say something intelligent. I felt bad but Joe Carp came over and grabbed him by the shirt and said leave him alone you lousy cracker or Ill break your neck. I didnt expect Joe to take my part so I guess hes really my friend.

Later Frank Reilly came over and said Charlie if anybody bothers you or trys to take advantage you call me or Joe and we will set em straight. I said thanks Frank and I got choked up so I had to turn around and go into the supply room so he wouldnt see me cry. Its good to have friends.

July 28   I did a dumb thing today I forgot I wasnt in Miss Kinnians class at the adult center any more like I use to be. I went in and sat down in my old seat in the back of the room and she looked at me funny and she said Charles. I dint remember she ever called me that before only Charlie so I said hello Miss Kinnian Im redy for my lesin today only I lost my reader that we was using. She startid to cry and run out of the room and everybody looked at me and I saw they wasnt the same pepul who used to be in my class.

Then all of a suddin I rememberd some things about the operashun and me getting smart and I said holy smoke

Make Inferences About Characters Why do you think Charlie's old coworkers treat him with respect now?

I reely pulled a Charlie Gordon that time. I went away before she come back to the room.

Thats why Im going away from New York for good. I dont want to do nothing like that agen. I dont want Miss Kinnian to feel sorry for me. Evry body feels sorry at the factery and I dont want that eather so Im going someplace where nobody knows that Charlie Gordon was once a genus and now he cant even reed a book or rite good.

Im taking a cuple of books along and even if I cant reed them Ill practise hard and maybe I wont forget every thing I lerned. If I try reel hard maybe Ill be a littel bit smarter than I was before the operashun. I got my rabits foot and my luky penny and maybe they will help me.

If you ever reed this Miss Kinnian dont be sorry for me Im glad I got a second chanse to be smart becaus I lerned a lot of things that I never even new were in this world and Im grateful that I saw it all for a littel bit. I dont know why Im dumb agen or what I did wrong maybe its becaus I dint try hard enuff. But if I try and practis very hard maybe Ill get a littl smarter and know what all the words are. I remember a littel bit how nice I had a feeling with the blue book that has the torn cover when I red it. Thats why Im gonna keep trying to get smart so I can have that feeling agen. Its a good feeling to know things and be smart. I wish I had it rite now if I did I would sit down and reed all the time. Anyway I bet Im the first dumb person in the world who ever found out something importent for sience. I remember I did somthing but I dont remember what. So I gess its like I did it for all the dumb pepul like me.

Good-by Miss Kinnian and Dr. Strauss and evreybody. And P.S. please tell Dr Nemur not to be such a grouch when pepul laff at him and he woud have more frends. Its easy to make frends if you let pepul laff at you. Im going to have lots of frends where I go.

P.P.S. Please if you get a chanse put some flowrs on Algernons grave in the bak yard . . .

BQ ▷ **BIG Question**

Why is Charlie leaving New York? Think about what really matters to Charlie and how it has changed since the beginning of the story.

Make Inferences About Characters Why does Charlie continue to want flowers for Algernon's grave?

After You Read

Respond and Think Critically

1. In your own words, describe the most significant events in this part of the story. [Summarize]

2. As Charlie's intelligence increases, he begins to lose his ability to communicate with people. Why do you think this happens? [Interpret]

3. When Charlie goes back to Miss Kinnian's class, why does she start to cry and then run out of the room? [Infer]

4. Charlie describes his own pain as his intelligence decreases. Do you think the author is suggesting that Charlie would have been better off if he had never had the operation? Why or why not? [Analyze]

5. As the story ends, Charlie is planning to leave New York. What do you think will happen to Charlie? Explain your thoughts. [Synthesize]

6. **BQ** **BIG Question** Think about what really matters to Charlie when he is a genius. Does this change as he loses his intelligence? Cite examples from the story. [Compare and Contrast]

Vocabulary Practice

On a separate sheet of paper, write the vocabulary word that correctly completes each sentence. If none of the words fits the sentence, write "none."

technique   cowered   petition   obscure   tangible

1. The window's dirt was thick enough to _____ the view.

2. The boy's friends called him a _____ because he wouldn't jump off the high-dive board.

3. The boxer's fighting _____ made him unbeatable.

4. The Quiz Bowl champions gave the principal a _____ for a day off from school.

5. The brightly shining sun helped _____ the tall mountains.

6. The fog was so thick it seemed quite _____.

7. During the hurricane, the family _____ in the basement.

Academic Vocabulary

In "Flowers for Algernon," doctors **modified** Charlie's brain to triple his intelligence. In the preceding sentence, *modified* means "changed." Write a few sentences about a behavior or situation in your life that you modified.

TIP

Interpreting
Here are some tips to help you interpret. Remember when you interpret, you are using your own understanding of the world to decide what the events or ideas in a text mean.

- Think about the times when Charlie, as a genius, has trouble communicating with people.

- Think about a similar situation when you or others were unable to communicate.

- Think about what you know about extremely intelligent people.

- Decide what the author is really saying about Charlie's ability to communicate when he is a genius.

 FOLDABLES **Study Organizer** Keep track of your ideas about the **BIG Question** in your unit Foldable.

 Literature Online

Selection Resources
For Selection Quizzes, eFlashcards, and Reading-Writing Connection activities, go to glencoe.com and enter QuickPass code GL39770u5.

Test Skills Practice

1. What is the significance of Algernon's sudden, violent behavior?

   A It is expected because Algernon was not a well-behaved mouse.

   B It is symbolic of Charlie laughing at the dishwasher days before.

   C It has no literary significance— sometimes mice bite when they are scared.

   D It hints that the experiment is a failure and Charlie will soon lose his intelligence.

Review: Voice

2. Throughout the story, Charlie's writing changes. In what ways do the words Charlie writes reveal his increasing intelligence? Support your answer with details and information from the story.

3. In what ways do the words Charlie writes toward the end of the story reveal the loss of his intelligence? Support your answer with details and information from the story.

Reading Strategy **Make Inferences About Characters**

4. Based on what you have read, what can you tell about Charlie Gordon's personality and values? Support your answer with details and information from the story.

5. What can you tell about the personalities and values of the other main characters— Dr. Strauss, Dr. Nemur, and Miss Kinnian? Support your answer with details and information from the story.

6. Choose one of the minor characters from the story. What clues do you have about this character's personality and values? Support your answer with details and information from the story.

Grammar Link

Commas with Relative Clauses A **relative clause** begins with a relative pronoun like *that, who,* or *which.* Essential relative clauses (those necessary to make the sentence's meaning clear) are **not** set off with commas. Use the relative pronoun *that* or *who* to begin an essential relative clause.

Nonessential relative clauses (those **not** necessary to make the sentence's meaning clear) are set off by commas. Use the relative pronoun *which* or *who* to begin a nonessential relative clause.

Essential: Daniel Keyes wrote a short story that won the Hugo Award.

Nonessential: "Flowers for Algernon," which is a short story, won the Hugo Award.

Essential: The author who wrote "Flowers for Algernon" is Daniel Keyes.

Nonessential: Daniel Keyes, who also wrote "Flowers for Algernon," is the author of *Algernon, Charlie,* and *I: A Writer's Journey.*

Practice Write two sentences with essential relative clauses and two with nonessential relative clauses. Be sure to punctuate each sentence correctly.

Research and Report

Internet Connection Use Internet sources and other research strategies to learn about humans using science to improve their minds. Try to include primary sources. Be sure all sources are reliable, such as university Web sites or encyclopedias. Then make a list of reading recommendations. Record the author, title, publication date, and number of pages for each source. Write a short blurb describing each story or article.

Comparing Literature

The Story of My Life and Letters of Annie Sullivan

BQ BIG Question

As you read these paired selections, think about what really matters in the lives of Helen Keller and Annie Sullivan.

Literary Element Tone

In writing, **tone** is the author's attitude toward his or her subject matter or audience. Authors convey tone through words and details that express emotions. *Sad, optimistic, serious,* and *humorous* are words that can describe different tones. When the situation within a piece of writing changes, the tone may change as well. For example, in the selections you are about to read, both women experience a range of emotions as they face challenges in their lives. Their unique experiences affect their attitude about life and their belief in other people. As you read, notice details that reveal each author's tone.

Reading Skill Compare and Contrast

As you know, comparing and contrasting is an important skill to use as you read. When you compare, you look for similarities. When you contrast, you look for differences.

Comparing tones in different pieces of writing—as well as within one selection—allows you to see how authors feel about various events, subjects, and people. You will be comparing and contrasting the tones of two selections—"The Story of My Life" and "Letters of Annie Sullivan." You may find it helpful to use a chart like the one below to organize your ideas as you read.

	Tone	Example
Helen Keller		
Annie Sullivan		

LOG ON ▶ **Literature** Online

Author Search For more about Helen Keller and Annie Sullivan, go to glencoe.com and enter QuickPass code GL39770u5.

Meet the Authors

Helen Keller

Scarlet fever left Helen Keller blind and deaf as a child. She devoted her adult life to helping blind and deaf people. Keller was born in 1880 and died in 1968.

Annie Sullivan

Annie Sullivan was Helen Keller's teacher and companion. Sullivan was born in 1866 and died in 1936.

⚜ ⚜ ⚜ ⚜

from
THE STORY *of* MY LIFE

HELEN KELLER

THE MOST IMPORTANT DAY I remember in all my life is the one on which my teacher, Anne Mansfield Sullivan, came to me. I am filled with wonder when I consider the immeasurable contrasts between the two lives which it connects. It was the third of March, 1887, three months before I was seven years old.

On the afternoon of that eventful day, I stood on the porch, dumb, expectant. I guessed vaguely from my mother's signs and from the hurrying to and fro in the house that something unusual was about to happen, so I went to the door and waited on the steps. The afternoon sun penetrated the mass of honeysuckle that covered the porch, and fell on my upturned face. My fingers lingered almost unconsciously on the familiar leaves and blossoms which had just come forth to greet the sweet southern spring. I did not know what the future held of marvel or surprise for me. Anger and bitterness had preyed upon me continually for weeks and a deep languor[1] had succeeded this passionate struggle.

Have you ever been at sea in a dense fog, when it seemed as if a tangible white darkness shut you in, and the great ship, tense and anxious, groped her way toward the shore with plummet and sounding-line,[2] and you waited with beating heart for something to happen? I was like that ship before my education began, only I was without compass or sounding-line, and had no way of knowing how near the harbor was. "Light! give me light!" was the wordless cry of my soul, and the light of love shone on me in that very hour.

I felt approaching footsteps. I stretched out my hand as I supposed to my mother. Someone took it, and I was caught up and held close in the arms of her who had come to reveal all things to me, and, more than all things else, to love me.

Comparing Literature
What tone toward Anne Sullivan does Helen Keller reveal in this paragraph?

---

1 *Languor* is the lack of spirit or interest; physical fatigue.

2 A *plummet and sounding-line* is the device used to measure the depth of water. A line of rope or cord is marked at intervals and has a weight, or *plummet*, at one end.

The morning after my teacher came she led me into her room and gave me a doll. The little blind children at the Perkins Institution had sent it and Laura Bridgman[3] had dressed it; but I did not know this until afterward. When I had played with it a little while, Miss Sullivan slowly spelled into my hand the word "d-o-l-l." I was at once interested in this finger play and tried to imitate it. When I finally succeeded in making the letters correctly I was flushed with childish pleasure and pride. Running downstairs to my mother I held up my hand and made the letters for doll. I did not know that I was spelling a word or even that words existed; I was simply making my fingers go in monkey-like imitation. In the days that followed I learned to spell in this uncomprehending[4] way a great many words, among them *pin, hat, cup,* and a few verbs like *sit, stand,* and *walk*. But my teacher had been with me several weeks before I understood that everything has a name.

One day, while I was playing with my new doll, Miss Sullivan put my big rag doll into my lap also, spelled "d-o-l-l," and tried to make me understand that "d-o-l-l" applied to both. Earlier in the day we had had a tussle over the words "m-u-g" and "w-a-t-e-r." Miss Sullivan had tried to impress it upon me that "m-u-g" is *mug* and that "w-a-t-e-r" is *water*, but I persisted in confounding[5] the two. In despair she had dropped the subject for the time, only to renew it at the first opportunity. I became impatient at her repeated attempts and, seizing the new doll, I dashed it upon the floor. I was keenly delighted when I felt the fragments of the broken doll at my feet. Neither sorrow nor regret followed my passionate outburst. I had not loved the doll. In the still, dark world in which I lived there was no strong sentiment or tenderness. I felt my teacher sweep

Comparing Literature What is Helen Keller's opinion of herself and her ability to spell? Consider her use of the phrase "monkey-like imitation."

---

3 *Laura Bridgman* (1829–1889), a student of Dr. Samuel G. Howe of the Perkins Institution for the Blind, was the first deaf, blind, and mute person to be successfully educated in the United States.

4 *Uncomprehending* means "without understanding."

5 Here, *confounding* means "confusing; mixing up; failing to understand."

the fragments to one side of the hearth, and I had a sense of satisfaction that the cause of my discomfort was removed. She brought me my hat, and I knew I was going out into the warm sunshine. This thought, if a wordless sensation may be called a thought, made me hop and skip with pleasure.

We walked down the path to the well-house, attracted by the fragrance of the honeysuckle with which it was covered. Some one was drawing water and my teacher placed my hand under the spout. As the cool stream gushed over one hand she spelled into the other the word *water*, first slowly, then rapidly. I stood still, my whole attention fixed upon the motions of her fingers. Suddenly I felt a misty consciousness as of something forgotten—a thrill of returning thought; and somehow the mystery of language was revealed to me. I knew then that "w-a-t-e-r" meant the wonderful cool something that was flowing over my hand. That living word awakened my soul, gave it light, hope, joy, set it free! There were barriers still, it is true, but barriers that could in time be swept away.

I left the well-house eager to learn. Everything had a name, and each name gave birth to a new thought. As we returned to the house every object which I touched seemed to quiver with life. That was because I saw everything with the strange, new sight that had come to me. On entering the door I remembered the doll I had broken. I felt my way to the hearth and picked up the pieces. I tried vainly to put them together. Then my eyes filled with tears; for I realized what I had done, and for the first time I felt repentance and sorrow.

I learned a great many new words that day. I do not remember what they all were; but I do know that *mother, father, sister, teacher* were among them—words that were to make the world blossom for me, "like Aaron's rod,[6] with flowers." It would have been difficult to find a happier child than I was as I lay in my

Comparing Literature
What tone, or attitude, do the words *awakened, light, hope,* and *joy* suggest?

---

6 In the Bible, ***Aaron's rod***, a wooden walking stick, miraculously blossoms and bears almonds.

Helen Keller reading braille.

crib at the close of that eventful day and lived over the joys it had brought me, and for the first time longed for a new day to come. . . .

I had now the key to all language, and I was eager to learn to use it. Children who hear acquire language without any particular effort; the words that fall from others' lips they catch on the wing, as it were, delightedly, while the little deaf child must trap them by a slow and often painful process. But whatever the process, the result is wonderful. Gradually from naming an object we advance step by step until we have traversed[7] the vast distance between our first stammered syllable and the sweep of thought in a line of Shakespeare.

BQ **BIG Question**

What does the author believe matters most in her world?

7 **Traversed** means "passed across or through."

At first, when my teacher told me about a new thing I asked very few questions. My ideas were vague, and my vocabulary was inadequate; but as my knowledge of things grew, and I learned more and more words, my field of inquiry broadened, and I would return again and again to the same subject, eager for further information. Sometimes a new word revived an image that some earlier experience had engraved on my brain.

I remember the morning that I first asked the meaning of the word, "love." This was before I knew many words. I had found a few early violets in the garden and brought them to my teacher. She tried to kiss me: but at that time I did not like to have anyone kiss me except my mother. Miss Sullivan put her arm gently round me and spelled into my hand, "I love Helen."

"What is love?" I asked.

She drew me closer to her and said, "It is here," pointing to my heart, whose beats I was conscious of for the first time. Her words puzzled me very much because I did not then understand anything unless I touched it.

I smelled the violets in her hand and asked, half in words, half in signs, a question which meant, "Is love the sweetness of flowers?"

"No," said my teacher.

Again I thought. The warm sun was shining on us.

"Is this not love?" I asked, pointing in the direction from which the heat came. "Is this not love?"

It seemed to me that there could be nothing more beautiful than the sun, whose warmth makes all things grow. But Miss Sullivan shook her head, and I was greatly puzzled and disappointed. I thought it strange that my teacher could not show me love.

A day or two afterward I was stringing beads of different sizes in symmetrical[8] groups—two large

Comparing Literature
Think about Helen Keller's words in this paragraph and her description of her actions. In what way does her tone change?

---

8 **Symmetrical** means "exactly agreeing in size, form, and arrangement on both sides of something."

beads, three small ones, and so on. I had made many mistakes, and Miss Sullivan had pointed them out again and again with gentle patience. Finally I noticed a very obvious error in the sequence and for an instant I concentrated my attention on the lesson and tried to think how I should have arranged the beads. Miss Sullivan touched my forehead and spelled with decided emphasis, "Think."

In a flash I knew that the word was the name of the process that was going on in my head. This was my first conscious perception of an abstract[9] idea.

For a long time I was still—I was not thinking of the beads in my lap, but trying to find a meaning for "love" in the light of this new idea. The sun had been under a cloud all day, and there had been brief showers; but suddenly the sun broke forth in all its southern splendor.

Again I asked my teacher, "Is this not love?"

"Love is something like the clouds that were in the sky before the sun came out," she replied. Then in simpler words than these, which at that time I could not have understood, she explained: "You cannot touch the clouds, you know; but you feel the rain and know how glad the flowers and the thirsty earth are to have it after a hot day. You cannot touch love either; but you feel the sweetness that it pours into everything. Without love you would not be happy or want to play."

The beautiful truth burst upon my mind—I felt that there were invisible lines stretched between my spirit and the spirits of others.

From the beginning of my education Miss Sullivan made it a practice to speak to me as she would speak to any hearing child; the only difference was that she spelled the sentences into my hand instead of speaking them. If I did not know the words and idioms[10] necessary to express my thoughts she supplied them, even suggesting

9 **Abstract** means "not concrete; unlike any specific example or thing."

10 **Idioms** are expressions that have a meaning different from the literal meaning of the words. Examples are "She's on the ball," "My stomach is in knots," and "The test was a piece of cake."

Comparing Literature What tone does the author express in this paragraph? Give examples of words, details, and actions that show this.

conversation when I was unable to keep up my end of the dialogue.

This process was continued for several years; for the deaf child does not learn in a month, or even in two or three years, the numberless idioms and expressions used in the simplest daily intercourse.[11] The little hearing child learns these from constant repetition and imitation. The conversation he hears in his home stimulates his mind and suggests topics and calls forth the spontaneous[12] expression of his own thoughts. This natural exchange of ideas is denied to the deaf child. My teacher, realizing this, determined to supply the kinds of stimulus[13] I lacked. This she did by repeating to me as far as possible, verbatim,[14] what she heard, and by showing me how I could take part in the conversation. But it was a long time before I ventured to take the initiative, and still longer before I could find something appropriate to say at the right time.

The deaf and the blind find it very difficult to acquire the amenities of conversation.[15] How much more this difficulty must be augmented in the case of those who are both deaf and blind! They cannot distinguish the tone of the voice or, without assistance, go up and down the gamut[16] of tones that give significance to words; nor can they watch the expression of the speaker's face, and a look is often the very soul of what one says. 🐚

Helen Keller with Annie Sullivan in 1888. Helen is eight years old in this photo.

Comparing Literature What does this paragraph reveal about the author's attitude toward people who are deaf and blind?

---

11 **Intercourse** is the exchange of thoughts, ideas, and feelings through conversation or other communication.

12 **Spontaneous** means "arising from a natural impulse or cause."

13 A **stimulus** is something that causes an action or effort.

14 **Verbatim** is Latin for "in exactly the same words."

15 By **amenities of conversation**, Keller means those things besides words, such as tone of voice or body language that help communicate meaning.

16 Here, **gamut** means the "entire series" or "entire range" of possible tones or sounds.

Letters of Annie Sullivan

Annie Sullivan

March 6, 1887 ○○○○○○○○○○○○

It was 6:30 when I reached Tuscumbia. I found
Mrs. Keller and Mr. James Keller waiting for me. They
said somebody had met every train for two days. The
drive from the station to the house, a distance of one
mile, was very lovely and restful. I was surprised to
find Mrs. Keller a very young-looking woman, not
much older than myself, I should think. Captain Keller
met us in the yard and gave me a cheery welcome and
a hearty handshake.

   My first question was, "Where is Helen?" I tried with
all my might to control the eagerness that made me
tremble so that I could hardly walk. As we approached
the house I saw a child standing in the doorway, and
Captain Keller said, "There she is. She has known all
day that some one was expected, and she has been wild
ever since her mother went to the station for you." I
had scarcely put my foot on the steps, when she rushed
toward me with such force that she would have thrown
me backward if Captain Keller had not been behind me.

Comparing Literature
Compare Annie Sullivan's
reaction to meeting Helen
Keller with Helen's own
response. What does each
author's tone about the
importance of this meeting
suggest about their
relationship?

She felt my face and dress and my bag, which she took out of my hand and tried to open. It did not open easily, and she felt carefully to see if there was a keyhole. Finding that there was, she turned to me, making the sign of turning a key and pointing to the bag. Her mother interfered at this point and showed Helen by signs that she must not touch the bag. Her face flushed, and when her mother attempted to take the bag from her, she grew very angry. I attracted her attention by showing her my watch and letting her hold it in her hand. Instantly the tempest subsided, and we went upstairs together.

Here I opened the bag, and she went through it eagerly, probably expecting to find something to eat. Friends had probably brought her candy in their bags, and she expected to find some in mine. I made her understand, by pointing to a trunk in the hall and to myself and nodding my head, that I had a trunk, and then made the sign that she had used for eating, and nodded again. She understood in a flash and ran downstairs to tell her mother, by means of emphatic signs, that there was some candy in a trunk for her. She returned in a few minutes and helped me put away my things. It was too comical to see her put on my bonnet and cock her head first to one side, then the other, and look in the mirror, just as if she could see.

Somehow I had expected to see a pale, delicate child—I suppose I got the idea from Dr. Howe's description of Laura Bridgman when she came to the Institution. But there's nothing pale or delicate about Helen. She is large, strong, and ruddy, and as unrestrained in her movements as a young colt. She has none of those nervous habits that are so noticeable and so distressing in blind children. Her body is well formed and vigorous, and Mrs. Keller says she has not been ill a day since the illness that deprived her of her sight and hearing. She has a fine head, and it is set on her shoulders just right. Her face is hard to describe. It is intelligent, but lacks mobility, or soul, or something.

Comparing Literature Is Annie Sullivan angry or amused at Helen Keller's actions? Support your answer with evidence from the text.

> *"I shall have to solve how to discipline and control her without breaking her spirit. I shall go rather slowly at first and try to win her love."*

Her mouth is large and finely shaped. You see at a glance that she is blind. One eye is larger than the other, and protrudes noticeably. She rarely smiles, indeed, I have seen her smile only once or twice since I came. She is unresponsive and even impatient of caresses from any one except her mother. She is very quick-tempered and wilful, and nobody, except her brother James, has attempted to control her.

The greatest problem I shall have to solve is how to discipline and control her without breaking her spirit. I shall go rather slowly at first and try to win her love. I shall not attempt to conquer her by force alone; but I shall insist on reasonable obedience from the start. One thing that impresses everybody is Helen's tireless activity. She is never still a moment. She is here, there, and everywhere. Her hands are in everything; but nothing holds her attention for long. Dear child, her restless spirit gropes in the dark. Her untaught, unsatisfied hands destroy whatever they touch because they do not know what else to do with things.

She helped me unpack my trunk when it came, and was delighted when she found the doll the little girls sent her. I thought it a good opportunity to teach her her first word. I spelled *d-o-l-l* slowly in her hand and pointed to the doll and nodded my head, which seems to be her sign for possession. Whenever anybody gives

Comparing Literature What is Annie's tone in her description of Helen's appearance and behavior?

her anything, she points to it, then to herself, and nods her head. She looked puzzled and felt my hand, and I repeated the letters. She imitated them very well and pointed to the doll. Then I took the doll, meaning to give it back to her when she had made the letters; but she thought I meant to take it from her, and in an instant she was in a temper, and tried to seize the doll. I shook my head and tried to form the letters with her fingers; but she got more and more angry. I forced her into a chair and held her there until I was nearly exhausted. Then it occurred to me that it was useless to continue the struggle—I must do something to turn the current of her thoughts. I let her go, but refused to give up the doll.

I went downstairs and got some cake (she is very fond of sweets). I showed Helen the cake and spelled *c-a-k-e* in her hand, holding the cake toward her. Of course she wanted it and tried to take it; but I spelled the word again and patted her hand. She made the letters rapidly, and I gave her the cake, which she ate in a great hurry, thinking, I suppose, that I might take it from her. Then I showed her the doll and spelled the word again, holding the doll toward her as I held the cake. She made the letters *d-o-l* and I made the other *l* and gave her the doll. She ran downstairs with it and could not be induced to return to my room all day.

> *"She looked puzzled and felt my hand, and I repeated the letters. She imitated them very well and pointed to the doll."*

Annie Sullivan reads to Helen Keller by spelling words into her hands.

April 5, 1887 ○ ○ ○ ○ ○ ○ ○ ○ ○ ○ ○ ○

I must write you a line this morning because something very important has happened. Helen has taken the second great step in her education. She has learned that *everything has a name, and that the manual alphabet is the key to everything she wants to know.*

In a previous letter I think I wrote you that *mug* and *milk* had given Helen more trouble than all the rest. She confused the nouns with the verb *drink*. She didn't know the word for *drink*, but went through the

Comparing Literature
Compare Annie's tone about Helen's progress with Helen's own attitude. How are their tones similar and different?

pantomime[1] of drinking whenever she spelled *mug* or *milk*. This morning, while she was washing, she wanted to know the name for *water*. When she wants to know the name of anything, she points to it and pats my hand. I spelled *w-a-t-e-r* and thought no more about it until after breakfast. Then it occurred to me that with the help of this new word I might succeed in straightening out the *mug-milk* difficulty.

We went out to the pump-house, and I made Helen hold her mug under the spout while I pumped. As the cold water gushed forth, filling the mug, I spelled *w-a-t-e-r* in Helen's free hand. The word coming so close upon the sensation of cold water rushing over her hand seemed to startle her. She dropped the mug and stood as one transfixed. A new light came into her face. She spelled *water* several times. Then she dropped on the ground and asked for its name and pointed to the pump and the trellis,[2] and suddenly turning round she asked for my name. I spelled *Teacher*. Just then the nurse brought Helen's little sister into the pump-house, and Helen spelled *baby* and pointed to the nurse. All the way back to the house she was highly excited, and learned the name of every object she touched, so that in a few hours she had added thirty new words to her vocabulary. Here are some of them: *Door, open, shut, give, go, come,* and a great many more.

P. S.—I didn't finish my letter in time to get it posted last night; so I shall add a line. Helen got up this morning like a radiant fairy. She has flitted from object to object, asking the name of everything and kissing me for very gladness. Last night when I got in bed, she stole into my arms of her own accord and kissed me for the first time, and I thought my heart would burst, so full was it of joy. 🖎

BQ **BIG Question**

What matters most to Annie Sullivan?

---

1 *Pantomime* is the technique of communicating meaning without speech through gestures, movements, and facial expressions.

2 A *trellis* is an open frame used as a support for growing vines.

Comparing Literature

BQ **BIG Question**

Now use the unit Big Question to compare and contrast Helen Keller's autobiography and Annie Sullivan's letters. With a group of classmates discuss questions such as,

- What does each author think really matters? Do the authors agree?

- What really matters to Helen Keller before she meets Annie Sullivan?

- Do you think what really matters to Annie Sullivan is the same before and after she meets Helen Keller?

Support each answer with evidence from the readings.

Literary Element Tone

Use the details you wrote in your graphic organizer to think about the tone in Helen Keller's "The Story of My Life" and Annie Sullivan's "Letters of Annie Sullivan." With a partner, answer the following questions:

1. Are the tones of the two pieces similar? Explain why or why not.

2. Look at both authors' description of the moment when Helen understands the meaning of the word *water*. How does each author make her tone clear? Give examples of the differences in the authors' tone about this discovery.

Write to Compare

Both selections describe the same incidents but from different perspectives. In one or two paragraphs, discuss how these two selections are alike and how they are different. You might want to focus on these ideas as you write.

- Describe the changing tones within each selection. Use examples from your graphic organizer.

- Include the differences in tone between the two selections and tell how the authors' attitudes reflect their unique experiences with the same situation.

- Explain how you think each author's tone affects readers and tell which author you think makes a stronger impression on the reader.

 Writing Tip

Direct Quotation As you write, use quotations—actual words from each selection set off by quotation marks—to help make your points about the tone of each work.

 Literature Online

Selection Resources For Selection Quizzes, eFlashcards, and Reading-Writing Connection activities, go to glencoe.com and enter QuickPass code GL39770u5.

Research Report

How do you decide what's really important in life? In this workshop, you will write a research report that will help you think about the Unit 5 Big Question: What Really Matters?

Review the writing prompt, or assignment, below. Then read the Writing Plan. It will tell you what you will do to write your research report.

Writing Assignment

In a research report you investigate a subject and present information on it, using a variety of reliable documented sources. Write a research report on a historical or contemporary person whose decisions and actions led that person to make a positive lasting impact on society or science. The audience should be your classmates and teacher.

Prewrite

How did the people you have read about in the biographies and autobiographies in this unit decide and act upon what really matters to society as a whole? Think about the biography of Mother Jones in "The March of the Mill Children." What other historical or contemporary person like her might be a good subject for your report?

Gather Ideas

Try any or all of the following activities to get ideas about people who have made a positive lasting impact on society or science:

- Talk with your friends and family.
- Look through your social studies and science textbooks, and check the library and the Internet.
- Watch the news or read newspapers and news magazines.

Use this research to create a list of people you'd like to write about.

Choose a Subject

Use your list to pick your subject. Consider the person's impact as well why the person interests you. Talk about your goal with a partner.

Partner Talk With a partner, follow these steps:

1. Decide which three people interest you the most and explain why.
2. Decide which three people have had the most positive important impact on society or science. Then complete the sentence below.

I will write about _____. I chose this person because _____.

Writing Plan

- Choose a focused subject or topic on which to develop a thesis.
- Draw upon reliable information from multiple sources.
- Incorporate relevant facts and details to support the main idea of the report.
- Organize the report in a logical sequence, concluding with a summary of the main idea.
- Include a list of sources (bibliography) and footnotes.

Plan and Conduct Your Research

Begin by asking specific questions about the positive impact of the person you have chosen. Questions that begin with *who, what, why, where, when,* and *how* can be especially helpful. Then look for answers to your questions on reliable Web sites and in encyclopedias, books, and magazines. Also use primary sources such as letters, diaries, and interviews, if they're available. Record the information you gather in a research chart like the one below. Number each piece of information and quote, summarize, or paraphrase it. Note whether the information is a fact or an opinion.

Source	Location of Info	Information	Fact or Opinion
1. Britannica Online	http://search.eb.com/eb/article-9109502	Only U.S. president elected to 4 terms	fact
2. New York Times	April 13, 1945, p. 16	"inspired free men in every part of the world"	opinion

Evaluate Your Information

Now evaluate the information you have gathered. Ask yourself how important the information is to what you want to say about this person. Then use the following criteria to determine which sources and information will be most dependable and useful.

- **Relevance** How does the information help you make your point?

- **Authority** Does the information come from an author or organization with a good reputation? Does the author have expert qualifications?

- **Accuracy** Can the information be verified with another source? Do grammatical or factual errors make the source seem questionable?

- **Conflict** Do different sources provide conflicting information? How does performing a multiple-step search resolve any conflicts?

- **Objectivity** Is the information a fact or an opinion? Is the source associated with an author or organization that is one-sided?

- **Currency** Is the information current or out-of-date?

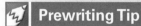

Prewriting Tip

Quotations While taking notes, put quotation marks around any words or phrases you copy directly from a source. Make sure the quote is accurate and that you give it correct and proper credit.

Literature Online

Writing and Research
For prewriting, drafting, and revising tools, go to glencoe.com and enter QuickPass code GL39770u5.

Drafting Tip

Check off each piece of information from your chart as you include it to make sure you use all the relevant ideas and support.

Get Organized

Create a working outline. Indicate the sources you will use from your research chart to support each main idea.

> I. Introduction—Franklin Delano Roosevelt's legacy to the world (1, 2)
> II. The Great Depression
>   A. Economic disaster (1)
>   B. FDR's response—New Deal (1)
> III. World War II

Draft

Now begin writing. Use the following skills to develop your draft.

Get It On Paper

- Review your research information. Look at your outline.
- Begin with an interesting fact or quotation that draws your readers in. Connect it to a statement that makes your purpose clear.
- For each body paragraph in your outline, write a topic sentence that supports your main idea. Then add the information from your research that supports the topic sentence.
- End your report by summarizing the main idea.
- Don't worry about paragraphs, spelling, grammar, or punctuation right now.
- When you're finished, read what you've written. Include more information if you need to.

Develop Your Draft

1. Write a **thesis statement** that summarizes the person's influence.

> Franklin D. Roosevelt had a tremendous impact on society, not only in the United States, but also throughout the world.

2. Include information from **multiple reliable sources.**

> Britain stood alone against the Nazis (Goodwin 100), and FDR thought the United States should help Britain defend democracy (Annual Message).

3. Support your main ideas with relevant **facts and details.**

> FDR rallied people when he told them "the only thing we have to fear is fear itself" (Inaugural).

4. Organize your report in a **logical sequence.**

> FDR proved to be as great a leader in wartime as he was during peacetime.

5. Include a list of sources in a **bibliography.**

> "Franklin D. Roosevelt." *New York Times* 13 April 1945: 16.

Apply Good Writing Traits:
Sentence Fluency

Fluency is the smooth flow of sentences. Good writing should sound graceful, not choppy. Sentences should be different lengths, and they should move from one idea to the next. Transitional words such as *then, after,* and *next* help sentences flow together.

Read the sentences below from "The March of the Mill Children" by Judith Pinkerton Josephson. What techniques does the author use to make her sentences flow?

> Pennsylvania, like many other states, had laws that said children under thirteen could not work. But parents often lied about a child's age. Poor families either put their children to work in the mills or starved.

As you draft your research report, vary the beginnings and lengths of your sentences. Use transitions such as *however* and *after* to connect ideas. Read your draft aloud and ask yourself if your writing has a smooth rhythm.

Analyze a Student Model

An era came to an end when President Franklin D. Roosevelt died in 1945. People across the country wept for the leader who "inspired free men in every part of the world to fight with greater hope and courage" (*New York Times* 18). Roosevelt, commonly known as FDR, is the only U.S. president elected to four terms (*Britannica*), which included major challenges at home and abroad. Franklin D. Roosevelt had a tremendous impact on society, not only in the United States, but also throughout the world.

The United States was in the third year of the Great Depression when FDR became president. Most of the banks had shut down. Almost half the country's workers were unemployed, and farmers were struggling to survive (Goodwin 98). FDR acknowledged the people's desperate situation and rallied the people when he told them that "the only thing we have to fear is fear itself" (*Inaugural*). He then acted quickly, passing the historic New Deal in his first hundred days in office. The New Deal was a program designed to help the country recover from the Depression. It put people to work and gave them hope for a better future (*Britannica*).

FDR proved to be as great a leader in war as he was in peace. While the United States was still trying to rebuild its economy, World War II broke out in Europe. Britain stood alone against the Nazis (Goodwin 100), and FDR thought the United States should help Britain defend democracy (Annual Message). Against opposition, he convinced Congress to give Britain "all aid short of war" (*Britannica*). In August 1941, he and British Prime Minister Winston Churchill issued the Atlantic Charter, pledging "the final destruction of Nazi tyranny" ("Atlantic Charter"). This document laid the foundation for the creation of the United Nations.

Thesis Statement

The writer ends the introduction with a clear statement of the report's main idea.

Multiple Sources

Information from several sources is included to give the report credibility.

Support

A direct quotation is used to support the thesis, explaining how the United States aided Britain at the start of the war.

On December 7, 1941, the Japanese attacked Pearl Harbor, Hawaii. The next day FDR persuaded Congress to declare war on Japan, and soon after, the United States was at war with Germany and Italy as well (*Britannica*). The United States had many military successes during the war. One of the most memorable was the Battle of Normandy, which began on D-Day, June 6, 1944. The largest invasion by sea in history, this Allied action began the liberation of Europe from Nazi occupation.

Unfortunately, President Franklin Delano Roosevelt did not live to see the end of the war he had fought so hard to win. During his presidency, he helped make the United States the most powerful country in the world and fought hard to make the world at large a safer place. Even his biggest opponent in Congress, Senator Robert Taft, had to acknowledge FDR's impact on the world: "The President's death removes the greatest figure of our time. . ." (Goodwin).

Organization
Information about FDR is presented in chronological order and the conclusion contains a summary of the thesis.

Works Cited

"The Atlantic Charter." Samuel Rosenman, ed., *Public Papers and Addresses of Franklin D. Roosevelt,* vol. 10 (1938–1950), 314.

"Franklin D. Roosevelt." *New York Times* 13 Apr. 1945: 16.

Franklin D. Roosevelt Annual Message to Congress, January 6, 1941; Records of the United States Senate; SEN 77A-H1; Record Group 46; National Archives.

Goodwin, Doris Kearns. "Franklin Delano Roosevelt." *Time* 31 Dec. 1999: 96–110.

Inaugural Addresses of the Presidents of the United States. Washington, D.C.: U.S. G.P.O.: for sale by the Supt. of Docs., U.S. G.P.O., 1989; Bartleby.com, 2001.

"Roosevelt, Franklin D." *Encyclopædia Britannica Online.* 2007. Encyclopædia Britannica Online. 31 Oct. 2007

Bibliography
Sources that were used are listed alphabetically.

Revise

Now it's time to revise your draft so your ideas really shine. Revising is what makes good writing great, and great writing takes work!

Peer Review Trade drafts with a partner. Use the chart below to review your partner's draft by answering the questions in the *What to do* column. Talk about your peer review after you have glanced at each other's drafts and written down the answers to the questions. Next, follow the suggestions in the *How to do it* column to revise your draft.

Revising Plan

What to do	How to do it	Example
Will readers know immediately why you wrote about this person?	State your thesis clearly in the introduction.	Franklin D. Roosevelt ~~was our 32nd president.~~ ^had a tremendous impact on society, not only in the United States, but also throughout the world.
Is your information accurate?	To make sure information is reliable, cite multiple sources in the text.	Britain stood alone against the Nazis (Goodwin 100), and FDR thought the United States should help Britain defend democracy. ^(*Annual Message*)
Does the information support your main ideas?	Use facts and details to support your thesis statement.	In August 1941, he and British Prime Minister Winston Churchill ~~vowed to fight.~~ ^issued the Atlantic Charter, pledging "the final destruction of Nazi tyranny" ("Atlantic Charter").
Is the report organized in a logical sequence?	Restate your main idea in your conclusion.	During his presidency, he helped make the United States the most powerful country in the world. ^and fought hard to make the world at large a safer place.
Will readers be able to find the sources you used?	Properly cite your sources at the end of your report.	~~Doris Goodwin, FDR, 1999.~~ ^Goodwin, Doris Kearns. "Franklin Delano Roosevelt." *Time* 31 Dec. 1999: 96–110.

Revising Tip

Be sure to cite the source of every piece of information in your report that is not common knowledge. For more information on summarizing, paraphrasing, and ethical, legal practices such as attributing sources to avoid plagiarism, see Media Workshop, page 229.

Edit and Proofread

For your final draft, read your research report one sentence at a time. The **Editing and Proofreading Checklist** inside the back cover of this book can help you spot errors. Use this resource to help you make any necessary corrections.

Grammar Focus: Commas in Dates and Place Names

Use commas to separate the various parts of a date, address, or geographical location within the text of your report. Do not use commas with dates in your bibliography. Below are examples of problems with comma placement and solutions from the Workshop Model.

Problem: Place names are confusing.

On December 7, 1941, the Japanese attacked Pearl Harbor Hawaii.

Solution: Separate the name of a city and state with a comma.

On December 7, 1941, the Japanese attacked Pearl Harbor, Hawaii.

Problem: A date is punctuated incorrectly in a bibliography.

"Franklin D. Roosevelt." New York Times 13, April, 1945: 16.

Solution: Write the day, month (abbreviated), and year with no commas separating them.

"Franklin D. Roosevelt." New York Times 13 Apr. 1945: 16.

Present

It's almost time to share your writing with others. Write your research report neatly in print or cursive on a separate sheet of paper. If you have access to a computer, type your research report on the computer and check your spelling. Save your document to a disk and print it out.

Grammar Tip

State Names In the text of your report, spell out the names of U.S. states (e.g., Pearl Harbor, Hawaii). Use the two-letter abbreviations in the bibliography (e.g., Pearl Harbor, HI: Harbor Books, 2007).

Presenting Tip

Use charts, maps, graphs, and other visuals in your report to capture the attention of your audience and clarify your ideas.

Literature Online

Writing and Research For editing and publishing tools, go to glencoe.com and enter QuickPass code GL39770u5.

Speaking, Listening, and Viewing Workshop

Oral Report

Activity

Connect to Your Writing Deliver an oral report to your classmates. You might want to adapt the research report you wrote for the Writing Workshop on pages 730–737. Remember that you focused on the Unit 5 Big Question: What Really Matters?

Plan Your Oral Report

Reread your research report and highlight the sections you want to include in your oral report. Just like your research report, your oral report should present well-researched information on a focused topic.

Rehearse Your Oral Report

Practice your oral report several times. Use an outline to help you organize your introduction, body paragraphs, and conclusion. Identify places where you should add transitions to connect ideas. Then use your outline to help you rehearse in front of a partner. Use feedback from your rehearsal partner to modify your organization and to make your meaning clearer by rearranging words and sentences.

Deliver Your Oral Report

- Use precise, detailed language and active voice instead of passive.
- Adjust your speaking style to add interest to the information you present.
- Change the vocal tone, pace, and volume of your speaking to help emphasize important information in your oral report.
- Use gestures and visual aids to direct the audience's attention to specific points and clarify your information.
- Use audience feedback to modify your report's organization.

Listening to Learn

Take notes as you listen to make sure you understand the topic. Use the following question frames to learn more about the interpretation from the presenter:

- I found this piece of information the most interesting: _____, because _____. What is the source of that information?
- To summarize the information in your oral report: _____. Is that correct?

Presentation Checklist

Answer the following questions to evaluate your presentation:

- ❏ Did you speak clearly and precisely—and with a style that distinguished your ideas from information you obtained from sources?
- ❏ Did you vary the tone, pace, and volume of your speaking to add emphasis?
- ❏ Did you use gestures and visual aids to clarify your information?
- ❏ Did you make eye contact with your audience?

LOG ON **Literature** Online

Speaking, Listening, and Viewing For project ideas, templates, and presentation tips, go to glencoe.com and enter QuickPass code GL39770u5.

Unit Challenge

Answer the BIG Question

In Unit 5, you explored the Big Question through reading, writing, speaking, and listening. Now it's time for you to complete one of the Unit Challenges below with your answer to the Big Question.

WHAT
Really Matters?

Use the notes you took in your Unit 5 **Foldable** to complete the Unit Challenge you have chosen.

Before you present your Unit Challenge, be sure it meets the requirements below. Use this first plan if you choose someone as a spokesperson to explain what really matters in life.

On Your Own Activity: Choose a Spokesperson

- ❏ Choose a person or character from one of the selections to be a spokesperson to explain what really matters in life.
- ❏ Write a speech he or she might give on what really matters.
- ❏ The speech should explain what really matters and provide, as support, one or more narrative stories.
- ❏ Use proper facial expressions and tone of voice to help get your message across to the class.

Use this second plan if you choose to write a newsletter containing articles about people who matter to others.

Group Activity: Create a Newsletter

- ❏ With a group, create a list of people and characters from the selections.
- ❏ Review the list and decide the person or character you will write about for the newsletter. Each writer should use narrative strategies such as dialogue, action, and description.
- ❏ Compile the articles into a newsletter titled "What Really Matters?" Distribute copies to the class.

Independent Reading

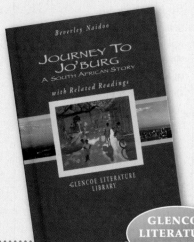

Fiction

To explore the Big Question in other works, choose one of these books from your school or local library.

Journey to Jo'burg: A South African Story

by Beverley Naidoo

In the late 1800s, thirteen-year-old Naledi and her younger brother Tiro walk three hundred miles to Johannesburg to fetch their mother after their baby sister becomes gravely ill. Read to discover how this journey changes Naledi's view of her world.

GLENCOE LITERATURE LIBRARY

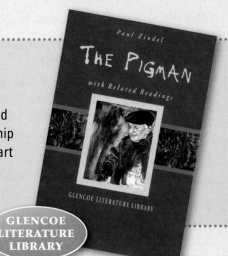

The Pigman

By Paul Zindel

Two alienated teenage boys set out to take advantage of a lonely old man with an awful secret, but instead they develop a warm friendship with him. When the old man dies, the teens are left to ponder the part he played in their lives and the part they may have played in his life and in his death.

GLENCOE LITERATURE LIBRARY

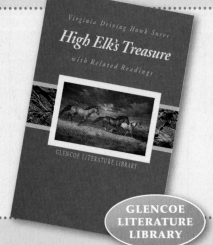

High Elk's Treasure

By Virginia Driving Hawk Sneve

Teenager Joe High Elk and his family are descendants of the Sioux, who defeated Custer at the Battle of Little Big Horn. They live on a South Dakota reservation in the early 1970s. A series of exciting events leads Joe into a new understanding of his people, their character, and their rich cultural heritage.

GLENCOE LITERATURE LIBRARY

Kira-Kira

by Cynthia Kadohata

In the 1950s, a Japanese American family moves to Georgia from Iowa. The adjustment is difficult for everyone, and Katie turns to her sister Lynn for help. When Lynn becomes seriously ill, Katie's strength is severely tested. *Kira-kira* means "glittering" in Japanese. Read to find out what it really means to Katie and her family.

Nonfiction

Jaime Escalante
by Ann Byers

This fascinating biography discusses the challenges faced and overcome by a gifted and determined teacher. Jaime Escalante is a Bolivian-born teacher who immigrated to the United States, where he inspired and motivated his inner city students to excel in mathematics. Escalante and his dedicated students proved to the world that hard work and desire can triumph over poverty and prejudice. The movie *Stand and Deliver* was based on this book.

Facing the Lion: Growing Up Maasai on the African Savanna
by Joseph Lemasolai-Lekuton

Joseph Lemasolai-Lekuton grew up in one of Kenya's poorest tribes. In this story of determination and courage, he tells about his childhood in Kenya, where he tended his family's herd of valuable cows, standing guard at night against lions. He describes his path from Kenya to the United States as well as the ties that still bind him to the Africa he loves.

Ryan White: My Own Story
by Ryan White and Ann Marie Cunningham

The young AIDS activist Ryan White tells his story, including how he got AIDS and how he fought for the right to attend school. When his hometown found out he had AIDS, they responded with fear and hate and told him he couldn't return to school. This moving book shares the voice of a young man who faced terrible circumstances, stood up for his beliefs, and made the whole world listen.

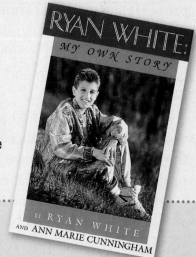

Keep a Reader Response Journal

Read one of these books. As you read, record journal entries about what you found interesting, unexpected, challenging, or exciting. Support your responses with specific examples from the text.

Assessment

Reading

This passage describes the author's experiences growing up in the 1930s. Read the passage and answer the questions. Write your answers on a separate sheet of paper.

---

from "Being Japanese American" by Yoshiko Uchida

Superstitions were not the only Japanese things in my life. A lot more of me was Japanese than I realized, whether I liked it or not.

I was born in California, recited the Pledge of Allegiance to the flag each morning at school, and loved my country as much as any other American—maybe even more.

Still, there was a large part of me that was Japanese simply because Mama and Papa had passed on to me so much of their own Japanese spirit and soul. Their own values of loyalty, honor, self-discipline, love, and respect for one's parents, teachers, and superiors were all very much a part of me.

There was also my name, which teachers couldn't seem to pronounce properly even when I shortened my first name to Yoshi. And there was my Japanese face, which closed more and more doors to me as I grew older.

How wonderful it would be, I used to think, if I had blond hair and blue eyes like Marian and Solveig. Or a name like Mary Anne Brown or Betty Johnson.

If only I didn't have to ask such questions as, "Can we come swim in your pool? We're Japanese." Or when we were looking for a house, "Will the neighbors object if we move in next door?" Or when I went for my first professional haircut, "Do you cut Japanese hair?"

Still, I didn't truly realize how different I was until the summer I was eleven. Although Papa usually went on business trips alone, bringing back such gifts as silver pins for Mama or charm bracelets for Keiko and me, that summer he was able to take us along, thanks to a railroad pass. . . .

For my mother, the high point of the trip was a visit to the small village of Cornwall, Connecticut. There she had her first meeting with the two white American pen pals with whom she had corresponded since her days at Doshisha University. She also visited one of her former missionary teachers, Louise DeForest, who had retired there. And it was there I met a young girl my age, named Cathy Sellew. We became good friends, corresponded for many years, and met again as adults when I needed a home and a friend.

Everyone in the village greeted us warmly, and my father was asked to say a few words to the children of the Summer Vacation Church School—which he did with great relish.

Most of the villagers had never before met a Japanese American. One smiling woman shook my hand and said, "My but you speak English so beautifully." She had meant to compliment me, but I was so astonished, I didn't know what to say. I realized she had seen only my outer self—my Japanese face—and addressed me as a foreigner. I knew then that I would always be different, even though I wanted so badly to be like my white American friends.

---

1. You can tell that this passage is autobiographical because

   A. it is about someone's life.
   B. it is about the author's own life.
   C. it tells more about the narrator than anyone else.
   D. it reveals the main character's thoughts.

2. The narrator points out that she recited the Pledge of Allegiance each morning to show

   A. how American she was.
   B. how much she wanted to be like other students.
   C. how obedient she was.
   D. how well she spoke English.

3. Read this sentence from the passage.

   And there was my Japanese face, which closed more and more doors to me as I grew older.

   The words <u>closed more and more doors</u> are closest in meaning to the words

   A. made people shut their doors to me.
   B. made me avoid other people.
   C. made opportunities unavailable to me.
   D. kept me from entering stores and restaurants.

4. As a child, why did the narrator wish she had a name like Mary Anne Brown?

   A. It would be harder to shorten to a nickname.
   B. It would be an unusual name for a Japanese American girl.
   C. It sounds more American than her real name.
   D. She wanted to have a middle name.

5. The narrator mentions having had to ask permission to swim in other people's pools to point out that

   A. her own family could not afford a pool.

   B. she was raised to be polite.

   C. she was overly protected.

   D. even as a child, she was aware of prejudice.

6. How is the description of the narrator's trip to Connecticut organized?

   A. problem and solution

   B. cause and effect

   C. order of importance

   D. a list of details

7. Read this sentence from the passage.

> **There she had her first meeting with the two white American pen pals with whom she had corresponded since her days at Doshisha University.**

What does the word <u>corresponded</u> mean?

   A. vacationed

   B. competed

   C. taken classes

   D. exchanged letters

8. The "smiling woman" in Connecticut probably assumed that

   A. the narrator had grown up in America.

   B. the narrator was showing off.

   C. the narrator was younger than she actually was.

   D. the narrator's primary language was Japanese.

9. Read this sentence from the passage.

> **We became good friends, corresponded for many years, and met again as adults when I needed a home and a friend.**

This sentence is an example of

   A. foreshadowing.

   B. irony.

   C. cultural context.

   D. historical context.

10. The narrator's visit to Connecticut at age eleven made her realize that she

   A. could feel at home only in California.

   B. did not speak English as well as she thought.

   C. would always be seen as being different.

   D. was as American as anyone anywhere.

11. How does the narrator develop her description of what it was like to be Japanese American during the 1930s?

   A. with facts and statistics

   B. with logical arguments

   C. with examples and anecdotes

   D. by quoting experts

Extended Answer

12. Based on the information in this passage and your own knowledge, explain what made Yoshiko Uchida a typical American child. Consider her experiences, emotions, and her reactions to other people.

Vocabulary Skills

On a separate sheet of paper, write the numbers 1–14. Next to each number, write the letter of the word or phrase that is closest in meaning to the underlined word.

1. ignoring their <u>taunts</u>
- **A.** whispers
- **B.** name calling
- **C.** questions
- **D.** appearance

2. some <u>internal</u> voice
- **A.** inner
- **B.** distant
- **C.** unexpected
- **D.** hopeful

3. to <u>sustain</u> a conversation
- **A.** cut short
- **B.** dislike
- **C.** keep up
- **D.** enjoy

4. <u>inhumane</u> treatment
- **A.** physical
- **B.** good-natured
- **C.** selfish
- **D.** cruel

5. our energy had <u>ebbed</u>
- **A.** rocketed
- **B.** faded
- **C.** not changed
- **D.** slowly grown

6. <u>tangible</u> support
- **A.** invisible
- **B.** solid
- **C.** puzzling
- **D.** unbelievable

7. speaking <u>solemnly</u>
- **A.** rapidly
- **B.** jokingly
- **C.** too loudly
- **D.** very seriously

8. <u>prosperity</u> for all
- **A.** hunger
- **B.** education
- **C.** hardships
- **D.** good times

9. the defendant's <u>petition</u>
- **A.** request
- **B.** opinion
- **C.** response
- **D.** case

10. a rarely used <u>technique</u>
- **A.** tool
- **B.** meaning
- **C.** procedure
- **D.** form of speech

11. a time of <u>turmoil</u>
- **A.** disbelief
- **B.** progress
- **C.** peace
- **D.** unrest

12. to <u>obscure</u> the image
- **A.** reveal
- **B.** block out
- **C.** feature
- **D.** complete

13. <u>barricades</u> of old furniture
- **A.** barriers
- **B.** loads
- **C.** sales
- **D.** collections

14. <u>treacherous</u> waves
- **A.** big
- **B.** imaginary
- **C.** unsafe
- **D.** gentle

LOG ON ▶ **Literature** Online

Assessment For additional test practice, go to glencoe.com and enter QuickPass code GL39770u5.

Writing Strategies

The following is a rough draft of part of a student's report. It contains errors. Read the passage. Then answer the questions on a separate sheet of paper.

---

(1) Everyone today <u>travels</u> by plane, but people used to take more <u>journeyes</u> by train. (2) My grandpa, an engineer for thirty years, often told us about his trips. (3) Everything about train travel <u>is seeming</u> fun to me. (4) I wish my parents who don't travel much would take us. (5) I think we'd enjoy <u>ourselves</u>.

1. What is the correct way to write the underlined words in sentence 1?

   A. travels, journeys
   B. travel, journeyes
   C. is traveling, journies
   D. Leave as is.

2. What is the correct way to punctuate sentence 2?

   A. My grandpa an engineer for thirty years, often told us about his trips.
   B. My grandpa, an engineer for thirty years often told us about his trips.
   C. My grandpa, an engineer, for thirty years often told us, about his trips.
   D. Leave as is.

3. What is the correct way to write the underlined words in sentence 3?

   A. seem
   B. seems
   C. was seeming
   D. Leave as is.

4. What is the correct way to punctuate sentence 4?

   A. I wish, my parents who don't travel much would take us.
   B. I wish my parents, who don't travel much, would take us.
   C. I wish my parents who don't travel much, would take us.
   D. Leave as is.

5. What is the correct way to write the underlined word in sentence 5?

   A. ourselfs
   B. ourselvs
   C. ourselfes
   D. Leave as is.

Writing Product

Read the assignment in the box below and follow the directions. Use one piece of paper as a planning sheet to jot down ideas and organize your thoughts. Then neatly write your final story on another sheet. You may not use a dictionary or other reference materials.

Writing Situation:

The law determines what makes a person a citizen of the United States. What makes a person a "true American," though, is less a matter of fact.

Directions for Writing:

Think about what, in your opinion, makes a person a "true American."

Now write to explain what characteristics, attitudes, and behaviors a "true American" has.

Keep these hints in mind when you write.

- Concentrate on what the prompt tells you to write.
- Organize the way you will present your ideas.
- Provide good, clear support for your ideas.
- Use different kinds of sentence structures.
- Use precise words that express your ideas clearly.
- Check your essay for mistakes in spelling, grammar, and punctuation.

HOW Do You Keep from Giving Up?

**American surfer
Bethany Hamilton**

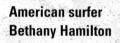 Survivor of a shark attack

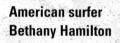 Winner of surfing contests

 ESPY Award for Best
Comeback Athlete

THE **BIG** Question

> *People can do whatever they want if they just set their heart to it, and just never give up, and just go out there and do it.*

—BETHANY HAMILTON

FOLDABLES®
Study Organizer

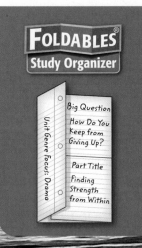

Unit Genre Focus: Drama

Big Question
How Do You Keep from Giving Up?

Part Title
Finding Strength from Within

Throughout Unit 6, you will read, write, and talk about the **BIG** Question—"How Do You Keep from Giving Up?" Use your Unit 6 **Foldable**, shown here, to keep track of your ideas as you read. Turn to the back of this book for instructions on making this **Foldable**.

HOW Do You Keep from Giving Up?

No matter how much you prepare for the future, there is always the chance an unexpected and unfortunate event or development can upset your plans. After suffering a difficult setback, it can be easy to become discouraged. You have read the advice of surfer Bethany Hamilton on page 749. Hamilton survived a shark attack, and she tells everyone, "just never give up." What do you do when faced with challenges? Explore how you can carry on through difficult times.

Think about this important way to help you keep from giving up during hard times:

○ Finding Strength from Within

What You'll Read

Reading about how other people stay positive during hard times will give you ideas about ways to stay strong and keep trying. In this unit, **drama**—any work of literature performed before an audience—is an excellent way to see how people get through hard times. You will also read a diary entry, poetry, and other texts that can lead you to discover answers to the Big Question.

What You'll Write

As you explore the Big Question, you'll write notes in your Unit **Foldable.** Later, you'll use these notes to complete two writing assignments related to the Big Question.

1. Write an Expository Essay

2. Choose a Unit Challenge

- **On Your Own Activity: Write a Narrative Poem**
- **Group Activity: Create a Newspaper Ad**

What You'll Learn

Literary Elements

act and scene

drama

stage directions

voice

speaker

Reading Skills and Strategies

analyze plot

make generalizations about theme

question

draw conclusions about author's perspective

preview

analyze text features

Bouncing Back

How to Get on Your Feet When Life Knocks You Down

from *Current Health* Magazine

Jan Farrington

When Beth Driscoll of Denton, Texas, was in middle school, she dreamed of following her friends to a private high school. Her family didn't have the money, so she went to the local public high school. Beth made it work. But in her senior year, she got more bad news—her dad had lost his job. Her parents told her they couldn't help pay for college.

You can see where this story line might go: Beth gives up, takes an unfulfilling[1] job, and maybe dives into drugs. But that didn't happen. Instead, she applied for student loans, took a part-time job, and rented a tiny room near campus, where she's now studying to be a special-education teacher.

Beth's life isn't perfect. She works too many hours to spend as much time studying as she'd like to. But Beth, now 21, is determined to earn her degree and make a good life for herself.

Six Tips for Taking Charge

When life knocks you down, do you have trouble getting off the ground? Or are you a resilient[2] teen with a gift for bouncing back, like Beth?

"Some kids come into this world and have an easier time being happy and dealing with stress," Robert Brooks of Harvard Medical School told *Current Health*. Brooks is a family psychologist and a coauthor of

---

1 **Unfulfilling** (un′fool fil′ing) means "not satisfying."

2 A **resilient** (ri zil′yənt) teen is one who is able to recover from or adjust easily to misfortune or change.

Set a Purpose for Reading

Read the article "Bouncing Back" to discover how some people kept from giving up when bad things happened to them.

BQ BIG Question

What did Beth do when she found out her family couldn't pay for her college education?

The Power of Resilience: Achieving Balance, Confidence, and Personal Strength in Your Life. For teens who don't handle stress well, Brooks says there are things that they can do to take charge of their problems and build better coping skills. He suggests the strategies[3] below.

1. **Surround yourself with people who make you stronger.** Having a few close friends can be a great source of strength, says Brooks. "But some teens with low self-esteem would rather have friends who make fun of them and get them in trouble than be ignored," he added. Bottom line: Don't put up with friends who put you down.

2. **Involve adults in your life.** "Resilient people almost always say there were one or two adults who really believed in them and stood by them" when they were teens, Brooks said. For many teens, parents fit the bill.[4] For other teens, those caring adults may be family friends or youth club leaders.

3. **Discover something you're good at.** By focusing on your strengths and talents, you can develop a sense of pride and dignity that will help you overcome obstacles in other areas of your life.

4. **Let yourself experience success.** "Success builds on success," noted Brooks. As you work toward a long-term goal, achieving smaller goals (making a speech in public, studying for 30 minutes longer each night) can give you a taste of success that will help you cope with bigger challenges ahead.

5. **Believe things will get better.** "Most of the problems that teens face are solvable," Brooks told *CH*. "But if [teens are] feeling down or incompetent,[5] it's easy for them to feel their whole life is going to be that way." Think about all the

BQ ⟩ **BIG Question**

Think about an adult on whom you can rely. In what ways does this person provide support for you?

---

3 **Strategies** (strat´ ə jēs) are plans for working through a problem or activity.

4 Here, to **fit the bill** means "to be right for a situation."

5 Someone who feels **incompetent** thinks that he or she is not able to do things correctly or successfully.

changes you've seen in your life, and you'll realize that a "rough spot" is only temporary.

6. **Put yourself out there.** Volunteer at a food bank, at a nursing home, or with the local Special Olympics program. "Teens who help others are less likely to feel depressed or angry," said Brooks. "Giving back to the community gives teens an opportunity to shine and to feel they're making a difference in the world."

Classroom Heroes

What does resilience look like? Sometimes it looks like the kid sitting next to you in math class.

Robin Regan, 18, and Patricia Calderon, 19, had shared a class at their Orange County, Calif., high school. But until both girls won the 2003 Julie Inman Courage Award, neither had discussed what the other was going through.

Regan's mother had broken her neck in an accident, and Regan was helping her mom learn to walk again. Calderon had an older sister who was dying of leukemia.[6] Both teens were taking care of younger siblings, tackling household chores, and keeping up with honors classes, school commitments, and volunteer projects. But that didn't stop the two girls from graduating from high school on time. Regan and Calderon are now thriving college students.

How did they manage? "I'm not going to lie," Regan said. "After Mom's accident, I was really angry. I thought, *This isn't fair; why did it have to happen just when I need her so much?*" she said. "But my parents' dream for me always was that I go to college. So I couldn't throw away all their hard work."

Calderon says she owes her strength to her sister. "She always told me to try my hardest. She didn't get to finish [her life], so I want to succeed not just for me but for her too."

BQ BIG Question

In what ways can any of these strategies be useful to you? Think about times you have used any of these strategies.

---

6 **Leukemia** (loō kē′ mē ə) is a deadly disease that affects blood cells.

As remarkable as their stories are, Regan and Calderon fit the profile of typical Inman award winners. The annual awards recognize teens who have earned their diplomas in spite of broken homes, illnesses, or other challenges. "Sometimes these kids are overlooked, and all we see are the athletes and scholars," said Julie Inman, the inspiration for the award. Inman herself knows a lot about resilience. After a skiing accident left her paralyzed at age 15, she went on to get a college degree with honors and has never abandoned her goal of someday walking again.

School of Hard Knocks

No one enjoys tough times. Still, there can be a surprising upside to life's downturns: They make you stronger. "I am not the same person I was before," Calderon told *CH*. "Before, I always had older sisters who looked after me. But then suddenly I had to pull myself together and take over."

"Little things don't bother me anymore," Regan added. "I had to grow up pretty quick, but in the long run, I think that will be good. When other tough things come up, I can tell myself that I've gotten through something tough before, and I can handle it."

Tough Times of the Rich and Famous

U.S. senator Barack Obama went through a rebellious phase[7] after his father left the family. Obama went so far as to experiment with alcohol and drugs. In his autobiography, *Dreams From My Father*, he writes that his mother's love and the support of some wonderful teachers and mentors[8] "pulled me out of it."

Country singer Shania Twain grew up in a destitute[9] family in a Canadian mining town. She was just 21 when her mother and stepfather were killed in a car

BQ BIG Question

How did Robin and Patricia cope with their problems? Think about how each girl found strength within herself.

BQ BIG Question

In what ways do tough times make people stronger? Think of a time in your life when a difficult situation made you stronger.

---

7 A *phase* (fāz) is a step in the development of a person or thing.

8 *Mentors* (men′tərz) are wise and trusted people who model good methods of coping with life.

9 A *destitute* (des′tə toot′) family is one that is lacking the necessities of life and is in a state of absolute need.

accident. Nonetheless, Twain took charge of raising her three younger siblings. "It was a difficult time," she told *Rolling Stone.* "But boy, oh boy, did I get strong."

Would You Survive . . . or Thrive?

When bad things happen, feeling upset can be a normal first response. But what's your second response? Do you move in a positive direction or in a negative one?

In the situations below, think honestly about how you'd react, and choose the letter for that response. We'll help you analyze the results.

1. **The referee doesn't call pass interference when an opposing player keeps you from connecting with a pass. You**

   a) rush the ref and yell in his or her face.

   b) spend the ride home talking about the bad call.

   c) tell yourself to get back in the game and play even harder and smarter than before.

2. **You think you did fine on an English exam, but the teacher gives it a grade of C minus. You**

   a) tell yourself that the test questions were confusing and blame your teacher.

   b) decide you won't study as hard for the next test, because it won't do any good.

   c) take a long walk and then ask the teacher for study suggestions.

If you have *a* or *b* answers, you probably have a hard time letting go of negative feelings. Having *c* answers means you're pretty resilient: When you hit a rough spot, you try to turn things in a more positive direction. *Do you need to work on resiliency skills?* Try some of the suggestions in the article, and remember: One of the best ways to get rid of negative emotions is to get involved in something outside yourself. Do something worthwhile—for your family, for your community, for your school—and you'll make yourself stronger too. 🐾

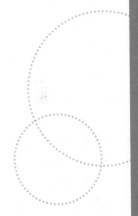

BQ BIG Question

Think about how you would answer the question "Do you need to work on resiliency skills?" What are some ways this article has taught you to find strength from within?

After You Read

Respond and Think Critically

1. What are the six tips from the article for handling stress? Restate them in your own words. [Summarize]

2. Why do you think the author includes celebrities as examples of resiliency? What can you infer about the author's beliefs about the influence of celebrities on people? [Infer]

3. Pick one of the people mentioned in "Bouncing Back." Which of the six strategies did the person use to take charge of his or her life? In your answer, include details from the person's life. [Analyze]

4. Do you think this article is successful in educating readers about how to cope with difficult times? Explain your opinion. [Evaluate]

Writing

Write a Summary Write a summary of the methods you rely on when dealing with difficult problems. You may want to begin your summary with this sentence:

"When times are rough, one way of coping that I use is _____."

Consider how you want to order this information for the reader. Does a numbered list of tips similar to the one used by this article's author work for your summary? Or does writing in a traditional essay form better suit your information?

Make sure you explain how the information you are summarizing has worked for you and why you think it could help others.

Learning Objectives

For page 756

In this assignment, you will focus on the following objectives:

Reading:
Analyzing and evaluating informational text.

Connecting to contemporary issues.

Writing: Writing a summary.

LOG ON ▶ **Literature** Online

Unit Resources For additional skills practice, go to glencoe.com and enter QuickPass code GL39770u6.

Finding Strength
from Within

Healing, 1996. Daniel Nevins. Oil on wood. Private Collection.

BQ ▶ **BIG Question How Do You Keep from Giving Up?**

In the painting *Healing,* the woman's pink heart could be viewed as a symbol of her inner strength. What does this image of a strong-willed woman suggest to you? Why do people often rely on their inner strength to stay hopeful?

The Diary of Anne Frank, Act One

Connect to the Drama

Think about a time in your life when you had to hide.
Quickwrite Write a brief paragraph describing the situation of hiding. Where and why did you hide? From whom did you hide? What was the result?

Build Background

Anne Frank's diary became famous in the 1950s. It tells Anne's story just before and during her family's hiding from Nazi forces.

- Anne Frank and her family were Jewish. They were living in Germany when Adolf Hitler came to power in 1933. Hitler's Nazi party blamed the Jews for Germany's economic and social problems. The Nazi government started restricting the Jews' freedoms. Soon, Hitler was moving Jews to ghettos and, later, to concentration camps where millions were eventually killed. Because of the increased danger, Anne's family moved to the Netherlands.

- When Germany invaded the Netherlands in May 1940, the Nazis continued discriminating against Jews in that country. Dutch officials shipped Jews to German and Austrian work camps. Anne's sister, Margot, received a call-up to go to Germany. Fearing for her life, the Frank family went into hiding.

Vocabulary

conspicuous (kən spik′ū əs) *adj.* easily seen, apparent (p. 765). *Her rainbow hat made her conspicuous.*

loathe (lōth) *v.* to regard with extreme disgust; hate (p. 776). *I loathe going to the dentist.*

aggravating (ag′rə vāt ing) *adj.* irritating; annoying (p. 784). *The child's constant complaining was aggravating.*

subdued (səb dōōd′) *adj.* quiet and restrained (p. 793). *The crowd became subdued when they heard the bad news.*

jubilation (jōō′bə lā′shən) *n.* great joy and excitement (p. 806). *The winner cried out in jubilation.*

Meet Frances Goodrich and Albert Hackett

"Anytime Frances talked about Anna, she cried. She kept saying, 'Where was I when this was happening?'"

—Albert Hackett

Drama Duo Frances Goodrich and her husband, Albert Hackett, spent two years writing their play based on *Anne Frank: The Diary of a Young Girl.* They met Anne's father and visited the building in Amsterdam where the Franks hid. The award-winning play was first performed in 1955.

Screenplays Goodrich and Hackett also wrote over thirty screenplays for Hollywood, including *The Thin Man.*

Goodrich was born in 1890 and died in 1984. Hackett was born in 1900 and died in 1995.

 Literature Online

Author Search For more about Frances Goodrich and Albert Hackett, go to glencoe.com and enter QuickPass code GL39770u6.

Set Purposes for Reading

BQ BIG Question

As you read, ask yourself, in what ways do Anne and her family find strength from within in the face of great danger?

Literary Elements Act and Scene

An **act** is a major division of a drama. An act usually focuses on one piece of the plot or theme of the play. An act is divided into **scenes,** or subdivisions. A scene presents action in one place or situation. Acts and scenes are usually numbered in a script.

Acts and scenes are important because they organize and add dramatic emphasis to the story. In live performance, you can identify a scene by a brief break in the story or blackout on the stage. Breaks between acts are much longer and often present major changes when the story resumes.

As you read, determine the effect the scene structure has on the story.

Reading Skill Analyze Plot

The **plot** is the sequence of events in a story, novel, or play. The plot begins with an **exposition**. The exposition introduces the characters, setting, and situation, and the **conflict**. The exposition provides important information for understanding the plot. The **rising action** follows and adds complications to the story until it reaches its point of greatest interest or suspense, the **climax**.

Analyzing plot is very important in order to understand what is happening and why. It can also reveal information about the characters' motivations, decisions, and development.

When you analyze plot, you

- identify important information in the exposition
- think about the potential consequences of the conflict and its effect on characters
- connect the conflict to events in the story

As you read, ask yourself what the consequences of the conflict are. You may find it helpful to use a graphic organizer like the one below.

Conflict	Between Whom?	Setting	Effect

Learning Objectives

For pages 758–813

In studying this text, you will focus on the following objectives:

Literary Study: Analyzing drama.

Reading: Analyzing plot.

TRY IT

Analyze Plot Think of a favorite fairy tale or fable. List the story's characters, setting, and conflict(s). Write a brief explanation of the primary conflict and the effects it has on the characters.

The rear exterior of the Anne Frank House, including a view of the attic, Amsterdam.

The **Diary** of **Anne Frank**

Frances Goodrich and Albert Hackett

ACT ONE—SCENE 1

CHARACTERS

Mr. Frank	Mr. Van Daan	Margot Frank	Mr. Kraler
Miep	Peter Van Daan	Anne Frank	Mr. Dussel
Mrs. Van Daan	Mrs. Frank		

[*The scene remains the same throughout the play. It is the top floor of a warehouse and office building in Amsterdam, Holland. The sharply peaked roof of the building is outlined against a sea of other rooftops, stretching away into the distance. Nearby is the belfry[1] of a church tower, the Westertoren, whose carillon rings out the hours. Occasionally faint sounds float up from below: the voices of children playing in the street, the tramp of marching feet, a boat whistle from the canal.*

The three rooms of the top floor and a small attic space above are exposed to our view. The largest of the rooms is in the center, with two small rooms, slightly raised, on either side. On the right is a bathroom, out of sight. A narrow steep flight of stairs at the back leads up to the attic. The rooms are sparsely furnished with a few chairs, cots, a table or two. The windows are painted over, or covered with makeshift blackout curtains.[2] In the main room there is a sink, a gas ring for cooking and a wood-burning stove for warmth.

---

1 A ***belfry*** is the tower of a church or other building in which a bell is hung.

2 ***Blackout curtains*** were used to hide room lights from enemy bombers.

Act and Scene Describe the setting of Scene 1.

The room on the left is hardly more than a closet. There is a skylight in the sloping ceiling. Directly under this room is a small steep stairwell, with steps leading down to a door. This is the only entrance from the building below. When the door is opened we see that it has been concealed on the outer side by a bookcase attached to it.

The curtain rises on an empty stage. It is late afternoon, November, 1945.

The rooms are dusty, the curtains in rags. Chairs and tables are overturned.

The door at the foot of the small stairwell swings open. MR. FRANK *comes up the steps into view. He is a gentle, cultured European in his middle years. There is still a trace of a German accent in his speech.*

He stands looking slowly around, making a supreme effort at self-control. He is weak, ill. His clothes are threadbare.[3]

Visual Vocabulary

A **rucksack** is a knapsack, or large carrying bag with straps worn on the back.

After a second he drops his **rucksack** *on the couch and moves slowly about. He opens the door to one of the smaller rooms, and then abruptly closes*

it again, turning away. He goes to the window at the back, looking off at the Westertoren as its carillon strikes the hour of six, then he moves restlessly on.

From the street below we hear the sound of a barrel organ and children's voices at play. There is a many-colored scarf hanging from a nail. MR. FRANK *takes it, putting it around his neck. As he starts back for his rucksack, his eye is caught by something lying on the floor. It is a woman's white glove. He holds it in his hand and suddenly all of his self-control is gone. He breaks down, crying.*

We hear footsteps on the stairs. MIEP GIES[4] *comes up, looking for* MR. FRANK. MIEP *is a Dutch girl of about twenty-two. She wears a coat and hat, ready to go home. She is pregnant. Her attitude toward* MR. FRANK *is protective, compassionate.*]

MIEP. Are you all right, Mr. Frank?

MR. FRANK. [*Quickly controlling himself.*] Yes, Miep, yes.

MIEP. Everyone in the office has gone home . . . It's after six. [*Then pleading.*] Don't stay up here, Mr. Frank. What's the use of torturing yourself like this?

MR. FRANK. I've come to say good-bye . . . I'm leaving here, Miep.

MIEP. What do you mean? Where are you going? Where?

---

3 Clothes that are ***threadbare*** are so old or worn that the threads can be seen.

Analyze Plot Why is it important for the audience to know about the bookcase? Think about the way in which this part of the exposition hints at the upcoming conflict.

---

4 ***Miep Gies*** (mēp gēs)

Act and Scene What has already happened in the past at the beginning of Act 1, Scene 1? Explain.

People can visit the restored house where Anne Frank and her family hid. In this photograph, notice how the bookcase hides the stairway to the rear of the building where the Franks hid.

MR. FRANK. I don't know yet. I haven't decided.

MIEP. Mr. Frank, you can't leave here! This is your home! Amsterdam is your home. Your business is here, waiting for you . . . You're needed here . . . Now that the war is over, there are things that . . .

MR. FRANK. I can't stay in Amsterdam, Miep. It has too many memories for me. Everywhere there's something . . . the house we lived in . . . the school . . . that street organ playing out there . . . I'm not the person you used to know, Miep. I'm a bitter old man.

[*Breaking off.*] Forgive me. I shouldn't speak to you like this . . . after all that you did for us . . . the suffering . . .

MIEP. No. No. It wasn't suffering. You can't say we suffered.

[*As she speaks, she straightens a chair which is overturned.*]

MR. FRANK. I know what you went through, you and Mr. Kraler.[5] I'll remember it as long as I live. [*He gives one last look around.*] Come, Miep.

5 **Kraler** (krä′lər)

The Diary of Anne Frank, Act One   **763**

[*He starts for the steps, then remembers his rucksack, going back to get it.*]

MIEP. [*Hurrying up to a cupboard.*] Mr. Frank, did you see? There are some of your papers here. [*She brings a bundle of papers to him.*] We found them in a heap of rubbish on the floor after . . . after you left.

MR. FRANK. Burn them.

[*He opens his rucksack to put the glove in it.*]

MIEP. But, Mr. Frank, there are letters, notes . . .

MR. FRANK. Burn them. All of them.

MIEP. Burn this?

[*She hands him a paperbound notebook.*]

MR. FRANK. [*Quietly.*] Anne's diary. [*He opens the diary and begins to read.*] "Monday, the sixth of July, nineteen forty-two." [*To* MIEP.] Nineteen forty-two. Is it possible, Miep? . . . Only three years ago. [*As he continues his reading, he sits down on the couch.*] "Dear Diary, since you and I are going to be great friends, I will start by telling you about myself. My name is Anne Frank. I am thirteen years old. I was born in Germany the twelfth of June, nineteen twenty-nine. As my family is Jewish, we emigrated to

Holland when Hitler came to power."[6]

[*As* MR. FRANK *reads on, another voice joins his, as if coming from the air. It is* ANNE'S *voice.*]

MR. FRANK AND ANNE. "My father started a business, importing spice and herbs. Things went well for us until nineteen forty. Then the war came, and the Dutch capitulation, followed by the arrival of the Germans.[7] Then things got very bad for the Jews."

[MR. FRANK'S *voice dies out.* ANNE'S *voice continues alone. The lights dim slowly to darkness. The curtain falls on the scene.*]

ANNE'S VOICE. You could not do this and you could not do that. They forced Father out of his business. We had to wear yellow stars.[8] I had to turn in my bike. I couldn't go to a Dutch school any more. I couldn't go to the movies, or ride in an automobile, or even on a streetcar, and a million other things. But somehow we children still managed to have fun. Yesterday Father told me we were going into hiding. Where, he wouldn't say. At five o'clock this morning

---

6 Thousands of German Jews left the country after Adolf Hitler became the head of government in 1933.

7 Germany began its invasion of the Netherlands on May 10, 1940, and, within a few days, forced the Dutch army's surrender, or **capitulation** (kə pich´ə lā´ shən).

8 The Nazis ordered Jews to wear **yellow stars** at all times for easy identification. The six-pointed Star of David is a religious symbol of the Jewish people.

Analyze Plot What important information do you learn from Anne's monologue?

Analyze Plot What does this detail tell you about the way the Franks left the attic room? Think about why this is an important part of the exposition.

BQ BIG Question What do you think gives Mr. Frank the strength to read Anne's diary?

Mother woke me and told me to hurry and get dressed. I was to put on as many clothes as I could. It would look too suspicious if we walked along carrying suitcases. It wasn't until we were on our way that I learned where we were going. Our hiding place was to be upstairs in the building where Father used to have his business. Three other people were coming in with us . . . the Van Daans and their son Peter . . . Father knew the Van Daans but we had never met them . . .

[*During the last lines the curtain rises on the scene. The lights dim on.* ANNE'S *voice fades out.*]

ACT ONE—SCENE 2

[*It is early morning, July, 1942. The rooms are bare, as before, but they are now clean and orderly.*

MR. VAN DAAN, *a tall, portly man in his late forties, is in the main room, pacing up and down, nervously smoking a cigarette. His clothes and overcoat are expensive and well cut.*

MRS. VAN DAAN *sits on the couch, clutching her possessions, a hatbox, bags, etc. She is a pretty woman in her early forties. She wears a fur coat over her other clothes.*

PETER VAN DAAN *is standing at the window of the room on the right, looking down at the street below. He is a shy, awkward boy of sixteen. He wears a cap, a raincoat, and long Dutch trousers, like "plus fours."*[1] *At his feet is a black case, a carrier for his cat.*

The yellow Star of David is **conspicuous** *on all of their clothes.*]

MRS. VAN DAAN. [*Rising, nervous, excited.*] Something's happened to them! I know it!

MR. VAN DAAN. Now, Kerli!

MRS. VAN DAAN. Mr. Frank said they'd be here at seven o'clock. He said . . .

MR. VAN DAAN. They have two miles to walk. You can't expect . . .

MRS. VAN DAAN. They've been picked up. That's what's happened. They've been taken . . .

[MR. VAN DAAN *indicates that he hears someone coming.*]

MR. VAN DAAN. You see?

[PETER *takes up his carrier and his schoolbag, etc., and goes into the main room as* MR. FRANK *comes up the stairwell*

Act and Scene In what way is Anne's diary entry an effective way to end Scene 1 and move on to Scene 2?

Act and Scene How does the setting here differ from Scene 1? Think about why this is important to know.

Analyze Plot What does the description of Mr. Van Daan suggest about his economic status? Why might this be important to the story?

---

1 **Dutch trousers** and **plus fours** are pants that end at or a few inches below the knees.

Analyze Plot What does Mrs. Van Daan's anxiety tell us about life in Amsterdam under Nazi occupation? What are you learning about the drama's main conflict?

Vocabulary ....

conspicuous (kən spik′ ū əs) *adj.* easily seen, apparent

from below. MR. FRANK looks much younger now. His movements are brisk, his manner confident. He wears an overcoat and carries his hat and a small cardboard box. He crosses to the VAN DAANS, shaking hands with each of them.]

MR. FRANK. Mrs. Van Daan, Mr. Van Daan, Peter. [*Then, in explanation of their lateness.*] There were too many of the Green Police[2] on the streets . . . we had to take the long way around.

[*Up the steps come MARGOT FRANK, MRS. FRANK, MIEP (not pregnant now), and MR. KRALER. All of them carry bags, packages, and so forth. The Star of David is conspicuous on all of the FRANKS' clothing. MARGOT is eighteen, beautiful, quiet, shy. MRS. FRANK is a young mother, gently bred, reserved. She, like MR. FRANK, has a slight German accent. MR. KRALER is a Dutchman, dependable, kindly. As MR. KRALER and MIEP go upstage[3] to put down their parcels, MRS. FRANK turns back to call ANNE.*]

MRS. FRANK. Anne?

[*ANNE comes running up the stairs. She is thirteen, quick in her movements, interested in everything, mercurial[4] in her emotions. She wears a cape, long wool socks and carries a schoolbag.*]

MR. FRANK. [*Introducing them.*] My wife, Edith. Mr. and Mrs. Van Daan [*MRS. FRANK hurries over, shaking hands with them.*] . . . their son, Peter . . . my daughters, Margot and Anne.

[*ANNE gives a polite little curtsy as she shakes MR. VAN DAAN's hand. Then she immediately starts off on a tour of investigation of her new home, going upstairs to the attic room. MIEP and MR. KRALER are putting the various things they have brought on the shelves.*]

MR. KRALER. I'm sorry there is still so much confusion.

MR. FRANK. Please. Don't think of it. After all, we'll have plenty of leisure to arrange everything ourselves.

MIEP. [*To MRS. FRANK.*] We put the stores of food you sent in here. Your drugs are here . . . soap, linen here.

MRS. FRANK. Thank you, Miep.

MIEP. I made up the beds . . . the way Mr. Frank and Mr. Kraler said. [*She starts out.*] Forgive me. I have to hurry. I've got to go to the other side of town to get some ration books[5] for you.

MRS. VAN DAAN. Ration books? If they see our names on ration books, they'll know we're here.

---

2 One branch of the Nazi police force was called the Green Police because its members wore green uniforms.

3 **Upstage** is toward the back of the stage; **downstage** is the front, near the audience.

4 Anne is described as **mercurial** (mər kyoorʹē əl) because her emotions change quickly and unpredictably, like the mercury in a thermometer.

---

5 **Ration books** contain coupons that people use to buy a limited amount of food and supplies.

Analyze Plot What does Mr. Frank mean when he says they will have plenty of leisure to arrange everything?

MR. KRALER. There isn't anything . . .

MIEP. Don't worry. Your names won't be on them. [*As she hurries out.*] I'll be up later.

MR. FRANK. Thank you, Miep.

MRS. FRANK. [*To MR. KRALER.*] It's illegal, then, the ration books? We've never done anything illegal.

MR. FRANK. We won't be living here exactly according to regulations.

[*As MR. KRALER reassures MRS. FRANK, he takes various small things, such as matches, soap, etc., from his pockets, handing them to her.*]

MR. KRALER. This isn't the black market, Mrs. Frank. This is what we call the white market[6] . . . helping all of the hundreds and hundreds who are hiding out in Amsterdam.

[*The carillon is heard playing the quarter-hour before eight. MR. KRALER looks at his watch. ANNE stops at the window as she comes down the stairs.*]

ANNE. It's the Westertoren!

MR. KRALER. I must go. I must be out of here and downstairs in the office before the workmen get here. [*He starts for the stairs leading out.*] Miep or I, or both of us, will be up each day to bring you food and news and find out what your needs are. Tomorrow I'll get you a better bolt for the door at the foot of the stairs. It needs a bolt that you can throw yourself and open only at our signal. [*To MR. FRANK.*] Oh . . . You'll tell them about the noise?

MR. FRANK. I'll tell them.

MR. KRALER. Good-bye then for the moment. I'll come up again, after the workmen leave.

MR. FRANK. Good-bye, Mr. Kraler.

MRS. FRANK. [*Shaking his hand.*] How can we thank you?

[*The others murmur their good-byes.*]

MR. KRALER. I never thought I'd live to see the day when a man like Mr. Frank would have to go into hiding. When you think—

[*He breaks off, going out. MR. FRANK follows him down the steps, bolting the door after him. In the interval before he returns, PETER goes over to MARGOT, shaking hands with her. As MR. FRANK comes back up the steps, MRS. FRANK questions him anxiously.*]

MRS. FRANK. What did he mean, about the noise?

MR. FRANK. First let us take off some of these clothes.

---

6 In the ***black market,*** goods were sold illegally, usually at very high prices. In the ***white market,*** which also violated Nazi laws, goods were donated by people who wanted to help the Jews.

BQ **BIG Question** What does Anne's response to hearing the church bells suggest about her personality?

[*They all start to take off garment after garment. On each of their coats, sweaters, blouses, suits, dresses, is another yellow Star of David.* MR. *and* MRS. FRANK *are underdressed quite simply. The others wear several things, sweaters, extra dresses, bathrobes, aprons, nightgowns, etc.*]

MR. VAN DAAN. It's a wonder we weren't arrested, walking along the streets . . . Petronella with a fur coat in July . . . and that cat of Peter's crying all the way.

ANNE. [*As she is removing a pair of panties.*] A cat?

MRS. FRANK. [*Shocked.*] Anne, please!

ANNE. It's all right. I've got on three more.

[*She pulls off two more. Finally, as they have all removed their surplus clothes, they look to* MR. FRANK, *waiting for him to speak.*]

MR. FRANK. Now. About the noise. While the men are in the building below, we must have complete quiet. Every sound can be heard down there, not only in the workrooms, but in the offices too. The men come at about eight-thirty, and leave at about five-thirty. So, to be perfectly safe, from eight in the morning until six in the evening we must move only when it is necessary, and then in stockinged feet. We must not speak above a whisper. We must not run any water. We cannot use the sink, or even, forgive me, the w.c.[7] The pipes go down through the workrooms. It would be heard. No trash . . . [MR. FRANK *stops abruptly as he hears the sound of marching feet from the street below. Everyone is motionless, paralyzed with fear.* MR. FRANK *goes quietly into the room on the right to look down out of the window.* ANNE *runs after him, peering out with him. The tramping feet pass without stopping. The tension is relieved.* MR. FRANK, *followed by* ANNE, *returns to the main room and resumes his instructions to the group.*] . . . No trash must ever be thrown out which might reveal that someone is living up here . . . not even a potato paring. We must burn everything in the stove at night. This is the way we must live until it is over, if we are to survive.

---

7 Short for "water closet," the ***w.c.*** is a bathroom.

Analyze Plot What complications are now added to the plot?

[There is silence for a second.]

MRS. FRANK. Until it is over.

MR. FRANK. [*Reassuringly.*] After six we can move about . . . we can talk and laugh and have our supper and read and play games . . . just as we would at home. [*He looks at his watch.*] And now I think it would be wise if we all went to our rooms, and were settled before eight o'clock. Mrs. Van Daan, you and your husband will be upstairs. I regret that there's no place up there for Peter. But he will be here, near us. This will be our common room, where we'll meet to talk and eat and read, like one family.

MR. VAN DAAN. And where do you and Mrs. Frank sleep?

MR. FRANK. This room is also our bedroom.

MRS. VAN DAAN. That isn't right. We'll sleep here and you take the room upstairs. ⎤
⎥— *Together*
MR. VAN DAAN. It's your place. ⎦

MR. FRANK. Please. I've thought this out for weeks. It's the best arrangement. The only arrangement.

MRS. VAN DAAN. [*To MR. FRANK.*] Never, never can we thank you. [*Then to MRS. FRANK.*] I don't know what would have happened to us, if it hadn't been for Mr. Frank.

Analyze Plot What are the playwrights suggesting with the silence following Mr. Frank's speech?

MR. FRANK. You don't know how your husband helped me when I came to this country . . . knowing no one . . . not able to speak the language. I can never repay him for that. [*Going to VAN DAAN.*] May I help you with your things?

MR. VAN DAAN. No. No. [*To MRS. VAN DAAN.*] Come along, liefje.[8]

MRS. VAN DAAN. You'll be all right, Peter? You're not afraid?

PETER. [*Embarrassed.*] Please, Mother.

[They start up the stairs to the attic room above. MR. FRANK turns to MRS. FRANK.]

MR. FRANK. You too must have some rest, Edith. You didn't close your eyes last night. Nor you, Margot.

ANNE. I slept, Father. Wasn't that funny? I knew it was the last night in my own bed, and yet I slept soundly.

MR. FRANK. I'm glad, Anne. Now you'll be able to help me straighten things in here. [*To MRS. FRANK and MARGOT.*] Come with me . . . You and Margot rest in this room for the time being.

[He picks up their clothes, starting for the room on the right.]

MRS. FRANK. You're sure . . . ? I could help . . . And Anne hasn't had her milk . . .

---

8 *Liefje* (lēf´ yə) is Dutch for "darling."

Analyze Plot What is the history of the relationship between Mr. Frank and Mr. Van Daan?

MR. FRANK. I'll give it to her. [*To* ANNE *and* PETER.] Anne, Peter . . . it's best that you take off your shoes now, before you forget.

[*He leads the way to the room, followed by* MARGOT.]

MRS. FRANK. You're sure you're not tired, Anne?

ANNE. I feel fine. I'm going to help Father.

MRS. FRANK. Peter, I'm glad you are to be with us.

PETER. Yes, Mrs. Frank.

[MRS. FRANK *goes to join* MR. FRANK *and* MARGOT.

During the following scene MR. FRANK *helps* MARGOT *and* MRS. FRANK *to hang up their clothes. Then he persuades them both to lie down and rest. The* VAN DAANS *in their room above settle themselves. In the main room* ANNE *and* PETER *remove their shoes.* PETER *takes his cat out of the carrier.*]

ANNE. What's your cat's name?

PETER. Mouschi.[9]

ANNE. Mouschi! Mouschi! Mouschi! [*She picks up the cat, walking away with it. To* PETER.] I love cats. I have one . . . a darling little cat. But they made me leave her behind. I left some food and a note for the neighbors to take care of her . . . I'm going to miss her terribly.

What is yours? A him or a her?

PETER. He's a tom. He doesn't like strangers.

[*He takes the cat from her, putting it back in its carrier.*]

ANNE. [*Unabashed.*[10]] Then I'll have to stop being a stranger, won't I? Is he fixed?

PETER. [*Startled.*] Huh?

ANNE. Did you have him fixed?

PETER. No.

ANNE. Oh, you ought to have him fixed—to keep him from—you know, fighting. Where did you go to school?

PETER. Jewish Secondary.

ANNE. But that's where Margot and I go! I never saw you around.

PETER. I used to see you . . . sometimes . . .

ANNE. You did?

PETER. . . . in the school yard. You were always in the middle of a bunch of kids.

[*He takes a penknife from his pocket.*]

ANNE. Why didn't you ever come over?

PETER. I'm sort of a lone wolf.

---

9 *Mouschi* (mōōs′ kē)

Act and Scene What relationship does this part of the scene introduce?

10 *Unabashed* means "not ashamed; bold."

Analyze Plot Why might Peter seem so gruff at first toward Anne?

Analyze Plot Why do you think Anne and Peter never knew each other at school?

Performance photographs are from a 1997
adaptation of *The Diary of Anne Frank.*

[*He starts to rip off his Star of David.*]

ANNE. What are you doing?

PETER. Taking it off.

ANNE. But you can't do that. They'll arrest you if you go out without your star.

[*He tosses his knife on the table.*]

PETER. Who's going out?

ANNE. Why, of course! You're right! Of course we don't need them any more. [*She picks up his knife and starts to take her star off.*] I wonder what our friends will think when we don't show up today?

PETER. I didn't have any dates with anyone.

ANNE. Oh, I did. I had a date with Jopie to go and play ping-pong at her house. Do you know Jopie de Waal?

PETER. No.

ANNE. Jopie's my best friend. I wonder what she'll think when she telephones and there's no answer? . . . Probably she'll go over to the house . . . I wonder what she'll think . . . we left everything as if we'd suddenly been called away . . . breakfast dishes in the sink . . . beds not made . . . [*As she pulls off her star, the cloth underneath shows clearly the color and form of the star.*] Look! It's still there! [*PETER goes over to the stove with his star.*] What're you going to do with yours?

PETER. Burn it.

ANNE. [*She starts to throw hers in, and cannot.*] It's funny, I can't throw mine away. I don't know why.

PETER. You can't throw . . . ? Something they branded you with . . . ? That they made you wear so they could spit on you?

ANNE. I know. I know. But after all, it is the Star of David, isn't it?

[*In the bedroom, right, MARGOT and MRS. FRANK are lying down. MR. FRANK starts quietly out.*]

PETER. Maybe it's different for a girl.

[*MR. FRANK comes into the main room.*]

MR. FRANK. Forgive me, Peter. Now let me see. We must find a bed for your cat. [*He goes to a cupboard.*] I'm glad you brought your cat. Anne was feeling so badly about hers. [*Getting a used small washtub.*] Here we are. Will it be comfortable in that?

PETER. [*Gathering up his things.*] Thanks.

MR. FRANK. [*Opening the door of the room on the left.*] And here is your room. But I warn you, Peter, you can't grow any more. Not an inch, or you'll have to sleep with your feet out of the skylight. Are you hungry?

PETER. No.

MR. FRANK. We have some bread and butter.

Analyze Plot Why does Anne have mixed feelings about throwing away her star? Think about the inner conflict this reveals.

PETER. No, thank you.

MR. FRANK. You can have it for luncheon then. And tonight we will have a real supper . . . our first supper together.

PETER. Thanks. Thanks.

[*He goes into his room. During the following scene he arranges his possessions in his new room.*]

MR. FRANK. That's a nice boy, Peter.

ANNE. He's awfully shy, isn't he?

MR. FRANK. You'll like him, I know.

ANNE. I certainly hope so, since he's the only boy I'm likely to see for months and months.

[MR. FRANK *sits down, taking off his shoes.*]

MR. FRANK. Annele,[11] there's a box there. Will you open it?

[*He indicates a carton on the couch.* ANNE *brings it to the center table. In the street below there is the sound of children playing.*]

ANNE. [*As she opens the carton.*] You know the way I'm going to think of it here? I'm going to think of it as a boarding house.[12] A very peculiar summer boarding house, like the one that we—[*She breaks off as she pulls out some photographs.*] Father! My movie stars! I was wondering where they were! I was looking for them this morning . . . and Queen Wilhelmina![13] How wonderful!

MR. FRANK. There's something more. Go on. Look further.

[*He goes over to the sink, pouring a glass of milk from a thermos bottle.*]

ANNE. [*Pulling out a pasteboard-bound book.*] A diary! [*She throws her arms around her father.*] I've never had a diary. And I've always longed for one. [*She looks around the room.*] Pencil, pencil, pencil, pencil. [*She starts down the stairs.*] I'm going down to the office to get a pencil.

MR. FRANK. Anne! No!

[*He goes after her, catching her by the arm and pulling her back.*]

ANNE. [*Startled.*] But there's no one in the building now.

MR. FRANK. It doesn't matter. I don't want you ever to go beyond that door.

---

11 Both **Annele** (än′ ə lə) and **Anneke**, which is used later, are affectionate nicknames.

BQ **BIG Question** In what way does Anne's idea show her strength of spirit?

12 A **boarding house** is like a small hotel in a private home. The owner provides rooms and meals to people who pay a weekly or monthly rent.

13 **Wilhelmina** (wil hel mē′ nə) was queen of the Netherlands from 1890 to 1948. She and her family escaped to England and then Canada at the time of the German invasion.

ANNE. [*Sobered.*] Never . . . ? Not even at nighttime, when everyone is gone? Or on Sundays? Can't I go down to listen to the radio?

MR. FRANK. Never. I am sorry, Anneke. It isn't safe. No, you must never go beyond that door.

[*For the first time* ANNE *realizes what "going into hiding" means.*]

ANNE. I see.

MR. FRANK. It'll be hard, I know. But always remember this, Anneke. There are no walls, there are no bolts, no locks that anyone can put on your mind. Miep will bring us books. We will read history, poetry, mythology. [*He gives her the glass of milk.*] Here's your milk. [*With his arm about her, they go over to the couch, sitting down side by side.*] As a matter of fact, between us, Anne, being here has certain advantages for you. For instance, you remember the battle you had with your mother the other day on the subject of overshoes? You said you'd rather die than wear overshoes? But in the end you had to wear them? Well now, you see, for as long as we are here you will never have to wear overshoes! Isn't that good? And the coat that you inherited from Margot, you won't have to wear that any more. And the piano! You won't have to practice on the piano. I tell you, this is going to be a fine life for you!

[ANNE's *panic is gone.* PETER *appears in the doorway of his room, with a saucer in his hand. He is carrying his cat.*]

PETER. I . . . I . . . I thought I'd better get some water for Mouschi before . . .

MR. FRANK. Of course.

[*As he starts toward the sink the carillon begins to chime the hour of eight. He tiptoes to the window at the back and looks down at the street below. He turns to* PETER, *indicating in pantomime*[14] *that it is too late.* PETER *starts back for his room. He steps on a creaking board. The three of them are frozen for a minute in fear. As* PETER *starts away again,* ANNE *tiptoes over to him and pours some of the milk from her glass into the saucer for the cat.* PETER *squats on the floor, putting the milk before the cat.* MR. FRANK *gives* ANNE *his fountain pen, and then goes into the room at the right. For a second* ANNE *watches the cat, then she goes over to the center table, and opens her diary.*]

In the room at the right, MRS. FRANK has sat up quickly at the sound of the carillon. MR. FRANK comes in and sits down beside her on the **settee,** his arm comfortingly around her.

Analyze Plot What does Anne's question reveal about her understanding of being in hiding? Consider the complications this might add to the plot.

---

14 Here, in **pantomime** (pant´ə mīm´) means in silent gestures instead of in words.

Upstairs, in the attic room, MR. and MRS. VAN DAAN *have hung their clothes in the closet and are now seated on the iron bed.* MRS. VAN DAAN *leans back exhausted.* MR. VAN DAAN *fans her with a newspaper.*

ANNE *starts to write in her diary. The lights dim out, the curtain falls.*

In the darkness ANNE'S *voice comes to us again, faintly at first, and then with growing strength.*]

ANNE'S VOICE. I expect I should be describing what it feels like to go into hiding. But I really don't know yet myself. I only know it's funny never to be able to go outdoors . . . never to breathe fresh air . . . never to run and shout and jump. It's the silence in the nights that frightens

me most. Every time I hear a creak in the house, or a step on the street outside, I'm sure they're coming for us. The days aren't so bad. At least we know that Miep and Mr. Kraler are down there below us in the office. Our protectors, we call them. I asked Father what would happen to them if the Nazis found out they were hiding us. Pim[15] said that they would suffer the same fate that we would . . . Imagine! They know this, and yet when they come up here, they're always cheerful and gay as if there were nothing in the world to bother them . . . Friday, the twenty-first of August, nineteen forty-two. Today I'm going to tell you our general news. Mother is unbearable. She insists on treating me like a baby, which I **loathe.** Otherwise things are going better. The weather is . . .

[*As* ANNE'S *voice is fading out, the curtain rises on the scene.*]

ACT ONE—SCENE 3

[*It is a little after six o'clock in the evening, two months later.* MARGOT *is in the bedroom at the right, studying.* MR. VAN DAAN *is lying down in the attic room above.*

The rest of the "family" is in the main room. ANNE *and* PETER *sit opposite each other at the center table, where they have been doing their lessons.* MRS. FRANK *is on the couch.* MRS. VAN DAAN *is seated with her fur coat, on which she has been sewing, in her lap. None of them are wearing their shoes.*

Their eyes are on MR. FRANK, *waiting for him to give them the signal which will release them from their day-long quiet.* MR. FRANK, *his shoes in his hand, stands looking down out of the window at the back, watching to be sure that all of the workmen have left the building below.*

After a few seconds of motionless silence, MR. FRANK *turns from the window.*]

MR. FRANK. [*Quietly, to the group.*] It's safe now. The last workman has left.

[*There is an immediate stir of relief.*]

ANNE. [*Her pent-up energy explodes.*] WHEE!

MRS. FRANK. [*Startled, amused.*] Anne!

MRS. VAN DAAN. I'm first for the w.c.

[*She hurries off to the bathroom.* MRS. FRANK *puts on her shoes and starts up to the sink to prepare supper.* ANNE *sneaks* PETER'S *shoes from under the table and hides them behind her back.* MR. FRANK *goes into* MARGOT'S *room.*]

MR. FRANK. [*To* MARGOT.] Six o'clock.

---

15 **Pim** is Anne's nickname for her father.

Act and Scene In what way is the reading from Anne's diary an effective way to end this scene? Explain.

Vocabulary ....

loathe (lōth) *v.* to regard with extreme disgust; hate

Act and Scene In what way are Anne's attitudes and actions different at the beginning of Scene 3 than at the end of Scene 2?

School's over.

[MARGOT *gets up, stretching.* MR. FRANK *sits down to put on his shoes. In the main room* PETER *tries to find his.*]

PETER. [*To* ANNE.] Have you seen my shoes?

ANNE. [*Innocently.*] Your shoes?

PETER. You've taken them, haven't you?

ANNE. I don't know what you're talking about.

PETER. You're going to be sorry!

ANNE. Am I?

[PETER *goes after her.* ANNE, *with his shoes in her hand, runs from him, dodging behind her mother.*]

MRS. FRANK. [*Protesting.*] Anne, dear!

PETER. Wait till I get you!

ANNE. I'm waiting! [PETER *makes a lunge for her. They both fall to the floor.* PETER *pins her down, wrestling with her to get the shoes.*] Don't! Don't! Peter, stop it. Ouch!

MRS. FRANK. Anne! . . . Peter!

[*Suddenly* PETER *becomes self-conscious. He grabs his shoes roughly and starts for his room.*]

ANNE. [*Following him.*] Peter, where are you going? Come dance with me.

PETER. I tell you I don't know how.

ANNE. I'll teach you.

PETER. I'm going to give Mouschi his dinner.

ANNE. Can I watch?

PETER. He doesn't like people around while he eats.

ANNE. Peter, please.

PETER. No!

[*He goes into his room.* ANNE *slams his door after him.*]

MRS. FRANK. Anne, dear, I think you shouldn't play like that with Peter. It's not dignified.[1]

ANNE. Who cares if it's dignified? I don't want to be dignified.

[MR. FRANK *and* MARGOT *come from the room on the right.* MARGOT *goes to help her mother.* MR. FRANK *starts for the center table to correct* MARGOT'S *school papers.*]

MRS. FRANK. [*To* ANNE.] You complain that I don't treat you like a grown-up. But when I do, you resent it.

ANNE. I only want some fun . . . someone to laugh and clown with . . . After you've sat still all day and hardly moved, you've got to have some fun. I don't know what's the matter with that boy.

MR. FRANK. He isn't used to girls. Give him a little time.

Act and Scene In what way has the relationship between Anne and Peter changed since Scene 1?

---

1 **Dignified** means "behaving in a calm, proper way."

ANNE. Time? Isn't two months time? I could cry. [*Catching hold of* MARGOT.] Come on, Margot . . . dance with me. Come on, please.

MARGOT. I have to help with supper.

ANNE. You know we're going to forget how to dance . . . When we get out we won't remember a thing.

[*She starts to sing and dance by herself.* MR. FRANK *takes her in his arms, waltzing with her.* MRS. VAN DAAN *comes in from the bathroom.*]

MRS. VAN DAAN. Next? [*She looks around as she starts putting on her shoes.*] Where's Peter?

ANNE. [*As they are dancing.*] Where would he be!

MRS. VAN DAAN. He hasn't finished his lessons, has he? His father'll kill him if he catches him in there with that cat and his work not done. [MR. FRANK *and* ANNE *finish their dance. They bow to each other with extravagant formality.*[2]] Anne, get him out of there, will you?

ANNE. [*At* PETER'S *door.*] Peter? Peter?

PETER. [*Opening the door a crack.*] What is it?

ANNE. Your mother says to come out.

PETER. I'm giving Mouschi his dinner.

MRS. VAN DAAN. You know what your father says.

[*She sits on the couch, sewing on the lining of her fur coat.*]

PETER. For heaven's sake, I haven't even looked at him since lunch.

MRS. VAN DAAN. I'm just telling you, that's all.

ANNE. I'll feed him.

PETER. I don't want you in there.

MRS. VAN DAAN. Peter!

PETER. [*To* ANNE.] Then give him his dinner and come right out, you hear?

[*He comes back to the table.* ANNE *shuts the door of* PETER'S *room after her and disappears behind the curtain covering his closet.*]

MRS. VAN DAAN. [*To* PETER.] Now is that any way to talk to your little girlfriend?

PETER. Mother . . . for heaven's sake . . . will you please stop saying that?

MRS. VAN DAAN. Look at him blush! Look at him!

PETER. Please! I'm not . . . anyway . . . let me alone, will you?

MRS. VAN DAAN. He acts like it was something to be ashamed of. It's nothing to be ashamed of, to have a little girlfriend.

---

2 In showing **extravagant formality,** Anne and her father make deep, formal bows, exaggerating the custom of bowing to one's partner at the end of a dance.

BQ **BIG Question** In what way does Anne's statement show an inner strength despite danger?

PETER. You're crazy. She's only thirteen.

MRS. VAN DAAN. So what? And you're sixteen. Just perfect. Your father's ten years older than I am. [*To* MR. FRANK.] I warn you, Mr. Frank, if this war lasts much longer, we're going to be related and then . . .

MR. FRANK. Mazeltov![3]

MRS. FRANK. [*Deliberately changing the conversation.*] I wonder where Miep is. She's usually so prompt.

[*Suddenly everything else is forgotten as they hear the sound of an automobile coming to a screeching stop in the street below. They are tense, motionless in their terror. The car starts away. A wave of relief sweeps over them. They pick up their occupations again.* ANNE *flings open the door of* PETER's *room, making a dramatic entrance. She is dressed in* PETER's *clothes.* PETER *looks at her in fury. The others are amused.*]

ANNE. Good evening, everyone. Forgive me if I don't stay.
[*She jumps up on a chair.*] I have a friend waiting for me in there. My friend Tom. Tom Cat. Some people say that we look alike. But Tom has the most beautiful whiskers, and I have only a little fuzz. I am hoping . . . in time . . .

PETER. All right, Mrs. Quack Quack!

ANNE. [*Outraged—jumping down.*] Peter!

PETER. I heard about you . . . How you talked so much in class they called you Mrs. Quack Quack. How Mr. Smitter made you write a composition . . . "'Quack, quack,' said Mrs. Quack Quack."

ANNE. Well, go on. Tell them the rest. How it was so good he read it out loud to the class and then read it to all his other classes!

PETER. Quack! Quack! Quack . . . Quack . . . Quack . . .

[ANNE *pulls off the coat and trousers.*]

ANNE. You are the most intolerable, insufferable[4] boy I've ever met!

[*She throws the clothes down the stairwell.* PETER *goes down after them.*]

PETER. Quack, quack, quack!

MRS. VAN DAAN. [*To* ANNE.] That's right, Anneke! Give it to him!

ANNE. With all the boys in the world . . . Why I had to get locked up with one like you! . . .

PETER. Quack, quack, quack, and from now on stay out of my room!

[*As* PETER *passes her,* ANNE *puts out her foot, tripping him. He picks himself up, and goes on into his room.*]

---

3 *Mazeltov* (mä´zəl täv) means "congratulations" or "best wishes" in Hebrew.

Analyze Plot Why do the authors periodically have the actors react in fear to noises from outside? Think about how this affects the rising action of the drama.

---

4 Both *intolerable* and *insufferable* mean "unbearable."

MRS. FRANK. [*Quietly.*] Anne, dear . . . your hair. [*She feels* ANNE'S *forehead.*] You're warm. Are you feeling all right?

ANNE. Please, Mother.

[*She goes over to the center table, slipping into her shoes.*]

MRS. FRANK. [*Following her.*] You haven't a fever, have you?

ANNE. [*Pulling away.*] No. No.

MRS. FRANK. You know we can't call a doctor here, ever. There's only one thing to do . . . watch carefully. Prevent an illness before it comes. Let me see your tongue.

ANNE. Mother, this is perfectly absurd.⁵

MRS. FRANK. Anne, dear, don't be such a baby. Let me see your tongue. [*As* ANNE *refuses,* MRS. FRANK *appeals to* MR. FRANK.] Otto . . . ?

MR. FRANK. You hear your mother, Anne.

[ANNE *flicks out her tongue for a second, then turns away.*]

MRS. FRANK. Come on—open up! [*As* ANNE *opens her mouth very wide.*] You seem all right . . . but perhaps an aspirin . . .

MRS. VAN DAAN. For heaven's sake, don't give that child any pills. I waited for fifteen minutes this morning for her to come out of the w.c.

ANNE. I was washing my hair!

MR. FRANK. I think there's nothing the matter with our Anne that a ride on her bike, or a visit with her friend Jopie de Waal wouldn't cure. Isn't that so, Anne?

[MR. VAN DAAN *comes down into the room. From outside we hear faint sounds of bombers going over and a burst of ack-ack.*⁶]

MR. VAN DAAN. Miep not come yet?

MRS. VAN DAAN. The workmen just left, a little while ago.

MR. VAN DAAN. What's for dinner tonight?

MRS. VAN DAAN. Beans.

MR. VAN DAAN. Not again!

MRS. VAN DAAN. Poor Putti! I know. But what can we do? That's all that Miep brought us.

[MR. VAN DAAN *starts to pace, his hands behind his back. anne follows behind him, imitating him.*]

ANNE. We are now in what is known as the "bean cycle." Beans boiled, beans *en casserole*, beans with strings, beans without strings . . .

---

5 **Absurd** means "not making sense, very silly."

Analyze Plot What does this interaction tell us about Anne's relationships with her mother and father?

---

6 **Ack-ack** was the slang name for anti-aircraft gunfire. It was the Allies who were bombing the Nazi-controlled Netherlands.

BQ **BIG Question** In what way does Anne keep her spirits up?

[PETER *has come out of his room. He slides into his place at the table, becoming immediately absorbed in his studies.*]

MR. VAN DAAN. [*To* PETER.] I saw you . . . in there, playing with your cat.

MRS. VAN DAAN. He just went in for a second, putting his coat away. He's been out here all the time, doing his lessons.

MR. FRANK. [*Looking up from the papers.*] Anne, you got an excellent in your history paper today . . . and very good in Latin.

ANNE. [*Sitting beside him.*] How about algebra?

MR. FRANK. I'll have to make a confession. Up until now I've managed to stay ahead of you in algebra. Today you caught up with me. We'll leave it to Margot to correct.

ANNE. Isn't algebra vile,[7] Pim!

MR. FRANK. Vile!

MARGOT. [*To* MR. FRANK.] How did I do?

ANNE. [*Getting up.*] Excellent, excellent, excellent, excellent!

MR. FRANK. [*To* MARGOT.] You should have used the subjunctive[8] here . . .

MARGOT. Should I? . . . I thought . . . look here . . . I didn't use it here . . .

[*The two become absorbed in the papers.*]

ANNE. Mrs. Van Daan, may I try on your coat?

MRS. FRANK. No, Anne.

MRS. VAN DAAN. [*Giving it to* ANNE.] It's all right . . . but careful with it. [ANNE *puts it on and struts with it.*] My father gave me that the year before he died. He always bought the best that money could buy.

ANNE. Mrs. Van Daan, did you have a lot of boyfriends before you were married?

MRS. FRANK. Anne, that's a personal question. It's not courteous to ask personal questions.

MRS. VAN DAAN. Oh I don't mind. [*To* ANNE.] Our house was always swarming with boys. When I was a girl we had . . .

MR. VAN DAAN. Oh, God. Not again!

MRS. VAN DAAN. [*Good-humored.*] Shut up! [*Without a pause, to* ANNE. MR. VAN DAAN *mimics[9]* MRS. VAN DAAN, *speaking the first few words in unison with her.*] One summer we had a big house in Hilversum. The boys came buzzing round like bees around a jam pot.

---

7 **Vile** (vīl) means "very bad or extremely unpleasant."

8 The **subjunctive** (səb jungk′tiv) is the verb form used to express wishes, possibilities, or things that are opposed to fact. In the sentence, "If I were you, I wouldn't go," *were* is the subjunctive form of *to be.*

Analyze Plot What does this accusation reveal about Mr. Van Daan?

---

9 Here, Mr. Van Daan **mimics,** or makes fun of by imitating or copying, Mrs. Van Daan.

Analyze Plot Why does Mrs. Van Daan tell Anne this story about her childhood?

And when I was sixteen! . . . We were wearing our skirts very short those days and I had good-looking legs. [*She pulls up her skirt, going to* MR. FRANK.] I still have 'em. I may not be as pretty as I used to be, but I still have my legs. How about it, Mr. Frank?

MR. VAN DAAN. All right. All right. We see them.

MRS. VAN DAAN. I'm not asking you. I'm asking Mr. Frank.

PETER. Mother, for heaven's sake.

MRS. VAN DAAN. Oh, I embarrass you, do I? Well, I just hope the girl you marry has as good. [*Then to* ANNE.] My father used to worry about me, with so many boys hanging round. He told me, if any of them gets fresh, you say to him . . . "Remember, Mr. So-and-So, remember I'm a lady."

ANNE. "Remember, Mr. So-and-So, remember I'm a lady."

[*She gives* MRS. VAN DAAN *her coat.*]

MR. VAN DAAN. Look at you, talking that way in front of her! Don't you know she puts it all down in that diary?

MRS. VAN DAAN. So, if she does? I'm only telling the truth!

[ANNE *stretches out, putting her ear to the floor, listening to what is going on below. The sound of the bombers fades away.*]

MRS. FRANK. [*Setting the table.*] Would you mind, Peter, if I moved you over to the couch?

ANNE. [*Listening.*] Miep must have the radio on.

[PETER *picks up his papers, going over to the couch beside* MRS. VAN DAAN.]

MR. VAN DAAN. [*Accusingly, to* PETER.] Haven't you finished yet?

PETER. No.

MR. VAN DAAN. You ought to be ashamed of yourself.

PETER. All right. All right. I'm a dunce. I'm a hopeless case. Why do I go on?

MRS. VAN DAAN. You're not hopeless. Don't talk that way. It's just that you haven't anyone to help you, like the girls have. [*To* MR. FRANK.] Maybe you could help him, Mr. Frank?

MR. FRANK. I'm sure that his father . . . ?

MR. VAN DAAN. Not me. I can't do anything with him. He won't listen to me. You go ahead . . . if you want.

BQ ▶ **BIG Question** Do you think Peter will have the strength to go on through hard times? Explain.

MR. FRANK. [*Going to* PETER.] What about it, Peter? Shall we make our school coeducational?[10]

MRS. VAN DAAN. [*Kissing* MR. FRANK.] You're an angel, Mr. Frank. An angel. I don't know why I didn't meet you before I met that one there. Here, sit down, Mr. Frank . . . [*She forces him down on the couch beside* PETER.] Now, Peter, you listen to Mr. Frank.

MR. FRANK. It might be better for us to go into Peter's room.

[PETER *jumps up eagerly, leading the way.*]

MRS. VAN DAAN. That's right. You go in there, Peter. You listen to Mr. Frank. Mr. Frank is a highly educated man.

[*As* MR. FRANK *is about to follow* PETER *into his room,* MRS. FRANK *stops him and wipes the lipstick from his lips. Then she closes the door after them.*]

ANNE. [*On the floor, listening.*] Shh! I can hear a man's voice talking.

MR. VAN DAAN. [*To* ANNE.] Isn't it bad enough here without your sprawling all over the place?

[ANNE *sits up.*]

MRS. VAN DAAN. [*To* MR. VAN DAAN.] If you didn't smoke so much, you wouldn't be so bad-tempered.

MR. VAN DAAN. Am I smoking? Do you see me smoking?

MRS. VAN DAAN. Don't tell me you've used up all those cigarettes.

MR. VAN DAAN. One package. Miep only brought me one package.

MRS. VAN DAAN. It's a filthy habit anyway. It's a good time to break yourself.

MR. VAN DAAN. Oh, stop it, please.

MRS. VAN DAAN. You're smoking up all our money. You know that, don't you?

MR. VAN DAAN. Will you shut up? [*During this,* MRS. FRANK *and* MARGOT *have studiously kept their eyes down. But* ANNE, *seated on the floor, has been following the discussion interestedly.* MR. VAN DAAN *turns to see her staring up at him.*] And what are you staring at?

ANNE. I never heard grown-ups quarrel before. I thought only children quarreled.

MR. VAN DAAN. This isn't a quarrel! It's a discussion. And I never heard children so rude before.

ANNE. [*Rising, indignantly.*[11]] I, rude!

MR. VAN DAAN. Yes!

MRS. FRANK. [*Quickly.*] Anne, will you get me my knitting? [ANNE *goes to get it.*] I must remember, when Miep comes, to ask her to bring me some more wool.

---

10 A *coeducational* school has both male and female students.

11 *Indignantly* (in dig′nənt lē) means "with anger in response to an insult or injustice."

Act and Scene How has the bickering between the Van Daans changed from earlier in the play?

MARGOT. [*Going to her room.*] I need some hairpins and some soap. I made a list.

[*She goes into her bedroom to get the list.*]

MRS. FRANK. [*To ANNE.*] Have you some library books for Miep when she comes?

ANNE. It's a wonder that Miep has a life of her own, the way we make her run errands for us. Please, Miep, get me some starch. Please take my hair out and have it cut. Tell me all the latest news, Miep. [*She goes over, kneeling on the couch beside MRS. VAN DAAN.*] Did you know she was engaged? His name is Dirk, and Miep's afraid the Nazis will ship him off to Germany to work in one of their war plants. That's what they're doing with some of the young Dutchmen . . . they pick them up off the streets—

MR. VAN DAAN. [*Interrupting.*] Don't you ever get tired of talking? Suppose you try keeping still for five minutes. Just five minutes.

[*He starts to pace again. Again ANNE follows him, mimicking him. MRS. FRANK jumps up and takes her by the arm up to the sink, and gives her a glass of milk.*]

MRS. FRANK. Come here, Anne. It's time for your glass of milk.

MR. VAN DAAN. Talk, talk, talk. I never heard such a child. Where is my . . . ? Every evening it's the same, talk, talk, talk. [*He looks around.*] Where is my . . . ?

MRS. VAN DAAN. What're you looking for?

MR. VAN DAAN. My pipe. Have you seen my pipe?

MRS. VAN DAAN. What good's a pipe? You haven't got any tobacco.

MR. VAN DAAN. At least I'll have something to hold in my mouth! [*Opening MARGOT's bedroom door.*] Margot, have you seen my pipe?

MARGOT. It was on the table last night.

[*ANNE puts her glass of milk on the table and picks up his pipe, hiding it behind her back.*]

MR. VAN DAAN. I know. I know. Anne, did you see my pipe? . . . Anne!

MRS. FRANK. Anne, Mr. Van Daan is speaking to you.

ANNE. Am I allowed to talk now?

MR. VAN DAAN. You're the most **aggravating** . . . The trouble with you is, you've been spoiled. What you need is a good old-fashioned spanking.

ANNE. [*Mimicking MRS. VAN DAAN.*] "Remember, Mr. So-and-So, remember I'm a lady."

Analyze Plot What is it about his situation that bothers Mr. Van Daan so much? Explain.

Vocabulary . . . .

aggravating (ag′rə vāt ing) *adj.* irritating; annoying

[*She thrusts the pipe into his mouth, then picks up her glass of milk.*]

MR. VAN DAAN. [*Restraining himself with difficulty.*] Why aren't you nice and quiet like your sister Margot? Why do you have to show off all the time? Let me give you a little advice, young lady. Men don't like that kind of thing in a girl. You know that? A man likes a girl who'll listen to him once in a while . . . a domestic[12] girl, who'll keep her house shining for her husband . . . who loves to cook and sew and . . .

ANNE. I'd cut my throat first! I'd open my veins! I'm going to be remarkable! I'm going to Paris . . .

MR. VAN DAAN. [*Scoffingly.*] Paris!

ANNE. . . . to study music and art.

MR. VAN DAAN. Yeah! Yeah!

ANNE. I'm going to be a famous dancer or singer . . . or something wonderful.

[*She makes a wide gesture, spilling the glass of milk on the fur coat in* MRS. VAN DAAN'S *lap.* MARGOT *rushes quickly over with a towel.* ANNE *tries to brush the milk off with her skirt.*]

---

12 Someone who is **domestic** (dō mes′ tik) likes to cook, clean, and care for the family.

Analyze Plot Given Mr. Van Daan's idea of the perfect wife, what can you conclude about his relationship with his own wife?

BQ BIG Question What is one way Anne finds strength from within while being confined to the hiding place?

MRS. VAN DAAN. Now look what you've done . . . you clumsy little fool! My beautiful fur coat my father gave me . . .

ANNE. I'm so sorry.

MRS. VAN DAAN. What do you care? It isn't yours . . . So go on, ruin it! Do you know what that coat cost? Do you? And now look at it! Look at it!

ANNE. I'm very, very sorry.

MRS. VAN DAAN. I could kill you for this. I could just kill you!

[MRS. *VAN DAAN goes up the stairs, clutching the coat.* MR. *VAN DAAN starts after her.*]

MR. VAN DAAN. Petronella . . . *liefje! Liefje!* . . . Come back . . . the supper . . . come back!

MRS. FRANK. Anne, you must not behave in that way.

ANNE. It was an accident. Anyone can have an accident.

MRS. FRANK. I don't mean that. I mean the answering back. You must not answer back. They are our guests.
We must always show the greatest courtesy to them. We're all living under terrible tension. [*She stops as* MARGOT *indicates that* VAN DAAN *can hear. When he is gone, she continues.*] That's why we must control ourselves . . . You don't hear

---

Analyze Plot What does the fur coat symbolize to Mrs. Van Daan? Think about the ways in which relationships are adding conflicts to the plot.

Margot getting into arguments with them, do you? Watch Margot. She's always courteous with them. Never familiar. She keeps her distance. And they respect her for it. Try to be like Margot.

ANNE. And have them walk all over me, the way they do her? No, thanks!

MRS. FRANK. I'm not afraid that anyone is going to walk all over you, Anne. I'm afraid for other people, that you'll walk on them. I don't know what happens to you, Anne. You are wild, self-willed. If I had ever talked to my mother as you talk to me . . .

ANNE. Things have changed. People aren't like that any more. "Yes, Mother." "No, Mother." "Anything you say, Mother." I've got to fight things out for myself! Make something of myself!

MRS. FRANK. It isn't necessary to fight to do it. Margot doesn't fight, and isn't she . . . ?

ANNE. [Violently rebellious.] Margot! Margot! Margot! That's all I hear from everyone . . . how wonderful Margot is . . . "Why aren't you like Margot?"

MARGOT. [Protesting.] Oh, come on, Anne, don't be so . . .

ANNE. [Paying no attention.] Everything she does is right, and everything I do is wrong! I'm the goat[13] around here! . . . You're all against me! . . . And you worst of all!

[She rushes off into her room and throws herself down on the settee, stifling[14] her sobs. MRS. FRANK sighs and starts toward the stove.]

MRS. FRANK. [To MARGOT.] Let's put the soup on the stove . . . if there's anyone who cares to eat. Margot, will you take the bread out? [MARGOT gets the bread from the cupboard.] I don't know how we can go on living this way . . . I can't say a word to Anne . . . she flies at me . . .

MARGOT. You know Anne. In half an hour she'll be out here, laughing and joking.

MRS. FRANK. And . . . [She makes a motion upwards, indicating the VAN DAANS.] . . . I told your father it wouldn't work . . . but no . . . no . . . he had to ask them, he said . . . he owed it to him, he said. Well, he knows now that I was right! These quarrels! . . . This bickering![15]

MARGOT. [With a warning look.] Shush. Shush.

[The buzzer for the door sounds. MRS. FRANK gasps, startled.]

MRS. FRANK. Every time I hear that sound, my heart stops!

MARGOT. [Starting for PETER's door.] It's Miep. [She knocks at the door.] Father?

[MR. FRANK comes quickly from PETER's room.]

---

13 A *goat* (or scapegoat) is one who is blamed or punished for other people's mistakes.

Analyze Plot Why is Anne so angry with her mother?

14 *Stifling* means "smothering; holding back."

15 *Bickering* is a quarrel or argument, especially about minor details.

MR. FRANK. Thank you, Margot. [*As he goes down the steps to open the outer door.*] Has everyone his list?

MARGOT. I'll get my books. [*Giving her mother a list.*] Here's your list. [*MARGOT goes into her and ANNE'S bedroom on the right. ANNE sits up, hiding her tears, as MARGOT comes in.*] Miep's here.

[*MARGOT picks up her books and goes back. ANNE hurries over to the mirror, smoothing her hair.*]

MR. VAN DAAN. [*Coming down the stairs.*] Is it Miep?

MARGOT. Yes. Father's gone down to let her in.

MR. VAN DAAN. At last I'll have some cigarettes!

MRS. FRANK. [*To MR. VAN DAAN.*] I can't tell you how unhappy I am about Mrs. Van Daan's coat. Anne should never have touched it.

MR. VAN DAAN. She'll be all right.

MRS. FRANK. Is there anything I can do?

MR. VAN DAAN. Don't worry.

[*He turns to meet MIEP. But it is not MIEP who comes up the steps. It is MR. KRALER, followed by MR. FRANK. Their faces are grave.[16] ANNE comes from the bedroom. PETER comes from his room.*]

MRS. FRANK. Mr. Kraler!

MR. VAN DAAN. How are you, Mr. Kraler?

MARGOT. This is a surprise.

MRS. FRANK. When Mr. Kraler comes, the sun begins to shine.

MR. VAN DAAN. Miep is coming?

MR. KRALER. Not tonight.

[*KRALER goes to MARGOT and MRS. FRANK and ANNE, shaking hands with them.*]

MRS. FRANK. Wouldn't you like a cup of coffee? . . . Or, better still, will you have supper with us?

MR. FRANK. Mr. Kraler has something to talk over with us. Something has happened, he says, which demands an immediate decision.

MRS. FRANK. [*Fearful.*] What is it?

[*MR. KRALER sits down on the couch. As he talks he takes bread, cabbages, milk, etc., from his briefcase, giving them to MARGOT and ANNE to put away.*]

MR. KRALER. Usually, when I come up here, I try to bring you some bit of good news. What's the use of telling you the bad news when there's nothing that you can do about it? But today something has happened . . . Dirk . . . Miep's Dirk, you know, came to me just now. He tells me that he has

---

16 *Grave* means very serious and concerned.

Analyze Plot Why are Miep's visits so important to the plot?

Analyze Plot What can you infer about Mr. Kraler from this statement?

a Jewish friend living near him. A dentist. He says he's in trouble. He begged me, could I do anything for this man? Could I find him a hiding place? . . . So I've come to you . . . I know it's a terrible thing to ask of you, living as you are, but would you take him in with you?

MR. FRANK. Of course we will.

MR. KRALER. [*Rising.*] It'll be just for a night or two . . . until I find some other place. This happened so suddenly that I didn't know where to turn.

MR. FRANK. Where is he?

MR. KRALER. Downstairs in the office.

MR. FRANK. Good. Bring him up.

MR. KRALER. His name is Dussel . . . Jan Dussel.[17]

MR. FRANK. Dussel . . . I think I know him.

MR. KRALER. I'll get him.

[*He goes quickly down the steps and out.* MR. FRANK *suddenly becomes conscious of the others.*]

MR. FRANK. Forgive me. I spoke without consulting you. But I knew you'd feel as I do.

MR. VAN DAAN. There's no reason for you to consult anyone. This is your place. You have a right to do exactly as you please. The only thing I feel . . . there's so little food as it is . . . and to take in another person . . .

[PETER *turns away, ashamed of his father.*]

MR. FRANK. We can stretch the food a little. It's only for a few days.

MR. VAN DAAN. You want to make a bet?

MRS. FRANK. I think it's fine to have him. But, Otto, where are you going to put him? Where?

PETER. He can have my bed. I can sleep on the floor. I wouldn't mind.

MR. FRANK. That's good of you, Peter. But your room's too small . . . even for you.

ANNE. I have a much better idea. I'll come in here with you and Mother, and Margot can take Peter's room and Peter can go in our room with Mr. Dussel.

MARGOT. That's right. We could do that.

MR. FRANK. No, Margot. You mustn't sleep in that room . . . neither you nor Anne. Mouschi has caught some rats in there. Peter's brave. He doesn't mind.

ANNE. Then how about this? I'll come in here with you and Mother, and Mr. Dussel can have my bed.

MRS. FRANK. No. No. No! Margot will come in here with us and he can have her bed. It's the only way.

---

17 *Jan Dussel* (yän doos′əl)

Analyze Plot What does Mr. Frank's response reveal about his character?

Margot, bring your things in here. Help her, Anne.

[MARGOT *hurries into her room to get her things.*]

ANNE. [*To her mother.*] Why Margot? Why can't I come in here?

MRS. FRANK. Because it wouldn't be proper for Margot to sleep with a . . . Please, Anne. Don't argue. Please.

[ANNE *starts slowly away.*]

MR. FRANK. [*To* ANNE.] You don't mind sharing your room with Mr. Dussel, do you, Anne?

ANNE. No. No, of course not.

MR. FRANK. Good. [ANNE *goes off into her bedroom, helping* MARGOT. MR. FRANK *starts to search in the cupboards.*] Where's the cognac?[18]

MRS. FRANK. It's there. But, Otto, I was saving it in case of illness.

MR. FRANK. I think we couldn't find a better time to use it. Peter, will you get five glasses for me?

[PETER *goes for the glasses.* MARGOT *comes out of her bedroom, carrying her possessions, which she hangs behind a curtain in the main room.* MR. FRANK *finds the cognac and pours it into the five glasses that* PETER *brings him.*]

MR. VAN DAAN *stands looking on sourly.* MRS. VAN DAAN *comes downstairs and looks around at all the bustle.*]

MRS. VAN DAAN. What's happening? What's going on?

MR. VAN DAAN. Someone's moving in with us.

MRS. VAN DAAN. In here? You're joking.

MARGOT. It's only for a night or two . . . until Mr. Kraler finds him another place.

MR. VAN DAAN. Yeah! Yeah!

[MR. FRANK *hurries over as* MR. KRALER *and* DUSSEL *come up.* DUSSEL *is a man in his late fifties, meticulous,[19] finicky . . . bewildered[20] now. He wears a raincoat. He carries a briefcase, stuffed full, and a small medicine case.*]

MR. FRANK. Come in, Mr. Dussel.

MR. KRALER. This is Mr. Frank.

DUSSEL. Mr. Otto Frank?

MR. FRANK. Yes. Let me take your things. [*He takes the hat and briefcase, but* DUSSEL *clings to his medicine case.*] This is my wife Edith . . . Mr. and Mrs. Van Daan . . . their son, Peter . . . and my daughters, Margot and Anne.

[DUSSEL *shakes hands with everyone.*]

---

18 Cognac is an aloholic drink.

BQ BIG Question What does the way the Frank family responds to the addition of another person suggest about their ability to deal with adversity?

---

19 **Meticulous** (mi tik′ yə ləs) means "careful about small details."

20 **Bewildered** (bi wil′ dərd) means "confused."

Analyze Plot Why do you think Mr. Dussel clings to his medicine case?

The Diary of Anne Frank, Act One **789**

MR. KRALER. Thank you, Mr. Frank. Thank you all. Mr. Dussel, I leave you in good hands. Oh . . . Dirk's coat.

[DUSSEL *hurriedly takes off the raincoat, giving it to* MR. KRALER. *Underneath is his white dentist's jacket, with a yellow Star of David on it.*]

DUSSEL. [*To* MR. KRALER.] What can I say to thank you . . . ?

MRS. FRANK. [*To* DUSSEL.] Mr. Kraler and Miep . . . They're our life line. Without them we couldn't live.

MR. KRALER. Please. Please. You make us seem very heroic. It isn't that at all. We simply don't like the Nazis. [*To* MR. FRANK, *who offers him a drink.*] No, thanks. [*Then going on.*] We don't like their methods. We don't like . . .

MR. FRANK. [*Smiling.*] I know. I know. "No one's going to tell us Dutchmen what to do with our damn Jews!"

MR. KRALER. [*To* DUSSEL.] Pay no attention to Mr. Frank. I'll be up tomorrow to see that they're treating you right. [*To* MR. FRANK.] Don't trouble to come down again. Peter will bolt the door after me, won't you, Peter?

PETER. Yes, sir.

MR. FRANK. Thank you, Peter. I'll do it.

MR. KRALER. Good night. Good night.

GROUP. Good night, Mr. Kraler.

We'll see you tomorrow, etc., etc.

[MR. KRALER *goes out with* MR. FRANK. MRS. FRANK *gives each one of the "grown-ups" a glass of cognac.*]

MRS. FRANK. Please, Mr. Dussel, sit down.

[MR. DUSSEL *sinks into a chair.* MRS. FRANK *gives him a glass of cognac.*]

DUSSEL. I'm dreaming. I know it. I can't believe my eyes. Mr. Otto Frank here! [*To* MRS. FRANK.] You're not in Switzerland then? A woman told me . . . She said she'd gone to your house . . . the door was open, everything was in disorder, dishes in the sink. She said she found a piece of paper in the wastebasket with an address scribbled on it . . . an address in Zurich.[21] She said you must have escaped to Zurich.

ANNE. Father put that there purposely . . . just so people would think that very thing!

DUSSEL. And you've been *here* all the time?

MRS. FRANK. All the time . . . ever since July.

[ANNE *speaks to her father as he comes back.*]

---

21 **Zurich** (zōōr′ik) is a city in Switzerland, a nation that remained neutral during the war.

Analyze Plot Why do you think Mr. Dussel clings to his medicine case?

ANNE. It worked, Pim . . . the address you left! Mr. Dussel says that people believe we escaped to Switzerland.

MR. FRANK. I'm glad. . . . And now let's have a little drink to welcome Mr. Dussel. [*Before they can drink,* MR. DUSSEL *bolts his drink.* MR. FRANK *smiles and raises his glass.*] To Mr. Dussel. Welcome. We're very honored to have you with us.

MRS. FRANK. To Mr. Dussel, welcome.

[*The* VAN DAANS *murmur a welcome. The "grown-ups" drink.*]

MRS. VAN DAAN. Um. That was good.

MR. VAN DAAN. Did Mr. Kraler warn you that you won't get much to eat here? You can imagine . . . three ration books among the seven of us . . . and now you make eight.

[PETER *walks away, humiliated.*[22] *Outside a street organ is heard dimly.*]

DUSSEL. [*Rising.*] Mr. Van Daan, you don't realize what is happening outside that you should warn me of a thing like that. You don't realize what's going on . . . [*As* MR. VAN DAAN *starts his characteristic pacing,* DUSSEL *turns to speak to the others.*] Right here in Amsterdam every day hundreds of Jews disappear . . .

They surround a block and search house by house. Children come home from school to find their parents gone. Hundreds are being deported . . . people that you and I know . . . the Hallensteins . . . the Wessels . . .

MRS. FRANK. [*In tears.*] Oh, no. No!

DUSSEL. They get their call-up notice . . . come to the Jewish theater on such and such a day and hour . . . bring only what you can carry in a rucksack. And if you refuse the call-up notice, then they come and drag you from your home and ship you off to Mauthausen.[23] The death camp!

MRS. FRANK. We didn't know that things had got so much worse.

DUSSEL. Forgive me for speaking so.

ANNE. [*Coming to* DUSSEL.] Do you know the de Waals? . . . What's become of them? Their daughter Jopie and I are in the same class. Jopie's my best friend.

DUSSEL. They are gone.

ANNE. Gone?

DUSSEL. With all the others.

ANNE. Oh, no. Not Jopie!

---

22 **Humiliated** means "embarrassed and ashamed."

Analyze Plot Think about the kind of person Mr. Van Daan is. What effects does he have on the conflict in this play?

---

23 **Mauthausen** (mout´hou zən) was a Nazi concentration camp in Austria.

Analyze Plot How has the outside world changed since Scene 1? Think about what part of the plot this represents and why.

[*She turns away, in tears.* MRS. FRANK *motions to* MARGOT *to comfort her.* MARGOT *goes to* ANNE, *putting her arms comfortingly around her.*]

MRS. VAN DAAN. There were some people called Wagner. They lived near us . . . ?

MR. FRANK. [*Interrupting, with a glance at* ANNE.] I think we should put this off until later. We all have many questions we want to ask . . . But I'm sure that Mr. Dussel would like to get settled before supper.

DUSSEL. Thank you. I would. I brought very little with me.

MR. FRANK. [*Giving him his hat and briefcase.*] I'm sorry we can't give you a room alone. But I hope you won't be too uncomfortable. We've had to make strict rules here . . . a schedule of hours . . . We'll tell you after supper. Anne, would you like to take Mr. Dussel to his room?

ANNE. [*Controlling her tears.*] If you'll come with me, Mr. Dussel?

[*She starts for her room.*]

DUSSEL. [*Shaking hands with each in turn.*] Forgive me if I haven't really expressed my gratitude to all of you. This has been such a shock to me.

I'd always thought of myself as Dutch. I was born in Holland. My father was born in Holland, and my grandfather. And now . . . after all these years . . . [*He breaks off.*] If you'll excuse me.

[DUSSEL *gives a little bow and hurries off after* ANNE. MR. FRANK *and the others are* **subdued**.]

ANNE. [*Turning on the light.*] Well, here we are.

[DUSSEL *looks around the room. In the main room* MARGOT *speaks to her mother.*]

MARGOT. The news sounds pretty bad, doesn't it? It's so different from what Mr. Kraler tells us. Mr. Kraler says things are improving.

MR. VAN DAAN. I like it better the way Kraler tells it.

[*They resume their occupations, quietly.* PETER *goes off into his room. In* ANNE'S *room,* ANNE *turns to* DUSSEL.]

ANNE. You're going to share the room with me.

DUSSEL. I'm a man who's always lived alone. I haven't had to adjust myself to others. I hope you'll bear with me until I learn.

ANNE. Let me help you. [*She takes his*

View the Photograph What is the mood of this photograph? Is this scene similar to the way you pictured it as you read about the Hannukah gathering? Explain.

Analyze Plot What is Mr. Dussel suggesting about the way he sees himself?

Vocabulary . . . .

subdued (səb dood´) *adj.* quiet and restrained

The Diary of Anne Frank, Act One **793**

briefcase.] Do you always live all alone? Have you no family at all?

DUSSEL. No one.

[*He opens his medicine case and spreads his bottles on the dressing table.*]

ANNE. How dreadful. You must be terribly lonely.

DUSSEL. I'm used to it.

ANNE. I don't think I could ever get used to it. Didn't you even have a pet? A cat, or a dog?

DUSSEL. I have an allergy for fur-bearing animals. They give me asthma.

ANNE. Oh, dear. Peter has a cat.

DUSSEL. Here? He has it here?

ANNE. Yes. But we hardly ever see it. He keeps it in his room all the time. I'm sure it will be all right.

DUSSEL. Let us hope so.

[*He takes some pills to fortify himself.*]

ANNE. That's Margot's bed, where you're going to sleep. I sleep on the sofa there. [*Indicating the clothes hooks on the wall.*] We cleared these off for your things. [*She goes over to the window.*] The best part about this room . . . you can look down and see a bit of the street and the canal. There's a houseboat . . . you can see the end of it . . . a bargeman lives there with his

family . . . They have a baby and he's just beginning to walk and I'm so afraid he's going to fall into the canal some day. I watch him. . . .

DUSSEL. [*Interrupting.*] Your father spoke of a schedule.

ANNE. [*Coming away from the window.*] Oh, yes. It's mostly about the times we have to be quiet. And times for the w.c. You can use it now if you like.

DUSSEL. [*Stiffly.*] No, thank you.

ANNE. I suppose you think it's awful, my talking about a thing like that. But you don't know how important it can get to be, especially when you're frightened . . . About this room, the way Margot and I did . . . she had it to herself in the afternoons for studying, reading . . . lessons, you know . . . and I took the mornings. Would that be all right with you?

DUSSEL. I'm not at my best in the morning.

ANNE. You stay here in the mornings then. I'll take the room in the afternoons.

DUSSEL. Tell me, when you're in here, what happens to me? Where am I spending my time? In there, with all the people?

ANNE. Yes.

DUSSEL. I see. I see.

ANNE. We have supper at half past six.

Analyze Plot What does Mr. Dussel's question suggest about the way in which he perceives himself?

DUSSEL. [*Going over to the sofa.*] Then, if you don't mind . . . I like to lie down quietly for ten minutes before eating. I find it helps the digestion.

ANNE. Of course. I hope I'm not going to be too much of a bother to you. I seem to be able to get everyone's back up.

[*DUSSEL lies down on the sofa, curled up, his back to her.*]

DUSSEL. I always get along very well with children. My patients all bring their children to me, because they know I get on well with them. So don't you worry about that.

[*ANNE leans over him, taking his hand and shaking it gratefully.*]

ANNE. Thank you. Thank you, Mr. Dussel.

[*The lights dim to darkness. The curtain falls on the scene. ANNE's voice comes to us faintly at first, and then with increasing power.*]

ANNE'S VOICE. . . . And yesterday I finished Cissy Van Marxvelt's latest book. I think she is a first-class writer. I shall definitely let my children read her. Monday the twenty-first of September, nineteen forty-two. Mr. Dussel and I had another battle yesterday. Yes, Mr. Dussel! According to him, nothing, I repeat . . . nothing, is right about me . . . my appearance, my character, my manners. While he was going on at me I thought . . . sometime I'll give you such a smack that you'll fly right up to the ceiling! Why is it that every grown-up thinks he knows the way to bring up children? Particularly the grown-ups that never had any. I keep wishing that Peter was a girl instead of a boy. Then I would have someone to talk to. Margot's a darling, but she takes everything too seriously. To pause for a moment on the subject of Mrs. Van Daan. I must tell you that her attempts to flirt with father are getting her nowhere. Pim, thank goodness, won't play.

[*As she is saying the last lines, the curtain rises on the darkened scene. ANNE's voice fades out.*]

Act and Scene In what way are the playwrights using these monologues from Anne's diary? Think about how effective this method is.

ACT ONE—SCENE 4

[*It is the middle of the night, several months later. The stage is dark except for a little light which comes through the skylight in* PETER'S *room.*]

Everyone is in bed. MR. *and* MRS. FRANK *lie on the couch in the main room, which has been pulled out to serve as a makeshift[1] double bed.*

MARGOT *is sleeping on a mattress on the floor in the main room, behind a curtain stretched across for privacy. The others are all in their accustomed rooms.*

From outside we hear two drunken soldiers singing "Lili Marlene." A girl's high giggle is heard. The sound of running feet is heard coming closer and then fading in the distance. Throughout the scene there is the distant sound of airplanes passing overhead.

A match suddenly flares up in the attic. We dimly see MR. VAN DAAN. *He is getting his bearings.[2] He comes quickly down the stairs, and goes to the cupboard where the food is stored. Again the match flares up, and is as quickly blown out. The dim figure is seen to steal back up the stairs.*

---

1 **Makeshift** means "used in place of the normal or proper thing."

2 When Mr. Van Daan is **getting his bearings,** he's figuring out his position in the dimly lit room.

Act and Scene How is the setting of Scene 4 different than the setting of Scene 3?

Analyze Plot What plot complications does this interaction show? Think about the ways in which these conflicts might affect a reader or the play's audience.

There is quiet for a second or two, broken only by the sound of airplanes, and running feet on the street below.

Suddenly, out of the silence and the dark, we hear ANNE *scream.*]

ANNE. [*Screaming.*] No! No! Don't . . . don't take me!

[*She moans, tossing and crying in her sleep. The other people wake, terrified.* DUSSEL *sits up in bed, furious.*]

DUSSEL. Shush! Anne! Anne, for God's sake, shush!

ANNE. [*Still in her nightmare.*] Save me! Save me!

[*She screams and screams.* DUSSEL *gets out of bed, going over to her, trying to wake her.*]

DUSSEL. For God's sake! Quiet! Quiet! You want someone to hear?

[*In the main room* MRS. FRANK *grabs a shawl and pulls it around her. She rushes in to* ANNE, *taking her in her arms.* MR. FRANK *hurriedly gets up, putting on his overcoat.* MARGOT *sits up, terrified.* PETER'S *light goes on in his room.*]

MRS. FRANK. [*To* ANNE, *in her room.*] Hush, darling, hush. It's all right. It's all right. [*Over her shoulder to* DUSSEL.] Will you be kind enough to turn on the light, Mr. Dussel? [*Back to* ANNE.] It's nothing, my darling. It was just a dream.

Analyze Plot What can you infer about Mr. Dussel's priorities from his comment?

[*DUSSEL turns on the light in the bedroom. MRS. FRANK holds ANNE in her arms. Gradually ANNE comes out of her nightmare, still trembling with horror. MR. FRANK comes into the room, and goes quickly to the window, looking out to be sure that no one outside has heard ANNE's screams. MRS. FRANK holds ANNE, talking softly to her. In the main room MARGOT stands on a chair, turning on the center hanging lamp. A light goes on in the VAN DAANS' room overhead. PETER puts his robe on, coming out of his room.*]

DUSSEL. [*To MRS. FRANK, blowing his nose.*] Something must be done about that child, Mrs. Frank. Yelling like that! Who knows but there's somebody on the streets? She's endangering all our lives.

MRS. FRANK. Anne, darling.

DUSSEL. Every night she twists and turns. I don't sleep. I spend half my night shushing her. And now it's nightmares!

[*MARGOT comes to the door of ANNE's room, followed by PETER. MR. FRANK goes to them, indicating that everything is all right. PETER takes MARGOT back.*]

MRS. FRANK. [*To ANNE.*] You're here, safe, you see? Nothing has happened.

[*To DUSSEL.*] Please, Mr. Dussel, go back to bed. She'll be herself in a minute or two. Won't you, Anne?

DUSSEL. [*Picking up a book and a pillow.*] Thank you, but I'm going to the w.c. The one place where there's peace!

[*He stalks out. MR. VAN DAAN, in underwear and trousers, comes down the stairs.*]

MR. VAN DAAN. [*To DUSSEL.*] What is it? What happened?

DUSSEL. A nightmare. She was having a nightmare!

MR. VAN DAAN. I thought someone was murdering her.

DUSSEL. Unfortunately, no.

[*He goes into the bathroom. MR. VAN DAAN goes back up the stairs. MR. FRANK, in the main room, sends PETER back to his own bedroom.*]

MR. FRANK. Thank you, Peter. Go back to bed.

[*PETER goes back to his room. MR. FRANK follows him, turning out the light and looking out the window. Then he goes back to the main room, and gets up on a chair, turning out the center hanging lamp.*]

Analyze Plot Why do you think Anne is becoming more and more restless in her sleep?

BQ **BIG Question** In what way does Mrs. Frank show an inner strength?

MRS. FRANK. [*To* ANNE.] Would you like some water? [ANNE *shakes her head.*] Was it a very bad dream? Perhaps if you told me . . . ?

ANNE. I'd rather not talk about it.

MRS. FRANK. Poor darling. Try to sleep then. I'll sit right here beside you until you fall asleep.

[*She brings a stool over, sitting there.*]

ANNE. You don't have to.

MRS. FRANK. But I'd like to stay with you . . . very much. Really.

ANNE. I'd rather you didn't.

MRS. FRANK. Good night, then. [*She leans down to kiss* ANNE. ANNE *throws her arm up over her face, turning away.* MRS. FRANK, *hiding her hurt, kisses* ANNE'S *arm.*] You'll be all right? There's nothing that you want?

ANNE. Will you please ask Father to come.

MRS. FRANK. [*After a second.*] Of course, Anne dear. [*She hurries out into the other room.* MR. FRANK *comes to her as she comes in.*] Sie verlangt nach Dir!

MR. FRANK. [*Sensing her hurt.*] Edith, Liebe, schau . . .

MRS. FRANK. Es macht nichts! Ich danke dem lieben Herrgott, dass sie sich wenigstens an Dich wendet, wenn sie Trost braucht! Geh hinein, Otto, sie

ist ganz hysterisch vor Angst. [*As* MR. FRANK *hesitates.*] Geh zu ihr.[3] [*He looks at her for a second and then goes to get a cup of water for* ANNE. MRS. FRANK *sinks down on the bed, her face in her hands, trying to keep from sobbing aloud.* MARGOT *comes over to her, putting her arms around her.*] She wants nothing of me. She pulled away when I leaned down to kiss her.

MARGOT. It's a phase . . . You heard Father . . . Most girls go through it . . . they turn to their fathers at this age . . . they give all their love to their fathers.

MRS. FRANK. You weren't like this. You didn't shut me out.

MARGOT. She'll get over it . . .

[*She smooths the bed for* MRS. FRANK *and sits beside her a moment as* MRS. FRANK *lies down. In* ANNE'S *room* MR. FRANK *comes in, sitting down by* ANNE. ANNE *flings her arms around him, clinging to him. In the distance we hear the sound of ack-ack.*]

ANNE. Oh, Pim. I dreamed that they came to get us! The Green Police! They broke down the door and grabbed me and started to drag me out the way they did Jopie.

---

3 The Franks' conversation in German translates as follows: MRS. FRANK. "She wanted to see you!" MR. FRANK. "Edith, dear, look. . ." MRS. FRANK. "It's all right! Thank God that at least she turns to you when she is in need of comfort. Go in, Otto, she is hysterical with fear. Go to her."

Analyze Plot Why does Anne respond to her mother in this way?

Analyze Plot In what way is the main conflict of the play beginning to change Anne's behavior? Explain.

MR. FRANK. I want you to take this pill.

ANNE. What is it?

MR. FRANK. Something to quiet you.

[She takes it and drinks the water. In the main room MARGOT turns out the light and goes back to her bed.]

MR. FRANK. [To ANNE.] Do you want me to read to you for a while?

ANNE. No. Just sit with me for a minute. Was I awful? Did I yell terribly loud? Do you think anyone outside could have heard?

MR. FRANK. No. No. Lie quietly now. Try to sleep.

ANNE. I'm a terrible coward. I'm so disappointed in myself. I think I've conquered my fear . . . I think I'm really grown-up . . . and then something happens . . . and I run to you like a baby . . . I love you, Father. I don't love anyone but you.

MR. FRANK. [Reproachfully.] Annele!

ANNE. It's true. I've been thinking about it for a long time. You're the only one I love.

MR. FRANK. It's fine to hear you tell me that you love me. But I'd be happier if you said you loved your mother as well . . . She needs your help so much . . . your love . . .

ANNE. We have nothing in common. She doesn't understand me.

Whenever I try to explain my views on life to her she asks me if I'm constipated.

MR. FRANK. You hurt her very much just now. She's crying. She's in there crying.

ANNE. I can't help it. I only told the truth. I didn't want her here . . . [Then, with sudden change.] Oh, Pim, I was horrible, wasn't I? And the worst of it is, I can stand off and look at myself doing it and know it's cruel and yet I can't stop doing it. What's the matter with me? Tell me. Don't say it's just a phase! Help me.

MR. FRANK. There is so little that we parents can do to help our children. We can only try to set a good example . . . point the way. The rest you must do yourself. You must build your own character.

ANNE. I'm trying. Really I am. Every night I think back over all of the things I did that day that were wrong . . . like putting the wet mop in Mr. Dussel's bed . . . and this thing now with Mother. I say to myself, that was wrong. I make up my mind, I'm never going to do that again. Never! Of course I may do something worse . . . but at least I'll never do *that* again! . . . I have a nicer side, Father . . . a sweeter, nicer side. But I'm scared to show it. I'm afraid that people are going to laugh at me if I'm serious.

So the mean Anne comes to the outside and the good Anne stays on the inside, and I keep on trying to switch them around and have the good Anne outside and the bad Anne inside and be what I'd like to be . . . and might be . . . if only . . . only . . .

[*She is asleep.* MR. FRANK *watches her for a moment and then turns off the light, and starts out. The lights dim out. The curtain falls on the scene.* ANNE'S *voice is heard dimly at first, and then with growing strength.*]

ANNE'S VOICE. . . . The air raids are getting worse. They come over day and night. The noise is terrifying. Pim says it should be music to our ears. The more planes, the sooner will come the end of the war. Mrs. Van Daan pretends to be a fatalist.[4] What will be, will be. But when the planes come over, who is the most frightened? No one else but Petronella! . . . Monday, the ninth of November, nineteen forty-two. Wonderful news! The Allies have landed in Africa. Pim says that we can look for an early finish to the war. Just for fun he asked each of us what was the first thing we wanted to do when we got out of here. Mrs. Van Daan longs to be home with her own things, her needle-point chairs, the Beckstein piano her father gave her . . . the best that money could buy. Peter would like to go to a movie. Mr. Dussel wants to get back to his dentist's drill. He's afraid he is losing his touch. For myself, there are so many things . . . to ride a bike again . . . to laugh till my belly aches . . . to have new clothes from the skin out . . . to have a hot tub filled to overflowing and wallow in it for hours . . . to be back in school with my friends . . .

The **Menorah** (mə nor´ə) is a candlestick with nine branches.

[*As the last lines are being said, the curtain rises on the scene. The lights dim on as* ANNE'S *voice fades away.*]

ACT ONE—SCENE 5

[*It is the first night of the Hanukkah celebration.* MR. FRANK *is standing at the head of the table on which is the* **Menorah.** *He lights the Shamos, or servant candle, and holds it as he says the blessing. Seated listening is all of the "family," dressed in their best. The men wear hats,* PETER *wears his cap.*[1]]

---

4 A **fatalist** (fā´ təl ist) is someone who believes that fate controls everything that happens.

Analyze Plot What is Anne's conflict with herself? Explain.

1 The eight-day Jewish holiday **Hanukkah** (hä´ nə kə) is celebrated in December. It honors the Jews' victory over Syrian enemies in 165 B.C. Jewish males wear some sort of hat during religious services and ceremonies. In the next few speeches, Mr. and Mrs. Frank read traditional Hanukkah blessings and prayers.

Act and Scene Why do you think this scene is short?

Analyze Plot Why do you think the playwrights included this Hanukkah scene?

MR. FRANK. [*Reading from a prayer book.*] "Praised be Thou, oh Lord our God, Ruler of the universe, who has sanctified us with Thy commandments and bidden us kindle the Hanukkah lights. Praised be Thou, oh Lord our God, Ruler of the universe, who has wrought wondrous deliverances for our fathers in days of old. Praised be Thou, oh Lord our God, Ruler of the universe, that Thou has given us life and sustenance and brought us to this happy season." [MR. FRANK *lights the one candle of the Menorah as he continues.*] "We kindle this Hanukkah light to celebrate the great and wonderful deeds wrought through the zeal with which God filled the hearts of the heroic Maccabees, two thousand years ago. They fought against indifference, against tyranny and oppression, and they restored our Temple to us.[2] May these lights remind us that we should ever look to God, whence cometh our help." Amen. [*Pronounced O-mayn.*]

ALL. Amen.

[MR. FRANK *hands* MRS. FRANK *the prayer book.*]

MRS. FRANK. [*Reading.*] "I lift up mine eyes unto the mountains, from whence cometh my help. My help cometh from the Lord who made heaven and earth.

He will not suffer thy foot to be moved. He that keepeth thee will not slumber. He that keepeth Israel doth neither slumber nor sleep. The Lord is thy keeper. The Lord is thy shade upon thy right hand. The sun shall not smite thee by day, nor the moon by night. The Lord shall keep thee from all evil. He shall keep thy soul. The Lord shall guard thy going out and thy coming in, from this time forth and forevermore." Amen.

ALL. Amen.

[MRS. FRANK *puts down the prayer book and goes to get the food and wine.* MARGOT *helps her.* MR. FRANK *takes the men's hats and puts them aside.*]

DUSSEL. [*Rising.*] That was very moving.

ANNE. [*Pulling him back.*] It isn't over yet!

MRS. VAN DAAN. Sit down! Sit down!

ANNE. There's a lot more, songs and presents.

DUSSEL. Presents?

MRS. FRANK. Not this year, unfortunately.

MRS. VAN DAAN. But always on Hanukkah everyone gives presents . . . everyone!

DUSSEL. Like our St. Nicholas' Day.[3]

[*There is a chorus of "no's" from the group.*]

---

2 It was the Maccabees, a family of Jewish patriots, who led the Jews in their fight against the Syrians' cruel and unjust use of power (**tyranny and oppression**).

BQ BIG Question How does recounting what the Maccabees did two thousand years ago give the people in the apartment strength?

---

3 In the Netherlands, Christian children receive gifts from **St. Nicholas** on December 6th.

MRS. VAN DAAN. No! Not like St. Nicholas! What kind of a Jew are you that you don't know Hanukkah?

MRS. FRANK. [*As she brings the food.*] I remember particularly the candles . . . First one, as we have tonight. Then the second night you light two candles, the next night three . . . and so on until you have eight candles burning. When there are eight candles it is truly beautiful.

MRS. VAN DAAN. And the potato pancakes.

MR. VAN DAAN. Don't talk about them!

MRS. VAN DAAN. I make the best *latkes*[4] you ever tasted!

MRS. FRANK. Invite us all next year . . . in your own home.

MR. FRANK. God willing!

MRS. VAN DAAN. God willing.

MARGOT. What I remember best is the presents we used to get when we were little . . . eight days of presents . . . and each day they got better and better.

MRS. FRANK. [*Sitting down.*] We are all here, alive. That is present enough.

ANNE. No, it isn't. I've got something . . .

[*She rushes into her room, hurriedly puts on a little hat improvised from the lamp shade, grabs a satchel bulging with parcels and comes running back.*]

MRS. FRANK. What is it?

ANNE. Presents!

MRS. VAN DAAN. Presents!

DUSSEL. Look!

MR. VAN DAAN. What's she got on her head?

PETER. A lamp shade!

ANNE. [*She picks out one at random.*] This is for Margot. [*She hands it to* MARGOT, *pulling her to her feet.*] Read it out loud.

MARGOT. [*Reading.*]

"You have never lost your temper.
You never will, I fear,
You are so good.
But if you should,
Put all your cross words here."
[*She tears open the package.*] A new crossword puzzle book! Where did you get it?

ANNE. It isn't new. It's one that you've done. But I rubbed it all out, and if you wait a little and forget, you can do it all over again.

MARGOT. [*Sitting.*] It's wonderful, Anne. Thank you. You'd never know it wasn't new.

[*From outside we hear the sound of a streetcar passing.*]

---

4 *Latkes* (lot′kəz) are potato pancakes.

Analyze Plot In what way does Mr. Dussel's comparison point out a major difference between him and the others?

Analyze Plot What does Anne's poem tell you about Anne?

ANNE. [*With another gift.*] Mrs. Van Daan.

MRS. VAN DAAN. [*Taking it.*] This is awful . . . I haven't anything for anyone . . . I never thought . . .

MR. FRANK. This is all Anne's idea.

MRS. VAN DAAN. [*Holding up a bottle.*] What is it?

ANNE. It's hair shampoo. I took all the odds and ends of soap and mixed them with the last of my toilet water.⁵

MRS. VAN DAAN. Oh, Anneke!

ANNE. I wanted to write a poem for all of them, but I didn't have time. [*Offering a large box to* MR. VAN DAAN.] Yours, Mr. Van Daan, is really something . . . something you want more than anything. [*As she waits for him to open it.*] Look! Cigarettes!

MR. VAN DAAN. Cigarettes!

ANNE. Two of them! Pim found some old pipe tobacco in the pocket lining of his coat . . . and we made them . . . or rather, Pim did.

MRS. VAN DAAN. Let me see . . . Well, look at that! Light it, Putti! Light it.

[MR. VAN DAAN *hesitates.*]

ANNE. It's tobacco, really it is! There's a little fluff in it, but not much.

[*Everyone watches intently as* MR. VAN DAAN *cautiously lights it. The cigarette flares up. Everyone laughs.*]

PETER. It works!

MRS. VAN DAAN. Look at him.

MR. VAN DAAN. [*Spluttering.*] Thank you, Anne. Thank you.

[ANNE *rushes back to her satchel for another present.*]

ANNE. [*Handing her mother a piece of paper.*] For Mother, Hanukkah greeting.

[*She pulls her mother to her feet.*]

MRS. FRANK. [*She reads.*] "Here's an I.O.U. that I promise to pay. Ten hours of doing whatever you say. Signed, Anne Frank."

[MRS. FRANK, *touched, takes* ANNE *in her arms, holding her close.*]

DUSSEL. [*To* ANNE.] Ten hours of doing what you're told? Anything you're told?

ANNE. That's right.

DUSSEL. You wouldn't want to sell that, Mrs. Frank?

MRS. FRANK. Never! This is the most precious gift I've ever had!

---

5 **Toilet water** is a lightly scented liquid used as a perfume.

Analyze Plot Why does Mr. Frank make a point of saying this?

Act and Scene How is the way the Van Daans react to Anne's gifts different than it would have been if it had happened earlier in Act 1?

Analyze Plot Why is Anne's gift so valuable to Mrs. Frank? Think about the conflict between Anne and her mother.

[*She sits, showing her present to the others.* ANNE *hurries back to the satchel and pulls out a scarf, the scarf that* MR. FRANK *found in the first scene.*]

ANNE. [*Offering it to her father.*] For Pim.

MR. FRANK. Anneke . . . I wasn't supposed to have a present!

[*He takes it, unfolding it and showing it to the others.*]

ANNE. It's a muffler . . . to put round your neck . . . like an ascot, you know. I made it myself out of odds and ends . . . I knitted it in the dark each night, after I'd gone to bed. I'm afraid it looks better in the dark!

MR. FRANK. [*Putting it on.*] It's fine. It fits me perfectly. Thank you, Annele.

[ANNE *hands* PETER *a ball of paper, with a string attached to it.*]

ANNE. That's for Mouschi.

PETER. [*Rising to bow.*] On behalf of Mouschi, I thank you.

ANNE. [*Hesitant, handing him a gift.*] And . . . this is yours . . . from Mrs. Quack Quack. [*As he holds it gingerly[6] in his hands.*] Well . . . open it . . . Aren't you going to open it?

PETER. I'm scared to. I know something's going to jump out and hit me.

ANNE. No. It's nothing like that, really.

MRS. VAN DAAN. [*As he is opening it.*] What is it, Peter? Go on. Show it.

ANNE. [*Excitedly.*] It's a safety razor!

DUSSEL. A what?

ANNE. A razor!

MRS. VAN DAAN. [*Looking at it.*] You didn't make that out of odds and ends.

ANNE. [*To* PETER.] Miep got it for me. It's not new. It's second-hand. But you really do need a razor now.

DUSSEL. For what?

ANNE. Look on his upper lip . . . you can see the beginning of a mustache.

DUSSEL. He wants to get rid of that? Put a little milk on it and let the cat lick it off.

PETER. [*Starting for his room.*] Think you're funny, don't you?

DUSSEL. Look! He can't wait! He's going in to try it!

PETER. I'm going to give Mouschi his present!

[*He goes into his room, slamming the door behind him.*]

MR. VAN DAAN. [*Disgustedly.*] Mouschi, Mouschi, Mouschi.

[*In the distance we hear a dog persistently barking.* ANNE *brings a gift to* DUSSEL.]

---

6 **Gingerly** means "lightly; cautiously."

Act and Scene In Scene 3, Anne made fun of Peter's "little fuzz" on his lip. What is Anne's intention in giving Peter this gift?

ANNE. And last but never least, my roommate, Mr. Dussel.

DUSSEL. For me? You have something for me?

[*He opens the small box she gives him.*]

ANNE. I made them myself.

DUSSEL. [*Puzzled.*] Capsules! Two capsules!

ANNE. They're ear-plugs!

DUSSEL. Ear-plugs?

ANNE. To put in your ears so you won't hear me when I thrash around at night. I saw them advertised in a magazine. They're not real ones . . . I made them out of cotton and candle wax. Try them . . . See if they don't work . . . see if you can hear me talk . . .

DUSSEL. [*Putting them in his ears.*] Wait now until I get them in . . . so.

ANNE. Are you ready?

DUSSEL. Huh?

ANNE. Are you ready?

DUSSEL. Good God! They've gone inside! I can't get them out! [*They laugh as MR. DUSSEL jumps about, trying to shake the plugs out of his ears. Finally he gets them out. Putting them away.*] Thank you, Anne! Thank you!

MR. VAN DAAN. A real Hanukkah!

MRS. VAN DAAN. Wasn't it cute of her?

} — *Together*

MRS. FRANK. I don't know when she did it.

MARGOT. I love my present.

ANNE. [*Sitting at the table.*] And now let's have the song, Father . . . please . . . [*To DUSSEL.*] Have you heard the Hanukkah song, Mr. Dussel? The song is the whole thing! [*She sings.*] "Oh, Hanukkah! Oh Hanukkah! The sweet celebration . . ."

MR. FRANK. [*Quieting her.*] I'm afraid, Anne, we shouldn't sing that song tonight. [*To DUSSEL.*] It's a song of **jubilation**, of rejoicing. One is apt to become too enthusiastic.

ANNE. Oh, please, please. Let's sing the song. I promise not to shout!

MR. FRANK. Very well. But quietly now . . . I'll keep an eye on you and when . . .

[*As ANNE starts to sing, she is interrupted by DUSSEL, who is snorting and wheezing.*]

DUSSEL. [*Pointing to PETER.*] You . . . You! [*PETER is coming from his bedroom, ostentatiously[7] holding a bulge in his coat as if he were holding his cat, and dangling ANNE's present before it.*] How many times . . . I told you . . . Out! Out!

---

7 When Peter holds his coat **ostentatiously** (os´ten tā´shəs lē), he does it in a showy way that's meant to attract attention.

Vocabulary . . . .

jubilation (jōō´bə lā´shən) *n.* great joy and excitement

Analyze Plot What is Anne's purpose for giving Mr. Dussel this gift? How might this affect the conflict between the two?

MR. VAN DAAN. [*Going to* PETER.] What's the matter with you? Haven't you any sense? Get that cat out of here.

PETER. [*Innocently.*] Cat?

MR. VAN DAAN. You heard me. Get it out of here!

PETER. I have no cat.

[*Delighted with his joke, he opens his coat and pulls out a bath towel. The group at the table laugh, enjoying the joke.*]

DUSSEL. [*Still wheezing.*] It doesn't need to be the cat . . . his clothes are enough . . . when he comes out of that room . . .

MR. VAN DAAN. Don't worry. You won't be bothered any more. We're getting rid of it.

DUSSEL. At last you listen to me.

[*He goes off into his bedroom.*]

MR. VAN DAAN. [*Calling after him.*] I'm not doing it for you. That's all in your mind . . . all of it! [*He starts back to his place at the table.*] I'm doing it because I'm sick of seeing that cat eat all our food.

PETER. That's not true! I only give him bones . . . scraps . . .

MR. VAN DAAN. Don't tell me! He gets fatter every day! Damn cat looks better than any of us. Out he goes tonight!

PETER. No! No!

ANNE. Mr. Van Daan, you can't do that! That's Peter's cat. Peter loves that cat.

MRS. FRANK. [*Quietly.*] Anne.

PETER. [*To* MR. VAN DAAN.] If he goes, I go.

MR. VAN DAAN. Go! Go!

MRS. VAN DAAN. You're not going and the cat's not going! Now please . . . this is Hanukkah . . . Hanukkah . . . this is the time to celebrate . . . What's the matter with all of you? Come on, Anne. Let's have the song.

ANNE. [*Singing.*] "Oh, Hanukkah! Oh, Hanukkah! The sweet celebration."

MR. FRANK. [*Rising.*] I think we should first blow out the candle . . . then we'll have something for tomorrow night.

MARGOT. But, Father, you're supposed to let it burn itself out.

MR. FRANK. I'm sure that God understands shortages. [*Before blowing it out.*] "Praised be Thou, oh Lord our God, who hast sustained us and permitted us to celebrate this joyous festival."

[*He is about to blow out the candle when suddenly there is a crash of something falling below. They all freeze in horror, motionless. For a few seconds there is complete silence.* MR. FRANK *slips off his shoes. The others*

Analyze Plot Why do you think Peter plays this joke?

Analyze Plot How would you describe the relationship between Peter and his father?

noiselessly follow his example. MR. FRANK turns out a light near him. He motions to PETER to turn off the center lamp. PETER tries to reach it, realizes he cannot and gets up on a chair. Just as he is touching the lamp he loses his balance. The chair goes out from under him. He falls. The iron lamp shade crashes to the floor. There is a sound of feet below, running down the stairs.]

MR. VAN DAAN. [*Under his breath.*] God Almighty! [*The only light left comes from the Hanukkah candle. DUSSEL comes from his room. MR. FRANK creeps over to the stairwell and stands listening. The dog is heard barking excitedly.*] Do you hear anything?

MR. FRANK. [*In a whisper.*] No. I think they've gone.

MRS. VAN DAAN. It's the Green Police. They've found us.

MR. FRANK. If they had, they wouldn't have left. They'd be up here by now.

MRS. VAN DAAN. I know it's the Green Police. They've gone to get help. That's all. They'll be back!

MR. VAN DAAN. Or it may have been the Gestapo,[8] looking for papers . . .

MR. FRANK. [*Interrupting.*] Or a thief, looking for money.

MRS. VAN DAAN. We've got to do something . . . Quick! Quick! Before they come back.

MR. VAN DAAN. There isn't anything to do. Just wait.

[*MR. FRANK holds up his hand for them to be quiet. He is listening intently. There is complete silence as they all strain to hear any sound from below. Suddenly ANNE begins to sway. With a low cry she falls to the floor in a faint. MRS. FRANK goes to her quickly, sitting beside her on the floor and taking her in her arms.*]

MRS. FRANK. Get some water, please! Get some water!

[*MARGOT starts for the sink.*]

MR. VAN DAAN. [*Grabbing MARGOT.*] No! No! No one's going to run water!

MR. FRANK. If they've found us, they've found us. Get the water. [*MARGOT starts again for the sink. MR. FRANK, getting a flashlight.*] I'm going down.

[*MARGOT rushes to him, clinging to him. ANNE struggles to consciousness.*]

MARGOT. No, Father, no! There may be someone there, waiting . . . It may be a trap!

MR. FRANK. This is Saturday. There is no way for us to know what has happened until Miep or Mr. Kraler comes on Monday morning. We cannot live with this uncertainty.[9]

---

8 The **Gestapo** (gə stä′pō) were the Nazi secret police.

Analyze Plot In what ways do Mrs. Van Daan and Mr. Frank react differently to this complication in the plot?

9 **Uncertainty** (ən surt′ən tē) is the state or condition of being unsure or not knowing.

Act and Scene What happened in Scene 4 that might help explain why Anne fainted?

MARGOT. Don't go, Father!

MRS. FRANK. Hush, darling, hush. [MR. FRANK *slips quietly out, down the steps, and out through the door below.*] Margot! Stay close to me.

[MARGOT *goes to her mother.*]

MR. VAN DAAN. Shush! Shush!

[MRS. FRANK *whispers to* MARGOT *to get the water.* MARGOT *goes for it.*]

MRS. VAN DAAN. Putti, where's our money? Get our money. I hear you can buy the Green Police off, so much a head. Go upstairs quick! Get the money!

MR. VAN DAAN. Keep still!

MRS. VAN DAAN. [*Kneeling before him, pleading.*] Do you want to be dragged off to a concentration camp? Are you going to stand there and wait for them to come up and get you? Do something, I tell you!

MR. VAN DAAN. [*Pushing her aside.*] Will you keep still!

[*He goes over to the stairwell to listen.* PETER *goes to his mother, helping her up onto the sofa. There is a second of silence, then* ANNE *can stand it no longer.*]

ANNE. Someone go after Father! Make Father come back!

PETER. [*Starting for the door.*] I'll go.

MR. VAN DAAN. Haven't you done enough?

[*He pushes* PETER *roughly away. In his anger against his father* PETER *grabs a chair as if to hit him with it, then puts it down, burying his face in his hands.* MRS. FRANK *begins to pray softly.*]

ANNE. Please, please, Mr. Van Daan. Get Father.

MR. VAN DAAN. Quiet! Quiet!

[ANNE *is shocked into silence.* MRS. FRANK *pulls her closer, holding her protectively in her arms.*]

MRS. FRANK. [*Softly, praying.*] "I lift up mine eyes unto the mountains, from whence cometh my help. My help cometh from the Lord who made heaven and earth. He will not suffer thy foot to be moved . . . He that keepeth thee will not slumber . . ."

[*She stops as she hears someone coming. They all watch the door tensely.* MR. FRANK *comes quietly in.* ANNE *rushes to him, holding him tight.*]

MR. FRANK. It was a thief. That noise must have scared him away.

MRS. VAN DAAN. Thank God.

MR. FRANK. He took the cash box. And the radio. He ran away in such a hurry that he didn't stop to shut the street door. It was swinging wide open. [*A breath of relief sweeps over them.*] I think it would be good to have some light.

Analyze Plot What does Mr. Van Daan mean by this comment?

Analyze Plot What do Peter's actions reveal about his true feelings toward his father?

MARGOT. Are you sure it's all right?

MR. FRANK. The danger has passed. [MARGOT *goes to light the small lamp.*] Don't be so terrified, Anne. We're safe.

DUSSEL. Who says the danger has passed? Don't you realize we are in greater danger than ever?

MR. FRANK. Mr. Dussel, will you be still!

[MR. FRANK *takes* ANNE *back to the table, making her sit down with him, trying to calm her.*]

DUSSEL. [*Pointing to* PETER.] Thanks to this clumsy fool, there's someone now who knows we're up here! Someone now knows we're up here, hiding!

MRS. VAN DAAN. [*Going to* DUSSEL.] Someone knows we're here, yes. But who is the someone? A thief! A thief! You think a thief is going to go to the Green Police and say . . . I was robbing a place the other night and I heard a noise up over my head? You think a thief is going to do that?

DUSSEL. Yes. I think he will.

MRS. VAN DAAN. [*Hysterically.*] You're crazy!

[*She stumbles back to her seat at the table.* PETER *follows protectively, pushing* DUSSEL *aside.*]

DUSSEL. I think some day he'll be caught and then he'll make a bargain with the Green Police . . . if they'll let him off, he'll tell them where some Jews are hiding!

[*He goes off into the bedroom. There is a second of appalled silence.*]

MR. VAN DAAN. He's right.

ANNE. Father, let's get out of here! We can't stay here now . . . Let's go . . .

MR. VAN DAAN. Go! Where?

MRS. FRANK. [*Sinking into her chair at the table.*] Yes. Where?

MR. FRANK. [*Rising, to them all.*] Have we lost all faith? All courage? A moment ago we thought that they'd come for us. We were sure it was the end. But it wasn't the end. We're alive, safe. [MR. VAN DAAN *goes to the table and sits.* MR. FRANK *prays.*] "We thank Thee, oh Lord our God, that in Thy infinite mercy Thou hast again seen fit to spare us." [*He blows out the candle, then turns to* ANNE.] Come on, Anne. The song! Let's have the song! [*He starts to sing.* ANNE *finally starts falteringly to sing, as* MR. FRANK *urges her on. Her voice is hardly audible at first.*]

ANNE. [*Singing.*]
  "Oh, Hanukkah! Oh, Hanukkah!
  The sweet . . . celebration . . ."

BQ **BIG Question** How does Mr. Frank encourage the others to keep from giving up and to hope for the best?

Analyze Plot Why does Mr. Frank suggest singing the Hanukkah song now when earlier he did not want to sing it?

Analyze Plot In what ways might the incident with the thief lead to more tension and conflict between the characters?

[*As she goes on singing, the others gradually join in, their voices still shaking with fear.* MRS. VAN DAAN *sobs as she sings.*]

GROUP. "Around the feast . . . we . . . gather
In complete . . . jubilation . . .
Happiest of sea . . . sons
Now is here.
Many are the reasons for good cheer."

[DUSSEL *comes from the bedroom. He comes over to the table, standing beside* MARGOT, *listening to them as they sing.*]

"Together
We'll weather
Whatever tomorrow may bring."

[*As they sing on with growing courage, the lights start to dim.*]

"So hear us rejoicing
And merrily voicing
The Hanukkah song that we sing.
Hoy!"

[*The lights are out. The curtain starts slowly to fall.*]

"Hear us rejoicing
And merrily voicing
The Hanukkah song that we sing."

[*They are still singing, as the curtain falls.*]

Act and Scene What is the effect of ending the scene and act with the characters singing?

After You Read

Respond and Think Critically

1. Why does Mr. Frank tell Miep he is leaving Amsterdam? How does he seem to feel about leaving? [Recall and Infer]

2. Based on what you've learned, what can you infer about life in the Franks' household before they went into hiding? Explain. [Infer]

3. Do you think Mr. and Mrs. Frank would like Anne to be more like Margot? Why or why not? Explain your thoughts. [Interpret]

4. What are the major differences between how the Franks, the Van Daans, and Mr. Dussel deal with the constant danger? [Compare]

5. A **flashback** is an interruption of the narrative that presents scenes that occurred before that point in the story. Why do you think the authors tell the Franks' story in flashback? [Analyze]

6. **BQ** BIG Question What are some things Anne does that help her find strength from within? [Analyze]

Vocabulary Practice

On a separate sheet of paper, write the vocabulary word that correctly completes each sentence. Write "none" if no word fits.

conspicuous   loathe   aggravating   subdued   jubilation

1. The shrieking car alarm became very _____.

2. People celebrated with _____ at the war's end.

3. The mood at the funeral was _____.

4. The _____ robber walked unnoticed past the police officer.

5. The large yellow hat she wore was very _____.

6. Getting the surprise gift was very _____.

7. Some parents _____ changing dirty diapers.

Academic Vocabulary

Mr. Frank apologized to the Van Daans because he didn't **confer** with them before telling Mr. Kraler that Mr. Dussel could live with them. In the preceding sentence, *confer* means "to discuss or plan together." *Confer* also has other meanings. For instance: The university will confer its highest degree on the senior official. What do you think *confer* means in the preceding sentence? What is the difference between the two meanings?

TIP

Interpreting
Here are some tips to help you interpret. Remember when you interpret, you use your own understanding of the world to decide what the events or ideas in a selection mean.

- Think about how Mr. and Mrs. Frank treat Margot.

- Think about how Mr. and Mrs. Frank treat Anne. Consider what frustrates the Franks about Anne.

- Make a general statement on the basis of these details.

FOLDABLES Keep track of your ideas about the **BIG Question** in your unit Foldable.

 Literature Online

Selection Resources
For Selection Quizzes, eFlashcards, and Reading-Writing Connection activities, go to glencoe.com and enter QuickPass code GL39770u6.

1. Why are the brief moments between scenes important in telling a story through a play? Support your answer with examples from *The Diary of Anne Frank*.

2. Do you think that the events at the end of Act One create an appropriate place to end the act before continuing to Act Two? Why or why not? Support your answer with examples from the play.

Review: Dialogue

Dialogue is conversation between characters in a literary work. Most of *The Diary of Anne Frank* is made up of dialogue. For example:

ANNE. I slept, Father. Wasn't that funny? I knew it was the last night in my own bed, and yet I slept soundly.

In some instances, a character gives a **monologue.** A monologue is a long uninterrupted speech by one character in a play.

3. What do you learn about Anne's personality from her dialogue throughout the play? Support your answer with at least two examples from the play.

4. Identify and describe two of Anne's monologues in Act One. For each example, explain what you learn about the character of Anne or about the plot.

Reading Skill Analyze Plot

5. Which of the following describes the main conflict that drives the plot?

    A. Anne Frank struggles with inner conflicts.

    B. Anne does not always get along well with her mother.

    C. Mr. Van Daan does not treat the others very well.

    D. The two families are hiding from the Nazis.

Grammar Link

Commas to Prevent Misreading or Confusion If the order of words in a sentence is confusing, the sentence may need a comma for clarity.

Unclear: Instead of calling Eric sent an e-mail to his brother.

Clear: Instead of calling, Eric sent an e-mail to his brother.

When a clause is introduced by the conjunction *for,* it is easy to misread *for* as a preposition. To prevent this, add a comma before the conjunction.

Unclear: She must love spaghetti for she ate two helpings.

Clear: She must love spaghetti, for she ate two helpings.

To prevent misreading a noun as part of the object of the preposition, add a comma after the prepositional phrase.

Unclear: Aboard the ship Jill tightened her life jacket.

Clear: Aboard the ship, Jill tightened her life jacket.

Practice Rewrite the following sentences, adding commas to prevent misreading:

1. Although he saw two there were actually three cars.

2. While cutting onions your eyes may water.

Listening and Speaking

Performance With a group, select a scene from Act One. Practice performing the scene and listen carefully for accurate emotion from each actor, as described in the stage directions. Try to recreate the body language and gestures the characters might have used.

Genre Focus:
Drama

A **drama,** or play, is a story performed for an audience. It is a type of entertainment that people have been performing and viewing since ancient times. Drama has many of the same elements as fiction, such as characters, plot, and theme. In drama, these elements are communicated through dialogue and the actions of the characters.

Comedies, tragedies, histories, satire, farce, and musicals are types of drama.

Elements of Drama

Plot The plot is the series of events in a narrative—what happens in a story. The plot usually revolves around a problem or conflict. The **rising action** develops the conflict and builds suspense. The **climax** is the point of greatest emotion and interest. The **falling action** reveals what happens to the characters after the climax. Sometimes the story will include a **flashback.** A flashback is an interruption in the narrative to show an event that happened earlier. Through information provided in the flashback, the audience can better understand the characters and their actions.

Characters A **character** is a person, animal, or other creature that appears in a literary work. The story is usually built around a **main character. Minor characters** move the action along by interacting with the main character.

Setting The **setting** is the time and place in which a story occurs. In a drama, the setting is conveyed through scenery (objects and decoration on the stage), costumes, and dialogue, including references to historical events.

Theme The **theme** is the main message of a story. In a play, the theme may be stated directly by a character. Often, the audience must figure out the theme by examining the characters, the plot, and other elements of the play.

Act In a play, an **act** covers a significant part of the plot. Acts are divided into **scenes,** which are comparable to the chapters of a book. A change in scene often indicates a change in time or place.

Stage Directions The **stage directions** in a drama describe the appearance of the stage, the sounds to be heard, and the clothing, movements, and expressions of the actors. Stage directions are like instructions for performers. Without stage directions, it would be difficult for directors and actors to understand what the playwright had in mind.

TRY IT

Using the diagram on the next page, identify the characteristics of a drama as you read Act Two of *The Diary of Anne Frank.*

Characteristics of the Genre

To better understand literary elements in drama, look at the diagram below, which addresses setting, plot, and theme. The diagram includes examples from Act One of *The Diary of Anne Frank.* As you continue reading the play, think about how you would fill in the missing sections of the diagram.

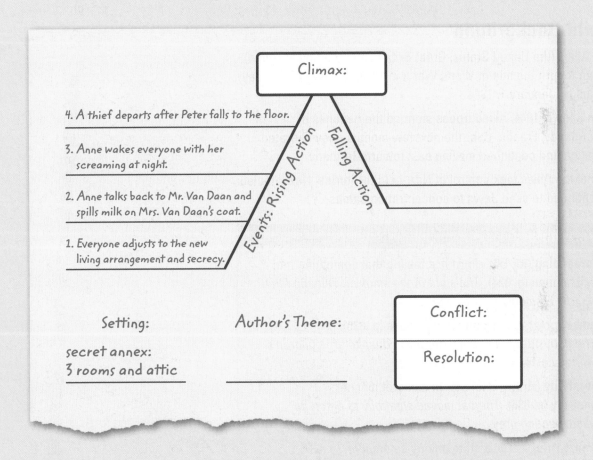

Climax:

4. A thief departs after Peter falls to the floor.

3. Anne wakes everyone with her screaming at night.

2. Anne talks back to Mr. Van Daan and spills milk on Mrs. Van Daan's coat.

1. Everyone adjusts to the new living arrangement and secrecy.

Events: Rising Action

Falling Action

Setting:
secret annex:
3 rooms and attic

Author's Theme:

Conflict:

Resolution:

The Diary of Anne Frank, Act Two

Connect to the Drama

Think about the plot of the first act of *The Diary of Anne Frank*.

Partner Talk With a partner, talk about what you think will happen in the second act. What events might occur? What changes might develop in the characters?

Build Background

The Allies (the United States, Great Britain, and the Soviet Union) began to turn the tide of World War II in 1943. Act Two of the play begins on January 1, 1944.

- On June 6, 1944, Allied troops stormed the beaches of Normandy, France. Over the next few months, they liberated France and continued moving east toward Germany.

- Until the Allies took control of Nazi-held territories, Nazi officials continued to send Jews to concentration camps.

Vocabulary

foreboding (fôr bō′ding) *n.* a feeling that something bad will happen (p. 824). *The sight of the smoking volcano filled nearby residents with foreboding.*

poise (poiz) *n.* self-control; calmness (p. 835). *The babysitter maintained her poise despite the children's wild behavior.*

stealthily (stelth′ə lē) *adv.* in a secret manner; sneakily (p. 836). *The cat moved stealthily to catch its unsuspecting prey.*

frenzy (fren′zē) *n.* a state of intense emotion (p. 837). *Late for a meeting, Mr. Brasher was in a frenzy as he looked for his lost car keys.*

Set Purposes for Reading

BQ ⟩ BIG Question

Read *The Diary of Anne Frank, Act Two,* to find out how the people living in the attic manage to keep going each day. As you read, ask yourself what you are learning about inner strength from this play.

Literary Elements Stage Directions

Stage directions are instructions in a drama that describe the characters, sets, costumes, and lighting.

Stage directions are important because they give readers insight into what the author intends for the visual aspects of settings and specific actions. Stage directions appear in italics offset by brackets.

As you read, think about the importance of the stage directions.

Reading Skill Make Generalizations About Theme

The **theme** of a literary work is its main idea. Some themes recur across many literary works, such as the theme "good will win out over evil." Often, the theme of a literary work is implied—not expressed in a statement but revealed gradually through elements such as plot, characters, point of view, setting, symbols, and irony. Thus, readers must **make generalizations** about theme.

When you make generalizations about theme, you make a broad statement based on story and character details. Doing this can help you understand the author's purpose.

When you generalize about theme, you

- notice details about characters, ideas, events, and conflicts
- think of a word or phrase that describes what the details you noticed might mean
- make sure the word or phrase you choose seems logical and makes sense

As you read, ask yourself how you can state the theme. You may find it helpful to use a graphic organizer like the one below.

Theme:	Story Support
Maintaining internal strength	Anne says: "What's the good of thinking of misery when you're already miserable? That's stupid!"

Learning Objectives

For pages 816–851

In studying this text, you will focus on the following objectives:

Literary Study: Analyzing drama.

Reading: Making generalizations about theme.

TRY IT

Generalize a possible theme from the story below.

Busy ants at an ant colony work hard gathering food. A lazy grasshopper ignores their advice to prepare for winter. When winter comes, the ants eat well, while the grasshopper starves.

The **Diary** of **Anne Frank**

Frances Goodrich and Albert Hackett

ACT TWO—SCENE 1

[*In the darkness we hear* ANNE'S *voice, again reading from the diary.*]

ANNE'S VOICE. Saturday, the first of January, nineteen forty-four. Another new year has begun and we find ourselves still in our hiding place. We have been here now for one year, five months, and twenty-five days. It seems that our life is at a standstill.

[*The curtain rises on the scene. It is late afternoon. Everyone is bundled up against the cold. In the main room* MRS. FRANK *is taking down the laundry which is hung across the back.* MR. FRANK *sits in the chair down left, reading.* MARGOT *is lying on the couch with a blanket over her and the many-colored knitted scarf around her throat.* ANNE *is seated at the center table, writing in her diary.* PETER, MR. *and* MRS. VAN DAAN, *and* DUSSEL *are all in their own rooms, reading or lying down. As the lights dim on,* ANNE'S *voice continues, without a break.*]

ANNE'S VOICE. We are all a little thinner. The Van Daans' "discussions" are as violent as ever. Mother still does not understand me. But then I don't understand her either. There is one great change, however. A change in myself. I read somewhere that girls of my age don't feel quite certain of themselves. That they become quiet within and begin to think of the miracle that is taking place in their bodies. I think that what is happening to me is so wonderful . . . not only what can be seen, but what is taking place inside. Each time it has happened I have a

Stage Directions What information is revealed by the stage directions that follow? Explain.

View the Photograph This photo shows Anne Frank's bedroom while she was in hiding. Today, this is part of the Anne Frank House Museum in Amsterdam. What details about the room or Anne's belongings surprise you the most?

feeling that I have a sweet secret. [*We hear the chimes and then a hymn being played on the carillon outside.*] And in spite of any pain, I long for the time when I shall feel that secret within me again.

[*The buzzer of the door below suddenly sounds. Everyone is startled,* MR. FRANK *tiptoes cautiously to the top of the steps and listens. Again the buzzer sounds, in* MIEP'S *V-for-Victory signal.*[1]]

MR. FRANK. It's Miep!

[*He goes quickly down the steps to unbolt the door.* MRS. FRANK *calls upstairs to the* VAN DAANS *and then to* PETER.]

MRS. FRANK. Wake up, everyone! Miep is here! [ANNE *quickly puts her diary away.* MARGOT *sits up, pulling the blanket around her shoulders.* MR. DUSSEL *sits on the edge of his bed, listening, disgruntled.*[2] MIEP *comes up the steps, followed by* MR. KRALER. *They bring flowers, books, newspapers, etc.* ANNE *rushes to* MIEP, *throwing her arms affectionately around her.*] Miep . . . and Mr. Kraler . . . What a delightful surprise!

---

1 The ***V-for-Victory signal*** was based on Morse Code for the letter *v*—three short buzzes followed by a long one.

2 ***Disgruntled*** (dis grunt′ əld) means "not pleased; in a bad humor."

Stage Directions What do you learn from the stage directions about how the characters react to Miep's arrival?

Make Generalizations About Theme How does this list of items reinforce the theme of finding strength in difficult times?

MR. KRALER. We came to bring you New Year's greetings.

MRS. FRANK. You shouldn't . . . you should have at least one day to yourselves.

[*She goes quickly to the stove and brings down teacups and tea for all of them.*]

ANNE. Don't say that, it's so wonderful to see them! [*Sniffing at* MIEP'S *coat.*] I can smell the wind and the cold on your clothes.

MIEP. [*Giving her the flowers.*] There you are. [*Then to* MARGOT, *feeling her forehead.*] How are you, Margot? . . . Feeling any better?

MARGOT. I'm all right.

ANNE. We filled her full of every kind of pill so she won't cough and make a noise.

[*She runs into her room to put the flowers in water.* MR. *and* MRS. VAN DAAN *come from upstairs. Outside there is the sound of a band playing.*]

MRS. VAN DAAN. Well, hello, Miep. Mr. Kraler.

MR. KRALER. [*Giving a bouquet of flowers to* MRS. VAN DAAN.] With my hope for peace in the New Year.

PETER. [*Anxiously.*] Miep, have you seen Mouschi? Have you seen him anywhere around?

MIEP. I'm sorry, Peter. I asked everyone in the neighborhood had they seen a gray cat. But they said no.

[MRS. FRANK *gives* MIEP *a cup of tea.* MR. FRANK *comes up the steps, carrying a small cake on a plate.*]

MR. FRANK. Look what Miep's brought for us!

MRS. FRANK. [*Taking it.*] A cake!

MR. VAN DAAN. A cake! [*He pinches* MIEP'S *cheeks gaily and hurries up to the cupboard.*] I'll get some plates.

[DUSSEL, *in his room, hastily puts a coat on and starts out to join the others.*]

MRS. FRANK. Thank you, Miepia. You shouldn't have done it. You must have used all of your sugar ration for weeks. [*Giving it to* MRS. VAN DAAN.] It's beautiful, isn't it?

MRS. VAN DAAN. It's been ages since I even saw a cake. Not since you brought us one last year. [*Without looking at the cake, to* MIEP.] Remember? Don't you remember, you gave us one on New Year's Day? Just this time last year? I'll never forget it because you had "Peace in nineteen forty-three" on it. [*She looks at the cake and reads.*] "Peace in nineteen forty-four!"

MIEP. Well, it has to come sometime, you know. [*As* DUSSEL *comes from his room.*] Hello, Mr. Dussel.

MR. KRALER. How are you?

MR. VAN DAAN. [*Bringing plates and a knife.*] Here's the knife, *liefje.* Now, how many of us are there?

MIEP. None for me, thank you.

MR. FRANK. Oh, please. You must.

MIEP. I couldn't.

MR. VAN DAAN. Good! That leaves one . . . two . . . three . . . seven of us.

DUSSEL. Eight! Eight! It's the same number as it always is!

MR. VAN DAAN. I left Margot out. I take it for granted Margot won't eat any.

ANNE. Why wouldn't she!

MRS. FRANK. I think it won't harm her.

MR. VAN DAAN. All right! All right! I just didn't want her to start coughing again, that's all.

DUSSEL. And please, Mrs. Frank should cut the cake.

MR. VAN DAAN. What's the difference? } —*Together*

MRS. VAN DAAN. It's not Mrs. Frank's cake, is it, Miep? It's for all of us.

DUSSEL. Mrs. Frank divides things better.

MRS. VAN DAAN. [*Going to* DUSSEL.] What are you trying to say? } —*Together*

MR. VAN DAAN. Oh, come on! Stop wasting time!

Stage Directions What does this direction tell you about Mr. Dussel?

Make Generalizations About Theme What possible theme does Miep's comment suggest?

MRS. VAN DAAN. [*To* DUSSEL.] Don't I always give everybody exactly the same? Don't I?

MR. VAN DAAN. Forget it, Kerli.

MRS. VAN DAAN. No. I want an answer! Don't I?

DUSSEL. Yes. Yes. Everybody gets exactly the same . . . except Mr. Van Daan always gets a little bit more.

[*VAN DAAN advances on* DUSSEL, *the knife still in his hand.*]

MR. VAN DAAN. That's a lie!

[*DUSSEL retreats before the onslaught of the* VAN DAANS.]

MR. FRANK. Please, please! [*Then to* MIEP.] You see what a little sugar cake does to us? It goes right to our heads!

MR. VAN DAAN. [*Handing* MRS. FRANK *the knife.*] Here you are, Mrs. Frank.

MRS. FRANK. Thank you. [*Then to* MIEP *as she goes to the table to cut the cake.*] Are you sure you won't have some?

MIEP. [*Drinking her tea.*] No, really, I have to go in a minute.

[*The sound of the band fades out in the distance.*]

PETER. [*To* MIEP.] Maybe Mouschi went back to our house . . . they say that cats . . . Do you ever get over there . . . ? I mean . . . do you suppose you could . . . ?

MIEP. I'll try, Peter. The first minute I get I'll try. But I'm afraid, with him gone a week . . .

DUSSEL. Make up your mind, already someone has had a nice big dinner from that cat!

[PETER *is furious, inarticulate.*[3] *He starts toward* DUSSEL *as if to hit him.* MR. FRANK *stops him.* MRS. FRANK *speaks quickly to ease the situation.*]

MRS. FRANK. [*To* MIEP.] This is delicious, Miep!

MRS. VAN DAAN. [*Eating hers.*] Delicious!

MR. VAN DAAN. [*Finishing it in one gulp.*] Dirk's in luck to get a girl who can bake like this!

MIEP. [*Putting down her empty teacup.*] I have to run. Dirk's taking me to a party tonight.

ANNE. How heavenly! Remember now what everyone is wearing, and what you have to eat and everything, so you can tell us tomorrow.

MIEP. I'll give you a full report! Good-bye, everyone!

MR. VAN DAAN. [*To* MIEP.] Just a minute. There's something I'd like you to do for me.

[*He hurries off up the stairs to his room.*]

MRS. VAN DAAN. [*Sharply.*] Putti, where are you going? [*She rushes up the stairs*

Stage Directions What does this stage direction tell you about Mr. Van Daan's mental state at this point in the play?

---

3 Peter is so angry that he becomes unable to speak (*inarticulate*).

after him, calling hysterically.] What do you want? Putti, what are you going to do?

MIEP. [*To* PETER.] What's wrong?

PETER. [*His sympathy is with his mother.*] Father says he's going to sell her fur coat. She's crazy about that old fur coat.

DUSSEL. Is it possible? Is it possible that anyone is so silly as to worry about a fur coat in times like this?

PETER. It's none of your darn business . . . and if you say one more thing . . . I'll, I'll take you and I'll . . . I mean it . . . I'll . . .

[*There is a piercing scream from* MRS. VAN DAAN *above. She grabs at the fur coat as* MR. VAN DAAN *is starting downstairs with it.*]

MRS. VAN DAAN. No! No! No! Don't you dare take that! You hear? It's mine! [*Downstairs* PETER *turns away, embarrassed, miserable.*] My father gave me that! You didn't give it to me. You have no right. Let go of it . . . you hear?

[MR. VAN DAAN *pulls the coat from her hands and hurries downstairs.* MRS. VAN DAAN *sinks to the floor, sobbing. As* MR. VAN DAAN *comes into the main room the others look away, embarrassed for him.*]

MR. VAN DAAN. [*To* MR. KRALER.] Just a little—discussion over the advisability[4]

---

4 **Advisability** means "the quality of being wise, fitting, or proper."

Stage Directions What do Mrs. Van Daan's actions reveal about her?

of selling this coat. As I have often reminded Mrs. Van Daan, it's very selfish of her to keep it when people outside are in such desperate need of clothing . . . [*He gives the coat to* MIEP.] So if you will please to sell it for us? It should fetch a good price. And by the way, will you get me cigarettes. I don't care what kind they are . . . get all you can.

MIEP. It's terribly difficult to get them, Mr. Van Daan. But I'll try. Good-bye.

[*She goes.* MR. FRANK *follows her down the steps to bolt the door after her.* MRS. FRANK *gives* MR. KRALER *a cup of tea.*]

MRS. FRANK. Are you sure you won't have some cake, Mr. Kraler?

MR. KRALER. I'd better not.

MR. VAN DAAN. You're still feeling badly? What does your doctor say?

MR. KRALER. I haven't been to him.

MRS. FRANK. Now, Mr. Kraler! . . .

MR. KRALER. [*Sitting at the table.*] Oh, I tried. But you can't get near a doctor these days . . . they're so busy. After weeks I finally managed to get one on the telephone. I told him I'd like an appointment . . . I wasn't feeling very well. You know what he answers . . . over the telephone . . . Stick out your tongue! [*They laugh. He turns to* MR. FRANK *as* MR. FRANK *comes back.*] I have some contracts here . . . I wonder if you'd look over them with me . . .

MR. FRANK. [*Putting out his hand.*] Of course.

MR. KRALER. [*He rises.*] If we could go downstairs . . . [*MR. FRANK starts ahead, MR. KRALER speaks to the others.*] Will you forgive us? I won't keep him but a minute.

[*He starts to follow MR. FRANK down the steps.*]

MARGOT. [*With sudden foreboding.*] What's happened? Something's happened! Hasn't it, Mr. Kraler?

[*MR. KRALER stops and comes back, trying to reassure MARGOT with a pretense of casualness.*]

MR. KRALER. No, really. I want your father's advice . . .

MARGOT. Something's gone wrong! I know it!

MR. FRANK. [*Coming back, to MR. KRALER.*] If it's something that concerns us here, it's better that we all hear it.

MR. KRALER. [*Turning to him, quietly.*] But . . . the children . . . ?

MR. FRANK. What they'd imagine would be worse than any reality.

Stage Directions What clues give Margot her sense of foreboding?

Make Generalizations About Theme Why does Mr. Frank suggest that the children can imagine something more frightening than reality?

Vocabulary ....

foreboding (fôr bō´ding) *n.* a feeling that something bad will happen

[*As MR. KRALER speaks, they all listen with intense apprehension.[5]*
MRS. VAN DAAN comes down the stairs and sits on the bottom step.]

MR. KRALER. It's a man in the storeroom . . . I don't know whether or not you remember him . . . Carl, about fifty, heavy-set, near-sighted . . . He came with us just before you left.

MR. FRANK. He was from Utrecht?[6]

MR. KRALER. That's the man. A couple of weeks ago, when I was in the storeroom, he closed the door and asked me . . . how's Mr. Frank? What do you hear from Mr. Frank? I told him I only knew there was a rumor that you were in Switzerland. He said he'd heard that rumor too, but he thought I might know something more. I didn't pay any attention to it . . . but then a thing happened yesterday . . . He'd brought some invoices to the office for me to sign. As I was going through them, I looked up. He was standing staring at the bookcase . . . your bookcase. He said he thought he remembered a door there . . . Wasn't there a door that used to go up to the loft? Then he told me he wanted more money. Twenty

---

5 **Apprehension** (ap´ri hen´shən) is the fear of what may happen.

6 **Utrecht** (ū´trekt) is a city in the central Netherlands.

guilders[7] more a week.

MR. VAN DAAN. Blackmail![8]

MR. FRANK. Twenty guilders? Very modest blackmail.

MR. VAN DAAN. That's just the beginning.

DUSSEL. [*Coming to* MR. FRANK.] You know what I think? He was the thief who was down there that night. That's how he knows we're here.

MR. FRANK. [*To* MR. KRALER.] How was it left? What did you tell him?

MR. KRALER. I said I had to think about it. What shall I do? Pay him the money? . . . Take a chance on firing him . . . or what? I don't know.

DUSSEL. [*Frantic.*] For God's sake don't fire him! Pay him what he asks . . . keep him here where you can have your eye on him.

MR. FRANK. Is it so much that he's asking? What are they paying nowadays?

MR. KRALER. He could get it in a war plant. But this isn't a war plant. Mind you, I don't know if he really knows . . . or if he doesn't know.

MR. FRANK. Offer him half. Then we'll soon find out if it's blackmail or not.

DUSSEL. And if it is? We've got to pay it, haven't we? Anything he asks we've got to pay!

MR. FRANK. Let's decide that when the time comes.

MR. KRALER. This may be all my imagination. You get to a point, these days, where you suspect everyone and everything. Again and again . . . on some simple look or word, I've found myself . . .

[*The telephone rings in the office below.*]

MRS. VAN DAAN. [*Hurrying to* MR. KRALER.] There's the telephone! What does that mean, the telephone ringing on a holiday?

MR. KRALER. That's my wife. I told her I had to go over some papers in my office . . . to call me there when she got out of church. [*He starts out.*] I'll offer him half then. Good-bye . . . we'll hope for the best!

[*The group call their good-bye's half-heartedly.* MR. FRANK *follows* MR. KRALER, *to bolt the door below. During the following scene,* MR. FRANK *comes back up and stands listening, disturbed.*]

---

7 The **guilder** (gil′dər) was the monetary unit of the Netherlands.

8 Here, **blackmail** is obtaining money by threat of exposure.

Stage Directions How might the actor who plays Mr. Dussel convey this stage direction?

DUSSEL. [*To* MR. VAN DAAN.] You can thank your son for this . . . smashing the light! I tell you, it's just a question of time now.

[*He goes to the window at the back and stands looking out.*]

MARGOT. Sometimes I wish the end would come . . . whatever it is.

MRS. FRANK. [*Shocked.*] Margot!

[ANNE *goes to* MARGOT, *sitting beside her on the couch with her arms around her.*]

MARGOT. Then at least we'd know where we were.

MRS. FRANK. You should be ashamed of yourself! Talking that way! Think how lucky we are! Think of the thousands dying in the war, every day. Think of the people in concentration camps.

ANNE. [*Interrupting.*] What's the good of that? What's the good of thinking of misery when you're already miserable? That's stupid!

MRS. FRANK. Anne!

[*As* ANNE *goes on raging at her mother,* MRS. FRANK *tries to break in, in an effort to quiet her.*]

ANNE. We're young, Margot and Peter and I! You grown-ups have had your chance! But look at us . . . If we begin thinking of all the horror in the world,

we're lost! We're trying to hold onto some kind of ideals . . . when everything . . . ideals, hopes . . . everything, are being destroyed! It isn't our fault that the world is in such a mess! We weren't around when all this started! So don't try to take it out on us!

[*She rushes off to her room, slamming the door after her. She picks up a brush from the chest and hurls it to the floor. Then she sits on the settee, trying to control her anger.*]

MR. VAN DAAN. She talks as if we started the war! Did we start the war?

[*He spots* ANNE'S *cake. As he starts to take it,* PETER *anticipates him.*]

PETER. She left her cake. [*He starts for* ANNE'S *room with the cake. There is silence in the main room.* MRS. VAN DAAN *goes up to her room, followed by* MR. VAN DAAN. DUSSEL *stays looking out the window.* MR. FRANK *brings* MRS. FRANK *her cake. She eats it slowly, without relish.* MR. FRANK *takes his cake to* MARGOT *and sits quietly on the sofa beside her.* PETER *stands in the doorway of* ANNE'S *darkened room, looking at her, then makes a little movement to let her know he is there.* ANNE *sits up, quickly, trying to hide the signs of her tears.* PETER *holds out the cake to her.*] You left this.

ANNE. [*Dully.*] Thanks.

[PETER *starts to go out, then comes back.*]

PETER. I thought you were fine just now. You know just how to talk to them. You know just how to say it. I'm

BQ **BIG Question** In what way does Anne show an inner strength that Margot lacks? Explain.

no good . . . I never can think . . . especially when I'm mad . . . That Dussel . . . when he said that about Mouschi . . . someone eating him . . . all I could think is . . . I wanted to hit him. I wanted to give him such a . . . a . . . that he'd . . . That's what I used to do when there was an argument at school . . . That's the way I . . . but here . . . And an old man like that . . . it wouldn't be so good.

ANNE. You're making a big mistake about me. I do it all wrong. I say too much. I go too far. I hurt people's feelings . . .

[DUSSEL *leaves the window, going to his room.*]

PETER. I think you're just fine . . . What I want to say . . . if it wasn't for you around here, I don't know. What I mean . . .

[PETER *is interrupted by* DUSSEL'S *turning on the light.* DUSSEL *stands in the doorway, startled to see* PETER. PETER *advances toward him forbiddingly.* DUSSEL *backs out of the room.* PETER *closes the door on him.*]

ANNE. Do you mean it, Peter? Do you really mean it?

PETER. I said it, didn't I?

ANNE. Thank you, Peter!

[*In the main room* MR. *and* MRS. FRANK *collect the dishes and take them to the sink, washing them.* MARGOT *lies down again on the couch.* DUSSEL, *lost, wanders into* PETER'S *room and takes up a book, starting to read.*]

PETER. [*Looking at the photographs on the wall.*] You've got quite a collection.

ANNE. Wouldn't you like some in your room? I could give you some. Heaven knows you spend enough time in there . . . doing heaven knows what . . .

PETER. It's easier. A fight starts, or an argument . . . I duck in there.

ANNE. You're lucky, having a room to go to. His lordship is always here . . . I hardly ever get a minute alone. When they start in on me, I can't duck away. I have to stand there and take it.

PETER. You gave some of it back just now.

ANNE. I get so mad. They've formed their opinions . . . about everything . . . but we . . . we're still trying to find out . . . We have problems here that no other people our age have ever had. And just as you think you've solved them, something comes along and bang! You have to start all over again.

PETER. At least you've got someone you can talk to.

ANNE. Not really. Mother . . . I never discuss anything serious with her. She doesn't understand. Father's all right.

Stage Directions In your own words, describe what you see Peter doing.

Make Generalizations About Theme What aspect of Anne's personality does her dialogue reveal?

We can talk about everything . . . everything but one thing. Mother. He simply won't talk about her. I don't think you can be really intimate[9] with anyone if he holds something back, do you?

PETER. I think your father's fine.

ANNE. Oh, he is, Peter! He is! He's the only one who's ever given me the feeling that I have any sense. But anyway, nothing can take the place of school and play and friends of your own age . . . or near your age . . . can it?

PETER. I suppose you miss your friends and all.

ANNE. It isn't just . . . [*She breaks off, staring up at him for a second.*] Isn't it funny, you and I? Here we've been seeing each other every minute for almost a year and a half, and this is the first time we've ever really talked. It helps a lot to have someone to talk to, don't you think? It helps you to let off steam.

PETER. [*Going to the door.*] Well, any time you want to let off steam, you can come into my room.

ANNE. [*Following him.*] I can get up an awful lot of steam. You'll have to be careful how you say that.

PETER. It's all right with me.

---

9 **Intimate** (in′tə mit) means "very close and personal; private."

Make Generalizations About Theme Why do you think this is so important to Anne and to the theme of inner strength?

ANNE. Do you mean it?

PETER. I said it, didn't I?

[*He goes out.* ANNE *stands in her doorway looking after him. As* PETER *gets to his door he stands for a minute looking back at her. Then he goes into his room.* DUSSEL *rises as he comes in, and quickly passes him, going out. He starts across for his room.* ANNE *sees him coming, and pulls her door shut.* DUSSEL *turns back toward* PETER's *room.* PETER *pulls his door shut.* DUSSEL *stands there, bewildered, forlorn.*]

The scene slowly dims out. The curtain falls on the scene. ANNE's *voice comes over in the darkness . . . faintly at first, and then with growing strength.*]

ANNE'S VOICE. We've had bad news. The people from whom Miep got our ration books have been arrested. So we have had to cut down on our food. Our stomachs are so empty that they rumble and make strange noises, all in different keys. Mr. Van Daan's is deep and low, like a bass fiddle. Mine is high, whistling like a flute. As we all sit around waiting for supper, it's like an orchestra tuning up. It only needs Toscanini to raise his baton and we'd be off in the Ride of the Valkyries. Monday, the sixth of March, nineteen forty-four. Mr. Kraler is in the hospital. It seems he has ulcers.[10] Pim

---

10 Arturo **Toscanini** (tə skə nē′nē) was an Italian conductor. **Ride of the Valkyries** is a passage from an opera by Richard Wagner, a German composer. Mr. Kraler's **ulcers** are sores on the lining of his stomach.

Stage Directions How do the stage directions reveal the relationship between Peter, Anne, and Dussel? Explain.

---

says we are his ulcers. Miep has to run the business and us too. The Americans have landed on the southern tip of Italy. Father looks for a quick finish to the war. Mr. Dussel is waiting every day for the warehouse man to demand more money. Have I been skipping too much from one subject to another? I can't help it. I feel that spring is coming. I feel it in my whole body and soul. I feel utterly confused. I am longing . . . so longing . . . for everything . . . for friends . . . for someone to talk to . . . someone who understands . . . someone young, who feels as I do . . .

[*As these last lines are being said, the curtain rises on the scene. The lights dim on.* ANNE'S *voice fades out.*]

ACT TWO—SCENE 2

[*It is evening, after supper. From outside we hear the sound of children playing. The "grown-ups," with the exception of* MR. VAN DAAN, *are all in the main room.* MRS. FRANK *is doing some mending,* MRS. VAN DAAN *is reading a fashion magazine.* MR. FRANK *is going over business accounts.* DUSSEL, *in his dentist's jacket, is pacing up and down, impatient to get into his bedroom.* MR. VAN DAAN *is upstairs working on a piece of embroidery in an embroidery frame.*

In his room PETER *is sitting before the mirror, smoothing his hair. As the scene goes on, he puts on his tie, brushes his coat and puts it on, preparing himself meticulously for a visit from* ANNE. *On his wall are now hung some of* ANNE'S *motion picture stars. In her room* ANNE *too is getting dressed. She stands before the mirror in her slip, trying various ways of dressing her hair.* MARGOT *is seated on the sofa, hemming a skirt for* ANNE *to wear. In the main room* DUSSEL *can stand it no longer. He comes over, rapping sharply on the door of his and* ANNE'S *bedroom.*]

ANNE. [*Calling to him.*] No, no, Mr. Dussel! I am not dressed yet. [DUSSEL *walks away, furious, sitting down and burying his head in his hands.* ANNE *turns to* MARGOT.] How is that? How does that look?

MARGOT. [*Glancing at her briefly.*] Fine.

ANNE. You didn't even look.

MARGOT. Of course I did. It's fine.

ANNE. Margot, tell me, am I terribly ugly?

MARGOT. Oh, stop fishing.

ANNE. No. No. Tell me.

MARGOT. Of course you're not. You've got nice eyes . . . and a lot of animation,[1] and . . .

Make Generalizations About Theme In what way or ways do Anne's feelings differ from what she presents to the people around her?

---

1 Here, *animation* means "liveliness."

Stage Directions What do Anne's actions reveal about her view of her meeting with Peter?

ANNE. A little vague, aren't you?

[*She reaches over and takes a brassière out of* MARGOT's *sewing basket. She holds it up to herself, studying the effect in the mirror. Outside,* MRS. FRANK, *feeling sorry for* DUSSEL, *comes over, knocking at the girls' door.*]

MRS. FRANK. [*Outside.*] May I come in?

MARGOT. Come in, Mother.

MRS. FRANK. [*Shutting the door behind her.*] Mr. Dussel's impatient to get in here.

ANNE. [*Still with the brassière.*] Heavens, he takes the room for himself the entire day.

MRS. FRANK. [*Gently.*] Anne, dear, you're not going in again tonight to see Peter?

ANNE. [*Dignified.*] That is my intention.

MRS. FRANK. But you've already spent a great deal of time in there today.

ANNE. I was in there exactly twice. Once to get the dictionary, and then three-quarters of an hour before supper.

MRS. FRANK. Aren't you afraid you're disturbing him?

ANNE. Mother, I have some intuition.[2]

MRS. FRANK. Then may I ask you this

much, Anne. Please don't shut the door when you go in.

ANNE. You sound like Mrs. Van Daan!

[*She throws the brassière back in* MARGOT's *sewing basket and picks up her blouse, putting it on.*]

MRS. FRANK. No. No. I don't mean to suggest anything wrong. I only wish that you wouldn't expose yourself to criticism . . . that you wouldn't give Mrs. Van Daan the opportunity to be unpleasant.

ANNE. Mrs. Van Daan doesn't need an opportunity to be unpleasant!

MRS. FRANK. Everyone's on edge, worried about Mr. Kraler. This is one more thing . . .

ANNE. I'm sorry, Mother. I'm going to Peter's room. I'm not going to let Petronella Van Daan spoil our friendship.

[MRS. FRANK *hesitates for a second, then goes out, closing the door after her. She gets a pack of playing cards and sits at the center table, playing solitaire. In* ANNE'S *room* MARGOT *hands the finished skirt to* ANNE. *As* ANNE *is putting it on,* MARGOT *takes off her high-heeled shoes and stuffs paper in the toes so that* ANNE *can wear them.*]

MARGOT. [*To* ANNE.] Why don't you two

---

2 **Intuition** is the ability to know things without having to reason them out.

Stage Directions What do Margot's actions reveal about how she views Anne? Explain.

talk in the main room? It'd save a lot of trouble. It's hard on Mother, having to listen to those remarks from Mrs. Van Daan and not say a word.

ANNE. Why doesn't she say a word? I think it's ridiculous to take it and take it.

MARGOT. You don't understand Mother at all, do you? She can't talk back. She's not like you. It's just not in her nature to fight back.

ANNE. Anyway . . . the only one I worry about is you. I feel awfully guilty about you.

[*She sits on the stool near* MARGOT, *putting on* MARGOT's *high-heeled shoes.*]

MARGOT. What about?

ANNE. I mean, every time I go into Peter's room, I have a feeling I may be hurting you. [MARGOT *shakes her head.*] I know if it were me, I'd be wild. I'd be desperately jealous, if it were me.

MARGOT. Well, I'm not.

ANNE. You don't feel badly? Really? Truly? You're not jealous?

MARGOT. Of course I'm jealous . . . jealous that you've got something to get up in the morning for . . . But jealous of you and Peter? No.

[ANNE *goes back to the mirror.*]

ANNE. Maybe there's nothing to be jealous of. Maybe he doesn't really like me. Maybe I'm just taking the place of his cat . . . [*She picks up a pair of short white gloves, putting them on.*] Wouldn't you like to come in with us?

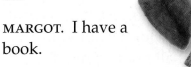

MARGOT. I have a book.

[*The sound of the children playing outside fades out. In the main room* DUSSEL *can stand it no longer. He jumps up, going to the bedroom door and knocking sharply.*]

DUSSEL. Will you please let me in my room!

ANNE. Just a minute, dear, dear Mr. Dussel. [*She picks up her Mother's pink* **stole** *and adjusts it elegantly over her shoulders, then gives a last look in the mirror.*] Well, here I go . . . to run the gauntlet.[3]

[*She starts out, followed by* MARGOT.]

DUSSEL. [*As she appears—sarcastic.*] Thank you so much.

[DUSSEL *goes into his room.* ANNE *goes toward* PETER's *room, passing* MRS. VAN DAAN *and her parents at the center table.*]

Make Generalizations About Theme What do Margot's words tell you about the theme of staying strong in difficult times? Explain.

---

3 To **run the gauntlet** is to endure opposition or difficulties.

MRS. VAN DAAN. My God, look at her! [ANNE *pays no attention. She knocks at* PETER'S *door.*] I don't know what good it is to have a son. I never see him. He wouldn't care if I killed myself. [PETER *opens the door and stands aside for* ANNE *to come in.*] Just a minute, Anne. [*She goes to them at the door.*] I'd like to say a few words to my son. Do you mind? [PETER *and* ANNE *stand waiting.*] Peter, I don't want you staying up till all hours tonight. You've got to have your sleep. You're a growing boy. You hear?

MRS. FRANK. Anne won't stay late. She's going to bed promptly at nine. Aren't you, Anne?

ANNE. Yes, Mother . . . [*To* MRS. VAN DAAN.] May we go now?

MRS. VAN DAAN. Are you asking me? I didn't know I had anything to say about it.

MRS. FRANK. Listen for the chimes, Anne dear.

[*The two young people go off into* PETER'S *room, shutting the door after them.*]

MRS. VAN DAAN. [*To* MRS. FRANK.] In my day it was the boys who called on the girls. Not the girls on the boys.

MRS. FRANK. You know how young people like to feel that they have secrets. Peter's room is the only place where they can talk.

MRS. VAN DAAN. Talk! That's not what they called it when I was young.

[MRS. VAN DAAN *goes off to the bathroom.* MARGOT *settles down to read her book.* MR. FRANK *puts his papers away and brings a chess game to the center table. He and* MRS. FRANK *start to play. In* PETER'S *room,* ANNE *speaks to* PETER, *indignant, humiliated.*]

ANNE. Aren't they awful? Aren't they impossible? Treating us as if we were still in the nursery.

[*She sits on the cot.* PETER *gets a bottle of pop and two glasses.*]

PETER. Don't let it bother you. It doesn't bother me.

ANNE. I suppose you can't really blame them . . . they think back to what they were like at our age. They don't realize how much more advanced we are . . . When you think what wonderful discussions we've had! . . . Oh, I forgot. I was going to bring you some more pictures.

PETER. Oh, these are fine, thanks.

ANNE. Don't you want some more? Miep just brought me some new ones.

PETER. Maybe later.

[*He gives her a glass of pop and, taking some for himself, sits down facing her.*]

ANNE. [*Looking up at one of the photographs.*] I remember when I got that . . . I won it. I bet Jopie that I could eat five ice-cream cones. We'd all been playing ping-pong . . . We used to have heavenly times . . . we'd finish up with ice cream at the Delphi, or the Oasis, where Jews were allowed . . . there'd always be a lot of boys . . . we'd laugh and joke . . . I'd like to go back to it for a few days or a week. But after that I know I'd be bored to death. I think more seriously about life now. I want to be a journalist . . . or something. I love to write. What do you want to do?

PETER. I thought I might go off some place . . . work on a farm or something . . . some job that doesn't take much brains.

ANNE. You shouldn't talk that way. You've got the most awful inferiority complex.[4]

PETER. I know I'm not smart.

ANNE. That isn't true. You're much better than I am in dozens of things . . . arithmetic and algebra and . . . well, you're a million times better than I am in algebra. [*With sudden directness.*] You like Margot, don't you? Right from the start you liked her, liked her much better than me.

PETER. [*Uncomfortably.*] Oh, I don't know.

[*In the main room* MRS. VAN DAAN *comes from the bathroom and goes over to the sink, polishing a coffee pot.*]

ANNE. It's all right. Everyone feels that way. Margot's so good. She's sweet and bright and beautiful and I'm not.

PETER. I wouldn't say that.

ANNE. Oh, no, I'm not. I know that. I know quite well that I'm not a beauty. I never have been and never shall be.

PETER. I don't agree at all. I think you're pretty.

ANNE. That's not true!

PETER. And another thing. You've changed . . . from at first, I mean.

ANNE. I have?

PETER. I used to think you were awful noisy.

ANNE. And what do you think now, Peter? How have I changed?

PETER. Well . . . er . . . you're . . . quieter.

[*In his room* DUSSEL *takes his pajamas and toilet articles and goes into the bathroom to change.*]

ANNE. I'm glad you don't just hate me.

PETER. I never said that.

ANNE. I bet when you get out of here you'll never think of me again.

PETER. That's crazy.

---

4 An *inferiority complex* is a general feeling of personal unworthiness and inadequacy.

Make Generalizations About Theme Make a generalization about theme based on Anne's statement.

Stage Directions What does this stage direction suggest about Peter's feelings for Margot and Anne?

ANNE. When you get back with all of your friends, you're going to say . . . now what did I ever see in that Mrs. Quack Quack.

PETER. I haven't got any friends.

ANNE. Oh, Peter, of course you have. Everyone has friends.

PETER. Not me. I don't want any. I get along all right without them.

ANNE. Does that mean you can get along without me? I think of myself as your friend.

PETER. No. If they were all like you, it'd be different.

[*He takes the glasses and the bottle and puts them away. There is a second's silence and then* ANNE *speaks, hesitantly, shyly.*]

ANNE. Peter, did you ever kiss a girl?

PETER. Yes. Once.

ANNE. [*To cover her feelings.*] That picture's crooked. [PETER *goes over, straightening the photograph.*] Was she pretty?

PETER. Huh?

ANNE. The girl that you kissed.

PETER. I don't know. I was blindfolded. [*He comes back and sits down again.*] It was at a party. One of those kissing games.

ANNE. [*Relieved.*] Oh. I don't suppose

that really counts, does it?

PETER. It didn't with me.

ANNE. I've been kissed twice. Once a man I'd never seen before kissed me on the cheek when he picked me up off the ice and I was crying. And the other was Mr. Koophuis,[5] a friend of Father's who kissed my hand. You wouldn't say those counted, would you?

PETER. I wouldn't say so.

ANNE. I know almost for certain that Margot would never kiss anyone unless she was engaged to them. And I'm sure too that Mother never touched a man before Pim. But I don't know . . . things are so different now . . . What do you think? Do you think a girl shouldn't kiss anyone except if she's engaged or something? It's so hard to try to think what to do, when here we are with the whole world falling around our ears and you think . . . well . . . you don't know what's going to happen tomorrow and . . . What do you think?

PETER. I suppose it'd depend on the girl. Some girls, anything they do's wrong. But others . . . well . . . it wouldn't necessarily be wrong with them. [*The carillon starts to strike nine o'clock.*] I've always thought that when two people . . .

ANNE. Nine o'clock. I have to go.

Stage Directions What are Anne's feelings, and why does she feel the need to conceal them?

5 *Koophuis* (koip′ hœs)

PETER. That's right.

ANNE. [*Without moving.*] Good night.

[*There is a second's pause, then* PETER *gets up and moves toward the door.*]

PETER. You won't let them stop you coming?

ANNE. No. [*She rises and starts for the door.*] Sometime I might bring my diary. There are so many things in it that I want to talk over with you. There's a lot about you.

PETER. What kind of things?

ANNE. I wouldn't want you to see some of it. I thought you were a nothing, just the way you thought about me.

PETER. Did you change your mind, the way I changed my mind about you?

ANNE. Well . . . You'll see . . .

[*For a second* ANNE *stands looking up at* PETER, *longing for him to kiss her. As he makes no move she turns away. Then suddenly* PETER *grabs her awkwardly in his arms, kissing her on the cheek.* ANNE *walks out dazed. She stands for a minute, her back to the people in the main room. As she regains her* **poise** *she goes to her mother and father and* MARGOT, *silently kissing them. They murmur their good nights to her. As she is about to open her bedroom door, she catches sight of*

MRS. VAN DAAN. *She goes quickly to her, taking her face in her hands and kissing her first on one cheek and then on the other. Then she hurries off into her room.* MRS. VAN DAAN *looks after her, and then looks over at* PETER'*s room. Her suspicions are confirmed.*]

MRS. VAN DAAN. [*She knows.*] Ah hah!

[*The lights dim out. The curtain falls on the scene. In the darkness* ANNE'*s voice comes faintly at first and then with growing strength.*]

ANNE'S VOICE. By this time we all know each other so well that if anyone starts to tell a story, the rest can finish it for him. We're having to cut down still further on our meals. What makes it worse, the rats have been at work again. They've carried off some of our precious food. Even Mr. Dussel wishes now that Mouschi was here. Thursday, the twentieth of April, nineteen forty-four. Invasion fever[6] is mounting every day. Miep tells us that people outside talk of nothing else. For myself, life has become much more pleasant. I often go to Peter's room after supper. Oh, don't think I'm in love, because I'm not. But it does make life more bearable to have someone with whom you can exchange views. No more tonight. P.S. . . . I must be honest.

---

6 ***Invasion fever*** refers to the widely held belief that the Allies would soon invade and take control of areas occupied by German forces.

Stage Directions What effect might this stage direction have on the reader? Think about how it might affect the theater audience in a different way.

Vocabulary

poise (poiz) *n.* self-control; calmness

I must confess that I actually live for the next meeting. Is there anything lovelier than to sit under the skylight and feel the sun on your cheeks and have a darling boy in your arms? I admit now that I'm glad the Van Daans had a son and not a daughter. I've outgrown another dress. That's the third. I'm having to wear Margot's clothes after all. I'm working hard on my French and am now reading La Belle Nivernaise.[7]

[*As she is saying the last lines—the curtain rises on the scene. The lights dim on, as* ANNE'S *voice fades out.*]

ACT TWO—SCENE 3

[*It is night, a few weeks later. Everyone is in bed. There is complete quiet. In the* VAN DAANS' *room a match flares up for a moment and then is quickly put out.* MR. VAN DAAN, *in bare feet, dressed in underwear and trousers, is dimly seen coming* **stealthily** *down the stairs and into the main room, where* MR. *and* MRS. FRANK *and* MARGOT *are sleeping. He goes to the food safe and again lights a match. Then he cautiously opens the safe, taking out a half-loaf of bread. As he closes the safe, it creaks.*

---

7 *La Belle Nivernaise* (lä bel′ nē′ vər nāz) was a book by a nineteenth-century French novelist.

BQ **BIG Question** What change has given Anne more strength?

Vocabulary ....

stealthily (stelth′ ə lē) *adv.* in a secret manner; sneakily

---

[*He stands rigid.* MRS. FRANK *sits up in bed. She sees him.*]

MRS. FRANK. [*Screaming.*] Otto! Otto! Komme schnell!

[*The rest of the people wake, hurriedly getting up.*]

MR. FRANK. Was ist los? Was ist passiert?

[DUSSEL, *followed by* ANNE, *comes from his room.*]

MRS. FRANK. [*As she rushes over to* MR. VAN DAAN.] Er stiehlt das Essen![1]

DUSSEL. [*Grabbing* MR. VAN DAAN.] You! You! Give me that.

MRS. VAN DAAN. [*Coming down the stairs.*] Putti . . . Putti . . . what is it?

DUSSEL. [*His hands on* VAN DAAN'S *neck.*] You dirty thief . . . stealing food . . . you good-for-nothing . . .

MR. FRANK. Mr. Dussel! For God's sake! Help me, Peter!

[PETER *comes over, trying, with* MR. FRANK, *to separate the two struggling men.*]

PETER. Let him go! Let go!

[DUSSEL *drops* MR. VAN DAAN, *pushing him away. He shows them the end of a loaf of bread that he has taken from* VAN DAAN.]

---

1 The Franks' conversation in German translates as follows: MRS. FRANK. "Come quickly!" MR. FRANK. "What's the matter? What happened?" MRS. FRANK. "He is stealing food!"

Make Generalizations About Theme What is surprising about Peter's reaction to Mr. Dussel's actions? What does it tell you about Peter?

DUSSEL. You greedy, selfish . . . !

[MARGOT *turns on the lights.*]

MRS. VAN DAAN. Putti . . . what is it?

[*All of* MRS. FRANK's *gentleness, her self-control, is gone. She is outraged, in a **frenzy** of indignation.*]

MRS. FRANK. The bread! He was stealing the bread!

DUSSEL. It was you, and all the time we thought it was the rats!

MR. FRANK. Mr. Van Daan, how could you!

MR. VAN DAAN. I'm hungry.

MRS. FRANK. We're all of us hungry! I see the children getting thinner and thinner. Your own son Peter . . . I've heard him moan in his sleep, he's so hungry. And you come in the night and steal food that should go to them . . . to the children!

MRS. VAN DAAN. [*Going to* MR. VAN DAAN *protectively.*] He needs more food than the rest of us. He's used to more. He's a big man.

[MR. VAN DAAN *breaks away, going over and sitting on the couch.*]

Stage Directions Think about the way the actress playing Mrs. Frank might act out this stage direction. What does this direction tell you about Mrs. Frank at this point in the story?

Vocabulary . . . .

frenzy (fren′zē) *n.* a state of intense emotion

MRS. FRANK. [*Turning on* MRS. VAN DAAN.] And you . . . you're worse than he is! You're a mother, and yet you sacrifice your child to this man . . . this . . . this . . .

MR. FRANK. Edith! Edith!

[MARGOT *picks up the pink woolen stole, putting it over her mother's shoulders.*]

MRS. FRANK. [*Paying no attention, going on to* MRS. VAN DAAN.] Don't think I haven't seen you! Always saving the choicest bits for him! I've watched you day after day and I've held my tongue. But not any longer! Not after this! Now I want him to go! I want him to get out of here!

MR. FRANK. Edith! ⎫
MR. VAN DAAN. Get out of ⎬ – *Together*
here? ⎭

MRS. VAN DAAN. What do you mean?

MRS. FRANK. Just that! Take your things and get out!

MR. FRANK. [*To* MRS. FRANK.] You're speaking in anger. You cannot mean what you are saying.

MRS. FRANK. I mean exactly that!

[MRS. VAN DAAN *takes a cover from the* FRANKS' *bed, pulling it about her.*]

MR. FRANK. For two long years we have lived here, side by side. We have respected each other's rights . . . we have managed to live in peace. Are we now going to throw it all away? I know this will never happen again, will it, Mr. Van Daan?

MR. VAN DAAN. No. No.

MRS. FRANK. He steals once! He'll steal again!

[MR. VAN DAAN, *holding his stomach, starts for the bathroom.* ANNE *puts her arms around him, helping him up the step.*]

MR. FRANK. Edith, please. Let us be calm. We'll all go to our rooms . . . and afterwards we'll sit down quietly and talk this out . . . we'll find some way . . .

MRS. FRANK. No! No! No more talk! I want them to leave!

MRS. VAN DAAN. You'd put us out, on the streets?

MRS. FRANK. There are other hiding places.

MRS. VAN DAAN. A cellar . . . a closet. I know. And we have no money left even to pay for that.

MRS. FRANK. I'll give you money. Out of my own pocket I'll give it gladly.

[*She gets her purse from a shelf and comes back with it.*]

MRS. VAN DAAN. Mr. Frank, you told Putti you'd never forget what he'd done for you when you came to Amsterdam. You said you could never repay him, that you . . .

MRS. FRANK. [*Counting out money.*] If my husband had any obligation to you, he's paid it, over and over.

MR. FRANK. Edith, I've never seen you like this before. I don't know you.

MRS. FRANK. I should have spoken out long ago.

DUSSEL. You can't be nice to some people.

MRS. VAN DAAN. [*Turning on* DUSSEL.] There would have been plenty for all of us, if you hadn't come in here!

MR. FRANK. We don't need the Nazis to destroy us. We're destroying ourselves.

[*He sits down, with his head in his hands.* MRS. FRANK *goes to* MRS. VAN DAAN.]

MRS. FRANK. [*Giving* MRS. VAN DAAN *some money.*] Give this to Miep. She'll find you a place.

ANNE. Mother, you're not putting Peter out. Peter hasn't done anything.

Make Generalizations About Theme Would you add these sentences to your chart to help make generalizations about theme? Why or why not?

Make Generalizations About Theme What does this sentence reveal about the hard times the characters are experiencing? Think about how this might affect your generalizatons about the play's theme.

MRS. FRANK. He'll stay, of course. When I say I must protect the children, I mean Peter too.

[PETER *rises from the steps where he has been sitting.*]

PETER. I'd have to go if Father goes.

[MR. VAN DAAN *comes from the bathroom. MRS. VAN DAAN hurries to him and takes him to the couch. Then she gets water from the sink to bathe his face.*]

MRS. FRANK. [*While this is going on.*] He's no father to you . . . that man! He doesn't know what it is to be a father!

PETER. [*Starting for his room.*] I wouldn't feel right. I couldn't stay.

MRS. FRANK. Very well, then. I'm sorry.

ANNE. [*Rushing over to* PETER.] No, Peter! No! [PETER *goes into his room, closing the door after him.* ANNE *turns back to her mother, crying.*] I don't care about the food. They can have mine! I don't want it! Only don't send them away. It'll be daylight soon. They'll be caught . . .

MARGOT. [*Putting her arms comfortingly around* ANNE.] Please, Mother!

MRS. FRANK. They're not going now. They'll stay here until Miep finds them a place. [*To* MRS. VAN DAAN.] But one thing I insist on! He must never come down here again! He must never come to this room where the food is stored!

Stage Directions What are Mrs. Van Daan's actions intended to convey to the audience about the Van Daans' relationship?

We'll divide what we have . . . an equal share for each! [DUSSEL *hurries over to get a sack of potatoes from the food safe.* MRS. FRANK *goes on, to* MRS. VAN DAAN.] You can cook it here and take it up to him.

[DUSSEL *brings the sack of potatoes back to the center table.*]

MARGOT. Oh, no. No. We haven't sunk so far that we're going to fight over a handful of rotten potatoes.

DUSSEL. [*Dividing the potatoes into piles.*] Mrs. Frank, Mr. Frank, Margot, Anne, Peter, Mrs. Van Daan, Mr. Van Daan, myself . . . Mrs. Frank . . .

[*The buzzer sounds in* MIEP'S *signal.*]

MR. FRANK. It's Miep!

[*He hurries over, getting his overcoat and putting it on.*]

MARGOT. At this hour?

MRS. FRANK. It is trouble.

MR. FRANK. [*As he starts down to unbolt the door.*] I beg you, don't let her see a thing like this!

MR. DUSSEL. [*Counting without stopping.*] . . . Anne, Peter, Mrs. Van Daan, Mr. Van Daan, myself . . .

MARGOT. [*To* DUSSEL.] Stop it! Stop it!

DUSSEL. . . . Mr. Frank, Margot, Anne, Peter, Mrs. Van Daan, Mr. Van Daan, myself, Mrs. Frank . . .

MRS. VAN DAAN. You're keeping the big ones for yourself! All the big ones . . . Look at the size of that! . . . And that! . . .

[DUSSEL *continues on with his dividing.* PETER, *with his shirt and trousers on, comes from his room.*]

MARGOT. Stop it! Stop it!

[*We hear* MIEP's *excited voice speaking to* MR. FRANK *below.*]

MIEP. Mr. Frank . . . the most wonderful news! . . . The invasion has begun!

MR. FRANK. Go on, tell them! Tell them!

[MIEP *comes running up the steps, ahead of* MR. FRANK. *She has a man's raincoat on over her nightclothes and a bunch of orange-colored flowers in her hand.*]

MIEP. Did you hear that, everybody? Did you hear what I said? The invasion has begun! The invasion!

[*They all stare at* MIEP, *unable to grasp what she is telling them.* PETER *is the first to recover his wits.*]

PETER. Where?

MRS. VAN DAAN. When? When, Miep?

MIEP. It began early this morning . . .

[*As she talks on, the realization of what she has said begins to dawn on them. Everyone goes crazy. A wild demonstration takes place.* MRS. FRANK *hugs* MR. VAN DAAN.]

MRS. FRANK. Oh, Mr. Van Daan, did you hear that?

[DUSSEL *embraces* MRS. VAN DAAN. PETER *grabs a frying pan and parades around the room, beating on it, singing the Dutch National Anthem.* ANNE *and* MARGOT *follow him, singing, weaving in and out among the excited grown-ups.* MARGOT *breaks away to take the flowers from* MIEP *and distribute them to everyone. While this pandemonium[2] is going on* MRS. FRANK *tries to make herself heard above the excitement.*]

MRS. FRANK. [*To* MIEP.] How do you know?

MIEP. The radio . . . The B.B.C.! They said they landed on the coast of Normandy![3]

PETER. The British?

MIEP. British, Americans, French, Dutch, Poles, Norwegians . . . all of them! More than four thousand ships! Churchill spoke, and General Eisenhower![4] D-Day they call it!

MR. FRANK. Thank God, it's come!

MRS. VAN DAAN. At last!

---

2 *Pandemonium* (pan′ də mō′ nē əm) is wild disorder and uproar.

3 *B.B.C.* stands for British Broadcasting Corporation. *Normandy* is a region in France across the English Channel from the southern coast of England.

4 Winston *Churchill* was the British prime minister, and Dwight D. *Eisenhower* commanded the Allied forces in Europe.

Stage Directions How would you describe the mood indicated by these stage directions?

Stage Directions Why do you think Mr. Dussel continues to count potatoes despite protests from Margot and Mrs. Van Daan?

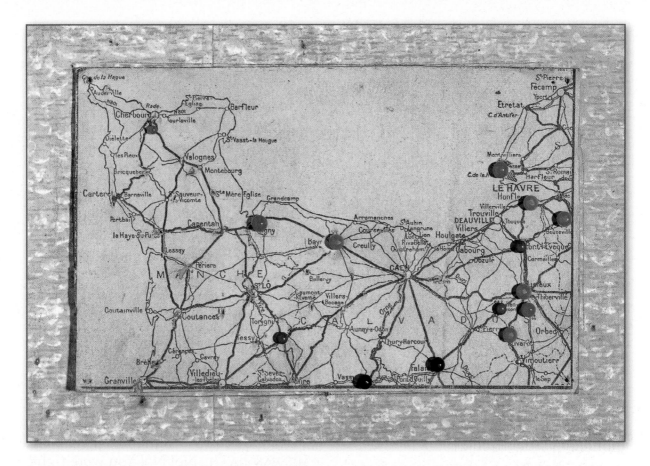

A map kept by Mr. Frank to chart the progress of the Allied forces after they landed in Normandy in 1944. Colored pins show the movement of the troops between Cherbourg and Le Havre in northwest France.

MIEP. [*Starting out.*] I'm going to tell Mr. Kraler. This'll be better than any blood transfusion.[5]

MR. FRANK. [*Stopping her.*] What part of Normandy did they land, did they say?

MIEP. Normandy . . . that's all I know now . . . I'll be up the minute I hear some more!

[*She goes hurriedly out.*]

MR. FRANK. [*To* MRS. FRANK.] What did I tell you? What did I tell you?

[MRS. FRANK *indicates that he has forgotten to bolt the door after* MIEP. *He hurries down the steps.*
MR. VAN DAAN, *sitting on the couch, suddenly breaks into a convulsive sob. Everybody looks at him, bewildered.*]

MRS. VAN DAAN. [*Hurrying to him.*] Putti! Putti! What is it? What happened?

---

5 A **blood transfusion** is the process of transferring blood from a healthy person to a sick person. Evidently, Mr. Kraler's ulcers have made him seriously ill.

MR. VAN DAAN. Please. I'm so ashamed.

[MR. FRANK *comes back up the steps.*]

DUSSEL. Oh, for God's sake!

MRS. VAN DAAN. Don't, Putti.

MARGOT. It doesn't matter now!

MR. FRANK. [*Going to* MR. VAN DAAN.] Didn't you hear what Miep said? The invasion has come! We're going to be liberated! This is a time to celebrate!

[*He embraces* MRS. FRANK *and then hurries to the cupboard and gets the cognac and a glass.*]

MR. VAN DAAN. To steal bread from children!

MRS. FRANK. We've all done things that we're ashamed of.

ANNE. Look at me, the way I've treated Mother . . . so mean and horrid to her.

MRS. FRANK. No, Anneke, no.

[ANNE *runs to her mother, putting her arms around her.*]

ANNE. Oh, Mother, I was. I was awful.

MR. VAN DAAN. Not like me. No one is as bad as me!

DUSSEL. [*To* MR. VAN DAAN.] Stop it now! Let's be happy!

MR. FRANK. [*Giving* MR. VAN DAAN *a glass of cognac.*] Here! Here! Schnapps! Locheim![6]

[VAN DAAN *takes the cognac. They all watch him. He gives them a feeble smile.* ANNE *puts up her fingers in a V-for-Victory sign. As* VAN DAAN *gives an answering V-sign, they are startled to hear a loud sob from behind them. It is* MRS. FRANK, *stricken with remorse. She is sitting on the other side of the room.*]

MRS. FRANK. [*Through her sobs.*] When I think of the terrible things I said . . .

[MR. FRANK, ANNE *and* MARGOT *hurry to her, trying to comfort her.* MR. VAN DAAN *brings her his glass of cognac.*]

MR. VAN DAAN. No! No! You were right!

MRS. FRANK. That I should speak that way to you! . . . Our friends! . . . Our guests!

[*She starts to cry again.*]

DUSSEL. Stop it, you're spoiling the whole invasion!

[*As they are comforting her, the lights dim out. The curtain falls.*]

ANNE'S VOICE. [*Faintly at first and then with growing strength.*] We're all in much better spirits these days. There's still

---

6 **Schnapps** (shnäps) is a type of cognac. **Locheim** (lə khä′yim) means "To Life!"

Make Generalizations About Theme What has Mr. Van Daan realized that makes him feel so ashamed? Think about ways in which you might connect his feeling of shame with the theme of the play.

Make Generalizations About Theme What does Mrs. Frank's expression of remorse reveal about her? What might it reveal about the theme of the play?

excellent news of the invasion. The best part about it is that I have a feeling that friends are coming. Who knows? Maybe I'll be back in school by fall. Ha, ha! The joke is on us! The warehouse man doesn't know a thing and we are paying him all that money! . . . Wednesday, the second of July, nineteen forty-four. The invasion seems temporarily to be bogged down. Mr. Kraler has to have an operation, which looks bad. The Gestapo have found the radio that was stolen. Mr. Dussel says they'll trace it back and back to the thief, and then, it's just a matter of time till they get to us. Everyone is low. Even poor Pim can't raise their spirits. I have often been downcast[7] myself . . . but never in despair. I can shake off everything if I write. But . . . and that is the great question . . . will I ever be able to write well? I want to so much. I want to go on living even after my death. Another birthday has gone by, so now I am fifteen. Already I know what I want. I have a goal, an opinion.

[*As this is being said—the curtain rises on the scene, the lights dim on, and* ANNE's *voice fades out.*]

ACT TWO—SCENE 4

[*It is an afternoon a few weeks later . . . Everyone but* MARGOT *is in the main room. There is a sense of great tension.*

---

7 *Downcast* means "sad; depressed."

BQ **BIG Question** In what way does Anne's expression of inner strength differ from her previous expressions? Explain.

Both MRS. FRANK *and* MR. VAN DAAN *are nervously pacing back and forth,* DUSSEL *is standing at the window, looking down fixedly at the street below.* PETER *is at the center table, trying to do his lessons.* ANNE *sits opposite him, writing in her diary.* MRS. VAN DAAN *is seated on the couch, her eyes on* MR. FRANK *as he sits reading. The sound of a telephone ringing comes from the office below. They all are rigid, listening tensely.* MR. DUSSEL *rushes down to* MR. FRANK.]

DUSSEL. There it goes again, the telephone! Mr. Frank, do you hear?

MR. FRANK. [*Quietly.*] Yes. I hear.

DUSSEL. [*Pleading, insistent.*] But this is the third time, Mr. Frank! The third time in quick succession! It's a signal! I tell you it's Miep, trying to get us! For some reason she can't come to us and she's trying to warn us of something!

MR. FRANK. Please. Please.

MR. VAN DAAN. [*To* DUSSEL.] You're wasting your breath.

DUSSEL. Something has happened, Mr. Frank. For three days now Miep hasn't been to see us! And today not a man has come to work. There hasn't been a sound in the building!

MRS. FRANK. Perhaps it's Sunday. We may have lost track of the days.

MR. VAN DAAN. [*To* ANNE.] You with the diary there. What day is it?

Stage Directions How do these characters' actions reflect the mood of the scene?

The Diary of Anne Frank, Act Two **843**

DUSSEL. [*Going to* MRS. FRANK.] I don't lose track of the days! I know exactly what day it is! It's Friday, the fourth of August. Friday, and not a man at work. [*He rushes back to* MR. FRANK, *pleading with him, almost in tears.*] I tell you Mr. Kraler's dead. That's the only explanation. He's dead and they've closed down the building, and Miep's trying to tell us!

MR. FRANK. She'd never telephone us.

DUSSEL. [*Frantic.*] Mr. Frank, answer that! I beg you, answer it!

MR. FRANK. No.

MR. VAN DAAN. Just pick it up and listen. You don't have to speak. Just listen and see if it's Miep.

DUSSEL. [*Speaking at the same time.*] For God's sake . . . I ask you.

MR. FRANK. No. I've told you, no. I'll do nothing that might let anyone know we're in the building.

PETER. Mr. Frank's right.

MR. VAN DAAN. There's no need to tell us what side you're on.

MR. FRANK. If we wait patiently, quietly, I believe that help will come.

[*There is silence for a minute as they all listen to the telephone ringing.*]

DUSSEL. I'm going down. [*He rushes down the steps.* MR. FRANK *tries ineffectually*[1] *to hold him.* DUSSEL *runs to the lower door, unbolting it. The telephone stops ringing.*

---

1 **Ineffectually** means "without effect; uselessly."

DUSSEL *bolts the door and comes slowly back up the steps.*] Too late. [MR. FRANK *goes to* MARGOT *in* ANNE'S *bedroom.*]

MR. VAN DAAN. So we just wait here until we die.

MRS. VAN DAAN. [*Hysterically.*] I can't stand it! I'll kill myself! I'll kill myself!

MR. VAN DAAN. For God's sake, stop it!

[*In the distance, a German military band is heard playing a Viennese waltz.*]

MRS. VAN DAAN. I think you'd be glad if I did! I think you want me to die!

MR. VAN DAAN. Whose fault is it we're here? [MRS. VAN DAAN *starts for her room. He follows, talking at her.*] We could've been safe somewhere . . . in America or Switzerland. But no! No! You wouldn't leave when I wanted to. You couldn't leave your things. You couldn't leave your precious furniture.

MRS. VAN DAAN. Don't touch me!

[*She hurries up the stairs, followed by* MR. VAN DAAN. PETER, *unable to bear it, goes to his room.* ANNE *looks after him, deeply concerned.* DUSSEL *returns to his post at the window.* MR. FRANK *comes back into the main room and takes a book, trying to read.* MRS. FRANK *sits near the sink, starting to peel some potatoes.* ANNE *quietly goes to* PETER'S *room, closing the door after her.* PETER *is lying face down on the cot.* ANNE *leans over him, holding him in her arms, trying to bring him out of his despair.*]

ANNE. Look, Peter, the sky. [*She looks*

up through the skylight.] What a lovely, lovely day! Aren't the clouds beautiful? You know what I do when it seems as if I couldn't stand being cooped up for one more minute? I think myself out. I think myself on a walk in the park where I used to go with Pim. Where the **jonquils** and the crocus and the violets grow down the slopes. You know the most wonderful part about thinking yourself out? You can have it any way you like. You can have roses and violets and chrysanthemums all blooming at the same time . . . It's funny . . . I used to take it all for granted . . . and now I've gone crazy about everything to do with nature. Haven't you?

PETER. I've just gone crazy. I think if something doesn't happen soon . . . if we don't get out of here . . . I can't stand much more of it!

ANNE. [*Softly.*] I wish you had a religion, Peter.

PETER. No, thanks! Not me!

ANNE. Oh, I don't mean you have to be Orthodox. . . or believe in heaven and hell and purgatory[2] and things . . . I just mean some religion . . . it doesn't matter what. Just to believe in something! When I think of all that's out there . . .

---

2 The **Orthodox** branch of Judaism is the most traditional, requiring strict obedience to ancient laws and customs. **Purgatory** is, some believe, a place of temporary punishment for the souls of the dead.

BQ **BIG Question** How does Anne's suggestion help show her inner strength?

the trees . . . and flowers . . . and seagulls . . . when I think of the dearness of you, Peter . . . and the goodness of the people we know . . . Mr. Kraler, Miep, Dirk, the vegetable man, all risking their lives for us every day . . . When I think of these good things, I'm not afraid any more . . . I find myself, and God, and I . . .

Visual Vocabulary

A **jonquil** is a yellow flower of a plant that resembles the daffodil.

[PETER *interrupts, getting up and walking away.*]

PETER. That's fine! But when I begin to think, I get mad! Look at us, hiding out for two years. Not able to move! Caught here like . . . waiting for them to come and get us . . . and all for what?

ANNE. We're not the only people that've had to suffer. There've always been people that've had to . . . sometimes one race . . . sometimes another . . . and yet . . .

PETER. That doesn't make me feel any better!

ANNE. [*Going to him.*] I know it's terrible, trying to have any faith . . . when people are doing such horrible . . . But you know what I sometimes think? I think the world may be going through a phase, the way I was with Mother. It'll pass, maybe not for hundreds of years, but someday . . .

I still believe, in spite of everything, that people are really good at heart.

PETER. I want to see something now . . . Not a thousand years from now!

[*He goes over, sitting down again on the cot.*]

ANNE. But, Peter, if you'd only look at it as part of a great pattern . . . that we're just a little minute in the life . . . [*She breaks off.*] Listen to us, going at each other like a couple of stupid grown-ups! Look at the sky now. Isn't it lovely? [*She holds out her hand to him.* PETER *takes it and rises, standing with her at the window looking out, his arms around her.*] Someday, when we're outside again, I'm going to . . .

[*She breaks off as she hears the sound of a car, its brakes squealing as it comes to a sudden stop. The people in the other rooms also become aware of the sound. They listen tensely. Another car roars up to a screeching stop.* ANNE *and* PETER *come from* PETER's *room.* MR. *and* MRS. VAN DAAN *creep down the stairs.* DUSSEL *comes out from his room. Everyone is listening, hardly breathing. A doorbell clangs again and again in the building below.* MR. FRANK *starts quietly down the steps to the door.* DUSSEL *and* PETER *follow him. The others stand rigid, waiting, terrified.*

In a few seconds DUSSEL *comes stumbling back up the steps. He shakes off* PETER's *help and goes to his room.* MR. FRANK *bolts the door below, and comes slowly back up the steps. Their eyes are all on him as he*

stands there for a minute. They realize that what they feared has happened.* MRS. VAN DAAN *starts to whimper.* MR. VAN DAAN *puts her gently in a chair, and then hurries off up the stairs to their room to collect their things.* PETER *goes to comfort his mother. There is a sound of violent pounding on a door below.*]

MR. FRANK. [*Quietly.*] For the past two years we have lived in fear. Now we can live in hope.

[*The pounding below becomes more insistent. There are muffled sounds of voices, shouting commands.*]

MEN'S VOICES. Auf machen! Da drinnen! Auf machen! Schnell! Schnell! Schnell![3] etc., etc.

[*The street door below is forced open. We hear the heavy tread of footsteps coming up.* MR. FRANK *gets two school bags from the shelves, and gives one to* ANNE *and the other to* MARGOT. *He goes to get a bag for* MRS. FRANK. *The sound of feet coming up grows louder.* PETER *comes to* ANNE, *kissing her good-bye, then he goes to his room to collect his things. The buzzer of their door starts to ring.* MR. FRANK *brings* MRS. FRANK *a bag. They stand together, waiting. We hear the thud of gun butts on the door, trying to break it down.*

ANNE *stands, holding her school satchel, looking over at her father and mother*

---

3 The voices are saying, in German: "Open up! Inside there! Open up! Quick! Quick! Quick!" The abbreviation *etc.* means "and so on." The actors are supposed to keep speaking until the curtain falls.

Make Generalizations About Theme How does this help us understand Anne's actions throughout the play?

Make Generalizations About Theme What does Mr. Frank mean?

with a soft, reassuring smile. She is no longer a child, but a woman with courage to meet whatever lies ahead.

The lights dim out. The curtain falls on the scene. We hear a mighty crash as the door is shattered. After a second ANNE'S voice is heard.]

ANNE'S VOICE. And so it seems our stay here is over. They are waiting for us now. They've allowed us five minutes to get our things. We can each take a bag and whatever it will hold of clothing.

Nothing else. So, dear Diary, that means I must leave you behind. Good-bye for a while. P.S. Please, please, Miep, or Mr. Kraler, or anyone else. If you should find this diary, will you please keep it safe for me, because some day I hope . . .

[*Her voice stops abruptly. There is silence. After a second the curtain rises.*]

BQ **BIG Question** In what way does Anne continue to show an inner strength despite knowing she will be captured?

ACT TWO—SCENE 5

[*It is again the afternoon in November, 1945. The rooms are as we saw them in the first scene.* MR. KRALER *has joined* MIEP *and* MR. FRANK. *There are coffee cups on the table. We see a great change in* MR. FRANK. *He is calm now. His bitterness is gone. He slowly turns a few pages of the diary. They are blank.*]

MR. FRANK. No more.

[*He closes the diary and puts it down on the couch beside him.*]

MIEP. I'd gone to the country to find food. When I got back the block was surrounded by police . . .

MR. KRALER. We made it our business to learn how they knew. It was the thief . . . the thief who told them.

[MIEP *goes up to the gas burner, bringing back a pot of coffee.*]

MR. FRANK. [*After a pause.*] It seems strange to say this, that anyone could be happy in a concentration camp. But Anne was happy in the camp in Holland where they first took us. After two years of being shut up in these rooms, she could be out . . . out in the sunshine and the fresh air that she loved.

MIEP. [*Offering the coffee to* MR. FRANK.] A little more?

MR. FRANK. [*Holding out his cup to her.*] The news of the war was good. The British and Americans were sweeping through France. We felt sure that they would get to us in time. In September we were told that we were to be shipped to Poland . . . The men to one camp. The women to another. I was sent to Auschwitz. They went to Belsen. In January we were freed, the few of us who were left. The war wasn't yet over, so it took us a long time to get home. We'd be sent here and there behind the lines where we'd be safe. Each time our train would stop . . . at a siding, or a crossing . . . we'd all get out and go from group to group . . . Where were you? Were you at Belsen? At Buchenwald?[4] At Mauthausen? Is it possible that you knew my wife? Did you ever see my husband? My son? My daughter? That's how I found out about my wife's death . . . of Margot, the Van Daans . . . Dussel. But Anne . . . I still hoped . . . Yesterday I went to Rotterdam.[5] I'd heard of a woman there . . . She'd been in Belsen with Anne . . . I know now.

[*He picks up the diary again, and turns the pages back to find a certain passage. As he finds it we hear* ANNE'S *voice.*]

ANNE'S VOICE. In spite of everything, I still believe that people are really good at heart.

[MR. FRANK *slowly closes the diary.*]

MR. FRANK. She puts me to shame.

[*They are silent.*]

THE CURTAIN FALLS 🙠

---

4 **Auschwitz** (oush′vits), **Belsen** (bel′zən), **Buchenwald** (book′ən wôld), and **Mauthausen** (mout′hou zən) were the sites of Nazi concentration camps in Poland, Austria, and Germany. These camps specialized in exterminating prisoners.

5 **Rotterdam** is a city in the southwestern Netherlands.

Stage Directions What might explain this change in Mr. Frank?

BQ ▶ **BIG Question** What is Mr. Frank saying here about Anne's refusal to give up through hard times?

After You Read

Respond and Think Critically

1. In your own words, recap the major events of the second act. Include specific details. [Summarize]

2. Anne tells Peter she believes "that people are really good at heart." What does this statement tell you about Anne's character? Support your answer with details from the play. [Infer]

3. What message do the authors seem to be sending with their description of Mr. and Mrs. Van Daan in the play? Explain. [Analyze]

4. Think about another story you have read or heard about a family or families facing hardship and crisis. What theme did that story convey? Compare and contrast that theme to the theme of *The Diary of Anne Frank*. [Compare and Contrast]

5. How believable is the description of Anne as a "woman with courage to meet whatever lies ahead"? Explain your opinion. [Evaluate]

6. **BQ** BIG Question What is the most impressive example of Anne's inner strength in Act Two? Explain your answer with references to the play. [Make Judgments]

TIP

Evaluating
Here are some tips to help you evaluate. When you evaluate, you make a judgment or form an opinion.

- Skim the selection and look for scenes in which Anne is confronted with extraordinary situations.

- Consider Anne's life compared to "normal" teen life.

- Form a judgment about the effects on a teen of stress and possible death.

 Keep track of your ideas about the **BIG Question** in your unit Foldable.

You're the Critic

"Destructibility" or "Life Force"?

Read these excerpts from reviews about *The Diary of Anne Frank*.

"The diary is not a song to life—rather it reveals the easy destructibility of the human spirit; it is the vehicle that has accomplished mankind's almost universal . . . [slowness in understanding] about the dark lessons of Auschwitz."

—Cynthia Ozick, *New Yorker*

"This play makes use of elements having mainly to do with human courage, faith, hope, brotherhood, love, and self-sacrifice. . . . [I]t was a play about . . . 'the life force.'"

—Garson Kanin, *New York Times*

Group Activity Discuss these questions. Refer to the excerpts and the play to support your answers.

1. The first excerpt says that the diary obscures lessons of the Holocaust. Do you agree or disagree? Explain.

2. The second excerpt states that the play has a universal message about humanity. Do you agree or disagree? Explain.

1. Some information appears only in stage directions. What is one example in Act Two? Briefly state the information and identify why it is given.

2. The second-to-last line of the script is this stage direction: [*They are silent.*] What reasons might the playwrights have had for including this?

Review: Conflict

As you learned on page 311, conflict is the struggle between opposing forces in a story or drama. An **external conflict** exists when a character struggles against some outside force, such as nature, society, fate, or another person. A character that is torn between opposing feelings or goals is experiencing an **internal conflict.**

Test Skills Practice

3. Which of the following is an example of internal conflict in *The Diary of Anne Frank*?
   A Mrs. Van Daan tries to stop Anne and Peter from seeing each other.
   B Mr. Van Daan steals food when everyone is asleep.
   C Anne struggles to believe in the goodness of people.
   D Mrs. Frank wants the Van Daans to leave.

Reading Skill
Make Generalizations About Theme

4. In one or two sentences, state what you think is the play's most prominent theme. Give an example of a specific detail that led you to make this generalization.

5. What other themes did you see in the play? State one or two of them and support your answer with details from the play.

Vocabulary Practice

Synonyms are words with the same or nearly the same meaning. Match each vocabulary word with its synonym to the right. Two of the words in the right-hand column will not have matches.

1. **foreboding**   a. composure
2. **poise**   b. openly
3. **stealthily**   c. secretly
4. **frenzy**   d. tranquility
                       e. misgiving
                       f. excitement

Academic Vocabulary

The Allied invasion of France challenged Nazi Germany's **dominance** of Europe. To become more familiar with the word *dominance*, fill out a graphic organizer like the one below.

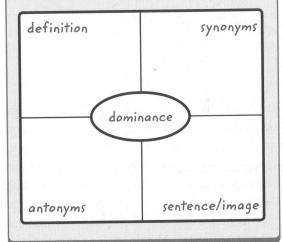

Literature Online

Selection Resources For Selection Quizzes, eFlashcards, and Reading-Writing Connection activities, go to glencoe.com and enter QuickPass code GL39770u6.

Respond Through Writing

Review

Convince an Audience Write a review that will convince an audience of the merits of the play *The Diary of Anne Frank*.

Understand the Task A **review** is a kind of **persuasive essay** that **summarizes** and **evaluates** a work of art, such as a play. It should persuade readers to experience (or not to experience) its subject.

Prewrite To begin getting ideas, read the review excerpts on page 850. Then think of elements of the play that you thought were effective. What details can you use to support your opinions? Keep track of your ideas in an organizer like the one below.

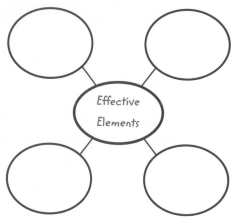

Effective Elements

Draft Before drafting, make an overall plan, one that can be accomplished in the time available. Remember that a review should include a summary of important events and an evaluation of the play. As you plan and write, differentiate between facts (events and quotations from the play) and opinions (your own evaluation). In addition, address possible counterarguments that your audience might have to your ideas. Your draft should include a thesis statement. This sentence frame might help you begin your draft:

I believe that *The Diary of Anne Frank* is _____ because _____, _____, and _____.

Revise Read your first draft to determine whether your paragraphs are in logical order. Rearrange as necessary. Ask yourself, "Will this convince readers of the play's merits?" Also be sure your arguments are consistent—not contradicting each other.

Edit and Proofread Proofread your paper, correcting errors in spelling, grammar, and punctuation. Try to incorporate at least one or two words from the Word Bank to the right in your review of the play.

> **Word Bank**

These words may be helpful in writing a review of *The Diary of Anne Frank*:

convincingly
crucial
enhanced
exceeding
inevitable
motivations
participation
psychological
transitions

from *Anne Frank: The Diary of a Young Girl*

Connect to the Diary

Many young people record their day-to-day experiences in a diary or journal. What kinds of things do you, or would you, write in your own diary?

List Make a list of the topics you might write about in a diary. What would your diary tell readers about you and your world if they had the opportunity to read it?

Build Background

Anne Frank recorded her daily life in a diary from June 1942 to July 1944. You are about to read two entries from her diary—one from before she went into hiding and another just one month before the Nazis found her family.

- During the Holocaust, two million Jewish children died.

- Both Anne and her sister Margot died of typhoid fever in the Bergen-Belsen concentration camp in Germany.

- Bergen-Belsen was liberated by British troops on April 15, 1945, just weeks after the Frank sisters died.

Vocabulary

melancholy (mel′ən kol′ ē) *adj.* sadly thoughtful (p. 856). *The girl's writing was characterized by a melancholy tone.*

superficial (soo pər fish′ əl) *adj.* lacking deep meaning; shallow; unimportant or unnecessary (p. 859). *Skimming the selection gave the student only a superficial understanding of what he was reading.*

prejudice (prej′ ə dis) *n.* an opinion formed without considering all sides of a question (p. 859). *After a lifetime of having cats as pets, the boy's mother had developed a prejudice against dogs.*

perturb (pər turb′) *v.* to disturb greatly (p. 861). *The constant chatter in the Reading Room will perturb the librarian.*

Meet Anne Frank

"I want to be useful or bring enjoyment to all people, even those I've never met. I want to go on living even after my death!"

—Anne Frank

A Legacy to the World Anne Frank was a teenager in the Netherlands in 1942, when her family went into hiding to escape persecution from the Nazis. Despite her confinement, Anne had hopes and dreams and a strong desire to be a writer. She kept a diary, which today is a classic of war literature.

The Diary *The Diary of a Young Girl* was first published in 1947. It has been translated into more than fifty languages.

Anne Frank was born in 1929 and died in 1945.

Literature Online

Author Search For more about Anne Frank, go to glencoe.com and enter QuickPass code GL39770u6.

Set Purposes for Reading

BQ BIG Question

Read the excerpts from *Anne Frank: The Diary of a Young Girl* to learn how Anne finds strength from within to keep from giving up.

Learning Objectives

For pages 853–864

In studying this text, you will focus on the following objectives:

Literary Study: Analyzing voice.

Reading: Questioning.

Literary Element | Voice

In literature, **voice** refers to an author's use of language that allows the reader to "hear" a distinctive personality. An author's choice of sentence structure, words, and tone all help to create a memorable voice.

Understanding the choices an author makes in his or her writing is important. Some writers rely on long sentences and sophisticated words, creating formal voices. Other writers prefer short sentences and ordinary words, making for conversational voices.

As you read, pay attention to the elements of sentence structure, word choice, and tone. Think about how they contribute to Anne's voice as a writer.

Reading Strategy | Question

Being an active reader involves asking questions as you read. When you **question** a text, you ask whether certain information is important or whether you understand what you've read.

Questioning is important to intelligent reading. Asking questions helps you increase your understanding of a selection. It also helps you remember it better.

When you question, you

- pause to ask yourself about confusing or difficult parts of the text

- read carefully and look for clues or answers that clear up your confusion

As you read, think of questions to ask yourself about the diary. Keep track of your questions and any answers or clues you may discover later in the text. You may find it helpful to use a graphic organizer like the one below.

TRY IT

Question With a classmate, take turns giving directions to your home or another location, like the local mall or the library. While you listen, question your partner to make sure you understand all the directions and could find the place.

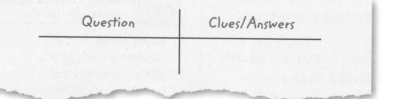

Question	Clues/Answers

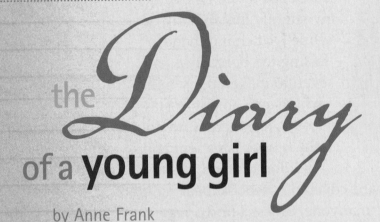

from ANNE FRANK:

the *Diary* of a **young girl**

by Anne Frank

Saturday, 20 June, **1942**

I haven't written for a few days, because I wanted first of all to think about my diary. It's an odd idea for someone like me to keep a diary; not only because I have never done so before, but because it seems to me that neither I—nor for that matter anyone else—will be interested in the unbosomings[1] of a thirteen-year-old schoolgirl.

---

1 *Unbosomings* are Anne's expressions, in her diary, of her most personal thoughts and feelings; in these writings, she "gets things off her chest."

Still, what does that matter? I want to write, but more than that, I want to bring out all kinds of things that lie buried deep in my heart.

There is a saying that "paper is more patient than man"; it came back to me on one of my slightly **melancholy** days, while I sat chin in hand, feeling too bored and limp even to make up my mind whether to go out or stay at home. Yes, there is no doubt that paper is patient and as I don't intend to show this cardboard-covered notebook, bearing the proud name of "diary," to anyone, unless I find a real friend, boy or girl, probably nobody cares. And now I come to the root of the matter, the reason for my starting a diary: it is that I have no such real friend.

Let me put it more clearly, since no one will believe that a girl of thirteen feels herself quite alone in the world, nor is it so. I have darling parents and a sister of sixteen. I know about thirty people whom one might call friends—I have strings of boy friends, anxious to catch a glimpse of me and who, failing that, peep at me through mirrors in class. I have relations, aunts and uncles, who are darlings too, a good home, no—I don't seem to lack anything. But it's the same with all my friends, just fun and joking, nothing more. I can never bring myself to talk of anything outside the common round. We don't seem to be able to get any closer, that is the root of the trouble. Perhaps I lack confidence, but anyway, there it is, a stubborn fact and I don't seem to be able to do anything about it.

Voice What is Anne's tone, or attitude, here? How does she show that her feelings are at odds with the facts?

Question You may be unfamiliar with the phrase "common round." What clues can you find in the surrounding text that will help you figure out its meaning?

---

2 *Enhance* (en hans′) means "to make greater."

Vocabulary

melancholy (mel′ ən kol′ ē) *adj.* sadly thoughtful

Hence, this diary. In order to enhance[2] in my mind's eye the picture of the friend for whom I have waited so long, I don't want to set down a series of bald facts in a diary like most people do, but I want this diary itself to be my friend, and I shall call my friend Kitty. No one will grasp what I'm talking about if I begin my letters to Kitty just out of the blue, so, albeit[3] unwillingly, I will start by sketching in brief the story of my life.

My father was thirty-six when he married my mother, who was then twenty-five. My sister Margot was born in 1926 in Frankfort-on-Main, I followed on June 12, 1929, and, as we are Jewish, we emigrated to Holland in 1933, where my father was appointed Managing Director of Travies N.V. This firm is in close relationship with the firm of Kolen & Co. in the same building, of which my father is a partner.

The rest of our family, however, felt the full impact of Hitler's anti-Jewish laws,[4] so life was filled with anxiety. In 1938 after the pogroms,[5] my two uncles (my mother's brothers) escaped to the U.S.A. My old grandmother came to us, she was then seventy-three. After May 1940 good times rapidly fled: first the war, then the capitulation,[6] followed by the arrival of the Germans, which is when the sufferings of us Jews really began. Anti-Jewish decrees followed each other in quick succession. Jews must wear a yellow star, Jews must hand in their bicycles, Jews are banned[7] from trams and are forbidden to drive. Jews are only allowed to do their shopping between three and five o'clock and then only in shops which bear the

Margot and Anne Frank in 1933.

3 **Albeit** is another way of saying "although" or "even if."

4 An **impact** is a strong effect. Anti-Jewish feelings increased sharply in Germany during the early 1930s, and many Jews left the country after Hitler came to power in 1933.

5 **Pogroms** (pō gromz′) were organized efforts to persecute and kill Jews. The Netherlands (also called Holland) tried to stay neutral early in the war, but Germany invaded the nation.

6 The surrender, or **capitulation** (kə pich′ ə lā′ shən), of the Dutch army came on May 14, 1940.

7 **Banned** means "outlawed or prohibited."

placard "Jewish shop." Jews must be indoors by eight o'clock and cannot even sit in their own gardens after that hour. Jews are forbidden to visit theaters, cinemas, and other places of entertainment. Jews may not take part in public sports. Swimming baths, tennis courts, hockey fields, and other sports grounds are all prohibited to them. Jews may not visit Christians. Jews must go to Jewish schools, and many more restrictions of a similar kind.

So we could not do this and were forbidden to do that. But life went on in spite of it all. Jopie[8] used to say to me, "You're scared to do anything, because it may be forbidden." Our freedom was strictly limited. Yet things were still bearable.

Granny died in January 1942; no one will ever know how much she is present in my thoughts and how much I love her still.

Anne in 1935.

In 1934 I went to school at the Montessori[9] Kindergarten and continued there. It was at the end of the school year, I was in form 6B, when I had to say good-bye to Mrs. K. We both wept, it was very sad. In 1941 I went, with my sister Margot, to the Jewish Secondary School, she into the fourth form and I into the first.

So far everything is all right with the four of us and here I come to the present day.

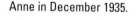

Anne in December 1935.

8 Anne's best friend was **Jopie deWaal** (yo′ pē də väl′).

9 A **Montessori** (mon′ tə sôr′ ē) school is a type of private school that encourages students to act, think, and speak freely.

Saturday, 15 July, **1944**

Dear kitty,

We have had a book from the library with the challenging title of: *What Do You Think of the Modern Young Girl?* I want to talk about this subject today.

The author of this book criticizes "the youth of today" from top to toe, without, however, condemning the whole of the young brigade as "incapable of anything good." On the contrary, she is rather of the opinion that if young people wished, they have it in their hands to make a bigger, more beautiful and better world, but that they occupy themselves with **superficial** things, without giving a thought to real beauty.

In some passages the writer gave me very much the feeling she was directing her criticism at me, and that's why I want to lay myself completely bare to you for once and defend myself against this attack.

I have one outstanding trait in my character, which must strike anyone who knows me for any length of time, and that is my knowledge of myself. I can watch myself and my actions, just like an outsider. The Anne of every day I can face entirely without **prejudice,** without making excuses for her, and watch what's good and what's bad about her. This "self-consciousness" haunts me, and every time I open my mouth I know as soon as I've spoken whether "that ought to have been different" or "that was right as it was." There are so many things about myself that I condemn; I couldn't begin to name them all. I understand more and more how true Daddy's words were when he said: "All children must look after their own upbringing."

Question Who is Kitty, and why is Anne addressing her diary to this person?

Anne in 1936.

Vocabulary

superficial (sōō pər fish′əl) *adj.* lacking deep meaning; shallow; unimportant or unnecessary

prejudice (prej′ə dis) *n.* an opinion formed without considering all sides of a question

Parents can only give good advice or put them on the right paths, but the final forming of a person's character lies in their own hands.

In addition to this, I have lots of courage, I always feel so strong and as if I can bear a great deal, I feel so free and so young! I was glad when I first realized it, because I don't think I shall easily bow down before the blows that inevitably come to everyone.

But I've talked about these things so often before. Now I want to come to the chapter of "Daddy and Mummy don't understand me." Daddy and Mummy have always thoroughly spoiled me, were sweet to me, defended me, and have done all that parents could do. And yet I've felt so terribly lonely for a long time, so left out, neglected, and misunderstood. Daddy tried all he could to check my rebellious spirit, but it was no use, I have cured myself, by seeing for myself what was wrong in my behavior and keeping it before my eyes.

How is it that Daddy was never any support to me in my struggle, why did he completely miss the mark when he wanted to offer me a helping hand? Daddy tried the wrong methods, he always talked to me as a child who was going through difficult phases. It sounds crazy, because Daddy's the only one who has always taken me into his confidence, and no one but Daddy has given me the feeling that I'm sensible. But there's one thing he's omitted: you see, he hasn't realized that for me the fight to get on top was more important than all else. I didn't want to hear about "symptoms of your age," or "other girls," or "it wears off by itself"; I didn't want to be treated as a girl-like-all-others, but as Anne-on-her-own-merits. Pim[10] didn't understand that. For that matter, I can't confide in anyone, unless they tell me a lot about themselves, and as I know very little

Anne in 1937.

Question Why does Anne feel she can't confide in anyone? Give details from the text.

___
10 *Pim* was a nickname Anne gave her father.

about Pim, I don't feel that I can tread upon more intimate ground with him. Pim always takes up the older, fatherly attitude, tells me that he too has had similar passing tendencies. But still he's not able to feel with me like a friend, however hard he tries. These things have made me never mention my views on life nor my well-considered theories to anyone but my diary and, occasionally, to Margot. I concealed from Daddy everything that **perturbed** me; I never shared my ideals[11] with him. I was aware of the fact that I was pushing him away from me.

I couldn't do anything else. I have acted entirely according to my feelings, but I have acted in the way that was best for my peace of mind. Because I should completely lose my repose[12] and self-confidence, which I have built up so shakily, if, at this stage, I were to accept criticisms of my half-completed task. And I can't do that even from Pim, although it sounds very hard, for not only have I not shared my secret thoughts with Pim but I have often pushed him even further from me, by my irritability.

This is a point that I think a lot about: why is it that Pim annoys me? So much so that I can hardly bear him teaching me, that his affectionate ways strike me as being put on, that I want to be left in peace and would really prefer it if he dropped me a bit, until I felt more certain in my attitude towards him. Because I still have a gnawing feeling of guilt over that horrible letter that I dared to write him when I was so wound up. Oh, how hard it is to be really strong and brave in every way!

Anne in 1938.

---

11 People's **ideals** involve the standards of excellence or perfection they believe in.

12 Anne's **repose** was her calm, relaxed manner.

Yet this was not my greatest disappointment; no, I ponder[13] far more over Peter[14] than Daddy. I know very well that I conquered him instead of he conquering me. I created an image of him in my mind, pictured him as a quiet, sensitive, lovable boy, who needed affection and friendship. I needed a living person to whom I could pour out my heart; I wanted a friend who'd help to put me on the right road. I achieved what I wanted, and slowly but surely, I drew him towards me. Finally, when I had made him feel friendly, it automatically developed into an intimacy which, on second thought, I don't think I ought to have allowed.

We talked about the most private things, and yet up till now we have never touched on those things that filled, and still fill, my heart and soul. I still don't know quite what to make of Peter, is he superficial, or does he still feel shy, even of me? But dropping that, I committed one error in my desire to make a real friendship: I switched over and tried to get at him by developing it into a more intimate relation, whereas I should have explored all other possibilities. He longs to be loved and I can see that he's beginning to be more and more in love with me. He gets satisfaction out of our meetings, whereas they just have the effect of making me want to try it out with him again. And yet I don't seem able to touch on the subjects that I'm so longing to bring out into the daylight. I drew Peter towards me, far more than he realizes. Now he clings to me, and for the time being, I don't see any way of shaking him off and putting him on his own feet. When I realized that he could not be a friend for my understanding, I thought I would at least try to lift him up out of his narrow-mindedness and make him do something with his youth.

"For in its innermost depths youth is lonelier than old age." I read this saying in some book and I've always remembered it, and found it to be true. Is it true then that grown-ups have a more difficult time here than we do? No. I know it isn't. Older people have formed

Question What is it about Peter that disappoints Anne?

Anne in 1940.

---

13 To **ponder** (pon'dər) is to think over carefully.

14 **Peter Van Daan** (fän dän) and his parents lived in hiding with the Franks. Peter and Margot were closer in age, but Peter and Anne became closer friends.

their opinions about everything, and don't waver[15] before they act. It's twice as hard for us young ones to hold our ground, and maintain our opinions, in a time when all ideals are being shattered and destroyed, when people are showing their worst side, and do not know whether to believe in truth and right and God.

Anyone who claims that the older ones have a more difficult time here certainly doesn't realize to what extent our problems weigh down on us, problems for which we are probably much too young, but which thrust themselves upon us continually, until, after a long time, we think we've found a solution, but the solution doesn't seem able to resist the facts which reduce it to nothing again. That's the difficulty in these times: ideals, dreams, and cherished hopes rise within us, only to meet the horrible truth and be shattered.

It's really a wonder that I haven't dropped all my ideals, because they seem so absurd[16] and impossible to carry out. Yet I keep them, because in spite of everything I still believe that people are really good at heart. I simply can't build up my hopes on a foundation consisting of confusion, misery, and death. I see the world gradually being turned into a wilderness, I hear the ever approaching thunder, which will destroy us too, I can feel the sufferings of millions and yet, if I look up into the heavens, I think that it will all come right, that this cruelty too will end, and that peace and tranquility[17] will return again.

In the meantime, I must uphold my ideals, for perhaps the time will come when I shall be able to carry them out.

Yours, Anne

Statue of Anne Frank. Mari Andriessen. Westermarkt, Amsterdam.

BQ **BIG Question**
How does Anne keep from giving up?

Voice How does Anne's voice change from the 1942 entry to the one from 1944? What elements are different?

---

15 When people *waver* (wā′ vər) before they act, they become uncertain. They falter.

16 *Absurd* means "silly" or "ridiculous."

17 *Tranquility* (trang kwil′ ə tē) means "the state or quality of being calm and free from disturbance."

After You Read

Respond and Think Critically

1. Why does Anne think that youth is lonelier than old age?
   [Recall and Identify]

2. What factors in Anne's life probably influence this belief about youth? **[Interpret]**

3. What can you infer about Anne from her desire to "shake off" Peter? **[Infer]**

4. **Literary Element** Voice Describe Anne's voice in these two diary entries. Which element—sentence structure, word choice, or tone—most clearly reveals her personality? **[Analyze]**

5. **Reading Strategy** Question Anne refers to criticisms of her "half-completed task." What do you think it is? What clues can you find in the text? **[Draw Conclusions]**

6. **BQ** BIG Question Anne finds the strength to keep going despite living in dangerous times. What would you do if you were trapped in a hopeless situation? How you would find strength? **[Connect]**

Vocabulary Practice

Respond to these questions.

1. Who would you more likely describe as **melancholy**—someone thinking about an upsetting event or a person celebrating his or her birthday?

2. Who would you describe as **superficial**—a person who takes time to get to know someone or one who judges people on appearances?

3. How would you describe **prejudice**—an opinion formed without any prior knowledge or an idea formed through research and careful thought?

4. How would you **perturb** somebody—by complimenting the person or by mocking him or her?

Writing

Write a Journal Entry Think about the ways your life has changed in the past couple of years. In what ways is being a teenager different from being a child? Write a journal entry reflecting on how you sort through your feelings about adolescence.

TIP

Interpreting
Here are some tips to help you interpret. Remember when you interpret, you use your own knowledge and understanding to decide what the events or ideas in a selection mean.

- Recall what Anne says about youth being a lonely time.

- Think about what you already know that you can relate to Anne's life.

- Combine details in the text with your experience to form an understanding of Anne's ideas.

FOLDABLES **Study Organizer** Keep track of your ideas about the **BIG Question** in your unit Foldable.

 Literature Online

Selection Resources
For Selection Quizzes, eFlashcards, and Reading-Writing Connection activities, go to glencoe.com and enter QuickPass code GL39770u6.

from **SKY** Hanneke Ippisch

Jefferson Cup Award

Learning Objectives

For pages 865–870

In studying this text, you will focus on the following objective:

Reading: Drawing conclusions about author's perspective.

Set a Purpose for Reading

Read to learn historical facts about the time period during which Anne Frank wrote her diary.

Build Background

Hanneke Ippisch was born in Holland in 1925. At the age of 17, she joined a secret group—known as the Resistance, or "underground"—to help Jews escape the Nazis.

Reading Strategy Draw Conclusions About Author's Perspective

To draw conclusions about **author's perspective**, first look for details that reveal the author's ideas. Then combine these details with your own knowledge to reach a conclusion—a general understanding about the author's viewpoint. As you read, use a chart like the one below to take notes on how the author views the events that are happening around her.

Details from Event	Author's Perspective

One night when I came home from Amsterdam during a break from my schooling, I once again overheard a conversation in my father's study, this one between him and an older woman. They were whispering, and I picked up the word "underground." Then I knew that my father was the kind of man who would be involved in the Resistance, and it made me feel very good. When the meeting ended and the woman left, I secretly followed her in the dark to her house. Maybe this was my chance to work against the enemy.

She lived across a bridge, on the other side of town, in a simple room behind a small vegetable store. I knocked on her door. When she opened it just a crack, I introduced myself, and she let me in.

I told her I wanted to join the underground forces. She looked at me and said, "I want you to go back to your studies and think about it for a long time. There is nothing adventurous or romantic about working against the enemy—it is incredibly hard work. Your life would not be yours anymore. Go back to your studies and maybe forget about it. You are very young." I left disappointed, her words resonating[1] in my mind, and returned to Amsterdam and my studies.

The situation became more grave[2] as the war continued. We students in Amsterdam heard stories about incidents involving not only Jewish people, but also about students being taken to Germany against their will, and about the executions of political leaders in Holland.

About three months after my first conversation with the older woman in the vegetable store, I went back to her and told her that there was no doubt in my mind, I still wanted to join the underground.

"Very well," she said. "Tomorrow you will meet Piet in the square in front of the Protestant Church at exactly nine A.M. He will wear a brown wool hat and a gray raincoat. He will have a newspaper under his right arm and a shopping basket in his left hand. You will introduce yourself as Ellie. Good luck and be careful. Do not ever talk about what you are doing, including to your own family."

After hearing those simple words, I left her. I did not sleep very well that night. I was repeating softly the things the old woman had told me: Nine A.M. in front of the Protestant Church, gray raincoat, brown hat, newspaper, shopping basket, Piet. Nine A.M. shopping basket, brown hat, Protestant Church, nine A.M. . . . Finally I fell asleep, but woke up early and paced the floor until it was time to go. I carried my books and my tennis racket with me, so my family would think I was going back to school.

Full of anticipation[3] and a little bit nervous, I headed for the square and spotted Piet immediately. He was indeed in the right place at the right time, wearing a gray raincoat, a brown hat, holding a newspaper under his right arm and a shopping basket in his left hand. He gave me my first assignment: I was to bring some identification papers and food coupons[4] to a Jewish family hidden in an old house in the town of Haarlem. He also handed me a falsified I.D.: My new name was Ellie Van Dyk.

---

1 Here, **resonating** (rez´ə nāt´ing) means "echoing; repeating."

2 Here, **grave** (grāv) means "very serious; likely to produce harm or danger."

3 **Anticipation** (an tis´ə pā´shən) means "the act of looking forward to; expectation."

4 There were food shortages because the war limited production and imports. **Food coupons** were, in effect, permission slips for buying food.

On that day my life changed completely. I rarely attended classes anymore. At night I was told where to meet my contact the next morning to receive new instructions, and which code words to use when approaching him or her. I was given a different assignment each day transporting Jewish people from one place to another, safer spot. Often we had to separate the children from their parents. I traveled with the children on trains and boats to the countryside, to the safer hiding places on farms, where the Germans rarely went. Quite a few of those children—unaware of their families' fate—stayed in the countryside until the end of the war in 1945. Many farmers' families "adopted" the Jewish children and treated them as their own. They went to school with the other children in the villages.

One problem was that clothing was getting scarce and the winter always seemed to get colder. Jewish people going into hiding ("underwater," as we called it) had to take the star off their coats. But cloth fades, and most old overcoats—which were so necessary during the cold winters—showed an obvious unfaded star-shaped spot. We always feared that star-shaped spot would be a dead giveaway and just hoped that it would not be noticed. Some women ingeniously took material from the inside hem of the old coats and sewed

The Dutch invasion by Nazi troops circa 1940. Nazi troops and armored divisions driving along a main street in Amsterdam, on a route from Central Station past the queen's palace.

pockets over the faded spot. Others wore wool scarves over their coats, while still others held a newspaper to hide the spot. Then there were people who did not take any of these precautions[5] and didn't get caught. Several times, however, while walking or traveling with us, Jews were arrested by some observant[6] German. If that happened, we had to pretend we did not know the arrested person. Other Resistance workers told me about tragic incidents,[7] but fortunately none of my Jewish traveling companions were ever caught.

Traveling to the Countryside, 1943

It was early in the morning and I dressed quickly and warmly. At seven A.M. I had to meet a Jewish

---

5 **Precautions** (pri kô´shənz) are actions taken to prevent difficulty before it happens.

6 **Observant** (əb zur´vənt) means "quick to notice or observe; alert; watchful."

7 Ippisch is probably referring to times when Jews were caught and killed on the spot.

couple, musicians who had played in the symphony in Amsterdam. I was to transport them to a village in the province of Friesland, where they were to be met and taken to a safe place on a farm.

When I arrived at the given address, I knocked three times hard and twice softly (a code knock) on the door. A smiling Dutch woman opened the door and let me in. "I will miss them," she said. "They have been good company for my husband and me, but there are too many German soldiers around lately walking the streets. It is better for our guests to move on." As she spoke I followed her up two flights of stairs, through a linen closet, which had a small door inside, and into a room, where the curtains in front of the windows were closed. A Jewish man and woman, both pale and nervous, were waiting.

"Hello," I said. "Are you ready to go?" They embraced their Dutch hostess and followed me through the linen closet, down the stairs, and out into the street. Each was carrying a small shopping basket in which they had packed all their belongings.

I walked ahead, pretending not to know them, and they followed. The wind was blowing hard, and the man's hat blew off. He had lots of grayish-black, curly, rather long hair, and the wind blew his hair high around his head. He ran after his hat, grabbed it, and put it firmly on his head, holding it with one hand so he wouldn't lose it again.

We rode a trolley car[8] to the Central Station, where I went to a ticket window and bought three round-trip tickets (the couple would only travel one way, but in case of a question they could say they were visiting a friend). I quickly handed their tickets to them, and we went to a platform where a train was waiting to take us to the northern part of the province of North Holland.

When we boarded the train we saw several compartments occupied by German officers. We walked through the corridors and finally found a compartment with only two older women sitting in it. The Jewish couple, immediately after sitting down, closed their eyes and pretended they were asleep. Suddenly a German officer opened the door of the compartment and hollered, "I.D. *bitte.*" ("I.D. please.") All of us pulled out our I.D. cards, he looked at them and looked at us, and compared photos with faces, and looked again. Though shaky inside, I pretended to be calm. The Jewish couple, however, seemed visibly shaken. How could the officer not detect our fear?

After what seemed an eternity, the German handed our I.D. cards back to us and said with a smile, "*Danke schön und gute Reise.*" ("Thank you very much and have a good trip.")

---

8 A *trolley car* runs along tracks laid in the street and is powered by electricity.

This is a typical passenger train of the kind used throughout Europe in the early 1940s.

View the Photograph How would you have felt if you were trying to escape while sharing a train with enemy soldiers?

Neither he nor the two older women in our compartment had noticed anything amiss.[9]

After about one hour the train stopped in the middle of some meadows. Passengers leaned out of the windows to see why the train had stopped. German soldiers were hollering and shouting commands. We heard that a small bridge had been slightly damaged, and the train could not safely cross it. We had to get out of the train and carefully walk, one after the other, over the damaged bridge.

All three of us dreaded[10] the watchful eyes of the German soldiers, but miraculously we crossed the bridge and boarded a waiting train on the other side without any problems.

We finally reached Enkhuizen, an ancient harbor town, where the brisk wind from the sea was blowing so hard that we had to hold on to hats, skirts, and scarves. We walked with farmers and their families to the ferry boat. The farmers were holding baskets full of chickens, purchased at the open-air market.

---

9 **Amiss** (ə mis´) means "wrong; not as it should be."

10 **Dreaded** (dred´ed) means "feared greatly."

Many fishermen who made the trip across the inland sea to sell fish at the Enkhuizen market walked toward the boat, their baskets now filled with fresh produce to bring home.

We boarded the ferry boat and settled down rather close to each other, but not together. We ate some pieces of bread, bought some imitation coffee, then closed our eyes. The wind was blowing hard, and the ferry boat bounced on the waves. The Jewish woman began to look gray-green, but never spoke. The passage on the inland sea was uneventful, and after two hours we reached the northeast coast of Holland.

We stepped ashore, again under the watchful eyes of German officers, and went to a small waiting room. I wore a bright blue scarf and red mittens and was approached by a young man who wore a red scarf and blue wool gloves.

The young man said, "Did you have a good trip? I am so happy to see you again. Come on, and we will have some coffee."

I told him, "The trip was good, and I brought my aunt and uncle with me, so they can see a little bit of the countryside."

"Great!" he said. "You are very welcome."

After our coffee, the four of us left the small waiting room and climbed on a farm cart pulled by a horse. After about fifteen minutes of silent travel, the young man looked around. Nobody was in sight, and he stopped. He let me off the cart and then continued on with the Jewish couple.

I returned to the ferry boat on foot and started my long journey back to Amsterdam, very relieved that all had gone well that day. ❧

Respond and Think Critically

1. Write a brief summary of the main events in this excerpt. For help in writing a summary, see page 185. [Summarize]

2. When Ippisch followed the older woman to her house, the woman cautioned Ippisch about joining the Resistance. Why did the woman respond this way? [Interpret]

3. Why was it important to get the Jews out of Amsterdam and into more rural areas? [Infer]

4. **Text-to-Text** What do you think Anne Frank and Hanneke Ippisch might have said to each other if they had met? [Connect]

5. **Reading Strategy** Draw Conclusions About Author's Perspective Why do you think Ippisch decided to join the Resistance? [Conclude]

6. **BQ** BIG Question How was Ippisch able to live such a dangerous life without giving up, even when she knew that she was up against so much? [Evaluate]

Set a Purpose for Reading

Read to discover how architects are making skyscrapers safer and stronger.

Preview the Article

1. Read the **title** and the **deck**, or the sentence below the title. What topics will be covered in the article?

2. Look at the **graphic images** and read the **captions**. What does this information tell you about the buildings described in the article?

Reading Skill

Analyze Text Features

To **analyze text features,** look for captions, images, and headings and determine how they help your understanding of the text. As you read, note what new information each feature provides.

TIME

STANDING TALL

Architects and engineers are working with new designs and materials that can make future skyscrapers sturdier and safer.

By **MICHAEL DOLAN**

The idea of building a tower to touch the sky goes back thousands of years. And during the past century, concrete, steel, and other materials have made it possible for architects and engineers to design and build structures that stand a quarter-mile high. These buildings are a tribute[1] to humankind's need to both test a structure's limits and solve problems such as overcrowding in cities.

But after September 11, 2001, skyscrapers are being seen in a whole new way. Terrorists hijacked[2] and crashed two planes into New York City's tallest buildings, causing the twin towers of the World Trade Center to collapse.[3] Skyscrapers around the world suddenly gained a new label: target.

---

1 Here, **tribute** (trib′ ūt) means "evidence of some good quality."

2 When a plane is **hijacked,** one or more people take control of it by force.

3 **Collapse** (kə laps′) means "to fall apart, cave in, or break down."

On September 11, 2001, terrorists crashed two planes into the twin towers of New York City's World Trade Center (two tallest buildings in center of photo), causing both to collapse.

Farrell Grehan/Corbis

That new label has inspired builders to work on a new goal—creating the safest tall building in the world. The smartest minds in architecture and structural engineering are working together to figure out how to construct a building that could survive threats of terrorism[4] and natural disasters.

One material that could help architects and engineers is concrete. New types of concrete are being developed to help resist the force of bomb blasts and the 2,000°F temperatures of jet fuel fires. For

example, one new type of concrete contains pieces of recycled stainless steel. The stainless steel increases the concrete's strength and its ability to stand up to a bomb blast or similar forces.

A skyscraper made with steel-supported concrete wouldn't shatter as much when attacked. Instead its concrete would cling together in larger chunks, making it less likely to collapse. Steel-mesh concrete was originally used as a way to keep tall buildings safe in parts of the world where earthquakes occur frequently. Now engineers are thinking

---

4 **Terrorism** is the use of violence, especially against non-military civilian targets, to try to make people or governments meet certain demands.

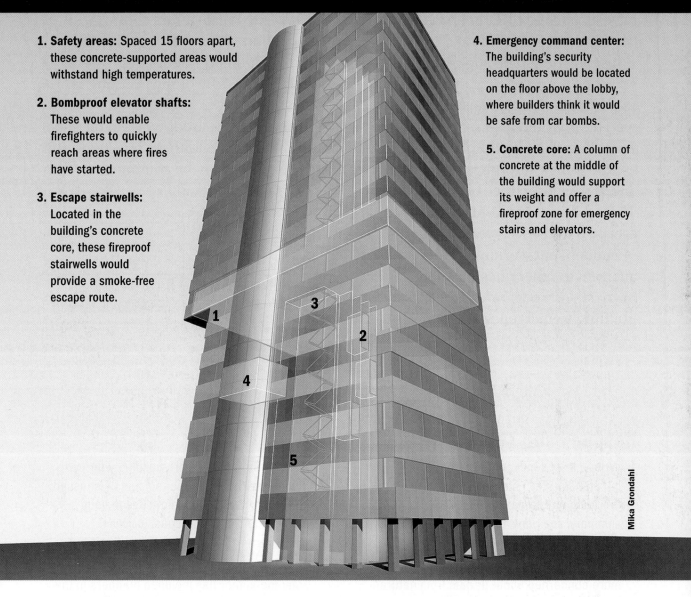

Skyscraper Self-defense Builders are exploring new ways to make office workers feel safe. Some ideas include steel-supported concrete, escape routes that could withstand[5] bomb blasts, safety floors where people could wait out a fire, and laser machines that could identify dangerous chemicals.

1. **Safety areas:** Spaced 15 floors apart, these concrete-supported areas would withstand high temperatures.

2. **Bombproof elevator shafts:** These would enable firefighters to quickly reach areas where fires have started.

3. **Escape stairwells:** Located in the building's concrete core, these fireproof stairwells would provide a smoke-free escape route.

4. **Emergency command center:** The building's security headquarters would be located on the floor above the lobby, where builders think it would be safe from car bombs.

5. **Concrete core:** A column of concrete at the middle of the building would support its weight and offer a fireproof zone for emergency stairs and elevators.

Mika Grondahl

of using this same material in all skyscrapers to protect against the force of airplane crashes and the fires they cause.

In addition to fire protection, various forms of concrete could make a skyscraper stronger and more stable.[6] Whereas the World Trade Center towers got most of their support from

---

5 To **withstand** something is to resist the effects of it or stand up against it.

6 Here, **stable** (stā′ bəl) means "firm and steady; long-lasting."

steel columns around the outside of the buildings, many engineers now think every future skyscraper should have a concrete core that runs down the center of the building.

Just as your spine supports much of your body, a concrete core would serve as a building's spine and support its weight. It would also serve as a safety zone. Designers could place emergency escape routes and fireproof elevators and stairwells in the concrete core. These features could help more people escape if a disaster were to occur.

Builders are working hard to find answers to other questions that could make skyscrapers safer. Could a building's emergency staff use sensitive laser machines to find harmful chemical materials before they even reach the building? Is it possible to create a fireproof evacuation system[7] that could help people on the top floors find safety when the middle of the building is in flames?

There's still a lot of work to be done, but the answers to these questions and many others may be coming soon to a skyscraper near you. 🐚

---

7 An **evacuation system** is a way to get people out of a building when there is an emergency. To **evacuate** is to clear out, or leave.

Respond and Think Critically

1. Write a brief summary of the main ideas in "Standing Tall" before you answer the following questions. For help on writing a summary, see page 185. [Summarize]

2. Based on the description of the designs for new skyscrapers, do you think builders are more concerned about threats from natural disasters or terrorist attacks? Explain. [Infer]

3. "Standing Tall" discusses how to make new skyscrapers safer. Do you think the technologies described in the article could be applied to existing skyscrapers? Why or why not? [Evaluate]

4. **Text-to-Self** If you were building your own home, are there any technologies discussed in the article that you might use in your design? Explain your ideas. [Connect]

5. Reading Skill Analyze Text Features Look at the labeled diagram on page 873. Explain why the author has included numbers in this diagram. In what way do they help you understand the information? [Analyze]

6. BQ BIG Question How might architects have "given up" after September 11, 2001? How does this article support the conclusion that they have not given up? [Draw Conclusions]

Vocabulary Workshop

Word Origins

Connection to Literature

"Saturday, 20 June, 1942

I haven't written for a few days, because I wanted first of all to think about my diary."

—Anne Frank, from *Anne Frank: The Diary of a Young Girl*

Knowing a word's history—or **etymology**—can help you understand when the word was first used and how its meaning has developed over time. The English language includes many words from Greek, Roman, and Anglo-Saxon mythology. For example, the word *Saturday* stems from Saturn, the Roman god of agriculture. In ancient Rome, this god's festival, the Saturnalia, was among the most important celebrations of the year. Today, *Saturday* refers to the seventh day of the week, a time often spent relaxing and having fun. Similarly, the word *Tuesday* comes from the word *Tiw*, the god of war in Anglo-Saxon mythology.

This chart shows the mythological origins of several English words.

Word	Origin	Meaning Today
fatal *(adj.)*	from the Fates, classical goddesses who determine the course of human life	something that causes death or destruction
museum *(n.)*	from the Muses, the Greek goddesses of literature and the arts	a place where valuable objects are shown
titanic *(adj.)*	from the Titans, giants of Greek mythology	large, enormous
volcanic *(adj.)*	from Vulcan, the Roman god of fire and metalworking	relating to or produced by a volcano

TRY IT: Using a dictionary, find the etymology for each of these words from mythology. On a separate sheet of paper, write the word's origin and meaning.

1. atlas
2. fury
3. jovial
4. mentor

Learning Objectives

For page 875

In this workshop, you will focus on the following objective:

Vocabulary: Understanding word origins.

Tip

Vocabulary Terms The origins of a word are usually presented in brackets within its dictionary entry.

Test-taking Tip Always apply your knowledge of word history when you encounter unfamiliar words while reading passages or choosing responses on a multiple-choice test.

 Literature Online

Vocabulary For more vocabulary practice, go to glencoe.com and enter QuickPass code GL39770u6.

Comparing Literature

Mother to Son and
Speech to the Young:
Speech to the Progress-Toward

BQ BIG Question

As you read the paired selections, ask yourself how the poems advise you to overcome difficulties and keep from giving up.

Literary Element Speaker

You remember that the speaker is the voice that communicates a poem's ideas, actions, descriptions, and feelings, similar to the narrator in fiction. Often, the speaker is unknown, but sometimes the speaker has a specific identity, like a character in a story. As you read each poem, analyze how the poet's choice of speaker contributes to the poem's overall mood and meaning.

Reading Skill Compare and Contrast

When you compare and contrast, you look for similarities and differences. For example, imagine you are deciding which movie you want to see. You might consider how the things that interest you about each movie are alike and how they are different.

You can understand poetry better when you compare how poets use literary elements such as the speaker of a poem. On the following pages you'll compare and contrast the speakers of "Mother to Son" and "Speech to the Young: Speech to the Progress-Toward." Use a comparison chart like the one below to keep track of details about each speaker.

Speaker	Hughes poem	Brooks poem
Character		
Mood		
Meaning		

Meet the Authors

Langston Hughes

Langston Hughes is best known for his poetry. Hughes was born in 1902 and died in 1967.

Gwendolyn Brooks

Gwendolyn Brooks, the first African American to win the Pulitzer Prize for poetry, was born in 1917 and died in 2000.

LOG ON **Literature** Online

Author Search For more about Langston Hughes and Gwendolyn Brooks, go to glencoe.com and enter QuickPass code GL39770u6.

MOTHER TO SON

Langston Hughes

Survivor, 1978. Elizabeth Catlett. Linocut, 10 7/8 x 9 7/8 in. Amistad Research Center, Tulane University, New Orleans, LA. Art ©Elizabeth Catlett/Licensed by VAGA, New York, NY.

Well, son, I'll tell you:
Life for me ain't been no crystal stair.
It's had tacks in it,
And splinters,
5 And boards torn up,
And places with no carpet on the floor—
Bare.
But all the time
I'se been a-climbin' on,
10 And reachin' landin's,
And turnin' corners,
And sometimes goin' in the dark
Where there ain't been no light.
So, boy, don't you turn back.
15 Don't you set down on the steps
'Cause you finds it kinder hard.
Don't you fall now—
For I'se still goin', honey,
I'se still climbin',
20 And life for me ain't been no crystal stair.

Comparing Literature What do lines 9 through 11 tell you about the speaker's life?

BQ ▶ **BIG Question**

For the speaker, not giving up is like what type of effort or activity?

SPEECH TO THE Young: SPEECH TO THE Progress-Toward

Woman in Calico, 1944. William H. Johnson. Oil on paperboard, 26 1/2 x 20 1/2 in. Gift of the Harmon Foundation. Smithsonian American Art Museum, Washington, DC.

View the Art Look at the art with each poem. Which piece's subject do you think better represents the speaker in the poem on its particular page? Why?

Gwendolyn Brooks

Say to them,
say to the down-keepers,
the sun-slappers,
the self-soilers,
5   the harmony-hushers,
"Even if you are not ready for day
it cannot always be night."
You will be right.
For that is the hard home-run.

10   Live not for battles won.
Live not for the-end-of-the-song.
Live in the along.

Comparing Literature The poem begins and ends with a series of repeated words. What does this repetition tell you about the speaker?

Comparing Literature

BQ BIG Question

Now use the unit Big Question to compare and contrast Hughes's and Brooks's poems. With a group of classmates discuss questions such as,

- What do each of these poems have to say about not giving up?

- How is each poem different in the way it discusses the difficulties a person faces? How is each poem similar in discussing how people can deal with difficulties?

- How could these poems help people keep going when faced with difficult times?

Support each answer with evidence from the poems.

Literary Element Speaker

Use the details you wrote in your graphic organizer to analyze the speakers in Langston Hughes's "Mother to Son" and Gwendolyn Brooks's "Speech to the Young: Speech to the Progress-Toward." With a partner, answer the following questions.

1. In what ways are the speakers different in the two poems? Think about who the speaker is in each poem—is it a specific character or an unidentified voice? Also think about who the speaker in each poem is addressing.

2. In what ways are the speakers of the two poems similar? Consider the message each speaker is trying to express and the attitude the speaker expresses toward the poem's subject.

3. How do the speakers contribute to the mood, or atmosphere, of each poem? Give examples from the poems to support your ideas.

Write to Compare

Imagine you are writing a short persuasive letter to encourage a friend not to give up on something. Use the messages and ideas from these poems to help make your point.

- Make references to what the speaker of each poem has to say about giving up.

- Explain why you think these references have meaning, and apply them to your own life, if possible.

- Try to include elements of each poem's specific style in your letter.

 Writing Tip

As you write, use direct quotes, or actual words from each poem, to help support your points.

 Literature Online

Selection Resources
For Selection Quizzes, eFlashcards, and Reading-Writing Connection activities, go to glencoe.com and enter QuickPass code GL39770u6.

Expository Essay

To get through tough times, people need strength. In this workshop, you will write an expository essay that will help you think about the Unit 6 Big Question: How Do You Keep from Giving Up?

Review the writing prompt, or assignment, below. Then read the Writing Plan. It will tell you what to do to write your expository essay.

Writing Assignment

An expository essay informs or explains or does both. Write an expository essay informing your readers about what teenagers can do to find strength to keep going when times are tough. The audience, those reading your essay, should be your classmates and teacher.

Prewrite

Think about the steps suggested by Dr. Robert Brooks in "Bouncing Back." What does he recommend? Do you know of other ways to keep going and overcome life's hurdles?

Gather Ideas

Think about the situations facing teenagers that are presented in this unit. Using prior knowledge, consider ways to deal with these troubles. With a small group, brainstorm different formats, or ways to organize, for presenting your ideas in an essay. Consider formats such as,

- ○ a step-by-step process for dealing with troubled times
- ○ a compare-and-contrast of resources that assist those in need
- ○ anecdotes that explain how or why a particular method works

Choose a Format

Look over the information you have collected and select a format for your essay. To get started, discuss your ideas with a partner.

Partner Talk With a partner, follow these steps:

1. Tell your partner what you would like to say about how teenagers can deal with tough times. Come up with a thesis, and discuss how each format could work with what you want to say.

2. Work together to write a sentence that briefly summarizes what you will discuss in your essay and how you will organize it.

I will discuss how teens can face hard times and not give up by _____, and I will present the information _____.

Writing Plan

- Present the thesis, or main idea, of the essay in the introduction.
- Organize the essay in an effective and appropriate pattern.
- Include examples to support and clarify ideas.
- Use language techniques to maintain reader interest.
- Conclude by linking back to the thesis of the essay.

🚀 Prewriting Tip

Your thesis can be stated directly or implied. For purposes of clarity, it is usually best to write it out directly to refer to as you write, even if it is only implied in your final essay.

Get Organized

Create an outline or graphic organizer that fits the format you chose. Include the introduction, body, and conclusion of the essay.

> I. Introduction
>   A. Positive attitude prevents giving up.
> II. Anecdotes of how positive thinking works
>   A. My mother
>   B. My brother
>   C. Anne Frank
> III. Conclusion

Draft

Organize your ideas and add more details to your writing. Use the following skills to develop your draft.

Get It On Paper

- Review your thesis and look at your outline or graphic organizer.

- Begin with something to interest your audience, such as an anecdote of a problem you will address. Connect it to your thesis.

- For each part of your outline, write a topic sentence that explains in what way the information can help teenagers in problem situations.

- End your essay by connecting to your thesis.

- Don't worry about spelling, grammar, or punctuation right now.

- When you're finished, read what you've written. Include more information if you need to.

Develop Your Draft

1. State your **thesis** in your introduction.

> When facing difficult situations or problems that feel overwhelming, positive thinking can help a person deal with these troubles.

2. Organize the body logically, perhaps step-by-step or in order of importance.

> But for me the strongest example of the power of a positive attitude is Anne Frank.

 Literature Online

Writing and Research For prewriting, drafting, and revising tools, go to glencoe.com and enter QuickPass code GL39770u6.

Drafting Tip

One way to elaborate on, or explain, an idea is to use an **analogy**—to compare it with something familiar. To explain how electricity moves through wires, for example, you might say it is like water moving through a hose.

TRY IT

Analyzing Cartoons
In this cartoon, why does the student hold a light bulb over her head? With a partner, discuss how she might find ideas for her essay.

3. Support and clarify your ideas with **examples**.

> Although she was always tired, she said she made sure to smile each day, which kept her mind off of how tough things were.

4. Use specific **language** that appeals to the senses.

> He realized that what he enjoyed most about basketball was sprinting down the court.

5. Refer back to your thesis in your essay's **conclusion**.

> Positive thinking helped them and it can help you too.

Apply Good Writing Traits: Ideas

Readers enjoy reading about ideas. Not only can these ideas be entertaining for them, but they can say something important and true that may stay with readers for a long time. As a writer, it's important to include ideas as you write. In this case, your ideas are your thoughts about how teenagers draw strength while facing tough situations or life struggles.

Read the sentences below from "Bouncing Back" by Jan Farrington. How do you think the author came up with her ideas?

> "Success builds on success," noted Brooks.

> "Little things don't bother me any more," Regan added. "I had to grow up pretty quick . . ."

> One of the best ways to get rid of negative emotions is to get involved in something outside yourself.

As you draft your essay, try to include new ideas that occur to you. After you finish, read your draft and ask yourself, "Have I stated my ideas clearly and organized them logically?"

Analyze a Student Model

Whenever times are tough, I recall a lesson I learned from people I've known and read about: the power of positive thinking. When facing difficult situations or problems that feel overwhelming, positive thinking can help a person deal with these troubles. Many have benefited from this healthy approach, and I'm sure it can also help teens deal with the challenges we all face.

I first learned about how useful a positive attitude could be from my mother. When she was younger, she wanted to become a nurse, but her family couldn't afford college. Instead of giving up, she worked as a secretary during the day and went to school at night. Although she was always tired, she said she made sure to smile each day, which kept her mind off of how tough things were.

For me, my brother is an even stronger reminder of the wonders of a positive attitude. When he learned he did not make the basketball team, he was angry and felt sorry for himself. But then he started focusing on the good things instead of the bad. He realized that what he enjoyed most about basketball was sprinting down the court. He tried out for the track team then, and became a star. By focusing on the positive, he found something that he enjoys and is really good at.

But for me the strongest example of the power of a positive attitude is Anne Frank. During World War II, she went into hiding with her family to escape from the Germans. They remained in a tiny, cramped attic for years. To keep up her spirits, Anne wrote in her diary. Although she faced the possibility of death daily, she never lost hope. "In spite of everything I still believe that people are really good at heart," she affirmed.

Everyone faces trouble in life, and the teen years can be especially challenging. If you ever feel like giving up, just think of my mother, my brother, and Anne Frank. Positive thinking helped them and it can help you too.

Thesis
The thesis statement is included in the introduction.

Organization
The writer uses the organizational pattern that works for the essay—in this case, organizing in the order of importance.

Supporting Examples
A specific example of how the writer's brother uses positive thinking supports the writer's idea.

Sensory Language
The phrase *tiny, cramped attic* creates a vivid image of the place Anne was living for a period of time.

Conclusion
The last paragraph links back to the thesis from the introduction.

Reading-Writing Connection Think about the writing techniques that you have just learned and try them out in an essay of your own.

One way to make your writing more interesting is to use allusion. An allusion is a reference to a well-known character, place, or situation from literature, music, art, or history.

Revise

Now it's time to revise your draft so your ideas really shine. Revising is what makes good writing great, and great writing takes work!

Peer Review Trade drafts with a partner. Use the chart below to review your partner's draft by answering the questions in the *What to do* column. Talk about your peer review after you have glanced at each other's drafts and written down the answers to the questions. Next, follow the suggestions in the *How to do it* column to revise your draft.

Revising Plan

What to do	How to do it	Example
Will readers know the main idea of your essay early on?	Clearly state your thesis in the first paragraph.	~~Positive thinking can be a good thing.~~ ₐWhen facing difficult situations or problems that feel overwhelming, positive thinking can help a person deal with these troubles.
Is the order of information clear?	Use words and phrases to show that the information is presented in order of importance. Make sure the transitions between your ideas are clear.	For me, my brother is an ~~example~~ ₐeven stronger reminder of the wonders of a positive attitude.
Are there enough specific examples to clarify and support ideas?	Include examples and explanations that help illustrate your ideas.	Although she was always tired, she ~~didn't think about~~ ₐsaid she made sure to smile each day, which kept her mind off of how tough things were.
Do your words create vivid images in readers' minds?	Replace vague language with specific sensory words.	He realized that what he enjoyed most about basketball was ~~running.~~ ₐsprinting down the court
Does your conclusion summarize your main idea?	Restate your thesis in different words in the conclusion.	If you ever feel like giving up, just think of my mother, my brother, and Anne Frank. ₐPositive thinking helped them and it can help you too.

Edit and Proofread

For your final draft, read your essay one sentence at a time. The **Editing and Proofreading Checklist** inside the back cover of this book can help you spot errors. Use this resource to help you make any necessary corrections.

Grammar Focus: Colons

Use a colon to introduce lists and long quotations (such as the opinions of authorities). Below are examples of problems with the use of colons and their solutions.

Problem: It's not clear where a list begins.

These people can all provide support grandparents, friends, and teachers.

Solution: Insert a colon at the end of the word before the list begins.

These people can all provide support: grandparents, friends, and teachers.

Problem: A long quotation has no introductory punctuation.

My mother put it this way "I had no idea how I was going to go to college, but just knew I had to find a way. I realized that if I got a job as a secretary, I could get paid well for my typing skills during the day.
I could then use the money to study for my degree in night school."

Solution: Insert a colon at the end of the word just before the quotation starts.

My mother put it this way: "I had no idea how I was going to go to college, but just knew I had to find a way. I realized that if I got a job as a secretary, I could get paid well for my typing skills during the day. I could then use the money to study for my degree in night school."

Present

It's almost time to share your writing with others. Write your essay neatly in print or cursive on a separate sheet of paper. If you have access to a computer, type your essay on the computer and check your spelling. Save your document to a disk and print it out.

Grammar Tip

Semicolons Be sure not to confuse the colon and semicolon. A semicolon is used to join the parts of a compound sentence when there is no coordinating conjunction, such as *and*. It can also be used to separate main clauses joined by a conjunctive adverb, such as *therefore*.

Presenting Tip

Make an extra copy of your essay to submit to any social service agencies in town that deal with teenage problems. They may even publish it!

Literature Online

Writing and Research For editing and publishing tools, go to glencoe.com and enter QuickPass code GL39770u6.

Speaking, Listening, and Viewing Workshop

Active Listening and Note-Taking

What Is Active Listening?

Active listening is concentrating on a speaker's message. It involves using your eyes and mind as well as your ears. Listening actively means thinking about what a person is saying and evaluating their ideas based on your own knowledge and experience. Then you share what you have heard with the speaker.

Why Is Active Listening Important?

Active listening is important because it helps you learn. By paying attention when others speak, you can find out information you might not have known. You may also learn why people believe what they do. In a small group discussion, you'll have a chance to express your own ideas as well. You may even discover that your opinions are affected once you hear something from another person's perspective.

How Do I Do It?

Taking part in a group discussion gives you a chance to practice active listening every time someone speaks. Here's what to do:

- Focus on the speaker's choice of words, tone, and pitch of voice.
- Watch the speaker's posture, gestures, and facial expressions.
- Notice the mood, or atmosphere, the speaker's presentation creates.
- Take notes on important information. Make an informal outline to organize what you hear and separate main ideas from supporting details. You might want to create a drawing, timeline, or other graphic organizer to help you clarify and remember the information.
- Write down questions and thoughts as they occur to you.

When each person is done speaking, the other members should tell the group what they thought the speaker said and ask questions for clarification. Here are some sentence frames you might consider using:

- I'm confused about _____. Will you explain that more clearly?
- I disagree with _____ because _____. Does what I said change your opinion? If so, how?
- Based on what you've said, _____ must be true. Do you agree?

Active Listening and Note-Taking Checklist

Answer the following questions to evaluate your active listening and note-taking:

- ❏ Did you identify the speaker's purpose?
- ❏ Did you understand the speaker's tone and body language?
- ❏ Did you write down the speaker's main points?
- ❏ Did you ask questions to clarify information?

LOG ON ▶ **Literature** Online

Speaking, Listening, and Viewing For project ideas, templates, and presentation tips, go to glencoe.com and enter QuickPass code GL39770u6.

Unit Challenge

Answer the Big Question

In Unit 6, you explored the Big Question through reading, writing, speaking, and listening. Now it's time for you to complete one of the Unit Challenges below with your answer to the Big Question.

HOW Do You Keep from Giving Up?

Learning Objectives

For page 887

In this assignment, you will focus on the following objectives:

Writing:
Writing a narrative poem.

Writing a persuasive ad.

Use the notes you took in your Unit 6 **Foldable** to complete the Unit Challenge you have chosen.

Before you present your Unit Challenge, be sure it meets the requirements below. Use this first plan if you choose to write a narrative poem about a person or a group of people who survived hard times.

On Your Own Activity: Write a Narrative Poem

❏ Write a narrative poem that relates an incident, event, or situation in which someone refuses to give up.

❏ Pick a speaker for your poem. Decide whether the speaker will be a disembodied voice or someone in the poem.

❏ Make sure the poem reveals your attitude about the importance of not giving up when times are tough.

❏ Use plot, detailed descriptions, figurative language, and dialogue to make your poem lively and engaging.

Use this second plan if you choose to write a newspaper ad persuading people to help a nearby community after a natural disaster.

Group Activity: Create a Newspaper Ad

❏ Clearly state your purpose in the ad—to persuade people to volunteer their time and energy to help those in need.

❏ Develop your argument by using detailed evidence to explain how the disaster has affected the community.

❏ Provide details that explain ways in which people can help.

❏ Emphasize the importance of helping others not give up.

Independent Reading

Fiction

To explore the Big Question in other works, choose one of these books from your school or local library.

A House for Mr Biswas

by V. S. Naipaul

A Hindu man tries to find a house of his own in the British colony of Trinidad in the Caribbean. In this humorous story he is forced to overcome people's prejudices against his culture to discover who he is inside and stick up for himself.

GLENCOE LITERATURE LIBRARY

The Glory Field

by Walter Dean Myers

This novel traces the lives of an African American family, beginning with the capture and enslavement of the first member in 1753. Each generation struggles against poverty and racism. But their love for one another and for their land keeps the members of the Lewis family strong.

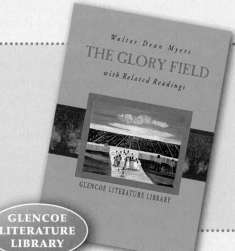

GLENCOE LITERATURE LIBRARY

Lupita Mañana

by Patricia Beatty

Lupita Torres is thirteen when she and her older brother decide to go to the United States. They need jobs there to support their widowed mother and younger siblings. But are they prepared for the dangers and difficulties of crossing a border illegally?

GLENCOE LITERATURE LIBRARY

Missing May

by Cynthia Rylant

Summer has had many homes, but when she joins her aunt and uncle, she is welcomed and deeply loved. Then Aunt May dies, and Summer and Uncle Ob must come to terms with their loss.

Nonfiction

Teens with the Courage to Give: Young People Who Triumphed Over Tragedy and Volunteered to Make a Difference

by Jackie Waldman

This book profiles thirty young people who overcame great personal odds to reach out and help others. With their stories, these teens take us to the depths of their struggles and the heights of their newfound sense of purpose and peace.

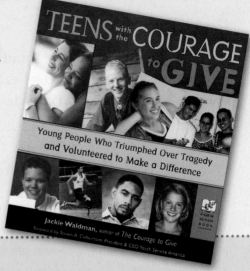

Chinese Cinderella

by Adeline Yen Mah

Adeline Yen Mah's autobiography, like the fairy tale "Cinderella," tells of a childhood dominated by a cruel stepmother. It is only when she wins a writing contest that her father finally notices Yen Mah and grants her wish to attend college. The book includes the legend of the original Chinese Cinderella.

And Still We Rise: The Trials and Triumphs of Twelve Gifted Inner-City High School Students

by Miles Corwin

Twelve seniors from an Advanced Placement English class in Los Angeles dream of going to college. This book deals with the hard realities of their lives and their struggle to achieve their dreams.

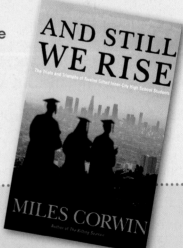

 Create a Book Cover

Create a new cover for the book you read. Your cover should be engaging and convey something important about the book. Ask a classmate who has read the book to critique the cover you created.

Assessment

Reading

In this excerpt from a play about a girl who is both blind and deaf, the girl's mother and new teacher meet each other for the first time. Read the passage and answer the questions. Write your answers on a separate sheet of paper.

---

from *The Miracle Worker,* **Act I,** by William Gibson

(. . . *The railroad sounds off left have mounted in a crescendo to a climax typical of a depot at arrival time, the lights come up on stage left, and we see a suggestion of a station. Here* ANNIE *in her smoked glasses and disarrayed by travel is waiting with her suitcase, while* JAMES *walks to meet her; she has a battered paper-bound book, which is a Perkins report, under her arm.*)

JAMES [*coolly*]: Miss Sullivan?

ANNIE [*cheerily*]: Here! At last, I've been on trains so many days I thought they must be backing up every time I dozed off—

JAMES: I'm James Keller.

ANNIE: James? (*The name stops her.*) I had a brother Jimmie. Are you Helen's?

JAMES: I'm only half a brother. You're to be her governess?

ANNIE [*lightly*]: Well. Try!

JAMES [*eying her*]: You look like half a governess. (KATE *enters,* ANNIE *stands moveless, while* JAMES *takes her suitcase.* KATE'S *gaze on her is doubtful, troubled.*) Mrs. Keller, Miss Sullivan. (KATE *takes her hand.*)

KATE [*simply*]: We've met every train for two days. (ANNIE *looks at* KATE'S *face, and her good humor comes back.*)

ANNIE: I changed trains every time they stopped, the man who sold me that ticket ought to be tied to the tracks . . . (KATE *is studying her face, and* ANNIE *returns the gaze; this is a mutual appraisal, southern gentlewoman and working-class Irish girl, and* ANNIE *is not quite comfortable under it.*) You didn't bring Helen, I was hoping you would.

KATE: No, she's home. . . . (*Now she voices part of her doubt, not as such, but* ANNIE *understands it.*) I expected—a desiccated spinster. You're very young.

ANNIE [*resolutely*]: Oh, you should have seen me when I left Boston. I got much older on this trip.

KATE: I mean, to teach anyone as difficult as Helen.

ANNIE: I mean to try. They can't put you in jail for trying!

KATE: Is it possible, even? To teach a deaf-blind child *half* of what an ordinary child learns—has that ever been done?

ANNIE: Half?

KATE: A tenth.

ANNIE [*reluctantly*]: No. (KATE'S *face loses its remaining hope, still appraising her youth.*) Dr. Howe did wonders, but—an ordinary child? No, never. But then I thought when I was going over his reports—(*She indicates the one in her hand*)—he never treated them like ordinary children. More like—eggs everyone was afraid would break.

KATE [*a pause*]: May I ask how old you are?

ANNIE: Well, I'm not in my teens, you know! I'm twenty.

KATE: All of twenty. (ANNIE *takes the bull by the horns, valiantly.*)

ANNIE: Mrs. Keller, don't lose heart just because I'm not on my last legs. I have three big advantages over Dr. Howe that money couldn't buy for you. One is his work behind me, I've read every word he wrote about it and he wasn't exactly what you'd call a man of few words. Another is to *be* young, why, I've got energy to do anything. The third is, I've been blind. (*But it costs her something to say this.*)

KATE [*quietly*]: Advantages.

ANNIE [*wry*]: Well, some have the luck of the Irish, some do not. (KATE *smiles; she likes her.*)

KATE: What will you try to teach her first?

ANNIE: First, last, and—in between, language.

KATE: Language.

ANNIE: Language is to the mind more than light is to the eye. Dr. Howe said that.

KATE: Language. (*She shakes her head.*) We can't get through to teach her to sit still. You *are* young, despite your years, to have such—confidence. Do you, inside? (ANNIE *studies her face; she likes her, too.*)

ANNIE: No, to tell you the truth I'm as shaky inside as a baby's rattle! (*They smile at each other, and* KATE *pats her hand.*)

KATE: Don't be. (JAMES *returns to usher them off.*) We'll do all we can to help, and to make you feel at home. Don't think of us as strangers, Miss Annie.

ANNIE [*cheerily*]: Oh, strangers aren't so strange to me. I've known them all my life! (KATE *smiles again,* ANNIE *smiles back, and they precede* JAMES *offstage.*)

1. This excerpt from Act 1 of the play is most likely part of the
   A. rising action.
   B. climax.
   C. falling action.
   D. resolution.

2. Annie's attitude in this scene is best described as
   A. quiet and gentle.
   B. angry and hostile.
   C. nervous and afraid.
   D. cheerful and determined.

3. Annie says that her goal is to teach Helen language. Kate's response to this suggests that Kate
   A. is thrilled by the idea.
   B. doubts that it's possible.
   C. doesn't think language is important.
   D. thinks only an older person could do this.

4. Stage directions in this scene serve mainly to communicate
   A. how the characters move.
   B. why the characters are talking.
   C. what the characters are wearing.
   D. what the characters' emotions are.

5. Kate seems to think it's a problem that Annie
   A. is so young.
   B. is from Boston.
   C. had been blind.
   D. appears to be confident.

6. Read this excerpt from the play.

   ANNIE: . . . The third is, I've been blind. (*But it costs her something to say this.*)

   The stage directions in this excerpt suggest that
   A. it is painful for Annie to remember being blind.
   B. Annie thinks that blindness is a shameful problem.
   C. Annie had to pay a lot of money to regain her sight.
   D. Annie will be paid less because she had been blind.

7. In what way might Annie's former blindness be an advantage?
   A. She won't expect much from Helen.
   B. She won't expect much from herself.
   C. She will work harder to prove herself.
   D. She will understand Helen's situation.

Extended Answer

8. Near the end of this scene, the stage directions reveal that Kate and Annie like each other. Why do you think they do?

Literature Online

Assessment For additional test practice, go to glencoe.com and enter QuickPass code GL39770u6.

Vocabulary Skills

On a separate sheet of paper, write the numbers 1–12. Next to each number, write the letter of the word or phrase that is closest in meaning to the underlined word.

1. conspicuous in the snow
   A. cold
   B. noticeable
   C. stuck
   D. buried

2. a very superficial discussion
   A. interesting
   B. valuable
   C. meaningless
   D. lengthy

3. a sense of foreboding
   A. happiness
   B. duty
   C. failure
   D. doom

4. fans in a frenzy
   A. wild excitement
   B. stunned silence
   C. hopeful mood
   D. cold fury

5. stealthily leaving the building
   A. secretly
   B. rapidly
   C. publicly
   D. noisily

6. wild jubilation
   A. hope
   B. energy
   C. joy
   D. grief

7. loathe peas but not carrots
   A. eat
   B. reject
   C. love
   D. hate

8. a melancholy story
   A. mind-boggling
   B. heartbreaking
   C. fascinating
   D. romantic

9. answering with poise
   A. great speed
   B. hesitation
   C. self-pity
   D. dignity

10. to perturb our neighbor
    A. upset
    B. amuse
    C. support
    D. dislike

11. aggravating music
    A. repetitious
    B. gorgeous
    C. irritating
    D. popular

12. his subdued response
    A. hushed
    B. rapid
    C. delayed
    D. exaggerated

Writing Strategies

Read and answer each question. Write your answers on a separate sheet of paper.

1. Read this sentence.

   If you like Joe could help you with your homework.

   What is the correct way to write this sentence?

   A. If you like Joe, could help you with your homework.
   B. If you like Joe could help you, with your homework.
   C. If you like, Joe could help you with your homework.
   D. Leave as is.

2. Read this sentence.

   If you train them dogs can become great pets.

   What is the correct way to write this sentence?

   A. If you train, them dogs can be great pets.
   B. If you train them, dogs can be great pets.
   C. If you train them, dogs, can be great pets.
   D. Leave as is.

3. In which sentence is a comma needed to prevent confusion?

   A. After eating my dog likes to take a nap.
   B. I finally got to meet my cousin Ricardo.
   C. A life without laughter seems unbearable.
   D. Training a dog properly can take a long time.

4. In which sentence is a comma needed to prevent confusion?

   A. After lunch we can take a walk.
   B. It can be difficult to get all the answers right.
   C. Who knows whether Jenny will be able to be here?
   D. We need a guest room for Grandma is coming to visit.

5. In which sentence is a comma needed to prevent confusion?

   A. While eating dinner we heard sirens.
   B. The homework on my desk is due tomorrow.
   C. Where are all the flowers that were in the garden?
   D. Before leaving her husband straightened up the house.

Writing Product

Read the prompt in the box below and follow the directions. Use one piece of paper to jot down ideas and organize your thoughts. Then neatly write your essay on another sheet. You may not use a dictionary or other reference materials.

Writing Situation:

People often talk fondly about the past. Sometimes they refer to "the good old days," suggesting that things were better then.

Directions for Writing:

Think about how life is different for you than it was for your grandparents. What are the advantages of growing up now? What are the disadvantages? Now write to describe one thing that you think is better or worse about life today. Explain the reason for your choice.

Keep these hints in mind when you write.

- Concentrate on what the prompt tells you to write.
- Organize the way you will present your ideas.
- Provide good, clear support for your ideas.
- Use different kinds of sentence structures.
- Use precise words that express your ideas clearly.
- Check your essay for mistakes in spelling, grammar, and punctuation.

Reference Section

Literary Terms Handbook

A

Act A major unit of a drama. A play may be subdivided into several acts. Many modern plays have two or three acts. A short play can be composed of one or more scenes but only one act.

See also Scene.

Alliteration The repetition of consonant sounds, usually at the beginnings of words or syllables. Alliteration gives emphasis to words. For example,

Over the cobbles he clattered and clashed

Allusion A reference in a work of literature to a well-known character, place, or situation in history, politics, or science or from another work of literature, music, or art.

Analogy A comparison between two things, based on one or more elements that they share. Analogies can help the reader visualize an idea. In informational text, analogies are often used to explain something unfamiliar in terms of something known. For example, a science book might compare the flow of electricity to water moving through a hose. In literature, most analogies are expressed in metaphors or similes.

See also Metaphor, Simile.

Anecdote A brief, entertaining story based on a single interesting or humorous incident or event. Anecdotes are frequently biographical and reveal some aspect of a person's character.

Antagonist A person or force that opposes the protagonist, or central character, in a story or a drama. The reader is generally meant not to sympathize with the antagonist.

See also Conflict, Protagonist.

Anthropomorphism Representing animals as if they had human emotions and intelligence. Fables and fairy tales often contain anthropomorphism.

Aside In a play, a comment made by a character that is heard by the audience but not by the other characters onstage. The speaker turns to one side, or "aside," away from the other characters onstage. Asides are common in older plays—you will find many in Shakespeare's plays—but are infrequent in modern drama.

Assonance The repetition of vowel sounds, especially in a line of poetry.

See also Rhyme, Sound devices.

Author's purpose The intention of the writer. For example, the purpose of a story may be to entertain, to describe, to explain, to persuade, or a combination of these purposes.

Autobiography The story of a person's life written by that person. *I Know Why the Caged Bird Sings* by Maya Angelou is an example of autobiography.

See also Biography, Memoir.

B

Ballad A short musical narrative song or poem. Folk ballads, which usually tell of an exciting or dramatic episode, were passed on by word of mouth for generations before being written down. Literary ballads are written in imitation of folk ballads.

See also Narrative poetry.

Biography The account of a person's life written by someone other than the subject. Biographies can be short or book-length.

See also Autobiography, Memoir.

C

Character A person in a literary work. (If a character is an animal, it displays human traits.) Characters who show varied and sometimes contradictory traits are called **round.** Characters who reveal only one personality trait are called **flat.** A **stereotype** is a flat character of a familiar and often-repeated type. A **dynamic** character changes during the story. A **static** character remains primarily the same throughout the story.

Characterization The methods a writer uses to develop the personality of the character. In **direct characterization,** the writer makes direct statements about a character's personality. In **indirect characterization,** the writer reveals a character's personality through the character's words and actions and through what other characters think and say about the character.

Climax The point of greatest emotional intensity, interest, or suspense in a narrative. Usually the climax comes at the turning point in a story or drama, the point at which the resolution of the conflict becomes clear. The climax in "Icarus and Daedalus" occurs when Icarus forgets his father's warnings and flies too high.

Comedy A type of drama that is humorous and has a happy ending. A heroic comedy focuses on the exploits of a larger-than-life hero. In American popular culture, comedy can take the form of a scripted performance involving one or more performers—either as a skit that is part of a variety show, as in vaudeville, or as a stand-up monologue.

See also Humor.

Conflict The central struggle between opposing forces in a story or drama. An **external conflict** exists when a character struggles against some outside force, such as nature, society, fate, or another person. An **internal conflict** exists within the mind of a character who is torn between opposing feelings or goals.

See also Antagonist, Plot, Protagonist.

Consonance A pleasing combination of sounds, especially in poetry. Consonance usually refers to the repetition of consonant sounds in stressed syllables.

See also Sound devices.

Couplet Two successive lines of verse that form a unit and usually rhyme.

D

Description Writing that seeks to convey the impression of a setting, a person, an animal, an object, or an event by appealing to the senses. Almost all writing, fiction and nonfiction, contains elements of description.

Details Particular features of things used to make descriptions more accurate and vivid. Authors use details to help readers imagine the characters, scenes, and actions they describe.

Dialect A variation of language spoken by a particular group, often within a particular region. Dialects differ from standard language because they may contain different pronunciations, forms, and meanings.

Dialogue Conversation between characters in a literary work.

See also Monologue.

Drama A story intended to be performed by actors on a stage or before movie or TV cameras. Most dramas before the modern period can be divided into two basic types: tragedy and comedy. The script of a drama includes dialogue (the words the actors speak) and stage directions (descriptions of the action and scenery).

See also Comedy, Tragedy.

E

Elegy A mournful or melancholy poem that honors someone who is dead. Some elegies are written in rhyming couplets that follow a strict metric pattern.

Epic A long narrative poem, written in a dignified style, that celebrates the adventures and achievements of one or more heroic figures of legend, history, or religion. *Beowulf* is an epic.

See also Narrative Poetry.

Essay A short piece of nonfiction writing on a single topic. The purpose of the essay is to communicate an idea or opinion. A **formal essay** is serious and impersonal. A **informal essay** entertains while it informs, usually in a light conversational style.

Exposition The part of the plot of a short story, novel, novella, or play in which the characters, setting, and situation are introduced.

Extended metaphor An implied comparison that continues through an entire poem.

See also Metaphor.

F

Fable A short, simple tale that teaches a moral. The characters in a fable are often animals who speak and act like people. The moral, or lesson, of the fable is usually stated outright.

Falling action In a play or story, the action that follows the climax.

See also Plot.

Fantasy A form of literature that explores unreal worlds of the past, the present, or the future.

Fiction A prose narrative in which situations and characters are invented by the writer. Some aspects of a fictional work may be based on fact or experience. Fiction includes short stories, novellas, and novels.

See also Novel, Novella, Short story.

Figurative language Language used for descriptive effect, often to imply ideas indirectly. Expressions of figurative language are not literally true but express some truth beyond the literal level. Although it appears in all kinds of writing, figurative language is especially prominent in poetry.

See also Analogy, Figure of speech, Metaphor, Personification, Simile, Symbol.

Figure of speech Figurative language of a specific kind, such as **analogy, metaphor, simile,** or **personification.**

First-person narrative. *See also* Point Of View.

Flashback An interruption in a chronological narrative that tells about something that happened before that point in the story or before the story began. A flashback gives readers information that helps to explain the main events of the story.

Folklore The traditional beliefs, customs, stories, songs, and dances of the ordinary people (the "folk") of a culture. Folklore is passed on by word of mouth and performance rather than in writing.

See also Folktale, Legend, Myth, Oral tradition.

Folktale A traditional story passed down orally long before being written down. Generally the author of a folktale is anonymous. Folktales include animal stories, trickster stories, fairy tales, myths, legends, and tall tales.

See also Legend, Myth, Oral tradition, Tall tale.

Foreshadowing The use of clues by an author to prepare readers for events that will happen in a story.

Free verse Poetry that has no fixed pattern of meter, rhyme, line length, or stanza arrangement.

See also Rhythm

G

Genre A literary or artistic category. The main literary genres are prose, poetry, and drama. Each of these is divided into smaller genres. For example: **Prose** includes fiction (such as novels, novellas, short stories, and folktales) and nonfiction (such as biography, autobiography, and essays). **Poetry** includes lyric poetry, dramatic poetry, and narrative poetry. **Drama** includes tragedy, comedy, historical drama, melodrama, and farce.

H

Haiku Originally a Japanese form of poetry that has three lines and seventeen syllables. The first and third lines have five syllables each; the middle line has seven syllables.

Hero A literary work's main character, usually one with admirable qualities. Although the word *hero* is applied only to males in traditional usage (the female form is *heroine*), the term now applies to both sexes.

See also Legend, Myth, Protagonist, Tall tale.

Historical fiction A novel, novella, play, short story, or narrative poem that sets fictional characters against a historical backdrop and contains many details about the period in which it is set.

See also Genre.

Humor The quality of a literary work that makes the characters and their situations seem funny, amusing, or ludicrous. Humorous writing can be as effective in nonfiction as in fiction.

See also Comedy.

I

Idiom A figure of speech that belongs to a particular language, people, or region and whose meaning cannot be obtained, and might even appear ridiculous, by joining the meanings of the words composing it. You would be using an idiom if you said you *caught* a cold.

Imagery Language that emphasizes sensory impressions to help the reader of a literary work see, hear, feel, smell, and taste the scenes described in the work.

See also Figurative language.

Informational text One kind of nonfiction. This kind of writing conveys facts and information without introducing personal opinion.

Irony A form of expression in which the intended meaning of the words used is the opposite of their literal meaning. *Verbal irony* occurs when a person says one thing and means another—for example, saying "Nice guy!" about someone you dislike. *Situational irony* occurs when the outcome of a situation is the opposite of what was expected.

J

Journal An account of day-to-day events or a record of experiences, ideas, or thoughts. A journal may also be called a diary.

L

Legend A traditional story, based on history or an actual hero, that is passed down orally. A legend is usually exaggerated and gains elements of fantasy over the years. Stories about Daniel Boone and Davy Crockett are American legends.

Limerick A light humorous poem with a regular metrical scheme and a rhyme scheme of *aabba*.

See also Humor, Rhyme scheme.

Local color The fictional portrayal of a region's features or peculiarities and its inhabitants' distinctive ways of talking and behaving, usually as a way of adding a realistic flavor to a story.

Lyric The words of a song, usually with a regular rhyme scheme.

See also Rhyme scheme.

Lyric poetry Poems, usually short, that express strong personal feelings about a subject or an event.

M

Main idea The most important idea expressed in a paragraph or an essay. It may or may not be directly stated.

Memoir A biographical or autobiographical narrative emphasizing the narrator's personal experience during a period or at an event.

See also Autobiography, Biography.

Metaphor A figure of speech that compares or equates seemingly unlike things. In contrast to a simile, a metaphor implies the comparison instead of stating it directly; hence, there is no use of connectives such as *like* or *as*.

See also Figure of speech, Imagery, Simile.

Meter A regular pattern of stressed and unstressed syllables that gives a line of poetry a predictable rhythm.

See also Rhythm.

Monologue A long speech by a single character in a play or a solo performance.

Mood The emotional quality or atmosphere of a story or poem.

See also Setting.

Myth A traditional story of unknown authorship, often involving goddesses, gods, and heroes, that attempts to explain a natural phenomenon, a historic event, or the origin of a belief or custom.

N

Narration Writing or speech that tells a story. Narration is used in prose fiction and narrative poetry. Narration can also be an important element in biographies, autobiographies, and essays.

Narrative poetry Verse that tells a story.

Narrator The person who tells a story. In some cases the narrator is a character in the story.

See also Point of view.

Nonfiction Factual prose writing. Nonfiction deals with real people and experiences. Among the categories of nonfiction are biographies, autobiographies, and essays.

See also Autobiography, Biography, Essay, Fiction.

Novel A book-length fictional prose narrative. The novel has more scope than a short story in its presentation of plot, character, setting, and theme. Because novels are not subject to any limits in their presentation of these elements, they encompass a wide range of narratives.

See also Fiction.

Novella A work of fiction shorter than a novel but longer than a short story. A novella usually has more characters, settings, and events and a more complex plot than a short story.

O

Ode A lyric poem, usually rhymed, often in the form of an address and usually dignified or lofty in subject.

See also Lyric poetry.

Onomatopoeia The use of a word or a phrase that actually imitates or suggests the sound of what it describes.

See also Sound Devices.

Oral tradition Stories, knowledge, customs, and beliefs passed by word of mouth from one generation to the next.

See also Folklore, Folktale, Legend, Myth.

P

Parallelism The use of a series of words, phrases, or sentences that have similar grammatical form. Parallelism emphasizes the items that are arranged in the similar structures.

See also Repetition.

Personification A figure of speech in which an animal, object, or idea is given human form or characteristics.

See also Figurative language, Figure of speech, Metaphor.

Plot The sequence of events in a story, novel, or play. The plot begins with **exposition,** which introduces the story's characters, setting, and situation. The plot catches the reader's attention with a **narrative hook.** The **rising action** adds complications to the story's conflict, or problem, leading to the **climax,** or point of highest emotional pitch. The **falling action** is the logical result of the climax, and the **resolution** presents the final outcome.

Plot twist An unexpected turn of events in a plot. A surprise ending is an example of a plot twist.

Poetry A form of literary expression that differs from prose in emphasizing the line as the unit of composition. Many other traditional characteristics of poetry—emotional, imaginative language; use of metaphor and simile; division into stanzas; rhyme; regular pattern of stress, or meter—apply to some poems.

Point of view The relationship of the narrator, or storyteller, to the story. In a story with **first-person point of view,** the story is told by one of the characters, referred to as "I." The reader generally sees everything through that character's eyes. In a story with a **limited third-person point of view,** the narrator reveals the thoughts of only one character, but refers to that character as "he" or "she." In a story with an **omniscient point of view,** the narrator reveals the thoughts of several characters.

Props Theater slang (a shortened form of *properties*) for objects and elements of the scenery of a stage play or movie set.

Propaganda Speech, writing, or other attempts to influence ideas or opinions, often through the use of stereotypes, faulty generalizations, logical fallacies, and/or emotional language.

Prose Writing that is similar to everyday speech and language, as opposed to poetry. Its form is based on sentences and paragraphs without the patterns of rhyme, controlled line length, or meter found in much poetry. Fiction and nonfiction are the major categories of prose. Most modern drama is also written in prose.

See also Drama, Essay, Fiction, Nonfiction.

Protagonist The central character in a story, drama, or dramatic poem. Usually the action revolves around the protagonist, who is involved in the main conflict.

See also Antagonist, Conflict.

Pun A humorous play on two or more meanings of the same word or on two words with the same sound. Today puns often appear in advertising headlines and slogans—for example, "Our hotel rooms give you suite feelings."

See also Humor.

R

Refrain A line or lines repeated regularly, usually in a poem or song.

Repetition The recurrence of sounds, words, phrases, lines, or stanzas in a speech or piece of writing. Repetition increases the feeling of unity in a work. When a line or stanza is repeated in a poem or song, it is called a refrain.

See also Parallelism, Refrain.

Resolution The part of a plot that concludes the falling action by revealing or suggesting the outcome of the conflict.

Rhyme The repetition of sounds at the ends of words that appear close to each other in a poem. **End rhyme** occurs at the ends of lines. **Internal rhyme** occurs within a single line. **Slant rhyme** occurs when words include sounds that are similar but not identical. Slant rhyme usually involves some variation of **consonance** (the repetition of consonant sounds) or **assonance** (the repetition of vowel sounds).

Rhyme scheme The pattern of rhyme formed by the end rhyme in a poem. Rhyme scheme is designated by the assignment of a different letter of the alphabet to each new rhyme. For example, one common rhyme scheme is *ababcb*.

Rhythm The pattern created by the arrangement of stressed and unstressed syllables, especially in poetry. Rhythm gives poetry a musical quality that helps convey its meaning. Rhythm can be regular (with a predictable pattern or meter) or irregular, (as in free verse).

See also Meter.

Rising action The part of a plot that adds complications to the problems in the story and increases reader interest.

See also Falling action, Plot.

S

Scene A subdivision of an act in a play. Each scene takes place in a specific setting and time. An act may have one or more scenes.

See also Act.

Science fiction Fiction dealing with the impact of real science or imaginary superscience on human or alien societies of the past, present, or future. Although science fiction is mainly a product of the twentieth century, nineteenth-century authors such as Mary Shelley, Jules Verne, and Robert Louis Stevenson were pioneers of the genre.

Screenplay The script of a film, usually containing detailed instructions about camera shots and angles in addition to dialogue and stage directions. A screenplay for an original television show is called a teleplay.

See also Drama.

Sensory imagery Language that appeals to a reader's five senses: hearing, sight, touch, taste, and smell.

See also Visual imagery.

Sequence of events The order in which the events in a story take place.

Setting The time and place in which the events of a short story, novel, novella, or play occur. The setting often helps create the atmosphere or mood of the story.

Short story A brief fictional narrative in prose. Elements of the short story include **plot, character, setting, point of view, theme,** and sometimes **symbol** and **irony.**

Simile A figure of speech using *like* or *as* to compare seemingly unlike things.

See also Figurative language, Figure of speech.

Sonnet A poem containing fourteen lines, usually written in iambic pentameter. Sonnets have strict patterns of rhyme and usually deal with a single theme, idea, or sentiment.

Sound devices Techniques used to create a sense of rhythm or to emphasize particular sounds in writing. For example, sound can be controlled through the use of **onomatopoeia, alliteration, consonance, assonance,** and **rhyme.**

See also Rhythm.

Speaker The voice of a poem—sometimes that of the poet, sometimes that of a fictional person or even a thing. The speaker's words communicate a particular tone or attitude toward the subject of the poem.

Stage directions Instructions written by the dramatist to describe the appearance and actions of characters, as well as sets, costumes, and lighting.

Stanza A group of lines forming a unit in a poem. Stanzas are, in effect, the paragraphs of a poem.

Stereotype A character who is not developed as an individual but as a collection of traits and mannerisms supposedly shared by all members of a group.

Style The author's choice and arrangement of words and sentences in a literary work. Style can reveal an author's purpose in writing and attitude toward his or her subject and audience.

Suspense A feeling of curiosity, uncertainty, or even dread about what is going to happen next. Writers increase the level of suspense in a story by giving readers clues to what may happen.

See also Foreshadowing, Rising action.

Symbol Any object, person, place, or experience that means more than what it is. **Symbolism** is the use of images to represent internal realities.

T

Tall tale A wildly imaginative story, usually passed down orally, about the fantastic adventures or amazing feats of folk heroes in realistic settings.

See also Folklore, Oral tradition.

Teleplay A play written or adapted for television.

Theme The main message of a story, poem, novel, or play, usually expressed as a general statement. Some works have a **stated theme,** which is expressed directly. More frequently works have an **implied theme,** which is revealed gradually through other elements such as plot, character, setting, point of view, symbol, and irony.

Third-person narrative. *See also* Point of view.

Title The name of a literary work.

Tone The attitude of the author toward the subject, ideas, theme, or characters. A factual article would most likely have an objective tone, while an editorial on the same topic could be argumentative or satiric.

Tragedy A play in which the main character suffers a downfall. That character often is a person of dignified or heroic stature. The downfall may result from outside forces or from a weakness within the character, which is known as a tragic flaw.

V

Visual imagery Details that appeal to the sense of sight.

Voice An author's distinctive style or the particular speech patterns of a character in a story.

See also Style, Tone.

Reading and Thinking with Foldables®

by Dinah Zike, M.Ed., Creator of Foldables®

Using Foldables® Makes Learning Easy and Enjoyable

As you read the selections in each unit, the following Foldables will help you keep track of your ideas about the Big Questions. Follow these directions to make your Foldable, and then use the directions on the Unit Opener for labeling your unit Foldable.

 Foldable 1 and Foldable 2—For Units 1 and 2

 Step ❶ Fold five sheets of paper into *hamburgers.*

 Step ❷ Cut the sheets of paper in half along the fold lines.

 Step ❸ Fold each section of paper into *hamburgers.* However, fold one side one-half inch shorter than the other side. This will form a tab that is one-half inch long.

 Step ❹ Fold this tab forward over the shorter side, and then fold it back the opposite way.

 Step ❺ Glue together to form an *accordion* by gluing a straight edge of one section into the *valley* of another section.

Step ❻ On the front cover, write the unit number and the **Big Question.** Turn the page. Across the top, write the selection title. To the left of the crease, write **My Purpose for Reading.** To the right of the crease, write **Big Question.** Repeat until you have all the titles from the Reading Workshops and the Comparing Literature Workshop in your Foldable.

 Foldable 3 and Foldable 5—For Units 3 and 5

 Step ❶ Stack three sheets of paper so that the bottom of each sheet is one inch higher than the sheet behind it.

 Step ❷ Fold down the tops of the paper to form six tabs. Align the edges so that all of the layers are about an inch apart.

 Step ❸ Crease the paper to hold the layers in place and then staple them together. Cut the bottom five layers up to the crease. Do not cut the top flap.

 Step ❹ On the top front flap, write the unit number and the **Big Question.** Write a selection title on the bottom of each flap. Then open each flap. Write **My Purpose for Reading** at the top of the flap and write **Big Question** below the crease.

Foldable 4 and Foldable 6—For Units 4 and 6

Step ❶ Fold a sheet of paper in half so that one side is one inch longer than the other side. Fold the one-inch tab over the short side to form a fold. On the fold, write the workshop number and the **Big Question.**

Step ❷ Cut the front flap in half toward the top crease to create two flaps. Write the title of the first selection in Reading Workshop 1 on the left flap and the title of the second selection on the right flap.

Step ❸ Open the flaps. At the very top of each flap, write **My Purpose for Reading.** Below each crease, write **Big Question.**

Step ❹ Repeat these steps for each remaining Reading Workshop and the Reading Across Texts or Comparing Literature Workshop.

Step ❺ Fold a 11 x 17 sheet of paper in half. Open the paper and fold up one of the long sides two inches to form a pocket. Glue the outer edges of the pocket. Refold the paper so that the pockets are on the inside. Keep your Foldables for the unit inside.

Functional Documents

Business Letter

In the business world, in school, and even at home, there are many standard types of documents that serve specific functions. Understanding these forms of writing will help you to be a better communicator in your everyday life.

The following business letter uses modified block style.

❶ 10 Pullman Lane
Cromwell, CT 06416
January 16, 2009

❷ Mr. Philip Fornaro
Principal
Cromwell School
179 West Maple St.
Cromwell, CT 06416

❸ Dear Mr. Fornaro:

❹ My friends and I in the seventh grade at Brimmer Middle School feel that there is not enough to do in Cromwell during the winter vacation week. Some students can afford to go away for vacation. Many families, however, cannot afford to go away, or the parents have to work.

❺ I would like to suggest that you keep the Brimmer Middle School gym open during the vacation week. If the gym were open, the basketball teams could practice. The fencing club could meet. We could meet our friends there instead of going to the mall.

❻ Thanks for listening to my request. I hope you will think it over.

❼ Sincerely,
Kim Goodwin
Kim Goodwin

❶ In the heading, write your address and the date on separate lines.

❷ In the inside address, write the name and address of the person to whom you are sending the letter.

❸ Use a colon after the greeting.

❹ In your introduction, say who you are and why you are writing.

❺ In the body of your letter, provide details concerning your request.

❻ Conclude by restating your purpose and thanking the person you are writing to.

❼ In the closing, use *Sincerely, Sincerely yours,* or *Yours truly* followed by a comma. Include both your signature and your printed or typed name.

Job Application

When applying for a job, you usually need to fill out a job application. Read the form carefully before beginning to fill it out. Write neatly and fill out the form completely, providing all information directly and honestly. If a question does not apply to you, indicate that by writing *n/a*, short for "not applicable." Keep in mind that you will have the opportunity to provide additional information in your résumé, in your letter of application, or during the interview process.

Please type or print neatly in blue or black ink.

Name: _____ Today's date: _____

Address: _____

Phone #: _____ Birth date: _____ Sex: _____ Soc. Sec. #: _____

****

Job History (List each job held, starting with the most recent job.)

1. Employer: _____ Phone #: _____

Dates of employment: _____

Position held: _____

Duties: _____

2. Employer: _____ Phone #: _____

Dates of employment: _____

Position held: _____

Duties: _____

****

Education (List the most recent level of education completed.)

_____

_____

****

Personal References:

1. Name: _____ Phone #: _____

Relationship: _____

2. Name: _____ Phone #: _____

Relationship: _____

❶ The application provides specific instructions.

❷ All of the information requested should be provided in its entirety.

❸ The information should be provided neatly and succinctly.

❹ Experience should be stated accurately and without embellishment.

Activity

Pick up a job application from a local business. Complete the application thoroughly. Be sure to pay close attention to the guidelines mentioned above.

Writing a Memo

A memo, or memorandum, is a brief, efficient way of communicating information to another person or group of people. It begins with a header that provides basic information. A memo does not have a formal closing.

TO: *Brimmer Banner* newspaper staff
FROM: Paul Francis
SUBJECT: Winter issue
DATE: January 18, 2009

Articles for the winter issue of the *Brimmer Banner* are due by February 1. Please see Terry about your assignment as soon as possible! The following articles or features have not yet been assigned:

Cafeteria Mess: Who Is Responsible?
Teacher Profile: Mr. Jinks, Ms. Magee
Sports roundup

Using Electronic Business Correspondence

Imagine that you ordered a game through a company's Web site. When you tried playing the game, you found that it didn't work well. You could send a letter to the company you bought the game from explaining your problem. But it's easier and faster to send an e-mail. Any business that operates on the Internet has a way for customers to reach them—either a hyperlink "button" that will take you to Customer Service, or an e-mail address such as *service@ gamecorp.com.*

Here are a few hints for effective business e-mails.

- Your e-mail window includes an area for the subject of your message. Think carefully and make your subject as clear and concise as possible. In a business e-mail you'll want your recipient to know right away your purpose for writing.

- Reread your message carefully before hitting the Send button. Check your grammar and spelling. Then double-check your spelling by using the spell-checker program on your computer.

- Your e-mail program probably offers options for how to send a message—for example: plain text, rich text, or HTML. If your letter contains some formatting (like italics or boldface) or special characters (such as a cursive typeface that looks like handwriting), choose rich text or HTML to avoid losing your formatting.

Technical Writing

Technical writing involves the use of very specific vocabulary and a special attention to detail. The purpose of technical writing is to describe a process clearly enough so that the reader can perform the steps and reach the intended goal, such as installing software, connecting a piece of equipment, or programming a device.

Instructions for Connecting DVD Player to HDTV

Your DVD player can be connected to an HDTV using RCA cables or, if available, an HDMI cable.

Connecting with RCA Cables

Step 1: Insert the ends of the red, white, and yellow cables into the jacks labeled "AUDIO/VIDEO OUT." **①** Be sure to match the color of the cable with the color of the jack.

②Step 2: Insert the other ends of the RCA cables into the jacks labeled "AUDIO/VIDEO IN" on your HDTV. These are usually located on the side or the back of the television. Again, be sure to match the colors of the cables with the colors of the jacks.

Connecting with HDMI Cable

Step 1: Insert one end of the HDMI cable into the HDMI port located on the back of the DVD player.

Step 2: Insert the other end of the HDMI cable into the HDMI port on your HDTV.

③Note: Your television may have more than one HDMI port. If so, be sure that you set your television to the correct input when viewing.

① Uses specific language to clearly describe the process

② Lists each step individually

③ Brings attention to possible variations the reader may encounter

Activity

Choose a device that you own or have access to, such as an mp3 player or a cell phone. Write brief step-by-step directions on how to perform a specific function on the device, so that someone else can follow your instructions and perform the function successfully.

Writing Handbook

Research Report Writing

When you write a research report, you explore a topic by gathering factual information from several different resources. Through your research, you develop a point of view or draw a conclusion. This point of view or conclusion becomes the main idea, or thesis, of your report.

Select a Topic

Because a research report usually takes time to prepare and write, your choice of topic is especially important. Follow these guidelines.

- Brainstorm a list of questions about a subject you would like to explore. Choose one that is neither too narrow nor too broad for the length of paper you will write. Use that question as your topic.

- Select a topic that genuinely interests you.

- Be sure you can find information on your topic from several different sources.

Conduct Research

Start by looking up your topic in an encyclopedia to find general information. Then find specific information in books, magazines, and newspapers, on CD-ROMs and the Internet, and from personal interviews when this seems appropriate. Use the computerized or card catalog in the library to locate books on your topic. Then search for up-to-date information in periodicals (magazines) or newspapers and from electronic sources, such as CD-ROMs or the Internet. If you need help in finding or using any of these resources, ask the librarian.

As you gather information, make sure each source you use relates closely to your topic. Also be sure that your source is reliable. Be extra careful if you are using information from the Internet. If you are not sure about the reliability of a source, consult the librarian or your teacher.

Conduct Internet Research

In order to conduct research on the Internet, you will need to use a search engine, a tool that allows you to use keywords to find information on the World Wide Web. There are many different search engines on the Internet, but most of them operate similarly.

First, choose a search engine. Somewhere near the top you'll find a white box into which you can type. Next to it will be a button that in most search engines says "Search." Try searching for Web sites about protecting animals in the wild. For keywords, try "endangered wildlife." The quotation marks tell the search engine to look for the whole phrase rather than for each word by itself. Click on the Search button and the engine will provide you with a list of sites that include the phrase "endangered wildlife." Visit a few of these sites by clicking on the underlined titles.

As you conduct your Internet search, you may want to narrow your search to something more specific, such as "wildlife preserves." Try different keywords to come up with additional sites dealing with your topic. Most search engines also have an advanced search feature, which allows you to be even more specific about your search.

Because there is such a huge amount of information on the Internet, you will have to visit many sites and evaluate which ones have the information you need, based on relevance and appropriateness.

Activity

Conduct an Internet search using the word "cooking" as a keyword. How many sites do you find? Now do a search to find a recipe for your favorite dessert. Think of exact phrases you could place in quotes to narrow your search.

Make Source Cards

For a research report, you must document the source or sources of your information. To keep track of your sources, write the author, title, publication information, and location of each source on a separate index card. Give each source card a number and write it in the upper right-hand corner. These cards will be useful for preparing a bibliography.

Sample Source Card

❶ Douglas, Marjory Stoneman   ❷ 15
❸ **The Everglades: River of Grass**
❹ **Marietta, Georgia: Mockingbird**
   Books, 1986. ❺

❻ Carrollton Public Library   ❼ 654.3 S2

❶ Author   ❺ Date of publication
❷ Source number   ❻ Location of source
❸ Title   ❼ Library call number
❹ City of publication/
   Publisher

Take Notes

As you read, you encounter many new facts and ideas. Taking notes will help you keep track of information and focus on the topic. Here are some helpful suggestions:

- Use a new card for each important piece of information. Separate cards will help you organize your notes.

- At the top of each card, write a key word or phrase that tells about the information. Also, write the number of the source you used.

- Write only details and ideas that relate to your topic.

- Summarize information in your own words.

- Write down a phrase or a quote only when the words are especially interesting or come from an important source. Enclose all quotes in quotation marks to make clear that the ideas belong to someone else.

This sample note card shows information to include.

Sample Note Card

❶ **Functions of Wetlands**   ❷ 15
Besides furnishing a home for a variety of wildlife, the wet, spongy soil of wetlands maintains the level of the water table.
p. 79 ❸

❶ Write a key word or phrase that tells you what the information is about.

❷ Write the source number from your source card.

❸ Write the number of the page or pages on which you found the information.

Develop Your Thesis

As you begin researching and learning about your topic, think about the overall point you want to make. Write one sentence, your *thesis statement*, that says exactly what you plan to report on.

Sample Thesis Statement

Everglades National Park is a beautiful but endangered animal habitat.

Keep your thesis in mind as you continue to do research and think about your topic. The thesis will help you determine what information is important. However, be prepared to change your thesis if the information you find does not support it.

Write an Outline

When you finish taking notes, organize the information in an outline. Write down the main ideas that you want to cover. Write your thesis statement at the beginning of your outline. Then list the supporting details. Follow an outline form like the one below.

1 Everglades National Park is a beautiful but endangered animal habitat.

   I. Special aspects of the Everglades

     2 A. Characteristics of wetlands

     B. Endangered birds and animals

   II. Pressures on the Everglades

     A. Florida agriculture

     B. Carelessness of visitors

  III. How to protect the Everglades

     A. Change agricultural practices

     B. Educate park visitors

       1. Mandatory video on safety for individuals and **3** environment

       2. Instructional reminders posted throughout the park

1 The thesis statement identifies your topic and the overall point you will make.

2 If you have subtopics under a main topic, there must be at least two. They must relate directly to your main topic.

3 If you wish to divide a subtopic, you must have at least two divisions. Each must relate to the subtopic above it.

Document Your Information

You must document, or credit, the sources of all the information you use in your report. There are two common ways to document information.

Avoid Plagiarism

Plagiarism is the act of presenting an author's words or ideas as if they were your own. This is not only *unethical*, it is also *illegal*. You must credit the source not only for material directly quoted but also for any facts or ideas obtained from the source. See the Media Workshop on Media Ethics (p. 229) for more information.

Create Footnotes

To document with footnotes, place a number at the end of the information you are documenting. Number your notes consecutively, beginning with number 1. These numbers should be slightly raised and should come after any punctuation. The documentation information itself goes at the bottom of the page, with a matching number.

In-text number for note:

The Declaration of Independence was read in public for the first time on July 6, 1776.[3]

Footnote at bottom of page:

   [3] John Smith, <u>The Declaration of Independence </u>(New York: DI, 2001) 221.

Use Parenthetical Documentation

In this method, you give the source for your information in parentheses at the end of the sentence where the information appears. You do not need to give all the details of the source. Just provide enough information for your readers to identify it. Here are the basic rules to follow.

- Usually it is enough to give the author's last name and the number of the page where you found the information.

   The declaration was first read in public by militia colonel John Nixon (Smith 222).

- If you mention the author's name in the sentence, you do not need to repeat it in the parentheses.

  According to Smith, the reading was greeted with wild applause (224).

- If your source does not identify a particular author, as in a newspaper or encyclopedia article, give the first word or two of the title of the piece.

The anniversary of the reading was commemorated by a parade and fireworks ("Reading Celebrated").

Full information on your sources goes in a list at the end of your paper.

Create a Works Cited List

At the end of your paper, list all the sources of information that you used in preparing your report. Arrange them alphabetically by the author's last name (or by the first word in the title if no author is mentioned) as shown below. Title this list *Works Cited*. (Use the term *bibliography* if all your sources are printed media, such as books, magazines, or newspapers.)

Works Cited **1**

2 Bertram, Jeffrey. "African Bees: Fact or Myth?" *Orlando Sentinel* 18 Aug. 1999: D2.

3 Gore, Rick. "Neanderthals." National Geographic. January 1996: 2–35. **8**

4 Gould, Stephen J. The Panda's Thumb. New York: W. W. Norton & Co., 1982.

5 "Governor Chiles Vetoes Anti-Everglades **9** Bills–5/13/98." Friends of the Everglades. May 1998. 26 Aug 1998 <http://www.everglades.org/pressrel_may28.htm>.

6 "Neanderthal man." The Columbia Encyclopedia. 5th Edition. New York: Columbia University Press, 1993.

7 Pabst, Laura (Curator of Natural History Museum), Interview. March 11, 1998.

1 Indent all but the first line of each item.

2 Newspaper article

3 Magazine article

4 Book with one author

5 Online article

6 Encyclopedia

7 Interview

8 Include page numbers for a magazine article but not for a book, unless the book is a collection of essays by different authors.

9 Include database (underlined), publication medium (online), computer service, and date of access.

Present Your Text

For readers to appreciate your writing fully, it is very important that you present it neatly, effectively, and according to the needs of your audience and the purpose of your writing. The following standard is how you should format most of your formal school papers.

Format Your Text

- The standard typeface setting for most school papers is Courier 12 point.

- Double-space your work so that it is easy to read.

- Leave one-inch margins on all sides of every page.

- Include the page number in the upper right-hand corner of each page.

- If you are including charts, graphs, maps, or other visual aids, consider setting them on their own page. This will allow you to show the graphic at a full size that is easy to read.

Activity

Look in the library or on the Internet to find style guides for various types of writing, such as short stories or magazine articles. Assess which format is right for your piece of writing and apply it.

Using a Computer for Writing

Use Word Processing Software

A word processor is a digital tool that lets you move your words and ideas around until you find the best way to present them. Each type of word processing software is a bit different, but they all help you plan, draft, revise, edit, and present properly formatted documents.

Menus, Toolbars, and Rulers

Open a word processing document. At the top of your screen, locate the menu bar, one or more toolbars, and a ruler.

Menu Bar Menus help you perform important processes. The Edit menu, for example, allows you to copy, paste, and find text within your document.

Toolbars There are two basic types of tools. **Function tools** perform some kind of computer function, such as printing a document or checking its spelling. **Formatting tools** are used to change the way a document looks—for example, changing its font (typeface) or paragraph style.

Ruler The ruler looks like a measuring stick with markers at each end. These markers control the margins of your document. Try changing the margins on your document. You can also put tabs on the ruler so that you can use the tab key on your keyboard to send your cursor to those positions.

Activity

Use the menu, toolbars, and ruler to properly format your document according to the guidelines on p. R17.

Multimedia Presentations

You can use digital technology, such as a computer with presentation software, to create a multimedia presentation of your work. Adding pictures, video, and sound to your presentation can attract and hold your audience's attention. However, it is important that you understand the rules and laws about using other people's creations in your work. See the Media Workshop on Media Ethics (p. 229) for more information.

Slides

In a multimedia presentation, each screen a viewer sees is called a slide. Generally, a slide consists of text—not too much of it—and an image of some kind. Each slide should be limited to a single idea with a few supporting details. Because you want to get your point across quickly, it's important that you choose your images and words carefully. An Internet search engine can help you find downloadable images to use in your presentation. Most computer images have the file extension *.gif* or *.jpeg*.

Video

For some types of presentations, adding video can have a big impact. For example, if you're presenting a report on an actor, what better way

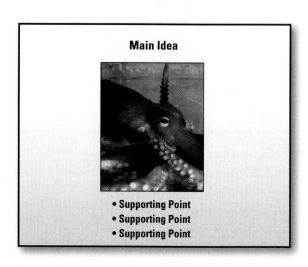

to illustrate his or her style than with movie clips? You can record video clips from your TV or download them from the Internet. Most movie files have the extensions *.avi, .mov,* or *.mpeg.*

You can add your images and video clips to your presentation using the Insert menu in your presentation software. Also, most presentation software has a "wizard" or templates that will help you put together your multimedia presentation.

Activity

Working with a partner, choose a movie or television show as the basis for a complete multimedia presentation. Include in your presentation at least six slides with pictures and text and two video clips. Don't forget about media ethics, and be careful not to plagiarize as you choose media for your presentation.

Databases

An electronic database is a software program that allows you to organize, store, and retrieve information. Data are organized into a table of columns and rows. Each single piece of information is called a field.

Once the information is in your database, you can recall it in a number of useful ways. For example, you can arrange an address-book database to show you all the names of people who live in a certain city or zip code.

Activity

Create a database of your research materials for a current or upcoming report. Enter fields for authors, titles, types of media, and key words describing useful information you found in each. Practice organizing the database in different ways. For example, organize your database to show how many magazine articles you used in your research.

Field Columns (Categories)

Record

Name	Address	City	State	Zip
Brown, Katie	12814 South Emerald	Chicago	IL	60601
Hauser, Sam	63 Taylor	Stamford	CT	06904
Marmalard, Greg	1001 Porterhouse	Laredo	TX	78040
O'Hare, Megan	140 Blossom	Shaker Heights	OH	44118
Trumbull, Ellen	302 St. Nicolas	Darien	CT	06820

Field

Language Handbook

Grammar Glossary

This glossary will help you quickly locate information on parts of speech and sentence structure.

A

Absolute phrase. *See* Phrase.

Abstract noun. *See* Noun chart.

Action verb. *See* Verb.

Active voice. *See* Voice.

Adjective A word that modifies a noun or pronoun by limiting its meaning. Adjectives appear in various positions in a sentence. **(The gray cat purred. The cat is gray.)**

Many adjectives have different forms to indicate degree of comparison. **(short, shorter, shortest)**

The positive degree is the simple form of the adjective. **(easy, interesting, good)**

The comparative degree compares two persons, places, things, or ideas. **(easier, more interesting, better)**

The superlative degree compares more than two persons, places, things, or ideas. **(easiest, most interesting, best)**

A predicate adjective follows a linking verb and further identifies or describes the subject. **(The child is happy.)**

A proper adjective is formed from a proper noun and begins with a capital letter. Many proper adjectives are created by adding these suffixes: *-an, -ian, -n, -ese,* and *-ish.* **(Chinese, African)**

Adjective clause. *See* Clause chart.

Adverb A word that modifies a verb, an adjective, or another adverb by making its meaning more specific. When modifying a verb, an adverb may appear in various positions in a sentence. **(Cats generally eat less than dogs. Generally, cats eat less than dogs.)** When modifying an adjective or another adverb, an adverb appears directly before the modified word. **(I was quite pleased that they got along so**

well.) The word *not* and the contraction *-n't* are adverbs. **(Mike wasn't ready for the test today.)** Certain adverbs of time, place, and degree also have a negative meaning. **(He's never ready.)**

Some adverbs have different forms to indicate degree of comparison. **(soon, sooner, soonest)**

The comparative degree compares two actions. **(better, more quickly)**

The superlative degree compares three or more actions. **(fastest, most patiently, least rapidly)**

Adverb clause. *See* Clause chart.

Antecedent. *See* Pronoun.

Appositive A noun or a pronoun that further identifies another noun or pronoun. **(My friend Julie lives next door.)**

Appositive phrase. *See* Phrase.

Article The adjective *a, an,* or *the.*

Indefinite articles **(a, an)** refer to one of a general group of persons, places, or things. **(I eat an apple a day.)**

The definite article **(the)** indicates that the noun is a specific person, place, or thing. **(The alarm woke me up.)**

Auxiliary verb. *See* Verb.

B

Base form. *See* Verb tense.

C

Clause A group of words that has a subject and a predicate and that is used as a sentence or part of a sentence. Clauses fall into two categories: main clauses, which are also called independent clauses, and subordinate clauses, which are also called dependent clauses.

Types of Subordinate Clauses

Clause	Function	Example	Begins with . . .
Adjective clause	Modifies a noun or pronoun	Songs that have a strong beat make me want to dance.	A relative pronoun such as *which, who, whom, whose,* or *that*
Adverb clause	Modifies a verb, an adjective, or an adverb	Whenever Al calls me, he asks to borrow my bike.	A subordinating conjuction such as *after, although, because, if, since, when,* or *where*
Noun clause	Serves as a subject, an object, or a predicate nominative	What Philip did surprised us.	Words such as *how, that, what, whatever, when, where, which, who, whom, whoever, whose,* or *why*

A main clause can stand alone as a sentence. There must be at least one main clause in every sentence. (**The rooster crowed, and the dog barked.**)

A subordinate clause cannot stand alone as a sentence. A subordinate clause needs a main clause to complete its meaning. Many subordinate clauses begin with subordinating conjunctions or relative pronouns. (**When Geri sang her solo, the audience became quiet.**) The chart on this page shows the main types of subordinate clauses.

Collective noun. *See* Noun chart.

Common noun. *See* Noun chart.

Comparative degree. *See* Adjective; Adverb.

Complement A word or phrase that completes the meaning of a verb. The four basic kinds of complements are direct objects, indirect objects, object complements, and subject complements.

A direct object answers the question *what* or *whom* after an action verb. (**Kari found a dollar. Larry saw Denise.**)

An indirect object answers the question *to whom, for whom, to what,* or *for what* after an action verb. (**Do me a favor. She gave the child a toy.**)

An object complement answers the question *what* after a direct object. An object complement is a noun, a pronoun, or an adjective that completes the meaning of a direct object by identifying or describing it. (**The director made me the understudy for the role. The little girl called the puppy hers.**)

A subject complement follows a subject and a linking verb. It identifies or describes a subject. The two kinds of subject complements are predicate nominatives and predicate adjectives.

A predicate nominative is a noun or pronoun that follows a linking verb and tells more about the subject. (**The author of "The Raven" is Edgar Allan Poe.**)

A predicate adjective is an adjective that follows a linking verb and gives more information about the subject. (**Ian became angry at the bully.**)

Complex sentence. *See* Sentence.

Compound preposition. *See* Preposition.

Compound sentence. *See* Sentence.

Compound-complex sentence. *See* Sentence.

Conjunction A word that joins single words or groups of words.

A coordinating conjunction **(and, but, or, nor, for, yet, so)** joins words or groups of words that are equal in grammatical importance. **(David and Ruth are twins. I was bored, so I left.)**

Correlative conjunctions **(both . . . and, just as . . . so, not only . . . but also, either . . . or, neither . . . nor, whether . . . or)** work in pairs to join words and groups of words of equal importance. **(Choose either the muffin or the bagel.)**

A subordinating conjunction **(after, although, as if, because, before, if, since, so that, than, though, until, when, while)** joins a dependent idea or clause to a main clause. **(Beth acted as if she felt ill.)**

Conjunctive adverb An adverb used to clarify the relationship between clauses of equal weight in a sentence. Conjunctive adverbs are used to replace *and* **(also, besides, furthermore, moreover)**, to replace *but* **(however, nevertheless, still)**, to state a result **(consequently, therefore, so, thus)**, or to state equality **(equally, likewise, similarly)**. **(Ana was determined to get an A; therefore, she studied often.)**

Coordinating conjunction. *See* Conjunction.

Correlative conjunction. *See* Conjunction.

D

Declarative sentence. *See* Sentence.

Definite article. *See* Article.

Demonstrative pronoun. *See* Pronoun.

Direct object. *See* Complement.

E

Emphatic form. *See* Verb tense.

F

Future tense. *See* Verb tense.

G

Gerund A verb form that ends in *-ing* and is used as a noun. A gerund may function as a subject, the object of a verb, or the object of a preposition. **(Smiling uses fewer muscles than frowning. Marie enjoys walking.)**

Gerund phrase. *See* Phrase.

I

Imperative mood. *See* Mood of verb.

Imperative sentence. *See* Sentence chart.

Indicative mood. *See* Mood of verb.

Indirect object. *See* Complement.

Infinitive A verb form that begins with the word *to* and functions as a noun, an adjective, or an adverb. **(No one wanted to answer.)** Note: When *to* precedes a verb, it is not a preposition but instead signals an infinitive.

Infinitive phrase. *See* Phrase.

Intensive pronoun. *See* Pronoun.

Interjection A word or phrase that expresses emotion or exclamation. An interjection has no grammatical connection to other words. Commas follow mild ones; exclamation points follow stronger ones. **(Well, have a good day. Wow!)**

Interrogative pronoun. *See* Pronoun.

Intransitive verb. *See* Verb.

Inverted order In a sentence written in inverted order, the predicate comes before the subject. Some sentences are written in inverted order for variety or special emphasis. **(Up the beanstalk scampered Jack.)** The subject also generally follows the predicate in a sentence that begins with *here* or *there*. **(Here was the solution to his problem.)** Questions, or interrogative sentences, are generally written in inverted order. In many questions, an auxiliary verb precedes the subject, and the main verb follows it. **(Has anyone seen Susan?)** Questions that begin with *who* or *what* follow normal word order.

Irregular verb. *See* Verb tense.

L

Linking verb. *See* Verb.

M

Main clause. *See* Clause.

Mood of verb A verb expresses one of three moods: indicative, imperative, or subjunctive.

The indicative mood is the most common. It makes a statement or asks a question. **(We are out of bread. Will you buy it?)**

The imperative mood expresses a command or makes a request. **(Stop acting like a child! Please return my sweater.)**

The subjunctive mood is used to express, indirectly, a demand, suggestion, or statement of necessity **(I demand that he stop acting like a child. It's necessary that she buy more bread.)** The subjunctive is also used to state a condition or wish that is contrary to fact. This use of the subjunctive requires the past tense. **(If you were a nice person, you would return my sweater.)**

N

Nominative pronoun. *See* Pronoun.

Noun A word that names a person, a place, a thing, or an idea. The chart on this page shows the main types of nouns.

Noun clause. *See* Clause chart.

Noun of direct address. *See* Noun chart.

Number A noun, pronoun, or verb is singular in number if it refers to one; plural if it refers to more than one.

O

Object. *See* Complement.

P

Participle A verb form that can function as an adjective. Present participles always end in *-ing*. **(The woman comforted the crying child.)** Many past participles end in *-ed*. **(We bought the beautifully painted chair.)** However, irregular verbs form their past participles in some other way. **(Cato was Caesar's sworn enemy.)**

Passive voice. *See* Voice.

Past tense. *See* Verb tense.

Perfect tense. *See* Verb tense.

Personal pronoun. *See* Pronoun, Pronoun chart.

Types of Nouns

Noun	Function	Example
Abstract noun	Names an idea, a quality, or a state	independence, energy
Collective noun	Names a group of things or persons	herd, troop, crowd, class
Common noun	Names a general type of person, place, thing, or idea	musician, city, building
Compound noun	Is made up of two or more words	checkerboard, parking lot, mother-in-law
Noun of direct address	Identifies the person or persons being spoken to	Maria, please stand.
Possessive noun	Shows possession, ownership, or the relationship between two nouns	my friend's room, my friend's brother
Proper noun	Names a particular person, place, thing, or idea	Cleopatra, Italy, Christianity

Phrase A group of words that acts in a sentence as a single part of speech.

An absolute phrase consists of a noun or pronoun that is modified by a participle or participial phrase but has no grammatical relation to the complete subject or predicate. **(The vegetables being done, we finally sat down to eat dinner.)**

An appositive phrase is an appositive along with any modifiers. If not essential to the meaning of the sentence, an appositive phrase is set off by commas. **(Jack plans to go to the jazz concert, an important musical event.)**

A gerund phrase includes a gerund plus its complements and modifiers. **(Playing the flute is her hobby.)**

An infinitive phrase contains the infinitive plus its complements and modifiers. **(It is time to leave for school.)**

A participial phrase contains a participle and any modifiers necessary to complete its meaning. **(The woman sitting over there is my grandmother.)**

A prepositional phrase consists of a preposition, its object, and any modifiers of the object. A prepositional phrase can function as an adjective, modifying a noun or a pronoun. **(The dog in the yard is very gentle.)** A prepositional phrase may also function as an adverb when it modifies a verb, an adverb, or an adjective. **(The baby slept on my lap.)**

A verb phrase consists of one or more auxiliary verbs followed by a main verb. **(The job will have been completed by noon tomorrow.)**

Positive degree. *See* Adjective.

Possessive noun. *See* Noun chart.

Predicate A verb or verb phrase and any objects, complements, or modifiers that express the essential thought about the subject of a sentence.

A simple predicate is a verb or verb phrase that tells something about the subject. **(We ran.)**

A complete predicate includes the simple predicate and any words that modify or complete it. **(We solved the problem in a short time.)**

A compound predicate has two or more verbs or verb phrases that are joined by a conjunction and share the same subject. **(We ran to the park and began to play baseball.)**

Predicate adjective. *See* Adjective; Complement.

Predicate nominative. *See* Complement.

Preposition A word that shows the relationship of a noun or pronoun to some other word in the sentence. Prepositions include *about, above, across, among, as, behind, below, beyond, but, by, down, during, except, for, from, into, like, near, of, on, outside, over, since, through, to, under, until, with.* **(I usually eat breakfast before school.)**

A compound preposition is made up of more than one word. **(according to, ahead of, as to, because of, by means of, in addition to, in spite of, on account of) (We played the game in spite of the snow.)**

Prepositional phrase. *See* Phrase.

Present tense. *See* Verb tense.

Progressive form. *See* Verb tense.

Pronoun A word that takes the place of a noun, a group of words acting as a noun, or another pronoun. The word or group of words that a pronoun refers to is called its antecedent. (In the following sentence, *Mari* is the antecedent of *she.* **Mari likes Mexican food, but she doesn't like Italian food.)**

A demonstrative pronoun points out specific persons, places, things, or ideas. **(this, that, these, those)**

An indefinite pronoun refers to persons, places, or things in a more general way than a noun does. **(all, another, any, both, each, either, enough, everything, few, many, most, much, neither, nobody, none, one, other, others, plenty, several, some)**

An intensive pronoun adds emphasis to another noun or pronoun. If an intensive pronoun is omitted, the meaning of the sentence will be the same. **(Rebecca herself decided to look for a part-time job.)**

An interrogative pronoun is used to form questions. **(who? whom? whose? what? which?)**

A personal pronoun refers to a specific person or thing. Personal pronouns have three cases: nominative, possessive, and objective. The case depends upon the function of the pronoun in a sentence. The first chart on this page shows the case forms of personal pronouns.

A reflexive pronoun reflects back to a noun or pronoun used earlier in the sentence, indicating that the same person or thing is involved. **(We told ourselves to be patient.)**

A relative pronoun is used to begin a subordinate clause. **(who, whose, that, what, whom, whoever, whomever, whichever, whatever)**

Proper adjective. *See* Adjective.

Proper noun. *See* Noun chart.

R

Reflexive pronoun. *See* Pronoun.

Relative pronoun. *See* Pronoun.

S

Sentence A group of words expressing a complete thought. Every sentence has a subject and a predicate. Sentences can be classified by function or by structure. The second chart on this page shows the categories by function; the following subentries describe the categories by structure. See also Subject; Predicate; Clause.

Personal Pronouns

Case	Singular Pronouns	Plural Pronouns	Function in Sentence
Nominative	I, you, she, he, it	we, you, they	subject or predicate nominative
Objective	me, you, her, him, it	us, you, them	direct object, indirect object, or object of a preposition
Possessive	my, mine, your, yours, her, hers, his, its	our, ours, your, yours, their, theirs	replacement for the possessive form of a noun

Types of Sentences

Sentence Type	Function	Ends with . . .	Examples
Declarative sentence	Makes a statement	A period	I did not enjoy the movie.
Exclamatory sentence	Expresses strong emotion	An exclamation point	The books are already finished!
Imperative sentence	Expresses a request or a demand	A period or an exclamation point	Please come to the party. Stop!
Interrogative sentence	Asks a question	A question mark	Is the composition due today?

A simple sentence has only one main clause and no subordinate clauses. **(Alan found an old violin.)** A simple sentence may contain a compound subject or a compound predicate or both. **(Alan and Teri found an old violin. Alan found an old violin and tried to play it. Alan and Teri found an old violin and tried to play it.)** The subject and the predicate can be expanded with adjectives, adverbs, prepositional phrases, appositives, and verbal phrases. As long as the sentence has only one main clause, however, it remains a simple sentence. **(Alan, rummaging in the attic, found an old violin.)**

A compound sentence has two or more main clauses. Each main clause has its own subject and predicate, and these main clauses are usually joined by a comma and a coordinating conjunction. **(Cats meow and dogs bark, but ducks quack.)** Semicolons may also be used to join the main clauses in a compound sentence. **(The helicopter landed; the pilot had saved four passengers.)**

A complex sentence has one main clause and one or more subordinate clauses. **(Since the movie starts at eight, we should leave here by seven-thirty.)**

A compound-complex sentence has two or more main clauses and at least one subordinate clause.
(If we leave any later, we may miss the previews, and I want to see them.)

Simple predicate. *See* Predicate.

Simple subject. *See* Subject.

Subject The part of a sentence that tells what the sentence is about.

A simple subject is the main noun or pronoun in the subject. **(Babies crawl.)**

A complete subject includes the simple subject and any words that modify it. **(The man from New Jersey won the race.)** In some sentences, the simple subject and the complete subject are the same. **(Birds fly.)**

A compound subject has two or more simple subjects joined by a conjunction. The subjects share the same verb. **(Firefighters and police officers protect the community.)**

Subjunctive mood. *See* Mood of verb.

Subordinate clause. *See* Clause.

Subordinating conjunction. *See* Conjunction.

Superlative degree. *See* Adjective; Adverb.

T

Tense. *See* Verb tense.

Transitive verb. *See* Verb.

V

Verb A word that expresses action or a state of being. **(cooks, seem, laughed)**

An action verb tells what someone or something does. Action verbs can express either physical or mental action. **(Crystal decided to change the tire herself.)**

A transitive verb is an action verb that is followed by a word or words that answer the question *what* or *whom*. **(I held the baby.)**

An intransitive verb is an action verb that is not followed by a word that answers the question *what* or *whom*. **(The baby laughed.)**

A linking verb expresses a state of being by linking the subject of a sentence with a word or an expression that identifies or describes the subject. **(The lemonade tastes sweet. He is our new principal.)** The most commonly used linking verb is *be* in all its forms **(am, is, are, was, were, will be, been, being).** Other linking verbs include *appear, become, feel, grow, look, remain, seem, sound, smell, stay, taste.*

An auxiliary verb, or helping verb, is a verb that accompanies the main verb to form a verb phrase. **(I have been swimming.)** The forms of *be* and *have* are the most common auxiliary verbs: **am, is, are, was, were, being, been; has, have, had, having.** Other auxiliaries include *can, could, do, does, did, may, might, must, shall, should, will, would.*

Verbal A verb form that functions in a sentence as a noun, an adjective, or an adverb. The three kinds of verbals are gerunds, infinitives, and participles. *See* Gerund; Infinitive; Participle.

Verb tense The tense of a verb indicates when the action or state of being occurs. All the verb tenses are formed from the four principal parts of a verb: a base form **(talk)**, a present participle **(talking)**, a simple past form **(talked)**, and a past participle **(talked)**. A regular verb forms its simple past and past participle by adding *-ed* to the base form **(climb, climbed)**. An irregular verb forms its past and past participle in some other way **(get, got, gotten)**.

In addition to present, past, and future tenses, there are three perfect tenses.

> The present perfect tense expresses an action or condition that occurred at some indefinite time in the past. This tense also shows an action or condition that began in the past and continues into the present. **(She has played the piano for four years.)**

> The past perfect tense indicates that one past action or condition began and ended before another past action started. **(Andy had finished his homework before I even began mine.)**

The future perfect tense indicates that one future action or condition will begin and end before another future event starts. Use *will have* or *shall have* with the past participle of a verb. **(By tomorrow, I will have finished my homework too.)**

The progressive form of a verb expresses a continuing action with any of the six tenses. Use the appropriate tense of the verb *be* with the present participle of the main verb. **(She is swimming. She has been swimming.)**

The emphatic form adds special force, or emphasis, to the present and past tense of a verb. For the emphatic form, use *do, does,* or *did* with the base form. **(Toshi did want that camera.)**

Voice The voice of a verb shows whether the subject performs the action or receives the action of the verb.

> A verb is in the active voice if the subject of the sentence performs the action. **(The referee blew the whistle.)**

> A verb is in the passive voice if the subject of the sentence receives the action of the verb. **(The whistle was blown by the referee.)**

Troubleshooter

Use the Troubleshooter to recognize and correct common writing errors.

Sentence Fragment

A sentence fragment does not express a complete thought. It may lack a subject, a verb, or both parts.

Problem: A fragment that lacks a subject

The lion paced the floor of the cage. Looked hungry. frag

Solution: Add a subject to the fragment to make a complete sentence.

The lion paced the floor of the cage. It looked hungry.

Problem: A fragment that lacks a predicate

I'm painting my room. The walls yellow. frag

Solution: Add a predicate to make the sentence complete.

I'm painting my room. The walls are going to be yellow.

Problem: A fragment that lacks both a subject and a predicate

We walked around the reservoir. Near the parkway. frag

Solution: Combine the fragment with another sentence.

We walked around the reservoir near the parkway.

Tip: When subject and verb are separated by a prepositional phrase, check for agreement by reading the sentence without the prepositional phrase.

Run-on Sentence

A run-on sentence is two or more sentences written incorrectly as one sentence.

Problem: Two main clauses separated only by a comma

Roller coasters make me dizzy, I don't enjoy them. run-on

Solution A: Replace the comma with a period or other end mark. Start the second sentence with a capital letter.

Roller coasters make me dizzy. I don't enjoy them.

Solution B: Replace the comma with a semicolon.

Roller coasters make me dizzy; I don't enjoy them.

Problem: Two main clauses with no punctuation between them

Acid rain is a worldwide problem there are no solutions in sight. run-on

Solution A: Separate the main clauses with a period or other end mark. Begin the second sentence with a capital letter.

Acid rain is a worldwide problem. There are no solutions in sight.

Solution B: Add a comma and a coordinating conjunction between the main clauses.

Acid rain is a worldwide problem, but there are no solutions in sight.

Problem: Two main clauses with no comma before the coordinating conjunction

Our chorus has been practicing all month but we still need another rehearsal. run-on

Solution: Add a comma before the coordinating conjunction.

Our chorus has been practicing all month, but we still need another rehearsal.

Lack of Subject-Verb Agreement

A singular subject calls for a singular form of the verb. A plural subject calls for a plural form of the verb.

Problem: A subject that is separated from the verb by an intervening prepositional phrase

The two policemen at the construction site looks bored. agr

The members of my baby-sitting club is saving money. agr

Solution: Make sure that the verb agrees with the subject of the sentence, not with the object of the preposition. The object of a preposition is never the subject.

The two policemen at the construction site look bored.

The members of my baby-sitting club are saving money.

Tip: When subject and verb are separated by a prepositional phrase, check for agreement by reading the sentence without the prepositional phrase.

Problem: A sentence that begins with *here* or *there*

Here come the last bus to Pelham Heights. agr

There is my aunt and uncle. agr

Solution: In sentences that begin with *here* or *there*, look for the subject after the verb. Make sure that the verb agrees with the subject.

Here comes the last bus to Pelham Heights.

There are my aunt and uncle.

Problem: An indefinite pronoun as the subject

Each of the candidates are qualified. agr

All of the problems on the test was hard. agr

Solution: Some indefinite pronouns are singular; some are plural; and some can be either singular or plural, depending on the noun they refer to. Determine whether the indefinite pronoun is singular or plural, and make sure the verb agrees with it.

Each of the candidates is qualified.

All of the problems on the test were hard.

Problem: A compound subject that is joined by *and*

Fishing tackle and a life jacket was stowed in the boat. agr

Peanut butter and jelly are delicious. agr

Solution A: If the compound subjects refer to different people or things, use a plural verb.

Fishing tackle and a life jacket were stowed in the boat.

Solution B: If the parts of a compound subject name one unit or if they refer to the same person or thing, use a singular verb.

Peanut butter and jelly is delicious.

Problem: A compound subject that is joined by *or* or *nor*

Either my aunt or my parents plans to attend parents' night. agr

Neither onions nor pepper improve the taste of this meatloaf. agr

Solution: Make the verb agree with the subject that is closer to it.

Either my aunt or my parents plan to attend parents' night.

Neither onions nor pepper improves the taste of this meatloaf.

Incorrect Verb Tense or Form

Verbs have different tenses to show when the action takes place.

Problem: An incorrect or missing verb ending

The Parks Department install a new water fountain last week. tense

They have also plant flowers in all the flower beds. tense

Solution: To form the past tense and the part participle, add *-ed* to a regular verb.

The Parks Department installed a new water fountain last week.

They have also planted flowers in all the flower beds.

Problem: An improperly formed irregular verb

Wendell has standed in line for two hours. tense

I catched the fly ball and throwed it to first base. tense

Solution: Irregular verbs vary in their past and past participle forms. Look up the ones you are not sure of.

Wendell has stood in line for two hours.

I caught the fly ball and threw it to first base.

Problem: Confusion between the past form and the past participle

The cast for The Music Man has began rehearsals. tense

Solution: Use the past participle form of an irregular verb, not its past form, when you use the auxiliary verb *have*.

The cast for The Music Man has begun rehearsals.

Problem: Improper use of the past participle

Our seventh grade <u>drawn</u> a mural for the wall of the cafeteria. tense

Solution: Add the auxiliary verb have to the past participle of an irregular verb to form a complete verb.

Our seventh grade <u>has drawn</u> a mural for the wall of the cafeteria.

Tip: Because irregular verbs vary, it is useful to memorize the verbs that you use most often.

Incorrect Use of Pronouns

The noun that a pronoun refers to is called its **antecedent.** A pronoun must refer to its antecedent clearly. Subject pronouns refer to subjects in a sentence. Object pronouns refer to objects in a sentence.

Problem: A pronoun that could refer to more than one antecedent

Gary and Mike are coming, but <u>he</u> doesn't know the other kids. ant

Solution: Substitute a noun for the pronoun to make your sentence clearer.

Gary and Mike are coming, but <u>Gary</u> doesn't know the other kids.

Problem: Personal pronouns as subjects

<u>Him</u> and John were freezing after skating for three hours. pro

Lori and <u>me</u> decided not to audition for the musical. pro

Solution: Use a subject pronoun as the subject part of a sentence.

<u>He</u> and John were freezing after skating for three hours.

Lori and <u>I</u> decided not to audition for the musical.

Problem: Personal pronouns as objects

Ms. Wang asked Reggie and <u>I</u> to enter the science fair. pro

Ms. Wang helped <u>he</u> and I with the project. pro

Solution: Use an object pronoun as the object of a verb or a preposition.

Ms. Wang asked Reggie and <u>me</u> to enter the science fair.

Ms. Wang helped <u>him</u> and me with the project.

Incorrect Use of Adjectives

Some adjectives have irregular forms: comparative forms for comparing two things and superlative forms for comparing more than two things.

Problem: Incorrect use of *good, better, best*

Their team is <u>more good</u> at softball than ours. adj

They have <u>more better</u> equipment too. adj

Solution: The comparative and superlative forms of good are better and best. Do not use more or most before irregular forms of comparative and superlative adjectives.

Their team is <u>better</u> at softball than ours.

They have <u>better</u> equipment too.

Problem: Incorrect use of *bad, worse, worst*

The flooding on East Street was the <u>baddest</u> I've seen. adj

Mike's basement was in <u>badder</u> shape than his garage. adj

Solution: The comparative and superlative forms of *bad* are *worse* and *worst*. Do not use *more* or *most* or the endings *-er* or *-est* with *bad*.

The flooding on East Street was the <u>worst</u> I've seen.

Mike's basement was in <u>worse</u> shape than his garage.

Problem: Incorrect use of comparative and superlative adjectives

The Appalachian Mountains are <u>more older</u> than the Rockies. adj

Mount Washington is the <u>most highest</u> of the Appalachians. ⌐adj

Solution: Do not use both *-er* and *more* or *-est* and *most* at the same time.

The Appalachian Mountains are <u>older</u> than the Rockies.

Mount Washington is the <u>highest</u> of the Appalachians.

Incorrect Use of Commas

Commas signal a pause between parts of a sentence and help to clarify meaning.

Problem: Missing commas in a series of three or more items

Sergio put <u>mustard catsup and bean sprouts</u> on his hot dog. ⌐com

Solution: If there are three or more items in a series, use a comma after each one, including the item preceding the conjunction.

Sergio put <u>mustard, catsup, and bean sprouts</u> on his hot dog.

Problem: Missing commas with direct quotations

"A little cold <u>water</u>" the swim coach <u>said</u> "won't hurt you." ⌐com

Solution: The first part of an interrupted quotation ends with a comma followed by quotation marks. The interrupting words are also followed by a comma.

"A little cold <u>water</u>," the swim coach <u>said</u>, "won't hurt you."

Problem: Missing commas with nonessential appositives

My sneakers <u>a new pair</u> are covered with mud. ⌐com

Solution: Determine whether the appositive is important to the meaning of the sentence. If it is not essential, set off the appositive with commas.

My sneakers, <u>a new pair</u>, are covered with mud.

Incorrect Use of Apostrophes

An apostrophe shows possession. It can also indicate missing letters in a contraction.

Problem: Singular possessive nouns

A <u>parrots</u> toes are used for gripping. ⌐poss

The <u>bus</u> color was bright yellow. ⌐poss

Solution: Use an apostrophe and an *s* to form the possessive of a singular noun, even one that ends in *s*.

A <u>parrot's</u> toes are used for gripping.

The <u>bus's</u> color was bright yellow.

Problem: Plural possessive nouns ending in *-s*

The <u>visitors</u> center closes at five o'clock. ⌐poss

The guide put several <u>tourists</u> luggage in one compartment. ⌐poss

Solution: Use an apostrophe alone to form the possessive of a plural noun that ends in *s*.

The <u>visitors'</u> center closes at five o'clock.

The guide put several <u>tourists'</u> luggage in one compartment.

Problem: Plural possessive nouns not ending in *-s*

The <u>peoples</u> applause gave courage to the young gymnast. ⌐poss

Solution: Use an apostrophe and an *s* to form the possessive of a plural noun that does not end in *s*.

The <u>people's</u> applause gave courage to the young gymnast.

Problem: Possessive personal pronouns

Jenny found the locker that was <u>her's</u>; she waited while her friends found <u>their's</u>. ⌐poss

Solution: Do not use apostrophes with possessive personal pronouns.

Jenny found the locker that was <u>hers</u>; she waited while her friends found <u>theirs</u>.

Incorrect Capitalization

Proper nouns, proper adjectives, and the first words of sentences always begin with a capital letter.

Problem: Words referring to ethnic groups, nationalities, and languages

Many <u>canadians</u> in the province of <u>quebec</u> speak <u>french</u>. cap

Solution: Capitalize proper nouns and adjectives that refer to ethnic groups, nationalities, and languages.

Many <u>Canadians</u> in the province of <u>Quebec</u> speak <u>French</u>.

Problem: Words that refer to a family member

Yesterday <u>aunt</u> Doreen asked me to baby-sit. cap

Don't forget to give <u>dad</u> a call. cap

Solution: Capitalize words that are used as part of or in place of a family member's name.

Yesterday <u>Aunt</u> Doreen asked me to baby-sit.

Don't forget to give <u>Dad</u> a call.

Tip: Do not capitalize a word that identifies a family member when it is preceded by a possessive adjective: My father bought a new car.

Problem: The first word of a direct quotation

The judge declared, "<u>the</u> court is now in session." cap

Solution: Capitalize the first word in a direct quotation.

The judge declared, "<u>The</u> court is now in session."

Tip: If you have difficulty with a rule of usage, try rewriting the rule in your own words. Check with your teacher to be sure you understand the rule.

Troublesome Words

This section will help you choose between words and expressions that are often confusing or misused.

accept, except

Accept means "to receive." *Except* means "other than."

Phillip walked proudly to the stage to <u>accept</u> the award.

Everything fits in my suitcase <u>except</u> my sleeping bag.

affect, effect

Affect is a verb meaning "to cause a change in" or "to influence." *Effect* as a verb means "to bring about or accomplish." As a noun, *effect* means "result."

Bad weather will <u>affect</u> our plans for the weekend.

The new medicine <u>effected</u> an improvement in the patient's condition.

The gloomy weather had a bad <u>effect</u> on my mood.

ain't

Ain't is never used in formal speaking or writing unless you are quoting the exact words of a character or a real person. Instead of using *ain't*, say or write *am not, is not, are not*; or use contractions such as *I'm not, she isn't*.

The pizza <u>is not</u> going to arrive for another half hour.

The pizza <u>isn't</u> going to arrive for another half hour.

a lot

The expression *a lot* means "much" or "many" and should always be written as two words. Some authorities discourage its use in formal writing.

A lot of my friends are learning Spanish.

Many of my friends are learning Spanish.

all ready, already

All ready, written as two words, is a phrase that means "completely ready." *Already,* written as one word, is an adverb that means "before" or "by this time."

By the time the fireworks display was all ready, we had already arrived.

all right, alright

The expression *all right* should be written as two words. Some dictionaries do list the single word *alright* but usually not as a preferred spelling.

Tom hurt his ankle, but he will be all right.

all together, altogether

All together means "in a group." *Altogether* means "completely."

The Minutemen stood all together at the end of Lexington Green.

The rebel farmers were not altogether sure that they could fight the British soldiers.

among, between

Use *among* for three or more people, things, or groups. Use *between* for two people, things, or groups.

Mr. Kendall divided the jobs for the car wash among the team members.

Our soccer field lies between the gym and Main Street.

amount, number

Use *amount* with nouns that cannot be counted. Use *number* with nouns that can be counted.

This recipe calls for an unusual amount of pepper.

A record number of students attended last Saturday's book fair.

bad, badly

Bad is an adjective; it modifies a noun. *Badly* is an adverb; it modifies a verb, an adjective, or another adverb.

The badly burnt cookies left a bad smell in the kitchen.

Joseph badly wants to be on the track team.

beside, besides

Beside means "next to." *Besides* means "in addition to."

The zebra is grazing beside a wildebeest.

Besides the zoo, I like to visit the aquarium.

bring, take

Bring means "to carry from a distant place to a closer one." *Take* means "to carry from a nearby place to a more distant one."

Please bring a bag lunch and subway money to school tomorrow.

Don't forget to take your art projects home this afternoon.

can, may

Can implies the ability to do something. *May* implies permission to do something.

You may take a later bus home if you can remember which bus to get on.

Tip: Although *can* is sometimes used in place of *may* in informal speech, a distinction should be made when speaking and writing formally.

choose, chose

Choose means "to select." *Chose*, the past tense of *choose*, means "selected."

Dad helped me choose a birthday card for my grandmother.

Dad chose a card with a funny joke inside.

doesn't, don't

The subject of the contraction *doesn't (does not)* is the third-person singular (*he* or *she*). The subject of the contraction *don't (do not)* is *I, you, we,* or *they.*

Tanya doesn't have any tickets for the concert.

We don't need tickets if we stand in the back row.

farther, further

Farther refers to physical distance. *Further* refers to time or degree.

Our new apartment is farther away from the school.

I will not continue this argument further.

fewer, less

Fewer is used to refer to things or qualities that can be counted. *Less* is used to refer to things or qualities that cannot be counted. In addition, *less* is used with figures that are regarded as single amounts.

Fewer people were waiting in line after lunch.

There is less fat in this kind of peanut butter.

Try to spend less than ten dollars on a present. [The money is treated as a single sum, not as individual dollars.]

good, well

Good is often used as an adjective meaning "pleasing" or "able." *Well* may be used as an adverb of manner telling how ably something is done or as an adjective meaning "in good health."

That is a good haircut.

Marco writes well.

Because Ms. Rodriguez had a headache, she was not well enough to correct our tests.

in, into

In means "inside." *Into* indicates a movement from outside toward the inside.

Refreshments will be sold in the lobby of the auditorium.

The doors opened, and the eager crowd rushed into the auditorium.

it's, its

Use an apostrophe to form the contraction of *it is.* The possessive of the personal pronoun *it* does not take an apostrophe.

It's hard to keep up with computer technology.

The computer industry seems to change its products daily.

lay, lie

Lay means "to place." *Lie* means "to recline."

I will lay my beach towel here on the warm sand.

Help! I don't want to lie next to a hill of red ants!

learn, teach

Learn means "to gain knowledge." *Teach* means "to give knowledge."

I don't learn very quickly.

My uncle is teaching me how to juggle.

leave, let

Leave means "to go away." *Let* means "to allow." With the word *alone,* you may use either *let* or *leave.*

Huang has to leave at eight o'clock.

Mr. Davio lets the band practice in his basement.

Leave me alone. Let me alone.

like, as

Use *like,* a preposition, to introduce a phrase of comparison. Use *as,* a subordinating conjunction, to introduce a subordinate clause. Many authorities believe that *like* should not be used before a clause in formal English.

Andy sometimes acts like a clown.

The detective looked carefully at the empty suitcase as she examined the room.

Tip: *As* can be a preposition in cases like the following: *Jack went to the costume party as a giant pumpkin.*

loose, lose

Loose means "not firmly attached." *Lose* means "to misplace" or "to fail to win."

If you keep wiggling that loose tooth, you might lose it.

raise, rise

Raise means to "cause to move up." *Rise* means "to move upward."

Farmers in this part of Florida raise sugarcane.

The hot air balloon began to rise slowly in the morning sky.

set, sit

Set means "to place" or "to put." *Sit* means "to place oneself in a seated position."

I set the tips of my running shoes against the starting line.

After running the fifty-yard dash, I had to sit down and catch my breath.

than, then

Than introduces the second part of a comparison. *Then* means "at that time" or "after that."

I'd rather go to Disney World in the winter than in the summer.

The park is too crowded and hot then.

their, they're

Their is the possessive form of *they. They're* is the contraction of *they are.*

They're visiting Plymouth Plantation during their vacation.

to, too, two

To means "in the direction of." *Too* means "also" or "to an excessive degree." *Two* is the number after one.

I bought two tickets to the concert.

The music was too loud.

It's my favorite group too.

who, whom

Who is a subject pronoun. *Whom* is an object pronoun.

Who has finished the test already?

Mr. Russo is the man to whom we owe our thanks.

who's, whose

Who's is the contraction of *who is. Whose* is the possessive form of *who.*

Who's going to wake me up in the morning?

The policeman discovered whose car alarm was making so much noise.

Mechanics

This section will help you use correct capitalization, punctuation, and abbreviations in your writing.

Capitalization

Capitalizing Sentences, Quotations, and Salutations

Rule: A capital letter appears at the beginning of a sentence.

Example: *Another gust of wind shook the house.*

Rule: A capital letter marks the beginning of a direct quotation that is a complete sentence.

Example: *Sabrina said, "The lights might go out."*

Rule: When a quoted sentence is interrupted by explanatory words, such as *she said,* do not begin the second part of the sentence with a capital letter.

Example: *"There's a rainbow," exclaimed Jeffrey, "over the whole beach."*

Rule: When the second part of a quotation is a new sentence, put a period after the explanatory words; begin the new part with a capital letter.

Example: *"Please come inside," Justin said. "Wipe your feet."*

Rule: Do not capitalize an indirect quotation.

Example: *Jo said that the storm was getting worse.*

Rule: Capitalize the first word in the salutation and closing of a letter. Capitalize the title and name of the person addressed.

Example: *Dear Dr. Menino*

Dear Editor

Sincerely

Capitalizing Names and Titles of People

Rule: Capitalize the names of people and the initials that stand for their names.

Example: *Malcolm X; J. F. K.; Robert E. Lee; Queen Elizabeth I*

Rule: Capitalize a title or an abbreviation of a title when it comes before a person's name or when it is used in direct address.

Example: *Dr. Salinas, "Your patient, Doctor, is waiting."*

Rule: Do not capitalize a title that follows or is a substitute for a person's name.

Example: *Marcia Salinas is a good doctor. He asked to speak to the doctor.*

Rule: Capitalize the names and abbreviations of academic degrees that follow a person's name. Capitalize *Jr.* and *Sr.*

Example: *Marcia Salinas, M.D.; Raoul Tobias, Attorney; Donald Bruns Sr.; Ann Lee, Ph.D.*

Rule: Capitalize words that show family relationships when used as titles or as substitutes for a person's name.

Example: *We saw Uncle Carlos.*

She read a book about Mother Teresa.

Rule: Do not capitalize words that show family relationships when they follow a possessive noun or pronoun.

Example: *Your brother will give us a ride.*

I forgot my mother's phone number.

Rule: Always capitalize the pronoun *I*.

Example: *After I clean my room, I'm going swimming.*

Capitalizing Names of Places

Tip: Do not capitalize articles and prepositions in proper nouns: *the Rock of Gibraltar, the Statue of Liberty.*

Rule: Capitalize the names of cities, counties, states, countries, and continents.

Example: *St. Louis, Missouri; Marin County; Australia; South America*

Rule: Capitalize the names of bodies of water and other geographical features.

Example: *the Great Lakes; Cape Cod; the Dust Bowl*

Rule: Capitalize the names of sections of a country and regions of the world.

Example: *East Asia; New England; the Pacific Rim; the Midwest*

Rule: Capitalize compass points when they refer to a specific section of a country.

Example: *the Northwest; the South*

Rule: Do not capitalize compass points when they indicate direction.

Example: *Canada is north of the United States.*

Rule: Do not capitalize adjectives indicating direction.

Example: *western Utah*

Rule: Capitalize the names of streets and highways.

Example: *Dorchester Avenue; Route 22*

Rule: Capitalize the names of buildings, bridges, monuments, and other structures.

Example: *Sears Tower; Chesapeake Bay Bridge*

Capitalizing Other Proper Nouns and Adjectives

Rule: Capitalize the names of clubs, organizations, businesses, institutions, and political parties.

Example: *Houston Oilers; the Food and Drug Administration; Boys and Girls Club*

Rule: Capitalize brand names but not the nouns following them.

Example: *Zippo brand energy bar*

Rule: Capitalize the names of days of the week, months, and holidays.

Example: *Saturday; June; Thanksgiving Day*

Rule: Do not capitalize the names of seasons.

Example: *winter; spring; summer; fall*

Rule: Capitalize the first word, the last word, and all important words in the title of a book, play, short story, poem, essay, article, film, television series, song, magazine, newspaper, and chapter of a book.

Example: *Not Without Laughter; World Book Encyclopedia; "Jingle Bells"; Star Wars; Chapter 12*

Rule: Capitalize the names of ethnic groups, nationalities, and languages.

Example: *Latino; Japanese; European; Spanish*

Rule: Capitalize proper adjectives that are formed from the names of ethnic groups and nationalities.

Example: *Shetland pony; Jewish holiday*

Punctuation

Using the Period and Other End Marks

Rule: Use a period at the end of a declarative sentence.

Example: *My great-grandfather fought in the Mexican Revolution.*

Rule: Use a period at the end of an imperative sentence that does not express strong feeling.

Example: *Please set the table.*

Rule: Use a question mark at the end of an interrogative sentence.

Example: *How did your sneakers get so muddy?*

Rule: Use an exclamation point at the end of an exclamatory sentence or a strong imperative.

Example: *How exciting the play was!*
Watch out!

Using Commas

Rule: Use commas to separate three or more items in a series.

> **The canary eats bird seed, fruit, and suet.**

Rule: Use commas to show a pause after an introductory word and to set off names used in direct address.

> **Yes, I offered to take care of her canary this weekend.**

> **Please, Stella, can I borrow your nail polish?**

Rule: Use a comma after two or more introductory prepositional phrases or when the comma is needed to make the meaning clear. A comma is not needed after a single short prepositional phrase, but it is acceptable to use one.

> **From the back of the balcony, we had a lousy view of the stage.**

> **After the movie we walked home. (no comma needed)**

Rule: Use a comma after an introductory participle and an introductory participial phrase.

> **Whistling and moaning, the wind shook the little house.**

Rule: Use commas to set off words that interrupt the flow of thought in a sentence.

> **Tomorrow, I think, our projects are due.**

Rule: Use a comma after conjunctive adverbs such as however, moreover, furthermore, nevertheless, and therefore.

> **The skating rink is crowded on Saturday; however, it's the only time I can go.**

Rule: Use commas to set off an appositive if it is not essential to the meaning of a sentence.

> **Ben Wagner, a resident of Pittsfield, won the first round in the golf tournament.**

Rule: Use a comma before a conjunction (*and, or, but, nor, so, yet*) that joins main clauses.

> **We can buy our tickets now, or we can take a chance on buying them just before the show.**

Rule: Use a comma after an introductory adverb clause.

> **Because I stayed up so late, I'm sleepy this morning.**

Rule: In most cases, do not use a comma with an adverb clause that comes at the end of a sentence.

> **The picnic will be canceled unless the weather clears.**

Rule: Use a comma or a pair of commas to set off an adjective clause that is not essential to the meaning of a sentence.

> **Tracy, who just moved here from Florida, has never seen snow before.**

Rule: Do not use a comma or pair of commas to set off an essential clause from the rest of the sentence.

> **Anyone who signs up this month will get a discount.**

Rule: Use commas before and after the year when it is used with both the month and the day. If only the month and the year are given, do not use a comma.

> **On January 2, 1985, my parents moved to Dallas, Texas.**

> **I was born in May 1985.**

Rule: Use commas before and after the name of a state or a country when it is used with the name of a city. Do not use a comma after the state if it is used with a ZIP code.

> **The area code for Concord, New Hampshire, is 603.**

> **Please forward my mail to 6 Madison Lane, Topsham, ME 04086**

Rule: Use commas or a pair of commas to set off an abbreviated title or degree following a person's name.

> **The infirmary was founded by Elizabeth Blackwell, M.D., the first woman in the United States to earn a medical degree.**

Rule: Use a comma or commas to set off *too* when *too* means "also."

We, too, bought groceries, from the new online supermarket.

Rule: Use a comma or commas to set off a direct quotation.

"My nose," exclaimed Pinocchio, "is growing longer!"

Rule: Use a comma after the salutation of a friendly letter and after the closing of both a friendly letter and a business letter.

Dear Gary,
Sincerely,
Best regards,

Rule: Use a comma when necessary to prevent misreading of a sentence.

In math, solutions always elude me.

Using Semicolons and Colons

Rule: Use a semicolon to join the parts of a compound sentence when a coordinating conjunction, such as *and, or, nor,* or *but,* is not used.

Don't be late for the dress rehearsal; it begins at 7 o'clock sharp.

Rule: Use a semicolon to join parts of a compound sentence when the main clauses are long and are subdivided by commas. Use a semicolon even if these clauses are already joined by a coordinating conjunction.

In the gray light of early morning, on a remote airstrip in the desert, two pilots prepared to fly on a dangerous mission; but accompanying them were a television camera crew, three newspaper reporters, and a congressman from their home state of Nebraska.

Rule: Use a semicolon to separate main clauses joined by a conjunctive adverb. Be sure to use a comma after the conjunctive adverb.

We've been climbing all morning; therefore, we need a rest.

Rule: Use a colon to introduce a list of items that ends a sentence. Use words such as *these, the following,* or *as follows* to signal that a list is coming.

Remember to bring the following items: a backpack, a bag lunch, sunscreen, and insect repellent.

Rule: Do not use a colon to introduce a list preceded by a verb or preposition.

Remember to bring a backpack, a bag lunch, sunscreen, and insect repellent. (No colon is used after bring.)

Rule: Use a colon to separate the hour and the minutes when you write the time of day.

My Spanish class starts at 9:15.

Rule: Use a colon after the salutation of a business letter.

Dear Dr. Coulombe:
Director of the Personnel Dept.:

Using Quotation Marks and Italics

Rule: Use quotation marks before and after a direct quotation.

"Curiouser and curiouser," said Alice.

Rule: Use quotation marks with both parts of a divided quotation.

"This gymnastics trick," explained Amanda, "took me three months to learn."

Rule: Use a comma or commas to separate a phrase such as *she said* from the quotation itself. Place the comma that precedes the phrase inside the closing quotation marks.

"I will be late," said the cable technician, "for my appointment."

Rule: Place a period that ends a quotation inside the closing quotation marks.

Scott said, "Thanks for letting me borrow your camping tent."

Rule: Place a question mark or an exclamation point inside the quotation marks when it is part of the quotation.

> **"Why is the door of your snake's cage open?" asked my mother.**

Rule: Place a question mark or an exclamation point outside the quotation marks when it is part of the entire sentence.

> **How I love "The Pit and the Pendulum"!**

Rule: Use quotation marks for the title of a short story, essay, poem, song, magazine or newspaper article, or book chapter.

> **short story: "The Necklace"**
> **poem: "The Fish"**
> **article: "Fifty Things to Make from Bottlecaps"**

Rule: Use italics or underlining for the title of a book, play, film, television series, magazine, newspaper, or work of art.

> **book: *To Kill a Mockingbird***
> **magazine: *The New Republic***
> **painting: *Sunflowers***

Rule: Use italics or underlining for the names of ships, trains, airplanes, and spacecraft.

> **ship: *Mayflower***
> **airplane: *Air Force One***

Using Apostrophes

Rule: Use an apostrophe and an *s* to form the possessive of a singular noun.

> **my brother's rock collection**
> **Chris's hat**

Rule: Use an apostrophe and an *s* to form the possessive of a plural noun that does not end in *s*.

> **the geese's feathers**
> **children's books**

Tip: If a thing is owned jointly by two or more individuals, only the last name should show possession: *Mom and Dad's car.* If the ownership is not joint, each name should show possession: *Mom's and Dad's parents are coming for Thanksgiving.*

Rule: Use an apostrophe alone to form the possessive of a plural noun that ends in *s*.

> **the animals' habitat**
> **the instruments' sound**

Rule: Use an apostrophe and an *s* to form the possessive of an indefinite pronoun.

> **everyone's homework**
> **someone's homework**

Rule: Do not use an apostrophe in a possessive pronoun.

> **The dog knocked over its dish.**
> **Yours is the best entry in the contest.**
> **One of these drawings must be hers.**

Rule: Use an apostrophe to replace letters that have been omitted in a contraction.

> **it + is = it's**
> **can + not = can't**
> **I + have = I've**

Rule: Use an apostrophe to form the plural of a letter, a figure, or a word that is used as itself.

> **Write three 7's.**
> **The word is spelled with two *m's.***
> **The sentence contains three *and's.***

Rule: Use an apostrophe to show missing numbers in a year.

> **the class of '02**

Using Hyphens, Dashes, and Parentheses

Rule: Use a hyphen to show the division of a word at the end of a line. Always divide the word between its syllables.

> **With the new recycling program, more residents are recycling their trash.**

Tip: One-letter divisions (for example, *e-lectric*) are not permissible. Avoid dividing personal names, if possible.

Rule: Use a hyphen in a number written as a compound word.

> **He sold forty-six ice creams in one hour.**

Rule: Use a hyphen in a fraction.

> **We won the vote by a two-thirds majority.**
> **Two-thirds of the votes have been counted.**

Rule: Use a hyphen or hyphens in certain compound nouns.

> **great-grandmother**
> **merry-go-round**

Rule: Hyphenate a compound modifier only when it precedes the word it modifies.

> **A well-known musician visited our school.**
> **The story was well written.**

Rule: Use a hyphen after the prefixes *all-, ex-,* and *self-* when they are joined to any noun or adjective.

> **all-star**
> **ex-president**
> **self-conscious**

Rule: Use a hyphen to separate any prefix from a word that begins with a capital letter.

> **un-American**
> **mid-January**

Rule: Use a dash or dashes to show a sudden break or change in thought or speech.

> **Daniel—he's kind of a pest—is my youngest cousin.**

Rule: Use parentheses to set off words that define or helpfully explain a word in the sentence.

> **The transverse flute (transverse means "sideways") is a wind instrument.**

Abbreviations

Rule: Abbreviate the titles *Mr., Mrs., Ms.,* and *Dr.* before a person's name. Also abbreviate any professional or academic degree that follows a name. The titles *Jr.* and *Sr.* are not preceded by a comma.

> **Dr. Stanley Livingston**
> **Luisa Mendez, M.A.**
> **Martin Luther King Jr.**

Rule: Use capital letters and no periods with abbreviations that are pronounced letter by letter or as words. Exceptions are *U.S.* and *Washington, D.C.,* which do use periods.

NAACP	**National Association for the Advancement of Colored People**
UFO	**unidentified flying object**
MADD	**Mothers Against Drunk Driving**

Rule: With exact times use A.M. (*ante meridiem,* "before noon") and P.M. (*post meridiem,* "after noon"). For years use B.C. (before Christ) and, sometimes, A.D. (*anno Domini,* "in the year of the Lord," after Christ).

> **8:15** A.M.   **6:55** P.M.
> **5000** B.C.   A.D. **235**

Rule: Abbreviate days and months only in charts and lists.

> **School will be closed on**
> **Mon., Sept. 3**
> **Wed., Nov. 11**
> **Thurs., Nov. 27**

Rule: In scientific writing abbreviate units of measure. Use periods with English units but not with metric units.

> **inch(es) in.**   **yard(s) yd.**
> **meter(s) m**   **milliliter(s) ml**

Rule: On envelopes only, abbreviate street names and state names. In general text, spell out street names and state names.

> **Ms. Karen Holmes**
> **347 Grandville St.**
> **Tilton, NH 03276**

> **Karen lives on Grandville Street in Tilton, New Hampshire.**

Writing Numbers

Rule: In charts and tables, always write numbers as numerals. Other rules apply to numbers not in charts or tables.

Student Test Scores

Student	Test 1	Test 2	Test 3
Lai, W.	82	89	94
Ostos, A.	78	90	86

Rule: Spell out a number that is expressed in one or two words.

We carried enough supplies for twenty-three days.

Rule: Use a numeral for a number of more than two words.

The tallest mountain in Mexico rises 17,520 feet.

Rule: Spell out a number that begins a sentence, or reword the sentence so that it does not begin with a number.

One hundred forty-three days later, the baby elephant was born.

The baby elephant was born 143 days later.

Rule: Write a very large number as a numeral followed by the word *million* or *billion.*

There are 15 million people living in or near Mexico City.

Rule: Related numbers should be written in the same way. If one number must be written as a numeral, use numerals for all the numbers.

There are 365 days in the year, but only 52 weekends.

Rule: Spell out an ordinal number (*first, second*).

Welcome to our fifteenth annual convention.

Rule: Use words to express the time of day unless you are writing the exact time or using the abbreviation A.M. or P.M.

My guitar lesson is at five o'clock. It ends by 5:45 P.M.

Rule: Use numerals to express dates, house and street numbers, apartment and room numbers, telephone numbers, page numbers, amounts of money of more than two words, and percentages. Write out the word *percent.*

August 5, 1999

9 Davio Dr.

Apartment 9F

24 percent

Spelling

The following rules, examples, and exceptions can help you master the spelling of many words.

Spelling *ie* and *ei*

Put *i* before *e* except when both letters follow *c* or when both letters are pronounced together as an *a* sound.

believe	**sieve**	**weight**
receive	**relieve**	**neighborhood**

It is helpful to memorize exceptions to this rule. Exceptions include the following words: *species, science, weird, either, seize, leisure,* and *protein.*

Spelling unstressed vowels

Notice the vowel sound in the second syllable of the word *won-d_r-ful.* This is the unstressed vowel sound; dictionary respellings use the schwa symbol (ə) to indicate it. Because any of several vowels can be used to spell this sound, you might find yourself uncertain about which vowel to use. To spell words with unstressed vowels, try thinking of a related word in which the syllable containing the vowel sound is stressed.

Unknown Spelling	Related Word	Word Spelled Correctly
wond_rful	wonder	wonderful
fort_fications	fortify	fortifications
res_dent	reside	resident

Suffixes and the silent *e*

For most words with silent *e*, keep the *e* when adding a suffix. When you add the suffix *-ly* to a word that ends in *l* plus silent *e*, drop the *-le*. Also drop the silent *e* when you add a suffix beginning with a vowel or a *y*.

> **wise + ly = wisely**
>
> **peaceful + ly = peacefully**

> **skate + ing = skating**
>
> **gentle + ly = gently**

There are exceptions to the rule, including the following:

> **awe + ful = awful**
>
> **judge + ment = judgment**
>
> **true + ly = truly**
>
> **noise + y = noisy**
>
> **dye + ing = dyeing**
>
> **mile + age = mileage**

Suffixes and the final *y*

When you are adding a suffix to words ending with a vowel + *y*, keep the *y*. For words ending with a consonant + *y*, change the *y* to *i* unless the suffix begins with *i*. To avoid having two *i*'s together, keep the *y*.

> **enjoy + ment = enjoyment**
>
> **merry + ment = merriment**
>
> **display + ed = displayed**
>
> **lazy + ness = laziness**
>
> **play + ful = playful**
>
> **worry + ing = worrying**

Note: For some words, there are alternate spellings:

> **sly + er = slyer or slier**
>
> **shy + est = shyest or shiest**

Adding prefixes

When you add a prefix to a word, do not change the spelling of the word.

> **un + done = undone**
>
> **re + schedule = reschedule**
>
> **il + legible = illegible**
>
> **semi + sweet = semisweet**

Doubling the final consonant

Double the final consonant when a word ends with a single consonant following one vowel and the word is one syllable, or when the last syllable of the word is accented both before and after adding the suffix.

sit + ing = sitting

rub + ing = rubbing

commit + ed = committed

confer + ed = conferred

Do not double the final consonant if the suffix begins with a consonant, if the accent is not on the last syllable, or if the accent moves when the suffix is added.

cancel + ing = canceling

commit + ment = commitment

travel + ed = traveled

defer + ence = deference

Do not double the final consonant if the word ends in two consonants or if the suffix begins with a consonant.

climb + er = climber

nervous + ness = nervousness

import + ance = importance

star + dom = stardom

When adding -*ly* to a word that ends in *ll*, drop one *l*.

hill + ly = hilly   **full + ly = fully**

Forming compound words

When forming compound words, keep the original spelling of both words.

home + work = homework

scare + crow = scarecrow

pea + nut = peanut

Forming Plurals

General Rules for Plurals		
If the noun ends in...	**Rule**	**Example**
s, ch, sh, x, or z	add -es	loss→losses, latch→latches, box→boxes, bush→bushes, quiz→quizzes
a consonant + y	change y to i and add -es	ferry→ferries, baby→babies, worry→worries
a vowel + y	add -s	chimney→chimneys, monkey→monkeys, toy→toys
a vowel + o	add -s	cameo→cameos, radio→radios, rodeo→rodeos
a consonant + o	add -es but sometimes add -s	potato→potatoes, echo→echoes photo→photos, solo→solos
f or ff	add -s but sometimes change f to v and add -es	proof→proofs, bluff→bluffs sheaf→sheaves, thief→thieves, hoof→hooves
lf	change f to v and add -es	calf→calves, half→halves, loaf→loaves
fe	change f to v and add -s	knife→knives, life→lives

Special Rules for Plurals

Rule	Example
To form the plural of most proper names and one-word compound nouns, follow the general rules for plurals.	Jones→Joneses, Thomas→Thomases, Hatch→Hatches
To form the plural of hyphenated compound nouns or compound nouns of more than one word, make the most important word plural.	credit card→credit cards mother-in-law→mothers-in-law district attorney→district attorneys
Some nouns have irregular plural forms and do not follow any rules.	man→men, foot→feet, tooth→teeth
Some nouns have the same singular and plural forms	deer→deer, species→species, sheep→sheep

Speaking, Listening, and Viewing Handbook

A large part of the school day is spent either listening or speaking to others. By becoming a better listener and speaker, you will know more about what is expected of you, and understand more about your audience.

Speaking Effectively

- Speak slowly, clearly, and in a normal tone of voice. Raise your voice a bit, or use gestures to stress important points.

- Pause a few seconds after making an important point.

- Use words that help your audience picture what you're talking about. Visual aids such as pictures, graphs, charts, and maps can also help make your information clear.

- Stay in contact with your audience. Make sure your eyes move from person to person in the group you're addressing.

Speaking informally

Most oral communication is informal. When you speak casually with your friends, family, and neighbors, you use informal speech. Human relationships depend on this form of communication.

- Be courteous. Listen until the other person has finished speaking.

- Speak in a relaxed and spontaneous manner.

- Make eye contact with your listeners.

- Do not monopolize a conversation.

- When telling a story, show enthusiasm.

- When giving an announcement or directions, speak clearly and slowly. Check that your listeners understand the information.

Presenting an oral report

The steps in preparing an oral report are similar to the steps in the writing process. Complete each step carefully and you can be confident of presenting an effective oral report.

Steps in preparing an Oral Report	
Prewriting	• Determine your purpose and audience. • Decide on a topic and narrow it.
Drafting	• Make an outline. • Fill in the supporting details. • Write the report.
Revising and Editing	• Review your draft. • Check the organization of ideas and details. • Reword unclear statements.
Practicing	• Practice the report aloud in front of a family member. • Time the report. • Ask for and accept advice.
Presenting	• Relax in front of your audience. • Make eye contact with your audience. • Speak slowly and clearly.

Practice

Pretend that you have been invited to give an oral report to a group of fifth graders. Your report will tell them what to expect and how to adjust to new conditions when they enter middle school. As you plan your report, keep your purpose and your audience in mind. Include lively descriptions and examples to back up your suggestions and hold your audience's attention. As you practice giving your report, be sure to give attention to your body language as well as your vocal projection. Ask a partner to listen to your report to give you feedback on how to improve your performance. Do the same for your partner after listening to his or her report.

Listening Effectively

Listening to instructions in class

Some of the most important listening in the school day involves listening to instructions. Use the following tips to help you.

- First, make sure you understand what you are listening for. Are you receiving instructions for homework or for a test? What you listen for depends upon the type of instructions being given.

- Think about what you are hearing, and keep your eyes on the speaker. This will help you stay focused on the important points.

- Listen for keywords, or word clues. Examples of word clues are phrases such as above all, most important, or the three basic parts. These clues help you identify important points that you should remember.

- Take notes on what you hear. Write down only the most important parts of the instructions.

- If you don't understand something, ask questions. Then if you're still unsure about the instructions, repeat them aloud to your teacher to receive correction on any key points that you may have missed.

Interpreting nonverbal clues

Understanding nonverbal clues is part of effective listening. Nonverbal clues are everything you notice about a speaker except what the speaker says. As you listen, ask yourself these questions:

- Where and how is the speaker standing?

- Are some words spoken more loudly than others?

- Does the speaker make eye contact?

- Does he or she smile or look angry?

- What message is sent by the speaker's gestures and facial expression?

Practice

Work with a partner to practice listening to instructions. Each of you should find a set of directions for using a simple device–for example, a mechanical tool, a telephone answering machine, or an DVD player. Study the instructions carefully. If you can bring the device to class, ask your partner to try to use it by following your step-by-step instructions. If you cannot have the device in class, ask your partner to explain the directions back to you. Then change roles and listen as your partner gives you a set of directions.

Viewing Effectively

Critical viewing means thinking about what you see while watching a TV program, newscast, film, or video. It requires paying attention to what you hear and see and deciding whether information is true, false, or exaggerated. If the information seems to be true, try to determine whether it is based on a fact or an opinion.

Fact versus opinion

A **fact** is something that can be proved. An opinion is what someone believes is true. **Opinions** are based on feelings and experiences and cannot be proved.

Television commercials, political speeches, and even the evening news contain both facts and opinions. They use emotional words and actions to persuade the viewer to agree with a particular point of view. They may also use faulty reasoning, such as linking an effect with the wrong cause. Think through what is being said. The speaker may seem sincere, but do his or her reasons make sense? Are the reasons based on facts or on unfair generalizations?

Commercials contain both obvious and hidden messages. Just as you need to discover the author's purpose when you read a writer's words, you must be aware of the purpose of nonverbal attempts to persuade you. What does the message sender want, and how is the sender trying to influence you?

For example, a magazine or TV ad picturing a group of happy teenagers playing volleyball on a sunny beach expresses a positive feeling. The advertiser hopes viewers will transfer that positive feeling to the product being advertised— perhaps a soft drink or a brand of beachwear. This technique, called **transfer,** is one of several propaganda techniques regularly used by advertisers to influence consumers.

Following are a few other common techniques.

Testimonial—Famous and admired people recommend or praise a product, a policy, or a course of action even though they probably have no professional knowledge or expertise to back up their opinion.

Bandwagon—People are urged to follow the crowd ("get on the bandwagon") by buying a product, voting for a candidate, or whatever else the advertiser wants them to do.

Glittering generalities—The advertiser uses positive, good-sounding words (for example, *all-American* or *medically proven*) to impress people.

Practice

Think of a television commercial that you have seen often or watch a new one and take notes as you watch it. Then analyze the commercial.

- What is the purpose behind the ad?
- What is expressed in written or spoken words?
- What is expressed nonverbally (in music or sound effects as well as in pictures and actions)?
- What methods does the advertiser use to persuade viewers?
- What questions would you ask the advertiser if you could?
- How effective is the commercial? Why?

Working in Groups

Working in a group is an opportunity to learn from others. Whether you are planning a group project (such as a class trip) or solving a math problem, each person in a group brings specific strengths and interests to the task. When a task is large, such as planting a garden, a group provides the necessary energy and talent to get the job done.

Small groups vary in size according to the nature of the task. Three to five students is a good size for most small-group tasks. Your teacher may assign you to a group, or you may be asked to form your own group. Don't work with your best friend if you are likely to chat too much. Successful groups often have a mix of student abilities and interests.

Individual role assignments give everyone in a group something to do. One student, the group recorder, may take notes. Another may lead the discussion, and another report the results to the rest of the class.

Roles for a Small Group	
Reviewer	Reads or reviews the assignment and makes sure everyone understands it
Recorder 1 (of the process)	Takes notes on the discussion
Recorder 2 (of the results)	Takes notes on the final results
Reporter	Reports results to the rest of the class
Discussion leader	Asks questions to get the discussion going; keeps the group focused
Facilitator	Helps the group resolve disagreements and reach a compromise

For a small group of three or four students, some of these roles can be combined. Your teacher may assign a role to each student in your group. Or you may be asked to choose your own role.

Tips for working in groups

- Review the group assignment and goal. Be sure that everyone in the group understands the assignment.

- Review the amount of time allotted for the task. Decide how your group will organize its time.

- Check that all the group members understand their roles in the group.

- When a question arises, try to solve it as a group before asking a teacher for help.

- Listen to other points of view. Be respectful as you point out mistakes a speaker might have made.

- When it is your turn to talk, address the subject and help the project move forward by building on the ideas of the previous speaker.

Glossary/Glosario

This glossary lists the vocabulary words found in the selections in this book. The definition given is for the word as it is used in the selection; you may wish to consult a dictionary for other meanings of these words. The key below is a guide to the pronunciation symbols used in each entry.

Pronunciation Key

a	at	ō	hope		ng	sing
ā	ape	ô	fork, all		th	thin
ä	father	oo	wood, put		th	this
e	end	ōō	fool		zh	treasure
ē	me	oi	oil		ə	ago, taken, pencil,
i	it	ou	out		ə	lemon, circus
ī	ice	u	up		′	primary stress
o	hot	ū	use		′	secondary stress

English

A

abate (ə bāt′) *v.* to reduce in amount, degree, or intensity; to lessen; **p. 551**

acute (ə kūt′) *adj.* sharp; strong or intense; **p. 232**

aggravating (ag′ rə vāt ing) *adj.* irritating; annoying; **p. 784**

agony (ag′ ə nē) *n.* intense physical or emotional suffering; **p. 550**

amiably (ā′ mē ə blē) *adv.* in a friendly, good-natured way; **p. 250**

aristocrat (ə ris′ tə krat) *n.* a member of the upper class; **p. 167**

assured (ə shoord′) *v.* told with certainty; **p. 358**

authentic (aw then′ tik) *adj.* not fake; real or genuine; **p. 41**

Español

A

abate/amainar *v.* reducir en cantidad, grado o intensidad; disminuir; **p. 551**

acute/agudo *adj.* cortante; fuerte o intenso; **p. 232**

aggravating/agravante *adj.* irritante; molesto; **p. 784**

agony/agonía *n.* sufrimiento emocional o físico intenso; **p. 550**

amiably/amablemente *adv.* de manera amistosa o de natural bueno; **p. 250**

aristocrat/aristócrata *n.* miembro de la clase alta; **p. 167**

assured/asegurado *v.* decir con certidumbre; **p. 358**

authentic/auténtico *adj.* no falso; real o genuino; **p. 41**

B

borne (bôrn) *v.* given birth to; **p. 33**

brazen (brā′ zən) *adj.* shameless, defiant; **p. 397**

C

competently (kom′ pət ənt lē) *adv.* done ably, with the necessary ability; **p. 170**

compromise (kom′ prə mīz′) *n.* a settlement of differences reached by each side giving in on certain demands; **p. 75**

conceived (kən sēvd′) *v.* planned; **p. 232**

congregation (kong′ grə gā′ shən) *n.* an assembly of persons who meet for worship; **p. 77**

conscious (kon′ shəs) *n.* the part of the mind that stores thoughts, feelings and experiences of which the mind is aware; **p. 681**

conspicuous (kən spik′ ū əs) *adj.* easily seen, apparent; **p. 765**

convey (kən vā′) *v.* to show or communicate by statement, gesture, or appearance; **p. 212**

cowered (kou′ ərd) *v.* moved away in fear or shame; **p. 700**

cunning (kun′ ing) *adj.* artfully shrewd or crafty; sly; **p. 331**

D

deftly (deft′ lē) *adv.* skillfully; **p. 397**

delinquent (di ling′ kwənt) *n.* a person who repeatedly breaks laws or social codes; **p. 550**

descendants (di sen′ dənts) *n.* people who come from a particular ancestor or group of ancestors; **p. 569**

diffused (di fūzd′) *v.* spread widely; dispersed; **p. 628**

B

borne/nació *v.* fue dado a luz; fue parido; **p. 33**

brazen/descarado *adj.* desvergonzado, desafiante; **p. 397**

C

competently/competentemente *adv.* hecho capazmente, con la habilidad necesaria; **p. 170**

compromise/compromiso *n.* acuerdo de diferencias logrado cuando cada lado concede ciertos deseos; **p. 75**

conceived/concebido *v.* planeado; **p. 232**

congregation/congregación *n.* asamblea de personas que se une para rezar; **p. 77**

conscious/consciente *adj.* se refiere a la parte de la mente que guarda pensamientos, sentimientos y experiencias de la que la mente está enterada; **p. 681**

conspicuous/conspicuo *adj.* fácilmente visto, aparente; **p. 765**

convey/transmitir *v.* mostrar o comunicar por aserción, gesto o apariencia; **p. 212**

cowered/se agachó *v.* se encogió de miedo o vergüenza; **p. 700**

cunning/astuto *adj.* hábil y diestro; **p. 331**

D

deftly/hábilmente *adv.* ágilmente; **p. 397**

delinquent/delincuente *n.* persona que repetidamente rompe leyes o códigos sociales; **p. 550**

descendants/descendientes *n.* personas que vienen de un antepasado particular o grupo de antepasados; **p. 569**

diffused/difuminó *v.* esparció ampliamente; diseminó; **p. 628**

E

ebbed (ebd) *v.* became less or weaker; declined; **p. 627**

ecological (ē′ kəl oj′ i kəl) *adj.* concerning the pattern of the relationship between living things and their environment; **p. 181**

embrace (em brās′) *v.* to clasp in the arms; hug; **p. 43**

endure (en door′) *v.* continue to be; last; **p. 507**

enterprise (en′ tər prīz′) *n.* a business organization; **p. 214**

extinction (iks tingk′ shən) *n.* the dying out of a plant or animal species; **p. 181**

F

foreboding (fôr bō′ ding) *n.* a feeling that something bad will happen; **p. 824**

frenzy (fren′ zē) *n.* a state of intense emotion; **p. 837**

G

gait (gāt) *n.* a particular manner of walking or stepping; **p. 549**

grimace (grim′ is) *n.* a twisted expression of the face; **p. 252**

H

horde (hôrd) *n.* a large crowd of people or animals; **p. 180**

E

ebbed/retrocedió *v.* disminuyó; decayó; **p. 627**

ecological/ecológico *adj.* perteneciente a la pauta de la relación entre entidades vivas y su ambiente; **p. 181**

embrace/abrazar *v.* apretar o estrechar entre los brazos; **p. 43**

endure/soportar *v.* continuar con; sobrevivir; perdurar; **p. 507**

enterprise/empresa *n.* una organización de negocios; **p. 214**

extinction/extinción *n.* morir de una especie animal o vegetal; **p. 181**

F

foreboding/aprensión *n.* sentimiento que algo malo va a pasar; **p. 824**

frenzy/frenesí *n.* estado de emoción intensa; **p. 836**

G

gait/modo de andar *n.* una manera particular de caminar o pisar; **p. 549**

grimace/mueca *n.* expresión torcida de la cara; **p. 252**

H

horde/horda *n.* muchedumbre grande de gente o animales; **p. 180**

I

immortality (im′ ôr tal′ ə tē) *n.* the state of living or lasting forever; **p. 313**

imprisoned (im priz′ ənd) *v.* put or kept in a prison; **p. 331**

impulse (im′ puls) *n.* a sudden urge to do something; **p. 395**

inaudible (in ô′ də bəl) *adj.* not able to be heard; **p. 259**

inconvenient (in′ kən vēn′ yənt) *adj.* not easy to do, use, or reach; **p. 77**

influx (in′ fluks) *n.* a continual flow; **p. 212**

intellect (int′ əl ekt′) *n.* power of mind to know, understand, and reason; **p. 33**

intercept (in′ tər sept′) *v.* to stop the course or progress of; **p. 250**

internal (in turn′ əl) *adj.* of, relating to, or existing on the inside; **p. 626**

intolerant (in tol′ ər ənt) *adj.* unwilling to allow or endure differences of opinion or practice; **p. 173**

invasive (in vā′ siv) *adj.* having a tendency to spread and have harmful effects; **p. 181**

J

jubilation (jōō′ bə lā shən) *n.* great joy and excitement; **p. 806**

I

immortality/inmortalidad *n.* estado de vivir o permanecer para siempre; **p. 313**

imprisoned/encarcelado *v.* puesto en una prisión; **p. 331**

impulse/impulso *n.* gana repentina de hacer algo; **p. 395**

inaudible/inaudible *adj.* incapaz de ser oído; **p. 259**

inconvenient/inconveniente *adj.* no fácil de hacer, usar o alcanzar; **p. 77**

influx/afluencia *n.* flujo contínuo; **p. 212**

intellect/intelecto *n.* capacidad de la cabeza de saber, entender y razonar; **p. 33**

intercept/interceptar *v.* detener el curso o progreso de; **p. 250**

internal/interno *adj.* relacionado con o que existe en el interior; **p. 626**

intolerant/intolerante *adj.* no dispuesto a permitir o soportar diferencias de opinión o práctica; **p. 173**

invasive/invasivo *adj.* que tiende a difundirse y tener efectos dañinos; **p. 181**

J

jubilation/júbilo *n.* gran alegría y ánimo; **p. 806**

L

laboratory (lab′ rə tôr′ ē) *n.* a room, building, or workshop for doing scientific experiments and tests; **p. 683**

lapse (laps) *v.* to slip or fall; **p. 396**

legitimately (li jit′ ə mit lē) *adv.* in a way that follows the rules; legally; **p. 315**

liable (lī′ ə bəl) *adj.* likely; apt; **p. 18**

loathe (lōth) *v.* to regard with extreme disgust; hate; **p. 776**

M

meditation (med′ ə tā′ shən) *n.* the act of thinking or reflecting deeply; **p. 396**

melancholy (mel′ ən kol′ ē) *adj.* sadly thoughtful; **p. 856**

mutely (mūt′ lē) *adj.* without speaking; silently; **p. 318**

mutilated (mūt′ əl āt′ ed) *adj.* severely deformed or injured; **p. 649**

N

nobly (nō′ blē) *adv.* in a worthy manner; courageously, bravely; **p. 507**

O

obliged (ə blījd′) *v.* to be grateful; **p. 33**

obscure (əb skyoor′) *adj.* not well known; **p. 213**

obscure (əb skyoor′) *v.* to hide; **p. 704**

oppressive (ə pres′ iv) *adj.* hard to bear; distressing; **p. 262**

L

laboratory/laboratorio *n.* cuarto, edificio o taller para experimentos y pruebas scientíficos; **p. 683**

lapse/decaer *v.* empeorar o bajar; **p. 396**

legitimately/legítimamente *adv.* de manera que sigue las reglas; legalmente; **p. 315**

liable/propenso *adj.* tener tendencia a; apto; **p. 18**

loathe/aborrecer *v.* mirar con gran desgusto; odiar; **p. 776**

M

meditation/meditación *n.* acto de pensar profundamente; **p. 396**

melancholy/melancolía *adj.* tristemente pensativo; **p. 856**

mutely/mudamente *adj.* sin hablar; en silencio; **p. 318**

mutilated/mutilado *adj.* deformado o dañido severamente; **p. 649**

N

nobly/noblemente *adv.* de manera digna; con valor, con coraje; **p. 507**

O

obliged/agradecido *v.* sentir gratitud; **p. 33**

obscure/oscuro *adj.* no bien conocido; **p. 213**

obscure/oscurecer *v.* esconder; **p. 704**

oppressive/opresivo *adj.* difícil de soportar; angustiante; **p. 262**

outskirts (out′ skurts′) *n. pl.* a part or an area away from the center; **p. 360**

overrunning (ō′ vər run′ing) *v.* overflowing or spreading over or throughout; **p. 568**

P

perish (per′ ish) *v.* to pass from existence; disappear; **p. 507**

persistently (pər sis′ tənt lē) *adv.* enduring; continuing for a long time; **p. 168**

perturbed (pər turbd′) *v.* disturbed greatly; **p. 861**

petition (pə tish′ ən) *n.* a formal request to a superior for some favor, privilege, or compensation for a loss or wrong; **p. 696**

plateau (pla tō′) *n.* a period of time or a stage where relatively little happens; p. 685

poise (poiz) *n.* relaxed and self-controlled composure; **p. 835**

prejudice (prej′ ə dis) *n.* an opinion formed without considering all sides of a question; **p. 859**

preliminary (pri lim′ ə ner′ ē) *adj.* preceding and leading up to the main event, subject, or action; **p. 568**

profound (prə found′) *adj.* showing great understanding, knowledge, or insight; **p. 233**

prosperity (pro-sper′ ə tē) *n.* the condition of having success, wealth, or good fortune; **p. 651**

publicity (pu blis′ ə tē) *n.* activities designed to increase public interest in something or somebody; **p. 649**

outskirts/afueras *n. pl.* parte o zona apartado del centro; **p. 360**

overrunning/desbordando *v.* extendiéndose sobre o através de; **p. 568**

P

perish/perecer *v.* morir; ruinarse o destruirse; **p. 507**

persistently/persistentemente *adv.* perdurablemente; continuando por un tiempo extendido; **p. 168**

perturb/fastidiar *v.* molestar enormemente; **p. 861**

petition/petición *n.* exigencia formal a un superior por algún favor, privilegio o compensación por una pérdida o un mal; **p. 696**

plateau/estancamiento/meseta *n.* períodos de tiempo o etapa cuando relativamente poco ocurre; **p. 685**

poise/desenvoltura *n.* compostura relajada y controlada; **p. 835**

prejudice/prejuicio *n.* opinión formada sin considerar todas las perspectivas de un asunto o cuestión; **p. 859**

preliminary/preliminar *adj.* precediendo y llegando hacia el evento, tema o acción principal; **p. 568**

profound/profundo *adj.* demostrando gran comprensión, conocimiento o percepción; **p. 233**

prosperity/prosperidad *n.* condición de tener éxito, riqueza o buena fortuna; **p. 651**

publicity/publicidad *n.* actividades diseñadas para aumentar el interés público en algo o en alguien; **p. 649**

Q

quench (kwench) *v.* satisfy; **p. 333**

R

rash (rash) *adj.* characterized by too great haste or lack of thought; **p. 332**

refrained (ri frānd´) *v.* kept oneself from doing or saying something; **p. 235**

reputation (rep´ yə tā´ shən) *n.* what people generally think about the character of a person or thing; good name; **p. 19**

resolute (rez´ ə lo͞ot´) *adj.* characterized by steady determination; **p. 317**

resolve (ri zolv´) *v.* to decide firmly; **p. 507**

retrieve (ri trēv´) *v.* to bring back; **p. 76**

rival (rī´ vəl) *adj.* describing two or more trying to achieve what only one can possess; **p. 214**

riveted (riv´ it id) *v.* fastened with threadless metal bolts; **p. 313**

S

sheepishly (shēp´ ish lē) *adv.* with embarrassment; with a feeling of being at fault; **p. 44**

sidekicks (sīd´ kik) *n.* close friends or companions; **p. 18**

sinister (sin´ is tər) *adj.* bad, evil, dishonest; **p. 259**

solemnly (sol´ əm lē) *adv.* in a grave or serious manner; **p. 654**

stately (stāt´ lē) *adj.* impressive or dignified; **p. 42**

static (stat´ ik) *n.* crackling or hissing sounds that interrupt normal sounds, such as those from a microphone; **p. 23**

Q

quench/saciar *v.* satisfacer; **p. 333**

R

rash/precipitado *adj.* imprudente, sin pensamiento o preocupación; **p. 332**

refrained/se abstuvo de *v.* se impidió de hacer o decir algo; **p. 235**

reputation/reputación *n.* lo que la gente piensa generalmente del carácter de una persona o cosa; buen nombre; **p. 19**

resolute/resuelto *adj.* caracterizado por determinación firme; **p. 317**

resolve/resolver *v.* decidir firmemente; **p. 507**

retrieve/rescatar *v.* recuperar; **p. 76**

rival/rival *adj.* describiendo a dos o más personas que intentan lograr lo que sólo uno puede poseer; **p. 214**

riveted/remachó *v.* sujetó con tornillos de metal sin rosca; **p. 313**

S

sheepishly/tímidamente *adv.* con vergüenza; con un sentimiento de culpabilidad; **p. 44**

sidekick/adlátere *n.* compañero o amigo íntimo; **p. 18**

sinister/siniestro *adj.* malo, corrupto, deshonesto; **p. 259**

solemnly/solemnemente *adv.* de manera grave o seria; **p. 654**

stately/majestuoso *adj.* impresionante o dignificado; **p. 42**

static/estática *n.* sonidos crujidos o silbsantes que interrumpen sonidos normales, como aquellos de un micrófono; **p. 23**

stealthily (stelth′ ə lē) *adv.* in a secret manner; sneakily; **p. 836**

stifled (stī′ fəld) *adj.* held back; muffled; **p. 234**

stricken (strik′ ən) *adj.* strongly affected or overwhelmed, as if by disease or sickness; **p. 360**

subconscious (sub kon′ shəs) *n.* the part of a person's mind that stores thoughts, feelings, and experiences of which the person is not aware; **p. 681**

subdued (səb dood′) *adj.* quiet and restrained; **p. 793**

superficial (soo′ pər fish′ əl) *adj.* lacking deep meaning; shallow; unimportant or unnecessary; **p. 859**

surveyor (sər vā′ ər) *n.* one whose work is to determine the shape, area, and boundaries of a region; **p. 567**

sustain (sə stān) *v.* keep going; keep in existence; **p. 625**

T

tangible (tan′ jə bəl) *adj.* able to be seen, touched, or felt; **p. 698**

technique (tek nēk′) *n.* a method used to perform an operation or achieve a goal; **p. 694**

tedious (tēd′ ē əs) *adj.* causing boredom or weariness; **p. 398**

treacherous (trech′ ər əs) *adj.* dangerously untrustworthy; **p. 649**

tremor (trem′ ər) *n.* a rapid shaking or vibrating movement; **p. 318**

stealthily/a hurtadillas *adv.* de manera secreta; furtivamente; **p. 836**

stifled/sofocado *v.* reprimido; ahogado; **p. 234**

stricken/aflijido *adj.* afectado o acosado fuertemente, como por enfermedad; **p. 360**

subconscious/subconsciente *n.* parte de la mente de una persona que guarda pensamientos, sentimientos y experiencias de la que el individuo no está enterado; **p. 681**

subdued/apagado *adj.* callado y restringido; **p. 793**

superficial/superficial *adj.* que carece de sentimiento profundo; poco profundo; sin importancia o necesidad; **p. 859**

surveyor/topógrafo *n.* uno cuyo trabajo es determinar la forma, área y fronteras de una región; **p. 567**

sustain/sostener *v.* soportar; mantener en existencia; **p. 625**

T

tangible/tangible *adj.* capaz de ser visto, tocado o sentido; **p. 698**

technique/técnica *n.* método usado para hacer una operación o lograr una meta; **p. 694**

tedious/tedio *adj.* que causa aburrimiento o cansancio; **p. 398**

treacherous/traicionero *adj.* peligrosamente indigno de confianza; **p. 649**

tremor/temblor *n.* movimiento rápido sacudiente o vibrante; **p. 318**

U

unforeseen (un´ fôr sēn´) *adj.* not known beforehand; unexpected; **p. 359**

V

vacancy (vā´ kən sē) *n.* unoccupied or empty space; **p. 333**

vexed (vekst) *adj.* annoyed or distressed; **p. 233**

W

wavered (wā´ vərd) *v.* moved unsteadily up and down or from side to side; swayed; **p. 332**

U

unforeseen/imprevisto *adj.* no sabido con antelación; inesperado; **p. 359**

V

vacancy/vacante *n.* espacio vacío; **p. 333**

vexed/desconcertado *adj.* irritado o afligido; **p. 233**

W

wavered/titubeó *v.* actuó con indecisión; vaciló; **p. 332**

Academic Word List

To succeed academically in high school and prepare for college, it is important to know academic vocabulary–special terms used in classroom discussion, assignments, and tests. These words are also used in the workplace and among friends to share information, exchange ideas, make decisions, and build relationships. Research has shown that the words listed below, compiled by Averil Coxhead in 2000, are the ones most commonly used in these ways. You will encounter many of them in the Glencoe Language Arts program. You will also focus on specific terms in connection with particular reading selections.

Note: The lists are ordered by frequency of use from most frequent to least frequent.

List One

analysis
approach
area
assessment
assume
authority
available
benefit
concept
consistent
constitutional
context
contract
create
data
definition
derived
distribution
economic
environment
established
estimate
evidence
export
factors
financial
formula
function
identified
income
indicate
individual
interpretation
involved
issues
labor
legal
legislation
major
method
occur
percent
period
policy
principle
procedure
process
required
research
response
role
section
sector
significant
similar
source
specific
structure
theory
variables

List Two

achieve
acquisition
administration
affect
appropriate
aspects
assistance
categories
chapter
commission
community
complex
computer
conclusion
conduct
consequences
construction
consumer
credit
cultural
design
distinction
elements
equation
evaluation
features
final
focus
impact
injury
institute
investment
items
journal
maintenance
normal
obtained
participation
perceived
positive
potential
previous
primary
purchase
range
region
regulations
relevant
resident
resources
restricted
security

select
site
sought
strategies
survey
text
traditional
transfer

List Three

alternative
circumstances
comments
compensation
components
consent
considerable
constant
constraints
contribution
convention
coordination
core
corporate
corresponding
criteria
deduction
demonstrate
document

dominant
emphasis
ensure
excluded
framework
funds
illustrated
immigration
implies
initial
instance
interaction
justification
layer
link
location
maximum
minorities
negative
outcomes
partnership
philosophy
physical
proportion
published
reaction
registered
reliance
removed
scheme
sequence
sex
shift
specified
sufficient
task
technical

techniques
technology
validity
volume

List Four

access
adequate
annual
apparent
approximated
attitudes
attributed
civil
code
commitment
communication
concentration
conference
contrast
cycle
debate
despite
dimensions
domestic
emerged
error
ethnic
goals
granted
hence
hypothesis
implementation
implications
imposed
integration
internal
investigation

job
label
mechanism
obvious
occupational
option
output
overall
parallel
parameters
phase
predicted
principal
prior
professional
project
promote
regime
resolution
retained
series
statistics
status
stress
subsequent
sum
summary
undertaken

List Five

academic
adjustment
alter
amendment
aware
capacity
challenge
clause

compounds
conflict
consultation
contact
decline
discretion
draft
enable
energy
enforcement
entities
equivalent
evolution
expansion
exposure
external
facilitate
fundamental
generated
generation
image
liberal
license
logic
marginal
medical
mental
modified
monitoring
network
notion
objective
orientation
perspective
precise
prime
psychology

pursue
ratio
rejected
revenue
stability
styles
substitution
sustainable
symbolic
target
transition
trend
version
welfare
whereas

List Six

abstract
accurate
acknowledged
aggregate
allocation
assigned
attached
author
bond
brief
capable
cited
cooperative
discrimination
display
diversity
domain
edition
enhanced
estate
exceed

expert
explicit
federal
fees
flexibility
furthermore
gender
ignored
incentive
incidence
incorporated
index
inhibition
initiatives
input
instructions
intelligence
interval
lecture
migration
minimum
ministry
motivation
neutral
nevertheless
overseas
preceding
presumption
rational
recovery
revealed
scope
subsidiary
tapes
trace
transformation
transport

underlying
utility

List Seven

adaptation
adults
advocate
aid
channel
chemical
classical
comprehensive
comprise
confirmed
contrary
converted
couple
decades
definite
deny
differentiation
disposal
dynamic
eliminate
empirical
equipment
extract
file
finite
foundation
global
grade
guarantee
hierarchical
identical
ideology
inferred
innovation

insert
intervention
isolated
media
mode
paradigm
phenomenon
priority
prohibited
publication
quotation
release
reverse
simulation
solely
somewhat
submitted
successive
survive
thesis
topic
transmission
ultimately
unique
visible
voluntary

List Eight

abandon
accompanied
accumulation
ambiguous
appendix
appreciation
arbitrary
automatically
bias
chart

clarity
conformity
commodity
complement
contemporary
contradiction
crucial
currency
denote
detected
deviation
displacement
dramatic
eventually
exhibit
exploitation
fluctuations
guidelines
highlighted
implicit
induced
inevitably
infrastructure
inspection
intensity
manipulation
minimized
nuclear
offset
paragraph
plus
practitioners
predominantly
prospect
radical
random
reinforced

restore
revision
schedule
tension
termination
theme
thereby
uniform
vehicle
via
virtually
visual
widespread

List Nine

accommodation
analogous
anticipated
assurance
attained
behalf
bulk
ceases
coherence
coincide
commenced
concurrent
confined
controversy
conversely
device
devoted
diminished
distorted
duration
erosion
ethical
format

founded
incompatible
inherent
insights
integral
intermediate
manual
mature
mediation
medium
military
minimal
mutual
norms
overlap
passive
portion
preliminary
protocol
qualitative
refine
relaxed
restraints
revolution
rigid
route
scenario
sphere
subordinate
supplementary
suspended
team
temporary
trigger
unified
violation
vision

List Ten

adjacent
albeit
assembly
collapse
colleagues
compiled
conceived
convinced
depression
encountered
enormous
forthcoming
inclination
integrity
intrinsic
invoked
levy
likewise
nonetheless
notwithstanding
odd
ongoing
panel
persistent
posed
reluctant
so-called
straightforward
undergo
whereby

Index of Skills

Literary Concepts

Prior knowledge 649

activating 57, 59, 60, 62, 67, 68, 649, 650, 652, 654, 655, 656, 659

Proposition-and-support text structure 469

Questioning 852, 856, 859, 860, 862

Recalling 53, 85, 90, 97, 183, 197, 215, 246, 345, 387, 400, 414, 474, 490, 502, 523, 545, 633, 668, 812

Recognizing

author's purpose 242, 246

bias 561, 563

Resolution 249

Responding 90, 363

to the Big Question 164

Rising action 249, 759

Scanning 199, 203, 206

Sequence, identifying 92, 94, 95, 96, 98

Setting 35, 70, 355, 646, 814

analyzing 355, 356, 357, 360, 364

Setting purpose for reading 2, 8, 14, 31, 35, 40, 57, 73, 82, 87, 92, 101, 147, 154, 159, 166, 179, 189, 199, 210, 218, 223, 231, 242, 249, 307, 311, 320, 324, 330, 339, 348, 355, 366, 369, 380, 385, 389, 394, 403, 411, 453, 459, 469, 477, 495, 505, 510, 516, 526, 533, 542, 548, 555, 561, 565, 601, 607, 624, 630, 634, 641, 649, 662, 667, 671, 690, 759, 817, 852, 865, 871

Short fiction 2, 70

Skimming 199, 200, 202, 203, 205

Static characters 73

Style 311

analyzing 311, 312, 314, 316, 317, 318, 319

Summarizing 6, 34, 38, 79, 97, 101, 103, 104, 105, 106, 152, 158, 159, 164, 176, 228, 239, 264, 308, 319, 323, 328, 334, 345, 352, 368, 378, 383, 387, 400, 408, 456, 474, 490, 502, 508, 515, 523, 531, 545, 554, 559, 563, 604, 620, 629, 633, 658, 668, 687, 712, 756, 849, 870, 874

Supporting details 87

determining 87, 90

Synthesizing 6, 12, 27, 152, 183, 264, 345, 510, 515, 712

the Big Question 474, 531

Text features, analyzing 871, 874

Text, informational 146

Text structure 671

analyzing 671, 672, 673, 677, 679, 683, 685, 686, 688

proposition-and-support 469

Theme 70, 646, 814, 817

analyzing 385, 386, 388

making generalizations about 817, 820, 821, 824, 827, 828, 829, 831, 832, 836, 837, 838, 840, 842, 845, 846, 850

Tone, analyzing 667, 668

Visualizing 35, 38, 223, 225, 227, 228

Vocabulary

Academic vocabulary 12, 28, 54, 67, 85, 98, 105, 176, 184, 197, 240, 264, 319, 334, 345, 352, 364, 387, 400, 408, 415, 474, 491, 502, 508, 524, 531, 545, 559, 621, 640, 659, 687, 712, 812, 850

Affix 287

Antonyms 474

Context clues 55

Dictionary skills 661

Idioms 493

Multiple-Meaning words 402

Prefix 287

Roots 287

Suffix 287

Synonyms 240, 364, 474, 850

Visual Vocabulary 22, 32, 42, 43, 59, 74, 122, 170, 173, 175, 182, 232, 234, 251, 254, 313, 331, 332, 370, 371, 395, 397, 460, 480, 499, 553, 567, 608, 616, 626, 653, 672, 695, 707, 761, 762

Word origins 875

Word parts 287

Writing

Analogy 882

Analyzing

a model 131, 291, 437, 585, 734, 883

plot 241

Arguing a position 525

Argument 583, 585

Speaking, Listening, and Viewing

Research, Test-Taking, and Study Skills

Interdisciplinary Activities

Index of Authors and Titles

Acknowledgments

Unit 1

"Miracle Man" by Sam Blair. Reprinted with permission of Sam Blair and *Boys' Life,* September 2006, published by the Boys Scouts of America.

"My Name" and "Bums in the Attic" from *The House on Mango Street.* Copyright © 1984 by Sandra Cisneros. Published by Vintage Books, a division of Random House, Inc., and in hardcover by Alfred A. Knopf in 1994. Reprinted by permission of Susan Bergholz Literary Services, New York, NY and Lamy, NM. All rights reserved.

"Raymond's Run" copyright © 1971 by Toni Cade Bambara, from *Gorilla, My Love* by Toni Cade Bambara. Used by permission of Random House, Inc.

From *Sojourner Truth: Ain't I a Woman?* By Patricia C. McKissack and Fredrick McKissack. Copyright © 1992 by Patricia McKissack. Reprinted by permission of Scholastic, Inc.

"Medicine Bag" by Virginia Sneve. Reprinted by permission of the author.

"Abuela Invents the Zero" from *An Island Like You: Stories of the Barrio* by Judith Ortiz Cofer. Scholastic Inc./Orchard Books. Copyright © 1995 by Judith Ortiz Cofer. Reprinted by permission.

"Saying Yes" by Diana Chang. Reprinted by permission of the author.

"Who Can Be Born Black" by Mari Evans. Reprinted by permission of the author.

"The People Could Fly" from *The People Could Fly: American Black Folktales* by Virginia Hamilton, illustrated by Leo and Diane Dillon, copyright © 1985 by Virginia Hamilton. Used by permission of Alfred A. Knopf, an imprint of Random House Children's Books, a division of Random House, Inc.

"Born Worker" from *Petty Crimes: Stories* by Gary Soto. Copyright © 1998 by Gary Soto. Reprinted by permission of Houghton Mifflin Harcourt Publishing Company. All rights reserved.

Unit 2

"There is no Frigate like a Book" reprinted by permission of the publishers and the Trustees of Amherst College from *The Poems of Emily Dickinson,* Thomas H. Johnson, ed., Cambridge, Mass.: The Belknap Press of Harvard University Press, Copyright © 1951, 1955, 1979, 1983 by the President and Fellows of Harvard College.

"Because of Libraries We Can Say These Things" from *Fuel,* copyright © 1998 by Naomi Shihab Nye. Reprinted by permission of the author.

From *I Know Why the Caged Bird Sings* by Maya Angelou, copyright © 1969 and renewed 1997 by Maya Angelou. Used by permission of Random House, Inc.

From "Huge, Freed Pythons Invade Florida Everglades" by Stefan Lovgren. *National Geographic,* June 3, 2004. Copyright © 2004 National Geographic Society. Reprinted by permission.

From *The Great Fire* by Jim Murphy. Copyright © 1995 by Jim Murphy. Reprinted by permission of Scholastic, Inc.

"Pretty Words" from *The Collected Poems of Elinor Wylie* by Elinor Wylie, copyright 1932 by Alfred A. Knopf, a division of Random House, Inc., copyright renewed 1960 by Edwina C. Rubenstein. Used by permission of Alfred A. Knopf, a division of Random House, Inc.

"Hollywood's Rise to Fame" by Robert D. San Souci, from *Cobblestone*'s January 2007 issue: *Hooray for Hollywood and the Rise of Motion Pictures,* © 2007, Carus Publishing Company, published by Cobblestone publishing, 30 Grove Street, Suite c, Peterborough, NH 03458. All rights reserved. Used by permission of the publisher.

"Introduction to Poetry" from *The Apple That Astonished Paris* by Billy Collins. Copyright © 1988 by Billy Collins. Reprinted by permission of the University of Arkansas Press.

From *Edgar Allan Poe* by Milton Meltzer. Copyright © 2003 by Milton Meltzer. Reprinted with the permission of Twenty-First Century Books, a division of Lerner Publishing Group, Inc. All rights reserved. No part of this excerpt may be used or reproduced in any manner whatsoever without the prior written permission of Lerner Publishing Group, Inc.

Unit 3

"Travel" copyright 1921, 1948 by Edna St. Vincent Millay.

"The Drummer Boy of Shiloh" by Ray Bradbury. Repritned by permission of Don Congdon Associates, Inc. Copyright © 1960 by the Curtis Publishing Company, renewed 1988 by Ray Bradbury.

"Exile" from *The Other Side/El Otro Lado*. Copyright © 1995 by Julia Alvarez. Published by Plume/Penguin, a division of Penguin Group (USA). Reprinted by permission of Susan Bergholz Literary Services, New York, NY and Lamy, NM. All rights reserved.

"The Lesson of the Moth" from *Archy and Mehitabel* by Don Marquis, copyright 1927 by Doubleday, a division of Random House, Inc. Used by permission of Doubleday, a division of Random House, Inc.

"The Oxcart" from *Sword and the Samurai: Adventure Stories from Japan* by Eric A. Kimmell. Copyright © 1999 by Eric A. Kimmell. Reprinted by permission of Houghton Mifflin Harcourt Publishing Company. All rights reserved.

From *Harriet Tubman: Conductor on the Underground Railroad* by Ann Petry. Reprinted by permission of Russell & Volkening as agents for the author. Copyright © 1955 by Ann Petry, renewed 1983 by Ann Petry.

"The Sound of Night" by Maxine Kumin, Copyright © 1961 by Maxine Kumin. Reprinted by permission of the author and The Anderson Literary Agency.

"Checkouts" from *A Couple of Kooks and Other Stories About Love* by Cynthia Rylant. Scholastic Inc./ Orchard Books. Copyright © 1990 by Cynthia Rylant. Reprinted by permission.

"Knoxville, Tennessee" from *Black Feeling, Black Talk, Black Judgment* by Nikki Giovanni. Copyright © 1968 1970 by Nikki Giovanni. Reprinted by permission of HarperCollins Publishers.

"Los New Yorks" from *Mainland (Poems)* by Victor Hernández Cruz, copyright © 1973 by Victor Hernández Cruz. Used by permission of Random House, Inc.

"Childhood" from *This Is My Century: New and Collected Poems* by Margaret Walker. Copyright © 1989 by Margaret Walker Alexander. Reprinted by permission of The University of Georgia Press.

From *Beowulf*, translated by Burton Raffel, copyright © 1963 renewed © 1991 by Burton Raffel. Used by permission of Dutton Signet, a division of Penguin Group (USA) Inc.

"Racing the Great Bear" from *Flying with the Eagle, Racing the Great Bear* by Joseph Bruchac. Copyright © 1993 by Joseph Bruchac. Repritned by permission of Barbara S. Kouts.

Unit 4

"Homeless," copyright © 1987 by Anna Quindlen, from *Living Out Loud* by Anna Quindlen. Used by permission of Random House, Inc.

Excerpt from *2 Minutes a Day for a Greener Planet,* by Marjorie Lamb. Copyright © 1990 by Marjorie Lamb. Reprinted by permission of the author.

"The Trouble with Television" by Robert MacNeil. Reprinted by permission of the author.

"The Treasure of Lemon Brown" by Walter Dean Myers. Reprinted by permission of Miriam Altshuler Literary Agency, on behalf of Walter Dean Myers. Copyright © 1983 by Walter Dean Myers.

Excerpt from *Lincoln: A Photobiography* by Russell Freedman. Copyright © 1987 by Russell Freedman. Reprinted by permission of Clarion Books, an imprint of Houghton Mifflin Company. All rights reserved.

"Ode to Thanks" from *Odes to Opposites* by Pablo Neruda. Copyright © 1995 by Pablo Neruda and Fundacion Pablo Neruda (Odes in Spanish); Copyright © 1995 by Ken Krabbenhoft (Odes in English); Copyright © 1995 by Ferris Cook (Illustrations and compilation). By permission of Little Brown & Company.

"Ode to Rain" copyright © 2006 by Pat Mora. Currently published in *Adobe Odes,* published by University of Arizona Press. Reprinted by permission of Curtis Brown, Ltd.

"Escaping" by Zdenko Slobodnik, from *Teen Ink: What Matters,* © 2003 The Young Authors Foundation, Inc. Reprinted by permission of Teenink.com and *Teen Ink* magazine.

"Napa, California" Copyright © 1995 by Ana Castillo. From *My Father Was a Toltec and Selected Poems,* published by Anchor Books, a division of Random

House, Inc. Originally published in *Otro Canto,* Alternativa Publications, Chicago in 1977. Reprinted by permission of Susan Bergholz Literary Services, New York, NY and Lamy, NM. All rights reserved.

"Working Hands" by Francisco X. Alarcón. From *Snake Poems,* copyright © 1992 by Francisco X. Alarcón. Used with permission of Chronicle Books LLC, San Francisco. Visit ChronicleBooks.com.

"I Have a Dream" Reprinted by arrangement with The Heirs to the Estate of Martin Luther King Jr., c/o Writers House as agent for the proprietor, New York, NY. Copyright 1963 Martin Luther King, Jr., copyright renewed 1991 Coretta Scott King.

"Harlem (s)", copyright 1951 by Langston Hughes, from *The Collected Poems of Langston Hughes* by Langston Hughes, edited by Arnold Rampersad with David Roessel, Associate Editor. Used by permission of Alfred A. Knopf, a division of Random House, Inc.

Unit 5

Excerpt from *The Book of Rock Stars: 24 Musical Icons that Shine Through History,* written by Kathleen Krull, art by Stephen Alcorn. Text copyright © 2003 by Kathleen Krull. Reprinted by permission of the author.

Reprinted with the permission of Simon & Schuster Books for Young Readers, an imprint of Simon & Schuster Children's publishing Division, from *Woodsong* by Gary Paulsen. Text copyright © 1990 by Gary Paulsen.

"My Father's Song" from *Woven Stone* by Simon J. Ortiz. Copyright © 1992 by Simon J. Ortiz. Reprinted by permission of the author.

"I Ask My Mother to Sing" from *Rose* by Li-Young Lee. Copyright © 1986 by Li-Young Lee. Reprinted by permission of Boa Editions.

"Mother Jones" by Judith Pinkerton Josephson. Copyright © 1997 by Judith Pinkerton Josephson. Reprinted with the permission of Twenty-First Century Books, a division of Lerner Publishing Group, Inc. All rights reserved. No part of this excerpt may be used or reproduced in any manner whatsoever without the prior written permission of Lerner Publishing Group, Inc.

"El Lucero de Dios" from *Elegy on the Death of Cesar Chavez,* copyright © 2000 by Rudolfo Anaya, published by Cinco Puntos Press, www.cincopuntos.com. Reprinted by permission.

"Flowers for Algernon" by Daniel Keyes. Copyright © 1959, 1966, renewed 1987 by Daniel Keyes. Reprinted by permission of the author. Available in book length, *Flowers for Algernon,* companion book, *Algernon, Charlie and I: A Writer's Journey.*

Unit 6

"Bouncing Back" by Jan Farrington. *Current Health,* March 2005. Special permission granted by *Weekly Reader,* published and copyrighted by Weekly Reader Corporation. All rights reserved.

The Diary of Anne Frank (Play) by Frances Goodrich and Albert Hackett, copyright © 1956 by Albert Hackett, Frances Goodrich and Otto Frank. Used by permission of Random House, Inc.

From *The Diary of Anne Frank: The Definitive Edition,* by Anne Frank, edited by Otto H. Frank and Mirjam Pressler, translated by Susan Massotty, translation copyright © 1995 by Doubleday, a division of Random House, Inc. Used by permission of Doubleday, a division of Random House, Inc.

Reprinted with the permission of Simon & Schuster Books for Young Readers, an imprint of Simon & Schuster Children's Publishing Division, from *Sky* by Hanneke Ippisch. Copyright © 1996 Hanneke Ippisch

"Mother to Son," copyright © 1994 by The Estate of Langston Hughes, from *The Collected Poems of Langston Hughes* by Langston Hughes, edited by Arnold Rampersad with David Roessel, Associate Editor. Used by permission of Alfred A. Knopf, a division of Random House, Inc.

"Speech to the Young: Speech to the Progress-Toward" by Gwendolyn Brooks. Reprinted by consent of Brooks Permissions.

End of Unit Assessments

"The Cloud-Mobile" by May Swenson. Reprinted with permission of the Literary Estate of May Swenson.

Reprinted with the permission of Simon & Schuster Books for Young Readers, an imprint of Simon & Schuster Children's Publishing Division from *The Invisible Thread* by Yoshiko Uchida. Copyright © 1991 by Yoshiko Uchida

Photo Credits

183 Brand X Pictures; **188** Arthur Cohen Photography; **190 193** North Wind/North Wind Picture Archives; **196** The Granger Collection, New York; **200** Stacy Gold/National Geographic/Getty Images; **201** Paul Thompson Images/Alamy Images; **202** Comstock/Alamy Images; **209** Courtesy Robert D. San Souci; **211** Bettmann/CORBIS; **212** Brand X/PunchStock; **213** Topical Press Agency/Getty Images; **214** Bettmann/CORBIS; **217** Fitzwilliam Museum, University of Cambridge, UK, ©DACS/Bridgeman Art Library; **218** (t)The Granger Collection, New York, (b)Lynn Goldsmith/CORBIS; **219** Private Collection/Bridgeman Art Library; **220** Kevin O'Shea/Illustraion Works/CORBIS; **222** (t)Bettmann/CORBIS, (b)Mary Evans Picture Library; **224** (t)North Wind Picture Archives/Alamy Images, (b)Getty Images; **226** Getty Images; **227** Museum of the City of New York; **230** Library of Congress; **232** (t)age fotostock/SuperStock, (b)Getty Images; **234** Ingram Publishing; **237** Sausage International/CORBIS; **239** Getty Images; **242** IT Stock Free/PunchStock (inset) American Library Association; **244** (l)The Granger Collection, New York, (r)Private Collection/Bridgeman Art Library; **247** Bettmann/CORBIS; **249** Doug Martin Photography; **251** bobo/Alamy Images; **253** Fine Arts Museums of San Francisco, CA; **254** Mark Steinmetz; **258** Fine Arts Museums of San Francisco, CA; **266** Bettmann/CORBIS; **267** (l)American Stock/Hulton Archive/Getty Images, (c)Getty Images, (r)Douglas Grundy/Getty Images; **268** (t)Douglas Grundy/Getty Images, (b)Ron Chapple/Thinkstock/JupiterImages/Comstock Images; **271** American Stock/Hulton Archive/Getty Images; **272** Mary Evans Picture Library; **273** MedioImages; **276** Mary Evans Picture Library; **277-285** Gary Gianni; **290** Zits Partnership. Reprinted with Permission of King Features Syndicate, Inc.; **296 297** Eclipse Studios; **300** Gaslight Advertising Archives, Inc.; **304-305** Gordon Wiltsie/National Geographic/Getty Images; **307** Ace Stock Limited/Alamy Images; **308** Getty Images; **309** Art Gallery of New South Wales, Sydney/Bridgeman Art Library; **310** Ralph Merlino/Shooting Star; **312** Library of Congress; **313** SuperStock/SuperStock; **314** Private Collection/Bridgeman Art Library; **318** First Image; **320** Bettmann/CORBIS; **321** Museum of Fine Arts, Houston, TX/Bridgeman Art Library; **322** Private Collection, James Goodman Gallery, NY/Bridgeman Art Library; **324** Hulton Archive/Getty Images; **325 326** Alamy Images; **327** Niall Benvie/CORBIS; **329** Radcliffe Archives, Radcliffe Institute, Harvard University; **331** (t)Private Collection/Bridgeman Art Library, (b)Jason Hawkes/CORBIS; **332** blickwinkel/Alamy Images; **333** Scala/Art Resource, NY. ©ARS, NY.; **338** (t)Michael Nicholson/CORBIS, (b)The McGraw-Hill Companies; **341** The Metropolitan Museum of Art, Arthur Hoppock Hearn Fund, 1950 (50.117). Photograph ©1988 The Metropolitan Museum of Art/Art ©Estate of Grant Wood/Licensed by VAGA, New York, NY; **342** SuperStock; **347** (t)Theo Westernberger, (b)Art Explosion; **349** Robert McIntosh/CORBIS; **354** Eric Kimmel; **356** Erich Lessing/Art Resource, NY; **358** R.P. Kingston/Index Stock; **359** Brooklyn Museum of Art, NY, Frank L. Babbott Fund/Bridgeman Art Library; **361** Victoria and Albert Museum, London/akg-Images; **363** (l)Getty Images, (r)Adoc-photos/Art Resource, NY; **366** Kamaria Greenfield; **367** Smithsonian American Art Museum, Washington, DC/Art Resource, NY; **369** age fotostock/SuperStock; **370** R.& N. Bowers/VIREO; **371** Raymond Bial; **372** The Granger Collection, New York; **375** North Wind Picture Archives; **376** The Art Archive/Philbrook Museum of Art Oklahoma/Laurie Platt Winfrey; **378** The Granger Collection, New York; **379** Private Collection/Bridgeman Art Library; **381** (t)Time for Kids, (b)Royal Geographic Society; **382** (t)Royal Geographic Society, (b)Bobby Model; **384** (t)Gordon Parks/Time & Life Pictures/Getty Images, (b)Art Explosion; **386** Museum of Fine Arts, Boston. Abraham Shuman Fund (1970.47); **389** Bettmann/CORBIS; **390** Private Collection/Bridgeman Art Library; **395** (tl tr)Elizabeth Whiting & Associates/Alamy Images, (b)Andre Jenny/Alamy Images; **396** Private Collection/Bridgeman Art Library; **397** (t)Private Collection/Bridgeman Art Library, (b)Neal and Molly Jansen/Alamy Images; **398** Private Collection/Bridgeman Art Library; **403** Judie Burstein/Globe Photos, Inc. 200; **404** Private Collection, Photo ©Christie's Images/Bridgeman Art Library; **406** Private Collection/Bridgeman Art Library; **410** CORBIS; **412** Antar Dayal/Illustration Works/CORBIS; **413** Henry Moore Foundation/